James Madison

International Library of Essays in the History of Social and Political Thought
Series Editor: Tom Campbell

Titles in the Series:

Hannah Arendt
Amy Allen

James Madison
Terence Ball

Charles-Louis de Secondat Montesquieu
David Carrithers

Emile Durkheim
Roger Cotterrell

Vilfredo Pareto
Joseph Femia

Jean Bodin
Julian H. Franklin

David Hume
Knud Haakonssen and Richard Whatmore

Edmund Burke
Iain Hampsher-Monk

Talcott Parsons
John Holmwood

Thomas Aquinas
John Inglis

Jűrgen Habermas, Volumes I and II
Christian Joerges, Klaus Guenther and Camil Ungureanu

Aristotle
George Klosko

Georg Hegel
Dudley Knowles

Thomas Paine
Bruce Kuklick

Max Weber
Peter Lassman

Mary Wollstonecraft
Jane Moore

T.H. Green
John Morrow

Martin Heidegger
Stephen Mulhall

Jean-Jacques Rousseau
Timothy O'Hagan

Michel Foucault
David Owen

John Rawls
David A. Reidy

Immanuel Kant
Arthur Ripstein

Jeremy Bentham
Frederick Rosen

Theodor Adorno
James Schmidt

Thomas Hobbes
Gabriella Slomp

Friedrich Nietzsche
Tracy Strong

James Madison

Edited by

Terence Ball

Arizona State University, USA

Routledge
Taylor & Francis Group
LONDON AND NEW YORK

First published 2008 by Ashgate Publishing

Reissued 2018 by Routledge
2 Park Square, Milton Park, Abingdon, Oxon, OX14 4RN
605 Third Avenue, New York, NY 10017

First issued in paperback 2021

Routledge is an imprint of the Taylor & Francis Group, an informa business

A Library of Congress record exists under LC control number: 2007050591

ISBN 13: 978-0-815-38990-3 (hbk)
ISBN 13: 978-1-351-15516-8 (ebk)
ISBN 13: 978-1-138-35822-5 (pbk)

DOI: 10.4324/9781351155168

Contents

PART IV REPUBLICAN OR DEMOCRAT?

PART V *THE FEDERALIST* AND FEDERALISM

PART VI MADISON'S BILL OF RIGHTS

PART VII RELIGIOUS LIBERTY

PART VIII POLITICAL PARTIES

Acknowledgements

I am grateful to Tom Campbell, the series editor, for inviting me to undertake this project and for his patience with my delays in delivering on my promise to complete it. I am also grateful to three undergraduate research assistants in my department's Junior Fellows programme – Joanna Kale, Dana Bersch and Venus Booth – who were tireless in tracking down sources, checking facts, photocopying and countless other chores in connection with this project. And, not least, for commenting critically and helpfully on my Introduction, I thank Tom Campbell, James Farr and, most especially, Russell Hanson.

The editor and publishers also wish to thank the following for permission to use copyright material.

Academy of Political Science for the essay: Neal Riemer (1954), 'The Republicanism of James Madison', *Political Science Quarterly*, **69**, pp. 45–64. Copyright © 1954 Academy of Political Science.

American Enterprise Institute for the essay: Jean Yarbrough (1987), 'Madison and Modern Federalism,' in Robert A. Goldwin and William A. Schambra (eds), *How Federal Is the Constitution?*, Washington DC: American Enterprise Institute, pp. 84–108.

Cambridge University Press for the essays: Robert J. Morgan (1981), 'Madison's Analysis of the Sources of Political Authority', *American Political Science Review*, **75**, pp. 613–25. Copyright © 1981 American Political Science Association; Robert A. Dahl (2005), 'James Madison: Republican or Democrat?', *Perspectives on Politics*, **3**, pp. 439–48. Copyright © 2005 American Political Science Association; Martin Diamond (1959), 'Democracy and *The Federalist*: A Reconsideration of the Framers' Intent', *American Political Science Review*, **69**, pp. 52–68. Copyright © 1959 American Political Science Association.

Copyright Clearance Center for the essays: Douglass Adair (1957), '"That Politics May be Reduced to a Science": David Hume, James Madison, and the Tenth *Federalist*', *Huntington Library Quarterly*, **20**, pp. 343–60. Copyright © 1957 University of California Press; Edmund S. Morgan (1986), 'Safety in Numbers: Madison, Hume, and the Tenth *Federalist*', *Huntington Library Quarterly*, **49**, pp. 95–112. Copyright © 1986 University of California Press; John Zvesper (1984), 'The Madisonian Systems', *Western Political Quarterly*, **37**, pp. 236–56. Copyright © 1984 Sage Publications, Inc.

Alan Gibson (1993), 'The Commercial Republic and the Pluralist Critique of Marxism: An Analysis of Martin Diamond's Interpretation of *Federalist* 10', *Polity*, **25**, pp. 497–528. Copyright © 1993 Alan Gibson.

Imprint Academic for the essay: Alan Gibson (1991), 'Impartial Representation and the Extended Republic: Towards a Comprehensive and Balanced Reading of the Tenth *Federalist* Paper', *History of Political Thought*, **12**, pp. 263–304. Copyright © 1991 Imprint Academic.

Douglas W. Jaenicke (1989), 'Madison v. Madison: The Party Essays v. The Federalist Papers', in Richard Maedment and John Zvesper (eds), *Reflections on the Constitution*, Manchester: Manchester University Press, pp. 116–47. Copyright © 1989 Douglas W. Jaenicke.

Joseph F. Kobylka and Bradley Kent Carter (1987), 'Madison, *The Federalist*, and the Constitutional Order: Human Nature and Institutional Structure', *Polity*, **20**, pp. 190–208. Copyright © 1987 Joseph F. Kobylka and Bradley Kent Carter.

Omohundro Institute of Early American History and Culture for the essays: Douglass Adair (1951), 'The Tenth Federalist Revisited', *William and Mary Quarterly*, 3rd Series, **8**, pp. 48–67; Irving Brant (1951), 'Madison on the Separation of Church and State', *William and Mary Quarterly*, **8**, pp. 3–24.

Princeton University Press for the essay: Douglass Adair (1946), 'James Madison', in Willard Thorp (ed.), *The Lives of Eighteen from Princeton*, Princeton NJ: Princeton University Press, pp. 137–57. Copyright © 1946 Princeton University Press.

Simon and Schuster, Inc for the essay: Charles A. Beard (1913), 'The Constitution as an Economic Document', in Charles A. Beard (ed.), *An Economic Interpretation of the Constitution of the United States*, New York: The Free Press, chapter VI, pp. 152–88.

University of California Press for the essay: Terence Ball (1992), 'Constitutional Interpretation and Conceptual Change', in Gregory Leyh (ed.), *Legal Hermeneutics: History, Theory, and Practice*, Berkeley CA: University of California Press, pp. 129–46. Copyright © 1992 Regents of the University of California.

University of Chicago Press for the essays: Paul Finkelman (1990), 'James Madison and the Bill of Rights: A Reluctant Paternity', *Supreme Court Review*, **9**, pp. 301–47. Copyright © 1990 University of Chicago Press; Robert A. Dahl (1956), 'Madisonian Democracy', in Robert A. Dahl *A Preface to Democratic Theory*, Chicago IL: University of Chicago Press, pp. 4–33.

William and Mary Law Review for the essay: Jack N. Rakove (1990), 'The Madisonian Theory of Rights', *William and Mary Law Review*, **31**, pp. 245–66. Copyright © 1990 William and Mary Law Review.

Every effort has been made to trace all the copyright holders, but if any have been inadvertently overlooked the publishers will be pleased to make the necessary arrangement at the first opportunity.

Series Preface

The International Library of Essays in the History of Social and Political Thought brings together collections of important essays dealing with the work of major figures in the history of social and political thought. The aim is to make accessible the complete text with the original pagination of those essays that should be read by all scholars working in that field. In each case, the selection is made from the extensive available literature by an established expert who has a keen sense of the continuing relevance of the history of social and political thought for contemporary theory and practice. The selection is made on the basis of the quality and enduring significance of the essays in question. Every volume has an introduction that places the selection made in the context of the wider literature, the historical period, the contemporary state of scholarship and the editor's particular interests.

TOM CAMPBELL
Series Editor
Centre for Applied Philosophy and Public Ethics (CAPPE)
Charles Sturt University
Canberra

Introduction

James Madison (1751–1836) was a man of singularly unimposing physical stature – a mere five feet, four inches tall in his stocking feet, and sickly to boot. But what he lacked in height and health he more than made up for in intellectual depth and vigour. In law, in political philosophy and history he could (and did) hold his own with his much taller friend and neighbour Thomas Jefferson, as well as the other eminent American Founders. Madison is today remembered as 'The Father of the American Constitution,' a title conferred posthumously by John Quincy Adams, and the sobriquet stuck and has held fast ever since. It is perhaps only a slight exaggeration to say that, without Madison, the Constitution of the United States of America might never have been drafted as it was and indeed it might not have been written – or, if written, ratified – at all. Nor would it have the Bill of Rights as its first ten amendments, drafted by Madison, proposed by the Congress in 1789 and ratified by the states in 1791. Nor would we know as much as we now do about the arguments, counterarguments and debates that went into the framing of the Constitution had Madison not kept careful and copious notes on the secret proceedings in Philadelphia during the sweltering summer of 1787. Moreover, Madison co-authored (with Alexander Hamilton and John Jay) *The Federalist*, the most complete and authoritative exposition and defence of the Constitution proposed by the Philadelphia convention in the autumn of 1787. And, as if that were not distinction enough, Madison served four terms as congressman from Virginia, as Secretary of State during the Jefferson administration, and – as his last act of conspicuous public service – two terms as President of the United States.

The present volume is concerned primarily with James Madison as a political (and particularly as a constitutional) thinker, theorist and writer – as a man of ideas more than as a man of action. Even so, the supposed dichotomy between ideas on the one hand and actions on the other – or, if you prefer, between 'theory' and 'practice' – is singularly inappropriate in Madison's case. And this is because his ideas were incorporated into the Constitution that created the institutions which have in turn shaped and channelled the course of political action in the United States from Madison's time until our own day. I begin by briefly describing Madison's career as a politician and public intellectual (as we say nowadays, although that designation seems somehow inadequate to describe Madison and his equally eminent contemporaries, including Jefferson, Adams, Hamilton and others). I next consider his contributions to political and constitutional theory, particularly in his *Federalist* essays, and most especially in the (in)famous tenth essay. This is followed by a discussion of Charles Beard's economic interpretation of the origin and meaning of the Constitution, and his critics' objections. I then discuss Madison's role in creating the prototype of the American party system. My Introduction concludes with a preview of the essays reprinted herein and a brief assessment of Madison's contributions to constitutional and political theory.

A Brief Biographical Sketch[1]

James Madison was born into a prominent family of planters in the early spring of 1751 in the British colony of Virginia. Montpelier, the Madison family plantation, grew tobacco and other crops planted and harvested by black slaves.[2] A sickly, shy and bookish boy, Madison was out of place in the cultural milieu of the rural Virginia gentry, which valued horse racing, heavy drinking, guns, gambling and girls over scholarly pursuits. Young James – always 'Jemmie' to his friends – was educated at home by personal tutors until the age of eleven, when he left to attend a local school for five years before returning to Montpelier and more home schooling. Two years later, in 1769, he enrolled in the College of New Jersey (now Princeton). There he had the extraordinary good fortune to be taught by Dr John Witherspoon, President of the college and a considerable intellect in his own right. President Witherspoon exposed young Jemmie to the ideas of Adam Smith, David Hume and other luminaries of the Scottish Enlightenment – ideas that were to have a profound and lasting impact on Madison's thinking about politics and the law, and thence on the drafting and defence of the Constitution of the United States.

Awarded the AB degree in 1771, Madison stayed on another year to pursue postgraduate studies under the personal tutelage of Dr Witherspoon, who had evidently recognized and wanted to nurture the young man's already remarkable mind and character. Returning home in 1772 Madison was at sixes and sevens, unsure of what he wanted to do with his life. He settled on a career in the law, though without much enthusiasm, until he agreed to take the case of a group of Baptist ministers who were being prosecuted by Anglican authorities for violating Virginia's laws requiring religious uniformity. Madison was incensed when they were imprisoned for following their consciences instead of (as he saw it) an unconscionable law. Although he did not know it at the time, he had acquired a loyal constituency among the growing sect of Baptists. This stood Madison in good stead when he decided to abandon the practice of law and pursue a political career as an outspoken opponent of an established church and religious tests for public office, a cause that he shared with his close friend and fellow Virginian, Thomas Jefferson.

In the mid-1770s, when revolutionary fervour filled the air of colonial Virginia, Madison's hopes of joining the local militia were dashed when he was deemed too sickly to be a soldier. His service to the revolutionary cause took a less direct and more political form, as he served on the local revolutionary committee in 1775 and a year later as a delegate to the Virginia Convention which was convened to design a new government for Virginia. It was then that Madison recognized where his real talents lay and the career for which his education had

---

1 The most comprehensive biography is Brant (1941–61). The best single-volume biography is Ketcham (1971). The best brief life is Adair (1946), reprinted as Chapter 1 in this volume.

2 Throughout his life Madison lived off the labour of slaves. He found this distasteful but he, like his friend and neighbour Thomas Jefferson, did so nonetheless. When writing *The Federalist* it fell to Madison – the only slave-owner among its three authors – to defend the proposed constitution's acceptance of slavery and its notorious three-fifths clause in particular (see *No. 54*). His co-authors, Alexander Hamilton and John Jay, were active in the anti-slavery cause and were in fact founders of the New York Society for the Manumission of Slaves. All three recognized, however, that the new constitution had no hope of adoption if it said (or even hinted at) anything against the Southern slave-holding interests or the institution of slavery itself.

prepared him. Madison's most conspicuous contribution to the Virginia Convention was to write into the new state constitution a provision that recognized freedom of religion as a fundamental and natural right.

In the following year Madison's pursuit of a political career suffered a setback when he lost his electoral bid to become a state legislator for Orange County. By all accounts Madison lost because he, unlike his opponent, had not plied his would-be constituents with enough (or indeed any) liquor – an unforgivable sin in that hard-drinking county. Happily, however, Madison was soon appointed by the legislature to serve in the governor's cabinet and, in 1779, as a delegate to the Continental Congress, where he served with distinction until 1783. After less than a year in private life Madison was again called to public service, this time as a member of the Virginia House of Delegates, the state legislature. Madison's earlier service in the Confederation Congress had convinced him that the Articles of Confederation (drafted in 1779 and ratified in 1781) were unsatisfactory and could create and maintain nothing more than a loose collection of quarrelsome and disunited states.[3] In 1786 he attended the Annapolis Convention, where he, Hamilton and others petitioned the Confederation Congress to call for a national constitutional convention to be held in Philadelphia the following year to revise the Articles of Confederation. In the event, the delegates decided to scrap the Articles and to draft an entirely new constitution.

Madison was characteristically conscientious and tireless in his preparations for the Philadelphia convention at which he served as delegate from Virginia. Before the convention he had done extensive and meticulous research on the histories of confederacies and republics, concluding that none supplied an adequate model and that a completely new kind of republic would be required for the already extensive and still-growing United States – an extensive federal republic in which a national or federal government divided and shared powers with the several states. By force of intellect, argument and hard work that nearly killed him, Madison persuaded his fellow delegates – at least those who had not left Philadelphia in a fury – to follow his plan, at any rate in rough outline, in drafting a new constitution.

Madison's views did not always prevail, however. He drafted the 'Virginia Plan' which proposed a national legislature consisting of an upper and a lower house, an executive and a judiciary. Members of the lower house would be elected directly by the people, and those of the upper house would be elected by the lower house from lists of nominees supplied by state legislatures. The membership of both bodies was to be determined by the populations of the several states: the more populous the state the more representatives it would send to Congress. Congress would in turn elect the President. Delegates from the less populous states feared that states with larger populations, such as Virginia, would dominate both houses of the legislature and would likewise have disproportionate influence in choosing the President. William Paterson countered by proposing the 'New Jersey Plan', according to which membership in a unicameral national legislature was to be divided equally among the states. The so-called 'Connecticut Compromise' or 'Great Compromise' that resulted was that membership in the lower house – the House of Representatives – was to be apportioned according to population and that of the upper body, the Senate, was to be divided equally among the several states. Every state would send two senators to the Senate. (The result of

3 For Madison's criticisms of the Articles of Confederation, see his memorandum 'Vices of the Political System of the United States' (April 1787), in Madison (1962–), vol. 9, pp. 345–58.

this less-than-great compromise is inegalitarian and undemocratic, inasmuch as the citizens of sparsely populated states such as Alaska and Wyoming are vastly overrepresented in the Senate relative to the representation of citizens in heavily populated states such as California and New York.)

When on 17 September 1787 the Constitutional Convention adjourned, Madison's Herculean labours were hardly over. Now began the strenuous and acrimonious debate over whether to ratify or reject the proposed constitution in state conventions called expressly for that purpose. Once again Madison entered the fray, this time as a Federalist (that is, pro-ratification) partisan and advocate. Madison was recruited by Hamilton to help write the series of 85 essays that became *The Federalist*. Meant mainly for audiences in New York, the pro-ratification arguments advanced in *The Federalist* also influenced a wider national audience, including Madison's native state of Virginia. So demanding and time-consuming was this writing assignment that Madison returned to Virginia exhausted and barely in time to take part in that state's ratifying convention and to prevail, against all odds and against the fiery anti-Federalist oratory of Patrick Henry. Virginia ratified the proposed constitution with a bare ten-vote majority out of 168 votes cast. The vote was even closer in New York, with 30 in favour of ratification and 27 against. Had either Virginia or New York voted against ratification, the constitution would have been as good as dead.[4] Both conventions were cliff-hangers until the very end, and the outcome the closest of close calls.

After ratification Madison had hoped to serve as senator from Virginia, but Henry, nursing the still-fresh wounds of defeat in the state ratifying convention, blocked that avenue of political advancement. Madison ran instead for the House of Representatives and, thanks largely to grateful Baptists, was elected to Congress in 1789. As a member of that body Madison drafted the constitutional amendments now known as the Bill of Rights and also served as a close advisor to President Washington. He and Hamilton became ever more estranged – Madison opposed Treasury Secretary Hamilton's scheme for a National Bank and other measures – even as he drew closer to Jefferson's Republican Party. When Jefferson became President in 1801 Madison served as his Secretary of State. Madison was elected President in 1808, succeeding Jefferson and serving two momentous terms. During the War of 1812 Washington DC was captured by British forces, the White House burned, and President Madison and his wife Dolley barely escaped capture.

Like Jefferson before him, Madison was offered, but declined, nomination for a third term. By the end of his many years in public service Montpelier was in physical and financial near-ruin. Madison spent his retirement years restoring his family plantation, giving advice to and corresponding with younger men and preparing his voluminous notes on the debates during the Constitutional Convention for publication after his death. Sickly all his life, he nonetheless outlived his healthier peers and, in 1836, was the last of the Founders to die.

[4] On the ratification debate in New York state, see Eubanks (1989) and De Pauw (1966). For Virginia, see Banning (1989). For state-by-state surveys, see Gillespie and Lienesch (1989).

Madison as Theorist: *The Federalist* [5]

Madison's most famous and conspicuous contributions to political and constitutional theory are his 29 essays in *The Federalist*, and most especially the brief but brilliant tenth essay in that series. Although *The Federalist* is imposing in its bulk – it is as long as Machiavelli's *Discourses* or Hobbes's *Leviathan* – it is not a systematic treatise on political theory. It is instead a collection of 85 newspaper editorials written at white-hot speed over a seven-month period (October 1787– May 1788) in defence of the newly drafted United States Constitution. Writing under the pseudonym 'Publius', its three authors hoped to persuade the citizens of New York State to ratify the proposed constitution. What was at first intended to be an ephemeral *pièce d'occasion* turned out to be America's most distinguished contribution to constitutional and political theory.

Had there been no *Federalist*, our understanding of the Constitution would today be greatly diminished. For the Constitution is a notoriously terse document, devoid of argument or explanation. *The Federalist* gives us a window into the minds of the Founders. As Madison remarked, *The Federalist* provides 'the most authentic exposition of the text of the Federal Constitution, as understood by the Body which prepared and the authority which accepted it'.[6] It explains why they found the Articles of Confederation unsatisfactory; why they sought to separate the powers of the several branches of the government; why they subdivided the national legislature into two houses; why they believed a federal court of final appeal to be both desirable and necessary; why they outlawed titles of nobility; why they believed a bill of rights to be an unnecessary addition – and why many other prescriptions and proscriptions were written into the Constitution or omitted entirely. As a contribution to the ratification debate, *The Federalist* is an extended exercise in exposition, explanation and political persuasion.

Although Hamilton designed *The Federalist* series and contributed the lion's share of the essays – 51 of 85 – Madison wrote some of the most memorable and important ones, including the justly famed *Federalist 10*. Madison's task, as he saw it, was to preserve and promote the liberty afforded by popular government while staving off majoritarian tyranny. He regarded himself as a thoroughgoing republican. And yet, contrary to classical republicanism's reliance on civic virtue to counter corruption and preserve liberty, Madison believed that individual virtue is a weak reed, not to be relied upon for very long, if at all.[7] Here he followed David Hume's advice to anyone who would draft a constitution:

> Political writers have established it as a maxim, that, in contriving any system of government, and fixing the several checks and controuls of the constitution, every man ought to be supposed a *knave*, and to have no other end, in all his actions, than private interest. By this interest we must govern him, and, by means of it, make him, notwithstanding his insatiable avarice and ambition, co-operate to public good. (Hume [1758] 1985, p. 42)

---

5 The literature on Madison as political theorist is enormous, and growing apace. See, *inter alia*, the following: Banning (1995) is a superb study of Madison's evolution as a political theorist; Matthews (1995) paints a darker picture of the thinker, the man and his motives. See further the superb study by Nedelsky (1990) and the insightful essays in Kernell (2003).

6 Madison to Jefferson, 8 February 1825, in Madison (1910), vol. IX, p. 218.

7 On this point Madison later changed his mind, maintaining that individual virtue is necessary but not sufficient to secure liberty and prevent corruption. See Banning (1988).

Or, to put Hume's (and Madison's) point in a more modern idiom: when writing a constitution it is prudent and wise to imagine a 'worst-case scenario' – that is, begin by assuming that men are not virtuous and public-spirited but, on the contrary, corrupt, ambitious, avaricious and self-interested; then design a system that will pit the interests of individuals, factions and government departments against one another. 'This policy of supplying by opposite and rival interests, the defect of better motives' informs and undergirds the new constitution (*Federalist 51*, p. 252).[8] As Madison elaborated:

> Ambition must be made to counteract ambition. The interest of the man must be connected with the constitutional rights of the place [that is, office or department]. It may be a reflection on human nature, that such devices should be necessary to controul the abuses of government. But what is government itself but the greatest of all reflections on human nature? If men were angels, no government would be necessary. If angels were to govern men, neither external nor internal controuls on government would be necessary. In framing a government which is to be administered by men over men, the great difficulty lies in this: You must first enable the government to controul the governed; and in the next place, oblige it to controul itself. (*Federalist*, p. 252).

The government to be created by the new Constitution would not, indeed could not, run on the high-octane fuel of civic virtue but on the low-octane fuel of factional and individual interest.

Madison begins *Federalist 10* conventionally enough by decrying the evils of 'faction', which he defines as 'a number of citizens, whether amounting to a majority or minority of the whole, who are united and actuated by some common impulse of passion, or of interest, adverse to the rights or other citizens, or to the permanent and aggregate interests of the community' (p. 41). A defining feature of any faction is its selfish character – that is, its members' willingness to pursue their own narrow interests to the detriment of others or, indeed, the public interest. A good constitution would 'break and control the violence of faction' (p. 40). This can be achieved in either of two ways. The first would be to eradicate factions by eliminating their causes; the second would be to allow factions to flourish and proliferate but to control their effects. The first remedy would be both draconian and impracticable, and would run counter to human nature, since 'the seeds of faction are ... sown in the nature of man' (p. 41). Men who own little or no property are naturally envious of those who own more. Thus the first solution would require the equal division of property – since envy is a primary source of faction – and the elimination of 'liberty, [which] is to faction what air is to fire, an aliment [that is, nutrient] without which it instantly expires'. But this, says Madison, would be 'folly,' for the 'remedy [would be] worse than the disease' (p. 41). The only reliable cure is to control the *effects* of faction. This is a remedy that democracy cannot supply and that only an *extended* republic can provide.

Madison drew a sharp – and controversial[9] – distinction between a democracy and a republic. A democracy, as Madison defines it, is what we would nowadays call participatory or direct democracy. Such a system requires rule by citizens who assemble periodically and in

8 Page references in parentheses refer to Hamilton, Madison and Jay (2003).

9 John Adams, for one, curtly dismissed the distinction between 'republic' and 'democracy': 'Mr. Madison's ... distinction between a republic and a democracy, cannot be justified. A democracy is really a republic as an oak is a tree, or a temple a building.' Quoted in Stourzh (1970), p. 55. Jefferson later

person to debate and deliberate about matters of common concern. When a vote is taken, the majority carries the day. A majority *can* be, but does not *have* to be, a faction. (The kinds of extraordinary majorities required to override presidential vetoes or to amend the Constitution presumably would not be factions in Madison's sense, because such majorities must reach out to and accommodate other interests. It is in this light that we must understand Madison's defence of an 'extended republic' in *Federalist 10* and the 'auxiliary precautions' against factious majorities in *Federalist 51*. Both are meant to block majority factions, without preventing legitimate – that is, non-factious – majorities from forming and ruling. This also has implications, as we shall see shortly, for his view of the role and function of political parties.) The most dangerous faction of all would be 'a majority ... of the whole, ... united by some common impulse or passion, or of interest, adverse to the rights of other citizens, or to the permanent and aggregate interests of the community' (*Federalist 10*, p. 41). The new Constitution was designed to prevent such a majoritarian faction from coming into existence in the first place. In any society the numerically largest faction will be made up of the poor and propertyless who, in a pure and unalloyed democracy, will rule in their own interest and to the detriment and disadvantage of an affluent minority. Far from promoting the interests of the public at large – as a non-factious majority would do – democracy promotes the interests of the largest faction. As a practical matter, moreover, democracy can operate only in a restricted territory containing a relatively small number of inhabitants – a description that most definitely did not fit the United States in the late eighteenth century.

By contrast, a republic, as Madison (re)defines it, is characterized by two key features. The first is its system of representation; the second is its enlarged extent. The former filters and refines the views of those whose interests are represented. The latter makes it impossible for citizens to assemble in person; they must instead turn to the former and elect representatives to speak and act on their behalf, and presumably in their interest. A large republic would take in a wide variety of interests, thus encouraging the proliferation of factions and reducing the likelihood that any single faction will predominate. To use the language of a later essay, 'the society itself will be broken into so many parts, interests and classes of citizens, that the rights of individuals or of the minority, will be in little danger from interested combinations of the majority' (*Federalist 51*, p. 254). By this Madison means that a potentially united and tyrannical majority will be subdivided into many smaller factions – regional (north versus south, east versus west, seaboard versus interior, rural versus urban, etc.), economic (skilled versus unskilled workers, affluent versus poor, etc.), and so on – which will in turn defuse the danger of majority tyranny.

A large or extended republic also has the added advantage of enlarging the pool of 'fit characters' from which representatives are to be chosen. And, by distancing representatives from direct influence by their constituents, a large republic would encourage representatives to develop an enlarged sensibility and to 'distill' and 'refine' their view of what the public interest is, and requires (*Federalist 10*, p. 44). It will also preclude the pursuit of such 'wicked and improper projects' as 'a rage for paper money, for an abolition of debts, for an equal division of property' (p. 46) – in other words, policies that would favour the interests of the poor majority over those of the wealthy minority. The system created by the Constitution

---

joined Adams in denying the validity of Madison's distinction: see Jefferson to John Taylor, 28 May 1816 in Jefferson (1999), p. 207. See further Hanson (1988).

would allegedly serve the public interest by protecting the property of the few from the predations of the many, and the many from themselves.

The Beard Thesis and its Critics

It was this ostensibly elitist and undemocratic conclusion that later led the Progressive muck-raking historian Charles Beard to read Madison's *Federalist 10* as a decoding device with whose aid we can expose the Constitution for the brazen sham that it is (see Chapter 4 in this volume). The 'real' reason that the Constitution was written and ratified was to protect the property interests of the rich. The evidence for this conclusion, Beard believed, had been hiding in plain sight for more than a century, in *Federalist 10*. In that essay (on Beard's reading) Madison sympathizes and sides with the wealthy. No surprise there, says Beard, since Madison, along with the other Founders, was himself a wealthy man. His wealth derived from land; the wealth of the others from banking, commerce and other capitalist enterprises. The Founders did not check their interests at the door of the constitutional convention. On the contrary, they brought these interests inside and drafted a document that would protect them and their heirs in perpetuity.

Beard's is a bold and challenging – and still-controversial – interpretation of the Framers' intent. But he gives the credit to Madison, who in *Federalist 10* formulated and articulated 'a masterly statement of the theory of economic determinism in politics' (Beard, 1913, p. 15). More than half a century before Karl Marx ever wrote a word, Madison had understood and underscored 'the economic basis of politics' (Beard, 1922). Politics is first and foremost about the protection and promotion of economic interests. The wealthy will support politicians who protect and promote their interests; workers will similarly attempt to protect and promote theirs. The problem, in Beard's view, is that the deck is constitutionally stacked against the working class. In a majoritarian democracy their interests would be represented, respected and protected; but that is not the kind of system that Madison and the Framers created with the Constitution. On the contrary, a politically unified and united working class is constitutionally precluded.

Beard was hardly alone in his harsh judgement. In his synoptic survey of American letters Vernon L. Parrington was highly critical of Madison's 'aristocratic' and 'antidemocratic' tendencies, as embodied in the United States Constitution and defended at length in *The Federalist*. The various *Federalist* papers, he contends, constitute a dreary compendium of anti-democratic thought. Following Beard, Parrington singles out *Federalist 10* as revealing the anti-democratic leanings of the Founders: 'the remarkable tenth number ... compresses within a few pages pretty much the whole Federalist theory of political science' (Parrington 1927, vol. I, p. 290).

Much has been written in criticism and defence of Beard's (in)famous economic interpretation of the Constitution. Once widely accepted as an authoritative account of the origins and import of the Constitution, the Beard thesis nowadays has a diminishing number of defenders[10] and a legion of critics (see, *inter alia*, Brown, 1956; Adair, 1974). Robert E.

[10] Many of Beard's modern-day defenders belong to the 'rational choice' school of political analysis which holds that self-interest motivates all rational actors; and since the Founders were rational they 'must' have been so motivated. See, for example, McGuire (2003).

Brown, for one, challenges the factual bases of Beard's interpretation, showing (for example) how he used questionable criteria in assessing and measuring the wealth of the members of the Constitutional Convention. Douglass Adair takes a rather different approach, criticizing Beard for ignoring the intellectual milieu of the Founders and for reading his Progressive preoccupation with ruthless robber-barons back into late eighteenth-century politics, and the politics of the drafting and ratification of the Constitution in particular.

If we are to understand Madison's thinking we must think as he thought, using the concepts and categories available to him. One of the most important of these, according to Adair, was *fame* – not in the sense of celebrity, but of an enduring reputation that is the closest thing to immortality to which humans can aspire. In the classical republican tradition the greatest and most enduring fame is accorded to founders of long-lived, peaceful and harmonious republics (Adair, 1974, ch. 1). Sir Francis Bacon's essay 'Of Honour and Reputation' (1625) constructs a hierarchy of honour and merit that accords 'first place [to] founders of states and commonwealths' (Bacon, 1955, p. 137). In so doing he merely restates a Renaissance and classical commonplace that connected lasting fame to the act of founding. Madison, Adams, Franklin and others in America's founding generation spoke unblushingly of 'the spur of fame', and in *Federalist 72* Hamilton wrote of 'the love of fame [which is] the ruling passion of the noblest minds' (p. 353). And from Aristotle and Cicero we learn that the noblest minds will not be motivated by monetary gain but by a love of honour and fame. A desire for fame motivated many (but by no means all) members of the founding generation to risk all in the Revolution and then to work so hard (Madison at grave cost to his health and even to the extent of endangering his life, as well as the wrack and ruin of Montpelier) to secure the gains of the Revolution by means of an ingenious Constitution. In short, Madison was not in it for the money but for the sort of lasting fame reserved for founders of long-lived republics.

Beard's hard-headed 'realism' and his muck-raking strategy of 'following the dollar' made him utterly deaf to the discourse of classical republicanism and especially its emphasis on fame and founding. He took no notice whatever, for example, of the significance of the ancient Greek and Roman pseudonyms adopted by Federalists and anti-Federalists alike during the debate over ratification. These included 'Solon', 'Phocion', 'Agrippa', 'Brutus', 'Cato' and – not least – 'Publius', which Hamilton took from the legendary Roman consul Publius Valerius, a founder and hero of the early Roman republic.[11] Madison and his co-authors rightly regarded themselves as founders no less illustrious than Publius, and believed that the glory of the American republic might one day rival Rome's.

Adair gives great credit to Beard for showing that many members of the revolutionary and founding generation were avaricious and less concerned with fame than with financial gain. Not so Madison, along with Hamilton, Adams, Jefferson, Washington and others. Fame, not gain, was their spur. Strange as it might seem, then, those of us now living participated as ghostly presences in the founding, for we constitute the posterity that the Founders aimed to impress by their labours. They live still in our memory and our veneration. Douglass Adair puts the point nicely: 'you and I, unborn in 1787, nevertheless played our part even then as an invisible audience that spurred some of the Fathers to nobility and political greatness' (Adair 1974, p. 34).

---

[11] Hamilton's source was probably Plutarch's chapter on 'Poplicola' (Publius Valerius) in his *Lives of the Noble Grecians and Romans* ([1683]; n.d.), pp. 117–30).

From Faction to Party

In his *Federalist* essays Madison uses the terms 'party' and 'faction' interchangeably, as when he writes of 'the most numerous party, or, in other words the most powerful faction' (*Federalist 10*, p. 42). The republic envisioned in his constitution was one in which factions and parties proliferated and prevented one another from gaining more than a modicum of power.[12] What Madison evidently did *not* foresee in the late 1780s was a *party system* in which various interests came together and were gathered under the aegis of stable and long-lived political parties. In the early 1790s, however, he began to think – and to act – in precisely these terms.

As he began to envision such a system Madison made three important moves. First, he effectively repudiated the equation of 'party' and 'faction' to which he had subscribed some five years earlier in his *Federalist* essays. In Madison's hands, party shed its negative associations and became instead a more or less neutral term for designating opposing political groups. Henceforth, it was not the term party *per se* that carries a negative (or positive) connotation, but the adjective specifying the *kind* of party to which one is referring. Second, Madison revised and rewrote the history of parties by periodizing that history in a novel way. Finally, and significantly, Madison came to refer to his own political association as a party. Let's look briefly at each of these argumentative moves.

'In every political society,' writes Madison in 'Parties' (1792), 'parties are unavoidable. A difference of interests, real or supposed, is the most natural and fruitful source of them'. Parties may be either 'natural' ones 'aris[ing] out of the nature of things', or 'artificial' ones resting upon unnatural divisions among men. Madison makes it clear that this is precisely the distinction to be drawn between his and Jefferson's party – 'the Republican party, as it may be termed' – and Hamilton's 'anti Republican party' (Madison 1962–, vol. 14, pp. 197–8).

Working with this new and non-pejorative understanding of 'party,' Madison in 'A Candid State of Parties' (1792) periodizes the political history of America in a novel fashion. 'The most interesting state of parties in the United States may', Madison says, 'be referred to three periods.' From 1776 to 1783, 'those who espoused the cause of independence and those who adhered to the British claims, formed the parties of the first period; *if, indeed, the disaffected class were considerable* [that is, numerous and important] *enough to deserve the name of a party*.' That is to say, the American revolutionaries constituted a party – a significant concession, and certainly one that neither Madison nor most of his contemporaries would have made several years earlier. 'From 1783 to 1787', he continues, 'there were parties in abundance, but being rather local than general, they are not within the present review.' The second significant period occurred in 1787– 88, the years of the ratification debate, which saw the contest between two new 'parties, the Federalists and the Antifederalists'. Now that this contest has been decided in favour of the former, these parties no longer exist. The third period, he says, began almost immediately after ratification when Hamilton's Federalist party began to be opposed by 'the Republican party' of Madison and Jefferson. Unlike earlier, short-lived divisions, the division between 'the anti Republican party, as it may be called' and 'the Republican party', he observes with wry understatement, 'is likely to be of some duration'

[12] This vision of power divided and subdivided into more or less distinct and competing 'interest groups' that modern political scientists call 'pluralism' or sometimes 'pluralist democracy'. See Dahl (1982).

(Madison 1962–, vol. 14, pp. 371–2). Note that Madison does not flinch from speaking of 'the Republican party', which he never once calls a faction. Nor, even more significantly, does he refer to Hamilton's 'anti Republican party' as a faction. Madison thus implicitly places both parties on a par – quarrelsome, contentious, but equal and animated by principle. In Madison's hands, party loses its older – and distinctly pejorative – connection with faction and becomes a legitimate form of political association and affiliation.[13]

This, however, is not as radical a break as it might first appear, if we recall Madison's view that a key defining feature of factions is their narrowly selfish character. A political party, being a broad coalition of various interests, is not narrowly selfish and is therefore not a faction, at least in Madison's meaning of the term. Thus did Madison in word and deed reconstitute the concept of party. In his parlance party became a relatively long-lived political organization devoted to furthering its members' aims and principles in peaceful and law-abiding opposition to other parties. And this, surely, is a conceptual innovation and a theoretical and practical shift of no small importance. Besides being the 'father of the constitution', then, Madison was the father of the prototype of the American party system as well. The two American political parties of Madison's day were based on elite competition rather than mass mobilization (the latter being typical of today's political parties). Not until the Jacksonian era do we witness the emergence of parties of the latter sort.

The Essays

The foregoing sketch – and it is only that – has, I hope, sufficed to suggest something of the depth, breadth and range of Madison's political and constitutional theorizing. Not surprisingly, much has been written about the man and his ideas and achievements. A collection of the best scholarly literature on Madison would fill many volumes. Here, however, I am required to fill only one. So I have been forced to be exceedingly stringent in selecting some of the very best of the best scholarly literature. Had I space to do so, I would have added selections by Samuel Kernell (2003), Jennifer Nedelsky (1990), Jack Rakove (1996), Lance Banning (1995), Michael Zuckert (1987) and other eminent Madison scholars. Here I shall have to be content with commending their splendid studies to the interested reader.

The lone essay comprising Part I is Douglass Adair's 'James Madison' (Chapter 1), a compact and delightfully readable biographical portrait of Madison that emphasizes his education and the ideas and ideals that animated his thinking and acting.

The essays in Part II deal with Madison's belief that there is a fairly fixed and stable human nature that would-be founders ignore at their great and grave peril. In Chapter 2 Robert J. Morgan examines the close connection between political authority and human nature as Madison conceives of it. Joseph F. Kobylka and Bradley Kent Carter (Chapter 3) offer a

---

[13] The extent to which the distinction between party and faction was now clearly and definitively drawn was dramatically underscored by Jefferson's fury at Hamilton for 'daring to call the republican party *a faction*'. See Jefferson to Madison, 29 June 1792, in Madison (1962–), vol. 14, p. 333. Jefferson, however, had no qualms about continuing to call Hamilton's Federalist Party a 'faction', and worse ('cabal' and so on). For a close and careful account of Madison's and Jefferson's sometimes-contrasting views of party, see Hofstadter (1970).

somewhat different, but complementary, exploration of Madison's conception of human nature and its implications for designing legal and political institutions.

The essays in Part III are concerned with Madison's most famous contribution to *The Federalist*, namely the tenth paper in that series. Charles A. Beard was the first scholar to attend closely (and critically, albeit appreciatively) to *Federalist 10*, the meaning and significance of which he interpreted, influentially but controversially, in 'economic' terms (Chapter 4). In Chapters 5 and 6 (actually a two-part article) Douglass Adair takes exception to Beard's interpretation which, he contends, ignores the *ideas* and the thinkers that motivated Madison in drafting his design for the United States Constitution. Adair asserts that Madison's arguments in defence of a large republic are almost certainly drawn from several of David Hume's political essays in his *Essays, Moral, Political, and Literary* (1758). Edmund S. Morgan argues that Adair has exaggerated Madison's intellectual debt to Hume and that Madison's design for an extended republic does not correspond at all possible points to Hume's 'Idea of a Perfect Commonwealth' (Chapter 7). In Chapter 8 Alan Gibson critically assesses and analyses the strengths and shortcomings of three approaches to interpreting *Federalist 10* – the Progressive (or quasi-Marxian) class-struggle interpretation advanced by Beard, the pluralist approach advocated by Robert Dahl and other political scientists, and the republican perspective adopted by Gordon Wood and other historians.

The essays in Part IV address the question of whether Madison was a 'republican' or a 'democrat'. Madison had (in)famously drawn a sharp distinction between the two in the tenth *Federalist*, and commentators have asked ever since whether this is a distinction with or without a difference (John Adams, for one, opting for the latter) and whether Madison was (as he claimed) a republican or (as Dahl and Diamond claim) a closet democrat. Neal Riemer weighs in by delineating the distinctively 'republican' features of Madison's political views (Chapter 9). Martin Diamond, by contrast, contends that Madison and the Founders were, for all practical purposes, democrats who appreciated democracy but also understood democracy's dangers and wisely legislated against its excesses (Chapter 10). In Chapter 11 Alan Gibson criticizes Diamond's interpretation as anachronistic and unduly narrow. In a formal reconstruction of the tenets of 'Madisonian democracy' Robert A. Dahl maintains that Madison, despite his protestations to the contrary, was a democrat of a rather narrow and restrictive stripe (Chapter 12). In Chapter 13, written half a century later, Dahl questions, criticizes and modifies his original thesis, adding that he is now both more admiring and more critical of Madison than he was originally.

The single essay by Jean Yarbrough in Part V (Chapter 14) addresses one of the most important and original contributions made by Madison and the other Founders to the theory and practice of modern governance: their idea of a 'federal' government in which power is divided and shared between the central government and the several states. She contends that the view of federalism that emerged from the constitutional convention was a hybrid born of compromise that differs in significant ways from modern understandings of federalism.

The essays in Part VI deal with Madison's conception of rights, and with his Bill of Rights in particular. The issue of rights was of pressing political importance since the proposed Constitution was ratified by several states on the condition that a bill of rights be added as soon as possible. The Bill of Rights – the first ten amendments to the new Constitution, drafted by Madison and adopted in 1791 – explicitly enumerated the rights to freedom of speech, press, assembly, and other protections. In Chapter 15 Jack N. Rakove sketches Madison's conception of rights and shows how it applied to the bill of rights he proposed. Taking a decidedly darker view of the matter, Paul Finkelman argues that Madison's 'paternity' of the Bill of Rights was at best 'reluctant', inasmuch as he had strong reservations about adding a list of enumerated rights to the new Constitution (Chapter 16).

Part VII deals with a matter particularly close to Madison's heart, from youth to old age – religious freedom and toleration. The clear and strong separation of church and state, as Irving Brant shows in Chapter 17, was Madison's lifelong passion and animated much of his political thinking in other spheres as well.

The essays in Part VIII deal with Madison's 'two systems'. The first was his view, advanced in *Federalist 10* and elsewhere, that 'party' and 'faction' are interchangeable terms and that either or both should proliferate and provide countervailing power within a constitutional republic. John Zvesper shows in Chapter 18 that Madison changed his mind in a most important way when he envisioned an alternative party system in which not short-lived factions but long-lived parties predominated. Building upon Zvesper's insight, Douglas W. Jaenicke shows how profound a perspectival shift this was (Chapter 19).

Finally, Part IX addresses the question of constitutional interpretation. Once it had been ratified and accepted as the law of the land, the Constitution awaited interpretation as to its meaning in particular instances and cases. One influential school of interpretation holds that the Constitution's meaning must be settled by appeals mainly or even exclusively to the Founders' intentions. Another holds that the United States Constitution is a living and evolving constitution and that appeals to its 'spirit' should trump (at least some) outdated original intentions of the Founders. In Chapter 20 Terence Ball assesses the arguments for and against an 'originalist' strategy of interpretation, and comes down decisively against originalism, citing none other than the Father of the Constitution himself as final arbiter and authority.

Conclusion

The essays reprinted in this volume assay only part of the range and richness of Madison's political and constitutional theorizing. But even to scratch the surface marks a beginning. If reading these essays prompts readers to further explore the scholarly literature – or, even better, to read Madison's works for themselves – it will have achieved its purpose. Although Madison's influence on legal theory and practice has been especially evident in the United States, it has also had some impact on legal thought and action abroad. Yet he was not, as some have claimed, a colossus – a modern Lycurgus or Solon – since he was hardly alone in drafting and defending the Constitution of the United States. He had help from his 'founding brothers' (Ellis, 2000). But within that eminent band of brothers Madison was arguably the first among equals.

References

Adair, Douglass (1974), *Fame and the Founding Fathers*, New York: W.W. Norton.

Bacon, Sir Francis (1955), 'Of Honour and Reputation', in Hugh G. Dick (ed.), *Selected Writings of Francis Bacon*, New York: Modern Library.

Ball, Terence and J.G.A. Pocock (eds) (1988), *Conceptual Change and the Constitution of the United States*, Lawrence, KS: University Press of Kansas.

Banning, Lance (1988), 'Some Second Thoughts on Virtue and the Course of Revolutionary Thinking', in Terence Ball and J.G.A. Pocock (eds), *Conceptual Change and the Constitution*, Lawrence, KS: University Press of Kansas, pp. 194–212

Banning, Lance (1989), 'Virginia: Sectionalism and the General Good', in Michael Allen Gillespie and Michael Lienesch (eds), *Ratifying the Constitution*, Lawrence, KS: University Press of Kansas, pp. 261– 99.

Banning, Lance (1995), *The Sacred Fire of Liberty: James Madison and the Founding of the Federal Republic*, Ithaca NY: Cornell University Press.

Beard, Charles A. (1913), *An Economic Interpretation of the Constitution of the United States*, New York: Macmillan.

Beard, Charles A. (1922), *The Economic Basis of Politics*, New York: Knopf.

Brant, Irving (1941–61), *James Madison*, 6 vols, Indianapolis, IN: Bobbs-Merrill.

Brown, Robert E. (1956), *Charles Beard and the Constitution: A Critical Analysis of 'An Economic Interpretation of the Constitution'*, Princeton, NJ: Princeton University Press.

Dahl, Robert A. (1982), *Dilemmas of Pluralist Democracy*, New Haven, CT: Yale University Press.

De Pauw, Linda Grant (1966), *The Eleventh Pillar: New York State and the Federal Constitution*, Ithaca NY: Cornell University Press.

Ellis, Joseph J. (2000), *Founding Brothers: The Revolutionary Generation*, New York: Knopf.

Eubanks, Cecil L. (1989), 'New York: Federalism and the Political Economy of Union', in Michael Allen Gillespie and Michael Lienesch (eds), *Ratifying the Constitution*, Lawrence, KS: University Press of Kansas, pp. 300–40.

Gillespie, Michael Allen and Lienesch Michael (eds) (1989), *Ratifying the Constitution*, Lawrence, KS: University Press of Kansas.

Hamilton, Alexander, Madison, James and Jay, John (2003), *The Federalist*, ed. Terence Ball, Cambridge: Cambridge University Press.

Hanson, Russell L. (1988), '"Commons" and "Commonwealth" at the American Founding: Democratic Republicanism as the New American Hybrid,' in Terence Ball and J.G.A. Pocock (eds), *Conceptual Change and the Constitution of the United States*, Lawrence, KS: University Press of Kansas.

Hofstadter, Richard (1970), *The Idea of a Party System*, Berkeley and Los Angeles CA: University of California Press.

Hume, David ([1758] 1985), *Essays, Moral, Political, and Literary*, Indianapolis IN: Liberty Fund.

Jefferson, Thomas (1999), *Jefferson: Political Writings*, eds. Joyce Appleby and Terence Ball, Cambridge: Cambridge University Press.

Kernell, Samuel (ed.) (2003), *James Madison: The Theory and Practice of Republican Government*, Stanford, CA: Stanford University Press.

Ketcham, Ralph (1971), *James Madison*, New York: Macmillan.

McGuire, Robert A. (2003), *To Form a More Perfect Union: A New Economic Interpretation of the Constitution of the United States*, Oxford and New York: Oxford University Press.

Madison, James (1910), *Writings of James Madison*, 9 vols, ed. Gaillard Hunt, New York: G.P. Putnam's Sons.

Madison, James (1962–), *Papers of James Madison*, ed. William T. Hutchinson, Robert Allen Rutland and William M.E. Rachal, 17 vols to date, Chicago IL: University of Chicago Press; and Charlottesville VA: University of Virginia Press.

Matthews, Richard K. (1995), *If Men Were Angels: James Madison and the Heartless Empire of Reason*, Lawrence KS: University Press of Kansas.

Nedelsky, Jennifer (1990), *Private Property and the Limits of American Constitutionalism*, Chicago IL: University of Chicago Press.

Parrington, Vernon L. (1927), *Main Currents of American Thought*, 3 vols, New York: Harcourt Brace & World.

Plutarch ([1683] n.d.), *Lives of the Nobel Grecians and Romans*, trans. John Dryden, New York : Modern Library

Rakove, Jack N. (1996), *Original Meanings: Politics and Ideas in the Making of the Constitution*, New York: Knopf.

Stourzh, Gerald (1970), *Alexander Hamilton and the Idea of Republican Government*, Stanford, CA: Stanford University Press.

Zuckert, Michael P. (1987), 'A System Without Precedent: Federalism in the American Constitution', in Leonard W. Levy and Dennis J. Mahoney (eds), *The Framing and Ratification of the Constitution*, New York: Macmillan.

Part I
Life and Times

[1]

James Madison [1751-1836]

BY DOUGLASS ADAIR

EVERY college tends to bask in the reflected glory of its famous alumni; alma mater naturally likes to hint that she is in large part responsible for the successful careers of her most illustrious sons. Yet any college which parades its distinguished graduates as proof that it is a nursery of genius lays itself open to a jibe made long ago by Adam Smith. That learned Scot complained in 1776 that educational institutions were always taking undeserved credit for the development of the talents of their students; a young man who starts his higher education "at seventeen or eighteen, and returns home at one and twenty, returns three or four years older . . . and at that age it is very difficult not to improve a good deal in three or four years."

It is safe to say, though, that for eighteen-year-old James Madison, junior, who entered Princeton six years before Smith made his cynical remark, the undergraduate years laid the foundation he was to build on all his days. And since James Madison became one of the chief architects of our political democracy, the "Father of the American Constitution," and President of our nation during its formative stage, his sojourn at Nassau Hall under the tutelage of the learned Dr. John Witherspoon was of incalculable importance to the destiny of the United States.

James Madison, junior, born March 5 (O.S.), 1751, was the oldest child of the leading family of Orange County, Virginia. His ancestors, planters in both the paternal and maternal lines, ranked, by his own description, "among the respectable though not the most opulent Class" of Virginia society. Orange County lies in the Piedmont between the fall-line and the Blue Ridge. The chief families of this region, the Madisons and the Jeffersons, while a little less wealthy and aristocratic than the great Tidewater families, demanded, and were accorded, the deference due to members of an established ruling class. The Madisons' wealth and political power were solidly based. James Madison, senior, was a justice of the peace and a vestryman in the

Anglican church—offices held only by men of ranking social position; he owned more than a hundred slaves, and the cultivated portion of the Montpelier plantation alone amounted to nearly two thousand acres. At birth, James junior entered a station of life that provided him with the values and opportunities esteemed most desirable by current Virginia standards.

Besides inherited wealth and position he had an advantage far more important—a first-rate brain. Although neither his father, nor his brothers, nor any other members of his immediate family or their descendants ever exhibited any particular intellectual distinction, James junior, through the mysterious alchemy of the genes, was endowed with a capacity for extraordinary intellectual accomplishment. Writing his autobiography at the age of eighty, he recorded as the first important incident of his life his intellectual delight in the discovery of *The Spectator*. He was then eleven years old. The memory of the profound impact of that literary classic led him to argue, seventy years later, that from "his own experience" it was a book "peculiarly adapted to inculcate just sentiments, an appetite for knowledge, and a taste for the improvement of the mind and manners." Madison, of course, put the cart before the horse. His natural "appetite for knowledge" was the cause of his excitement over *The Spectator*, not an effect of it.

Madison's failure to become conscious until he was nearly twelve of his own "taste" for mental improvement reveals the somewhat restricted intellectual opportunities available even to a member of the Virginia aristocracy in the eighteenth century. Though born for "the intellectual pleasures of the closet," Madison grew up in an open-air society where guns and horses, dogs and stirrup-cups were treated as far more important adjuncts of life than books. It was a gracious way of living but it was also profoundly frustrating for the development of the mind and spirit. A description of colonial Virginia by George Tucker, which was read and approved by Madison himself, speaks of the gentry as generally "open handed and open hearted; fond of society, indulging in all its pleasures, and practicing all its courtesies. But these social virtues also occasionally ran into the kindred vices of love of show, haughtiness, sensuality—and many of the wealthier class were to be seen seeking relief from the vacuity of idleness not merely in the allowable pleasures of the chase and the turf, but in the debasing ones of cock-fighting, gaming, and drinking. Literature was neglected, or cultivated, by the small number . . . rather as an accomplishment and mark of distinction than for the substantial benefits it confers." When existence is as easy and pleasant as it was for the first gentlemen in the Old Dominion there can be little of the discipline necessary for sustained creative thought; the mind of upper-class Virginia, like that of most aristocracies, was marked by dilettantism and philistinism. The pleasant tyranny of social life with its endless rounds of dinners, barbecues, fish-frys, and riding parties could only be resisted by a major effort of the will; and even among the best minds of Virginia there were few who succeeded in emancipating themselves. Add to these distractions the provincial nature of life on the scattered country-seats, the lack of scholarly companionship to provide what Madison termed "mutual emulation and mutual inspection," and it is understandable why Virginia's colonial culture was relatively so barren of intellectual accomplishment. An individual like young James Madison could only begin to realize his own potentialities after he was exposed to ideas and scholarly habits alien to the complacency of his native state.

Madison's initiation into the larger world of ideas occurred in 1762 when he entered the school established in King and Queen County by Donald Robertson, who had emigrated to Virginia from Scotland some ten years earlier. Madison describes Robertson as "a man of extensive learning and a distinguished Teacher." Under his direction for five years the young Virginian "studied the Latin and Greek languages, was taught to read but not speak French, and besides Arithmetic & Geography, made some progress in Algebra & Geometry. Miscellaneous literature was also embraced by the plan of the School." Within this comprehensive curriculum, Robertson's standards of performance were strict; but Madison's affectionate references to his teacher in later life show that this introduction to learning was viewed as an adventure rather than a task. Here, in the Scotch classicist's library, the first of any scope to which young Madison had access, he began to discover for himself the resources hidden in books.

In 1767 the boy left Robertson's school to study under a new teacher, the Reverend Thomas Martin of New Jersey, who had become rector of the Brick Church in Orange County. Since there were now four Madison children of school age, Mr. Martin agreed to live at Montpelier and supervise their lessons. Under this arrangement the young minister tutored James for two years. Martin had been graduated from Princeton in the class of 1764. His praise of Nassau Hall influenced the Madisons to select it as the place to which James should go for his higher education. Their choice was also determined by the reputation Princeton was rapidly acquiring under its new president, the famous Dr. Witherspoon, as the most progressive college in America.

2

When James Madison rode north to Princeton in the summer of 1769, a vastly important chapter of his life began. He set out, an eager intelligent boy, with no clear idea of what calling he would follow or where his talents would lead him. He returned home some three years later with his A.B. degree, a mature young man who had fully developed the rigorous habits of thought that were to mark him always, and to make him the most scholarly of American statesmen. At Princeton, the direction of his thinking was finally set; his mind henceforward would be continually preoccupied with the analysis and understanding of society and of principles of government. The Princeton years helped also to determine the goals of his thought, and to crystallize the standards and values that were to govern his political theorizing. At Nassau Hall he was immersed in the liberalism of the Enlightenment, and converted to eighteenth-century political radicalism. From then on James Madison's theories would advance the rights and happiness of man, and his most active efforts would serve devotedly the cause of civil and political liberty.

The twenty-three-year-old college at Princeton which Madison entered in 1769 was dominated by its new president, Dr. Witherspoon. This learned cleric, who lived in a perpetual storm center of ecclesiastical and political controversy, was a vigorous rather than a profound thinker, markedly dogmatic in questions of politics, religion, and philosophy, but always dramatic and provocative in his dogmatism. His reputation as a great teacher rests on the testimony of a whole generation of undergraduates whose mental life was aroused and guided by contact with him. In the case of eighteen-year-old James Madison, Witherspoon fully satisfied the need that most young men have in their formative years for a friend and confidant in whom they feel both wisdom and authority. Stimulated by Witherspoon's aggressive intellect, Madison's own mind bloomed. His joyous kindling to the new ideas and the scholarly discipline offered him at Princeton led the Virginian to carry double the normal load of classes, finishing the required four-year course in a little over two years. This necessitated, as Madison reports in his autobiography, "an indiscreet experiment of the minimum of sleep and the maximum of application which the constitution would bear. The former was reduced for some weeks to less than five hours in the twenty-four."

Madison was awarded his A.B. degree in the autumn of 1771. Then, as if to demonstrate that his accelerated program was the result of a voluntary and happy absorption in learning rather than a desire to finish his schooling quickly and return home, he insisted on staying on at Princeton for postgraduate work. During the winter of 1771-1772 he continued under Witherspoon's guidance, devoting his time to "miscellaneous studies" including some law, and "to acquiring a slight knowledge of the Hebrew, which was not among the regular College Studies."

It was, however, in the regular senior course labeled "Moral Philosophy" that Madison encountered the ideas which were to affect his life most significantly. The syllabus of Witherspoon's lectures in this course, which has been preserved with the list of recommended readings, explains the conversion of the young Virginian to the philosophy of the Enlightenment.

Because the French Revolution was a great drama, many people still think of the Enlightenment as a peculiarly French development connected primarily with the theories and ideas of such *philosophes* as Montesquieu, Voltaire, Diderot, and their circle. Actually the Enlightenment was international in scope. Every European nation produced its crop of philosophers. Moreover, while the Parisian salons were probably the chief center of advanced social thinking, the Scotch universities after 1750 were almost equally important in systematizing and disseminating the revolutionary ideas of the age. The great names in this sudden flowering of the Scotch intellect are David Hume,

Francis Hutcheson, Adam Smith, Thomas Reid, Lord Kames, and Adam Ferguson. Their books formed the core of the moral philosophy course at Princeton, and it was in these works treating of history, ethics, politics, economics, psychology, and jurisprudence, always from the modern and enlightened point of view, that Madison received his "very early and strong impressions in favor of Liberty both Civil & Religious."

A description of Madison's character as a statesman written in 1789 by Fisher Ames, when the Virginian was at the peak of his fame, shows how thoroughly he had assimilated at Princeton the ideals of the Scotch thinkers, and how profoundly they conditioned his lifelong approach to politics. Ames, a political opponent, noted that Madison was "well-versed in public life, was bred to it, and has no other profession." Yet, Ames complained, politics "is rather a science than a business, with him." In this statement he paid unconscious tribute to the great Scotch philosophers Madison studied at college.

Hutcheson, Hume, Smith, and others among the eighteenth century philosophers had conceived the bold and noble dream of reducing politics, economics, law, and sociology to a science. Their great model was Newton, who had demonstrated a century earlier that reason could discover the natural laws of the physical universe. Now in their turn the Scots aspired to use reason to discover the immutable laws of human nature. If the science of man and society was once established, it would allow reformers to reshape political, social, and economic institutions progressively so as to bring them into harmony with nature's divine plan, and thus create a new social order which would guarantee liberty, equality, and happiness to all men. It was this vision that fascinated young Madison while he studied at Nassau Hall. It was to this dream that he dedicated his life. The scholarly treatises of Ferguson, Hume, and Kames, which Madison read in Witherspoon's course, did not appear to him as dusty academic exercises, but rather as thrilling manifestoes in a program of political and social regeneration. To him the arguments of the philosophers became the slogans of a fighting faith. If the social scientist could gain, by the study of history, sure knowledge of the anatomy of political society, he would be able to diagnose and cure its ills. This high concept of the function of the scholar-statesman was Princeton's greatest gift to James

Madison. His complete acceptance of it throughout his life made him, with Franklin and Jefferson, one of the great American representatives of the Enlightenment.

Princeton also gave James Madison his first opportunity for intimacy with a congenial circle of friends. Nor was this a minor benefit. Like many diffident individuals the Virginian, throughout his life, showed a deep emotional need for affection. His manner tended toward stiffness and reserve, and he did not make friends easily. Even after he had become a famous statesman his self-confidence was not proof against the least suspicion of indifference or hostility in others. The comments of that famous Washington hostess Mrs. Margaret Bayard Smith are revealing in this connection. Writing of a visit made to Montpelier in 1828, she describes the brilliance of Madison's talk, "which was a stream of history . . . so rich in sentiments and facts, so enlivened by anecdotes and epigrammatic remarks, so frank and confidential as to opinions on men and measures, that it had an interest and charm, which the conversation of few men now living could have." Nevertheless, she adds: "This entertaining, interesting, and communicative personage, had a single stranger or indifferent person been present, would have been mute, cold and repulsive." Only a sympathetic environment could release Madison's deep capacity for friendship. Orange County had not provided such an environment in his youth. There is no record of any warm feeling toward his fellows at Robertson's school, nor any evidence that his relations with his brothers and numerous cousins were particularly close. When he arrived at Princeton, however, he entered as an equal member a brilliant group of young men whose tastes and talents were similar to his own. In William Bradford, Philip Freneau, and Hugh Henry Brackenridge—all of whom were to distinguish themselves in the arts and professions after leaving college—Madison discovered a trio of friends he would cherish all his life.

It was with this group, the leaders of the recently organized American Whig Society, that Madison found what he termed "recreation and release from business and books" while at Nassau Hall. With them he took part in those "Diversions" and "Foibles" of student life so charmingly described in the diary of Philip Fithian who entered college during Madison's last term. As Fithian speaks of the undergraduate practices of "giving each other *names* & *characters*; Meeting & Shoving in the dark entries; Knocking at Doors & going off without entering; Strowing the entries in the night with greasy Feathers; freezing the Bell; Ringing it at late Hours of the Night," one smiles at the conventionality through the centuries of student mischief, in which young Madison presumably shared. We do know certainly that he participated in another contemporary custom mentioned by Fithian: the "writing witty pointed anonymous Papers, in *Songs, Confessions, Wills, Soliliques, Proclamations, Advertisements* &c."[1] Preserved among the Bradford manuscripts in the Historical Society of Pennsylvania is a series of Whig satires in verse on the members of the rival Cliosophic Society. Among them are several of Madison's which indicate that, although he was a limping poet, he had already developed the taste for ribald jokes which was to scandalize a British ambassador when the Virginian was Secretary of State.

3

When Madison left Princeton and returned home in 1772 he entered the unhappiest period of his life. After the exciting years at Nassau Hall, Montpelier seemed an "obscure corner" of the world and inexpressibly lonely. Madison's letters to William Bradford written at this time are almost pitiful in their nostalgia to breathe "again . . . your free air." To add to his spiritual desolation his health had finally cracked from the strain of overstudy; for a time he believed he had epilepsy and was oppressed with a morbid expectation of an early death. Then, as his strength slowly came back under a regimen that balanced

[1] The remainder of Fithian's catalogue of undergraduate "Foibles" is worth printing if only to round out the picture of student mores at Princeton in Madison's day. Fithian continues: "Picking from the neighborhood now & then a plump fat Hen or Turkey for the private entertainment of the Club. . . . Parading bad Women, Burning Curse-John, Darting Sun-Beams upon the Town-People, Reconnoitering Houses in the Town, & ogling Women with the Telescope—Making Squibs, & other frightful compositions with Gun-Powder, & lighting them in the Rooms of timorous Boys, & new *comers* —the various methods used in naturalizing Strangers, of incivility in the Dining Room to make them bold; writing them sharp & threatening Letters to make them smart; leading them at first with long Lessons to make them industrious—And trying them by Jeers and Repartee in order to make them choose their Companions &c &c."

reading with exercise, the problem of his future career filled him with doubts and hesitations. Madison was strongly inclined to a profession that would provide a "decent and independent" income as an alternative to plantation ownership for, from principle, he wished "to depend as little as possible on the labour of slaves." Yet the practice of law, toward which his intellectual interests pointed, required physical strength and ability in public speaking which he did not possess. His voice, like Jefferson's, was abnormally weak, and his self-assurance completely failed him in large public gatherings. So although Madison, during 1772-1773, started "a course of reading which mingled miscellaneous subjects with the studies intended to qualify him for the Bar . . . he never formed any . . . determination" to become a professional pleader. From the books he was buying for his library and from the comments in his letters to Bradford we rather see that his chief preoccupation at this time continued to be public law, or, as he described it to his friend, "the principles and modes of government [which] are too important to be disregarded by an inquisitive mind."

It was at this time, too, that James Madison first translated his enlightened principles into political practice. A group of Baptist preachers in Orange and Culpeper counties, whose growing congregations had attracted the unfriendly notice of the Anglicans, were prosecuted under the religious laws of Virginia and jailed for nonconformity. Although admitting that the "enthusiasm" of these dissenters "rendered them obnoxious to sober opinion," Madison could not stomach this denial of religious liberty. To quote his own words, he "squabbled and scolded, abused and ridiculed," first "to save them from imprisonment," and when that failed "to promote their release from it." This action on his part was to have an unexpected effect on his political fortunes for, as he reports in his autobiography, "this interposition tho' a mere duty prescribed by his conscience obtained for him a lasting place in the favours of that particular sect." Consequently when the Anglican church was disestablished in Virginia and the dissenters were allowed to vote, Madison discovered that he could count on a solid bloc of Baptist supporters in his home district, no matter who ran against him, a decided advantage for a political philosopher who never became a colorful campaigner on the hustings.

The outbreak of the Revolution ended Madison's worries both over his future career and his poor health as "he entered with the prevailing zeal into the American Cause." Prevented from joining the army by "the discouraging feebleness of his constitution," he served during 1775 on the revolutionary Committee that ruled Orange County. Then in the spring of 1776, mainly through his family connections, he was chosen as a delegate to the Convention whose task it was to establish a new government for Virginia. When he journeyed to Williamsburg in May 1776 and took his seat in this Convention he found at last the profession for which talent and his training at Princeton had prepared him. Henceforth his life was devoted to the public service and, as one of the master builders of a new nation, he played a major part in framing the political institutions of the United States in accordance with the generous and humanistic creed of the Enlightenment.

Madison's role in the famous Virginia Convention of 1776 provides a striking example of the part political theory plays in revolutions. Every successful political revolution is to a large extent theoretical, since revolutionists faced with the hateful conditions that breed rebellion are forced to appeal from what is to what ought to be. They must attack current corrupt practices from the standpoint of an ideal system which they are struggling to establish. Theory, which etymologically means "vision," provides the new points of reference that replace the old norms; without theory to chart a visionary road into the uncertain future, revolt becomes no more than an incandescent blaze of unreasoning and destructive violence. The radical principles which directed the Virginia convention's work of state building were set forth in the famous Declaration of Rights drawn up by George Mason. But it was James Madison who revised Mason's clause respecting religious freedom, and in so doing made his first major contribution to American democracy.

Mason's theory of religious liberty originally written into the Declaration of Rights was revolutionary by eighteenth-century standards: "that religion . . . can be governed only by reason and conviction, not by force or violence; and, therefore, that all men should enjoy the fullest toleration in the exercise of religion, according to the dictates of conscience." Madison, viewing the problem on the basis of his reading at Princeton and his studies since leaving college, objected on principle to the inclusion of the word "toleration" in the Declaration of Rights, for it implied that freedom of conscience was a privilege that the state could grant or withhold as it saw fit. He viewed freedom of conscience as a *"natural and absolute* right," and hence completely outside the jurisdiction of government. So, while the delegate from Orange, "being young and in the midst of distinguished and experienced members," did not open his mouth during the debates in the Convention, he did play an important part in its proceedings, for he prevailed on Mason to amend the clause on religious liberty in accordance with his own more advanced theory.

Thus, through James Madison's intervention, it was proclaimed for the first time in any body of law drawn up in a Christian commonwealth that freedom of conscience is a substantive right, a right which could only be secured by a complete separation of church and state. In 1776 this separation was still only an ideal; even in Virginia church and state were not divorced. Nevertheless the public and official acceptance of Madison's theory clearly defined the issue thenceforth for all revolutionary America, and designated the field of battle where the struggle for religious freedom would be fought. In 1786 Madison at last had the satisfaction of seeing his ideal subscribed to in its entirety by the Virginia legislature. In 1789 he himself was to embody the principle in the federal Bill of Rights. By the time he died in 1836 the complete separation of church and state had become the established norm throughout the United States.

Unfortunately for Madison his constituents did not appreciate his silent services in the Virginia Convention. When he sought election to the legislature in 1777 he was defeated. The austerity of the campaign principles which he conceived necessary to maintain the "purity" of republican government also contributed to this setback; for he refused to recommend himself to the voters in the traditional fashion by providing them with "spirituous liquors, and other treats." This defiance of custom was too shocking for the Orange voters; Madison's constituents, well plied with drinks by his opponents, attributed his "abstinence" to "pride or parsimony." While thus excluded for a time from elective office, the young Virginian still continued active in public life. In November 1777 he was appointed by the Assembly to the Virginia Council of State, whose eight members served as the governor's cabinet. He remained a member of this body until 1779 when, Thomas Jefferson being governor, he was appointed by the legislature one of the Virginia delegates to the Continental Congress, in which he served until November 1783.

Madison's six years of appointive office in the Virginia Council of State and in the Confederation Congress supplemented his theories of government with that subtle form of political wisdom that can come only from experience. As a councilor of state he came to know all the foremost Virginia leaders, and entered upon a deep and lasting friendship with that other enlightened philosopher, Thomas Jefferson. As a Congressman he met and cooperated with distinguished men from other states, and grew steadily in awareness of the common interests shared by all thirteen.

Gradually Madison came to take a leading part in the congressional business relating to finances, national defense, trade, western lands, and international relations. Theory and experience now went hand in hand. Though his auditors still agreed that "he speaks low, his person is little and ordinary," nevertheless as they marked him in action they found that his "sense, reading, address, and integrity" made him remarkably persuasive. "His language is very pure, perspicuous, and to the point. . . . He states a principle and deduces consequences, with clearness and simplicity." Above all, his fellow statesmen were struck by his scholarly industry and marvelous grasp of fact; "he is a studious man, devoted to public business, and a thorough master of every public question that can arise, or he will spare no pains to become so, if he happens to be in want of information." It is no wonder then that on the termination of his service in Congress James Madison returned to Virginia with a national reputation as "one of the ablest Members that ever sat in that Council."

During these years in Congress he became more than a Virginia statesman, representing as he did a national point of view that transcended class and sectional interests. Madison had entered politics with a less provincial attitude than most of his contemporaries. Now, taught by his years in congressional service, he became with Washington the most continental-

JAMES MADISON
From A Painting By Asher B. Durand

minded of all the Virginia leaders. By the nature of his associations and work at Philadelphia he had been under tremendous pressure to think in national terms concerning the general welfare. When he returned home in 1783 the young statesman had gained a mature perspective which identified the cause of the American Union with the cause of liberty throughout the world.

4

Madison's return to private life was brief. In 1784 he was elected to the Virginia House of Delegates and at once became the leader of the radical party in the place of Jefferson, who had been appointed American minister to France. During the next three years he was instrumental in finally disestablishing the Anglican church, enacting a large portion of Jefferson's revised code of laws, and strengthening the basis of state finances. Moreover, while strenuously working to make his own state a model of enlightened administration, he was increasingly aware of the larger problems confronting the nation. During these years in the Virginia legislature he steadily urged that the powers of the Confederation be strengthened. It was largely on his initiative that Virginia participated in the series of interstate conferences that led ultimately to the Philadelphia Convention of 1787.

The Convention of 1787 provided the Princeton-trained political philosopher with the opportunity of rendering his greatest service to his country. In recognition of Madison's role in the Philadelphia meeting historians have named him "the Father of the Constitution." By 1787 the Confederation had declined into impotence; government credit was desperate; Congress, unable to maintain order or even to protect itself, was powerless in the face of treaty violation and foreign commercial discrimination. As the powers of Congress declined, the center of political gravity shifted to the states which soon were engaged in a series of bitter local rivalries. Inside each of these petty sovereignties, postwar depression and deflation touched off virulent class struggles between debtors and creditors as each group strove to control the state machinery in order to protect its own economic interests. In one quarter ominous voices were heard to declare that America was geographically too large and too heterogeneous to continue under a single government; while in another it was openly stated, for the first time since 1776, that the only cure for the ills of the new nation was to liquidate the republican experiment and establish an American monarchy. It seemed to thoughtful Americans in every section that the Union, which had been the instrument of victory in winning political liberty from England, was doomed to dissolve under the tensions of postwar disagreement. Against this background of economic distress, sectional quarrels, class conflict, and ideological confusion the Convention called to reform the Confederation met at Philadelphia in May 1787.

Long before he journeyed to Philadelphia Madison had become convinced that the fate of republican government in America and hence throughout the world hung in the balance. As early as 1785 he had begun to warn his fellow citizens that unless the Union was strengthened there would be a competitive system of jealous sovereign states, involving "an appeal to the sword in every petty squabble, standing armies, and perpetual taxes." Internal weakness would make the disunited states "the sport of foreign politics," threaten the very existence of liberty, and "blast the glory of the Revolution." In view of the decay of the Confederation, Madison had already taken steps to approach the problem scientifically. Since Jefferson in Paris had access to the book stalls of all Europe, Madison recruited his aid in building up an extensive collection of "treatises on the ancient or modern Federal Republics." In preparation for the Philadelphia meeting he was therefore able to study in his own library the structure and principles of all the confederations described in history. The result embodied in two memoranda, entitled respectively "Notes of Ancient and Modern Confederacies" and "Vices of the Political System of the United States," is probably the most fruitful piece of scholarly research ever carried out by an American.

Madison's reading of the accounts of historic confederations, such as the Lycian League, Amphictyonic Council, the United Netherlands, was discouraging; as precedents they furnished "no other light than that of beacons, which give warnings of the course to be shunned, without pointing out that which ought to be pursued." His studies confirmed his belief, steadily growing as he watched the American Confederation totter toward "imbecility," that it would be impossible to establish a stable federal system based on any principles tried in the past. Madison's reading underlined a further point. Never in all the history of the world had it been possible to organize a republican state in a territory as vast as America; never in the past had it been possible to frame a popular government for a population of such heterogeneous elements as those inhabiting the United States. As he discovered in his books, and as Alexander Hamilton was later to argue in the Convention, all political theorists agreed that a stable republic promoting the general welfare of a varied population could be established only in a small country. Stable empires of vast extent had been organized in the past, but they had all been held together from above by the power of a king.

It is James Madison's greatest glory as a philosopher-statesman that he accepted the challenge of the impossible. He transcended the impossible by inventing a completely new type of federal state, which while solidly resting on majority rule at the same time provided adequate safeguards for the rights of minority groups. From his reading and experience he evolved an original theory of republican federalism differing completely from the principles of any of the historic confederations. A full month before the Convention met he had elaborated his novel scheme in his memoranda and in letters to Jefferson, Randolph, and Washington. He had also commenced work on the blueprint of a governmental structure that would institutionalize this theory. It was a brilliant intellectual achievement which won for the thirty-five-year-old Madison the right to be called the philosopher of the American Constitution. His theory, embodied in the structure of the American Union, was to prove also the greatest triumph in practical application of the Enlightenment's ideal of scientific political research.

The story of Madison's labors to get his theory elaborated into the document known as the United States Constitution is too familiar to be detailed here. The Virginian played a decisive part in every phase of constitutional creation. On the basis of his theory, which he submitted to Washington's careful inspection, he was able to persuade the General that the Convention was not doomed to impotence before it opened, and that he should attend as a delegate. Washington's prestige, both at Philadelphia and during the struggle for ratification, proved of major significance in the outcome. It was Madison's theory too that provided the basis of the Virginia Plan which, after it was worked over by the assembled delegates for nearly four months, emerged as the new constitution. During the long summer days in the Convention, Madison, in the words of a fellow delegate, "took the lead in the management of every great question"; one of three debaters who were heard most frequently, he spoke from the floor 161 times. Whether in committee or in open session it was reported that "he always comes forward the best informed man on any point in debate. The affairs of the United States, he perhaps, has the most correct knowledge of, of any Man in the Union." Finally, marvelous to relate, it was James Madison, "the profound politician" blended "with the scholar," who somehow managed to find the extra energy necessary to write out daily a meticulous report of all the debates in the Convention. Although this exacting task almost killed him, as he later admitted, still he was determined that future political philosophers should have the "Debates" as scientific data requisite to carry forward the study of republican government.

Madison's labors for the Constitution did not end with the adjournment of the Convention. Almost at once the long bitter struggle to secure ratification began. During the winter of 1787-1788 the Virginian collaborated with Alexander Hamilton and John Jay in writing *The Federalist,* the classic exposition of the Constitution and the most important American contribution to the world's political literature. In the spring of 1788, elected a member of the Virginia ratifying convention, he acted as leader of the pro-constitution party, and matched himself against the great Patrick Henry who was chief of the opposition. Until the final vote was taken the issue hung in doubt, and with it the question of whether the Constitution would be given a trial. Virginia being both the largest and the most populous of the thirteen states, her rejection would have proved fatal to the plan. In the most dramatic episode of his career, Madison faced the fiery, passionate oratory of Henry and smothered it with his quiet, lucid reasoning. When the final vote was taken the logic of Madison and the constitutional party had caused eight members of the opposition to disregard the express wishes of their constituents, and two more to vote contrary to specific instructions. As a result the Constitution was approved by the narrow margin of 10 out of 168 votes.

5

Although the new Constitution was finally ratified in 1788, it was still merely a blueprint; the task remained of transforming its paper provisions into the institutions of a functioning government. To this delicate operation the first Congress addressed itself. Madison almost missed sharing in this labor: Patrick Henry's hatred first blocked his election to the new Senate, and then attempted to prevent his choice as a member of the House. Luckily for Madison his loyal Baptist supporters remembered their ancient debt and backed him solidly; and so in 1789 he began the first of his four terms as a Virginia representative in Congress. From the day he took his seat he was the leading member of the lower house. There was no act of legislative business during the first session in which he did not participate with his customary erudition. He sponsored the first ten amendments to the Constitution which make up the federal Bill of Rights, introduced the first revenue bill, helped organize the executive department, and acted as President Washington's congressional adviser and ghost writer. It was a strenuous period full of "delays and perplexities" arising in large part from the complete "want of precedents." Many times Madison felt that "we are in a wilderness, without a single footstep to guide us." Yet the task was accomplished. By the end of the first session of the first Congress, "the more perfect union" had successfully made the transition from paper to practice.

Before the new government had been in operation a year, Madison became deeply disturbed over the trend of events in the national capital. In his view, the trouble lay in the activities and policies of Alexander Hamilton, Secretary of the Treasury. To the New Yorker, no federal scheme could provide a sufficiently centralized authority to subsist in so large a country; and even worse was "the disease" of democracy which afflicted America. Hamilton, therefore, seized the opportunity during the formative stage of the new government to "administer" it —the term is Madison's—so that it would more closely approach his ideal of a consolidated oligarchy. With devious brilliance,

Hamilton set out, by a program of class legislation, to unite the propertied interests of the eastern seaboard into a cohesive administration party, while at the same time he attempted to make the executive dominant over the Congress by a lavish use of the spoils system. In carrying out his scheme, though he personally was above corruption, Hamilton transformed every financial transaction of the Treasury Department into an orgy of speculation and graft in which selected senators, congressmen, and certain of their richer constituents throughout the nation participated. As Madison watched Hamilton's program develop, he became disillusioned and bitter. In the Convention he had fought to create a Constitution under which "the interests and rights of every class of citizens should be duly represented and understood." Now he saw the machinery of his new government being used to exploit the mass of the people in the interest of a small minority.

Before the end of the first Congress, Madison, therefore, began to attack the Hamiltonian program as "unconstitutional" no less than antirepublican. In so doing, he probably saved the Constitution from being abrogated by the rising mass of injured citizens, and guaranteed that the American experiment in democratic government should continue on a national basis.

Hamilton's system of class government, while brilliantly successful in enlisting the loyalty of "the rich, the wise, and the well born" for the Constitution, in truth contained a major threat to American nationalism. During the struggle for ratification, a majority of the people had opposed the Constitution as containing a potential threat to their liberties. Living in an almost self-sufficient agrarian economy, they were content with the security provided by the system of independent states and saw little need for a stronger union. This majority was still deeply suspicious of the national government at its birth in 1789. Every device that Hamilton used to win the loyalty of the propertied elite tended to confirm the suspicions of the yeoman farmers and middle class groups and to erode their faith in the new government.

Not the least of James Madison's services to American nationalism was to put himself at the head of this potentially dangerous opposition and thus guarantee that it would remain loyal to the Union. Thomas Jefferson was to prove the great organizer and symbol of the anti-Hamiltonians; but Madison had already formulated the principles of the opposition before Jefferson assumed the role of party chief. In speeches, letters, and a series of essays contributed to the newspaper edited by his fellow Princetonian, Philip Freneau, "the father of the Constitution" stressed again and yet again that it was not the federal Union that was at fault but the individuals at its head. The Constitution itself was sound; the evil lay in Hamilton's perverted "interpretation" of the document.

Thus, an aroused party which might well have developed revolutionary tendencies was marshaled by Madison under the banner of a higher loyalty and a stricter veneration of the Constitution. Once again the Virginia theorist and political philosopher had played a decisive part in fixing the pattern of future political behavior in America. Following Madison's lead, discontented groups in the United States, even though out of power, have traditionally looked to the Constitution for the protection of their rights, and thus has been maintained that amazing balance between stability and change which has characterized our national existence. Certainly, this developed pattern of loyal opposition made the election of Thomas Jefferson and the reversal of national policies in 1800 a coup which, although "revolutionary," was still strictly constitutional.

During Jefferson's two terms as president, Madison served officially as his Secretary of State, and unofficially as his dearest friend and most trusted adviser. Since the President was a widower, it also came about that Madison's wife, the famous and attractive Dolly, whom he had married in his forty-fifth year, became the official hostess for the administration. As Secretary of State, James Madison shared fully in the two great triumphs of Jefferson's first term: the program of domestic reform that finally identified the Union as a people's government, and the Louisiana Purchase which extended the bounds of the republican experiment clear to the Pacific. In like manner, Madison was a leader in the unsuccessful attempt during Jefferson's second administration to develop through the Embargo a system of economic sanctions to replace the use of force in our foreign relations. In 1808, through Jefferson's influence, Madison was chosen to succeed him as president.

6

As chief executive, James Madison added few laurels to his reputation. He inherited from his predecessor the insoluble problem of preserving American neutrality in the midst of the titanic struggle between England and Napoleon. Before the beginning of his second administration the Virginian had become convinced that there was no alternative to war against England, if the United States was to maintain its maritime rights and its economic independence. Unfortunately, the talents of the philosopher statesman were designed for peace rather than war; after the opening of hostilities Madison's inadequacies as a military chieftain soon became apparent. Throughout the conflict, he was hampered in exerting executive leadership by his theory that Congress should take the initiative in determining policy.

As it turned out the United States was fortunate to emerge from the struggle territorially intact. Not a single American war aim was achieved; Washington was captured and the President was forced to flee to the Virginia woods for safety; and only the unexpected victories of the final months of the conflict—at Baltimore, Plattsburg, New Orleans—allowed his contemporaries to set down "Mr. Madison's War" as an American triumph. Yet the sentiment of national unity, which Madison had labored so long to inculcate by rational appeal, flowered under the irrational emotions released by the war; and the last remnants of antirepublicanism were swept away in the flood of patriotic pride. Soon after the treaty of peace, James Madison's presidential term ended and put a period to his forty years of public service.

After his retirement to Montpelier, Madison "devoted himself to his farm and his books, with much avocation, however, from both by an extensive and often laborious correspondence which seems to be entailed on Ex-Presidents." A large part of his time was spent in arranging his letters, and editing for the enlightenment of posterity the carefully preserved "Notes" on the debates in the Constitutional Convention. He was closely associated with Jefferson in the founding of the University of Virginia, and became its rector after Jefferson's death in 1826. When he had almost reached his eightieth birthday he reluctantly served as a member, but took no important part, in the Virginia Constitutional Convention of 1829. It was about this time that he dictated his short autobiography, nearly a fifth of which deals with his happy years at Princeton.

As Madison grew older, he withdrew as far as possible from politics. When pressed in 1830 for his opinion on a current controversial topic he wrote: "A man whose years have but reached the canonical three-score-and-ten . . . should distrust himself, whether distrusted by his friends or not, and should never forget that his arguments, whatever they may be, will be answered by allusions to the date of his birth." Yet, on the two issues of slavery and state rights which were eventually to threaten the existence of his beloved union, his principles forced him to break his silence. Until his death, he lent his active support to the African Colonization Society from an awareness that the "dreadful calamity" of Negro bondage was incompatible with the republican principles of liberty and equality. On one other subject also he would not hold his peace. When the South Carolinians, during the tariff controversy, tried to use his name and Jefferson's to support their doctrines of nullification and seccession, he repeatedly and publicly denounced their position as constitutional heresy.

James Madison lived on peacefully to the age of eighty-six, deeply happy in his marriage, still full of "inexhaustible faith" in the future of the great democratic commonwealth he had done so much to establish. On the morning of June 28, 1836, he died quietly in his easy-chair. It is reported that even his slaves wept when he was buried in the Montpelier graveyard.

Part II
Human Nature and Politics

[2]

Madison's Analysis of the Sources of Political Authority

ROBERT J. MORGAN
University of Virginia

James Madison believed that political institutions are not the effects of conflicts among private groups in society. He traced political authority to human nature. It is the ultimate source of both public opinion and the motives which impel some individuals to hold government offices. Prudently contrived governmental institutions can moderate the countervailing tendencies arising from these two sources of authority, although they are necessarily in a state of continuing tension. Strict accountability of representatives to the whole range of diverse opinion in society is in conflict with the tendency of government to become autonomous. The latter tendency follows from government's using its power to establish the fiscal and military institutions required to wage war. By doing so a government may create a new political equilibrium which is masked by apparent adherence to established constitutional balance and is then independent of the balance of private property.

My purpose is to present James Madison's analysis of the sources of governmental authority in order to challenge two dominant interpretations of his political theory. The more systematic of the two portrays him as the Founders' prophet who forecast that ruling majorities will be restrained because their power depends on the opinions and interests of diverse and numerous groups in the extended American republic. The other one pictures him as advocate of constitutional checks created and used by a ruling class bent on curbing democratic majorities. Both images are based almost exclusively on the tenth and fifty-first *Federalist* papers separately without any effort to perceive the significant linkages between them and anything else Madison wrote about politics. Scholars have ignored completely Madison's highly significant argument in these papers and elsewhere that governmental authority and the restraints upon it are both derived from the same ultimate and penultimate causes. The first cause is human nature and the proximate cause is opinion.

My thesis is that Madison's political theory follows from his perception of the fundamental dilemma involved in tracing both governmental power and restraints on it through opinion to original human nature. His consciousness of this problem led him to conclude that there is a natural, inescapable and enduring tension between accountability and autonomy in the American republic. That is why on various occasions he distinguished between a government which is self-controlled by the forms in which its power is distributed and a second type which is ruled by "a will independent of the community" (*Federalist* 51, pp. 339, 341; *Papers,* Vol. 9, p. 299; *Writings,* Vol. 9, pp. 231-33, 520-28). Consequently, he was moved to explain why the forms of the American republic resting on opinion and human nature offer a reasonable prospect, even if not an absolute certainty, of securing accountability.

My thesis is developed in three main sections. Each part elaborates successively Madison's ideas concerning: (1) the implications of basing the power and limits of republican government on public opinion; (2) the reasons why republican government tends to become autonomous in the performance of its protective functions; and (3) the process which is likely to enable the government to transform itself radically without appearing to do so. First, however, it is necessary to comment on the two prevailing interpretations of Madison's political theory.

Both portrayals dismiss Madison's prescription of governmental forms and his reasons for doing so because political institutions are now regarded as reflections of underlying groups or a dominant class seeking to curb majority rule. J. Allen Smith popularized the class image by claiming that Madison's tenth *Federalist* was proof of the undemocratic characteristics of the Constitution. It promised to break and control the violence of faction. This essay revealed Madison's determination to curb the "supremacy of public opinion" effectuated through elected, responsible political parties unimpeded by any limits on majority rule. The tenth paper was proof that Madison advocated constitutional checks to curb "the people, but not the government," in the interest of a propertied class (1965, pp. 40-42, 205). This image based on scanty evidence and tendentious proof has been very durable. It has been used to perpetuate the belief that Madison opposed majority rule and political parties, especially as they function in the British model.[1] James M. Burns' claim

[1]It was spread widely by Parrington (1931, Vol. 1, pp. 286-89) and has been repeated in the influential works

is typical: "Madison railed against the spirit of party" (1967, p. 27).

Charles A. Beard created the other durable image of Madison: the founder and prophet of an American science of politics. Beard did so by applying Bentley's group theory of politics to the framing of the Constitution and by claiming that Madison's tenth *Federalist* was the first American statement of such a theory (Beard, 1913, p. 6; Bentley, 1967, pp. 200-22). Beard used the tenth *Federalist* to impute to Madison the theory that economic group interest was the "impelling motive" of the Framers of the Constitution. This theory was proved by connecting provisions of the document, like any law, with the interests of the economic groups which advanced or opposed them. Beard claimed, also, that the scientific character of Madison's analysis in the tenth paper was certified by the power of his predictions, among which two are notable: (1) in the future the overbearing majority most to be dreaded, Madison "prophesied," will be the landless, urban proletariat; and (2) it will be difficult to form governing majorities because "the very size of the union will enable the inclusion of more interests" within them. It was Madison who provided us with proof that (1) the Constitution was not deduced from general "principles" applied to particular cases; (2) the motives of those who framed it were not a love of justice, the desire to advance the general welfare, or to protect the nation from foreign enemies; and (3) that the "superstructure" of government is simply an "incidental" reflex of underlying group conflicts (Beard, 1913, pp. 6-9, 14-18, 154-58). By claiming that the Constitution reflects the activities of groups moved by *economic motives,* Beard departed significantly from Bentley's paradigm (1967, pp. 212, 258-97, 453-60, 473, 477). Otherwise, Beard remained faithful to it and identified Madison with it.

Beard's transmogrification of Madison into a neo-Bentleyan group theorist reinforced Smith's thesis that Madison advocated constitutional checks to protect a propertied class from party government unimpeded by any limits on the will of popular majorities composed of leveling democrats. But Beard's Madisonian image has been used to support the contrary claim that (1) he prophesied the moderating effects of a large and socially diverse nation on political parties; or (2) he was the first American to state a pluralist theory of politics. Neither of the latter two, it is confidently believed, was developed "in connection with governmental structure" (Wright, 1949, p. 17). Several scholars have applied a superficial gloss to Beard's image despite the obvious contradictions involved.[2] Hartz tried to demolish Beard's neo-Marxist class theory, but left the Bentleyan paradigm untouched (1956, pp. 29-34).

Neither Hartz nor others paid any attention to Beard's extremely revealing recantation of his economic theory of politics. This theory omitted considerations of any "human motivation" except economic interest and treated that one as the *sole* and *independent cause* of all "political actions and institutions." Therefore, the theory omitted any consideration of the pursuit of unlimited power "as an end in itself, or as a means to class, national and imperialistic ends." So it ignored the degree to which this phenomenon makes *economic man dependent* on political and military man. His great error, Beard admitted, was to universalize a theory of politics which was relevant only between 1815 and 1914, but he consoled himself with the thought that Marxists and Liberals had made the same mistake. They had not paid enough attention to war, so they failed to realize that the effort to isolate economic activities as the cause of politics was doomed at a very early state of social development. The influences of these two kinds of activities on one another are reciprocal (1945, pp. 71-75, 90-91, 101-14).

Beard did not venture to say how his great error affects our understanding of Madison's political theory or the founding of the republic. I venture to do so in the course of challenging the prevailing Smith-Beard image of Madison.

Opinion, Majority Rule and Accountable Government

Madison's analysis of the dilemma facing the Founders started with his identification of the republican cause with self-government and his

of Schattschneider (1942, pp. 1-3), and Ranney (1975, pp. 22-24).

[2]Holcombe combined the first and second of these propositions and retained Beard's economic interpretation (1950, pp. 23-27, 78-80). Dahl first played Mark Antony to Madison by *restating* the extended sphere proposition in his Madisonian model which was not an analysis of the historical Madison (1956, pp. 5-7, 15-17); but later praised the tenth paper for being the first statement of the new concept of political pluralism in keeping with Bentley's paradigm (1967, pp. 40-42). See also Bourke (1975, pp. 271-95) for other pluralist readings of Madison. Authors who have combined the class and extended sphere arguments without embracing Beard's economic determinism include Riemer (1967, p. 132), Burns (1967, pp. 13-14, 18-23), Burns (1968, pp. 38, 94-98), and Wood (1969, pp. 501-06). The extended sphere proposition was restated by Wright (1949, pp. 17-25), Ketcham (1957, pp. 20-25) and Adair (1957, p. 348).

premise that it is founded on "opinion" like every other government, despotic or free (*Federalist* 51, p. 341; 49, p. 329). Yet wherever liberty is accepted as the *precondition* essential to political life, nothing is more evident from experience than its "natural diversity" (*Papers,* Vol. 5, p. 467; Vol. 10, p. 208) and the "zeal" with which different opinions about the theory and practice of religion, government and other subjects are expressed (*Federalist* 10, p. 55). Because opinion is the source of both the power and stability of governments as well as the security for individual rights (*Writings,* Vol. 6, pp. 70, 85), some political theorists friendly to democracy have prescribed social homogeneity as the condition essential for democratic self-government. They have claimed that if all persons were to be reduced to perfect political equality, then all would be "perfectly equalized and assimilated in their possessions . . . opinions, and passions" (*Federalist* 10, pp. 58-59). In fact, however, no society has ever been a homogeneous mass, not even a primitive one (*Papers,* Vol. 10, p. 212). This social condition can only be a postulate of utopian fantasies (*Writings,* Vol. 9, p. 527). It is no guide to the founder of a republic.

Diversity of opinion exists and makes all societies necessarily heterogeneous because it is rooted in human nature. Mankind's self-love, fallible reason, and diverse faculties combine to create differences of opinion. The rights of property originate in these differences of opinion. Although it is the first object of government to protect the diverse faculties and opinions out of which the rights of property originate, its efforts to do so divide society into different interests and parties (*Federalist* 10, p. 55). It is clear that he who would extinguish parties would extinguish liberty first (*Federalist* 50, p. 335). Thus, as long as human beings enjoy liberty, they will naturally hold and express diverse opinions and form parties which arise out of the actions of government. This truth is well illustrated by recent American history. The first parties divided after 1776 over the cause of independence; after 1783 parties were "in abundance," but they were local; the proposed constitution gave rise to a second and interesting division between its opponents and supporters among whom some may have entertained other secret objectives (*Writings,* Vol. 6, pp. 106-12). In free societies, "parties arise out of the nature of things, and the great art of politicians lies in making them checks and balances to each other" (*Writings,* Vol. 6, p. 86).

Opinion, Madison observed, is malleable as well as naturally diverse. He warned that, because the American people occupy an extended territory, they are likely to be influenced for some time to come by the "misrepresentations" of "interested men" (*Federalist* 63, p. 410). Three years later he repeated this warning, saying, the "larger a country is, the less easy for its real opinion to be ascertained, and the less difficult for it to be counterfeited" (*Writings,* Vol. 6, p. 70). His own legislative experience convinced Madison that political opinion, especially about policy issues, was commonly manipulated behind political masks and disguises. He had seen legislators enact "base and selfish measures masked by pretexts of the public good." Clever persons had made dupes of both the public and other honest but gullible legislators by "veiling . . . and varnishing sophistical arguments" in order to disguise their real objectives (*Papers,* Vol. 9, p. 354). It was scarcely worth the effort to reform Congress, if the people chose their own representatives only to find eventually that a clever, enterprising and "moneyed few" profited personally from every new regulation of commerce and finance at a cost paid by the "industrious and uninformed mass" (*Federalist* 62, p. 406). In subsequent private correspondence Madison lamented more than once the difficulty of informing people spread over a large area. The "towns . . . for a time . . . always set public opinion," so that the country is too much uninformed to match cities in this regard (*Letters,* Vol. 1, pp. 515, 596). The people cannot be informed properly much of the time because the aims of parties are often a "game behind the curtain." A party often wears a "mask" (*Letters,* Vol. 2, pp. 7, 114; see also pp. 121-22, 126). Madison even found himself blinded on one occasion, when the projects of our own "foreign Department are under a veil, not a corner of which I have been able to lift" (*Letters,* Vol. 2, p. 109). On the other hand, he conceded freely the need to deceive foreign governments; one occasion called for a diplomat "wearing a mercantile mask" (*Writings,* Vol. 6, p. 134; see also *Papers,* Vol. 9, p. 277).

The manipulation and counterfeiting of opinion with masks and gamesmanship are unavoidable, but censorship or legislation curbing the flow of free opinion is not. In 1794, Madison feared that a proposed tax on newspapers would obstruct the free flow of information *to* the public. Every government tends to want censorship to hide its own abuses. In ours, where members are so far removed from the "eye of their constituents," it is essential to have a prompt and easy circulation of newspapers throughout the whole of society and representatives traveling between their constituents and the government. Together they are the "equivalent to a contraction of territorial limits" in making true public opinion known (*Letters,* Vol. 1, p. 572; *Writings,* Vol. 6, p. 70). In addition: "Opinions are not the [proper] objects of legislation." The opinions expressed by associations formed freely and voluntarily to express their positions on public issues are not properly the subject of any notice whatsoever from the government of the United States. The democratic societies' beliefs will stand or fall by "public opinion. . . . In a Republic, light will prevail over darkness, truth over error" and Madison was confident of this principle (*Writings*, Vol. 6, pp. 222, 223). Subsequently, he applied the same reasoning to the Sedition Act of 1798, which made publication of political opinions a punishable offense if they held elected officials' conduct in contempt, disrepute or hatred. By making the truth of the utterance a defense, the law subjects opinions and conjectures to the same test as facts in court. When vigorously enforced, it effectively destroys the right of electing the members of the government. The exercise of this right includes the opportunity to express opinions which castigate elected public officers who discharge their responsibilities unfaithfully or defectively. The Constitution presupposes this right, which is the "very essence of a free and responsible government" (*Writings*, Vol. 6, pp. 386-89, 394-98).

Despite its natural diversity, opinion is, and must be, more or less fixed as the mind or sense of the community which has "full agency" in a republic (*Papers*, Vol. 12, p. 373). A republican consensus must support the Constitution with enlightened conviction, affection and that degree of veneration which only time can bestow. The fixed opinions to which Madison was committed as analyst and ardent advocate were the heritage of the American Revolution. It was made, he said in 1783, in the name of the rights of mankind with the promise that the "unadulterated forms" of republican government would more than merely "fulfill the ends of government." They would "ennoble national character," give exemplary and unprecedented support to liberty as well as other rights and prove that such goods are the consequences of our political establishments (*Papers*, Vol. 6, p. 494). The federal republic established by the Constitution of 1787, also, promised to meet the test of utility by serving the common good. It would preserve self-government by protecting the nation from foreign enemies, advance its commerce, relieve it of the Old World's burden of standing military establishments, restrain factions (the bane of the ancient republics), and promote domestic freedom, tranquility, happiness and the pursuit of justice. When government does so, it is supported by a degree of popular veneration which is essential to its stability (*Federalist* 14, p. 79; 20, p. 124; 51, p. 341; 62, pp. 404, 407).

The stability of the republic cannot rest upon enlightened opinion alone; it requires a sentimental attachment as well. Affection must be developed over time and must be so widely shared as to be rooted in sentiment rather than pure reason alone. The latter's fallibility is great enough to require the support of the "prejudices" of the community. The strength of every individual's *opinions*, and "*its practical influence on his conduct*," depends on both the number of persons one believes to have shared them and the long duration of time over which they have been held (*Federalist* 49, p. 329, emphasis added; see also *Papers*, Vol. 13, p. 22). As he explained in "Public Opinion," the sheer extent of the country also magnifies this problem: "the more extensive a country the more insignificant is each individual in his own eyes" (*Writings*, Vol. 6, p. 70). The Bill of Rights, Madison hoped, would provide precisely the kind of reinforcement of popular opinion by embodying certain maxims of free government in "national sentiment." An official declaration of rights embodied in the Constitution should have a tendency over time to establish public opinion in their favor and rouse the whole community against attempted violations of rights by a ruling majority. In the short run, such a declaration conforms with the prevailing opinion in the United States that there should be limits to all the "forms" of government. It ought, also, to base the Constitution on more than the mere acquiescence of a dissenting minority by assuring them that the Constitution's supporters are truly devoted to liberty and the republican cause (*Papers*, Vol. 12, pp. 198, 203, 204-05).

Madison's general conclusion was that a stable political system is one in which government acquires the "moral and political authority emanating from the actual possession of power, and a just and beneficial exercise of it" in conformity with political values deeply rooted and widely shared as the sense of the community (*Writings*, Vol. 9, p. 359). This perception of the effects of popular affection on political authority undoubtedly explains Madison's unease over any congruence between party cleavages and basic constitutional doctrines. When he expressed this concern in *Federalist* 49, he had good reason to be anxious about the durability of the young republic (*Writings*, Vol. 9, p. 318). This disquietude prompted him to publish his essays in the *National Gazette* in 1791-1792 and later to urge Washington privately to run for a second term. Under Washington's continued leadership, public opinion favoring republican government and its administration would be better decided as long as the parties were divided over these issues (*Writings*, Vol. 6, pp. 108-09). He conceded many years later, however, that such divisions are unavoidable whether a constitution is written or prescriptive (*Letters*, Vol. 3, pp. 442, 601).

Madison labored for a constitutional consensus which takes the form of "plain and general truths" instead of a collection of provisions desired or opposed by particular interests. Every attempt at the latter is "fallacious," when the object of action is to establish a "general system" of government for people who are divided by a "contrariety of opinions" and local attachments. No such system can be established, if people are inflexibly tenacious in defending individual opinions even to the point of opposing particular constitutional provisions out of secret motives plausibly inferred. The same difficulty is created when some interests demand provisions which they foolishly think will serve to protect them. For example, many southerners wanted a provision prohibiting Congress from enacting commercial regulations or maintaining a standing army without a favorable vote by two-thirds of the states. Why, Madison asked, should the "northern states most competent to their own safety bind themselves" with such provisions to the southern states which lack competent means of their own self-defense? In contrast, the provisions of the Bill of Rights and the constitutional prefix which Madison proposed unsuccessfully were truths so plain and general that they ought to serve all Americans for generations to come as the maxims of free government. Among these none is more important in establishing a general system of government than the idea of the sovereignty of the people. It means that the people of the United States established the Constitution by "compact" and can change it by the same means, if they please. While it is in force, however, all have an obligation to observe its terms despite the variety of opinions which the residents of some areas hold in contradiction to the sense of the community (*Papers,* Vol. 11, pp. 166, 173, 176; Vol. 12, pp. 200-03; *Writings,* Vol. 9, pp. 527-28).

One of the obligations incurred by compact is tacit obedience by all to the majority authorized to rule in a republic created to serve the public good and the private rights of all. In such governments the legislature commands the moral and physical force of the community so there is no appeal to any other sovereign than public opinion to sustain the maxims of free government on behalf of an injured minority. Experience gives no assurance that legislative majorities will be *self-controlled* by the restraints of religious convictions, by the desire to be respected for their integrity, or by conscience which is flawed by "unconscious bias." In short, a legislative majority, no matter how numerous, is in practice the author of its own standards of conduct so long as it is the voice of the majority in the body of the people (*Papers,* Vol. 9, pp. 354-56; Vol. 10, pp. 33-34, 213-14; Vol. 11, pp. 298-300; Vol. 12, p. 204; Vol. 13, pp. 22-24; *Writings,* Vol. 9, p. 361). In short, whenever a legislative majority, regardless of its size, mirrors and becomes the agent of a dominant interest in society, the majority principle fails to protect minor interests among the population. The state legislatures perfectly exemplified this truth, Madison pointed out. In most of them the landed and mercantile interests, sometimes mixed with creditors and debtors, as well as friends and foes of paper currency, alternated in power frequently enough to change the laws according to their respective interests to the detriment of stable policy. This truth, he reminded the Convention of 1787, was apparent in both large and small states. His congressional experience had convinced him, however, that, when a legislature is composed of members from all states, the number and variety of interests to which they are accountable and must respond collectively is greatly increased (*Papers,* Vol. 5, p. 467; Vol. 6, p. 495; Vol. 10, pp. 32-33). To this degree, American experience confirmed Hume's theory that extension of the territory of a political system embraces a greater variety and number of opinions than a small one. It thereby hinders political association based on shared interests (Ketcham, 1957, pp. 20-25; Adair, 1957, pp. 348-50). Madison insisted, however, that this theory is subject to one extremely important qualification. The natural diversity of opinion in free societies does not, ipso facto, restrain *legislative majorities.* The ease with which opinions are communicated and associations are formed to act on them *"result[s] from the structure of government itself"* and it is this premise which leads to a prudential remedy in the form of a federal republic (*Federalist* 10, pp. 55, 58, emphasis added; 51, p. 340; 63, p. 410; *Papers,* Vol. 10, pp. 208, 212-13).

Three generations of neo-Bentleyan scholars have turned a blind eye to Madison's definition of the most important problems facing the Framers and his remedies for them. The major question was whether republican government which is necessarily dominated by a legislature responsive to prevailing public opinion can be made so self-controlled as to serve all interests in a diverse society, or whether it must be controlled by the latter's dominant natural majority. Madison believed that self-control could be achieved only through constructive use of the *forms of governmental institutions.* His prescription to the Convention of 1787 was "enlarge the sphere" (from state to nation) by framing a "republican system on such a scale & in such a form as will control all the evils [which] have been experienced" in the states (*Papers,* Vol. 10, pp. 33-34).

These forms should include large districts from which to elect representatives chosen for three-year terms. These two choices are possible because an "extensive country" is suited to the creation of a federal republic which retains representative bodies in the states and creates a new one concerned with aggregate national interests. The two forms are necessary to secure election of representatives who have knowledge of interests in all the states as well as those of their own. The result should be that every representative will have a "*diffusive sympathy with the whole society.*" In time this attitude will be reinforced by a growing complexity in the social and economic structures of all states—an "assimilating" trend (*Federalist* 10, pp. 59-60; 56, p. 358; 58, p. 382; 63, p. 413; *Papers,* Vol. 9, p. 357; Vol. 10, p. 214; Vol. 12, p. 142; *Writings,* Vol. 9, pp. 520-28).

It is notable that Hamilton agreed with Madison's diagnosis of the issue, but not with his prognosis. Circumstances may dispose some members of the House to have some regard for the diversity of interests and differences of ranks within society, but competition for control of the new government will occur between "landed men and merchants." Large landowners will represent small farmers and merchants will represent manufacturers and mechanics. The crucial question will be whether those who control the new government will be partial to the "landed . . . moneyed . . . mercantile . . . or manufacturing interest" (*Federalist* 35, pp. 213-16; 60, pp. 390-92).

Madison believed that prevailing public opinion favored not only popular sovereignty and majority rule moderated by representation, but also responsible, accountable government. "I believe no principle is more clearly laid down in the Constitution than responsibility" (*Papers,* Vol. 12, p. 227). It must be limited to objects within the power of the responsible functionary and it must be made "effectually answerable" to the public. Periodic elections provide that means, no matter how imperfectly they may function. At least, regular reviews of performance with the prospect of returning offenders to private status prompt persons of talent and distinction who have a "great regard for public opinion" to perform any task for which they have pledged their reputations (*Federalist* 49, p. 330; 57, p. 371; 63, pp. 408-09; *Papers,* Vol. 10, p. 211; Vol. 12, p. 262).

One final word is helpful in judging Madison's commitment to the sovereignty of public opinion. Undoubtedly, his assertion that every kind of government is founded on opinion was derived from Hume. It is equally certain that Madison had read and reflected upon Hume's essays as Henry May has concluded (1976, pp. 3-65). Nevertheless, Madison did not simply mimic Hume with whom he often disagreed either explicitly or implicitly. Madison went far beyond Hume in perceiving the complex dimensions of public opinion in the American republic and he disagreed positively with the Scot in regard to other conclusions. The first of these is the doctrine that all legitimate political authority is founded ultimately on compact, an idea which Hume was most explicit in denying. The second difference is Madison's belief that legitimizing principles are of the essence of a constitutional consensus which ought to be largely beyond party strife and observed as an essential condition of free political union. Hume said that opinions of "right," consisting of the kind of "speculative principles" which Whigs and Tories had espoused in Britain, were needed to sustain authority, but they were really masks obscuring practical or party objectives. With regard to two ideas Madison followed Hume closely. First, Madison agreed that political institutions acquire a degree of autonomous moral and political authority over a long period of time, if power is used to serve the public interest as it is commonly understood. Second, stable institutions require veneration, affection and the prejudices of the community on their side. Consequently, party divisions over the legitimizing principles of the regime are deadly threats to political stability. Madison's qualified agreements with Hume regarding these matters show how he used the unique conservatism of Hume which Sheldon Wolin has delineated (1954, pp. 1001-14). Madison did so, paradoxically, to support the radical doctrine of popular sovereignty and accountable republican government which Hume abhorred. Like Hume, but under different circumstances, Madison wished to convert the heresy of revolutionary principles into the orthodoxy of constitutional consensus.

Power, Property and Governmental Autonomy

One of the most important elements missing from the prevailing interpretations of Madison is any explanation of his observation that operation of the majority principle in Congress ought to prevent rule by a minority which "masks" its actions behind the "forms of the Constitution" (*Federalist* 10, p. 57). His meaning requires elaboration of two general propositions which explain why governments tend to become autonomous even to the point of transforming themselves without appearing to do so. From experience Madison concluded that there is always some danger that "artful and ambitious rulers" will gradually erect an "independent Government" on the foundation of a self-governing one. This prospect is real because every government, once it has attained "a certain degree of energy," has a "tendency" to increase its power. Furthermore, a "*self-directed course* . . . is the natural propensity of every government" (*Papers,* Vol. 11, p. 299; *Writings,* Vol. 6, p. 67). Therefore, founders who establish a self-controlled republic and wish it to endure must understand how the energy of government increases its power at a certain point and why its tendency toward autonomy is natural.

The explanation of these two tendencies starts with knowledge of human nature and, particularly, the motives which impel individuals to seek governmental offices. Madison perceived three: "1. ambition 2. personal interest 3. public good. Unhappily the first two are proved by experience to be the most prevalent." The major object of constitutional reform, therefore, is to "meliorate" the form of republican government so as to attract from society individuals who "feel most strongly the proper motives" to hold public offices. The only combination consistent with human nature is one composed of ambition and a desire to serve the public good. If personal interest, by which Madison meant avarice, is accepted as a motive for holding office in the American republic, it will not be self-controlled. It will be ruled by a will independent of the desires of any social majority which ought "ultimately to give the law" (*Papers,* Vol. 9, pp. 354-55, 357; *Federalist* 51, p. 337).

Undoubtedly, Madison drew these inferences from personal observations, but they served only to confirm *some* of the conclusions reached by Hume in his new science of politics (Wolin, 1954, pp. 1004-06; Adair, 1957, pp. 343-44, 353-55). Significantly, Madison rejected Hume's conclusion that political authority is (and, therefore, ought to be) founded not only on opinion, but also, on the personal interest of rulers seeking to gratify their avarice as well as their ambition. Moreover, Hume argued, in a society where opinion favors the right to private property and accepts personal interest as the motive for holding office, rulers can establish a new and controlling equilibrium of power independent of: (1) the distribution of private wealth in society, and (2) the "forms" by which power is distributed in the constitution. This change can be effected because the self-interest of rulers can "determine, limit or alter" the operation of the elements of opinion which are the primary foundations of power. In Britain the shift from an original constitutional equilibrium to a new balance of power was effected by maintaining a semblance of old form, in accordance with Machiavelli's advice to keep up the appearance of unchanged institutions (1965, Vol. 1, p. 252). The interest relied upon to make rulers cooperate for the common good, despite their insatiable ambition and avarice, is property created by government—offices and, notably, shares in a growing public debt incurred to defer the costs of wars of imperial rivalry.

English experience since 1690 convinced Hume that Harrington was wrong in saying "the balance of power depends upon that of [private] property" (1770, Vol. 1, pp. 42-44). It is evident that a government can endure for a long period despite an imbalance between governmental power and private property. Locke (1946, pars. 157-59) was equally in error in supposing that the establishment of parliamentary supremacy necessarily entailed the redistribution of representation from underpopulated rural areas to the new and growing cities. When Hume published his essays, there was still a great disparity between the weight of property owned by commoners and their share of power under the constitution. The latter endured, nevertheless, Hume explained, because the government created and distributed a critical mass of property out of the public treasury. The latter took the traditional forms of honorable and often lucrative offices and a strikingly novel one, shares in the permanent national debt. By making it the private, or personal, interest of members of Parliament to acquire these forms of property, the government avoided the necessity of overtly redistributing representation and resolving the crisis which it would effect. The skillful distribution of the Crown's offices, Hume declared, "creates a much greater dependency than the same property dispersed" among many private owners. This public property creates an even greater "influence" than forms privately created, Hume concluded, because the persons who distribute it are "antecedently . . . invested with a public character." He approved of Parliament's *"corruption and dependency"* on the Crown, its consequent loss of direct accountability to particular constituencies and the mutation of the mixed and balanced constitution into a fiction—all on utilitarian grounds. The establishment of cabinet government maintained the prescriptive authority of the ancient constitution and, therefore, served the public interest in the highest sense. Furthermore, the appeal to the private interest of rulers is in the public interest. No nation such as Hume's contemporary Britain can exceed the Romans in greatness, if it limits the behavior of its rulers by the moral standards applied to private individuals (1770, Vol. 1, pp. 26, 40-49).

On the other hand, Hume was emphatically opposed to the new practice of permitting "the highest officers of the state to be commonly the public creditors." This policy threatened to become the characteristic cause of the "degeneracy" of free governments. It was a particular manifestation of the one universal truth of political science which he thought was beyond challenge: in free governments legislators enact measures of trade and revenue from which they expect to gain personally. A significant example is the distinctly modern policy of creating a national debt in order to defer payments of the cost of war by entailing it on posterity. This artificial policy is a "poison" for two major reasons. This "precarious" form of property tends to be located in cities, particularly the capital, thereby "making the head too large for the body." It concentrates the government's influence there to the neglect of the countryside and spells the doom of the "middle power." The "landowners will be utterly unable" to resist the growing power of the owners of this new property which is derived *exclusively* "from the commission of the sovereign" (1770, Vol. 1, pp. 107-08; Vol. 2, pp. 43-44, 121-22, 133-54). Shortly before his death in 1776, Hume bitterly denounced the "century of licentiousness" which had transformed Englishmen into "vile beasts" with the rise to power of "financiers" (Marshall, 1954, pp. 247-57; Forbes, 1975, Ch. 6). The equally dreadful consequence of linking wars of imperial rivalry with the expansion of this new form of governmental influence would surely be the destruction of free government due to excessive military conquests, as the ultimate fate of the Roman Republic proved. Unfortunately, the debt was popular with merchants and manufacturers who expanded their enterprises with this new form of capital. Obviously, Hume predated Marx, to say the least, in understanding this phenomenon (1770, Vol. 2, p. 350; Marx, 1930, Vol. 2, pp. 833, 836-39). Montesquieu shrewdly observed that this "fictitious" property is metamorphosed into a "real" form only by making those who acquire it the *dependent* supporters of a government which must endure in order for their property and liberty to be secure (1949, Vol. 1, Bk. 19, Ch. 27; Bk. 22, Chs. 17-18).

The American Founders were deeply divided over Hume's paradoxical and ironic analysis of political authority in the British model. Sophisticated owners of land found his prophecy foreboding. Hume presented the paradox of political authority prescriptively derived from ancient institutions and ironically maintained in appearance rather than reality by a radically new conception of civic virtue which transforms the avarice of rulers into a proper motive for public service. On the one hand, Hume insisted that in a modern commercial society avarice must be praised and encouraged no less than it was condemned by the ancient moral philosophers. Avarice must energize the aggrandizement of private property on which the wealth and power of the state depends (1770, Vol. 2, pp. 2-23, 30-31, 80-111, 127). The rulers of such a society cannot be expected to forego the fruits of avarice and to be held to higher standards of behavior than those prevailing in society. Hume was unwilling, however, to apply this rule without exception. He approved of the acquisition of lucrative offices under the Crown because it maintained the fiction of a fixed constitution. He denounced the acquisition of shares in the public debt by such officers because the dependence of the owners of this artificial property on the sovereign state would destroy the countervailing power of the owners of other forms of property. A civic morality based on avarice cuts two ways. "Social" indoctrination (Dahl, 1956, p. 18) of rulers would not be enough to save the ancient constitution in the long run.

As heirs to this British legacy of ideas and institutions, many of the Framers believed that the new American republic must derive its authority from the acquisitive drives of its rulers. They could not be held to self-denying standards of behavior contrary to those prevailing in a commercial society. Mercer was the purest disciple of Hume in espousing this position at the convention in 1787. "It is a first principle of political science . . . [that] public measures are calculated for the benefit of the Governors, not of the people." No change of government can alter this universal constant of political behavior. The executive must be armed with "influence," therefore, in order to counterbalance the "speculating legislatures" which had been plundering the American people (Farrand, ed., Vol. 2, pp. 284-85, 289). To this extent Mercer agreed with Hamilton who invoked "Hume's opinion" against republican purists who "reprobate the danger of influence in the British government" because they do not understand its necessity. Government must be established and maintained by appealing to "avarice, ambition, interest [the passions] which govern most individuals and all public bodies." Hamilton insisted, however, that interest must include that which Hume denounced as the certain cause of degeneracy in free governments: an "active and continuing interest" in public "debts and particular plans of finance." Together with force, these were the sources of the authority of the British constitution, the only good model available for imitation (Farrand, ed., Vol. 1, pp. 284-86, 288-89, 373, 376, 378-79, 381). Mason, who strongly objected to making the interest of rulers the foundation of authority in a republic, conceded nevertheless that in "the present state of American morals and manners" any plan of government which paid "premiums to a mercenary and depraved ambition" was not likely to lose many friends (Farrand, ed., Vol. 2, p. 284).

Madison was a leader among delegates who believed that the authority of republican government ought not to be derived from its rulers' personal interest in acquiring property in the form of public office. He worked, therefore, to make the narrowest possible application of Hume's doctrine of interest. He believed that republican government cannot be maintained by persons indoctrinated to act merely according to the mores of an acquisitive society. He labored, therefore, to find constitutional language which would prevent

American imitation of influence copied from the British model as it operated both at home and in the former American colonies. Exponents of the British model insisted that interest in holding *executive* office is essential to the energy of government and the accomplishment of great purposes. They were utterly contemptuous of the idea that any person of talent can ever be satisfied with a legislative career. Consequently, they opposed all explicit constitutional barriers to the appointment of ambitious legislators to offices which they vote to create or to compensate with increased emoluments or accept as rewards for supporting the government (Farrand, ed., Vol. 1, pp. 373-74, 386, 388, 390; Vol. 2, p. 405; see also pp. 484-92, 613-14). Madison supported such restrictions because they are essential to republican government. They encourage persons of talent to seek a legislative career, provided they are amply compensated by law and subject to scrutiny by the electorate. They do not bar them from eventual appointment to executive office but they imply that the conception of office as a form of property in which its holder has a personal interest is to be replaced with the idea that office is a public trust in which its holder can have no more than a psychological interest. This change can be effected even though it is necessary to rely on pride, vanity and ambition to move representatives to seek election and reelection to office. They will be tied to their constituents through sympathy and dependency, except for a few who seek other ends through "innovations" which subvert electoral authority (*Federalist* 57, pp. 372-73). For the same reason, Madison argued that Congress is constitutionally prohibited from sharing the president's power to remove executive officers. If Congress did so, it would soon create offices to serve as sinecures for favorites and pensioners (*Papers,* Vol. 12, pp. 255-56).

These restrictions on legislative power were not intended to curb democracy. They were designed to reinforce accountability to the electorate. So long as it is commonly believed that self-government (liberty) requires functional differentiation among governing institutions, it is necessary to show that this goal is consistent with the prevailing theory of political motivation. The members of institutions must have the motives to support their independence and functional integrity, but in the course of doing so their own behavior is so modified from its raw, natural state as to serve the public good. Private and public interest are made perfectly congruent.

The Convention's action to bar imitations of the British model of traditional governmental influence contrasts with its refusal to adopt language barring members of the government from having a personal interest in treasury operations. It was not the result of a plot, but of the opposition of members to provisions excluding particular categories of the population from serving in Congress. Even before the patronage issue was finally settled, Mason proposed to require the ownership of land as a qualification for membership in Congress and to disqualify all persons having unsettled accounts with, or debts to, the United States. The proposal to restrict membership to landowners brought on an immediate charge that it was "a scheme of the landed against the monied interest." Several members reminded all concerned that "the monied interest" is essential "in particular emergencies to the public safety," when a government is dependent on the willingness of the citizens to become its creditors. All apparently agreed that merchants were the most likely creditors during war. This assumption was unjustified because many farmers and planters, Madison noted in a later debate, had property "taken at the point of the bayonet, and a certificate presented in the same manner." It was clear that interest in what critics called "stock-jobbing" can be created only by government which does so only in consequence of waging war. Therefore, it is only a temporary interest, existing until war debt is liquidated. The monied interest was defined in this very narrow sense; it did not refer to other kinds of capital nor to wealth in general as has been supposed. Mason's other proposal was viewed by some delegates as hostile to "the commercial and manufacturing" interests and likely, as well, to cause more mischief than it would cure. Madison opposed Mason on the ground that, despite the solid evidence of abuses in state legislatures, every interest and part of the American community ought to be effectively and sympathetically represented in Congress. When he was challenged in 1788 to defend Congress' power to incur a public debt, Madison responded that war provides the sole occasion for its creation according to European experience. Consequently, we must provide for such "extraordinary emergencies" unless we assume that all wars are avoidable (Farrand, ed., Vol. 2, pp. 121-26, 290, 489-92; *Papers,* Vol. 11, p. 86; Vol. 13, pp. 48-49).

Madison was fully aware of the far-reaching implications of the decision to erect no constitutional barriers to legislative service by public creditors and officers of the armed forces. Conflict among the exponents and opponents of governmental power derived from the personal interest of rulers would undoubtedly continue after the establishment of the new government because the delegates authorized it to assume the obligation of the congressional war debt. The struggle would continue because the supporters of governmental energy derived from the personal interest of rulers regarded republican government as an impediment to the use of public debt for this purpose. The opponents of personal interest as a source of power considered republicanism to be the bulwark of liberty. In this conflict the public debt was like a political coin having obverse and reverse sides. Its exponents insisted that it must constitute one source of a permanent personal interest in order for the government to hold the balance of power in accordance with Hume's analysis of the British model. Opponents of interest such as Madison and Jefferson wanted to liquidate the war debt as soon as possible in order to deny the government its use to create interests which it can employ as the critical mass needed to control the balance of power constitutionally and politically. Both agreed that, if Hume were correct, any government which creates and manipulates the monied interest and its identical twin, the military interest, in order to make them its chosen instruments of power, forces the landed interest into conflict with both of these and the commercial interest as well.

This conflict had existed since 1780, when Madison served his first term in Congress. Madison had not been in Congress long before he became aware that certain members opposed the republican Confederation because it lacked financial powers needed to wage war independent of the wills of the several states. He wished, therefore, for the states to make an explicit grant of such authority to serve this end. It would "reconcile the army and everybody else to our republican forms of government; the principle inconveniences which are imputed to these being really the fruit of defective revenues" (*Papers,* Vol. 2, p. 166). In 1783 he justified his advocacy of an appeal to the states to support a plan for restoring the credit of the United States in order to disprove the charge that unadulterated republican governments will not meet the financial obligations incurred to fight a war of liberation. Americans should do so in particular because their revolutionary struggle had not been a war of "ambition and vain glory" of the sort which had entailed the burdens of public debt on other nations. This distinction between the kinds of wars which generate public debt did not mollify landowners like Mercer who charged that it would "establish and perpetuate a monied interest" which would gain "ascendancy" over the "landed interest" and by its "influence become dangerous to our republican institutions." Madison agreed that if the debt were not liquidated "within the shortest possible time," it would, indeed, "administer poison" to our republican institutions (*Papers,* Vol. 6, pp. 278, 492). Jefferson, also, expressed his concern in January 1787 that the war debt would be chained on our "necks in perpetuum." He outlined for Madison a plan for retiring it. In September 1789 he offered a philosophical doctrine to serve as a restraint on the government in the absence of an explicit constitutional bar to permanent debt and the anti-republican consequences of this omission. No law ought to be contrary to the principle of nature which forbids each generation to entail obligations on posterity. Applied to the war debt, this axiom would place "natural limits" on the borrowing power and thereby "bridle the spirit of War" to which "money-lenders" had excessively free recourse. The incorporation of this axiom into the principles of republican government would perfectly complement the constitutional provision which had transferred the power of making war from the executive to the legislative branch (*Papers,* Vol. 9, p. 284; Vol. 11, pp. 34-35; Vol. 12, pp. 382-87).

Madison agreed that the rule ought to be of particular value, when applied to the debt, but it was unacceptable to Congress as then constituted. He tried, but failed, to secure a "speedy and effectual" provision for the liquidation of the war debt (*Papers,* Vol. 13, p. 65). When this legislative effort proved barren, he used Rousseau's plan for international peace as a text for expounding Jefferson's axiom in order to state the republican doctrine that creation of a permanent war debt clearly distinguishes a government "independent of the will of the people" from governments depending upon the "will of the community." Not even the latter can prevent all wars, but republics offer the best hope of doing so provided they adopt "permanent and constitutional maxims" which forbid a government to entail the "accumulated interest of its perpetual debts" on posterity. Government instigates war, spends for it and "reaps its benefits" unless "avarice" is compelled to "calculate the expenses of ambition" and to make the latter publicly known. This argument was fully consistent with the conviction which Madison expressed before the Constitutional Convention of 1787, during it (*Papers,* Vol. 9, p. 350; Farrand, ed., Vol. 1, p. 318) and afterwards. No republic can endure for long if ruled by an elite consisting of persons combining "the skill and habits of military life and such as possess the great pecuniary resources" of society. The republican theory which vests both "right and power . . . in the majority" cannot hold this circumstance (*Federalist* 43, p. 284).

The bill to establish the Bank of the United States also provoked Madison to believe that its purpose was to extend a permanent monied interest to include working majorities in Congress so as to substitute the personal interest of members of the government in treasury operations for a proper sense of public duty. The covert objective of these operations was, in Madison's judgment, to undercut the constitutional balance so as to render the advantage of different independent branches useless. The bank's supporters assumed that

> the energetic administration of this government is . . . connected with this institution. Mr. M. here stated the principles on which he conceived this government ought to be administered; and added, other gentlemen have had other ideas on the subject, and may have consented to the ratification of the Constitution on different principles or expectations; but he considered the enlightened opinion and affections of the people the only solid basis of support for this government (*Writings*, Vol. 6, pp. 27, 37, 41; *Letters*, Vol. 4, pp. 485-86, 492, 494).

Defeated in Congress, Madison appealed to public opinion in a series of essays which portrayed significant differences between certain models of government and the American republic. The latter was designed to: (1) secure the right to "natural" property in opinions and goods of every variety instead of redistributing it through the artifice of monopolies created by law; (2) derive its "energy" from the "will," enlightened opinions and interests of every "occupation" in every state; it does not substitute private interest for public duty, reward supporters and bribe opponents through the treasury, nor hire persons to use their tongues and pens to sustain the "terror of the sword" so as to enable the few to rule the many despite the latter's "apparent liberty"; and (3) it relies on natural parties to become political checks on each other instead of using the "insinuating" monied interest, emoluments and the "tenor" of military force to "maintain the equilibrium of power." In order to make it clear that he had reference to real events, he asserted that the famous equilibrium of the British constitution, if it ever really existed, does not now depend upon "the form in which its powers are distributed" according to the theory that it is mixed and balanced (*Writings*, Vol. 6, pp. 86-87, 93-94, 101-04, 113-19).

By August 1791 Madison was thoroughly dismayed that his efforts to deny personal interest as a source of the new government's authority had failed. The legislative maneuvers and votes on the funding and bank bills had proved Mason to have been correct at the convention. They were evidence of

> the daring depravity of the times. The stock-jobbers will become the pretorian [*sic*] band of the Government, at once its tool and its tyrant; bribed by its largess, and overwhelming it by its clamours and combinations (*Letters*, Vol. 1, p. 541).

The natural tendency of government to increase its power by basing its energy on personal interest and performing its protective function had been set by artful design upon a self-directed course.

The Metamorphosis of Republican Government

There was a second general reason why Madison believed that the Constitution might become a mask for minority rule. "Measures mold governments" was the rule learned from British experience and confirmed by Hume. The tendency toward autonomy ends in the government's self-transformation even as it maintains the shadows of established forms. Madison based his analysis of constitutional change, one which originated with Machiavelli, on three premises: (1) Like causes produce like effects; war is the cause of all "vigorous and high toned" governments. (2) The "genius" of a government depends on its "system of policy"; hence there should be no introduction of "heterogeneous" (foreign) laws, and certainly not the English common law, unless agreed to expressly because the latter includes numerous "antirepublican doctrines." (3) The relationship between principles and facts can be perceived, just as Hume claimed, through "the eye of the Philosophical Legislator," long before it is "visible to the naked eye of the ordinary politician." The natural principle that one generation cannot bind another is a proposition of this sort. Philosophical insight enables some observers to determine when political actors are disguising their true objectives by manipulating appearances as substitutes for reality. Consequently, the correct "principles ought to govern" both political analysis and decisions because they are "so connected with facts" (Farrand, ed., Vol. 1, pp. 464-65; *Papers*, Vol. 10, p. 197; Vol. 12, p. 373; Vol. 13, p. 25).

Madison's belief that the genius of a government can be affected by its system of policy had a meaning now largely lost to us. He used it in a classical sense to mean that there are known first principles on which the institutions of every kind of regime are founded and they are guides for their proper functioning. They are tutelary. He used "genius" in a second sense derived from the new psychology of politics. It was synonymous with "spirit" in Montesquieu's sense: the springs, the characteristic motivating, energizing forces supporting each type of government. No system can be reduced to only one, however (*Writings*, Vol. 6, p. 93), because the American system properly rests on both ambition and the desire to serve the public good.

Madison repeatedly applied the two categories, system of policy and heterogeneous laws contrary to the genius of republicanism, to the actions of his political opponents in the 1790s. They all tended either to assimilate our institutions to the

British model covertly, or to "warp" public opinion openly in favor of it (*Letters*, Vol. 2, p. 156). Hamilton's financial statutes were a "system of measures more accommodated to" hereditary forms of government than to the "true genius" of ours (*Writings*, Vol. 6, p. 104). The pursuit of "national splendor and glory" by means of wars of ambition ought never to be our primary objective because war appeals to, and generously rewards, the strongest passions, avarice and ambition, as well as the most dangerous weaknesses of human nature, and links them in the use of force (*Papers*, Vol. 11, p. 97; *Writings*, Vol. 6, p. 174). No people were ever given a greater opportunity to understand the danger of intrigues between "political and military leaders," but whether they would profit from the instructive history of less fortunate people Madison was unsure (*Letters*, Vol. 2, p. 156).

Madison was quite explicit about the metamorphosing effects of introducing certain antirepublican principles of the English common law. First, the Constitution created a republican government and every effort to read into that document the common-law prerogative of war and assign it to the president is contrary to its "first principles" and inconsistent with its "forms." If it were to be accepted, then no citizen could any longer even guess the "character of the government under which he lives," nor could even the most learned jurist predict the extent of the "constructive prerogative" (*Writings*, Vol. 6, pp. 149, 151). Second, constructive incorporation of the common law of sedition would strike with equal force at the first principles of our republican government. Punishment for the utterance of political opinion not only destroys the very essence of a free government, but also converts it into a system of rule independent of the will of the majority of the community. When both of these anti-republican doctrines are constructively incorporated and combined, the design is clear. In 1798 Madison was convinced by Adams' war measures and support of the Sedition Act that it was his intention to transform the United States into "the makeweight of the European Balances of Power" in accordance with his theory of constitutional equilibrium and his love of the "maxims" of the British constitution. We have now long forgotten that the Virginia Assembly justified its resolutions of December, 1798, and Madison's exposition of its meaning and intended effect with another resolution. It declared that "the policy of the United States forbids a war of aggression" and the standing military forces needed to wage it. This warning was based on the proposition that "measures can mold governments," especially when they are "pretexts for power afforded by war." Once such transforming measures are added to "constructive perversions of the Constitution," Madison added, "our code of laws" will determine the "form as well as the powers of Government" (*Writings*, Vol. 6, pp. 310, 321, 327-28, 333, 338, 340, 407).

Conclusions

Madison was neither an opponent of majority rule and political parties responsive to public opinion nor a pluralist. The objective of his political theory was to show that limited government can be founded on human nature which interacts with stable institutions to serve the common good. This prospect is realistic so long as political authority rests on enlightened public opinion and the limited personal interest of rulers in the gratification derived from public service. Authority based on these two sources tends, however, to create a tension between strict accountability to a diverse society and governmental autonomy once an initial degree of support has been established. Thereafter, the balance of political authority is not based solely on the constitutional text nor on the balance of private property. War, in particular, enables government to alter this balance and it is likely to do so, given human nature and the gratification provided it by wars calculated to extend hegemony over others. The only countervailing force opposing such a change is appeal to public opinion to sustain the first principles and forms of accountable, representative government. Over time the moral and political authority of such a government is derived in great measure from the common belief that it has used power for beneficial purposes.

References

Adair, Douglas (1957). " 'That Politics May Be Reduced to a Science': David Hume, James Madison and the Tenth Federalist." *Huntington Library Quarterly* 20: 343-59.

Beard, Charles A. (1913). *An Economic Interpretation of the Constitution*. New York: Macmillan.

——— (1945). *The Economic Basis of Politics*. New York: Knopf.

Bentley, Arthur F. (1967; first published in 1908). *The Process of Government*. Cambridge, Mass.: Belknap Press, Harvard University Press.

Bourke, Paul T. (1975). "The Pluralist Reading of James Madison's Tenth *Federalist.*" *Perspectives in American History*, Vol. 9. Cambridge, Mass.: Harvard University Press, pp. 271-95.

Burns, Edward M. (1968). *James Madison Philosopher of the Constitution*. New York: Octagon Books.

Burns, James M. (1967). *Deadlock of Democracy*. Englewood Cliffs, N.J.: Prentice-Hall.

Dahl, Robert A. (1956). *A Preface to Democratic Theory*. Chicago: University of Chicago Press.

______ (1967). *Pluralist Democracy in the United States*. Chicago: Rand McNally.

Farrand, Max, ed. (1913). *The Records of the Federal Convention of 1787*, 4 vols. New Haven, Conn.: Yale University Press.

Forbes, Duncan (1975). *Hume's Philosophical Politics*. Cambridge: Cambridge University Press.

Hamilton, Alexander, John Jay and James Madison (1937). *The Federalist*. Introduction by Edward M. Earle. New York: Modern Library.

Hartz, Louis (1955). *The Liberal Tradition in America*. New York: Harcourt, Brace & World.

Hofstadter, Richard (1972). *The Idea of a Party System*. Berkeley: University of California Press.

Holcombe, Arthur M. (1950). *Our More Perfect Union*. Cambridge, Mass.: Harvard University Press.

Hume, David (1770). *Essays and Treatises on Several Subjects*, New Edition, 6 vols. London: T. Cadell.

Ketcham, Ralph L. (1957). "Notes on James Madison's Sources for the Tenth Federalist Paper." *Midwest Journal of Politics* 1: 20-25.

Locke, John (1946). *The Second Treatise of Civil Government*. Edited with an introduction by J. W. Gough. Oxford: Basil Blackwell.

Machiavelli, Niccolò (1965). *The Chief Works*, 3 vols. Translated by Allan Gilbert. Durham, N.C.: Duke University Press.

Madison, James (1884). *Letters and other Writings of James Madison*, 4 vols. New York: Worthington.

______ (1900-1910). *The Writings of James Madison*, 9 vols. Edited by Gaillard Hunt. New York: Putnam.

______ (1962 to date). *The Papers of James Madison*, 13 vols. to date. Edited by William T. Hutchinson, William M. E. Rachal, Robert A. Rutland and others. Chicago: University of Chicago Press; Charlottesville: University Press of Virginia.

Marshall, G. (1954). "David Hume and Political Scepticism." *The Philosophical Quarterly* 4: 247-57.

Marx, Karl (1930). *Capital*, 2 vols. Introduction by G. D. H. Cole. Translated by Eden and Cedar Paul. London: J. P. Dent.

May, Henry F. (1976). *The Enlightenment in America*. New York: Oxford University Press.

Montesquieu, Charles Louis de Secondat, Baron de (1949). *The Spirit of the Laws*, 2 vols. New York: Hafner.

Parrington, Vernon L. (1930). *Main Currents in American Thought*, 3 vols. New York: Harcourt, Brace.

Ranney, Austin (1975). *Curing the Mischiefs of Faction*. Berkeley: University of California Press.

Riemer, Neal (1967). *The Democratic Experience*. New York: Van Nostrand.

Schattschneider, E. E. (1942). *Party Government*. New York: Farrar and Rinehart.

Smith, J. Allen (1965: first published 1907). *The Spirit of American Government*. Cambridge, Mass.: Belknap Press, Harvard University Press.

White, Morton (1956). *Social Thought in America*. Boston: Beacon Press.

Wolin, Sheldon (1954). "Hume and Conservatism." *American Political Science Review* 47: 999-1016.

Wood, Gordon (1969). *The Creation of the American Republic*. New York: Norton.

Wright, Benjamin F. (1949). "The Federalist and the Nature of Political Man." *Ethics* 59, Pt. 2: 1-31.

[3]

Madison, *The Federalist,* & the Constitutional Order: Human Nature & Institutional Structure

Joseph F. Kobylka
Southern Methodost University, and

Bradley Kent Carter
Southern Methodist University

Interpretations of James Madison have tended to ignore his complex conception of human nature and how it colors his understanding of the plan for the Constitution. This article argues that Madison did not see human nature as either unstintingly Hobbesian or unambiguously virtuous, but rather as containing elements of both. Madison builds "auxiliary precautions" into the American system as defenses against the dark side of human nature, but at the same time rests the "primary controul of government" on the virtue of the people. To miss this duality in Madison's understanding of human nature, the authors argue, is to miss both the sophistication of Madison's defense of the Constitution and the normative core of his thought.

Joseph F. Kobylka is Assistant Professor of Political Science at Southern Methodist University. He has published in areas of public law, as well as American political thought. Bradley Kent Carter is an Associate Professor of Political Science at Southern Methodist University. A specialist in political theory, he and Kobylka have collaborated on several studies of the thought of James Madison.

The founding period has captivated Americans. A cascade of works explicate *the* theory of the Founders, *the* intellectual tradition they represent, *the* politics they would champion were they yet alive. James Madison has played an especially important role in this story, which is easily understood given the role he played at the Constitutional Convention and in explaining its product. Attempts to explicate his argument, however, have too often been made by drawing on secondary sources and a few primary works, or by refusing to take him at his word. These approaches slight Madison's complex formulation of human nature and its crucial relationship to his political thought.

Many interpretations of Madison ascribe to him a Hobbesian view of human nature that posits human beings who act solely from selfish motives, are incapable of understanding the interests of others, fear domination by others, and lust after power for themselves. Passages in *Federalist* 10 and 51 and some of his other writings lend support to this interpretation. Indeed, a government ordered on checks and balances seems to be premised on Hobbesian concerns: why check power if it is not subject to abuse by those who wield it? Moreover, the paramount foe of popular government, faction, is caused by a desire of a portion of the citizenry to dominate all citizens. This is what the Madisonian system is designed to combat. If humans were not Hobbesian, the problem of faction would not arise.

There is a superficial plausibility to labeling Madison's conception of human nature Hobbesian, but close analysis of his work demonstrates the contrary. His argument is premised on a variable human nature among and within individuals. This makes him more difficult to categorize, but considerably richer as a political thinker. It also suggests that the system defended in *The Federalist* is not understood in Madison's terms when it is treated as acting on, and being run by, Hobbesians.

Many of Madison's interpreters have done disservice to his thought. They have bent it to reflect analytic concerns not shared by the Virginian. They have read his writings through their eyes, not his. This problem can be lessened by paying close attention to primary texts and relying less on their interpretation by others. This approach avoids a problem that has plagued many students of Madison, who see in his writings only that conception of human nature they were taught was there and who ignore language and arguments that suggest the contrary.[1] This has served also to cloud their understanding of his defense of the constitutional system.

Madison asserts that government is "but a reflection on human

1. Some argue that non-Hobbesian references to human nature in Madison's *Federalist Papers* are merely included to distract from the core of his analysis and placate potential opponents. While *The Federalist* was produced as propaganda, it is dangerous to discard parts of it when trying to reconstruct its argument faithfully. On this point, see David F. Epstein, *The Political Theory of The Federalist* (Chicago: University of Chicago Press, 1984). Madison may have *meant* what he said when referring to things such as the capacity to act virtuously. It may be that as "moderns" we can reject, as does Robert Dahl, such references as "dubious and probably false;" Dahl, *Preface to Democratic Theory* (Chicago: University of Chicago Press, 1956), p. 17. However, to dismiss them because we think them naive is to read less of Madison and more of ourselves. For a sensitive treatment of the problem of interpretation, see Albert Furtwangler, *The Authority of Publius* (Ithaca, NY: Cornell University Press, 1985), chapter 5.

nature." While "auxiliary precautions" of institutional checks and pluralism are defended in light of human nature, he contends that a "dependence on the people . . . is the primary controul on government." The link between a variable human nature and the functioning of government is the key to understanding his defense of the institutional arrangements established by the Constitution. Madison envisions a political system that will operate in different ways depending on the present character of American citizens—a complex machine with backup mechanisms to forestall the disasters to which popular government is prone.

I. Madison's Reflections on Human Nature

Madison's thought has generated a wide variety of interpretations—e.g., economic,[2] pluralist,[3] and "depolitization"[4]—but the common thread through them all is their attribution to him of a Hobbesian conception of human nature. Louis Hartz argues that Madison possessed a "pessimistic view of human nature" grounded in "Hobbesian universalism."[5] Vernon Parrington contends that his goal was to "overcome universal selfishness" through the domination of government.[6] Sheldon Wolin sees him "appealing to self-interest and economic motives."[7] Nor-

2. Charles A. Beard, *An Economic Interpretation of the Constitution of the United States* (New York: The Macmillan Company, 1913); Vernon L. Parrington, *Main Currents in American Political Thought* (New York: Harcourt, Brace & Co., 1927).

3. See Louis Hartz, *The Liberal Tradition in America* (New York: Harcourt, Brace, Jovanovich, 1955); Dahl, *Preface to Democratic Theory,* chapter 1; Hannah Pitkin, *The Concept of Representation* (Berkeley, CA: University of California Press, 1967); and David Truman, *The Governmental Process* (New York: Alfred A. Knopf, Inc., 1951). Although Martin Diamond does not cite Dahl, his version of Madison's polity is not unlike the latter's polyarchy. See Diamond, *"The Federalist,"* in *History and Political Philosophy,* ed. Leo Strauss and James Cropsey, 2nd ed. (Chicago: Rand McNally, 1972), pp. 631–51.

4. See Norman Jacobson, "Political Science and Political Education," *American Political Science Review,* 62 (September 1963): 561–69; Sheldon Wolin, *Politics and Vision* (Boston: Little, Brown, and Company, 1960); Wolin, "The People's Two Bodies," *Democracy,* 1 (January 1981): 9–24; Gordon S. Wood, *Creation of the American Republic* (Chapel Hill, NC: University of North Carolina, 1969); Mason Drukman, *Community and Purpose in America* (New York: McGraw Hill, 1971); Terrance Ball, "The Ontological Presuppositions and Political Consequences of a Social Science," in *Changing Social Science,* ed. Daniel Sabia, Jr., and Jerald Wallulis (Albany, NY: State University of New York Press, 1983), pp. 31–51.

5. Hartz, *The Liberal Tradition,* pp. 80, 82.

6. Parrington, *Main Currents,* p. 290.

7. Wolin, "The People's Two Bodies," p. 14.

man Jacobson holds him to be fearful of human nature: "[He] anticipated little good, but mainly evil."[8] However, it is Robert Dahl who best summarizes the prevailing understanding of Madison's conception of human nature:

> These axioms are Hobbesian in character and run something like this: Men are instruments of their desires. They pursue their desires to satiation if given the opportunity. One such desire is the desire for power over other individuals, for not only is power directly satisfying but it also has great instrumental value because a wide variety of satisfactions depend upon it.[9]

This reading of Madison draws on comments of some of his contemporaries, his association with Hamilton, secondary scholarly sources, and some passages in his *Federalist Papers,* of which the following are best known:

> The latent causes of faction are thus sown in the nature of man . . . and render them much more disposed to vex and oppress each other, than to co-operate for their common good. So strong is this propensity of mankind to fall into mutual animosities, that where no substantial occasion presents itself, the most frivolous and fanciful distinctions have been sufficient to kindle their unfriendly passions, and excite their most violent conflicts *(Federalist* 10, p. 44).[10]

> Ambition must be made to counter ambition . . . If men were angels, no government would be necessary. If angels were to govern men, neither external nor internal controuls on government would be necessary. In framing a government which is to be administered by men over men, the great difficulty lies in this: You must first enable the government to controul the governed; and in the next place oblige it to controul itself *(Federalist* 51, p. 262).

These are not the words of a starry-eyed idealist. At a minimum, Madison sees selfishness and other dangerous elements in human nature. The question is, does he see them to be its defining elements?

Not all of Madison's interpreters view his concept of human nature as Hobbesian. J. G. A. Pocock sees a concern for virtue in Madison's work

8. Jacobson, "Political Science and Political Education," p. 562.

9. Dahl, *Preface,* p. 8.

10. There are numerous editions of *The Federalist.* All citations in this text are to Garry Wills, ed., *The Federalist* (New York: Bantam Books, 1982).

that was not fully translated into the Constitution.[11] Martin Edelman finds Hobbesian aspects in his writings, but argues that Madison and the other framers "did not see virtue and self-interest to be mutually exclusive." Reason would constrain selfishness thus serving as a "substitute for the virtuous citizenry of classical republican theory."[12] David Epstein sees a passionate sense of honor as performing the task Edelman has Madison assign to reason. However, since Madison does not stress reason as a check to faction, Edelman's argument is poorly supported by text. Epstein is closer to the mark, although love of honor is only a portion of what Madison calls virtue. His discussion also misses the variability Madison sees to be a part of human nature.

Garry Wills contends that Madison was a theorist of virtue.[13] While problematic on a number of scores,[14] his analysis of *The Federalist* points to much in that text that was previously ignored. He argues that Madison was no Hobbesian and can only be understood in the context of the Scottish Enlightenment. Seeing in Madison the arguments of David Hume, Wills contends that he had an "optimistic view of human nature" and understood the constitutional system in this light.[15] By finding in Madison an animating concern for virtuous behavior, Wills strongly challenges interpretations premised on Hobbesian assumptions. He contends that all prior attempts to come to grips with Madison's thought have been wrong. This bold claim is in part supportable, but only in part.

Madison's analysis in *The Federalist* and other texts suggests that he did not see human nature to be a constant. While he occasionally uses language that seems Hobbesian, he also argues that humans are benevolent and capable of transcending private interests when addressing public problems. *Federalist* 55[16] notes that,

11. Pocock, *The Machiavellian Moment* (Princeton, NJ: Princeton University Press, 1975), chapter 15.

12. Edelman, *Democratic Theories and the Constitution* (Albany, NY: State University of New York Press, 1984), p. 298.

13. Wills, *Explaining America* (Garden City, NY: Doubleday, 1980).

14. For example, Wills sees David Hume as Madison's sole teacher on the art and science of politics. This is questionable intellectual history, but that does not wholly negate the thrust of his insights into the Madisonian corpus. For critiques of Wills's argument, see Edmund S. Morgan, "Refining the Public Spirit," *The New Republic,* 24 January 1981, pp. 26–30, and Gordon S. Wood, "Heroics," *New York Review of Books,* 2 April 1981, pp. 16–18.

15. Wills, *Explaining America,* p. 189.

16. There is some confusion as to who wrote this paper, but both Wills and Clinton Rossiter, ed., *The Federalist* (New York: New American Library, 1961), attribute it to Madison. For the difficulties involved in such attribution, see Furtwangler, *The Authority of Publius,* pp. 30-32.

> As there is a degree of depravity in mankind which requires a certain degree of circumspection and distrust: So there are other qualities in human nature, which justify a certain portion of esteem and confidence. ***Republican government presupposes the existence of these qualities in a higher degree than any other form*** (p. 284; emphasis added).

For Madison, the nature of people is neither universal nor constant, but variable and malleable.[17] One nature allows republican governance; another invites despotism. The aspects of human nature that "justify a certain portion of esteem and confidence" are present in Americans of his day. He calls these characteristics "virtue."

The first task in analyzing Madison's concept of virtue is to examine the ways in which he uses the term. Wills contends that Madison's understanding is drawn from Montesquieu's classical conception of public virtue which saw it as preferring the good of the whole to that of the self.[18] This linkage is found in Madison's discussion of republican legitimacy: "No man is allowed to be a judge in his own cause; because his interest would certainly bias his judgment, and, not improbably, corrupt his integrity" *(Federalist* 10, p. 44). This is not Madison's sole reference to this idea in *The Federalist.* In *Federalist* 37, he speaks of the republican need for "a deep conviction of the necessity of sacrificing private opinions and partial interest to the public good" (pp. 181–82).[19] In a later paper he writes that questions of public policy should

> . . . turn on the true merits of the question . . . [instead of being] connected with the spirit of pre-existing parties, or of parties springing out of the question itself . . . [In this case] the ***passions*** therefore not ***the reason,*** of the public, would sit in judgment. But it is the reason of the public alone that ought to controul and regulate the government *(Federalist* 49, p. 258; emphasis in original).

17. This passage, as well as others in his text, demonstrates that Madison does not hold to a universalistic Hobbesian perspective on questions of human nature. See, for example, his 1792 essay "Who Are the Best Keepers of the People's Liberties" where he writes ". . . the people ought to be enlightened, awakened . . ." (Gaillard Hunt, *The Writings of James Madison,* 9 vols. (New York: G.P. Putnam and Sons, 1902–10), vol. VI, pp. 120, 121. Subsequent references to this work appear as (Hunt, volume, page).

18. Wills, *Explaining America,* Chapter 22.

19. Many Anti-Federalists argued that the system established by the Constitution relied too heavily on virtue. See Herbert J. Storing, *What the Anti-Federalists Were For* (Chicago: University of Chicago Press, 1981), p. 51.

The text of Madison's argument shows that his conception of political action is based on a vision of the public good. Faction is the obverse of virtue. The concept implies its opposite: governance in the interest of the whole. Faction is dangerous to popular government because it places private over public interests. It allows the public interest to be "sacrifice[d] to temporary or partial considerations" *(Federalist* 10, p. 47). While the "latent causes of faction are sown into human nature" (ibid., p. 44), Madison is clear that at least some people are able to overcome its impulse and act in a way consonant with "individual rights and the permanent and aggregate interests of the whole" (ibid., p. 43).

Madison assumed that American citizens were potentially virtuous. In *Federalist* 39 he argues that the "genius of the people of America" was republican and that any proposed government must be consistent with this "republican character" (p. 189). At various points in *The Federalist* he asserts the capacity for virtue in the citizenry. He writes in *Federalist* 49 that Americans possess "virtue and intelligence" (p. 256), and in number 57 that a "vigilant and manly spirit . . . actuates the people of America, a spirit which nourishes freedom, and in return is nourished by it" (p. 291). He further suggests that a virtuous people will zealously guard against legislative encroachments on their liberty *(Federalist* 55, p. 282). Without virtue, attempts at self-government will decay into despotism *(Federalist* 55, p. 284). In sum, a virtuous citizenry is required to make "a dependence on the people . . . the primary controul on the government" *(Federalist* 51, p. 262).

Madison's relative optimism about the nature of the American citizenry is not unbounded. While republican virtue is the present character of Americans, it is not their sole trait. Human nature is multifaceted. He underscored this theme before the Virginia Convention of 1830: ". . . but man is known to be a selfish as well as a social being" (Hunt, IX, p. 361). Many of his words in *The Federalist* note the human capacity for selfishness and tyranny. *Federalist* 10 roots faction in human nature, and in no way suggests that Americans are wholly immune to it. It is the danger to which most experiments in popular government succumb, and its ills were seen by Madison to have poisoned many of the state governments. The domination of selfish interests is the bane of all popular governments and must be guarded against: "It is well known that interest leads to injustice" (Hunt, V, p. 287). But Madison holds that propensity to faction can be overcome. While he notes the "infirmities and depravities of the human character," he speaks in the same paper of the "deep conviction of the necessity of sacrificing private opinions and partial interest to the public good" that made possible the success of the Convention *(Federalist* 37, pp. 181–82).

Madison's political and intellectual life was devoted to guarding against the selfishness of faction. He worked in the public realm promoting an informed citizenry and republican governance. He ministered to human nature without creating a fully developed theory of it. As Furtwangler notes, he never saw himself as a systematic philosopher.[20] He knew that humans could act in accordance with interests larger than their own, just as they could behave factiously. He did believe that a disposition to republican virtue was "the *present* genius of the people of America," but this suggests the possibility of its change *(Federalist* 55, p. 282). His task was not to devise a theory that explained this ambivalence, but to construct political institutions that check the ignoble and promote the noble.

The institutions defended by Madison reflected his understanding of this task. They lent themselves to description and analysis in terms of the mechanical metaphors popular in his day. Madison's constitutional machine is complete with primary systems to promote and facilitate the expression of public virtue and "auxiliaries" to prevent the destruction of the virtuous whole should public virtue occasionally wane. No machine is foolproof, but Madison argues in *The Federalist* that the structures and processes articulated in the Constitution make its machinery the best that can be assembled for republican self-governance. Its preservation was his dying wish, the theme of his political testament, "Advice to My Country."[21]

II. Public Virtue, Private Interest, and Madisonian Structures

Madison's conception of human nature is central to his explanation of the Constitutional machine; *". . . what is government itself but the greatest of all reflections on human nature?" (Federalist* 51, p. 262; emphasis added). He repeatedly stresses that the people are the only "legitimate fountain of power" *(Federalist* 49, p. 255; Hunt, VI, p. 120) and that it is essential to republican government that its powers derive from "the great body of the society, not from an inconsiderable portion, or favored class of it" *(Federalist* 39, p. 190). Because Madison believes that the nature of a people determines the type of government compatible with them, a republican government requires a republican citizenry.

As Madison sees a multifaceted human nature, so too he prescribes a multidimensional institutional arrangement that takes into account its

20. Furtwangler, *The Authority of Publius,* p. 43.

21. Irving Brant, *James Madison: Father of the Constitution,* in 6 vols. (New York: Bobbs-Merrill Co., 1950), vol. VI, p. 530.

various possibilities. His discussion of the way the institutions of government are to work parallels his treatment of human nature and is therefore neither clear nor simple. Attention to his complex notion of human nature helps to avoid an overly simplified reconstruction of his understanding of the constitutional system.

Representation

For Madison, simple democracy would not preclude factious control of the national government.

> A common passion or interest will, in almost every case, be felt by a majority of the whole . . . there is nothing to check the inducements to sacrifice the weaker party, or an obnoxious individual. Hence it is that such Democracies have ever been spectacles of turbulence and contention . . . and have in general been as short in their lives, as they have been violent in their deaths *(Federalist* 10, p. 45).

Republicanism, another species of popular government, improves upon democracy by adding the principle of representation which in turn permits expansion of the territory incorporated into the system. Representation and space are crucial aspects of the system he defends as that best fitted to the "republican genius" of the American people.

Wills, extending Douglas Adair's insight,[22] contends that the goal of Madison's representational plan was to keep faction *out* of government by election of non-factious, disinterested, and virtuous representatives. This flies in the face of pluralist readings of Madison which see representation introducing factions into the legislature to facilitate compromise. Superficially, it is more in line with the depolitization thesis implicit in Charles Beard and made manifest by the Berkeley School: Sheldon Wolin, Norman Jacobson, Terrance Ball, et al. These scholars see his plan as an attempt to keep faction out of government, but, for them, faction is the property-less majority. In essence, then, Madison's system is designed to install a faction of wealth over the unpropertied; his representatives are trustees of the economic elite.

The latter interpretation has its difficulties. First, while noting that property and wealth are "the most common and durable source of faction" *(Federalist* 10, p. 44), Madison does not limit faction to them. He notes such additional sources as religion, political views, and attachment to different leaders. The logic of his argument does not allow a distinc-

22. Adair, *Fame and the Founding Fathers* (New York: Norton, 1974).

tion between factious and non-factious groups on the basis of economic differences; people of wealth are as liable to faction as any other. Finally, adherents to this interpretation have never satisfactorily explained why Madison, if a champion of privilege, was allied politically with Thomas Jefferson for all of his life. In fact, Jefferson, a champion of the people from this perspective, supported ratification of the Constitution with only a few reservations.[23] Madison's argument is not an attempt to enshrine the propertied class.

Wills argues correctly that Madison's plan of representation was intended to put virtuous individuals into the legislature. The capacity for virtuous governance could be realized if a representational plan was constructed to promote election of the right kind of representatives. Thus, the "fundamental principle" of republican government was that citizens must choose virtuous representatives to act as their agents *(Federalist* 57, pp. 291-92). The way this is to be done is the heart of Madison's theory of representations. Wills errs, however, in seeing this as the whole of Madison's protection against faction.

Madison suggests that some people in society achieve a higher level of virtue than others and argues that they should hold office in the national legislature. Like the delegates to the Constitutional Convention, they would seek to promote the interest of the whole by focusing on the "true merits of a question" *(Federalist* 49, p. 258). Their characteristics are noted at various points in *The Federalist.* Number 10 refers to representatives who will deliberate with "a sole regard to justice and the public good" (p. 45) and "whose enlightened views and virtuous sentiments render them superior to local prejudices, and to schemes of injustice" (p. 48). He also contends that a large republic is "most favorable to the election of proper guardians of the public weal" (p. 47). In *Federalist* 53, he points out that a "competent legislator" will have "an upright intention and a sound judgment" (p. 272). Finally, Madison argues in *Federalist* 57 that

> The aim of every Constitution is or ought to be first to obtain for rulers, men who possess most wisdom to discern, and most virtue to pursue the common good of the society; and in the next place, to take the most effectual precautions for keeping them virtuous, whilst they hold their public trust (p. 289).

23. See Jefferson's letters to Alexander Donald, 7 Feb. 1788 in *The Political Writings of Thomas Jefferson,* ed. Edward Dumbauld (New York: The Liberal Arts Press, 1955), p. 137; Edward Carrington, 27 May 1788 (ibid., p. 138); James Madison, 31 July 1788 in *The Portable Thomas Jefferson,* ed. Merrill Peterson (New York: Penguin Books, 1975), p. 141; and John Norvell, 14 June 1807 (ibid., p. 504).

The former is achieved by a properly constructed representational scheme, the latter by periodic elections. In the same paper, he articulates a rule by which citizens can measure the fitness of candidates who present themselves for office.

> Who are to be the objects of popular choice? Every citizen whose merit may recommend him to the esteem and confidence of his country. No qualification of wealth, of birth, of religious faith, or of civil profession, is permitted to fetter the judgment or disappoint the inclination of the people (p. 290).

Madison's ideal legislator is the embodiment of the republican virtue of his constituency.[24]

How are such virtuous people to be elected? Wills's concoction argument, drawn from Madison's supposed obeisance to David Hume, cannot be supported. Despite references to "refining" the public's view through the representational system, there is no concoctions analysis in Madison's writings. Wills demonstrates that James Wilson made such an analysis at the Constitutional Convention,[25] but Wilson is not Madison. Wills is right about the ends of the scheme, but wrong about its means. The election of virtuous agents is not Humean; Madison suggests a more practical, less theory-bound approach.

In *Federalist* 55, Madison argues that republican virtue enables citizens to select representatives best qualified to act as "guardians of the people" (p. 284). Elections

> *refine and enlarge the public views* by passing them through the medium of a chosen body of citizens, whose wisdom may best discern *the true interest* of their country and whose patriotism and love of justice *will be least likely to sacrifice it to temporary or partial considerations (Federalist* 10, pp. 46–7; emphasis added).

Because of the wisdom and virtue of these representatives, Madison contends it is *possible* that their actions "will be more consonant to the public good than if pronounced by the people themselves, convened for

24. Dahl contends that Madison's descriptions of wise, etc., representatives and their availability in an extended republic is "extremely dubious and probably false" *(Preface to Democratic Theory,* p. 16). However, this assertion—an important one given the descriptive language Madison uses throughout *The Federalist*—is not supported by any evidence. It may be that Dahl does not believe, as is also true of Gordon Wood *(Creation of the American Republic* and "Heroes"), that there are such people. However, the opinions of these scholars need not coincide with those of Madison.

25. Wills, *Explaining America,* chapter 28.

that purpose'' (ibid., 47). If representation alone facilitates this end, he has solved the problem of faction, but it does not. State legislatures operated on a principle of representation, but he contends that factions had gained control of them as a result of small and homogeneous electoral districts. This made appeal to the partial interests of the electorate profitable: factious candidates were able to address narrow interests and gain election.

Space, extent of territory, is the final ingredient in the Madisonian solution. The size of legislative districts is crucial. In commenting on Jefferson's proposed Constitution for Virginia, Madison notes that small districts elect representatives who ''are everywhere observed to lose sight of the aggregate interests of the community, and even to sacrifice them to the interests and prejudices of their respective constituents'' (Hunt, V, p. 285). If few enough representatives are parceled out over a great enough space, individual electoral districts will contain more and different interests. The more interests in a district, the less likely the existence of a majority interest to which a demagogue could appeal. This encourages candidates to appeal to general, not factious interests. Large districts thus encourage a virtuous exercise of the ballot by the citizenry. Freeing the electorate from attachment to their selfish interests makes them ''more likely to center on men who possess the most attractive merit and the most diffusive and established characters'' (*Federalist* 10, p. 47). As this process produces virtuous representatives, it also exercises the virtue of the citizenry and reinforces their republican genius.

Madison's representation plan is calculated to ensure, insofar as possible, that those Jefferson termed the ''natural aristocracy'' would be elected. Wills calls this virtual representation, but Madison's argument is more subtle and complex. Wills contends that his aim was to have representatives wholly escape local influence, but Madison argues they must balance local and national interests. This is suggested in his discussion of the proper size for a legislative district.

> By enlarging too much the number of electors, you render the representative too little acquainted with all their local circumstances and lesser interests; as by reducing it too much, you render him unduly attached to these, and too little fit to comprehend and pursue great and national objects (*Federalist* 10, p. 47).

Wills's interpretation would also preclude the representative's role in cultivating the virtue of his constituency. This ignores the educative nature of electoral campaigns. Candid, non-factious argument elevates the public just as factious argument debases it. Good political debate was important to Madison: "if an early & well digested effort for calling out the real sense of the people be not made, there is room to apprehend they may in many places be misled" (Hunt, VI, 179).

Madison's linking of private interest, public virtue, space, and representation suggests that the republican genius of Americans was the wellspring of his constitutional theory. Seeing the system as premised on the potential for human virtue is contrary to standard interpretations of his thought. This is, in large measure, the contribution of Wills to the debate over Madison, but it is not the end of an interpretive effort. Madison's discussion does not end with representation, nor does it ignore the dangers posed by selfishness in the public realm. Different levels of public virtue exist in society at different times. Creation of an enduring Constitution requires attention to the possibility for change in the genius of the citizenry. Madison's system is structured to deal with this possibility.

Institutional Arrangement: The "Auxiliary Precautions"

Madison believed that he lived in a time of widespread public virtue. The nation had just emerged from a war of independence that required sacrifice to the common good. The debates of the Constitutional Convention were only successful, according to him, because of the virtue of its participants. He also knew people who had sacrificed their private interests and devoted much of their lives to public service. Washington was foremost among them,[26] but there were also, for example, Jefferson, Hamilton, Franklin, and Adams. But Madison knew too that the distribution of virtue could wax and wane. Governmental forms had to be created with this in mind.

Madison's representation scheme is the primary check against faction in government. However, while necessary, it is not sufficient. The malleability of human nature can lead to a decline in the virtue required for its successful operation. As a result,

> It is vain to say that enlightened statesmen will be able to adjust these clashing interests, and render them all subservient to the public good. Enlightened statesmen will not always be at the helm (*Federalist* 10, p. 45).

The plan of representation can fail to check faction. Virtuous citizens can be duped by "unworthy candidates [who] practise with success the

26. For the contemporary view of Washington see Garry Wills, *Cincinnatus: George Washington and the American Enlightenment* (Garden City, NY: Doubleday, 1984).

vicious arts, by which elections are too often carried'' (ibid., p. 47). They can also lose virtue temporarily and elect factious representatives. Because of this, precautions are necessary to maintain a stable base to await a reemergence of republican virtue. These precautions are not failsafe, but they are the best a virtuous founder can construct "without violating the principles [of popular government] to which he is attached'' (ibid., p. 42).

Madison's machine contains three "auxiliary precautions'' to protect popular government. One, federalism, is a product of historical development and political compromise at the convention.[27] It serves to check faction because,

> In the compound republic of America, the power surrendered by the people is first divided between two distinct governments, and then the portion allotted to each, subdivided among distinct and separate departments. Hence a double security arises to the rights of the people. The different governments will controul each other, at the same time that each will be controulled by itself *(Federalist* 51, p. 264).

A second "auxiliary precaution'' is the separation of powers in the national government. Wills suggests that, for Madison, separation of powers is independent of checks and balances.[28] This argument is problematic. Wills's difficulties stem from a too close textual analysis of *Federalist* 51, a desire to see Hume working through Madison's pen, and a failure to comprehend the structural significance of Madison's complex notion of human nature. Wills is correct to argue that the only check explicitly mentioned in number 51 is bicameralism. Indeed, papers 62 and 63 demonstrate the importance Madison placed on it. The latter speaks of the ability of a Senate in which virtue reigns to halt a factious House where virtue has lost its place: such an institution may be sometimes necessary, as a defense for the people against their own delusions. However, Madison's stress on the bicameral check should not blind us to the rest of his argument, nor to the structural relationships of the institutions he was defending.

While the focus of the discussion in *Federalist* 51 is separation of powers, its argument clearly points to the ability of the separate branches to stymie factious actions of the others. At the outset of the paper, Madison asks,

27. See Andrew C. McLaughlin, "The Background of American Federalism," *American Political Science Review,* 12 (May 1918): 215–40.

28. Wills, *Explaining America,* chapters 12, 13.

> To what expedient then shall we finally resort for maintaining in practice the necessary partition of power among the several departments, as laid down in the constitution? The only answer that can be given is, that as all these exterior provisions are found to be inadequate, the defect must be supplied, by so contriving the interior structure of the government, as that its several constituent parts may, by their mutual relations, be the means of keeping each other in their proper places (p. 261).

Thus, "some minimum deviations from the principle [separated powers] must be admitted" (p. 262). He suggests that

> . . . the great security against a gradual concentration of the several powers in the same department, consists in giving to those who administer each department the necessary constitutional means, and personal motives, to resist encroachments of the others (ibid.).

He then launches into the "ambition must be made to counteract ambition" argument that concludes with the assertions that, first, government must reflect human nature, and second, "reliance on the people is *no doubt* the primary controul on the government; but experience has taught mankind the *necessity* of auxiliary precautions" (p. 262; emphasis added). One of these precautions is the checking function of individual departments of the national government, and it is to operate when the check of the people, because infected with partial interest, does not adequately stand "centinel over the public rights" (p. 263). This arrangement, an "invention of prudence" (ibid.), is required to minimize the dangers if faction captures parts of the government. Institutional checks are a backup to preserve virtuous governance should its primary source—the people—momentarily fail. Wills fails to see this because of the assumptions that guide his analysis.

The institutional arrangement Madison defends, in addition to his argument in *Federalist* 51, further supports the contention that he saw institutional checks to be among the "auxiliary precautions" required to protect popular government. The presidential veto, the role of the Senate in ratifying treaties and confirming judicial nominations, and the power of judicial review are all present in the Constitution Madison was defending. To isolate, as Wills does, those aspects of the proposed government from the analysis offered in *Federalist* 51 is to miss the supplementary part of Madison's argument. He was aware of the whole of the system he was discussing in that paper, and this must be considered in a construction of its argument.

While Madison intends to keep faction out of government by means of the representational system, federalism, and the institutional safety valves, the extended federal republic provides a final auxiliary precaution. The spirit of faction—its narrowness and selfishness—militates against the possibility of a permanent majority faction. If the other checks fail, faction can check faction because an extended sphere and a pluralism of interests "renders factious combinations less to be dreaded" *(Federalist* 10, p. 48). Madison does not celebrate a politics of faction, but sees its potential to neutralize its danger in anticipation of a return to virtue *(Federalist* 57, p. 291).

In the end, popular government rests on the people (Hunt, IX, p. 351). Madison argues that for it to survive free of factious policies its citizenry must retain virtue. When "there is not sufficient virtue amoung men for self-government . . . nothing less than the chains of despotism can restrain them from destroying and devouring one another" *(Federalist* 55, p. 284). He helped frame a republican government that would allow for virtuous governance. Separation of powers and the checks it made possible was his primary "auxiliary precaution." However, should public virtue absolutely disappear, republican government would fail. As republican government is made possible by the character of the people, so too is despotism. The system was to promote and maintain the former, but no auxiliary precautions would stop the latter if the people failed. If a sustained and broadly based majority faction came into being, it would win. This is the irony of popular government. The government Madison defends has an open texture which admits of many possibilities, as human nature admits of many possibilities. Auxiliary precautions are used only to provide time to minister to the open texture of human nature and society, to restore society and its citizens to an attachment to the common weal. Madison's system allows many possibilities, the possibility of renewal being not the least of them.

III. Conclusion

A major obstacle to understanding Madison's political theory may be the theory itself. Sheldon Wolin tells us that the aim of theory is to see, explain, and alter the world.[29] We expect political theory to be based on a philosophical system that makes consistent and coherent judgment on questions of human nature, the origin of society and state, political

29. Wolin, "Political Theory: Trends and Goals," in *International Encyclopedia of the Social Sciences* (The Macmillan Company and the Free Press, 1968), pp. 318–31.

obligation, community, power, the ends of society, and the preferred structure of government. We expect that system to generate perspectives by which we can understand the political world as well as to generate prescriptions for altering and perfecting society.

This understanding of theory comes more from the work of Thomas Hobbes and Karl Marx than that of Madison. Madison was an English liberal nurtured in the American colonial political experience. His work reflects the Anglo-Saxon temperament. His philosophical system seems incomplete: he has no absolute concept of human nature; his Utopia is more one of structure than of goals. The decisions made under the new Constitution will provide prescriptions for a world in flux, but those decisions are left to posterity. The questions of human happiness and even a sense of community are largely removed from politics: his structure makes it possible to achieve happiness and community, but gives us neither. We are left to pursue them on our own. Madison's agenda, the creation of a stable popular government, did not lead him to offer a detailed perspective for analyzing and describing society. His task was simpler than that of Hobbes.

Madison's failure to offer a new epistemology or to construct a new Utopia does not, however, make his work merely descriptive. It is wrong to assume, with Dahl, that his normative vocabulary had no meaning. It is equally wrong to assume, with Wolin, that his aim "was not to educate men, but to deploy them, not to alter their moral character, but to arrange institutions in such a manner that human drives would cancel each other out. . . ."[30] Both Dahl and Wolin seem to assume that Madison, like Hobbes, believed reality to be coexistent with the political world and values to be simply the objects of passion.

Madison's Republic, unlike Plato's, was not a good order wholly transcending the empirical world. But neither was it altogether observable, empirical, when he helped design it. He had seen virtuous men. He imagined a state based on virtue, but not on perfect virtue. Madison was a normative theorist: the act of foundation was an act of imagination. The imagination used by the founders was shrewd and prudent. The success of the polity based on that imagination, for Dahl, obscured its normative basis, which he then rejected. Thus, it is easier to understand Dahl's approach than Wolin's. Wolin portrays the polity of *The Federalist* as one designed not to achieve but to prevent—Hobbesian, mechanistic, without purpose. To substantiate the first and third charges he overlooks

30. Wolin, *Politics and Vision,* p. 389.

the argument based on virtue; to substantiate the second he rejects all of liberalism as theory.

We cannot know, because Madison never addressed the subject, if he would have agreed with de Tocqueville's belief that political education could be found in secondary associations. But we do know that those associations existed in his time and that his system allowed them to continue and flourish, providing a school for citizenship.[31] No nation-state can meet Wolin's requirements. His concept of politics is confined to and by the polis. Madison's continental republic is not a polis, hence it is not political. Thus, Madison cannot satisfy the criteria of Wolin and the Berkeley School. The practice of virtue, as they understand it, can only take place in the assembly of the city state. Rousseau, not Madison, is their ideal eighteenth century theorist.[32] By making assumptions about Madison similar to those of the pluralists, the Berkeley School has been forced to reject the foundation. It cannot appeal to the founders in its invocation of a politics of community and virtue. It rejects the whole of the American liberal tradition in its determination to read *The Federalist* as a nineteenth century work.

Madison is liberal in seeing the state as an instrument based on claims of individuals. This does represent a departure from classical theory. But he belonged to the early liberal tradition, a tradition that assumed the will of man to be good, and assured that reason and conscience could guide the citizen. It was the nineteenth century, not the eighteenth, that replaced reason and conscience with pure self-interest. Madison belonged to the former tradition. At the Virginia ratifying convention he argued:

> I go on this great republican principle, that the people will have virtue and intelligence to select men of virtue and wisdom. Is there no virtue among us? If there be not, we are in a wretched situation. No theoretical checks, no form of government can render us secure. To suppose that any form of government will secure liberty or happiness without any virtue in the people is a chimerical idea. If there be sufficient virtue and intelligence in the community, it will be exercised in the selection of these men; so that we do not depend on

31. See Alexis de Tocqueville, *Democracy in America* (numerous editions), Vol II, Bk II, chs. 2–4; also see Mary Parker Follett, *The New State* (New York: Longman, Green, and Co., 1920), p. 179.

32. See Robert Pranger, *The Eclipse of Civilization* (New York: Holt, Rinehart, and Winston, 1968).

their virtue, or put confidence in our rules, but in the people who are to choose them.[33]

By placing Madison in the later liberal tradition, the Berkeley School lost a founder but created a foil.

By an equally narrow reading, pluralists have claimed Madison as one of their own. By ignoring his rejection of faction and his call for virtue, and by reading him as a nineteenth century liberal, they have made him the father of interest group pluralism. This invites all opposed to that approach to make Madison the great villain of American political thought.

The interests of Madison's day were few in number. The power of wealth was limited. The emergence of capitalist industrialism led to far greater changes than he could have imagined. The result has been that faction is a greater problem now than then, and conversely the technique of allowing faction to check faction is a greater temptation today than in his time. The pluralist approach can be seen as a contemporary strategy that grows out of Madison's work, but it makes a primary argument of that which was to Madison a secondary safety valve. To him, selfishness was contrary to virtue. It was the ultimate enemy of the Republic, not its foundation. It is here that the pluralists stray; their system fixes on Madison's auxiliary precautions and ignores his normative theory.

Wills, Pocock, and others have forced us to reconsider the actual foundation, to review what the founders saw as problems, and to reconsider their answers. At the very least this reexamination affords an historically richer account of American political thought. It also enables the founders to be our allies both in nurturing the republic and in the constant drama of incremental refoundation. It is not particularly important to rehabilitate James Madison. It is important, however, to understand the fullness and complexity of his explanation of the foundation—what he wanted for us, what he gave us—for therein lies our best hope of understanding, and potentially recovering, his contribution to our political inheritance.

33. Elliot's *Debates* quoted in Wills, *Explaining America,* p. xxi. This paragraph was shaped by the argument of John Hallowell in his *Main Currents in Modern Political Thought* (New York: Holt, Rinehart and Winston, 1950), pp. 112–15. Hallowell addresses liberalism in general; we have made the specific application to Madison.

Part III
The (In)famous Tenth *Federalist*

[4]

THE CONSTITUTION AS AN ECONOMIC DOCUMENT

Charles A. Beard

It is difficult for the superficial student of the Constitution, who has read only the commentaries of the legists, to conceive of that instrument as an economic document. It places no property qualifications on voters or officers; it gives no outward recognition of any economic groups in society; it mentions no special privileges to be conferred upon any class. It betrays no feeling, such as vibrates through the French constitution of 1791; its language is cold, formal, and severe.

The true inwardness of the Constitution is not revealed by an examination of its provisions as simple propositions of law; but by a long and careful study of the voluminous correspondence of the period,[1] contemporary newspapers and pamphlets, the records of the debates in the Convention at Philadelphia and in the several state conventions, and particularly, *The Federalist,* which was widely circulated during the struggle over ratification. The correspondence shows the exact character of the evils which the Constitution was intended to remedy; the records of the proceedings in the Philadelphia Convention reveal the succes-

[1] A great deal of this valuable material has been printed in the *Documentary History of the Constitution,* Vols. IV and V; a considerable amount has been published in the letters and papers of the eminent men of the period; but an enormous mass still remains in manuscript form. Fortunately, such important papers as those of Washington, Hamilton, Madison, and others are in the Library of Congress; but they are not complete, of course.

sive steps in the building of the framework of the government under the pressure of economic interests; the pamphlets and newspapers disclose the ideas of the contestants over the ratification; and *The Federalist* presents the political science of the new system as conceived by three of the profoundest thinkers of the period, Hamilton, Madison, and Jay.

Doubtless, the most illuminating of these sources on the economic character of the Constitution are the records of the debates in the Convention, which have come down to us in fragmentary form; and a thorough treatment of material forces reflected in the several clauses of the instrument of government created by the grave assembly at Philadelphia would require a rewriting of the history of the proceedings in the light of the great interests represented there.[1] But an entire volume would scarcely suffice to present the results of such a survey, and an undertaking of this character is accordingly impossible here.

The Federalist, on the other hand, presents in a relatively brief and systematic form an economic interpretation of the Constitution by the men best fitted, through an intimate knowledge of the ideals of the framers, to expound the political science of the new government. This wonderful piece of argumentation by Hamilton, Madison, and Jay is in fact the finest study in the economic interpretation of politics which exists in any language; and whoever would understand the Constitution as an economic document need hardly go beyond it. It is true that the tone of the writers is somewhat modified on account of the fact that

[1] From this point of view, the old conception of the battle at Philadelphia as a contest between small and large states — as political entities — will have to be severely modified. See Professor Farrand's illuminating paper on the so-called compromises of the Constitution in the *Report of the American Historical Association, 1903*, Vol. I, pp. 73 ff. J. C. Welling, "States' Rights Conflict over the Public Lands," *ibid.* (1888), pp. 184 ff.

they are appealing to the voters to ratify the Constitution, but at the same time they are, by the force of circumstances, compelled to convince large economic groups that safety and strength lie in the adoption of the new system.

Indeed, every fundamental appeal in it is to some material and substantial interest. Sometimes it is to the people at large in the name of protection against invading armies and European coalitions. Sometimes it is to the commercial classes whose business is represented as prostrate before the follies of the Confederation. Now it is to creditors seeking relief against paper money and the assaults of the agrarians in general; now it is to the holders of federal securities which are depreciating toward the vanishing point. But above all, it is to the owners of personalty anxious to find a foil against the attacks of levelling democracy, that the authors of *The Federalist* address their most cogent arguments in favor of ratification. It is true there is much discussion of the details of the new frame-work of government, to which even some friends of reform took exceptions; but Madison and Hamilton both knew that these were incidental matters when compared with the sound basis upon which the superstructure rested.

In reading the pages of this remarkable work as a study in political economy, it is important to bear in mind that the system, which the authors are describing, consisted of two fundamental parts — one positive, the other negative:

I. A government endowed with certain positive powers, but so constructed as to break the force of majority rule and prevent invasions of the property rights of minorities.

II. Restrictions on the state legislatures which had been so vigorous in their attacks on capital.

Under some circumstances, action is the immediate interest of the dominant party; and whenever it desires to make an economic gain through governmental functioning, it must have, of course, a system endowed with the requisite powers.

Examples of this are to be found in protective tariffs, in ship subsidies, in railway land grants, in river and harbor improvements, and so on through the catalogue of so-called "paternalistic" legislation. Of course it may be shown that the "general good" is the ostensible object of any particular act; but the general good is a passive force, and unless we know who are the several individuals that benefit in its name, it has no meaning. When it is so analyzed, immediate and remote beneficiaries are discovered; and the former are usually found to have been the dynamic element in securing the legislation. Take for example, the economic interests of the advocates who appear in tariff hearings at Washington.

On the obverse side, dominant interests quite as often benefit from the prevention of governmental action as from positive assistance. They are able to take care of themselves if let alone within the circle of protection created by the law. Indeed, most owners of property have as much to fear from positive governmental action as from their inability to secure advantageous legislation. Particularly is this true where the field of private property is already extended to cover practically every form of tangible and intangible wealth. This was clearly set forth by Hamilton: "It may perhaps be said that the power of preventing bad laws includes that of preventing good ones. . . . But this objection will have little weight with those who can properly estimate the mischiefs of that inconstancy and mutability in the laws which form the greatest blemish in the character and genius of our governments. They will consider every institution calculated to restrain the excess of law-making, and to keep things in the same state in which they happen to be at any given period, as more likely to do good than harm. . . . The injury which may possibly be done by defeating a few good laws will be amply compensated by the advantage of preventing a number of bad ones." [1]

THE UNDERLYING POLITICAL SCIENCE OF THE CONSTITUTION [2]

Before taking up the economic implications of the structure of the federal government, it is important to ascertain what, in the opinion of *The Federalist*, is the basis of all government. The most philosophical examination of the foundations of political science is made by Madison in the tenth number. Here he lays down, in no uncertain language, the principle that the first and elemental concern of every government is economic.

1. "The first object of government," he declares, is the protection of "the diversity in the faculties of men, from which the rights of property originate." The chief business of government, from which, perforce, its essential nature must be derived, consists in the control and adjustment of conflicting economic interests. After enumerating the various forms of propertied interests which spring up inevitably in modern society, he adds: "The regulation of these various and interfering interests forms the principal task of modern legislation, and involves the spirit of party and faction in the ordinary operations of the government." [3]

2. What are the chief causes of these conflicting political forces with which the government must concern itself? Madison answers. Of course fanciful and frivolous distinctions have sometimes been the cause of violent conflicts; "but the most common and durable source of factions has

[1] *The Federalist*, No. 73.

[2] See J. A. Smith, *The Spirit of American Government*.

[3] See Noah Webster's consideration of the subject of government and property; Ford, *Pamphlets on the Constitution*, pp. 57 ff.

been the various and unequal distribution of property. Those who hold and those who are without property have ever formed distinct interests in society. Those who are creditors, and those who are debtors, fall under a like discrimination. A landed interest, a manufacturing interest, a mercantile interest, a moneyed interest, with many lesser interests grow up of necessity in civilized nations, and divide them into different classes actuated by different sentiments and views."

3. The theories of government which men entertain are emotional reactions to their property interests. "From the protection of different and unequal faculties of acquiring property, the possession of different degrees and kinds of property immediately results; *and from the influence of these on the sentiments and views of the respective proprietors, ensues a division of society into different interests and parties.*" Legislatures reflect these interests. "What," he asks, "are the different classes of legislators but advocates and parties to the causes which they determine." There is no help for it. "The causes of faction cannot be removed," and "we well know that neither moral nor religious motives can be relied on as an adequate control."

4. Unequal distribution of property is inevitable, and from it contending factions will rise in the state. The government will reflect them, for they will have their separate principles and "sentiments"; but the supreme danger will arise from the fusion of certain interests into an overbearing majority, which Madison, in another place, prophesied would be the landless proletariat,[1] — an overbearing majority which will make its "rights" paramount, and sacrifice the "rights" of the minority. "To secure the public good," he declares, "and private rights against the

[1] Farrand, *Records*, Vol. II, p. 203.

danger of such a faction and at the same time preserve the spirit and the form of popular government is then the great object to which our inquiries are directed."

5. How is this to be done? Since the contending classes cannot be eliminated and their interests are bound to be reflected in politics, the only way out lies in making it difficult for enough contending interests to fuse into a majority, and in balancing one over against another. The machinery for doing this is created by the new Constitution and by the Union. (*a*) Public views are to be refined and enlarged "by passing them through the medium of a chosen body of citizens." (*b*) The very size of the Union will enable the inclusion of more interests so that the danger of an overbearing majority is not so great. "The smaller the society, the fewer probably will be the distinct parties and interests composing it; the fewer the distinct parties and interests, the more frequently will a majority be found of the same party. . . . Extend the sphere, and you take in a greater variety of parties and interests; you make it less probable that a majority of the whole will have a common motive to invade the rights of other citizens; or if such a common motive exists, it will be more difficult for all who feel it to discover their strength and to act in unison with each other."

Q. E. D., "in the extent and proper structure of the Union, therefore, we behold a republican remedy for the diseases most incident to republican government." [1]

[1] This view was set forth by Madison in a letter to Jefferson in 1788. "Wherever the real power in a Government lies, there is the danger of oppression. In our Governments the real power lies in the majority of the Community, and the invasion of private rights is *chiefly* to be apprehended, not from acts of Government contrary to the sense of its constituents, but from acts in which the Government is the mere instrument of the major number of the constituents. This is a truth of great importance, but not yet sufficiently attended to, and is probably more strongly impressed upon my mind by facts, and reflections suggested by them, than on yours which has contemplated abuses of power issuing from a very different quarter. Wherever there is an interest and power to do wrong, wrong will

I. THE STRUCTURE OF GOVERNMENT OR THE BALANCE OF POWERS

The fundamental theory of political economy thus stated by Madison was the basis of the original American conception of the balance of powers which is formulated at length in four numbers of *The Federalist* and consists of the following elements:

1. No mere parchment separation of departments of government will be effective. "The legislative department is everywhere extending the sphere of its activity, and drawing all power into its impetuous vortex. The founders of our republic . . . seem never for a moment to have turned their eyes from the danger to liberty from the overgrown and all-grasping prerogative of an hereditary magistrate, supported and fortified by an hereditary branch of the legislative authority. They seem never to have recollected the danger from legislative usurpations, which, by assembling all power in the same hands, must lead to the same tyranny as is threatened by executive usurpations."[1]

2. Some sure mode of checking usurpations in the government must be provided, other than frequent appeals to the people. "There appear to be insuperable objections against the proposed recurrence to the people as a provision in all cases for keeping the several departments of power within their constitutional limits."[2] In a contest between the legislature and the other branches of the government, the former would doubtless be victorious on account of the ability of the legislators to plead their cause with the people.

3. What then can be depended upon to keep the govern-

generally be done, and not less readily by a powerful and interested party than by a powerful and interested prince." *Documentary History of the Constitution*, Vol. V, p. 88.

[1] *The Federalist*, No. 48. [2] *Ibid.*, No. 49.

ment in close rein? "The only answer that can be given is, that as all these exterior provisions are found to be inadequate, the defect must be supplied by so contriving the interior structure of the government as that its several constituent parts may, by their mutual relations, be the means of keeping each other in their proper places. . . . It is of great importance in a republic not only to guard the society against the oppression of its rulers, but to guard one part of the society against the injustice of the other part. Different interests necessarily exist in different classes of citizens. If a majority be united by a common interest, the rights of the minority will be insecure."[1] There are two ways of obviating this danger: one is by establishing a monarch independent of popular will, and the other is by reflecting these contending interests (so far as their representatives may be enfranchised) in the very structure of the government itself so that a majority cannot dominate the minority — which minority is of course composed of those who possess property that may be attacked. "Society itself will be broken into so many parts, interests, and classes of citizens, that the rights of individuals, or of the minority, will be in little danger from interested combinations of the majority."[2]

4. The structure of the government as devised at Philadelphia reflects these several interests and makes improbable any danger to the minority from the majority. "The House of Representatives being to be elected immediately by the people, the Senate by the State legislatures, the President by electors chosen for that purpose by the people, there would be little probability of a common interest to cement these different branches in a predilection for any particular class of electors."[3]

5. All of these diverse interests appear in the amend-

[1] *The Federalist*, No. 51. [2] *Ibid.*, No. 51. [3] *Ibid.*, No. 60.

ing process but they are further reinforced against majorities. An amendment must receive a two-thirds vote in each of the two houses so constituted and the approval of three-fourths of the states.

6. The economic corollary of this system is as follows: Property interests may, through their superior weight in power and intelligence, secure advantageous legislation whenever necessary, and they may at the same time obtain immunity from control by parliamentary majorities.

If we examine carefully the delicate instrument by which the framers sought to check certain kinds of positive action that might be advocated to the detriment of established and acquired rights, we cannot help marvelling at their skill. Their leading idea was to break up the attacking forces at the starting point: the source of political authority for the several branches of the government. This disintegration of positive action at the source was further facilitated by the differentiation in the terms given to the respective departments of the government. And the crowning counterweight to "an interested and over-bearing majority," as Madison phrased it, was secured in the peculiar position assigned to the judiciary, and the use of the sanctity and mystery of the law as a foil to democratic attacks.

It will be seen on examination that no two of the leading branches of the government are derived from the same source. The House of Representatives springs from the mass of the people whom the states may see fit to enfranchise. The Senate is elected by the legislatures of the states, which were, in 1787, almost uniformly based on property qualifications, sometimes with a differentiation between the sources of the upper and lower houses. The President is to be chosen by electors selected as the legislatures of the states may determine—at all events by an authority one degree removed from the voters at large. The judiciary is to be chosen by the President and the Senate, both removed from direct popular control and holding for longer terms than the House.

A sharp differentiation is made in the terms of the several authorities, so that a complete renewal of the government at one stroke is impossible. The House of Representatives is chosen for two years; the Senators for six, but not at one election, for one-third go out every two years. The President is chosen for four years. The judges of the Supreme Court hold for life. Thus "popular distempers," as eighteenth century publicists called them, are not only restrained from working their havoc through direct elections, but they are further checked by the requirement that they must last six years in order to make their effects felt in the political department of the government, providing they can break through the barriers imposed by the indirect election of the Senate and the President. Finally, there is the check of judicial control that can be overcome only through the manipulation of the appointing power which requires time, or through the operation of a cumbersome amending system.

The keystone of the whole structure is, in fact, the system provided for judicial control — the most unique contribution to the science of government which has been made by American political genius. It is claimed by some recent writers that it was not the intention of the framers of the Constitution to confer upon the Supreme Court the power of passing upon the constitutionality of statutes enacted by Congress; but in view of the evidence on the other side, it is incumbent upon those who make this assertion to bring forward positive evidence to the effect that judicial control was not a part of the Philadelphia programme.[1] Certainly, the authors of *The Federalist* entertained no doubts on the point, and they conceived it to be such an excellent principle that they were careful to explain it to the electors to whom they addressed their arguments.

After elaborating fully the principle of judicial control over legislation under the Constitution, Hamilton enumerates the advantages to be derived from it. Speaking on the point of tenure during good behavior, he says: "In a monarchy it is an excellent barrier to the despotism of the prince; in a republic it is no less an excellent barrier to the encroachments and oppressions of the representative body. . . . If, then, the courts of justice are to be considered as the bulwarks of a limited Constitution against legislative encroachments, this consideration will afford a strong argument for the permanent tenure of judicial offices, since nothing will contribute so much as this to that independent spirit in the judges which must be essential to the faithful performance of so arduous a duty. . . . But it is not with a view to infractions of the Constitution only that the independence of the judges may be an essential safeguard against the effects of occasional ill humors in the society. These sometimes extend no farther than to the injury of private rights of particular classes of citizens, by unjust and partial laws. Here also the firmness of the judicial magistracy is of vast importance in mitigating the severity and confining the operation of such laws. It not only serves to moderate the immediate mischiefs of those which may have been passed, but it operates as a check upon the legislative body in passing them; who, perceiving that obstacles to the success of iniquitous intention are to be ex-

[1] Beard, *The Supreme Court and the Constitution*. See also the criticisms of this work by Professor W. F. Dodd, in the American Historical Review for January, 1913.

pected from the scruples of the courts, are in a manner compelled, by the very motives of injustice they meditate, to qualify their attempts. This is a circumstance calculated to have more influence upon the character of our governments than but few may be aware of." [1]

Nevertheless, it may be asked why, if the protection of property rights lay at the basis of the new system, there is in the Constitution no provision for property qualifications for voters or for elected officials and representatives. This is, indeed, peculiar when it is recalled that the constitutional history of England is in a large part a record of conflict over the weight in the government to be enjoyed by definite economic groups, and over the removal of the property qualifications early imposed on members of the House of Commons and on the voters at large. But the explanation of the absence of property qualifications from the Constitution is not difficult.

The members of the Convention were, in general, not opposed to property qualifications as such, either for officers or voters. "Several propositions," says Mr. S. H. Miller, "were made in the federal Convention in regard to property qualifications. A motion was carried instructing the committee to fix upon such qualifications for members of Congress. The committee could not agree upon the amount and reported in favor of leaving the matter to the legislature. Charles Pinckney objected to this plan as giving too much power to the first legislature. . . . Ellsworth objected to a property qualification on account of the difficulty of fixing the amount. If it was made high enough for the South, it would not be applicable to the Eastern States. Franklin was the only speaker who opposed the proposition to require property on principle, saying that 'some of the

[1] Number 78.

greatest rogues he was ever acquainted with were the richest rogues.' A resolution was also carried to require a property qualification for the Presidency. Hence it was evident that the lack of all property requirements for office in the United States Constitution was not owing to any opposition of the convention to such qualifications per se." [1]

Propositions to establish property restrictions were defeated, not because they were believed to be inherently opposed to the genius of American government, but for economic reasons — strange as it may seem. These economic reasons were clearly set forth by Madison in the debate over landed qualifications for legislators in July, when he showed, first, that slight property qualifications would not keep out the small farmers whose paper money schemes had been so disastrous to personalty; and, secondly, that landed property qualifications would exclude from Congress the representatives of "those classes of citizens who were not landholders," *i.e.* the personalty interests. This was true, he thought, because the mercantile and manufacturing classes would hardly be willing to turn their personalty into sufficient quantities of landed property to make them eligible for a seat in Congress.[2]

The other members also knew that they had most to fear from the very electors who would be enfranchised under a slight freehold restriction,[3] for the paper money party was everywhere bottomed on the small farming class. As Gorham remarked, the elections at Philadelphia, New York, and Boston, "where the merchants and mechanics vote, are at least as good as those made by freeholders only." [4] The fact emerges, therefore, that the personalty interests

[1] *American Historical Association Report* (1899), Vol. I, p. 108.
[2] Farrand, *Records*, Vol. II, pp. 123–124.
[3] *Ibid.*, pp. 201 ff.
[4] *Ibid.*, p. 216.

reflected in the Convention could, in truth, see no safeguard at all in a freehold qualification against the assaults on vested personalty rights which had been made by the agrarians in every state. And it was obviously impossible to establish a personalty test, had they so desired, for there would have been no chance of securing a ratification of the Constitution at the hands of legislatures chosen by freeholders, or at the hands of conventions selected by them.

A very neat example of this antagonism between realty and personalty in the Convention came out on July 26, when Mason made, and Charles Pinckney supported, a motion imposing landed qualifications on members of Congress and excluding from that body "persons having unsettled accounts with or being indebted to the United States." In bringing up this motion Mason "observed that persons of the latter descriptions had frequently got into the state legislatures in order to promote laws that might shelter their delinquencies; and that this evil had crept into Congress if report was to be regarded."[1]

Gouverneur Morris was on his feet in an instant. If qualifications were to be imposed, they should be laid on electors, not elected persons. The disqualification would fall upon creditors of the United States, for there were but few who owed the government anything. He knew that under this rule very few members of the Convention could get into the new government which they were establishing. "As to persons having unsettled accounts, he believed them to be pretty many. He thought, however, that such a discrimination would be both odious and useless and in many instances unjust and cruel. The delay of settlement had been more the fault of the public than of individuals. What will be done with those patriotic Citizens who have

[1] Farrand, *Records*, Vol. II, p. 121.

lent money or services or property to their country, without having been yet able to obtain a liquidation of their claims? Are they to be excluded?" On thinking it over, Morris added to his remarks on the subject, saying, "It was a precept of great antiquity as well as of high authority that we should not be righteous overmuch. He thought we ought to be equally on our guard against being wise overmuch. . . . The parliamentary qualifications quoted by Colonel Mason had been disregarded in practice; and was but a scheme of the landed against the monied interest." [1]

Gerry thought that the inconvenience of excluding some worthy creditors and debtors was of less importance than the advantages offered by the resolution, but, after some reflection, he added that "if property be one object of government, provisions for securing it cannot be improper." King sagely remarked that there might be a great danger in imposing a landed qualification, because "it would exclude the monied interest, whose aids may be essential in particular emergencies to the public safety."

Madison had no confidence in the effectiveness of the landed qualification and moved to strike it out, adding, "Landed possessions were no certain evidence of real wealth. Many enjoyed them to a great extent who were more in debt than they were worth. The unjust laws of the states had proceeded more from this class of men than any others. It had often happened that men who had acquired landed property on credit got into the Legislatures with a view of promoting an unjust protection against their Creditors. In the next place, if a small quantity of land should be made the standard, it would be no security; if a large one, it would exclude the proper representatives of those classes of Citizens who were not landholders." For these

[1] *Ibid.*, pp. 121–122.

and other reasons he opposed the landed qualifications and suggested that property qualifications on the voters would be better.[1]

The motion to strike out the "landed" qualification for legislators was carried by a vote of ten to one; the proposition to strike out the disqualification of persons having unsettled accounts with the United States was carried by a vote of nine to two. Finally the proposition to exclude persons who were indebted to the United States was likewise defeated by a vote of nine to two, after Pinckney had called attention to the fact that "it would exclude persons who had purchased confiscated property or should purchase Western territory of the public and might be some obstacle to the sale of the latter."

Indeed, there was little risk to personalty in thus allowing the Constitution to go to the states for approval without any property qualifications on voters other than those which the state might see fit to impose. Only one branch of new government, the House of Representatives, was required to be elected by popular vote; and, in case popular choice of presidential electors might be established, a safeguard was secured by the indirect process. Two controlling bodies, the Senate and Supreme Court, were removed altogether from the possibility of popular election except by constitutional amendment. Finally, the conservative members of the Convention were doubly fortified in the fact that nearly all of the state constitutions then in force provided real or personal property qualifications for voters anyway, and radical democratic changes did not seem perilously near.[2]

[1] Debate in Farrand, *Records*, Vol. II, pp. 123–124.

[2] See above, pp. 65 ff. The members of the Convention could not foresee the French Revolution which was to break out just as the new federal government was being put into operation in 1789.

II. THE POWERS CONFERRED UPON THE FEDERAL GOVERNMENT

1. The powers for positive action conferred upon the new government were few, but they were adequate to the purposes of the framers. They included, first, the power to lay and collect taxes; but here the rural interests were conciliated by the provision that direct taxes must be apportioned among the states according to population, counting three-fifths of the slaves. This, in the opinion of contemporaries eminently qualified to speak, was designed to prevent the populations of the manufacturing states from shifting the burdens of taxation to the sparsely settled agricultural regions.[1]

In a letter to the governor of their state, three delegates from North Carolina, Blount, Spaight, and Williamson, explained the advantage of this safeguard on taxation to the southern planters and farmers: "We had many things to hope from a National Government and the chief thing we had to fear from such a Government was the risque of unequal or heavy Taxation, but we hope you will believe as we do that the Southern states in general and North Carolina in particular are well secured on that head by the proposed system. It is provided in the 9th section of article the first that no Capitation or direct Tax shall be laid except in proportion to the number of inhabitants, in which number five blacks are only counted as three. If a land tax is laid, we are to pay the same rate; for example, fifty citizens of North Carolina can be taxed no more for all their Lands than fifty Citizens in one of the Eastern States. This must be greatly in our favour, for as most of their farms are small

[1] It was a curious turn of fortune that this provision prevented the agrarians and populists in 1894 from shifting a part of the burden of taxes to the great cities of the East. Thus the *Zweck im Recht* is sometimes reversed.

and many of them live in Towns we certainly have, one with another, land of twice the value that they possess. When it is also considered that five Negroes are only to be charged the same Poll Tax as three whites, the advantage must be considerably increased under the proposed Form of Government. The Southern states have also a better security for the return of slaves who might endeavour to escape than they had under the original Confederation."[1]

The taxing power was the basis of all other positive powers, and it afforded the revenues that were to discharge the public debt in full. Provision was made for this discharge in Article VI to the effect that "All debts contracted and engagements entered into before the adoption of this Constitution shall be valid against the United States under this Constitution as under the Confederation."

But the cautious student of public economy, remembering the difficulties which Congress encountered under the Articles of Confederation in its attempts to raise the money to meet the interest on the debt, may ask how the framers of the Constitution could expect to overcome the hostile economic forces which had hitherto blocked the payment of the requisitions. The answer is short. Under the Articles, Congress had no power to lay and collect taxes immediately; it could only make requisitions on the state legislatures. Inasmuch as most of the states relied largely on direct taxes for their revenues, the demands of Congress were keenly felt and stoutly resisted. Under the new system, however, Congress is authorized to lay taxes on its own account, but it is evident that the framers contemplated placing practically all of the national burden on the consumer. The provision requiring the apportionment of direct taxes on a basis of population obviously implied that such taxes were to be viewed

[1] Clark, *The Records of North Carolina*, Vol. XX, p. 778.

as a last resort when indirect taxes failed to provide the required revenue.

With his usual acumen, Hamilton conciliates the freeholders and property owners in general by pointing out that they will not be called upon to support the national government by payments proportioned to their wealth.[1] Experience has demonstrated that it is impracticable to raise any considerable sums by direct taxation. Even where the government is strong, as in Great Britain, resort must be had chiefly to indirect taxation. The pockets of the farmers "will reluctantly yield but scanty supplies, in the unwelcome shape of impositions on their houses and lands; and personal property is too precarious and invisible a fund to be laid hold of in any other way than by the imperceptible agency of taxes on consumption." Real and personal property are thus assured a generous immunity from such burdens as Congress had attempted to impose under the Articles; taxes under the new system will, therefore, be less troublesome than under the old.

2. Congress was given, in the second place, plenary power to raise and support military and naval forces, for the defence of the country against foreign and domestic foes. These forces were to be at the disposal of the President in the execution of national laws; and to guard the states against renewed attempts of "desperate debtors" like Shays, the United States guaranteed to every commonwealth a republican form of government and promised to aid in quelling internal disorder on call of the proper authorities.

The army and navy are considered by the authors of *The Federalist* as genuine economic instrumentalities. As will be pointed out below, they regarded trade and commerce as the fundamental cause of wars between nations; and the

[1] *The Federalist*, Number 12.

source of domestic insurrection they traced to class conflicts within society. "Nations in general," says Jay, "will make war whenever they have a prospect of getting anything by it";[1] and it is obvious that the United States dissevered and discordant will be the easy prey to the commercial ambitions of their neighbors and rivals.

The material gains to be made by other nations at the expense of the United States are so apparent that the former cannot restrain themselves from aggression. France and Great Britain feel the pressure of our rivalry in the fisheries; they and other European nations are our competitors in navigation and the carrying trade; our independent voyages to China interfere with the monopolies enjoyed by other countries there; Spain would like to shut the Mississippi against us on one side and Great Britain fain would close the St. Lawrence on the other. The cheapness and excellence of our productions will excite their jealousy, and the enterprise and address of our merchants will not be consistent with the wishes or policy of the sovereigns of Europe. But, adds the commentator, by way of clinching the argument, "if they see that our national government is efficient and well administered, our trade prudently regulated, our militia properly organized and disciplined, our resources and finances discreetly managed, our credit re-established, our people free, contented, and united, they will be much more disposed to cultivate our friendship than provoke our resentment."[2]

All the powers of Europe could not prevail against us. "Under a vigorous national government the natural strength and resources of the country, directed to a common interest, would baffle all the combinations of European jealousy to restrain our growth. . . . An active commerce, an ex-

[1] *The Federalist*, No. 4. [2] *Ibid.*

tensive navigation, and a flourishing marine would then be the offspring of moral and physical necessity. We might defy the little arts of the little politicians to control or vary the irresistible and unchangeable course of nature."[1] In the present state of disunion the profits of trade are snatched from us; our commerce languishes; and poverty threatens to overspread a country which might outrival the world in riches.

The army and navy are to be not only instruments of defence in protecting the United States against the commercial and territorial ambitions of other countries; but they may be used also in forcing open foreign markets. What discriminatory tariffs and navigation laws may not accomplish the sword may achieve. The authors of *The Federalist* do not contemplate that policy of mild and innocuous isolation which was later made famous by Washington's farewell address.[2] On the contrary — they do not expect the United States to change human nature and make our commercial classes less ambitious than those of other countries to extend their spheres of trade. A strong navy will command the respect of European states. "There can be no doubt that the continuance of the Union under an efficient government would put it within our power, at a period not very distant, to create a navy which, if it could not vie with those of the great maritime powers, would at least be of respectable weight if thrown into the scale of either of two contending parties. . . . A few ships of the line sent opportunely to the reinforcement of either side, would often be sufficient to decide the fate of a campaign, on the event of which interests of the greatest mag-

[1] *The Federalist*, No. 11.

[2] Washington's farewell address which was partially written by Hamilton is one of the most ingenious partisan documents ever written. It, too, has its economic interpretation.

nitude were suspended. Our position is, in this respect, a most commanding one. And if to this consideration we add that of the usefulness of supplies from this country, in the prosecution of military operations in the West Indies, it will be readily perceived that a situation so favorable would enable us to bargain with great advantage for commercial privileges. A price would be set not only upon our friendship, but upon our neutrality. By a steady adherence to the Union, we may hope, ere long, to become the arbiter of Europe in America, and to be able to incline the balance of European competitions in this part of the world as our interest may dictate." [1]

As to dangers from class wars within particular states, the authors of *The Federalist* did not deem it necessary to make extended remarks: the recent events in New England were only too vividly impressed upon the public mind. "The tempestuous situation from which Massachusetts has scarcely emerged," says Hamilton, "evinces that dangers of this kind are not merely speculative. Who can determine what might have been the issue of her late convulsions, if the malcontents had been headed by a Cæsar or by a Cromwell." [2] The strong arm of the Union must be available in such crises.

In considering the importance of defence against domestic insurrection, the authors of *The Federalist* do not overlook an appeal to the slave-holders' instinctive fear of a servile revolt. Naturally, it is Madison whose interest catches this point and drives it home, by appearing to discount it. In dealing with the dangers of insurrection, he says: "I take no notice of an unhappy species of population abounding in some of the states who, during the calm of regular government are sunk below the level of men; but who, in

[1] *The Federalist*, No. 11. [2] *Ibid.*, No. 21.

the tempestuous scenes of civil violence, may emerge into human character and give a superiority of strength to any party with which they may associate themselves." [1]

3. In addition to the power to lay and collect taxes and raise and maintain armed forces on land and sea, the Constitution vests in Congress plenary control over foreign and interstate commerce, and thus authorizes it to institute protective and discriminatory laws in favor of American interests,[2] and to create a wide sweep for free trade throughout the whole American empire. A single clause thus reflects the strong impulse of economic forces in the towns and young manufacturing centres. In a few simple words the mercantile and manufacturing interests wrote their *Zweck im Recht;* and they paid for their victory by large concessions to the slave-owning planters of the south.[3]

While dealing with commerce in *The Federalist*[4] Hamilton does not neglect the subject of interstate traffic and intercourse. He shows how free trade over a wide range will be to reciprocal advantage, will give great diversity to commercial enterprise, and will render stagnation less liable by offering more distant markets when local demands fall off. "The speculative trader," he concludes, "will at once perceive the force of these observations and will acknowledge that the aggregate balance of the commerce of the United States would bid fair to be much more favorable than that of the thirteen states without union or with partial unions."

4. Another great economic antagonism found its expression in the clause conferring upon Congress the power to dispose of the territories and make rules and regulations for their government and admission to the Union. In this contest, the interests of the states which held territories came

[1] *The Federalist*, No. 43. [2] *Ibid.*, No. 35.
[3] See the entire letter of Blount, Spaight, and Williamson, cited above, p. 169.
[4] No. 11.

prominently to the front; and the ambiguity of the language used in the Constitution on this point may be attributed to the inability of the contestants to reach precise conclusions.[1] The leaders were willing to risk the proper management of the land problem after the new government was safely launched; and they were correct in their estimate of their future political prowess.

These are the great powers conferred on the new government: taxation, war, commercial control, and disposition of western lands. Through them public creditors may be paid in full, domestic peace maintained, advantages obtained in dealing with foreign nations, manufactures protected, and the development of the territories go forward with full swing. The remaining powers are minor and need not be examined here. What implied powers lay in the minds of the framers likewise need not be inquired into; they have long been the subject of juridical speculation.

None of the powers conferred by the Constitution on Congress permits a direct attack on property. The federal government is given no general authority to define property. It may tax, but indirect taxes must be uniform, and these are to fall upon consumers. Direct taxes may be laid, but resort to this form of taxation is rendered practically impossible, save on extraordinary occasions, by the provision that they must be apportioned according to population — so that numbers cannot transfer the burden to accumulated wealth. The slave trade may be destroyed, it is true, after the lapse of a few years; but slavery as a domestic institution is better safeguarded than before.

Even the destruction of the slave trade had an economic basis, although much was said at the time about the ethics

[1] J. C. Welling, "States' Rights Conflict over the Public Lands," *Report of the American Historical Association* (1888), pp. 174 ff.

of the clause. In the North where slavery, though wide-spread, was of little economic consequence, sympathy with the unfortunate negroes could readily prevail. Maryland and Virginia, already overstocked with slaves beyond the limits of land and capital, had prohibited the foreign trade in negroes, because the slave-holders, who predominated in the legislatures, were not willing to see the value of their chattels reduced to a vanishing point by excessive importations. South Carolina and Georgia, where the death rate in the rice swamps and the opening of adjoining territories made a strong demand for the increase of slave property, on the other hand, demanded an open door for slave-dealers.

South Carolina was particularly determined,[1] and gave northern representatives to understand that if they wished to secure their commercial privileges, they must make concessions to the slave trade. And they were met half way. Ellsworth said: "As slaves multiply so fast in Virginia and Maryland that it is cheaper to raise than import them, whilst in the sickly rice swamps foreign supplies are necessary, if we go no farther than is urged, we shall be unjust towards South Carolina and Georgia. Let us not intermeddle. As population increases; poor laborers will be so plenty as to render slaves useless." [2]

General Pinckney taunted the Virginia representatives in the Convention, some of whom were against slavery as well as importation, with disingenuous interestedness. "South Carolina and Georgia cannot do without slaves. As to Virginia she will gain by stopping the importations. Her slaves will rise in value and she has more than she wants. It would be unequal to require South Carolina and Georgia to confederate on such unequal terms."

[1] Farrand, *Records*, Vol. II, p. 371.
[2] *Ibid.*, p. 371.

III. RESTRICTIONS LAID UPON STATE LEGISLATURES

Equally important to personalty as the positive powers conferred upon Congress to tax, support armies, and regulate commerce were the restrictions imposed on the states.[1] Indeed, we have the high authority of Madison for the statement that of the forces which created the Constitution, those property interests seeking protection against omnipotent legislatures were the most active.

In a letter to Jefferson, written in October, 1787, Madison elaborates the principle of federal judicial control over state legislation, and explains the importance of this new institution in connection with the restrictions laid down in the Constitution on laws affecting private rights. "The mutability of the laws of the States," he says, "is found to be a serious evil. The injustice of them has been so frequent and so flagrant as to alarm the most steadfast friends of Republicanism. I am persuaded I do not err in saying that the evils issuing from these sources contributed more to that uneasiness which produced the Convention, and prepared the public mind for a general reform, than those which accrued to our national character and interest from the inadequacy of the Confederation to its immediate objects. A reform, therefore, which does not make provision for private rights must be materially defective." [2]

Two small clauses embody the chief demands of personalty against agrarianism: the emission of paper money is pro-

[1] There are, of course, some restrictions on Congress laid down in the Constitution; but the powers of the national legislature are limited and the restrictions are not of the same significance. Radical action on the part of the national legislature was anticipated in the structure of the government itself, but specific provision had to be made against the assaults of popular majorities in state legislatures on property rights.

[2] *Writings of James Madison* (1865), Vol. I, p. 350. This entire letter deserves careful study by anyone who would understand the Constitution as an economic document.

hibited and the states are forbidden to impair the obligation of contract. The first of these means a return to a specie basis — when coupled with the requirement that the gold and silver coin of the United States shall be the legal tender. The Shays and their paper money legions, who assaulted the vested rights of personalty by the process of legislative depreciation, are now subdued forever, and money lenders and security holders may be sure of their operations. Contracts are to be safe, and whoever engages in a financial operation, public or private, may know that state legislatures cannot destroy overnight the rules by which the game is played.

A principle of deep significance is written in these two brief sentences. The economic history of the states between the Revolution and the adoption of the Constitution is compressed in them. They appealed to every money lender, to every holder of public paper, to every man who had any personalty at stake. The intensity of the economic interests reflected in these two prohibitions can only be felt by one who has spent months in the study of American agrarianism after the Revolution. In them personalty won a significant battle in the conflict of 1787–1788.

The authors of *The Federalist* advance in support of these two clauses very substantial arguments which bear out the view here expressed. "The loss which America has sustained since the peace, from the pestilential effects of paper money on the necessary confidence between man and man, on the necessary confidence in the public councils, on the industry and morals of the people, and on the character of republican government, constitutes an enormous debt against the States chargeable with this unadvised measure, which must long remain unsatisfied; or rather an accumulation of guilt which can be expiated no otherwise than by a voluntary sacrifice on the altar of justice of the power which has been the instrument of it." Speaking on the contract clause — that "additional bulwark in favor of personal security and private rights" — Madison is sure that the "sober people of America are weary of the fluctuating policy which has directed the public councils," and will welcome a reform that will "inspire a general prudence and industry and give a regular course to the business of society." [1]

Hamilton on several occasions laid great stress on the contract clause as one of the features of the Constitution which had warmly commended it to its supporters. In a communication to Washington, dated May 29, 1790, he wrote: "This, to the more enlightened part of the community, was not one of the least recommendations of that Constitution. The too frequent intermeddlings of the state legislatures in relation to private contracts were extensively felt and seriously lamented; and a Constitution which promised a preventative was, by those who felt and thought in that manner, eagerly embraced." [2]

There was not a little discussion of the obligation of contract clause in the contemporary press during the period of ratification, and there can be no doubt that it was favorably viewed by the supporters of the Constitution as an added safeguard against paper money and stay laws. A writer in the New Hampshire Spy, on November 3, 1787, in commending the new frame of government to his fellow citizens, calls particular attention to this provision: "It also expressly prohibits those destructive laws in the several states which alter or impair the obligation of contracts; so that in future anyone may be certain of an exact fulfilment

[1] *The Federalist*, No. 44.

[2] Ms. Library of Congress: *Treasury Department Letters, 1789–1790* (Washington Papers), folio 297.

of any contract that may be entered into or the penalty that may be stipulated for in case of failure."

Another writer of the period approves the same principle with more vigor. "My countrymen, the devil is among you. Make paper as much as you please. Make it a tender in all *future* contracts, or let it rest on its own credit — but remember that *past* contracts are sacred things — and that legislatures have no right to interfere with them— they have no right to say, a debt shall be paid at a discount, or in any manner which the parties never intended. . . . To pay *bona fide* contracts for cash, in paper of little value, or in old horses, would be a dishonest attempt in an individual: but for legislatures to frame laws to support and encourage such detestable villainy, is like a judge who should inscribe the arms of a rogue over the seat of justice." [1]

The full import of the obligation of contract clause was doubtless better understood by Chief Justice Marshall than by any man of that generation. He had taken an active part in the adoption of the Constitution in his state, and he had studied long and arduously the history of the period for his classic defence of Federalism, *The Life of Washington.* In more than one decision he applied the clause with great effect, and voiced the views of his Federalist contemporaries on this point, explaining the deep-seated social antagonism which is reflected in it.[2] And when at length, in his declining years, he saw it attacked in the legislatures by Jacksonian democracy, and beheld the Supreme Court itself surrendering the position which he had earlier taken, he spread on record in a dissenting opinion a warning and a protest which for cogency and vigor equals any of his great dissertations delivered in the name of the Court.

In the case of Ogden *v.* Saunders, decided in the January

[1] *The American Museum*, Vol. I, p. 118.

[2] See below, p. 295.

term of 1827, the Supreme Court was compelled to pass upon the issue: "Does a bankrupt law which applies to contracts made *after* its passage impair the obligation of those contracts?" The newer school on the bench, Washington, Johnson, Trimble, and Thompson were of opinion that such a law did not impair the obligation of contract and was valid. Marshall, Duvall, and Story dissented. The Chief Justice took the high ground that the obligation of a contract inhered in the contract itself, and could not be changed by any external legislation whatever. Therefore, obviously, legislation affecting adversely the obligation of future contracts was just as unconstitutional as legislation attacking contracts already made. In other words, Marshall, who ought to have known what the framers of the Constitution intended better than any man on the supreme bench, believed that it was designed to bring under the ban substantially all legislation which affected personalty adversely—in other words that it was similar in character to the due process clause of the Fourteenth Amendment.

Speaking on the contract clause he said with great solemnity: "We cannot look back to the history of the times when the august spectacle was exhibited of the assemblage of the whole people by their representatives in convention, in order to unite thirteen independent sovereignties under one government, so far as might be necessary for the purposes of union, without being sensible of the great importance attached to the tenth section of the first article. The power of changing the relative situation of debtor and creditor, of interfering with contracts, a power which comes home to every man, touches the interest of all, and controls the conduct of every individual in those things which he supposes to be proper for his own exclusive management, had been used to such an excess by the state legislatures as to break in upon the ordinary intercourse of society, and destroy all confidence between man and man. The mischief had become so great, so alarming as not only to impair commercial intercourse, and threaten the existence of credit, but to sap the morals of the people, and destroy the sanctity of private faith. To guard against the continuance of the evil was an object of deep interest with all the truly wise, as well as virtuous, of this great community, and was one of the important benefits expected from a reform of the government." [1]

THE ECONOMICS OF INTERNATIONAL POLITICS

The authors of *The Federalist* carry over into the field of international politics the concept of economic antagonisms which lie at the basis of their system of domestic politics. Modern wars spring primarily out of commercial rivalry, although the ambitions of princes have often been a source of international conflict. "Has commerce hitherto done anything more than change the objects of war?" asks Hamilton. "Is not the love of wealth as domineering and enterprising a passion as that of power or glory? Have there not been as many wars founded upon commercial motives, since that has become the prevailing system of nations, as were before occasioned by the cupidity of territory or dominion? Has not the spirit of commerce, in many instances, administered new incentives to the appetite, both for the one and for the other?" [2] Let history answer. Carthage, a commercial republic, was an aggressor in a war that ended in her destruction. The furious contests of Holland and England were over the dominion of the sea. Commerce has been for ages the predominant pursuit of England, and she has been constantly engaged in wars.

[1] Ogden *v.* Saunders, 12 Wheaton, pp. 213 ff. [2] *The Federalist*, No. 6.

Even the Hapsburg-Bourbon wars have in a large measure grown out of commercial considerations.

In this world-wide and age-long conflict of nations for commercial advantages, the United States cannot expect to become a non-resistant, an idle spectator. Even were pacific ideals to dominate American policy, she could not overcome the scruples of her ambitious rivals. In union, therefore, is strength against aggression and in support of offensive operations. Moreover, the Union will be better able to settle disputes amicably because of the greater show of power which it can make. "Acknowledgements, explanations, and compensations are often accepted as satisfactory from a strong united nation, which would be rejected as unsatisfactory if offered by a state or a confederacy of little consideration or power." [1]

Turning from the material causes of foreign wars the authors of *The Federalist* examine the possible sources of danger from domestic discord among the states, regarded as independent sovereignties. And how may such domestic discord arise? The North will probably grow strong and formidable and be tempted to despoil the South: nor "does it appear to be a rash conjecture," says Jay, "that its young swarms might often be tempted to gather honey in the more blooming fields and milder air of their luxurious and more delicate neighbors." [2]

Then the apple of discord may be thrown among the states by foreign countries if several confederacies take the place of union. And what is this apple of discord? Each of the proposed confederacies, says Jay, "would have its commerce with foreigners to regulate by distinct treaties; and as their productions and commodities are different and proper for different markets, so would those treaties

[1] *The Federalist*, No. 3. [2] *Ibid.*, No. 5.

be essentially different." Treaties are subject to the law of greatest economic pressure. "Different commercial concerns," he continues, "must create different interests, and of course different degrees of political attachment to and connection with different foreign nations."[1] The degrees of political attachment also follow the law of greatest economic pressure; and if foreign nations come to blows among themselves, their allies in America are likely to be drawn into the conflict. Thus domestic discord may arise among the states indirectly through their material connections with other countries.

But internecine warfare will more probably arise from causes operating within the states; and what may be the real sources of such conflict? asks Hamilton.[2] They are numerous: lust for power and dominion, the desire for equality and safety, the ambitions of leaders. Has it not invariably been found, he adds, "that momentary passions, and immediate interests have a more active and imperious control over human conduct than general and remote considerations of policy, utility, or justice? . . . Has commerce hitherto done anything more than change the objects of war? Is not the love of wealth as domineering and enterprizing a passion as that of power or glory? Have there not been as many wars founded upon commercial motives since that has become the prevailing system of nations, as were before occasioned by the cupidity of territory or dominion?"

Of course such acute observers as the authors of *The Federalist* do not omit to remark that the personal ambitions of monarchs have been a cause of wars, and the passions of men for leadership have been a source of domestic insurrections. But they are quick to add that the ag-

[1] *Ibid.* [2] *Ibid.*, No. 6.

grandizement and support of their particular families are among the motives that have led monarchs to undertake wars of conquest;[1] and as to personal element in domestic insurrections, Hamilton expresses a doubt whether Massachusetts would recently have been plunged into civil war "if Shays had not been a *desperate debtor*."[2]

Turning from the question as to the extent of the economic motive in the personal element, Hamilton makes an inquiry into the more probable sources of wars among the states in case a firmer union, endowed with adequate powers, is not established. These he enumerates:[3]

1. "Territorial disputes have at all times been found one of the most fertile sources of hostility among nations." The several states have an interest in the Western Territories, and "to reason from the past to the future, we shall have good ground to apprehend that the sword would sometimes be appealed to as the arbiter of their differences."

2. "The competitions of commerce would be another fruitful source of contention." Each state will pursue a policy conducive to its own advantage, and "the spirit of enterprize, which characterizes the commercial part of America, has left no occasion of displaying itself unimproved. It is not at all probable that this unbridled spirit would pay much respect to those regulations of trade by which particular states might endeavor to secure exclusive benefits to their own citizens." The economic motive will thus probably override all considerations of interstate comity and all considerations of international law. But that is not all; says Hamilton, in italics, "*We should be ready to denominate injuries those things which were in reality the justifiable acts of independent sovereignties consulting a distinct interest.*" Com-

[1] *The Federalist*, No. 4.
[2] *Ibid.*, No. 6.
[3] *Ibid.*, No. 7.

merce will have little respect for the right of other peoples to protect their interests, and it will stigmatize as an "injury" anything which blocks its enterprise.

3. "The public debt of the Union would be a further cause of collision between the separate states or confederacies." Some states would oppose paying the debt. Why? Because they are "less impressed with the importance of national credit, or because their citizens have little, if any, immediate interest in the question." But other states, "a numerous body of whose citizens are creditors to the public beyond the proportion of the state in the total amount of the national debt, would be strenuous for some equitable and effective provision." In other words, citizens who had nothing at stake would be indifferent, and those who had something to lose would clamor. Foreign powers also might intervene, and the "double contingency of external invasion and internal contention" would be hazarded.

4. "Laws in violation of private contracts, as they amount to aggressions on the rights of those states whose citizens are injured by them, may be considered as another probable source of hostility." Had there not been plenty of evidence to show that state legislatures, if unrestrained by some higher authority, would attack private rights in property? And had there not been a spirit of retaliation also? "We reasonably infer that in similar cases, under other circumstances, a war, not of *parchment*, but of the sword, would chastise such atrocious breaches of moral obligation and social justice."

These, then, are the four leading sources of probable conflict among the states if not united into a firm union: territory, commerce, the national debt, and violations of contractual rights in property — all as severely economic as could well be imagined.

To carry the theory of the economic interpretation of the Constitution out into its ultimate details would require a monumental commentary, such as lies completely beyond the scope of this volume. But enough has been said to show that the concept of the Constitution as a piece of abstract legislation reflecting no group interests and recognizing no economic antagonisms is entirely false. It was an economic document drawn with superb skill by men whose property interests were immediately at stake; and as such it appealed directly and unerringly to identical interests in the country at large.

[5]

The Tenth Federalist Revisited

Douglass Adair

ALTHOUGH James Madison wrote the *Tenth Federalist* in 1787 it was not until 1913, one hundred and twenty five years later, that Charles A. Beard made this particular essay famous for students of the United States Constitution. Before Beard published *An Economic Interpretation of the Constitution* practically no commentator on *The Federalist* or the Constitution, none of the biographers of Madison, had emphasized *Federalist 10* as of special importance for understanding our "more perfect union"; after Beard's book appeared the *Tenth Federalist* became the essay most often quoted to explain the philosophy of the fathers, and thus the "ultimate meaning" of the United States Constitution itself.

A sampling of the evidence for this generalization not only makes clear Beard's role in generating this latter-day fame for Madison's essay, but also shows the peculiar twist that the historian gave to that fame—a twist, a perspective, an interpretation that still governs to a remarkable degree the contemporary view of *Federalist 10,* Madison, and the Constitution.

To note this fact is to acknowledge the special greatness of Charles Beard as a scholar and to recognize the long shadow that his *Economic Interpretation* still casts over a crucial area of the American thought about the past. Nor is the word "shadow" inexact; for although Beard's research threw a brilliant beam of light on certain facets of the Constitution, his aim was selective, and by high-lighting special features of the document he thereby cast others into deep obscurity. Judged in terms of its effect on the thought of a whole generation, Beard's famous book is certainly the most significant piece of modern scholarship on the Constitution of 1787.[1]

[1] A survey of the text books used today in college courses on United States history shows the powerful influence still exerted by Beard's monograph of 1913. Perhaps the most succinct statement of the questions posed by Beard and still debatable can be seen in the Amherst readings in "Problems in American Civilization," Earl Latham, ed., *The Declaration of Independence and the Constitution* (New York, 1949), vi: "What was it the Founding Fathers did in Philadelphia in 1787? Were they selfless patriots bent upon establishing a new and enduring form of government that would save the fruits of a successful Revolution which were threatened by the inadequacies of the confederation government? Or were they self-seekers bent instead upon protecting the material advantage of the propertied class at the expense

It was also, when it appeared in 1913, the most important party tract of the Progressive Era that used scholarship as a weapon for twentieth-century politics.

The fact that Madison's *Tenth Federalist* was first widely publicized in this way and at this time in a monograph with a very special modern bias has had a curious after-effect. The peculiar anachronisms of the Beardian school have effectively diverted attention from what are, *prima facie,* the most obvious questions to ask about Madison's exercise in political theory: what did the theory of *Federalist 10* mean in 1787 when the Virginian enunciated it? What function did Madison's abstract theoretical speculations serve in the creation of the Constitution?

It will be the aim of the first section of this study to show, by describing the intellectual climate in which Charles Beard "discovered" *Federalist 10,* why the historian was only slightly concerned with Madison's theory as theory, but found in the Virginian's essay one element—the doctrine of class struggle—which, lifted out of context, served admirably the political causes of 1913 dear to Beard's heart. We shall see, as a result, that Beard was led to argue persuasively, but falsely, that Madison's *Federalist* theory expounded the doctrine that theories are unimportant in politics.

It will be the aim of the second half of this study to show by tracing the development of Madison's theory as he thought it out in the spring of 1787, before the Philadelphia Convention met and a year and a half before *Federalist 10* was written, that Madison subscribed to no such naive doctrine. Furthermore it will then be shown that Madison's theory as ab-

---

of the political rights of the many? Did the Constitution of 1787 reaffirm or reject the doctrine of the Declaration of Independence?"

Since historians, even in writing text books, do not always express their position with complete clarity and precision, it is difficult to fit their writings into completely exclusive neat categories on this point. Certainly the volumes of Billington, Loewenberg and Bockunier, Chitwood and Owsley, Faulkner, Harlow, Hicks, and Hockett state or imply that the Constitution rejected the doctrines of the Declaration. Most of these texts also imply or state with differing degrees of emphasis that the fathers were intent on protecting the property of the few at the expense of the political rights of the many. All of them absolve the fathers of being entirely motivated by desire "to line their own pockets" (Harlow's words), but seemingly subscribe to Chitwood and Owsley's belief that it is "impossible" to say exactly "to what extent the framers were influenced by these selfish motives." The texts of Dumond, Rae and Mahoney, and Wellborn argue that the fathers undoubtedly were patriots intent on saving the fruits of the Revolution, and that the Constitution was a consummation of the Declaration. Craven and Johnson, Morison and Commager, Saville and Barck, Wakefield and Lefler call them patriots but leave the relation of the Constitution to the Declaration unclear.

stract speculative thought played a significant role in the writing and ratification of the United States Constitution.

During the nineteenth century, the *Tenth Federalist* was generally ignored by commentators, nor is the reason difficult to discover, for it is a truism apparent to everyone who has reflected on American history that every generation sees mirrored in the Constitution its own deepest political interests. When James Madison died in 1836—just one year before the fiftieth anniversary of the Philadelphia Convention—the burning political issues of that day centered on the powers and structure of the federal union and its relation to the state governments. In this atmosphere the Federalist essays which seemed of most importance were those that dealt with the powers of Congress; the relationship between the President, the Congress, the Judiciary; and increasingly as the year 1860 drew closer, the rights of the states to nullify or otherwise protect themselves against obnoxious legislation. The *Tenth Federalist* was not directly in point in the fierce debates that raged over these issues before the Civil War; so although thousands of Americans must have read the essay while seeking to obtain light on the meaning of the Constitution, practically no one in this era publicly signaled it out for especial praise or comment.

The editors of the twelve editions of the *Federalist* published between 1818 and 1860 ignored Number 10, but indicated by reprinting Madison's *Helvidius* essays and Hamilton's *Pacificus* as an appendix to Publius, that Publius' most important topics related to the "strict" or "liberal" interpretation of the Constitution's powers.[2] The most able foreign interpreter of American democracy, De Tocqueville, describing *The Federalist* as an "excellent book, which ought to be familiar to the statesmen of all countries," specifically referred to more than fifty of the essays, but Madison's *Tenth* was not among them.[3] The two chief historians of the formation of the Constitution who were read during this generation, Hildreth and Curtis, in like manner silently bypassed the essay.[4] Not even the stylistic

[2] The editions of *The Federalist* printed before the Civil War are listed in Henry Cabot Lodge, ed., *The Federalist* (New York, 1886), xxxv-xlii. The Gideon edition of 1818 set the precedent, followed by almost every early editor, of including the Pacificus and Helvidius essays.

[3] Alexis de Tocqueville, *Democracy in America* (New York, 1841. Fourth Ed.), I, 115-145, *passim*. For quotation, see 119*n*.

[4] Richard Hildreth ignores *The Federalist*, but George Ticknor Curtis, *History of the Origin, Formation and Adoption of the Constitution* (New York, 1854) speaks of the work in some detail. See I, 417-418.

pains that Madison took with *Federalist 10* gained the paper inclusion in Griswold's famous anthology of *The Prose Writers of America;* Madison was indeed represented, but it was *Federalist 37* that Griswold chose to show the Virginian as a literary artist.[5]

It is true that the two pre-Civil War biographies of Madison do mention *Federalist 10,* but the casualness of the reference is perhaps the most convincing proof that during the first half of the nineteenth century this essay was taken for granted and held to be of less immediate significance than other of the Virginian's commentaries on the Constitution. The first of these biographies written in 1836 by John Quincy Adams—who here first baptized Madison "the father of the Constitution"[6]—discusses at some length the writing of all *The Federalist,* but Adams' analysis stresses lack of unity to be seen in Hamilton's and Madison's joint enterprise. "In examining closely the points selected by these two great co-operators . . . and their course of argument . . . it is not difficult to perceive that diversity of genius and character which afterwards separated them. . . ." Adams then offers as an example *Federalist* Numbers 9 and 10 where "the advantages of a confederated republic . . . to control [faction] . . . are insisted upon with equal energy in both—but the ninth number, written by Hamilton, draws its principal illustrations from the history of the Grecian Republics; while the tenth, written by Madison, searches for the disease and its remedies in the nature and faculties of MAN."[7] Adams, however, did not bother to elaborate on his praise or quote from Number 10; with manifest destiny looming on the political horizon he turned his attention

[5] Rufus Wilmot Griswold, *The Prose Writers of America* (New York, 1847).

[6] John Quincy Adams, "Eulogy on James Madison," in *The Lives of James Madison and James Monroe* (Buffalo, 1851). This sketch was delivered in a condensed form as a speech at Boston, September 27, 1836; printed the same year, it was widely circulated. Adams did an immense amount of research in preparing it, and it still stands as an able, but dated, short biography. Adams' bestowal of the title of "Father of the Constitution" on Madison was due largely to the recognition of the Virginian's great role in 1787-1788, but the use of the title was not divorced from Adams' strategy in using Madison's authority in the biography to belabor as Constitutional heresies Jefferson's Kentucky Resolution of 1798 and the South Carolina nullification theories of 1831. Adams, who believed Madison to be "a greater and far more estimable man" than Jefferson, expected his treatment of the Alien and Sedition Acts to cause controversy since Madison's "party friends" considered his conduct of 1798-99 "perhaps the greatest of his merits and services." Adams also expected attacks from idolators of Jefferson because of the "very explicit terms" in which he played Madison's theories off against Jefferson; see C. F. Adams, ed., *Memoirs of John Quincy Adams* (Philadelphia, 1876), IX, 305-310.

[7] Adams, "Eulogy," 42.

and most of his space to discussion and gloss of Number 14, dealing with the maximum extent of territory that can be ruled by a republican government, "a question" which he felt in 1836 was of "transcendant interest, and of fearful portent to the people of the Union," who were even then eyeing the "alluring spoils" of Canada and Mexico.

Even more negative is the treatment of Madison's second biographer, William C. Rives. In his outline of all of the Virginian's essays, he cursorily praises Number 10 in one sentence for its "power of analysis" and its "abstract reasoning," and then devotes fifteen pages (with lengthy quotation) to *Federalists* 37-51, "that division of the work," according to Rives, "which was . . . peculiarly his [Madison's] own."[8] Moreover, if Rives's biography had carried Madison's career past 1796 he would probably have indicated that, with Adams, he felt Madison's most significant commentary on the Constitution was not any of the *Federalist* essays. For Adams, by allotment of space in his biography, showed clearly that he thought Madison's most crucial comment on the more perfect union lay in his exegesis of the Tenth Amendment in the *Virginia Resolutions* of 1798-1799—those Resolutions which figured so prominently in the nullification crisis of the 1830's and which were featured in every Democratic Party platform from 1852 to 1860.

Madison was still "Father" of the Constitution after Appomattox, for such tags once rooted in the text books seem impossible to eradicate; but he was a parent treated with increasing disrespect—a parent to be apologized for—by the most authoritative commentators who wrote on *The Federalist* and the Constitution between the Civil War and the end of the nineteenth century. The most widely read biography of the Virginian written during this period, Gay's, treated him with contempt and scorn; Henry Adams, in the great history of Madison's administration, etched his portrait of the President with the acid of irony.[9] Henry Cabot Lodge, P. L. Ford and Goodwin Smith in the process of editing *The Federalist* stole—the word is exact—twelve of the essays written by Madison and attributed them to Hamilton, who all these editors agreed was the greatest of the founding fathers.[10] It was no wonder, then, that in 1900 when a poll

[8] William C. Rives, *Life and Times of James Madison* (Boston, 1866), II, 487 ff.

[9] S. H. Gay, *James Madison* (Boston, 1884); Henry Adams, *History of the United States during the Administrations of Jefferson and Madison* (New York, 1890-1891).

[10] The Lodge, Ford and Goodwin Smith editions of *The Federalist* appeared

was taken by the promoters of the newly-founded American Hall of Fame to determine which of our dead statesmen were worthy of enshrinement there, Madison ignobly failed to qualify.[11] By 1900 the Virginian's "fatherhood" of the Constitution was being explained by sophisticated historical experts as an accidental phenomenon. Madison's skill as a stenographer in reporting the Convention debates had misled the vulgar into attributing to him the paternity of the Constitution—so ran the argument—but this skill of a reporter was not to be compared with the truly great political genius that Hamilton exhibited at Philadelphia.[12]

One of the greatest triumphs of Charles Beard in 1913 thus, was to re-establish Madison's reputation as a major statesman of the Convention rather than as its mere "reporter." Beard's magnification of Madison, however, was essentially a by-product of the strategy in *An Economic Interpretation* of using the *Tenth Federalist* as a bomb to shatter the post-Appomattox interpretation of the Constitution—Alexander Hamilton's "Constitution"—which was proclaimed by conservatives and utilized by them in the party battles of the turn of the century.

The story of the historical revisionism which from the 1870's until the Progressive Era had devalued Madison's role in the creation of the Constitution while glorifying Alexander Hamilton's is too complicated to be told here in any detail. It is enough to note that the ruling groups in the new nation that emerged from the Civil War—a nation with its new pattern of industry, its deification of the business man and the banker as the country's most valuable citizens—found the traditional agrarian interpretation of the Constitution—an interpretation personified by Madison

respectively in 1886, 1898, 1901. For a discussion of the devices by which fifteen numbers by Madison were stolen and allocated to Hamilton, see Douglass Adair, "The Authorship of the Disputed Federalist Papers," *William and Mary Quarterly,* 3d. ser., I (1944), 94-122.

[11] The anonymous author of the sketch of Madison in Lamb's *Biographical Dictionary of the United States* (Boston, 1903), comments on the Hall of Fame vote and on the shameful neglect at that time of Madison's grave at Montpelier.

[12] W. C. Ford, "Hamilton's Notes in the Federal Convention of 1787," *American Historical Review,* X (1904), 97. Ford, contrasting the forceful personality of Hamilton with the negative character of the Virginian, notes that "Madison's studies had produced almost a colorless attitude of mind, in which his learning threatened to neutralize his energy. . . . His influence in the convention was small in spite of the many times he took part in the debates, and it was exerted rather through others than through himself. This attitude made him the best possible recorder of the debates as he was in a receptive frame of mind . . . ready to study what others had to propose."

and Jefferson and dominant from 1800 to 1860—politically and emotionally unsatisfactory.

The symbolic figure of Alexander Hamilton and a neo-Hamiltonian Constitutional philosophy, in contrast, suited the emotional needs and the political interests of the most potent social classes of America's Gilded Age. It was Hamilton's "Report on Manufactures" that with prophetic insight had first painted the vision of a powerful and rich industrialized nation—a vision that this generation of Americans, aided by tariffs and railroad subsidies, was turning into an actuality. To an age that applauded Carnegie's "gospel of wealth" and merged Darwinian biology with Spencerian sociology to justify the new rich as the most "fit" and the "best," Hamilton's eighteenth-century glorification of men of property as those best fitted to rule the state also seemed inspired social thinking. Finally Hamilton's pro-English orientation—his desire that the American Constitution approach the British in form and function, and above all his bitter denunciation of the French Revolution and "Gallic democracy" —appeared wholly admirable in an era when the bloody work of the Paris Commune of 1871 seemed to prove once again the lesson of Robespierre's "Reign of Terror": pure majority-rule democracy—the Rousseauistic "tyranny of numbers"—inevitably would end in social anarchy and open class war.

It was this proletarian threat to the status quo—still small in the United States but nevertheless a recognized danger after the great railroad strikes of the 70's and the Haymarket Riot of 1886—that gave added emotional appeal to the message preached by such historians as Von Holst, Henry Cabot Lodge, John Bach MacMaster, Paul Leceister Ford, Theodore Roosevelt, William Graham Sumner, and dozens of lesser scholars and publicists: the greatest glory of the American system established by the Constitution was its political and economic conservatism. The *ethos* of this document, thanks to the "racial" wisdom of Hamilton and other of the fathers, exemplified "the Anglo-Saxon" love of order, respect for the sacredness of property, and recognition that the only true liberty was the liberty of minority groups to be protected in their rights against the envy and malice of tyrannical majorities. This was the theme of Von Holst's ponderous volumes.[13] This was the point of Gladstone's famous praise of

[13] Herman Von Holst, *The Constitutional and Political History of the United States* (Chicago, 1877); see especially I, Chap. 2, "The Worship of the Constitution, and its Real Character."

the Constitution as "the most wonderful work ever struck off at a given time by the hand and purpose of man," and his comparison of the document with the British Constitution.[14] In spite of the fact, Gladstone says, in spite of the fact that the American Constitution is an *artificial* creation, written in the age of *a priori* theory, of Rousseau and Tom Paine, of Voltaire and Jefferson, it has created a political society as stable, and orderly, and *natural* as that established by the English Constitution "which has proceeded from the womb and long gestation of progressive history."

In this climate of opinion, in which top American scholars vied with the most distinguished foreign commentators to sing the glories of the Constitution as an instrument of conservatism, even statesmen and students whose inherited allegiance was to Jefferson's and Madison's Democratic Party echoed the philosophy of neo-Hamiltonianism. Grover Cleveland, the only Democrat to be President during the last half of the nineteenth century, in a speech made during the Centennial Celebration of the Constitution at Philadelphia, September 16, 1887, called for "business men" to participate more actively "in political affairs" and thus directly to help the nation follow policies that would advance prosperity. This counsel, Cleveland recognized, "might be considered at first a departure that would cause a diminution in personal profit," but the example of 1787 showed the reverse was true: the Constitution—"a triumph of patriotism over selfishness"—indicated that if the fathers by public service sacrificed the quick cash rewards of private business their eventual repayment came from a sound government under which business, and, consequently, all lesser interests flourished magnificently.[15] Hamilton's ghost could applaud such a sentiment; and it could applaud equally the remark, two years later, of a still unknown young Democrat named Woodrow Wilson: "Ever since I have had independent judgements of my own," said Wilson,

[14] W. E. Gladstone, "Kin Beyond the Sea," *North American Review,* CCLXIV (1878), 179-212. The famous quotation sentence can be found on p. 185, but the whole essay should be read, with its distinction between Anglo-American "ordered liberty" and the "autocracy" of Russia and France, and its warning to Americans in the concluding paragraph against "the proposal to tamper with the true monetary creed which the Tempter lately presented to the nation in the Silver Bill."

[15] Hampton L. Carson, ed., *History of the Celebration of the Hundredth Anniversary of the Promulgation of the Constitution of the United States* (Philadelphia, 1889), I, 375. For the sporadic comments on anarchism that periodically appeared during the celebration, see the speech of John A. Kasson, the President of the Centennial Committee (I, 323); and the remarks of the French Consul at Philadelphia, M. Voission, on the celebration (I, 447).

Virginia-born, Georgia-raised and educated at Madison's and Jefferson's colleges, "I have been a Federalist."[16]

It is necessary to remember this almost unanimous chorus of voices during the 1870's and 80's, hymning the sacred conservatism of the Constitution, in order to evaluate the originality of Charles Beard's study of 1913. Clearly when Beard then called the "fathers" conservative he was stating no novel doctrine; nor was there originality in his exhibiting Alexander Hamilton as "the colossal genius of the new system."[17] The shock quality of Beard's study of 1913 arose from two things: first, the shift in the political climate of opinion between 1887 and 1913 had turned the adjective "conservative" from a word of praise to one of censure; and, secondly, Beard was vastly original in offering, explicitly and by innuendo, historical evidence on the *motives* for the father's conservatism. In short, Beard told a generation that gloried in calling itself "progressive" why the Constitution was the antithesis of progressivism.

The beginning of this major shift away from political conservatism, so evident by 1913, was first conspicuous during the great depression of 1893, at which time the pocket-slapping complacency that characterized the 1887 Centennial Celebration of the Constitution had evaporated, not to reappear in America until the Coolidge "normalcy" of the 1920's. Agrarian unrest in the South and West exploded into Populism; in the great industrial centers of the country an unprecedented number of strikes were marked with scenes of terrorism, violence, and class war reminiscent of the Paris Commune. Cleveland's invitation to businessmen to take a more active part in running the government (applauded generally in 1887 as an appeal to men of virtue and probity) now took on a sinister sound in circles listening to Tom Watson denounce the "Vampires of Wall Street" or reading Henry Demerest Lloyd's *Wealth v Commonwealth.* As the economic disaster deepened and became more and more catastrophic, fear and hatred manifested themselves at every level of American society

[16]Letter to Albert Bushnell Hart, June 3, 1889, quoted in Arthur S. Link, *Wilson, the Road to the White House* (Princeton, 1947), 22.

[17]Charles A. Beard, *An Economic Interpretation of the Constitution of the United States* (New York, 1913), 100. Obviously, in reacting against certain features of the standpat Republican interpretation of the Constitution, Beard did not react against all of them. Most conspicuously he emphasized even more than Lodge, *et al.*, Alexander Hamilton's role at Philadelphia. Indeed in the key chapter, "The Economic Interests of the Members of the Convention" in which Beard proves that the fathers were not "disinterested," approximately one-fifth of the discussion is concerned solely with Hamilton and the Hamilton connection.

as the poor made the acquaintance of starvation and the rich shuddered to think what the starving might do.

Then from the 1895 spring term of the Supreme Court issued the three famous decisions on the sugar monopoly, on the Pullman strike injunction, and on the income tax, which cast the Constitution and Alexander Hamilton's *Federalist 78,* justifying judicial review, squarely into the very storm center of contemporary politics. The Court, the Constitution, and the writings of Publius were to stay there until the entrance of the United States in World War I diverted public attention from domestic reform.

The Debs and the Sugar Trust decisions seemed to outraged radicals and reformers to indicate that the Constitution, as interpreted by the Supreme Court, established a double standard of justice between labor and capital. The income tax decision appeared even more portentious. No matter if an overwhelming majority of the American people wished their representatives in Congress to tax the overgrown income of the wealthy, the words of the founding fathers inscribed in the Constitution forbad it; so said the Court. The economic expediency of an income tax, its justification as an equitable levy, all the arguments from public policy, were irrelevant weighed against those ghostly phrases of 1787.[18] Inevitably the Justices were subjected to what the historian of the Court describes as "violent criticism" and "bitter attack."[19]

This Constitutional crisis of 1895 and the years following, like the similar crises touched off by the Dred Scott opinion and the Court's overruling of New Deal legislation in 1936, produced two different reactions among critics of the decisions. There were some who accepted the court's edicts as bad policy, but good Constitutional law; others cried they were bad policy and bad law. In the first group was Debs himself, who spent

[18] For a fascinating contemporary report of Joseph H. Choate's oral argument before the Court attacking the constitutionality of the income tax, see David Graham Phillips' news story written for the New York *World,* printed in Edward S. Martin, *The Life of Joseph Hodges Choate* (New York, 1920), 7-15. See especially Phillips' conclusion: Choate "paid small attention to the arguments from public policy, from political economy with which his adversaries dealt so admirably. He kept close to the Constitution, and addressed himself to the interpreting of constitutional principles. And when he sat down everyone there present felt that . . . the income tax had had its worst blow."

[19] Charles Warren, *The Supreme Court in United States History* (Boston, 1937. Rev. Ed.), II, 701-702. For Beard's contemporary criticism of the Court's policy from 1877 to 1914, see his *Contemporary American History* (New York, 1914), 6-7, 13-19, 54-84, 219-220, 313-314; for his sardonic comments on the Debs and income tax cases, see 152-161.

his jail term reading socialist literature and came to the conclusion that his conviction did represent capitalist justice—the only kind of justice available under a capitalist constitution—and that the whole system should be revolutionized. By 1912 nearly a million Americans followed Debs to the polls and gave him their votes for President. Far more numerous, however, was the group who insisted that the Court had "usurped" power not granted it under the Constitution in order to twist that document's phrases to annul the intent of Congress and the wishes of the American people. This was the position taken by the Democratic Platform in 1896; this was the semi-official position of the Bull Moose Party that rallied behind Theodore Roosevelt in 1912. And in the years between 1895 and 1912 hundreds of scholars, publicists, and politicians explored American constitutional history, re-read *The Federalist,* and disputed over the intentions of the founding fathers in order either to justify demands for reform or to fortify the conservative position whose strongest inner citadel was the the United States Constitution, as interpreted by Chief Justice Fuller's Court.[20] Charles Beard's *An Economic Interpretation of the Constitution* published in 1913 was the climactic product of the left wing of "progressive" scholarship—a work whose artful selectivity dealt with those particular features of the Constitution which were most distressing to the American radicals of the first decade of the twentieth century.

Beard, before addressing himself to the meaning of the Constitution as a whole, had first explored the possibility that the Supreme Court of his day *was* "usurping" power not granted by the fathers in overruling Congressional legislation and thwarting the will of the people. His researches convinced him that there was no usurpation, that a majority of the fathers approved of "judicial control," of majority will, and that the anti-democratic principle of judicial supremacy was in harmony with the whole spirit of the Constitution.[21] As Beard was to argue in *An Economic In-*

[20] A short but representative bibliography of the attacks on the Court from 1895 to 1912 can be found in the references listed in Warren's footnotes, II, 703, 713, 743.

[21] Beard's study in its earliest form appeared in the *Political Science Quarterly,* XXVII (1912), 1-35, with the title "The Supreme Court—Usurper or Grantee." The quotation is in the lead paragraph. The study was also published as a book in expanded detail the same year, *The Supreme Court and the Constitution* (New York, 1912). For evidence of Beard's view that "judicial control" was essentially and inevitably anti-democratic, see the way he uses the approval of the doctrine as the yardstick to measure the liberal or reactionary complexion of members of the Convention in *An Economic Interpretation:* Gunning Bedford of Delaware—of all

terpretation "the keystone" of the whole constitutional structure of 1787 was the Court whose position allowed it to use "the sanctity and mystery of the law" to "foil" democracy. It was thus historically impossible, in Beard's words, to give "the color of legality, so highly prized by revolutionaries as well as by apostles of law and order" to any movement "designed to strip the court of their political function."

What course was then open to radicals and reformers? Their project for making over America into a land where social justice prevailed was denied even the color of legality, not by a usurping court, but by the sacred words of the Constitution of 1787. Beard's answer in *An Economic Interpretation* was to expose the nature of that Constitution, to unmask its hidden features in order to show that it deserved no veneration, no respect, and should carry no authority to democratic Americans of the twentieth century. Indeed, by what amounted to a stroke of tactical genius, Beard divined that the most devastating attack on the Court of 1913, the most powerful thrust against the whole conservative political position, could be made by a "purely historical" study.[22] This approach would exclude explicit discussion of contemporary issues in order to strip "the sanctity and mystery" from that venerable Constitution on which the Court and the old guard was standing pat.[23]

The contemporary reform issues that were agitating the progressives were, of course, all treated in Beard's book by indirection—the theme of

---

people—and R. D. Spaight of North Carolina can by "inference" (the word is Beard's) be called democrats because they disapproved "judicial control" (pp. 191, 214), while George Wythe is set down as conservative on the bare evidence that he was a "warm advocate" of the doctrine (p. 216), and James Wilson, although "he took a democratic view on several matters" in the Convention, is flatly denied the title of "democrat" for the same reason (pp. 215-216).

[22] For a sketch of Beard's early political orientation by a student-disciple who became a close friend, see Matthew Josephson, "Charles A. Beard: A Memoir," *Virginia Quarterly Review*, XXV (1949), 593-595. For a brilliant analysis of Beard's political values as they are revealed in *The Development of Modern Europe* (1907, written with H. J. Robinson) and in his *Contemporary American History* (1914), see Morton G. White, *Social Thought in America: the Revolt against Formalism* (New York, 1949), 32-58.

[23] Beard's book ostentatiously masquerades throughout as a dull monograph whose findings will be of interest only to professional scholars. See, for example, the preface statement of the modest aim of the work as merely "designed to suggest new lines of historical research" and to encourage "a few of this generation of scholars . . . to turn away from barren 'political' history." Note how in his summary Beard speaks of the importance "for political science" of the conclusions warranted by "this long and arid survey."

social justice, the unholy and corrupt alliance of business and politics that made economic injustice a regular feature of the American system, and, at greatest length, the sabotage of majority rule by a conspiracy of predatory minority groups concealing their operations behind the rhetorical false-face of "We, the people." After Beard had had his say it became extremely difficult for even the most naive conservatives to glorify the Constitution in quite the manner of Paul Leicester Ford in 1898, who in the introduction to his edition of *The Federalist* congratulated the American people on their great good luck that their "Federal compact was the first deliberate attempt and assent of a majority to tie its own hands."

This same indirection conditioned the use to which Beard put James Madison and the *Tenth Federalist.* All the evidence we have—and it will remain incomplete until we have an adequate biography of Charles Beard —indicates that the historian discovered Madison a good deal later than he discovered Karl Marx.[24] Certainly Beard's use of the concept of "economic determinism" in his famous study of 1913 is in many ways more Marxian than Madisonian. In fact, when Beard paraphrases from *Federalist 10* what he calls Madison's "masterly statement of the theory" his method is to quote one passage of that essay incompletely; to change subtly, but decisively, a key element in Madison's theory into Marxian terms; and then to buttress this misstatement of Madison's "economic determinism" with a footnote which is almost a verbatim transcription of a paragraph by Engels.[25]

[24] Matthew Josephson reports that Beard first read the Communist Manifesto while at DePauw College, 1895-1898, at a time when the future historian, deeply stirred by the free silver campaign, was defending as a college debater, the federal income tax and labor's right to organize. His post-graduate work in England, where he helped found Ruskin College, the first labor college at Oxford, threw Beard into close contact with young Socialist intelligentsia as well as English trade-union leaders. Certainly by 1907 when Beard published, with Robinson, *Development of Modern Europe,* he was familiar with the theories of Marx which are adequately covered in that volume. Josephson reports that Beard later described himself as "almost-a-socialist." If my reading of Beard's *Contemporary American History* is correct the immediate program of reform that he desired to see carried through was the advancement of "direct democracy" (p. 284 ff.) by preferential primaries, the initiative, referendum, and recall, as a first step in what he and Robinson had called in 1908 the "war on poverty."

[25] The section of *Federalist 10* omitted in both of Beard's paraphrases is the elaborate catalogue of non-economic factions; the misstatement of Madison's theory is the denial of Madison's explicit point that "opinions concerning government" can be causes of "violent conflicts" which becomes in Beard's restatement: "The theories of government which men entertain are emotional reactions to their property interests." (*Economic Interpretation,* 157, 15-16); the footnote quotation from Seligman's *The Economic Interpretation of History* quoted by Beard (p. 15) is as Morton

Apparently Beard's use of Madison's *Tenth Federalist* was, in part at least, a matter of political strategy—a device, quite self-consciously adopted, of wrapping himself in the American flag as he muckraked the motives of the founding fathers and, by implication, pointed to the Constitution as an instrument of class exploitation. My economic interpretation, Beard claimed, "is based upon the political science of James Madison, the father of the Constitution and later President of the Union he had done so much to create. . . .Those who are inclined to repudiate the hypothesis of economic determinism as a European importation [i.e. Marxism] must therefore revise their views on learning that one of the earliest and certainly one of the clearest statements of it came from a profound student of politics who sat in the convention that framed our fundamental law."[26]

It would be possible to show in detail how this special version of "economic determinism," created by Beard's grafting of Marx on Madison, colored the general conclusions reached in *An Economic Interpretation of the Constitution.* For the purposes of this paper, however, it is more important to note the ambiguous effect of Beard's book on Madison's reputation. Clearly, Beard's acclaim of *Federalist 10,* his praise of this essay's "master theory" of the Constitution publicized the essay and its author spectacularly among American historians. Scholars, following Beard's lead, almost all came to subscribe, with varying degrees of enthusiasm, to an economic interpretation of history during the 1920's and 1930's.[27] In this period, particularly after 1930, the *Tenth Federalist* became the most frequently quoted and most regularly anthologized essay of Publius.[28]

But what of Madison himself, the "master theorist" of 1787? Perhaps

White points out verbatim from Engels. For White's acute discussion of the hybrid nature of Beard's "determinism" see *Social Thought in America,* 119-127.

[26] Beard, *Economic Interpretation,* 14-16. I myself doubt very much if Beard was ever a through-going Marxist in his analysis; certainly his books were reformist rather than revolutionary in their mood. In effect then his stress on "economic determinism" and "the class struggle" was to call attention to legislation that would give disadvantaged groups in American society (women, Negroes, labor, etc.) more political power and consequently more favorable legislative treatment. It should be noted further that the connotations of the term "Marxist" are different in 1913 and 1951.

[27] Henry S. Commager, *The American Mind* (New Haven, 1950), Chapter XIII, makes this point in his account of the transition in the style and content of historical writing that came in America after the 1890's. Commager also suggests reasons for the popularity of an economic interpretation during the 1920's (p. 307) in his estimate of Beard's mushrooming influence during that decade.

[28] Many of the pre-Beard anthologies and "libraries of American literature" make no mention of Madison or *The Federalist.* Among those that do, including the

the most equivocal feature of Beard's latter-day revival of Madison's fame lies in the fact that the historian's major thesis about the Constitution can be taken to imply that "theory" played little or no part in the creation of the Federal Union. The fathers, as pictured by Beard, were "practical" men who, knowing exactly what they wanted in the way of concrete economic privileges, were willing to stage a "coup d'etat" to gain their ends.[29] Collectively they were exhibited as being adepts in the use of force, fraud, and false propaganda.[30] Beard gives no hint, however, that political theory played any consequential role in creating the Constitution; speculation there was in plenty in the Convention, but it was land and debt speculation, not speculative thought.[31] Indeed, if it is possible to determine an individual's political motives by cataloguing his property, the irrelevance of theory should be apparent. It was thus easy to deduce from Beard's study—though he did not himself go on to make that deduction—that Madison's "master theory" merely revealed him as a writer who was indiscreet enough to reveal in the *Tenth Federalist* the grinning death's head of economic exploitation concealed behind the decorous and misleading phrases of the Constitution. Certainly, this was the deduction made by Vernon Louis Parrington, Beard's most distinguished and influential disciple.

Parrington, in the fragment of autobiography entitled "A Chapter in American Liberalism," telling of the intellectual influences which shaped

collections edited by E. C. Stedman, E. C. Alderman, J. C. Harris, and W. P. Trent, *Federalist* essays by Madison are printed but never Number 10. Even as late as 1918 the author of the essay on the political writings of the critical period published in *The Cambridge History of American Literature* dismisses all of Madison's Publius essays as written under the influence of Hamilton (I, 148). In amusing contrast, thirty years later when *Federalist 10* had been printed and reprinted, Bernard Smith, anthologizing documents for *The Democratic Spirit* (New York, 1941), almost apologizes for not reprinting *Federalist 10* but for substituting an essay of Madison on religious liberty—a "phase" of Madison's thinking "not widely enough known."

[29] Beard, *Economic Interpretation,* 62-63.

[30] *Ibid.,* Chapter VIII, "The Process of Ratification." For fraud in Massachusetts see the heavy irony—"they are all—all honorable men"—with which King, Gorham, and Strong are treated (p. 228); for force in Pennsylvania see pp. 231-232; for false propaganda see Beard's explicit linking of "exaggeration of danger" characteristic of contemporary tariff propaganda with the federalist talk of commercial depression in 1787 (p. 41); and finally the hypothesis tentatively advanced (pp. 47-48) that the "critical period" was "but a phantom of the imagination produced by some undoubted evils which could have been remedied without a political revolution."

[31] In Beard's *Economic Interpretation,* 189-190, it is significant that Beard does not speak of political theories of the members of the Convention but describes what he calls their "doctrines."

his early thinking, describes the explosive impact of Beard's volume.[32] First, he remembers, had come the muckrakers—Steffens, Russell, Tarbell, Myers, and Sinclair—blazing across the political sky like "the tail of a comet," indoctrinating Parrington and his fellow progressives "in the elementary principles of political realism," revealing the "hidden cess pool . . . fouling American life . . . not one cess pool but many, under every city hall and beneath every state capitol—dug secretly by politicians in the pay of respectable business men." During this first period of education, Parrington reports, he hoped in vain that "a democratic electorate would speedily democratize" America. But the muckraking died off, and as the reform movement entered its second stage, Parrington and his fellow liberals passed from political to economic programs. In Parrington's judgment "Professor Beard's notable study *An Economic Interpretation of the Constitution* (1913), was the greatest intellectual achievement" of this second phase.[33] Beard's book offered "a discovery that struck home like a submarine torpedo—the discovery that the drift toward plutocracy was not a drift away from the spirit of the Constitution, but an inevitable unfolding from its premises; that instead of having been conceived by the fathers as a democratic instrument, it had been conceived in a spirit designedly hostile to democracy; that it was in fact, a carefully formulated expression of eighteenth-century property consciousness, erected as a defense against the democratic spirit that had got out of hand during the Revolution. . . ." This, Parrington learned from Beard, was the secret of the continual frustration of American democracy—"the source of the weakness of the democratic principal in governmental practice." America had never been a democracy, Parrington believed, "for the sufficient reason that too many handicaps had been imposed upon the majority will. The democratic principle had been bound with withes like Sampson and had become a play thing for the Philistines. From the beginning . . . democracy and property had been at odds. . . ." Moreover "in this ceaseless struggle between the man and the dollar, between democracy and property

[32] Parrington's fragment of autobiography is printed as an addenda to Volume III of *Main Currents in American Thought* (New York, 1927-1930), 401-403; all quotations in this paragraph are from this fragment.

[33] The other piece of scholarly writing on the Constitution praised by Parrington, but rated below Beard, is J. Allen Smith, *The Spirit of American Government* (New York, 1907). *Main Currents* was dedicated to Smith, whose book is one of the earliest scholarly tracts during this period to contrast the "reactionary" Constitution with the "democratic" Declaration.

the reasons for the persistant triumph of property" could be found in the provisions of that Constitution which James Madison had fathered.

Converted to "realism" by the dazzling light that Beard had thrown on the nature of the Constitution, Parrington labored for twenty years to document the never-ending struggle "between the man and the dollar" throughout American history. Taking as the positive liberal pole of American experience Jefferson's Declaration of Independence—"it seemed incredible that honest men [before Beard] could have erred so greatly in confusing the Constitution and the Declaration"—Parrington set up in sharp contrast the Constitution as the negative pole of black reaction; and in his great *Main Currents in American Thought* he showed how all American history from colonial times to his own day had vibrated between the doctrines of these two documents.[34]

Parrington's discussion of Madison the theorist and author of *Federalist 10* in *Main Currents in American Thought* illustrates the dilemma of a conscientious scholar carrying to a logical conclusion the half-hints, the deliberate ambiguities left unresolved by Beard. Parrington, of course, could not evade the problem as his master had done, for *Main Currents* was intellectual history. But Parrington's conclusion, oddly enough, while giving lip service to Madison as "a profound political thinker," resolutely denied that *Federalist 10* represented original or profound thought, or even accurate political observation.

The tone of Parrington's estimate of Madison is set by the first sentence of the chapter—"The Great Debate"—in which he analyzes the creation of the Constitution.[35] "When one considers the bulk of the commentary that has grown up about the Constitution," the historian notes, "It is surprising how little abstract political speculation accompanied its makeup and adoption. . . . It was the work of able lawyers and men of affairs confronting a definite situation, rather than of political philosophers; and it was accompanied by none of that searching examination of fundamental rights and principles which made the earlier Puritan and later French debate—so rich in creative speculation."

In Parrington's view it was unfortunate that in 1787 the seventeenth-century doctrines of the "Commonwealth Levelers"—manhood suffrage

[34] This contrast was not a unique phenomenon of the Progressive era, but is the normal product of every major and prolonged Constitutional crisis in American history, namely 1793ff., 1854ff., 1896ff., 1935ff.

[35] V. L. Parrington, *Main Currents in American Thought,* I, 279-291. All the quotations from Parrington that follow are taken from this chapter.

and annual parliaments—were "buried too deep under Tory obloquy to be resurrected" and "French democratic theory still awaited the rise of Jacobinism to clarify its principles." Consequently "the authorities bandied to and fro in the great debate" were such conservative English theorists as Hobbes, Locke, Harrington, Milton, Sidney, Halifax, Hume, and Blackstone, and a handful of continental writers, Machiavelli, Vattel, Pufendorf, and Montesquieu.[36] Every one of these authorities "either distrusted or violently condemned democracy, yet they provided the major body of theory made use of by the Federalists." Actually, Parrington argued, the antidemocratic nature of these authorities relied on by the fathers was relatively unimportant in the first debate at Philadelphia, where "in the privacy of the convention the speakers were free to express interests openly acknowledged." Indeed "in elaborating a system of checks and balances the members of the convention were influenced by the practical considerations of economic determinism more than by the theories of Montesquieu." But in the second debate—the debate over ratification in 1788—when the case for the Constitution was argued "before the generality of voters without doors," the lack of the democratic theory which would have been available after the French Revolution put the opponents of the Constitution at a great disadvantage. It was in this theoretical vacuum (Parrington felt) that the sophistries of Madison's *Federalist 10* proved so harmful to the democratic cause.

Parrington was frank to admit that despite the fame of *The Federalist* he could not value it as a truly great classic of political theory. In substance it was "the work of able lawyers, with whom was joined a notable political thinker," but, "designed as a frankly partizan argument," it is "in very large part . . . of interest only to students of early constitutional practice." Yet the one essay of Publius that Parrington bothers to quote and analyze is "the remarkable tenth number, which compresses within a few pages pretty much the whole Federalist theory of political science."

In Parrington's analysis of this "remarkable" essay he finds three aspects of Madison's argument worth comment: the Virginian's theory of faction, his explanation of the cause of faction, and the false conclusions that Parrington feels Madison drew in favor of minority rule. No theory, Parring-

[36] It should be noticed that although Parrington as an intellectual historian is presumably aware of the great differences between the theories of Locke and Hobbes, for example, and the practical consequences of those theoretical differences in politics, he is content to lump crudely the whole group together in the simple and misleading category "anti-democratic."

ton believes, "is more representative of the time than the theory of faction" which served the purpose in 1787 of "a first line of defense thrown up against the advancing democratic movement" by giving political parties an evil name. In 1787, Parrington argues, "in a world moving inevitably towards manhood suffrage, a sharp alignment of parties with definite platforms was greatly feared by the minority, for the organization of the rank and file of the voters must end in majority control. An honest appeal to the people was the last thing desired by the Federalists, and the democratic machinery of recalls and referendums and rotation in office, which had developed during the war, was stigmatized as factional devices which in the end must destroy good government." As a good progressive democrat Parrington could be contemptuous of such biased and faulty reasoning.

Madison, in the historian's view, was more intelligent in tracing "political parties to economic sources." The Virginian, however, was not original or unusually perspicacious in this insight which was apparent to "the greater political thinkers of the past"; nor was he original or even logical in deducing from this premise the need for "a republican rather than a democratic form of government." In this conclusion, Parrington felt sure, Madison was merely "adapting to his purpose the views of Milton and other seventeenth century republicans" whose fear of the people led them to attempt "to manacle the native libertie of mankinde." Then in a summary that practically stripped from the Father of the Constitution all pretensions to profundity Parrington dismissed the theory of *Federalist 10* with the remark, "it has long since become a commonplace of political observation that the minority and not the majority is the more dangerous to the common well-being, for it is the minority that most frequently uses government to its own ends."[37]

The surprising feature of Parrington's analysis of Madison as a thinker is not the derogatory conclusions reached—these, indeed, were implicit in any analysis that followed Beard's hints to a logical end or that allowed the Progressive Era's value judgments on political and economic democracy to

[37] Entirely logical from Parrington's point of view was the final argument that R. H. Lee's anti-Constitution pamphlet, *Letters from a Federal Farmer,* was superior to *The Federalist* as political analysis and "in its frank and disinterested examination" of the Constitution. One of the curious, but not entirely logical, results of the Progressives' attack on the Constitution as "anti-democratic" was the tendency to label anyone who opposed the Constitution a great democrat; see, for example, Beard on Luther Martin, Parrington on Patrick Henry.

be smuggled into the discussion—but the fact that in the forty years since Beard first publicized the *Federalist 10* and in the twenty years since Parrington's feeble attempt at dissection, no scholar has examined directly *all* the theoretical elements of the essay or studied the part played by the theories during the *whole* period of constitutional creation. In regard to this second point it should be noted that the closely-knit parts of *Federalist 10* were not, as Parrington assumes, hastily worked up by Madison after the Convention was over, merely as an argument for ratification. All the ideas, the whole thesis of the essay we know as *Federalist 10,* had been systematically worked out as part of a research project by the Virginian immediately before the Philadelphia meeting. What was Madison's purpose in this? What place did he think a complicated piece of speculative political philosophy would have in a Convention of hard-headed "practical" men? And finally what of the separate but related themes of Madison's essay? Beard and his followers fixed on Madison's discussion of property and faction, calling it a theory of "economic determinism." How did Madison envision the relation of economic factions with those that he is careful to distinguish as growing out of non-economic roots? What of the essay's obvious pre-occupation with "justice"?

These are not merely hypothetical questions that have remained unanswered because they are unanswerable. Because of the special cast of Madison's personality, because of the special school of political philosophy to which he gave his intellectual allegiance, he has left ample evidence which makes it possible to trace the development of his theory from its "first shoots"—the phrase is Madison's own—until its final flowering in the *Tenth Federalist.* In the process of studying the evolution of Madison's ideas it will become apparent that it is highly anachronistic to tag his theory "anti-democratic" in the nineteenth- or twentieth-century meaning of the term. Madison's *Tenth Federalist* is eighteenth-century political theory directed to an eighteenth-century problem; and it is one of the great creative achievements of that intellectual movement that later ages have christened "Jeffersonian democracy."

To these points will be addressed the last half of this discussion which will appear in a later issue of the *Quarterly.*

[6]

"That Politics May Be Reduced to a Science": David Hume, James Madison, and the Tenth *Federalist**

By Douglass Adair

In June 1783, the war for American independence being ended, General Washington addressed his once-famous circular letter to the state governors with the hopeful prophecy that if the Union of the States could be preserved, the future of the Republic would be both glorious and happy. "The foundation of our Empire was not laid in the gloomy age of Ignorance and Superstition," Washington pointed out, "but at an Epocha when the rights of mankind were better understood and more clearly defined, than at any former period; the researches of the human mind after social happiness, have been carried to a great extent, the treasures of knowledge, acquired by the labours of Philosophers, Sages, and Legislators, through a long succession of years, are laid open for our use, and their collected wisdom may be happily applied in the Establishment of our forms of Government . . . At this auspicious period, the United States came into existence as a Nation, and if their Citizens should not be completely free and happy, the fault will be intirely their own."

The optimism of General Washington's statement is manifest; the reasons he advances for this optimism, however, seem to modern Americans a century and a half later both odd and naive, if not slightly un-American. For Washington here argues in favor of "the Progress of the Human Mind." Knowledge gradually acquired through "researches of the human mind" about the nature of man and government—knowledge which "the gloomy age of Ignorance and Superstition" did not have—gives Americans in 1783 the power to new-model their forms of government according to the precepts

*Delivered at the Conference of Early American History at the Henry E. Huntington Library, February 9, 1957.

of wisdom and reason. The "Philosopher" as Sage and Legislator, General Washington hopes, will preside over the creation and reform of American political institutions.

"Philosopher" as written here by Washington was a word with hopeful and good connotations. But this was 1783. In 1789 the French Revolution began; by 1792 "philosophy" was being equated with the guillotine, atheism, the reign of terror. Thereafter "philosopher" would be a smear-word, connoting a fuzzy-minded and dangerous social theorist—one of those impractical Utopians whose foolish attempts to reform society according to a rational plan created the anarchy and social disaster of the Terror. Before his death in 1799 Washington himself came to distrust and fear the political activities of philosophers. And in time it would become fashionable among both French conservatives and among all patriotic Americans to stress the sinister new implications of the word "philosophy" added after 1789 and to credit the French philosophers with transforming the French Revolution into a "bad" revolution in contrast to the "good" non-philosophical American Revolution. But this ethical transformation of the word still lay in the future in 1783. Then "philosophy" and "philosopher" were still terms evoking optimism and hopes of the high tide of Enlightenment on both sides of the Atlantic.

Dr. Johnson in his *Dictionary* helps us understand why Washington had such high regard for philosophy as our war for independence ended. "Philosophy," according to the lexicographer, was "knowledge natural or moral"; it was "hypothesis or system upon which natural effects are explained." "To philosophize," or "play the philosopher," was "to search into nature; to enquire into the causes of effects." The synonym of "Philosophy" in 1783 then was "Science"; the synonym of "Philosopher" would be our modern word (not coined until 1840) "Scientist," "a man deep in knowledge, either moral or natural."

Bacon, Newton, and Locke were the famed trinity of representative great philosophers for Americans and all educated inhabitants of Western Europe in 1783. Francis Bacon, the earliest prophet of philosophy as a program for the advancement of learning, had preached that "Knowledge is Power" and that Truth discovered by

Reason through observation and free inquiry is as certain and as readily adapted to promote the happiness of human life, as Truth communicated to mankind through God's direct revelation. Isaac Newton, "the first luminary in this bright constellation," had demonstrated that Reason indeed could discover the laws of physical Nature and of Nature's God, while John Locke's researches into psychology and human understanding had definitely channeled inquiry toward the discovery of the immutable and universal laws of Human Nature. By the middle of the eighteenth century a multitude of researchers in all the countries of Europe were seeking, in Newtonian style, to advance the bounds of knowledge in politics, economics, law, and sociology. By the middle of the century the French judge and *philosophe* Montesquieu had produced a compendium of the behavioral sciences, cutting across all these fields in his famous study of *The Spirit of the Laws*.

However, Washington's assurance that already scientific knowledge about government had accumulated to such an extent that it could be immediately applied to the uses of "Legislators," pointed less toward France than toward Scotland. There, especially in the Scottish universities, had been developed the chief centers of eighteenth-century social science research and publication in all the world. The names of Francis Hutcheson, David Hume, Adam Smith, Thomas Reid, Lord Kames, Adam Ferguson, the most prominent of the Scottish philosophers, were internationally famous. In America the treatises of these Scots, dealing with history, ethics, politics, economics, psychology, and jurisprudence in terms of "system upon which natural effects are explained," had become the standard textbooks of the colleges of the late colonial period. At Princeton, at William and Mary, at Pennsylvania, at Yale, at King's, and at Harvard, the young men who rode off to war in 1776 had been trained in the texts of Scottish social science.

The Scottish system, as it had been gradually elaborated in the works of a whole generation of researchers, rested on one basic assumption, had developed its own special method, and kept to a consistent aim. The assumption was "that there is a great uniformity among the actions of men, in all nations and ages, and that human nature remains still the same, in its principles and operations. The same motives always produce the same actions; the same events follow from the same causes. . . . Would you know the sentiments, inclinations, and course of life of the Greeks and Romans? Study well the temper and actions of the French and English . . ."—thus David Hume, presenting the basis of a science of human behavior. The method of eighteenth-century social science followed from this primary assumption—it was historical-comparative synthesis. Again Hume: "Mankind are so much the same, in all times and places, that history informs us of nothing new or strange in this particular. Its chief use is only to discover the constant and universal principles of human nature, by showing men in all varieties and situations, and furnishing us with materials from which we may form our observations and become acquainted with the regular springs of human action and behavior."[1] Finally, the aim of studying man's behavior in its comparative-historical manifestations was for the purpose of prediction—philosophy would aid the legislator in making correct policy decisions. Comparative-historical studies of man in society would allow the discovery of the constant and universal principle of human nature, which, in turn, would allow at least some safe predictions about the effects of legislation "almost as general and certain . . . as any which the mathematical sciences will afford us." "Politics" (and again the words are Hume's) to some degree "may be reduced to a science."

By thus translating the abstract generalizations about "philosophy" in Washington's letter of 1783 into the concrete and particular type of philosophy to which he referred, the issue is brought into new focus more congenial to our modern under-

[1]David Hume, "Of Liberty and Necessity," in *An Enquiry Concerning Human Understanding* (London, 1748). An examination of the social theory of the Scottish school is to be found in Gladys Bryson, *Man and Society: The Scottish Inquiry of the Eighteenth Century* (Princeton, 1945). Miss Bryson seems unaware both of the position held by Scottish social science in the curriculum of the American colleges after 1750—Princeton, for example, where nine members of the Constitutional Convention of 1787 graduated, was a provincial carbon-copy, under President Witherspoon, of Edinburgh—and of its influence on the revolutionary generation. For a brilliant analysis of Francis Hutcheson's ideas and his part in setting the tone and direction of Scottish research, as well as the trans-Atlantic flow of ideas between Scotland and the American colonies in the eighteenth century, with a persuasive explanation of why the Scots specialized in social science formulations that were peculiarly congenial to the American revolutionary elite, see Caroline Robbins, "When It Is That Colonies May Turn Independent," *William and Mary Quarterly*, 3d ser., Vol. XI (April, 1954), pp. 214-251.

standing. On reviewing the specific body of philosophical theory and writing with which Washington and his American contemporaries were familiar, we immediately remember that "the collected wisdom" of at least some of the Scottish academic philosophers was applied to American legislation during the nineteenth century. It is obvious, for example, that the "scientific predictions," based on historical analysis, contained in Professor Adam Smith's *An Inquiry into the Nature and Causes of the Wealth of Nations* (London, 1776), concerning the role of free enterprise and economic productivity, was of prime significance in shaping the relations of the state with the American business community, especially after 1828. Washington's expectations of 1783 were thus accurate in the long-run view.[1a]

It is the purpose of this paper, however, to show that Washington's immediate expectations of the creative role of "philosophy" in American politics were also accurate in the period in which he wrote. It is thus the larger inference of the following essay that "philosophy," or "the science of politics" (as defined above), was integral to the whole discussion of the necessity for a *more* perfect Union that resulted in the creation of the American Constitution of 1787.

It can be shown, though not in this short paper, that the use of history in the debates both in the Philadelphia Convention and in the state ratifying conventions is not mere rhetorical-historical window-dressing, concealing substantially greedy motives of class and property. The speakers were making a genuinely "scientific" attempt to discover the "constant and universal principles" of any republican government in regard to liberty, justice, and stability.

In this perspective the three hundred pages of comparative-historical research in John Adams's *Defence of the Constitutions of the United States* (1787), and the five-hour closely argued historical analysis in Alexander Hamilton's Convention Speech of June 18, 1787, were both "scientific" efforts to relate the current difficulties

[1a]The theoretical and prophetic nature of Adam Smith's classic when it was published in 1776 is today largely ignored by both scholars and spokesmen for the modern American business community. In 1776, however, Smith could only theorize from scattered historical precedents as to how a projective free enterprise system might work, because nowhere in his mercantilist world was a free enterprise system of the sort he described on paper actually operating.

of the thirteen American republics to the universal tendencies of republicanism in all nations and in all ages. History, scientifically considered, thus helped *define* both the nature of the crisis of 1787 for these leaders and their audience, and also determined in large part the "reforms" that, it could be predicted, would end the crisis. To both Adams and Hamilton history proved (so they believed) that sooner or later the American people would have to return to a system of mixed or limited monarchy—so great was the size of the country, so diverse were the interests to be reconciled that no other system could be adequate in securing both liberty and justice. In like manner Patrick Henry's prediction, June 9, 1788, in the Virginia Ratifying Convention, "that one government [i.e., the proposed constitution] cannot reign over so extensive a country as this is, without absolute despotism" was grounded upon a "political axiom" scientifically confirmed, so he believed, by history.

The most creative and philosophical disciple of the Scottish school of science and politics in the Philadelphia Convention was James Madison. His effectiveness as an advocate of a new constitution, and of the particular constitution that was drawn up in Philadelphia in 1787, was certainly based in large part on his personal experience in public life and his personal knowledge of the conditions of America in 1787. But Madison's greatness as a statesman rests in part on his ability quite deliberately to set his limited personal experience in the context of the experience of men in other ages and times, thus giving extra reaches of insight to his political formulations.

His most amazing political prophecy, formally published in the tenth *Federalist,* was that the size of the United States and its variety of interests could be made a guarantee of stability and justice under the new constitution. When Madison made this prophecy the accepted opinion among all sophisticated politicians was exactly the opposite. It is the purpose of the following detailed analysis to show Madison, the scholar-statesman, evolving his novel theory, and not only using the behavioral science techniques of the eighteenth century, but turning to the writings of David Hume himself for some of the suggestions concerning an extended republic.

It was David Hume's speculations on the "Idea of a Perfect Commonwealth," first published in 1752, that most stimulated James

Madison's thought on factions.[2] In this essay Hume disclaimed any attempt to substitute a political Utopia for "the common botched and inaccurate governments" which seemed to serve imperfect men so well. Nevertheless, he argued, the idea of a perfect commonwealth "is surely the most worthy curiosity of any the wit of man can possibly devise. And who knows, if this controversy were fixed by the universal consent of the wise and learned, but, in some future age, an opportunity might be afforded of reducing the theory to practice, either by a dissolution of some old government, or by the combination of men to form a new one, in some distant part of the world." At the very end of Hume's essay was a discussion that could not help being of interest to Madison. For here the Scot casually demolished the Montesquieu small-republic theory; and it was this part of his essay, contained in a single page, that was to serve Madison in new-modeling a "botched" Confederation "in a distant part of the world." (I, 480-481, 492.)

Hume concluded his "Idea of a Perfect Commonwealth" with some observations on "the falsehood of the common opinion, that no large state, such as France or Great Britain, could ever be modelled into a commonwealth, but that such a form of government can only take place in a city or small territory." The opposite seemed to be true, decided Hume. "Though it is more difficult to form a republican government in an extensive country than in a city; there is more facility, when once it is formed, of preserving it steady and uniform, without tumult and faction."

The formidable problem of first unifying the outlying and various segments of a big area had thrown Montesquieu and like-minded theorists off the track, Hume believed. "It is not easy, for the distant parts of a large state to combine in any plan of free government; but they easily conspire in the esteem and reverence for a single person, who, by means of this popular favour, may seize the power, and forcing the more obstinate to submit, may establish a monarchical government." (I, 492.) Historically, therefore, it is

[2]David Hume, *Essays, Moral, Political, and Literary* (London, 1875). Madison apparently used the 1758 edition, which was the most complete printed during the Scot's lifetime, and which gathered up into two volumes what he conceived of as the final revised version of his thoughts on the topics treated. Earlier versions of certain of the essays had been printed in 1742, 1748, 1752; there are numerous modern editions of the 1758 printing. All page references to Hume in this article are to the 1875 edition.

the great leader who has been the symbol and engine of unity in empire building. His characteristic ability to evoke loyalty has made him in the past a mechanism both of solidarity and of exploitation. His leadership enables diverse peoples to work for a common end, but because of the power temptations inherent in his strategic position he usually ends as an absolute monarch.

And yet, Hume argued, this last step is not a rigid social law as Montesquieu would have it. There was always the possibility that some modern leader with the wisdom and ancient virtue of a Solon or of a Lycurgus would suppress his personal ambition and found a free state in a large territory "to secure the peace, happiness, and liberty of future generations." ("Of Parties in General," I, 127.) In 1776–the year Hume died–a provincial notable named George Washington was starting on the career that was to justify Hume's penetrating analysis of the unifying role of the great man in a large and variegated empire. Hume would have exulted at the discovery that his deductive leap into the future with a scientific prediction was correct: all great men who consolidated empires did not necessarily desire crowns.

Having disposed of the reason why monarchies had usually been set up in big empires and why it still was a matter of free will rather than necessity, Hume then turned to the problem of the easily founded, and unstable, small republic. In contrast to the large state, "a city readily concurs in the same notions of government, the natural equality of property favours liberty,[3] and the nearness of habitation enables the citizens mutually to assist each other. Even under absolute princes, the subordinate government of cities is commonly republican. . . . But these same circumstances, which facilitate the erection of commonwealths in cities, render their constitution more frail and uncertain. Democracies are turbulent. For however the people may be separated or divided into small parties, either in their votes or elections; their near habitation in a

[3]Hume seems to be referring to the development in cities of a specialized product, trade, or industrial skill, that gives the small area an equal interest in a specific type of economic activity. All the inhabitants of Sheffield from the lowly artisan to the wealthiest manufacturer had an interest in the iron industry; every dweller in Liverpool had a stake in the prosperity of the slave trade. It was this regional unity of occupation that Hume was speaking of, not equality of income from the occupation, as is shown by the latter part of his analysis.

city will always make the force of popular tides and currents very sensible. Aristocracies are better adapted for peace and order, and accordingly were most admired by ancient writers; but they are jealous and oppressive." (I, 492.) Here, of course, was the ancient dilemma that Madison knew so well, re-stated by Hume. In the city where wealth and poverty existed in close proximity, the poor, if given the vote, might very well try to use the power of the government to expropriate the opulent. While the rich, ever a self-conscious minority in a republican state, were constantly driven by fear of danger, even when no danger existed in fact, to take aggressive and oppressive measures to head off the slightest threat to their power, position, and property.

It was Hume's next two sentences that must have electrified Madison as he read them: "In a large government, which is modelled with masterly skill, there is compass and room enough to refine the democracy, from the lower people, who may be admitted into the first elections or first concoction of the commonwealth, to the higher magistrates, who direct all the movements. At the same time, the parts are so distant and remote, that it is very difficult, either by intrigue, prejudice, or passion, to hurry them into any measures against the public interest." (I, 492.) Hume's analysis here had turned the small-territory republic theory upside down: *if* a free state could once be established in a large area, it would be stable and safe from the effects of faction. Madison had found the answer to Montesquieu. He had also found in embryonic form his own theory of the extended federal republic.

Madison could not but feel that the "political aphorisms" which David Hume scattered so lavishly in his essays were worthy of his careful study. He re-examined the sketch of Hume's perfect commonwealth: "a form of government, to which," Hume claimed, "I cannot in theory discover any considerable objection." Hume suggested that Great Britain and Ireland—"or any territory of equal extent"—be divided into a hundred counties, and that each county in turn be divided into one hundred parishes, making in all ten thousand minor districts in the state. The twenty-pound freeholders and five-hundred-pound householders in each parish were to elect annually a representative for the parish. The hundred parish representatives in each county would then elect out of themselves one "senator" and ten county "magistrates." There would thus be in "the whole commonwealth, 100 senators, 1100 [*sic*] county magistrates, and 10,000 . . . representatives." Hume would then have vested in the senators the executive power: "the power of peace and war, of giving orders to generals, admirals, and ambassadors, and, in short all the prerogatives of a British King, except his negative." (I, 482-483.) The county magistrates were to have the legislative power; but they were never to assemble as a single legislative body. They were to convene in their own counties, and each county was to have one vote; and although they could initiate legislation, Hume expected the senators normally to make policy. The ten thousand parish representatives were to have the right to a referendum when the other two orders in the state disagreed.

It was all very complicated and cumbersome, but Hume thought that it would allow a government to be based on the consent of the "people" and at the same time obviate the danger of factions. He stated the "political aphorism" which explained his complex system.

> The lower sort of people and small proprietors are good judges enough of one not very distant from them in rank or habitation; and therefore, in their parochial meetings, will probably chuse the best, or nearly the best representative: But they are wholly unfit for county-meetings, and for electing into the higher offices of the republic. Their ignorance gives the grandees an opportunity of deceiving them.[4]

This carefully graded hierarchy of officials therefore carried the system of indirect elections to a logical conclusion.

Madison quite easily traced out the origin of Hume's scheme. He found it in the essay entitled "Of the First Principles of Government." Hume had been led to his idea of fragmentizing election districts by his reading of Roman history and his contemplation of the historically verified evils incident to the direct participation of every citizen in democratical governments. The Scotsman had little

[4]*Essays*, I 487. Hume elaborated his system in great detail, working out a judiciary system, the methods of organizing and controlling the militia, etc. The Scot incidentally acknowledged that his thought and theories on the subject owed much to James Harrington's *Oceana* (London, 1656), "the only valuable model of a [perfect] commonwealth that has yet been offered to the public." For Hume thought that Sir Thomas More's *Utopia* and Plato's *Republic* with all other utopian blueprints were worthless. "All plans of government, which suppose great reformation in the manners of mankind," he noted, "are plainly imaginary." Ibid., 481.

use for "a pure republic," that is to say, a direct democracy. "For though the people, collected in a body like the Roman tribes, be quite unfit for government, yet when dispersed in small bodies, they are more susceptible both of reason and order; the force of popular currents and tides is, in a great measure, broken; and the public interest may be pursued with some method and constancy." (I, 113.) Hence, Hume's careful attempts to keep the citizens with the suffrage operating in thousands of artifically created electoral districts. And as Madison thought over Hume's theoretic system, he must suddenly have seen that in this instance the troublesome corporate aggressiveness of the thirteen American states could be used to good purpose. There already existed in the United States local governing units to break the force of popular currents. There was no need to invent an artificial system of counties in America. The states themselves could serve as the chief pillars and supports of a new constitution in a large-area commonwealth.

Here in Hume's *Essays* lay the germ for Madison's theory of the extended republic. It is interesting to see how he took these scattered and incomplete fragments and built them into an intellectual and theoretical structure of his own. Madison's first full statement of this hypothesis appeared in his "Notes on the Confederacy" written in April 1787, eight months before the final version of it was published as the tenth *Federalist*.[5] Starting with the proposition that "in republican Government, the majority, however composed, ultimately give the law," Madison then asks what is to restrain an interested majority from unjust violations of the minority's rights? Three motives might be claimed to meliorate the selfishness of the majority: first, "prudent regard for their own good, as involved in the general . . . good"; second, "respect for character"; and finally, religious scruples.[6] After examining each in its turn Madison concludes that they are but a frail bulwark against a ruthless party.

In his discussion of the insufficiency of "respect for character" as

[5] *Federalist*, X, appeared in *The New York Packet*, Friday, Nov. 23, 1787. There are thus three versions of Madison's theoretic formulation of how a properly organized republic in a large area, incorporating within its jurisdiction a multiplicity of interests, will sterilize the class conflict of the rich versus the poor: (1) the "Notes" of Apr. 1787; (2) speeches in the convention during June 1787; and (3) the final polished and elaborated form, in the *Federalist*, Nov. 1787.

[6] James Madison, *Letters and Other Writings*, 4 vols. (Philadelphia, 1867), I, 325-326.

a curb on faction, Madison again leans heavily upon Hume. The Scot had stated paradoxically that it is "a just *political* maxim *that every man must be supposed a knave*: Though at the same time, it appears somewhat strange, that a maxim should be true in *politics*, which is false in *fact* . . . men are generally more honest in their private than in their public capacity, and will go greater lengths to serve a party, than when their own private interest is alone concerned. Honour is a great check upon mankind: But where a considerable body of men act together, this check is, in a great measure, removed; since a man is sure to be approved of by his own party . . . and he soon learns to despise the clamours of adversaries."[7] This argument, confirmed by his own experience, seemed to Madison too just and pointed not to use, so under "Respect for character" he set down: "However strong this motive may be in individuals, it is considered as very insufficient to restrain them from injustice. In a multitude its efficacy is diminished in proportion to the number which is to share the praise or the blame. Besides, as it has reference to public opinion, which, within a particular society, is the opinion of the majority, the standard is fixed by those whose conduct is to be measured by it."[8] The young Virginian readily found a concrete example in Rhode Island, where honor had proved to be no check on factious behavior. In a letter to Jefferson explaining the theory of the new constitution, Madison was to repeat his category of inefficacious motives,[9] but in formally presenting his theory to the world in the letters of Publius he deliberately excluded it.[10] There was a certain disadvantage in making derogatory remarks to a majority that must be persuaded to adopt your arguments.

In April 1787, however, when Madison was writing down his first thoughts on the advantage of an extended government, he had

[7]"Of the Independency of Parliament," *Essays*, I, 118-119.

[8]*Letters*, I, 326.

[9]Ibid., p. 352. To Thomas Jefferson, Oct. 24, 1787.

[10]In Madison's earliest presentation of his thesis certain other elements indicating his debt to Hume appear that have vanished in the *Federalist*. In the "Notes on the Confederacy" the phrase "notorious factions and oppressions which take place in corporate towns" (*Letters*, I, 327) recalls the original starting point of Hume's analysis in the "Perfect Commonwealth." Also the phraseology of the sentence: "The society becomes broken into a greater variety of interests . . . which check each other . . ." (ibid.), varied in the letter to Jefferson to: "In a large society, the people are broken into so many interests" (ibid., 352), is probably a parallel of Hume's "The force of popular currents and tides is, in a great measure, broken." ("First Principles of Governments," *Essays*, I, 113.)

still not completely thought through and integrated Hume's system of indirect elections with his own ideas. The Virginian, nevertheless, had not dismissed the subject from his thoughts. He had taken a subsidiary element of Hume's "Perfect Commonwealth" argument and developed it as the primary factor in his own theorem; but he was also to include Hume's major technique of indirect election as a minor device in the constitution he proposed for the new American state. As the last paragraph of "Notes on the Confederacy" there appears a long sentence that on its surface has little organic relation to Madison's preceding two-page discussion of how "an extensive Republic meliorates the administration of a small Republic."

> An auxiliary desideratum for the melioration of the Republican form is such a process of elections as will most certainly extract from the mass of the society the purest and noblest characters which it contains; such as will at once feel most strongly the proper motives to pursue the end of their appointment, and be most capable to devise the proper means of attaining it.[11]

This final sentence, with its abrupt departure in thought, would be hard to explain were it not for the juxtaposition in Hume of the material on large area and indirect election.

When Madison presented his thesis to the electorate in the tenth *Federalist* as justification for a more perfect union, Hume's *Essays* were to offer one final service. Hume had written a scientific analysis on "Parties in General" as well as on the "Parties of Great Britain." In the first of these essays he took the position independently arrived at by Madison concerning the great variety of factions likely to agitate a republican state. The Virginian, with his characteristic scholarly thoroughness, therefore turned to Hume again when it came time to parade his arguments in full dress. Hume had made his major contribution to Madison's political philosophy before the Philadelphia Convention. Now he was to help in the final polishing and elaboration of the theory for purposes of public persuasion in print.

Madison had no capacity for slavish imitation; but a borrowed word, a sentence lifted almost in its entirety from the other's essay, and above all, the exactly parallel march of ideas in Hume's "Parties"

[11]*Letters,* I, 328.

and Madison's *Federalist*, X, show how congenial he found the Scot's way of thinking, and how invaluable Hume was in the final crystallizing of Madison's own convictions. "Men have such a propensity to divide into personal factions," wrote Hume, "that the smallest appearance of real difference will produce them." (I, 128.) And the Virginian takes up the thread to spin his more elaborate web: "So strong is this propensity of mankind to fall into mutual animosities, that where no substantial occasion presents itself, the most frivolous and fanciful distinctions have been sufficient to kindle their unfriendly passions and excite their most violent conflicts."[12] Hume, in his parallel passage, presents copious examples. He cites the rivalry of the blues and the greens at Constantinople, and recalls the feud between two tribes in Rome, the Pollia and the Papiria, that lasted three hundred years after everyone had forgotten the original cause of the quarrel. "If mankind had not a strong propensity to such divisions, the indifference of the rest of the community must have suppressed this foolish animosity [of the two tribes], that had not any aliment of new benefits and injuries. . . ." (I, 128-129.) The fine Latinity of the word "aliment"[13] apparently caught in some crevice of Madison's mind, soon to reappear in his statement, "Liberty is to faction what air is to fire, an aliment, without which it instantly expires."[14] So far as his writings show, he

[12]*The Federalist*, ed. Max Beloff (Oxford and New York, 1948), No. X, p. 43. Hereafter page references to the *Federalist* will be to this edition.

[13]L. *alimentum*, fr. *alere* to nourish. Food; nutriment; hence, sustenance, means of support.—SYN. see PABULUM. This word is not a common one in 18th century political literature. Outside of *The Federalist* and Hume's essay I have run across it only in Bacon's works. To the man of the 18th century even the cognate forms "alimentary" (canal), and "alimony," so familiar to us in common speech, were still highly technical terms of medicine and law.

[14]*Federalist*, p. 42. Compare Hume's remarks: "In despotic governments, indeed, factions often do not appear; but they are not the less real; or rather, they are more real and more pernicious, upon that very account. The distinct orders of men, nobles and people, soldiers and merchants, have all a distinct interest; but the more powerful oppresses the weaker with impunity and without resistance; which begets a seeming tranquility in such governments." (I, 130.) Also see Hume's comparison of faction to "weeds . . . which grow most plentifully in the richest soil; and though absolute governments be not wholly free from them, it must be confessed, that they rise more easily, and propagate themselves faster in free governments, where they always infect the legislature itself, which alone could be able, by the steady application of rewards and punishments, to eradicate them" (I, 127-128); and notice Madison's "The regulation of these various and interfering interests forms the principal task of modern legislation, and involves the spirit of party and faction in the necessary and ordinary operations of the government." (*Federalist*, p. 43.)

never used the word again; but in this year of 1787 his head was full of such words and ideas culled from David Hume.

When one examines these two papers in which Hume and Madison summed up the eighteenth century's most profound thought on party, it becomes increasingly clear that the young American used the earlier work in preparing a survey on faction through the ages to introduce his own discussion of faction in America. Hume's work was admirably adapted to this purpose. It was philosophical and scientific in the best tradition of the Enlightenment. The facile damnation of faction had been a commonplace in English politics for a hundred years, as Whig and Tory vociferously sought to fasten the label on each other. But the Scot, very little interested as a partisan and very much so as a social scientist, treated the subject therefore in psychological, intellectual, and socio-economic terms. Throughout all history, he discovered, mankind has been divided into factions based either on personal loyalty to some leader or upon some "sentiment or interest" common to the group as a unit. This latter type he called a "Real" as distinguished from the "Personal" faction. Finally he subdivided the "real factions" into parties based on "interest," upon "principle," or upon "affection." Hume spent well over five pages dissecting these three types; but Madison, while determined to be inclusive, had not the space to go into such minute analysis. Besides, he was more intent now on developing the cure than on describing the malady. He therefore consolidated Hume's two-page treatment of "personal" factions, and his long discussion of parties based on "principle and affection" into a single sentence. The tenth *Federalist* reads: "A zeal for different opinions concerning religion, concerning government, and many other points, as well of speculation as of practice;[15] an attachment to different leaders ambitiously contending for pre-eminence

[15]This clause of Madison's refers to Hume's "parties from *principle*, especially abstract speculative principle," in the discussion of which he includes "different political principles" and "principles of priestly government . . . which has . . . been the poison of human society, and the source of the most inveterate factions." Hume, in keeping with his reputation as the great sceptic, feels that while the congregations of persecuting sects must be called "factions of principle," the priests, who are "the prime movers" in religious parties, are factious out of "interest." The word "speculation" that appears in Madison is rendered twice as "speculative" in Hume. (I, 130-132.)

and power;[16] or to persons of other descriptions whose fortunes have been interesting to the human passions,[17] have, in turn, divided mankind into parties, inflamed them with mutual animosity, and rendered them much more disposed to vex and oppress each other than to cooperate for their common good."[18] It is hard to conceive of a more perfect example of the concentration of idea and meaning than Madison achieved in this famous sentence.

It is noteworthy that while James Madison compressed the greater part of Hume's essay on factions into a single sentence, he greatly expanded the quick sketch of the faction from "interest" buried in the middle of the philosopher's analysis. This reference, in Madison's hands, became the climax of his treatment and is the basis of his reputation in some circles as the progenitor of the theory of economic determinism. Hume had written that factions from interest "are the most reasonable, and the most excusable. When two orders of men, such as the nobles and people, have a

[16]Here is Hume's "Personal" faction, "founded on personal friendship or animosity among such as compose the contending parties." Hume instances the Colonesi and Orsini of modern Rome, the Neri and Bianchi of Florence, the rivalry between the Pollia and Papiria of ancient Rome, and the confused mass of shifting alliances that marked the struggle between Guelfs and Ghibellines. (I, 128-129.)

[17]This phrase, which is quite obscure in the context, making a separate category of a type of party apparently just covered under "contending leaders," refers to the loyal bitter-end Jacobites of 18th-century England. These sentimental irreconcilables of the Squire Western ilk made up Hume's "party from *affection*." Hume explains: "By parties from affection, I understand those which are founded on the different attachments of men towards particular families and persons, whom they desire to rule over them. These factions are often very violent [Hume was writing only three years before Bonnie Prince Charlie and the clans had frightened all England in '45]; though, I must own, it may seem unaccountable, that men should attach themselves so strongly to persons, with whom they are no wise acquainted, whom perhaps they never saw, and from whom they never received, nor can ever hope for any favour." (I, 133.)

The fact that Madison includes this category in his paper satisfies me that, when he came to write the tenth *Federalist* for publication, he referred directly to Hume's volume as he reworked his introduction into its final polished form. One can account for the other similarities in the discussion of faction as a result of Madison's careful reading of Hume's works and his retentive memory. But the inclusion of this "party from affection" in the Virginian's final scheme where its ambiguity indeed detracts from the force of the argument, puts a strain on the belief that it resulted from memory alone. This odd fourth classification, which on its face is redundant, probably was included because Hume's book was open on the table beside him, and because James Madison would leave no historical stone unturned in his effort to make a definitive scientific summary.

[18]*Federalist*, X, pp. 42-43.

distinct authority in a government, not very accurately balanced and modelled, they naturally follow a distinct interest; nor can we reasonably expect a different conduct, considering that degree of selfishness implanted in human nature. It requires great skill in a legislator to prevent such parties; and many philosophers are of opinion, that this secret, like the *grand elixir*, or *perpetual motion*, may amuse men in theory, but can never possibly be reduced to practice." (I, 130.) With this uncomfortable thought Hume dismissed the subject of economic factions as he fell into the congenial task of sticking sharp intellectual pins into priestly parties and bigots who fought over abstract political principles.

Madison, on the contrary, was not satisfied with this cursory treatment. He had his own ideas about the importance of economic forces. All that Hume had to say of personal parties, of parties of principle, and of parties of attachment, was but a prologue to the Virginian's discussion of "the various and unequal distribution of property," throughout recorded history. "Those who hold, and those who are without property, have ever formed distinct interests in society. Those who are creditors, and those who are debtors, fall under a like discrimination. A landed interest, a manufacturing interest, a mercantile interest, a moneyed interest, with many lesser interests, grow up of necessity in civilized nations, and divide them into different classes actuated by different sentiments and views."[19] Here was the pivot of Madison's analysis. Here in this multiplicity of economic factions was "the grand elixir" that transformed the ancient doctrine of the rich against the poor into a situation that a skillful American legislator might model into equilibrium. Compound various economic interests of a large territory with a federal system of thirteen semi-sovereign political units, establish a scheme of indirect elections which will functionally bind the extensive area into a unit while "refining" the voice of the people, and you will have a stable republican state.

This was the glad news that James Madison carried to Philadelphia. This was the theory which he claimed had made obsolete the necessity for the "mixed government" advocated by Hamilton and Adams. This was the message he gave to the world in the

[19]*Federalist*, X, p. 43.

first *Federalist* paper he composed. His own scientific reading of history, ancient and modern, his experience with religious factions in Virginia, and above all his knowledge of the scientific axiom regarding man and society in the works of David Hume, ablest British philosopher of his age, had served him and his country well. "Of all men, that distinguish themselves by memorable achievements, the first place of honour seems due to Legislators and founders of states, who transmit a system of laws and institutions to secure the peace, happiness, and liberty of future generations." (I, 127.)

[7]

Safety in Numbers: Madison, Hume, and the Tenth *Federalist*

by Edmund S. Morgan

James Madison has long been known as the father of the United States Constitution. The document that emerged from the 1787 Convention was based in large part on the so-called "Virginia Plan," of which he was probably the principal author. Although he was distressed by the modifications made in the plan by the Convention, he and his allies, John Jay and Alexander Hamilton, defended the result so ably in *The Federalist* that Madison's reputation as a political thinker rests as much on that defense as it does on the Constitution itself.

The most celebrated number of *The Federalist* in the present century has been number 10, in which Madison explained the advantages of a large republic over a small one.[1] It was commonly supposed in the eighteenth century that republican government was suited only to small countries. Madison argued the opposite. In small countries the wide participation in government offered by a republic resulted in destructive factional disputes within the government among groups pursuing differing private interests. In a large country, Madison pointed out, it was fortunately impossible for all the people to assemble for purposes of government. Instead, they were obliged to elect a few of the wisest and best of their number to act as representatives of the rest. The larger the territory the larger would be the number of the wise and good they would have to choose from and the more likely therefore that those chosen would be wiser and better than in a small republic. More importantly, perhaps, the larger the territory the more difficult it would be for selfishly motivated groups (factions) to form the political alliances that would give them a commanding majority of the representative body and thus enable them to oppress a minority. Hence the government provided for the whole United States by the Constitution would overcome the defects of the small republics that had hitherto been united only in the ineffectual Continental Congress under the Articles of Confederation of 1781.

The validity of Madison's argument and its applicability to the government that developed under the Constitution have been the subject of a great deal of dispute, and its originality has been shown to be less than was once supposed. In 1957 Douglass Adair pointed out that Madison's analysis of the causes of faction was derived in large part from the essays of David Hume, particularly the essays "Of the First Principles of Government," "Of Parties in General," "Of the Independency of Parliament," "Of the Parties of Great Britain," and "Idea of a Perfect Commonwealth."[2] Factions were a familiar evil in the eighteenth century, and political thinkers, Hume and Madison included, agreed that republican governments were particularly afflicted by them. Madison, in the tenth *Federalist,* defined faction as "a number of citizens, whether amounting to a majority or minority of the whole, who are united and actuated by some common impulse of passion, or of interest, adverse to the rights of other citizens, or to the permanent and aggregate interests of the community" (57). Hume had outlined the manifold human sentiments, interests, passions, and principles that brought people together in these undesirable combinations, and in the tenth *Federalist* Madison clearly borrowed from Hume in a similar outline. But the insight that lent distinction to the tenth *Federalist* did not lie in Madison's borrowed discussion of the causes of faction; it lay in the reasons he advanced for believing that factions were less of a menace in a large country under republican government than in a small one. Hume too, in "Idea of a Perfect Commonwealth," had proposed a government for a large republic and had argued its advantages over a small one. The question is how much Madison's argument for a large republic depended on Hume's.

Adair in his 1957 essay suggested a large dependence, and Garry Wills has more recently made the suggestion more explicit.[3] Neither Adair nor Wills has anything but admiration for Madison, who remains for them as for other students of the period the most astute political thinker among the founding fathers. It scarcely detracts from his stature that he owed an intellectual debt to David Hume, perhaps the most astute political thinker of the century. It may nevertheless be worth examining again just what Hume's idea of a perfect commonwealth was and whether or how it contributed to Madison's thinking either in the Constitution or in the tenth *Federalist.*

Hume's perfect commonwealth was an adaptation and revision of the one that James Harrington had proposed a century earlier in *Oceana.*[4] Harrington had described in ridiculous detail an imaginary society in which property was widely distributed and kept that way by an "agrarian" law preventing the accumulation of more than the value of £2000 a year in one person's hands. The large numbers of property holders were to be divided and subdivided into various territorial units and, by a complex series of successive elections and assemblies, would produce a central parliament with a house of commons of more than a thousand and a senate of three hundred. In the passage of laws the senate would have the sole power to initiate, and the commons, acting for the people, would be restricted to accepting or rejecting without amendment whatever laws the senate proposed. Both the members of this legislature and the magistrates who administered the government would rotate in office.

In "Idea of a Perfect Commonwealth" Hume expresses the opinion that Harrington's was "the only valuable model of a commonwealth" (272) yet devised, but he found fault with three of its provisions. The agrarian law, he thought, would be unenforceable. Rotation in office would be "inconvenient." And the limitation to the senate of the power to initiate laws would endanger popular rights and liberties by giving an aristocratic group not merely a veto on legislation but an advance veto, preventing even the consideration by the lower house of laws needed to correct abuses. Hume accordingly outlined a government that would eliminate these shortcomings. It was in explaining the advantages of his own plan that he offered his observations about its suitability to a large country (the size of England or France).

What Hume proposed, in only slightly less bewildering detail than Harrington, was to divide the whole country into 100 counties, each of which would be "a kind of republic within itself" (275). Each county would be in turn divided into 100 parishes. Once a year the propertyholders of each parish would elect a representative, and two days later the 100 representatives of the county would assemble and elect ten county magistrates (corresponding to English justices of the peace) and one senator, who would also have the local powers of a magistrate. There would thus be a total of 10,000 county representatives, 1100 magistrates (including the senators), and 100 senators. The senators would meet in a single body in the capital and elect from their own number a protector (to preside over their sessions) and several councils (in effect committees) to deal with different foreign and domestic affairs.

All this is not far different from Harrington's scheme. Where it differs is in the powers and functions assigned the different bodies and in the peculiar structure of the legislative power. The 10,000 county representatives, Hume tells us, "possess the whole legislative power of the commonwealth" (273). The distinguishing characteristic of this legislature is that it never meets in one body: none of the representatives ever leaves his county. The national legislative power is thus dispersed into 100 legislative bodies, one in each county. The senate, though not a part of the legislature, is nevertheless given an influence in legislation, because every new law "must first be debated in the senate" (273), before being submitted to the county legislatures. The operative word here is "debated," for, if the majority of the senate reject the proposed law, a minority of ten is sufficient to send it on to the counties. Whenever a majority of the counties accepts it, it becomes a law, with no veto possible by the senate, or protector, or anyone else.

The senate in Hume's scheme, apart from its function in proposing laws, is a purely executive body, taking the place of a king and his privy council. It possesses "the whole executive power of the commonwealth; the power of peace and war, of giving orders to generals, admirals, and ambassadors; and, in short, all the prerogatives of a British King, except his negative" (273). Hume's protector, then, was not modeled on the English protectorate of the 1650s. He was merely the presiding officer in a plural executive, with no significant powers of his own.

Hume was evidently fearful of centralized power. He was unwilling to have a central legislature at all and defended his central executive (the senate) on the ground of "the small power they are allowed" (277). Even in those areas, particularly foreign affairs, where he gave his senate power, he justified it by virtue of the fact that "the legislative power being always superior to the executive, the magistrates or representatives [in the dispersed county assemblies] may interpose, whenever they think proper" (278).

The central feature of Hume's system, as opposed to Harrington's, was the dispersion of the legislative power. That dispersion was both complicated and emphasized by another provision that drastically qualified the local authority of the county assemblies. Besides voting on the national laws sent down to them by the senate, each county assembly was empowered to make "bye-laws," which would operate only within its own borders. But every such bye-law was subject to veto, not only by the senate but by any one of the ninety-nine other counties. The objective was to prevent any county from undertaking legislation that impinged on the interests of the rest.

It is hard to say what the effect of so drastic a veto power would have been. It would certainly have restricted severely the authority of individual counties over their internal affairs. And since no comparable power was given to the counties over national legislation, which a simple majority of the constituent counties could enact, with no veto of any kind, the effect might have been in favor of stronger national than local government. On the other hand, the dispersion of the national legislature into a hundred local legislatures would have tilted overwhelmingly in the opposite direction. On balance, the total effect of the provision is difficult to assess, and a situation in which it could have come into existence is difficult to imagine. If each county was a "kind of republic within itself," what kind of republic would be likely to agree to a veto over its internal legislation by another republic, let alone by any one of ninety-nine other republics? The possibility of a national veto over local legislation is another matter and, as we shall see, one that Madison considered quite feasible.

Hume provided many more details for the operation of his ideal commonwealth, but these are the features most relevant to his argument for the viability of a large republic. Before examining that argument and the effect it may have had on Madison's argument, it is necessary to consider the context in which Madison's argument, whether or not borrowed from Hume, was evoked. In doing so we turn from an imaginary world of ideal republics to a real world of ailing republics. While Hume sought to correct the faults he found in Harrington's theoretical thinking, Madison sought to correct the faults he found in the practicing republics among which he lived.

Madison was a firm believer in republican government, and he was also a firm believer in the union that had grown out of the American Revolution. Like many other Americans of the time he felt that not only the union but republican government itself was threatened by the performance of the state governments under the Articles of Confederation of 1781. As the threat expanded during the 1780s, he began to cast about for solutions. The search took him to a study of other confederacies, past and present; and in the spring of 1786 he analyzed the distribution of power in each and the vices exhibited in them. These could be summed up, as with the Achaean Confederacy, in "the defect of subjection in the members to the general authority."[5] In most cases the member states were theoretically supposed to defer to a general, central authority, but as in the Belgic Confederacy, on which his notes were extensive, he found "the practice very different from the Theory."[6]

In April 1787, a year after making his notes on other confederacies, Madison composed a more finished analysis of the "Vices of the Political System of the United States,"[7] in which he detailed the failings both of the state governments and of the way they were joined in the Continental Congress. In Madison's view, factions had taken possession of the thirteen state governments of America and were leading them into fraud and foolishness. The state legislatures passed too many laws, undigested, unfair, and unjust. By placing impediments on the collection of debts by English creditors they violated the treaty to which they owed recognition of their independence. By making devalued paper money a legal tender they deprived all creditors of their property. By ignoring their commitments to the Confederation and failing to furnish it with funds, they disabled it from performing the functions they assigned it. Even within their own respective borders they could not enforce their authority when defied by mobs that closed their courts. All in all, their actions brought the viability of republican government into question, disgraced the country in the eyes of Europeans, and prompted respectable people to think of monarchy as the only means of restoring the security of property for which the Revolution had been fought.[8]

That the central government of the United States was inadequate—if it could be called a government at all—was apparent to Madison as to other Americans. But Madison seems to have worried about the weakness of the central government less because of its intrinsic defects or its incompetence to perform its own functions than because of its inability to restrain the factions that controlled the state governments. Writing to Jefferson after the 1787 Convention, he spoke for himself when he observed of the laws passed by the state governments that "The injustice of them has been so frequent and so flagrant as to alarm the most stedfast friends of Republicanism. I am persuaded I do not err in saying that the evils issuing from these sources contributed more to that uneasiness which produced the Convention, and prepared the public mind for a general reform, than those which accrued to our national character and interest from the inadequacy of the Confederation to its immediate objects."[9]

Madison's answer to the evils of the state governments was the national government which he had his colleague Edmund Randolph propose to the Philadelphia Convention on 29 May 1787.[10] If Madison was influenced in this "Virginia Plan" by Hume's "Idea of a Perfect Commonwealth," he did not say so; and with the exception of one feature it would be difficult to show any resemblance to Hume's ideal commonwealth, either in Madison's plan or in the

Constitution as finally adopted. There was, on the other hand, a considerable resemblance between Hume's commonwealth and the political system of the United States, whose vices Madison had indicted and which he was seeking to replace.

The thirteen states of the union, like Hume's hundred counties, were republics within themselves. Their representative assemblies, in both cases, possessed the whole legislative power of the larger republic. Hume's senate corresponded closely to the Continental Congress under the Articles of Confederation. Neither was a legislative body; neither was elected by the qualified voters among the people. Both were indirectly elected by the legislative assemblies of the constituent republics; both were designedly weak. Similarly Hume's protector is comparable to the president of the Continental Congress, who was also merely a presiding officer, with none of the powers given to the president under the Constitution of 1787.

The comparison is heightened when we consider that Americans of the 1780s commonly viewed the Continental Congress as a "Supreme Executive," not as a national representative assembly. Precisely because it was not composed of elected representatives, Americans declined to give it powers of taxation or legislation. John Adams called it "not a legislative assembly, not a representative assembly, but only a diplomatic assembly." The powers assigned it by the Articles of Confederation were said to be "as extensive as the *prerogatives* of the crown of Great Britain," just as Hume's senate had "all the prerogatives of a British King, except his negative." (Hume's senate had a negative over county bye-laws but not over national laws.)[11]

The central feature of the government that Madison proposed in the Virginia plan was a national legislature designed to overcome the dispersion of power that prevailed both in the United States under the Articles of Confederation and in Hume's perfect commonwealth. Madison's national legislature would meet in one central location. It would include a house of representatives directly elected by the people, and it would operate directly on the people, not through the state governments. Madison was so determined to give it a dominant position over the state governments that he endowed it, in the Virginia plan, with an absolute veto over all state legislation, the kind of veto that Hume had assigned his executive senate over local bye-laws.

It is impossible to say whether Madison took the initial idea of a national veto from Hume. It was not, in any case, a difficult idea for anyone observing the American scene to invent, and Madison was not the only one to whom it occurred.[12] Madison first advanced it in a letter to Jefferson on 19 March 1787, insisting that it must apply *"in all cases whatsoever."* At the Convention Madison argued for it strenuously. When the Convention finally rejected it, he believed they had rendered the success of the whole enterprise highly doubtful. Without it, he feared, the states would overpower the national government and continue their irresponsible actions, ridden as they were by local factions. Republican government, he was convinced, could overcome factions and operate safely and decently, in the United States at least, only on a national scale.[13]

Madison had adumbrated his reasons for thinking so before the Convention met, he had expounded them during the Convention, and he finally gave classic expression to them in the tenth *Federalist.*[14] In that document Madison was defending a national legislature weaker than he wanted, but vastly more powerful than Hume's dispersed and virtually nonexistent one. If we now compare his arguments with Hume's and with the scheme of government Hume was defending, it will be apparent that Madison's insight into the advantages of a large republic bears only a superficial resemblance to Hume's.

Superficially the resemblance is obvious. Both men offer two reasons for the superiority of a large republic. For both, the first reason is the greater likelihood in a large republic of electing wise and disinterested citizens to government office; and for both the second reason is the greater difficulty that a large republic poses to the formation of factions. But Madison's ideas about the way these two advantages will be attained in a large republic are not borrowed from Hume.

Hume's prescription for putting the right people in office was a succession of elections of the kind he had described for "a large government, which is modelled with masterly skill" (280). He would have admitted only freeholders of substantial property to vote, and he would have allowed them to vote only for representatives in the county legislatures, who would in turn elect the local magistrates and the national senate. The senate, finally, would elect the protector and the several councils of state. Such a scheme, Hume thought, would give "room enough to refine the democracy, from the lower people, who may be admitted into the first elections or first concoction of the commonwealth, to the higher magistrates, who direct all the movements" (280). But this refinement had to be attained through institutions that would keep the lower people from sharing in matters beyond their comprehension:

> The lower sort of people and small proprietors are good enough judges of one not very distant from them in rank or habitation; and therefore, in their parochial meetings will probably chuse the best, or nearly the best representative: But they are wholly unfit for county meetings, and for electing into the higher offices of the republic. (276)

Hume's way of getting the right people into office in a large republic thus depended on excluding the lower sort of people from any direct choice of their rulers.

Madison may have begun to think about elections with something of the same sort in mind.[15] His analysis of the "Vices of the Political System of the United States," written just before the Convention met, closes with a single sentence on the subject that fails to indicate precisely what he wanted:

> An auxiliary desideratum for the melioration of the Republican form is such a process of elections as will most certainly extract from the mass of the Society the purest and noblest characters which it contains; such as will at once feel most strongly the proper motives to pursue the end of their appointment, and be most capable of devising the proper means of attaining it.[16]

In the Virginia Plan, as presented to the Convention by Randolph, Madison called for the election of the senate by the national house of representatives and of the president by "the National Legislature," that is, by the senate and the house of representatives.[17] Madison probably continued to favor this mode of electing the senate. He was dead set against election by the state legislatures, which resembled Hume's election by the county assemblies. The other members agreed with him that a principal reason for a powerful national legislature was to restrain the state legislatures, but they nevertheless proceeded not only to reject Madison's national veto on the states but also to make the state legislatures the electors of the national senate. Madison protested strenuously: "Nothing can be more contradictory," he pointed out, "than to say that the National Legislature without a proper check, will follow the example of the State Legislatures, and in the same breath, that the State Legislatures are the only proper check."[18]

Madison seems not to have agreed with his ally James Wilson that the senate should be elected directly by the people.[19] He probably continued to prefer election by the lower house. But with regard to the president, who was given much larger powers than Hume's protector, Madison abandoned his original proposal of election by the national legislature. By 19 July he had come to believe that direct election by the people was the best method, because "The people generally could only know and vote for some Citizen whose merits had rendered him an object of general attention and esteem." He hesitated to advocate such a method, because the right to vote was "much more diffusive in the Northern than the Southern States" and so might eliminate a southern candidate.[20] But by 25 July, "With all its imperfections he liked this best." The southern states, he now thought, would gradually relax their voting laws under the influence of republican principles and thus give themselves more votes.[21]

For the most powerful office in the United States, then, Madison favored direct popular election and favored it because of the large number of voters. Again, the Convention had less confidence in the people than he did and devised an indirect election by electoral college. When Madison came to defend the Constitution in the *Federalist* he was defending a document in which only the national representatives in Congress were elected in the way he thought proper. And a careful reading of the tenth *Federalist* will show that the greater likelihood he saw of electing good men to office in a large republic did not rest, as in Hume's case, on successive elections in which popular views were filtered through an ascending hierarchy of smaller bodies (though the Convention itself had evidently favored such a scheme more than he).

In the tenth *Federalist* Madison begins his discussion of the question in words that sound as though he were about to defend successive elections. A republic, he says, is superior to a democracy, because it is able "to refine and enlarge the public views, by passing them through the medium of a chosen body of citizens, whose wisdom may best discern the true interest of their country, and whose patriotism and love of justice, will be least likely to sacrifice it to temporary or partial considerations" (62). This is very similar to the fragmentary last sentence in his earlier analysis of the "Vices of the Political System of the United States." But it quickly becomes apparent that the "chosen body of citizens" are simply the popularly elected representatives of the national legislature and that the advantage of a large republic over a small for getting the right people into the government lies not in any further set of elections of higher officials but simply in the different considerations that will prevail among the people at large in their original election of this chosen body.

For Madison it is size alone, in and of itself, that gives the advantage, and he explains why. First, assuming that "the proportion of fit characters" will be the same regardless of the number involved, the greater number to choose from in a large republic "will present a greater option, and consequently a greater probability of a fit choice" (63). Second, a large number of voters, in Madison's view, will make it "more difficult for unworthy candidates to practice with success the vicious arts, by which elections are too often carried" (63). Madison did not expand on this statement, but it was well enough known that the vicious arts employed in elections included the expenditure of large sums of money in bribery of one sort or another. It went without saying that it was more difficult to bribe a large number of people than to bribe a few. Madison therefore sought safety in numbers, in large numbers of people voting.

Hume, in direct contrast, relied on reducing the numbers. In his perfect commonwealth he located the principal danger from factions in his senate, since he had dispersed the representative assemblies widely enough, in his view at least, to disarm them. To overcome faction in the senate he relied not only, as already mentioned, on "the small power they are allowed" (277), but also on their annual election "not by an undistinguishing rabble, like the English electors, but by men of fortune and education" (277) who had already been elected to the county assemblies. Hume offered a way to overcome the disadvantages of a large electorate, but Madison saw the largeness of the electorate as itself an advantage.

Madison did acknowledge that the electorate for a single representative could become too large:

> By enlarging too much the number of electors, you render the representative too little acquainted with all their local circumstances and lesser interests; as by reducing it too much, you render him unduly attached to these, and too little fit to comprehend and pursue great and national objects.(63)

But the danger from enlarging the electorate in the United States would be countered by the continuance of the state legislatures, where local and lesser interests might properly prevail, once the states were restrained to their proper sphere by the national government. Madison wanted the same sort of people in his national legislature that Hume wanted in his national executive, men of large vision, men known because they cut a figure beyond their local neighborhoods, men who would not stoop to the base tricks by which local politicians prevailed over narrow-minded people of their own kind. But Madison was confident that simply enlarging the size of the electorate who chose representatives would achieve this end.

By the same token Madison counted on a comparatively small body of national representatives. The Constitution as finally drafted and adopted called for no more than one representative for every 30,000 persons in each state. Madison would have been content to double the number of representatives,[22] but he never envisaged a body of the size of the British House of Commons with its 558 members. The first United States House of Representatives contained 65 members, fewer than in most of the state legislatures, fewer even than in Hume's plural executive.

The opponents of the Constitution were quick to agree that a large electorate and a small House would produce the kind of representatives Madison wanted, natural aristocrats. But such representatives, they feared, would not share in, and would therefore betray, the interests of the ordinary people who chose them.[23] Madison, of course, wanted precisely the men who would not be moved by local interests, but he sought to reassure the opponents of the Constitution in the Virginia ratifying convention by explaining that large electoral districts would at least be more likely than small to elect honest men. Expanding on what he had said in the tenth *Federalist,* he argued that "the greatest degree of treachery in representatives, is to be apprehended where they are chosen by the least number of electors; because there is a greater facility of using undue influence, and because the electors must be less independent." As proof he offered the example of Great Britain, where the most corrupt members of parliament, in Madison's as in most people's view at the time, were those from "small towns and districts." "The supporters of liberty," he maintained, "are from the great counties." It followed "that our representatives being chosen by such extensive districts, will be upright and independent."[24]

Modern historians may have reservations about Madison's logic and about his understanding of British electoral politics, and Antifederalists at the time continued to fear that representation on the scale provided by the Constitution would make the representatives too remote from their constituents. Hume's system of keeping the representatives close to home in local assemblies would probably have pleased many Antifederalists, but it embodied the very vices that Madison sought to cure. Safety lay not in a hierarchical structure of elections and dispersion of the legislative power, but in direct elections by large numbers and concentration of the legislative power. That was the advantage Madison, in direct contract to Hume, saw in a large republic, as far as electing the right men to public office was concerned.

The other advantage that Madison and Hume both claimed for a large republic lay in the obstacles it could place in the way of factions. Here the resemblance between their ideas is somewhat closer than in the case of the electoral process, but the two men were addressing different problems and projected different solutions.

Hume was engaged in an intellectual exercise: he could not have supposed that his plan of government would actually be followed in Great Britain. He was seeking to improve on Harrington's ideal model, which provided for a central representative assembly of 1000. Harrington had recognized that this was too large a body to carry on debate effectively and had therefore confined it to accepting or rejecting what his smaller senate proposed. Hume thought that this restricted the popular role in government too severely. So he made his representative body much larger and thus more popular, but divided and dispersed it into 100 parts. In doing so he quoted Cardinal de Retz to the effect that all numerous assemblies were "mere mob, and swayed in their debates by the least motive" (227). But, Hume went on, "Separate this great body; and tho' every member be only of middling sense, 'tis not probable, that any thing but reason can prevail over the whole" (277). Hume's logic is as dubious as Madison's, but his scheme, in any event, is fanciful. It proposes to correct the defects of one imaginary commonwealth by the imaginary institutions of another. And it is in defense of these imaginary institutions that Hume offers his argument for the viability of large republics.

The defense comes at the end of a paragraph explaining why republican government is easy to start and difficult to maintain in a small territory, but difficult to start and easy to maintain in a large one. In a small territory "popular tides and currents" bring disorder and destroy the government. In a large territory, on the other hand, "there is more facility, when once it [republican government] is formed, of preserving it steady and uniform, without tumult and faction" (270). The reason lies not merely in size but in the institutions that size permits:

> In a large government, which is modelled with masterly skill, there is compass and room enough to refine the democracy,

> from the lower people, who may be admitted into the first elections or first concoction of the commonwealth, to the higher magistrates, who direct all the movements. At the same time, the parts are so distant and remote, that 'tis very difficult, either by intrigue, prejudice, or passion, to hurry them into any measures against the public interest. (280)

In Hume's argument, then, the popular tides and currents that destroy small republics can be avoided in a large one not only by successive elections but also by having "the parts" so remote that they cannot be hurried "into any measures against the public interest." The syntax demands attention. It is difficult to hurry who or what into measures against the public interest? The answer would seem to be the "parts" of the large republic. But what kind of large republic? One "modelled with masterly skill," in other words, one modeled like the one Hume has just described, one in which the legislative power is dispersed among a hundred county assemblies. These are the parts that will not be hurried by intrigue, prejudice, and passion. These are the parts that will not be subject to the force of popular tides and currents. Even if Hume meant by "parts" something more general than his county assemblies, his words make sense only as applied to institutions of government capable of enacting "measures against the public interest." Hume had not had Madison's unhappy experience with dispersed legislative institutions. Such institutional dispersement, made possible by a large territory, lay at the center of Hume's argument.

Not only in the "Idea of a Perfect Commonwealth" but in his other political essays Hume looks to institutions to overcome the weaknesses of human nature, insofar as they can be overcome at all. It is no use telling us, he says, that whatever form of government is best administered is best. There has to be some advantage of one form over another. Otherwise there is no point in trying to think about the problem.[25] If you have a large country and if you want to have a republican government, and if you can succeed in establishing one, here is the kind to establish, in order to overcome the defects which attend all republics but which can be defeated by the proper institutions ("modelled with masterly skill") in a large one.

There were not nearly so many "ifs" in Madison's situation. He had a large country, divided into thirteen small republics, in which the government was not working because each state had fallen a prey to factions. He had devised a new republican government for the whole, and he was trying to persuade people that it would work better than their state governments and also improve the state governments themselves. Although he was proposing a new set of institutions, the force of his argument in the tenth *Federalist,* in contrast to Hume's, is not directed to the superiority of those institutions but to the beneficial effect of mere size. It was not the dispersion of the legislative power that would save republican government in America: the legislative power was already dispersed and not working. The supreme national legislature that Madison proposed would differ from the state legislatures (and from Hume's county assemblies) and escape their vices by virtue simply of its scale. It was the dispersion of the people themselves that would save the national republican government from control by factions, as the concentration of people had doomed the state governments.

If we return now to the way the two men thought about faction, the contrast will be more apparent. Adair and Wills have shown how indebted Madison was to Hume in his analysis of the causes of factions. Where the two parted was in the proposed treatment. Hume wanted, so far as possible, to keep factions from forming. He does not locate the superiority of a large republic in its control of factions but in the greater likelihood "of preserving it steady and uniform, without tumult and faction" (279). Not in spite of faction but *without* faction. Though he rooted factions in human nature, he emphasized prevention rather than control, uniformity rather than diversity. Here is his most explicit denunciation:

> As much as legislators and founders of states ought to be honoured and respected among men, as much ought the founders of sects and factions to be detested and hated; because the influence of factions is directly contrary to that of laws. Factions subvert government, render laws impotent, and beget the fiercest animosities among men of the same nation, who ought to give mutual assistance and protection to each other. And what should render the founders of parties more odious is, the difficulty of extirpating these parties, when once they have taken rise in any state. They naturally propagate themselves for many centuries, and seldom end but by the total dissolution of that government, in which they are planted.[26]

Factions, in Hume's view, were thus destructive of government, and the only solution was to prevent them from forming. Hume recognized sadly that England had them, and the effect was to "confound and distract our government."[27] His idea of a perfect commonwealth was an imaginary one where they could be eliminated by carefully designed institutions, institutions that bore small resemblance to any that existed in Hume's England.

Madison, on the other hand, confronting the factions he identified all around him, was ready to accept them as inevitable in a free society. The problem was to disarm them, and the solution lay not so much in institutions as in the obstacles that mere size posed to their operation. Safety, once again, lay in numbers, not in extirpating or preventing factions but in multiplying them, not in uniformity but in diversity. Simply by extending the sphere of the republic and thus increasing the number and variety of factions within it, the likelihood was reduced that any one of them could attain a majority or that any number of them could combine to control the government and oppress the others:

> Extend the sphere, and you take in a greater variety of parties and interests; you make it less probable that a majority of the whole will have a common motive to invade the rights of other citizens; or if such a common motive exists, it will be more difficult for all who feel it to discover their own strength, and to act in unison with each other. (64)

In sum, Madison agreed with Hume that republican government could operate more suitably in a large republic than in a small, and the general idea may first have come to him from Hume. But Madison's reasoning on the subject was different from Hume's, in some ways the direct opposite of Hume's. And while Hume may well have been in other areas a far more daring thinker than Madison, in this one Madison was the bolder and more original of the two. In order to overcome the narrow vision of representatives in his republic, Hume would have limited their election to a select body of voters. Madison instead prescribed a larger number of voters than had ever chosen a representative in an American legislature or in any but one or two constituencies of the British house of commons. Hume would have overcome factions by trying to prevent their formation. Madison, instead, made a virtue of their abundance. In devising a republican government for the whole United States, he sought to overwhelm the people of the several states with the people of the United States. The result was not quite what he intended, but that is the usual fate of political thinkers who leave the realm of speculation.

Yale University

NOTES

1. On the reputation of the tenth Federalist, see Douglass Adair, "The Tenth Federalist Revisited," *William and Mary Quarterly*, third series, 8 (1951): 48-67, reprinted in Adair, *Fame and the Founding Fathers*, ed. Trevor Colbourn (New York, 1974), 75-92. The authoritative edition of *The Federalist* is that edited by Jacob E. Cooke (Middletown, Ct., 1961). References in parentheses following quotations by Madison are to page numbers of this edition, in which number 10 occupies pages 56-65.

2. Douglass Adair, " 'That Politics May be Reduced to a Science,' David Hume, James Madison, and the Tenth Federalist," *Huntington Library Quarterly*, 20 (1957): 343-360, reprinted in Adair, *Fame and the Founding Fathers*, 93-106. Hume's essays were printed in various editions during the eighteenth century. They are all included in *Essays and Treatises on Several Subjects* (London, 1758). All references are to this edition. The crucial essay in question is "Idea of a Perfect Commonwealth," at pages 271-280. Unless otherwise noted, page numbers following quotations by Hume are to this essay.

3. Garry Wills, *Explaining America: The Federalist*, (New York, 1981).

4. *The Commonwealth of Oceana* (London, 1656). Reprinted in *The Political Works of James Harrington*, ed. J. G. A. Pocock (Cambridge, 1977), 155-359.

5. *The Papers of James Madison*, ed. W. T. Hutchinson, Robert A. Rutland, et al. (Chicago, 1962-), 9:8.

6. *Papers of James Madison*, 9:96.

7. *Papers of James Madison*, 9:345-358.

8. In addition to his formal analysis in "Vices of the Political System of the United States," Madison expressed his views extensively in his correspondence during the year preceding the Convention. *Papers of James Madison*, 9:74, 144, 154, 159, 186, 205, 295, 297, 301, 359, 396.

9. 24 October 1787. *Papers of James Madison*, 10: 212.

10. *Papers of James Madison*, 10:12-18; *The Records of the Federal Convention of 1787*, ed. Max Farrand (New Haven, 1911, 1937) 1:20-23.

11. Jack N. Rakove, *The Beginnings of National Politics: An Interpretive History of the Continental Congress* (New York, 1979), 383.

12. Tench Coxe proposed it in a pamphlet entitled *An Enquiry into the Principles of a Commercial System* (Philadelphia, 1787), advertised for sale on 19 May. *The Documentary History of the Ratification of the Constitution;* ed. Merrill Jensen, J. P. Kaminski, and G. P. Saladino (Madison, Wi., 1976-) 13:102-104. Cf. James McClurg to Madison, 5 and 22 August 1787, *Papers of James Madison*, 10:135, 154.

13. *Papers of James Madison*, 9:318. Madison repeated the point before the Convention met in letters to Edmund Randolph on 8 April (9:370) and to Washington on 16 April (9:383). For his arguments on it at the Convention see 10:41-42, 102-103; Farrand, *Records*, 1:164-165; 2:27-28. For his pessimism on failing to achieve it see his letters to Jefferson, 6 September and 24 October 1787, in which he attaches his defense of it to his argument for the advantages of a large republic. *Papers of James Madison*, 10:164-164, 205-206, 209-214. See also Charles F. Hobson, "The Negative on State Laws: James Madison and the Crisis of Republican Government," *William and Mary Quarterly*, third series, 36 (1979):215-235.

14. *Papers of James Madison,* 9:354-357; 10:32-34; Farrand, *Records,* 1:134-136.

15. Madison would not have had to derive the idea of successive elections from Hume. Hugh Peter proposed such a scheme for reform of the English Parliament in *A Word for the Armie. And Two Words to the Kingdome* (London, 1647), as did the anonymous author of *Chaos: or, A Discourse . . .* (London, 1659), 38. The earl of Shaftesbury offered a similar scheme in the posthumous *Some Observations Concerning the Regulating of Elections for Parliament, Found among the Earl of Shaftesbury's Papers after his Death . . .* (London, 1689), 15-18. Closer to home, in 1781 the provincial Congress of New Hampshire had (unsuccessfully) proposed successive elections as a way of producing a more enlightened state legislature. *Town Papers: Documents and Records relating to Towns in New Hampshire,* ed. Nathaniel Bouton (Concord, 1875), 9:849.

16. *Papers of James Madison,* 9:357.

17. *Papers of James Madison,* 10:16; Farrand, *Records,* 1:21.

18. *Papers of James Madison,* 10:40; Farrand, *Records,* 1:154.

19. *Papers of James Madison,* 10:19-20; Farrand, *Records,* 1:49-50. On 7 June Madison indicated that he preferred election of the Senate "by the people, or thro' any other channel than the State Legislatures," but the Virginia delegation (and every other state except Pennsylvania) voted against Wilson's motion for popular election. *Papers of James Madison,* 10:40; Farrand, *Records,* 1:154-155.

20. *Papers of James Madison,* 10:108; Farrand, *Records,* 2:56-57.

21. *Papers of James Madison* 10:116-117; Farrand, *Records,* 2:111.

22. *Papers of James Madison,* 10:97; Farrand, *Records,* 1:569.

23. For examples see *The Complete Anti-Federalist,* ed. Herbert J. Storing (Chicago, 1981), 2:142, 235, 264-269, 282, 379-382; 4:27-28, 141-142; 5:89-91; 6:153-163.

24. *Papers of James Madison,* 11:114-115; Jonathan Elliot, *The Debates in the Several State Conventions* (Washington, D.C., 1836), 3:256.

25. "That Politics May be Reduced to a Science," *Essays and Treatises on Several Subjects,* 11-19.

26. "Of Parties in General," *Essays and Treatises,* 36.

27. "Of the Parties of Great Britain," *Essays and Treatises,* 44.

[8]

IMPARTIAL REPRESENTATION AND THE EXTENDED REPUBLIC: TOWARDS A COMPREHENSIVE AND BALANCED READING OF THE TENTH *FEDERALIST* PAPER

Alan Gibson

> A certain degree of impartiality or the appearance of it is necessary in the most despotic Governments. In republics, this may be considered the vital principle of the Administration. And in a federal Republic founded on local distinctions involving local jealousies, it ought to be attended to with a still more scrupulous exactness.
>
> *James Madison*[1]

I
Three Traditions of Interpretation: From Progressivism to Pluralism to Republicanism

Since Charles Beard first focused attention upon it in 1913, the Tenth *Federalist* Paper has been at the centre of the debate concerning the foundations of the American republic. Specifically, there have been three primary interpretations of this document. Each corresponds to one of the three major traditions of interpretation that have dominated the study of American political thought in the twentieth century. Each also points towards and has been evoked in the service of drastically different political philosophies.

The first of these interpretations — the Progressive or Marxist interpretation of the Tenth *Federalist* Paper — is exemplified in Beard's monumental study, *An Economic Interpretation of the Constitution*. Here, the Tenth *Federalist* Paper served as the foundation for Beard's two-pronged interpretation of the Constitution. First, Beard fastened onto Madison's analysis of the causes of faction and argued that it was a 'masterly statement of the theory of economic determinism in politics'. As Beard noted, Madison had stated in the Tenth *Federalist* Paper that factions were inevitable in modern societies and formed principally around the various and unequal divisions of property, that political views were influenced by property holdings, and that the regulation of economic interests was the 'principal task of modern legislation' and involved the 'spirit of party and faction in the necessary and ordinary operations of the government'. From these statements, Beard deduced that Madison believed that politics and constitutional law were 'inevitably a reflex' of competing interests.[2] Most important, this reading of Madison's analysis of the causes of faction

1 Madison to Edmund Pendleton, 20 October 1788, *The Papers of James Madison*, ed. William T. Hutchinson, *et al.* (Chicago and Charlottesville, VA, 1962–), XI, pp. 306–7 (hereafter cited as *PJM*).

2 Charles Beard, *An Economic Interpretation of the Constitution of the United States* (New York, 1952, (1st edition 1913)), pp. 14–16, 156–8 for Beard's analysis of the Tenth *Federalist* Paper. Quotes are on p. 15 and p. 16.

served as the theoretical foundation for Beard's famous thesis that the Constitution was the product of a class struggle between the holders of personalty (primarily urban creditors and capitalists) on the one side and the holders of realty (non-slaveholding farmers and debtors) on the other.

Second, Beard also cited the Tenth *Federalist* Paper in support of his contention that the Constitution was an 'economic' and undemocratic document which benefitted the owners of personalty who had drafted it. In the Tenth *Federalist* Paper, Madison of course argued that expanded electoral districts would help insure the election of representatives who would refine the public views and that an extended republic would contain a diversity of economic interests which would act as a barrier to the formation and concert of majority factions. To Beard these mechanisms, in addition to judicial review and the system of checks and balances set up in the Constitution, were evidence that the Constitution had been designed to 'break up the attacking forces' of popular majorities. This 'disintegration of positive action' by the citizenry in turn was central to the Framers, according to Beard, because it provided protection for the property rights of capitalists and because it allowed property interests to secure advantageous legislation.[3]

Although Beard pointed to an important truth when he stressed Madison's emphasis on the centrality of economic conflict in politics, both prongs of Beard's interpretation of the Tenth *Federalist* Paper have been critically wounded by subsequent scholarship. First, as several scholars have observed, Madison was not an economic determinist — Beard selectively quoted Madison's analysis of the causes of faction and ignored a series of noneconomic causes that Madison had identified.[4] Second, Madison can hardly be cited in support of Beard's thesis that the Constitution was the product of a class struggle or that it reflects the will of an interested minority. In fact, Madison argued throughout the ratification process that the Constitution was the offspring of the whole people and reflected their will.[5] This was of course precisely the 'juristic' interpretation that Beard sought to refute. Third, as Douglass Adair has observed, Beard's reading of the Tenth *Federalist* Paper amounts to saying that Madison was indiscreet enough to publicly announce the self-interested motives of the Framers.[6] Adair's better interpretation is that this document was a 'complicated

[3] *Ibid.*, p. 161.

[4] See Robert E. Brown, *Charles Beard and the Constitution: A Critical Analysis of 'An Economic Interpretation of the Constitution'* (Princeton, 1956), pp. 29–30; Douglass Adair, 'The Tenth *Federalist* Revisited', in *Fame and the Founding Fathers: Essays by Douglass Adair*, ed. Trevor Colbourn (New York, 1974), p. 86 and n. 25; Garry Wills, *Explaining America: The Federalist* (Garden City, 1981), pp. xiv–xv, 212–13; Joseph F. Kobylka and Bradley Kent Carter, 'Madison, *The Federalist*, & the Constitutional Order: Human Nature & Institutional Structure', *Polity*, XX (1987), pp. 198–9; Morton White, *Philosophy, The Federalist, and the Constitution* (New York, 1987), pp. 55–81.

[5] See especially *The Federalist*, Nos. 39 and 40. In *The Federalist*, No. 40, for example, Madison wrote: 'It is *essential* to such a government (a republic) that it be derived from the great body of the society, *not from an inconsiderable proportion or a favored class of it.*' *The Federalist Papers*, ed. Jacob Cooke (Middletown, Connecticut, 1961), pp. 260–7. Quote is on p. 251. Subsequent citations are to this edition of *The Federalist Papers*.

[6] Adair, 'The Tenth *Federalist* Revisited', p. 88.

piece of speculative political philosophy', which was heavily influenced by the political essays of David Hume, and was designed to refute Montesquieu's small republic thesis, not to foreshadow Marx's doctrine of economic determinism. Fourth, as Adair also pointed out, Beard's use of Madison, rather than Marx, as the principal proponent of the theory of economic determinism was part of a broader political strategy. To borrow Adair's oft-quoted phrase, Beard evoked Madison as a means of 'wrapping himself in the American flag as he muckraked the motives of the Founding Fathers and, by implication, pointed to the Constitution as an instrument of class exploitation'.[7] Finally, Beard's contention that Madison sought to use expanded electoral districts and extent of territory to prevent rule by popular majorities systemically dissolves, rather than addresses, the central problem posed in the Tenth *Federalist* Paper. Madison did hope to use extent of territory to break up the attacking forces of majority *factions*. This remedy probably was designed to diminish the role of popular majorities in the normal operations of government. Still, it is neither fair nor subtle to simply dismiss Madison's system of constitutionalism as anti-democratic without qualification. As we will see, the 'Madisonian model' rested on a conception of popular sovereignty and he sought to reconcile the sovereignty of the people with the protection of private rights and the impartial promotion of the public good.

A second interpretation of the Tenth *Federalist* Paper — the pluralist reading — remains much more popular.[8] This reading, which is either implicitly or explicitly linked to both the Lockean or liberal interpretation of American political thought and the pluralist critique of Marxism, focuses upon Madison's argument that an extended republic embraces a multiplicity of interests and religious sects which check each other, hindering the formation and concert of majority factions and providing protection for minority and individual rights. Scholars who hold this reading also stress that Madison maintained that the spirit of faction was unavoidably

[7] *Ibid.* Quotes are on p. 92, p. 86. For the Hume–Madison connection see Adair's other classic article on the Tenth *Federalist* Paper, ' "That Politics May Be Reduced to a Science": David Hume, James Madison, and the Tenth *Federalist*', in *Fame and the Founding Fathers*, ed. Colbourn, pp. 93–106. See, however, Edmund Morgan, 'Safety in Numbers: Madison, Hume, and the Tenth *Federalist*', *Huntington Library Quarterly*, XLIX (1986), pp. 95–112 for a challenge to the Hume–Madison connection.

[8] The pluralist reading, however, is still deeply entrenched in political science literature. For examples see Martin Diamond, *The Founding of the Democratic Republic* (Itasca, Illinois, 1981), pp. 70–8, especially p. 71, pp. 77–8; Judith Shklar, 'Publius and the Science of the Past', *The Yale Law Journal*, LXXXVI (1977), pp. 1291–2; Robert Dahl, *A Preface to Democratic Theory* (Chicago, 1956), pp. 1–33. For an analysis of the intellectual context in which the pluralist reading was first set forth see Paul F. Bourke, 'The Pluralist Reading of the Tenth *Federalist* Paper', *Perspectives in American History*, IX (1975), pp. 271–95. When I argue in this paper that Madison was not a pluralist, I do not mean that he shared no common ground with modern pluralists. Like modern pluralists, Madison believed that modern societies were composed of competing interests and that a multiplicity of factions could help prevent the violation of individual and minority rights and help promote social stability. But as I point out throughout this essay, what Madison could never have accepted was the pluralists' account of the purpose and nature of representation, their dismissal of the idea of a common interest, their defence of the formation of legislation through coalition building, or their belief that a social equilibrium naturally emerged from interest group competition.

present in the legislative process and point to his contention in the *Federalist* No. 51 that in an extended republic containing a multiplicity of interests a majority coalition could only take place on principles of justice and the public good.[9] From these points of interpretation, scholars who hold this reading conclude that Madison expected that the multiplicity of interests present in the extended republic would be channelled into Congress through representatives who were acting as advocates for the particular interests of their constituents. But because no group would have a majority in Congress, public policies would be formed in a *process* in which representatives were forced to bargain with each other, to moderate their demands in order to build coalitions, and shifting and heterogenous legislative majorities were formed from the coalescing of interests. Together, these propositions are often closely linked with the broader belief that Madison and the Framers hoped to establish a modern, liberal state which would secure limited and universally accepted ends (especially self-preservation, the protection of property rights and commercial prosperity) and would promote moderate competition between interest groups as an alternative to ideological conflict and the class struggle.[10]

Beginning in 1974, however, a third interpretation of the Tenth *Federalist* Paper began to be established. In opposition to pluralist theorists, Harold Schultz, Robert Morgan, Gordon Wood, Garry Wills, Lance Banning, David Epstein, Neal Reimer, George Carey and Isaac Kramnick[11] have argued that Madison hoped to establish

[9] *The Federalist*, No. 10, p. 59; No. 51, p. 353.

[10] The fusion of the Lockean interpretation of foundations of the Constitution and the pluralist interpretation of the Tenth *Federalist* Paper to form a critique of Marxism is especially evident in Diamond's works. See especially Diamond's essay 'Politics and Ethics: The American Way', in *The Moral Foundations of the American Republic*, ed. Robert Horwitz (Charlottesville, 1986), pp. 75–108. I criticize this interpretation in 'Martin Diamond, the Commercial Republic, and the Pluralist Critique of Marxism', a paper presented at the Midwest Political Science Conference, 6 April 1990, Chicago, Illinois.

[11] Harold S. Schultz, *James Madison* (New York, 1970), pp. 59, 97–100; H.S. Schultz, 'James Madison: Father of the Constitution?', *The Quarterly Journal of the Library of Congress*, XXXVII (1980), p. 218; Robert Morgan, 'Madison's Theory of Representation in the Tenth *Federalist*', *Journal of Politics*, XXXVII (1974), pp. 852–85; R. Morgan, *James Madison on the Constitution and the Bill of Rights* (New York, 1988), pp. 13–18, 56–71; Gordon Wood, 'Interests and Disinterestedness in the Making of the Constitution', in *Beyond Confederation: Origins of the Constitution and American National Identity*, ed. Richard Beeman, Stephen Botein and Edward C. Carter (Chapel Hill, 1987), pp. 91–3; G. Wood, 'Heroics', Review of Garry Wills' *Explaining America: The Federalist*, in *New York Review of Books* (2 April 1981), pp. 17–18; Garry Wills, *Explaining America: The Federalist* (Garden City, 1981), pp. 179–264; G. Wills, 'Introduction', *The Federalist Papers*, ed. Garry Wills (New York, 1988), pp. xxi–xxiv; Lance Banning, 'The Hamiltonian Madison: A Reconsideration', *Virginia Magazine of History and Biography*, LXII (1984), pp. 12–15, p. 24 and notes 14–17; L. Banning, 'The Practicable Sphere of a Republic: James Madison, the Constitutional Convention, and the Emergence of Revolutionary Federalism', in *Beyond Confederation*, pp. 183–7; L. Banning, 'James Madison and the Dynamics of the Constitutional Convention', *The Political Science Reviewer*, XVII (1987), p. 41, n. 102; David Epstein, *The Political Theory of The Federalist* (Chicago, 1984), pp. 81–8; Neal Reimer, *James Madison: Creating the American Constitution* (Washington, DC, 1986), pp. 31–5, 37–9, 42, 103–30; John Murrin, 'Gordon S. Wood and the Search for Liberal America', *The William and Mary Quarterly*, XLIV (1987), p. 600 (*The William and Mary Quarterly* is hereafter cited as *WMQ*); George W. Carey, *The Federalist: Design for a Constitutional Republic* (Urbana, 1989), pp. 9–44; G.W. Carey, 'Republicanism and *The Federalist*', *The Political Science Reviewer*, XIX (1990), pp. 107–43, especially p. 134; Isaac Kramnick, 'The "Great

Congress as a 'disinterested and dispassionate umpire'[12] between the claims of interests, not a forum for the negotiations of partisan representatives. With only one important exception, the adoption of what I will call the 'disinterested umpire', 'impartial arbiter', or 'impartial representation' reading of the Tenth *Federalist* Paper has served to emphasize the centrality of republicanism in Madison's political philosophy and helped to further erode the liberal interpretation of the foundations of the American republic.[13] In particular, most of the scholars who hold this interpretation have made four closely related and ultimately decisive criticisms of the pluralist reading. First, they have emphasized that Madison wrote before the legitimation of interest group politics and thus that he still believed that 'factions' and 'interests' were the enemy of the public good. Second, they emphasized that, unlike pluralists, Madison did not conceive of the public good as the unintended aggregation of interest groups in Congress, but instead saw it as an independent and objective standard against which the claims of factions should be judged. Third, they have shown that Madison did not conceive of representatives as mere brokers for the interests of their constituents, but instead was fastened to a republican tradition which stressed that the citizenry should be deferential to socially established élites and that these élites were capable of exercising disinterested political leadership. Fourth, they have shown that Madison hoped that legislation would be formed based on deliberations between representatives about which policies were in the common interest, not through a process of bargaining and coalition building.[14]

National Discussion'': The Discourse of Politics in 1787', *WMQ*, XLV (1988), pp. 6, 12–14, 30–1; I. Kramnick, 'Editor's Introduction', in *The Federalist Papers* (New York, 1987), pp. 41–3, 46, 54–5. Other essays which have contributed to the critique of the pluralist reading include: Joseph M. Bessette, 'Deliberative Democracy: The Majority Principle in Republican Government', in *How Democratic is the Constitution?*, ed. Robert A. Goldwin and William A. Schambra (Washington, 1980), pp. 102–16; Kobylka and Carter, 'Madison & Constitutional Order', pp. 190–207, especially pp. 198–202; Cass Sunstein, 'Interest Groups in American Public Law', *Stanford Law Review*, XXXVIII (1985), pp. 29–48; Jean Yarbrough, 'Representation and Republicanism: Two Views', *Publius*, IX (1979), pp. 88–98; Jack N. Rakove, 'The Madisonian Moment', *University of Chicago Law Review*, LV (1988), p. 476, pp. 480–4; Charles Kesler, '*Federalist* 10 and American Republicanism', in *Saving the Revolution: The Federalist Papers and the American Founding*, ed. Charles Kesler (New York, 1987), pp. 13–39; Ralph Ketcham, 'Publius: Sustaining the Republican Principle', *WMQ*, XLIV (1987), pp. 580–1. Each of these scholars is also consciously indebted to Adair's two classic articles 'The Tenth *Federalist* Revisited' and ' ''That Politics May Be Reduced to a Science'': James Madison, David Hume, and the Tenth *Federalist*', in *Fame and the Founding Fathers*.

12 The phrase 'disinterested and dispassionate umpire' is from Madison to George Washington, 16 April 1787, *PJM*, IX, p. 384.

13 The exception to this generalization is found in the essays of Isaac Kramnick. Kramnick has stressed the similarity of Madison's goal to establish the state as a disinterested umpire and Locke's desire to establish a limited state which serves as a neutral protector of rights. Kramnick, 'The ''Great National Discussion'' ', pp. 12–14, 30–1 and Kramnick, 'Editor's Introduction', pp. 41–3, 46, 54–5. I discuss this interpretation in the conclusion of this essay.

14 Collectively, these points constitute a republican reading of the Tenth *Federalist* Paper which scholars are now beginning to use as a foundation for critiques of pluralism. See for example Sunstein, 'Interest Groups and American Public Law', pp. 29–87 and Sunstein, 'Beyond the Republican Revival', *The Yale Law Journal*, XCVII (1988), pp. 1539–90.

But while the scholars who hold the 'disinterested umpire' interpretation generally agree on these points, they are nevertheless also divided over a series of questions. Most important, these scholars disagree on just how Madison hoped to establish Congress as an impartial umpire. In their efforts to repudiate the pluralist reading and to establish the classical republican heritage of the Framers, Robert Morgan, Garry Wills and Gordon Wood have emphasized Madison's scheme for electing disinterested representatives from large electoral districts. According to these scholars, Madison believed that large electoral districts would help insure the election of enlightened and virtuous representatives whose wisdom and attachment to the public good would elevate them above selfish interests, allow them to refine public views, and qualify them to serve as impartial judges between the nation's factions. This — the 'filtration' of talent argument — has become to these scholars the central component of Madison's 'noble vision'[15] of 'heroic impartiality in the people's representatives'.[16] Morgan, Wills and Wood have either ignored, misinterpreted, or diminished the importance of Madison's argument that an extended republic would contain a greater variety of interests and religious sects which would check each other, protecting individual and minority rights and preventing the formation of majority factions. This argument, they seem to assume, is inseparably linked to a pluralist interpretation of the document and therefore must be de-emphasized.

In direct opposition to this interpretation, Lance Banning has recently maintained that electing representatives from expanded electoral districts was only a 'secondary and subsidiary' point of Madison's argument.[17] Madison, according to Banning, did believe that electing representatives from expanded electoral districts would improve the quality of representatives and the content of their decisions. Nevertheless, Banning asserts, Madison 'neither expected nor wished for federal representatives who would not reflect the character and interests of their constituents'. The principal argument of the Tenth *Federalist* Paper, according to Banning, is Madison's argument that a large republic would embrace such a variety of interests as to render unlikely the formation of majority factions and thus would provide protection for the rights of individuals and minorities. The reasoning behind this argument, Banning claims, would collapse if the legislature did not reflect the diversity of interests in the republic. Still, Banning asserts, 'a large republic would break the force of majority interest without endangering majority rule because a large variety of concerns would

[15] Wood, 'Heroics', p. 17.

[16] Wills, 'Introduction', p. xxiv.

[17] Quote is from Banning, 'The Hamiltonian Madison', p. 13. George Carey has also recently emphasized that Madison's scheme for electing representatives from expanded electoral districts was not the central point of his argument for an extended republic. Carey's analysis is the most judicious interpretation of the Tenth *Federalist* Paper in print. This essay builds and expands upon several points in Carey's analysis, especially the general goal of showing the relationship of extent of territory to impartial administration. Carey, *The Federalist: Design for a Constitutional Republic*, especially p. 23, p. 26 for his statements on the centrality of extent of territory and the multiplicity of interests in Madison's argument.

be represented in a Congress whose authority would not extend beyond those national subjects of which its members would adequately reflect their constituents' desires'.[18]

Although Banning has not yet fully explained this interpretation, he seems to suggest that Madison believed that Congressional authority would be limited to specific national concerns and that the people's will would be carefully divided between the states and the national government in such a way as to ensure majority rule without factional representation. In this way, Banning suggests, Congress could serve as a disinterested umpire, even though representatives mirrored the interests of their constituents. What is most important here is that, while he at least ostensibly holds the 'disinterested umpire' interpretation, Banning returns the debate on the Tenth *Federalist* Paper back to Madison's argument for extent of territory and a multiplicity of interests.[19]

The contemporary debate on the Tenth *Federalist* Paper now concerns this dispute over how Madison hoped to establish Congress as a disinterested umpire and a series of additional questions of interpretation and emphasis. What was the relationship between the two parts of Madison's argument? Have Morgan, Wood and Wills been correct in suggesting that Madison's scheme for using expanded electoral districts to help promote the election of enlightened and virtuous statesmen was the core of his argument for impartial representation, or is Lance Banning correct in maintaining that the principal argument in the Tenth *Federalist* Paper is that an extended republic will contain a multiplicity of economic interests and religious sects? What relationship did Madison believe that representatives should have to the interests and views of their constituents? Should they act merely as agents for their constituents' interests or should they consider these claims in relation to the collective interest of the nation? Did Madison consider the distance between representatives and their constituents important for establishing the independence of representatives? What was Madison's conception of impartial representation? What did Madison mean when he said that factions would serve as checks on each other? Is Banning correct in suggesting that Madison's argument for a multiplicity of interests only makes sense if the pluralistic structure of the extended republic is reflected into the national councils by representatives supporting particular interests? How did Madison hope that the 'greater obstacles'[20] to the formation and concert of factious majorities posed by the extended republic would not also prevent the formation of majorities based on justice and the public good? How did Madison expect legislative majorities to be formed within Congress? In general, what implications does Madison's aspiration for disinterested arbitration of factional disputes have on our understanding of his political philosophy? Does the impartial representation reading of the Tenth *Federalist* Paper really

[18] Banning, 'The Hamiltonian Madison', pp. 13–15 and notes 14–16. See also Banning, 'The Practicable Sphere', pp. 183–7.

[19] Banning, 'The Hamiltonian Madison', p. 15.

[20] *The Federalist*, No. 10, p. 64.

reinforce the republican interpretation of Madison's political philosophy or does it also point us back to a Lockean or liberal dimension of Madison's thought?

In what follows, I address these questions and attempt to establish a comprehensive and balanced reading of the Tenth *Federalist* Paper. The 'impartial representation' reading is clearly the most accurate and intriguing interpretation of this document. I hope to reinforce this reading by presenting an interpretation which incorporates, but also moves beyond, the insights of the scholars who have emphasized Madison's plan for securing the election of disinterested representatives and the criticisms that Lance Banning has made of this interpretation. In general, I will argue that Wood, Morgan and Wills have correctly argued that Madison hoped that representatives would be impartial guardians of the public good and that he hoped to promote impartial representation by electing representatives from expanded electoral districts. Nevertheless, the importance of this component of Madison's thought has clearly been over-emphasized. As Banning has suggested, the principal argument of the Tenth *Federalist* Paper is that an extended republic would contain a multiplicity of interests and religious sects which would help prevent the formation and concert of majority factions and thus provide protection for individual and minority rights. Still, Banning presents an interpretation of this component of Madison's argument which returns scholars to the reasoning of the pluralist interpretation and thus to the problems of this reading. In contrast to Banning, I will present an interpretation of Madison's argument for extent of territory which links it directly to his goal of impartial representation. In short, my interpretation of the Tenth *Federalist* will neither unduly emphasize Madison's argument for the benefits of elections from large districts nor will it fall back into the assumptions of the pluralist interpretation.

More specifically, my thesis is that *both* components of Madison's argument for an extended republic were designed to reconcile impartial representation with popular sovereignty. Expanded electoral districts were designed to promote the election of noble and disinterested representatives and to prevent the election of representatives who would either become partisan to legislation which would advance their own interests or who would become unduly attached to their constituents' interests. Instead, these representatives would act impartially by equally protecting the rights of all citizens, equally distributing public burdens and benefits between interests, and impartially advancing the public good when choices between interests had to be made. Extent of territory, however, was the primary mechanism which Madison believed would promote the impartial resolution of factional disputes and protect individuals' rights. Extent of territory was central to impartial representation because the greater space, greater number of citizens, greater variety of interests and civic or public consciousness that were present in the extended republic would help prevent majority factions from forming and coordinating the election of a majority of interested representatives. Preventing an interested majority from gaining control of Congress in turn provided protection for the rights of individuals and minorities and helped to establish conditions under which impartial majorities could be formed within Congress. Together, expanded electoral districts and extent of territory were designed to help ensure that the best representatives were elected to Congress and that, as much as possible, factions were purged from the public councils. This in turn made it more likely that legislative majorities would be formed by disinterested representatives and that public policies would be the product of deliberations about the common interest and mutual sacrifices towards this end.

II
Expanded Electoral Districts and Impartial Representation

Much of the scholarship which has led to the establishment of the disinterested umpire interpretation has focused on Madison's plan for electing élite representatives from large electoral districts; and indeed, this was a significant component of Madison's argument for an extended republic. In general, the proposition which acted as the foundation for this 'scheme of representation' was that the proportion of representatives to constituents does not have to be as great in a large republic as in a small republic.[21] More concretely, what this meant is that Madison believed that the number of representatives who would serve in the national government under the new Constitution could be proportionally much smaller than the number who had served in the state governments during the mid-1780s.[22] In his writings and speeches in the two years surrounding the formation of the Constitution, Madison identified four principal benefits which he hypothesized — and as Robert Morgan and Jack Rakove have stressed these were only predictions — would result from this 'moderate' representation and the election of representatives from large electoral districts.[23]

First, Madison argued that large electoral districts would help promote the election of the 'purest and noblest characters' in the society.[24] Such representatives, he maintained, would constitute a 'chosen body of citizens, whose wisdom may best discern the true interest of their country, and whose patriotism and love of justice,

[21] *The Federalist*, No. 10, pp. 62–3. Quote is on p. 62.

[22] Consider two comparisons. The total number of representatives in all of the state governments in 1787 was between 1600 and 1700. In contrast, only sixty-five federal representatives were elected under the new Constitution. *The Documentary History of the Ratification of the Constitution*, ed. Merrill Jensen (Madison, 1978), III, p. 392, n.8 (I owe this citation to Professor Walter Pratt, Notre Dame Law School). According to Madison, there were between three- and four-hundred representatives in Massachusetts alone. This state, however, elected only eight representatives under the new Constitution. *The Federalist*, No. 55, p. 373. At the Constitutional Convention, Madison motioned to double (from sixty five — the number eventually accepted) the number of national representatives. He also later seconded a motion to increase representation in the House of Representatives. See 'Speech of 10 July 1787', In Constitutional Convention, *Notes of Debates in the Federal Convention of 1787 Reported By James Madison*, ed. Adrienne Koch (reissued, New York, 1987), p. 263; Banning, 'Madison and the Dynamics of the Constitutional Convention', p. 41. Still, as the figures above indicate, even if these efforts to increase the number of representatives would have been successful, the powers of the national government would have been lodged in the hands of substantially fewer representatives than had been the case in the state governments during the mid-1780s.

[23] Rakove, 'The Madisonian Moment', p. 479; Morgan, 'Madison's Theory of Representation', p. 860. The phrase 'moderate' representation is from *The Federalist*, No. 56, p. 381.

[24] Madison, 'Vices of the Political System of the United States', *PJM*, IX, p. 357.

will be least likely to sacrifice it to temporary or partial considerations'.[25] This hypothesis — the so-called filtration or distillation of talent component of Madison's scheme of representation — rested on the premise that since fewer representatives would be necessary in a large republic than in a small republic, the large republic would create a 'greater option' and insure the greater probability of a 'fit' candidate for office because a fixed number of qualified candidates would compete for fewer offices.[26] Garry Wills provides a concise description of this argument:

> Madison's point, however, is that the more extensive the republic the higher the ratio between the constituents and delegates must become if the assembly is not to be unmanagably large. Thus, with proportionally fewer offices to fill, but a proportionally stable pool of virtuous men to draw from, extent will 'create a greater option, and consequently a greater probability of a fit choice'.[27]

More abstractly, Madison and his Federalist colleagues sought to secure the election of the members of a *natural aristocracy* through the *procedure* of electing representatives from large electoral districts. This procedure served as an alternative to trying to secure the election of élite representatives by writing *formal* qualifications into the Constitution which either restricted eligibility for membership in the House of Representatives or which limited the size of the electorate.[28] Such qualifications could have been formulated easily. The Framers might, for example,

[25] *The Federalist*, No. 10, p. 64.

[26] *Ibid*., pp. 62–3.

[27] Wills, *Explaining America*, p. 218.

[28] But while the Federalists did not try to secure the election of élite representatives by writing formal qualifications for holding public office into the Constitution, their use of expanded electoral districts to achieve this same goal contains at least three assumptions about the nature of the electorate which are often not noticed. First, Madison and his Federalist colleagues, assumed that the nation's élite would be at least somewhat evenly distributed across the sixty-five electoral districts. An even distribution of qualified candidates was of course made more likely by the use of large electoral districts. Still, the Federalists obviously assumed that an over-abundance of élite candidates would not be present in a few districts, since this would mean that several of the best candidates would be eliminated and several unqualified candidates might be elected.

Second, and more important, Madison and his Federalist colleagues assumed that the electorate would have the intelligence to identify the members of the natural aristocracy and the virtue to defer to their leadership. Indeed, as Madison doubtless realized, reducing the number of national representatives and creating large electoral districts not only makes a greater number of qualified candidates compete for fewer offices, it also ensures that a greater number of citizens who are *not* qualified candidates will be present in each district. Thus, if expanded electoral districts are to result in the election of élite representatives, it is only because the electorate has the intelligence to identify wise and virtuous representatives and the willingness to vote for them. See 'Speech of 20 June 1788', In Virginia Ratifying Convention, *PJM*, XI, p. 163. For additional analyses of the assumptions that the Federalists made about the intelligence, virtue and deference of the people see Kesler, '*Federalist* 10 and American Republicanism', pp. 36–7; Wood, *The Creation of the American Republic*, pp. 489, 518; Edmund S. Morgan, *Inventing the People: The Rise of Popular Sovereignty in England and America* (New York, 1988), p. 286. Contrast Madison's comments and these discussions with Thomas Pangle's recent criticisms of the Federalists for not making adequate provision for the recruitment, cultivation and selection of élite leaders. Thomas Pangle, *The Spirit of Modern Republicanism: The Moral Vision of the American Founders and the Philosophy of Locke* (Chicago and London, 1988), pp. 104–11.

have sought to secure the election of élite representatives by tying eligibility for office or the right to vote directly to wealth or property holdings, family status or education. Instead, as Jack Ravoke has recently observed,[29] the Federalists ensured that formal criteria for membership in the House of Representatives were easily met — representatives had only to be twenty-five years old and seven years a citizen of the United States. No property qualifications were required for membership in the House, representatives had only to be 'inhabitants' of the districts they represented (not residents), and salaries were paid to members of Congress (there was no presumption that national office holders would be wealthy). Similarly, no property qualifications or other restrictions were passed which limited the right of suffrage.[30] In short, although Madison and the Federalists greatly reduced the number of representatives who would serve in the national government and thus created large electoral districts, they also ensured that eligibility requirements for voting and for holding office were easily met. Their hope was that together open access and fewer offices would cause greater competition and consequently the election of better representatives. In this manner, the republican concern for formal equality and openness of opportunity was not sacrificed in order to meet the republican commitment to rule by the natural élite.

Third, Madison assumed that there was a direct relationship in free governments between reputation or recognition and merit. In other words, individuals who were widely known, according to Madison, were likely to be enlightened statesmen, not demagogues. Madison's belief that a 'diffusive and established' reputation was the concomitant of excellence was illustrated in his statement that large electoral districts would result in the election of the best representatives because 'in free Governments merit and notoriety of character are rarely separated'. Madison's hope, then, was that the attention of voters would centre on such widely known candidates. This would help keep lesser candidates from dividing the vote to gain office. Quote is from 'Observations on Jefferson's Draft of a Constitution for Virginia', *PJM*, XI, p. 286. This assumption doubtless seems counter-intuitive today when recognition and fame often seem to have no relationship to merit. Among Madison's contemporaries, Hamilton already questioned this notion. In his notes to Madison's important 6 June 1787 speech in the Constitutional Convention, Hamilton noted that expanded electoral districts might *not* lead to the election of the virtuous representatives because 'an influential demagogue will give an impulse to the whole [district]. Demagogues are not always *inconsiderable* persons'. Quoted at 'Speech of 6 June 1787', In Constitutional Convention, *PJM*, X, p. 34, n. 2.

[29] This discussion draws heavily on Jack N. Rakove, 'The Structure of Politics at the Accession of George Washington', in *Beyond Confederation*, ed. Beeman *et al.*, pp. 267–71.

[30] Madison maintained that 'the definition of the right of suffrage is very justly regarded as a fundamental article of republican government'. *The Federalist*, No. 52, p. 354. In the Convention, he also noted that 'a republic may be converted into an aristocracy or oligarchy as well by limiting the number capable of being elected, as the number authorised to elect'. 'Speech of 10 August 1787', In Constitutional Convention, *Notes of Debates in the Federal Convention*, p. 427. Madison therefore consistently argued that qualifications for suffrage should be written into the Constitution so that they could not be altered at the whim of Congress or the state legislatures. He also firmly held that qualifications for suffrage and candidacy should be easily met. Indeed, with the exception of one speech in which he spoke favourably of a freehold requirement for suffrage, Madison opposed such artificial restrictions on the electorate and on membership in the House of Representatives. For Madison's views on a freehold requirement see 'Speech of 7 August 1787', In Constitutional Convention, *ibid.*, pp. 403–4. Earlier, however, Madison had opposed a freehold requirement for eligibility for office. See 'Speech of 26 July 1787', In Constitutional Convention, *ibid.*, pp. 375–6. See also *The Federalist*, No. 52, pp. 354–5; No. 57, pp. 385, 387–8.

The second benefit that Madison expected to result from elections from large electoral districts was that they would help prevent interested electors and ambitious and unworthy candidates from using unjust electoral practices to win elections. Madison made this point in the Virginia Ratifying Convention when he said: 'The greatest degree of treachery in representatives is to be apprehended where they are chosen by the least number of electors; because there is a greater facility of using undue influence, and because the electors must be less independent . . . We may therefore conclude, that our representatives being chosen by such extensive districts, will be upright and independent'.[31] Here, Madison addressed the problems of demagogues rousing public passions in order to get elected and of rich candidates and electors using bribes to influence elections. The first of these problems had of course characterized the state administrations during the mid-1780s. During this period, candidates for office were often those who sought election in order to influence or enact legislation that directly affected their interests. Land speculators, for example, had often first acquired large handholdings on debt, then attempted to win election to the assembly in order to pass laws against their creditors.[32] Such 'sinister designs'[33] led Madison in 1784 to conclude that measures in the Virginia assembly were 'being propagated with more zeal & pains by those who have a particular interest to serve, than proper answers are by those who regard the general interest only'.[34] But if representatives were elected from large districts, Madison and other Federalists hypothesized, then unqualified and interested candidates would have more difficulty using the 'vicious arts' to gain election to the national government and to promote their selfish interests under the guise of pursuing the public good.[35]

A third hypothesis that Madison made for expansive electoral districts was that if representatives were elected from a large and reasonably diverse constituency, they would be less likely to become unduly attached to local interests. Here, Madison looked at the problem of interest and local prejudice from a different perspective. Whereas in his second hypothesis Madison noted that representatives sometimes become unduly attached to their personal interests at the expense of the public good, here he noted that representatives might also become unduly attached to the interests and views of their constituents. 'The most effectual remedy' for this 'local bias' in representatives, Madison argued in 'Observations on Jefferson's Draft of a Constitution for Virginia', was to elect them from a larger and more diverse segment of the

[31] 'Speech of 11 June 1788', In Virginia Ratifying Convention, *PJM*, XI, p. 114.

[32] See 'Speech of 26 July 1787', In Constitutional Convention, *Notes of Debates in the Federal Convention*, p. 375. See also Madison to Washington, 24 December 1786, *PJM*, IX, p. 225, for another example of Madison's frustrations with 'interested' candidates. For an excellent discussion of the political activity in the state legislatures during the mid-1780s and its influence on Madison and other Federalists see Wood, 'Interests and Disinterestedness', pp. 73–7.

[33] *The Federalist*, No. 10, p. 62.

[34] Madison to Jefferson, 20 August 1784, *PJM*, VIII, p. 103.

[35] *The Federalist*, No. 10, p. 63.

society. This would 'impress upon the mind' of the representative an attention to a greater part of the society by making him responsible to a greater number of voters. In fact, Madison believed that local bias in representatives would diminish in 'direct proportion to the number of electors to which they were responsible'.[36]

Fourth, Madison argued that reducing the number of representatives to a moderate number would make it more likely that laws would be formed within Congress through a process of deliberation and mutual concessions rather than through the accommodation of particular interests. Underlying this hypothesis was a more general theory that Madison held about the relationship between the size of legislative assemblies and the nature of their internal operations. Specifically, Madison argued that large legislative assemblies often produced inconsistent and even contradictory legislation, contained many members who had limited capabilities, were ruled by a few members (usually demagogues), were actuated by passion and thus were often oligarchic in their operations, failed to insure that representatives were held accountable for their policies, and often reflected the factional divisions that were present in the electorate. In contrast, he believed that if there were too few representatives in the assembly, the interests of the nation would not be adequately represented, the likelihood that the representatives could be corrupted or would establish an interest independent of the people was increased, and the confidence between the people and their representatives that was necessary to stability in republican governments was undermined. Against these opposing tendencies, Madison sought to find the correct number of representatives so as to secure information about all the interests of the nation, to prevent the assembly from simply mirroring the divisions of the electorate, to prevent Congress from being corrupted or bribed, to maintain the confidence of the electorate and responsibility in representatives, and finally to enhance free and constructive debate about what policies would best promote the common interest.[37]

Together, Madison's four hypotheses form an integrated defence of elections from expanded electoral districts as a means of promoting disinterested or impartial representation and of addressing the problems that had characterized the state administrations during the mid-1780s. If the scheme worked as Madison and other Federalists predicted, then the men who were elected to Congress under the new Constitution would have greater intelligence, greater abilities and nobler character. They would also, he predicted, be less likely to be unduly attached to either their personal interests or the interests of their constituents. Finally, the legislature was less likely to be a forum for the accommodation of particularistic interests and more likely to be a forum for constructive deliberation and impartial representation.

But what did Madison mean by impartial or disinterested representation? Briefly, Madison's conception of impartial representation can be broken into three concrete

[36] 'Observations On Jefferson's Draft of a Constitution for Virginia', *PJM*, XI, p. 286.

[37] See especially 'Vices of the Political System of the United States', *PJM*, IX, pp. 353–7; 'Speech of 7 June 1787', In Constitutional Convention, *PJM*, X, pp. 39–40; *The Federalist*, No. 44, pp. 301–2; *The Federalist*, No. 55, pp. 373–4; *The Federalist*, No. 58, pp. 395–6; *The Federalist*, No. 62, pp. 419–22; 'Amendments to the Constitution', In Congress, *PJM*, XII, p. 336.

goals: to protect equally the rights of each individual, interest, class and geographic region; to distribute equally public burdens and benefits among the interests of the nation; to advance impartially the public good or 'permanent and aggregate interest'[38] when choices had to be made between interests. Each of these goals required the representative to perform a different function. Each of them also presupposed that representatives would share a common understanding of the public good and a common conception of the rights that should be protected.

The first of these goals — commitment to the protection of property and other individual rights — was of course a key aspect of Madison's political philosophy. Here, Madison presented a theory of representation which conflated the division, standard to modern liberalism, between adjudication and legislation. 'What are many of the most important acts of legislation', he wrote in the Tenth *Federalist* Paper, 'but so many judicial determinations, not indeed concerning the rights of single persons, but concerning the rights of large bodies of citizens.'[39] By 1787, in other words, it had become clear to Madison that when representatives drafted laws concerning private debts, commerical regulations, or even navigation rights, their role would be that of a judge as well as a legislator. They would thus have to protect the rights of each interest and region while simultaneously trying to advance the public interest.[40]

Specifically, Madison argued that a just government had to secure the property of every citizen 'impartially'. Here, Madison defined property broadly to include not merely possessions, but also the faculties of the mind and the body. Indeed, to Madison the faculties of the mind, which included the rights of conscience and the communication of opinions, were 'the most sacred of all property'.[41] A just representative therefore would not violate the rights of conscience or the communications of opinions by imposing penalties, tests or taxes. Nor would an impartial representative allow the rights of conscience or the communications of opinions to be violated by a part (including the majority) of the society.[42] Protecting the faculties of labour, meanwhile, meant that representatives should not through 'arbitrary restrictions, exemptions, and monopolies' prevent individuals from freely using their

[38] *The Federalist*, No. 10, p. 57.

[39] *Ibid.*, p. 59.

[40] Madison made several statements in which he noted the judicial component of representation. As early as October 1785, he lamented that an adequate power over commerce would never be added to the Confederation Congress because such a power 'requires in those who are to decide it the spirit of impartial judges, whilst the spirit of those who compose Congress is rather that of advocates for the respective interests of their constituents' (Madison to Thomas Jefferson, 3 October 1785, *PJM*, VIII, p. 374). Also, in *The Federalist*, No. 43, he wrote: 'In cases where it may be doubted on which side justice lies, what better umpires could be desired by two violent factions, flying to arms and tearing a State to pieces, than the representatives of confederated States not heated by the local flame? To the impartiality of Judges they would unite the affection of friends.' (*The Federalist*, No. 43, p. 294). In general, a good discussion of Madison's understanding of 'legislative judging' can be found in Epstein, *The Political Theory of The Federalist*, pp. 81–8.

[41] 'Property', 27 March 1792, in *PJM*, XIV, p. 267.

[42] *Ibid.*, pp. 266–7; 'Memorial and Remonstrance against Religious Assessment', in *PJM*, VIII, pp. 300–2.

faculties of labour or freely choosing their occupations because these 'not only constitute their property in the general sense of the word; but are the means of acquiring property strictly so called'. Finally, according to Madison, an impartial government would protect possessions principally by not imposing unequal, arbitrary or excessive taxes.[43]

The second goal of impartial representation was to ensure that public burdens and benefits were distributed with a 'just and equal hand'[44] among the different interests and geographic regions of the nation. To achieve this end, the representative had to develop an empirical understanding of the 'aggregate interest'.[45] This could be done, Madison maintained, by using the information gathered in the census[46] and by making deductions from a 'just and fair comparison of local interests'.[47] The representative then had to act as an arbiter between the many interests of the nation, effecting a just balance between them. This aspect of impartial representation was illustrated by Madison in the debate on raising revenue that took place in the First Congress. Here, Madison tried to distribute impost duties impartially among the nation's many interests. This could be achieved, Madison argued, if a 'system' of duties was devised which laid taxes on a variety of items, each of which affected some geographic region and interest. Thus, even though no particular tax would affect each interest equally, in general the 'system' would be fair because all interests would bear a proportion of the public burden that was equal to their number, their ability to pay it, or the benefit they would receive from it.[48] Similarly, Madison hoped that representatives would impartially distribute public benefits among the many interests of the nation. Clearly, every interest had an equal right to be protected — through regulations such as protective tariffs or tonnage duties on foreign vessels — to the degree that it had developed in the community and thus had become a part of the aggregate interest. Thus, even though Madison was a Jeffersonian agrarian, he argued that 'the states that are most advanced in population and ripe for manufacturers, ought to have their particular interest attended to in some degree. The persons who had these interests had accepted the Constitution under the pretense that it would attend to their interests and they could not be disappointed.'[49]

Nevertheless, Madison understood that protecting the rights of each interest and equally distributing public burdens and benefits among them did not exhaust the kinds of decisions that representatives would have to make. As the discussion in the

43 'Property', pp. 266–8. Quotes are on p. 267.

44 'Speech of 17 April 1789', In Congress, *PJM*, XII, p. 87.

45 *The Federalist*, No. 10, p. 57.

46 'Speech of 25 January 1790', In Congress, *PJM*, XIII, pp. 8–9; and 'Speech of 2 February 1790', *ibid.*, pp. 15–16.

47 Madison to Edmund Randolph, 3 December 1782, *PJM*, V, p. 357.

48 See especially 'Speech of 9 April 1789', In Congress, *PJM*, XII, pp. 69–74; 'Speech of 17 April 1789', *ibid.*, p. 87; and 'Speech of 28 April 1789', *ibid.*, pp. 114–19.

49 'Speech of 9 April 1789', In Congress, *PJM*, XII, p. 70.

Tenth *Federalist* indicates,[50] Madison understood that representatives would often have to make decisions between interests. Here, as David Epstein has noted, the principle of equally protecting the rights of all interests 'does not provide a standard by which to choose between or even to compromise between two incommensurable faculties'.[51] Instead, Madison expected that disinterested or impartial representatives would use the 'public good' or 'the permanent and aggregate interest' as a standard for formulating regulations that would actively advance certain interests. But what did the the public good mean to Madison?

Giving content to Madison's conception of the 'public good' is of course a difficult and lengthy task. For the purposes of this article, however, Madison's conception of the public good — a conception which he apparently (but erroneously) believed would be shared by his colleagues[52] — may be briefly described as that of a Jeffersonian and land expansion agrarian. In general, this meant that Madison hoped to exploit the natural advantages that the United States had in agricultural interests. Specifically, as Drew McCoy has shown,[53] Madison hoped to combine commerical discrimination to open foreign markets for America's agricultural products with land expansion to perpetuate an agrarian society and to forestall the development of large-scale public manufacturing. The United States, in other words, should settle its western lands and sell its surplus agricultural products to Europe in exchange for manufactured goods which in turn would not have to be produced in the United States. This plan required a strong national government that could protect American navigation rights on the Mississippi, promote internal improvements in order to make surplus crops available for market, and engage in whatever commercial retaliations were necessary to open international markets for America's agricultural surpluses.

[50] This is especially evident in the following statement: 'Shall domestic manufactures be encouraged, and in what degree, by restrictions on foreign manufactures? are questions which would be differently decided by the landed and the manufacturing classes; and probably by neither, with a sole regard to justice and the public good.' (*The Federalist*, No. 10, p. 60.)

[51] Epstein, *The Political Theory of the Federalist*, pp. 83–4. Quote is on p. 84.

[52] This expectation was probably based on Madison's belief that representatives representing agricultural interests would control Congress from its first meeting and that trends in population growth would continue to strengthen the position of landed interests. See Lance Banning, 'Virginia: Sectionalism and the General Good'', in *Ratifying the Constitution*, ed. Allen Gillespie and Michael Lienesch (Lawrence, 1989), pp. 276, 282, 288–9; Drew McCoy, 'James Madison and Visions of American Nationality in the Confederation Period: A Regional Perspective', in *Beyond Confederation*, ed. Beeman *et al.*, especially pp. 245–50.

[53] McCoy's interpretation of Madison's political economy can be found in D. McCoy, *The Elusive Republic: Political Economy in Jeffersonian America* (Chapel Hill, 1980), pp. 120–35; D. McCoy, 'Jefferson and Madison on Malthus: Population Growth in Jeffersonian Political Economy', *The Virginia Magazine of History and Biography*, LXXXVIII (1980), pp. 259–76; D. McCoy, 'Republicanism and American Foreign Policy: James Madison and the Political Economy of Commercial Discriminations, 1789 to 1794', *WMQ*, XXXI (1974), pp. 633–46; D. McCoy, 'James Madison and Visions of American Nationality', pp. 226–58; D. McCoy, 'An Unfinished Revolution: The Quest for Economic Independence in the Early Republic', in *The American Revolution: Its Character and Limits*, ed. Jack P. Greene (New York, 1987), pp. 131–48.

It did not, however, require such policies as the direct promotion of public manufacturers. Indeed, as McCoy has shown, from Madison's perspective such policies had the effect of impelling the society into an unduly advanced and ultimately anti-republican stage of development. Most important, this conception of the public good provided, in Madison's estimation, a standard for making regulations about interests which should be actively advanced (agricultural) and which should be attended to only to the degree that they had already developed in the society (manufacturing).

Obviously, within this conception of impartial or disinterested representation, representatives could neither be mere agents for the immediate desires of their constituents nor could they establish an interest independent of the people. Specifically, three consistent and closely related teachings emerge from the statements that Madison made between 1782 and 1792 about the relationship of representatives to their constituents. First, Madison believed that representatives should try to advance the interests of their immediate constituents only so far as these were consistent with the common or aggregate interest. Second, Madison believed that representation provided a mechanism for calming the passions of the people and educating them about what policies were in their 'true' or 'permanent' interests without violating the ultimate sovereignty of the people.[54] Third, Madison believed that the popular foundation of the government would prevent representatives from establishing an interest independent of the society and that there would be a 'general' congruence between the interests of the citizenry and their representatives.[55]

First, as numerous points in the above discussion suggest, Madison consistently argued that representatives should remain attached to the permanent and aggregate interests of the nation and not sacrifice these to any temporary or partial considerations.[56] This enlarged vision of representation, Madison's writings and speeches suggest, required that representatives be given an *initial* independence from their immediate constituents in order to form a mature judgment about what policies were in the public good. This independence would be achieved in part because representatives were placed further away from their constituents in a large republic than they were in a small one.[57] This would make the instruction of representatives difficult.[58] Still, this does not mean that Madison believed that representatives should

54 These terms are found throughout *The Federalist* Papers. See for example *The Federalist*, No. 10, pp. 57, 62; *The Federalist*, No. 42, p. 283; *The Federalist*, No. 46, pp. 320–1.

55 *The Federalist*, No. 52, p. 355.

56 See especially Madison to Thomas Jefferson, 3 October 1785, *PJM*, VIII, p. 373; *The Federalist*, No. 10, pp. 62, 64; *The Federalist*, No. 57, p. 384; 'Speech of 11 June 1788', In Virginia Ratifying Convention, *PJM*, XI, pp. 109–10; 'Observations on Jefferson's Draft of a Constitution for Kentucky', 15 October 1788, *PJM*, XI, pp. 286–7; 'Notes on William Loughton Smith's *Politicks and Views*', *c*. 4 November 1792, *PJM*, XIV, pp. 398–9.

57 For statements which suggest that the greater distance between representatives and their constituents was one aspect of Madison's argument for extent of territory see *The Federalist*, No. 43, p. 294; and 'Public Opinion', 19 December 1791, *PJM*, XIV, p. 170.

58 Garry Wills has argued that the principal point of extent of territory was that the greater distance would prevent the instruction of representatives. Wills, *Explaining America*, pp. 223–4. Clearly, one aspect of

ignore or abnegate the views or interests of their constituents. Madison spoke of refining and enlarging the public views (not of displacing them) and of relating particular interests to the common interest (not of ignoring them). But it does mean that Madison believed that representatives should compare partial interests to each other and to the common interest and reject any claims — even those of their constituents — which violated the common interest.[59] To restate this point differently, for Madison one of the principal functions of representation was to ensure that the interests and rights of all citizens were 'felt and understood in the public councils'.[60] Every interest formed a part of the common interest. Thus, representatives had to make the interests of their constituents known in Congress.[61] Beyond this, however, the representative had to engage in deliberation about the goals or ends of public policy,[62] to remain conscious of the views and interests represented by other Congressmen, and to advance the views and interests of their constituents only to the degree that they were congruent with the public good.[63] In

Madison's argument for extent of territory was that it would place representatives away from their constituents and thus help to secure the initial independence that they need for making mature decisions. Still, Wills' conclusion is far too strong. As I argue in detail later in this essay, the principal point of extent of territory is that it prevents factions from forming the alliances which would give them a majority in the legislative body.

For Madison's opposition to the idea that constituents could bind representatives with instructions see 'Notes on Debates', In Confederation Congress, 28 January 1783, *PJM*, VI, p. 147; *Annals of Congress*, I Cong. I Sess., I, pp. 738–9. For a similar statement by Madison written late in his life (1836) see Adrienne Koch, *The American Enlightenment: The Shaping of the American Experiment and a Free Society* (New York, 1965), p. 483.

[59] See 'Observations on Jefferson's Draft of a Constitution for Kentucky', 15 October 1788, *PJM*, XI, pp. 286–7; 'Notes on William Loughton Smith's *Politicks and Views*', p. 399

[60] 'Qualifications for Holding National Office', Speech of 26 July 1787, In Constitutional Convention, *PJM*, X, p. 117.

[61] Madison consistently spoke of the representative's role as a dual trust. He repeatedly suggested that representatives had an obligation to represent the views and interests of their constituents, but that they also had an obligation to the common interest which trumped their obligation to their constituents. In addition to his discussions about instruction cited above see 'Impost on Tonnage Duties', Speech of 9 April 1789, In Congress, *PJM*, XII, p. 70.

[62] Madison's understanding of the purposes of deliberation is discussed in Bessette, 'Deliberative Democracy: The Majority Principle in Republican Government', pp. 102–16; Larry Arnhart, 'The Deliberative Rhetoric of *The Federalist*', *The Political Science Reviewer*, XIX (1990), pp. 49–86.

[63] My understanding of this continuous process of relating partial views and interests to the common interest has been influenced by Lance Banning's recent essay 'Some Second Thoughts on Virtue and the Course of Revolutionary Thinking'. In this article, Banning discusses how revolutionary leaders expected individuals to advance their own interests, but also to remain conscious of the interests and views of others. This underlying logic, I would suggest, is also true of Madison's understanding of representation. 'Disinterested' representation did not require representatives to completely transcend or abnegate the particular views and interests of their constituents, but to place them in proper relationship with the common interest. See 'Some Second Thoughts on Virtue and the Course of Revolutionary Thinking', in *Conceptual Change and the Constitution* , ed. Terence Ball and J.G.A. Pocock (Lawrence, 1988), pp. 194–212.

short, as Jack Rakove has said, Madison favoured a 'legislature composed of disinterested men who could speak intelligently for the needs and views of their constituents but then vote on the basis of some larger notion of the public good'.[64]

Second, Madison sometimes defended this conception of representation as a means of educating the citizenry about what was in their 'true' or 'permanent' interests. Here Madison drew upon the set of assumptions about 'the people' that was present in the eighteenth-century understanding of mixed government. The people, Madison believed, honestly pursued their interests and could never wilfully betray them. They were, however, easily fooled, misled or mistaken about their interests.[65] But if representatives temporarily blocked the passions of the people, then 'reason, justice, and truth' would have a chance to 'regain their authority over the public mind' and the reason, the '*cool* and *deliberate* sense' of the people would be heeded. Simultaneously, the people would often recognize that they had been wrong. Given time they would often agree that their best interests had been identified by their representatives.[66] In this manner, fidelity to the common interest was ensured without violating the ultimate sovereignty of the people.

Third, despite this enlarged vision of the purposes and effects of representation, it is also important to establish that Madison certainly did *not* hope that representatives would try to establish a personal interest independent of the people. Again, fidelity to the common interest meant that representatives would neither unduly advance the partial interests of their constituents nor establish an interest independent of the people. Madison focused on the second of these two points in *The Federalist*, No. 53 and Nos. 55–58. Here he replied to anti-federalist charges that the House of Representatives did not contain an adequate number of representatives and thus would establish a will independent of the society with carefully worded arguments which maintained that the 'government *in general* should have a common interest with the people'.[67] This general congruence of interests was secured, according to Madison, because representatives were elected, because there was an adequate number of them to ensure a 'diffusive sympathy with the whole society',[68] and because they would be 'acquainted' with the interests of their constituents and would relay a 'knowledge' of them into the public councils.[69] The interests of the people and their representatives would remain the same as long as an adequate number of representatives were added with increases in population, the length of terms of

64 Rakove, 'The Madisonian Moment', p. 483.

65 Madison reveals his acceptance of this understanding of the people in *The Federalist*, No. 63, p. 426. For a general discussion of the relationship of the eighteenth-century conception of democracy to the assumptions of mixed government see Douglass Adair, 'Clio Bemused', in *Fame and the Founding Fathers*, pp. 296–305.

66 *The Federalist*, No. 63, p. 425. Emphasis added. See also *The Federalist*, No. 49, p. 343.

67 *The Federalist*, No. 52, p. 355. Emphasis added.

68 *The Federalist*, No. 58, p. 396.

69 *The Federalist*, No. 56, pp. 378–9.

representatives was kept moderate, and the 'responsibility' of representatives was ensured during elections.[70]

III
Extent of Territory, Public Opinion and Impartial Majorities

So far this essay has repeated and further developed the line of interpretation given by scholars who have emphasized the 'filtration of talent' component of Madison's scheme of representation. Nevertheless, the election of élite representatives from expanded electoral districts and the filtration of the public's views simply were not the central points of Madison's argument for an extended republic.[71] Nor did Madison's argument rest on 'hope for a heroic impartiality in the people's representatives'.[72] Instead, Madison understood that 'enlightened statesmen will not always be at the helm'[73] and he sought to structure the new government so that impartial administration was possible even in the absence of heroic representatives. Equally important, Madison's principal concern — his 'Great Desideratum' — was to ensure the reconciliation of popular sovereignty with the protection of private rights and the impartial or disinterested promotion of public good.[74] Madison's chief solution to this problem was not the election of élite representatives from expanded electoral districts.[75]

Instead, Madison's resolution of the problem of reconciling majority rule with impartial administration and the protection of individual rights can be found in the central argument of the Tenth *Federalist* Paper. This section reads:

> The other point of difference is, the greater number of citizens and extent of territory which may be brought within the compass of Republican, than of

[70] For Madison's conception of responsibility see *The Federalist*, No. 52, pp. 353–9; *The Federalist*, No. 55, pp. 372–8; *The Federalist*, No. 56, pp. 378–83; *Annals of Congress* (Washington, 1834–6), I Sess., I Cong., I, p. 605. For Madison's understanding of sympathy see *The Federalist*, No. 57, pp. 386–7; *The Federalist*, No. 58, p. 396; 'Speech of 26 July 1787', In Constitutional Convention, *PJM*, X, p. 117; 'Speech of 16 December 1790', In Congress, *PJM*, XIII, p. 323.

[71] Using carefully chosen words, Lance Banning calls the 'filtration of talent' component of Madison's argument in the Tenth *Federalist* a 'secondary and subsidiary point' which was 'more than an afterthought, but much less than the vital core of Madison's thinking'. Banning notes first that the filtration of talent argument was clearly presented as a secondary argument in the text of the Tenth *Federalist* and that it appeared as an 'auxiliary desideratum' in 'Vices of the Political System of the United States'. Banning also notes that this component of Madison's argument does not even appear in Madison's important 24 October 1787 letter to Thomas Jefferson. Banning, 'The Hamiltonian Madison', pp. 13–15 and ns. 15 and 16. Quotes are on p. 13.

[72] Wills, 'Introduction', p. xxiv.

[73] *The Federalist*, No. 10, p. 60.

[74] See note 12, above, for the various ways that Madison stated this problem.

[75] This is especially noticeable in the 24 October 1787 letter to Jefferson. Here, Madison explicitly addresses the question of how the general government can serve as an impartial administrator without itself violating the republican principle of popular sovereignty; but he doesn't even mention the scheme for electing élite representatives from expanded electoral districts. Madison to Jefferson, 24 October 1787, *PJM*, X, pp. 212–14.

> Democratic Government; and *it is this circumstance principally which renders factious combinations less to be dreaded in the former, than in the latter*. The smaller the society, the fewer probably will be the distinct parties and interests composing it; the fewer the distinct parties and interests, the more frequently will a majority be found of the same party; and the smaller the number of individuals composing a majority, and the smaller the compass within which they are placed, the more easily will they concert and execute their plans of oppression. Extend the sphere, and you take in a greater variety of parties and interests; you make it less probable that a majority of the whole will have a common motive to invade the rights of other citizens; or if such a common motive exists, it will be more difficult for all who feel it to discover their own strength and to act in unison with each other. *Besides other impediments, it may be remarked, that where there is a consciousness of unjust and dishonorable purposes, communication is always checked by distrust, in proportion to the number whose concurrence is necessary.*[76]

With the exceptions of Lance Banning and George Carey, scholars who hold the 'impartial representation' interpretation of the Tenth *Federalist* Paper have apparently believed that emphasizing this argument would re-establish Madison as a pluralist. Unfortunately, they have therefore understated the importance of the central argument of the Tenth *Federalist* Paper. Meanwhile, Banning has argued that this argument only makes sense if the 'pluralistic structure of American society' is mirrored in the 'character and conduct' of its representatives.[77] Actually, extent of territory is the principal argument of the Tenth *Federalist*; but it is the principal argument for impartial administration, not for pluralism. More specifically, Madison argued that extent of territory would raise four principal 'obstacles' or 'impediments' to the communication, consolidation and concert of majority factions.[78] These were the greater space or distance (which I read to include both the greater distance between citizens and the distance between citizens and their representatives), the greater number of citizens, the greater variety of interests and religious sects, and the public or civic consciousness which Madison maintained would be embedded in

[76] *The Federalist*, No. 10, pp. 63–4. Emphases added. This paragraph of the Tenth *Federalist* is often quoted by pluralists. Nevertheless, they omit the last sentence (italicized above) and infer that Madison hoped that the multiplicity of interests in the extended republic would be reflected in Congress. They then quote Madison's statement in the Fifty First *Federalist* Paper that 'among the great variety of interests, parties and sects which it embraces, a coalition of a majority of the whole society could seldom take place on any other principles than those of justice and the general good' as evidence that he held a 'process' theory of coalition building. See Diamond, *Founding of the Democratic Republic*, pp. 71, 77–8 for an example of how the pluralist interpretation is constructed. There are several problems with this. First, when the final sentence in this paragraph is added it illustrates that Madison hoped to neutralize factions before they were able to communicate their designs to Congress. Second, as I argue throughout the second section of this essay, Madison did not believe that representatives should be the mere brokers for the interests of their constituents. Third, as I point out below, Madison did not accept the pluralist theory of coalition building.

[77] Quotes are from Banning, 'The Hamiltonian Madison', pp. 14, 24.

[78] Quotes are from *The Federalist*, No. 10, p. 64.

the society and would act as a barrier to the open communication of factious schemes. Together, these obstacles were designed to help prevent the consolidation of a majority faction or, if such a faction formed, to its ability to coordinate the election of a majority of factious representatives. Most important, Madison believed that if majority factions could be prevented from gaining control of Congress, then impartial or non-factious majorities could be formed within Congress, and impartial administration could be secured and the rights of individuals and minorities could be protected.

To understand this interpretation of extent of territory more fully, let us consider each of its two prongs separately. Consider first how Madison believed that extent of territory would establish a set of obstacles which would break the force of majority factions. To do this, we must first consider this argument in connection with the eighteenth-century conception of public opinion. Although it has never been comprehensively analysed, by 1787 Madison and many of his colleagues had a fully-developed conception of public opinion as a theory about group behaviour and an explanation of how institutions were formed, supported and ultimately controlled.[79] Specifically, two points within this idea of the sovereignty of opinion are important for understanding Madison's argument for extent of territory.

First, Madison and other Federalists had developed a theory of mass psychology and group behaviour based on the belief that men were public or 'political knaves'.[80] This theory suggested simply that political actors were often spurred by the opinions of others to boldly perform actions in public which reason did not dictate and 'against which their consciences would revolt if proposed to them under the like sanction, separately in their closets'.[81] When, for example, individuals acted in factions or large legislative assemblies, the reinforcing opinion of others led them to perform rash acts. But this dynamic was thought to be reversed when political actors were censured by their peers or when they were simply uncertain of the feelings of others.[82] When

[79] Several studies examine the development of the concepts of public opinion and popular sovereignty. These include: Edmund Morgan, *Inventing the People*; Robert Morgan, 'Madison's Analysis of the Sources of Political Authority', *American Political Science Review*, LXXV (1981), pp. 613–25; Paul A. Palmer, 'The Concept of Public Opinion in Political Theory' (unpublished doctoral dissertation, Harvard University, 1934), pp. 1–61; Paul A. Palmer, 'The Concept of Public Opinion in Political Theory', *Essays in History and Political Theory in Honor of Charles McIlwain*, ed. Carl Wittke (New York, 1936), pp. 230–57; Judith N. Shklar, *Men and Citizens: A Study of Rousseau's Social Theory* (Cambridge, 1969), pp. 75–103; Hans Speier, 'Historical Development of Public Opinion', *American Journal of Sociology*, LV (1949–50), pp. 376–88; Ernst Vollrath, 'That All Governments Rest on Opinion', *Social Research*, XL (1976), pp. 46–61; Wills, *Explaining America*, pp. 24–41; Gordon S. Wood, 'The Democratization of Mind in the American Revolution', in *The Moral Foundations of the American Republic*, ed. Robert Horwitz (Charlottesville, 1986), pp. 109–35.

[80] The phrase 'political knave' is a paraphrase from David Hume. Hume, 'Of the Independency of Parliament', in *The Philosophical Works of David Hume* (4 vols., Edinburgh, 1826), III, pp. 42–4. For quote from Madison see 'Vices of the Political System of the United States', *PJM*, IX, p. 356.

[81] 'Vices of the Political System of the United States', *PJM*, XI, p. 356.

[82] The idea that individuals lose confidence and are hesitant to act when they are censored by others can be traced back to Madison's earliest correspondence. In 1774, Madison wrote: 'Union of religious sentiments begets a surprising confidence and ecclesiastical establishments tend to great ignorance and

the force of reinforcing sentiments was broken, political actors would be sceptical, cautious, and thus hesitant to act. In general, the force of opinion was thought to depend upon the number of individuals who shared the same opinion and were aware of it. This is what Madison meant when he wrote in the Forty-Ninth *Federalist* Paper that 'the strength of opinion in each individual, and its practical influence on his conduct, depend much on the number which he supposes to have entertained the same opinion. The reason of man, like man himself, is timid and cautious, when left alone and acquires firmness and confidence, in proportion to the number with which it is associated.'[83]

Second, Madison and other Federalists also believed that governments 'rest on the opinion of the governed'.[84] Briefly what this meant was that governments had to be supported by the good opinion, the respect or the affection of the citizenry in order to be stable and to secure a gentle form of obedience. This respect would be gained by, among other means, just administration and confidence in the character and capabilities of political leaders. Conversely, no government could rely on force to secure obedience, since the latent force of the community was always on the side of the governed. Most important, when this opinion was present in the community, it signified that a public or civic consciousness was in place in support of the government and its laws and in opposition to factious coalitions. The more individuals who shared this view, the greater would be the confidence in and support for the government.[85]

In general, the 'public mind', as Madison referred to public opinion, was simply a public consciousness formed from the aggregation of individual sentiments.[86] In it, individual minds censured the behaviour of each other based on shared standards. Collectively, the sovereign mind of the community served as the support for the government, a spring for its actions, and a barrier beyond which it could not exceed. The opinion of the governed, in other words, made the power exercised by the government legitimate and it simultaneously set the bounds of that power.

The link between the sovereignty of opinion and the principal argument of the Tenth *Federalist* Paper can be readily established. Madison consistently held that factions — whether they have formed as a result of differences in opinions concerning religion and government, attachments to different leaders, or the influence of the various and unequal distributions of property on the views of individuals —

corruption all of which facilitate the execution of mischievous projects.' Madison to William Bradford, 24 January 1774, *PJM*, I, p. 105.

83 *The Federalist*, No. 49, p. 340.

84 *Ibid.*

85 In addition to the citations in note 86, below, see Hannah Arendt, *On Violence* (New York, 1969), pp. 40–56, for an excellent discussion of these points.

86 Madison uses the phrase 'public mind' or 'mind of the community' throughout his writings. Madison used the term 'public mind' twice in the 24 October 1787 letter alone. Madison to Jefferson, 24 October 1787, *PJM*, X, pp. 216–17. The term 'mind of the community' is taken from 'Location of the Capital', 4 September 1789, *PJM*, XII, p. 373.

manifested themselves as opinions or sentiments.[87] Furthermore, he believed that the behaviour of factions could be explained as a result of the group or mass psychology that I have explained above. Once these links are made, it can be understood that the 'obstacles' posed by the extended republic were designed to prevent the communication and contagion of a majority of factious motives and opinions. This, Madison hoped, would in turn isolate discontent and invert the dynamic of mass psychology that would take place if individuals of the same motives, opinions and interests were placed within a small geographic area. More specifically, as scholars have repeatedly emphasized, the structure of many of the state governments during the mid-1780s had included small electoral districts, numerous representatives who served short terms, and a small geographic area with a population of homogeneous interests. This organization of government made for the ready flow of factious sentiments, the easy communication and concert of factious schemes, and passionate behaviour in both the community and the legislature.[88]

But an extended republic, Madison argued, would be different. A factious majority might still be present. The difference between a small republic and a large republic was *not* that a factious majority, common unjust motive or factious sentiment was necessarily less likely to exist in the large republic.[89] The principal difference was that in a 'large society the people are broken into so many interests and parties that a common *sentiment* is less likely to be felt, and the requisite concert less likely to be formed by a majority of the whole'.[90] Madison believed, in other words, that in an extended republic the distance between citizens would make them unaware that they share a common factious sentiment or unjust motive. Since the reason of men is timid and cautious when left alone, citizens are more hesitant to act for factious causes and are more likely to be submissive to the common interest.

Two of the other 'obstacles' to the communication and concert of majority factions posed by the extended republic — a greater number of individuals and a greater variety of interests and religious sects — also break apart the impulses and unjust

[87] That all forms of faction manifest themselves as opinions is illustrated by the adjectives that Madison used to qualify interests. For Madison, interests opposed to the permanent and aggregate interest were 'apparent', 'imaginary' and 'supposed'. See *The Federalist*, No. 10, pp. 58–9, for Madison's discussion of the causes of faction. See 'Vices of the Political System of the United States', *PJM*, XI, p. 355; 'Notes on the Influence of Extent of Territory on Government', *PJM*, XIV, p. 132; 'Consolidation', *PJM*, XIV, p. 138 for the quotes above. I do not, however, mean to imply here that Madison believed that all opinions were simply projections of underlying interests. Quite the contrary, Madison clearly believed that some opinions had genuine validity. On this point see Kesler, '*Federalist* 10 and American Republicanism', pp. 13–39.

[88] For the structure and problems of the state governments see Wood, *Creation of the American Republic*, pp. 393–429.

[89] In 'Vices of the Political System of the United States', Madison wrote: 'If an enlargement of the sphere is found to lessen the insecurity of private rights, it is *not* because the impulse of a common interest or passion is less predominant in this case with the majority; but because a common interest or passion is less apt to be felt and the requisite combinations less easy to be formed by a great than by a small number.' 'Vices of the Political System of the United States', *PJM*, IX, p. 357 (emphasis added).

[90] Madison to Jefferson, 24 October 1787, *PJM*, X, p. 214.

motives present in majority factions, make it more difficult for them to realize that a common unjust motive is present in the society, and establish barriers to their opportunities to concert their 'plans of oppression'.[91] This, in turn, acts to reverse the psychological dynamic of group behaviour present in majority factions, to restore the opinion on which government rests, and to influence citizens to act for the common interest. A greater number of individuals included in the extended republic makes each individual a less important part of the whole and thus also makes them hesitant to oppose the common interests or the government.[92] Finally, the greater variety of interests present in the extended republic act as buffers between interests. This prevents a majority faction from becoming aware that it has a common interest contrary to the interest of the whole or, if it becomes aware of this, makes it more difficult for it to reveal its plans and to act in concert. Here, one of the central points of extent of territory emerges. An extended republic is heterogeneous. This variety of interests is the primary 'obstacle' to the formation, communication and concert of the 'plans of oppression' of an interested majority. Indeed, the greater variety of interests in the extended republic serve as a natural and *lasting* barrier to the formation of majority factions. Since 'enlightened statesmen will not always be at the helm',[93] the greater variety of interests and religous sects supply 'opposite and rival interests the defect of better motives'.[94] Interest checks interest. Vice checks vice. The very selfishness of the groups prevent them from combining for unjust purposes. The nation's many factions and interests, which are woven throughout the

[91] *The Federalist*, No. 10, p. 61. The importance of extent of territory as a means of separating the motives for unjust actions from the opportunity of committing them can be further understood by applying the perceptive discussion recently given by Morton White. According to White, Madison and the other authors of *The Federalist* Papers held a theory of individual and group behaviour which suggested that every human action required *both* a motive and an opportunity for acting on that motive. In the various versions of his theory of the extended republic, Madison explicitly rejected trying to reform the motives of majority factions or to appeal to 'better motives' that might be present in the group. Neither a prudent regard for the public good, respect for character, or religion could restrain majority factions. Indeed, these 'internal' restraints lost their efficacy to the degree that they were necessary. With this in mind, Madison formulated a solution that was congruent with his theory of action — he sought to use extent of territory to prevent majority factions from realizing that they shared a common unjust motive and prevented them from having the opportunity for unified action. Together, the greater distance, diversity, and the greater number individuals present in the extended republic were designed to prevent majority factions from realizing that they had a motive for action and raising impediments to their opportunity to action. Without both the motives and the opportunities for action, majority factions would not act. White, *Philosophy, The Federalist, and the Constitution*, pp. 131–71.

[92] This is implicit in the logic of Madison's statement that 'the strength of opinion in each individual, and its practical influence on his conduct, depend much on the number which he supposes to have entertained the same opinion. The reason of man, like man himself is timid and cautious when left alone and requires firmness and confidence in proportion to the number with which it is associated.' *The Federalist*, No. 49, p. 340. Madison also made this point explicitly in 1791. In an essay entitled 'Public Opinion', Madison argued that it was easy to 'counterfeit' public opinion in a larger country because 'the more extensive a country, the more insignificant is each individual in his own eyes'. 'Public Opinion', 19 December 1791, *PJM*, XIV, p. 170.

[93] *The Federalist*, No. 10, p. 60.

[94] *The Federalist*, No. 51, p. 349.

extended republic, serve as checks or censors, condemning or approving the actions of others depending on whether they are factious or in the common interest.[95] In short, the multiplicity of interests, like the multiplicity of religious sects, 'secure the national Councils' from a majority faction.[96]

When the connection between public opinion and extent of territory is grasped, it is also possible to understand the fourth impediment Madison mentions to the consolidation and concert of a majority faction. The obscure sentence after Madison observes that an extended republic will contain a greater variety of interests and religious sects reads: 'Besides other impediments, where there is a consciousness of unjust and dishonorable purposes communication is always checked by distrust in proportion to the number whose concurrence is necessary.'[97] This sentence rests on a submerged metaphor — 'the public mind' or the 'mind of the community'.[98] As I noted above, the public mind is a metaphor for public opinion, for an aggregate and civic consciousness. As long as the opinion of the citizenry continues to support the government, this civic consciousness acts as a barrier to the open communications of the 'secret wishes' and 'plans of oppression' of an unjust majority.[99] If individuals try to plot and concert a factional conspiracy, then their communications will be checked or 'censored' when they are 'discovered' or 'revealed' to other citizens who support the government or who have different interests and will not support the conspiracy.[100] This does not mean that all communications between citizens are checked. An 'idea of justice and equal right', Madison argued in 1789, is embedded in the public mind.[101] The opinion of the public, in other words, has a stable content. This underlying consensus allows citizens to openly communicate and form coalitions which have the principles of right, of reason and of the Constitution on their side.[102]

More technically, this sentence about a consciousness of unjust purposes also reveals the premises behind Madison's belief that there is 'safety in numbers'.[103] Earlier in this paragraph, Madison argued that an extended republic would contain a

[95] Madison's argument that the multiplicity of interests in the extended republic would check or censor each other is similar to Jefferson's argument that the numerous religious sects would perform the office of 'censor morum' (censor of morals) over each other. See Dumas Malone, *Thomas Jefferson and His Times* (6 vols., Boston, 1948–81), I, p. 277 and n. 9.

[96] *The Federalist*, No. 10, p. 65.

[97] *Ibid.*, p. 64.

[98] See note 86, above.

[99] Quotes are from *The Federalist*, No. 10, p. 64.

[100] I am indebted to Garry Wills for pointing out that the word 'discover' as Madison uses it in the critical paragraph of the Tenth *Federalist* means 'reveal'.

[101] 'Location of the Capital', 4 September 1789, *PJM*, XII, p. 373.

[102] In *The Federalist*, No. 58, p. 393, Madison indicates that he believes that the public mind will be inculcated with principles of right, of reason and of the Constitution.

[103] See Morgan, 'Safety in Numbers: Madison, Hume, and the Tenth *Federalist*', pp. 95–112 on this point.

greater number of citizens and thus that the number that made up a majority — 'the number whose concurrence is necessary' — would increase. Here, he argued that the coordination of unjust actions by the majority would become more difficult as its number increases.[104] The principal reason for this is that the members of unjust majority factions do not trust each other. Aware that they are acting unjustly, they find no basis for trust in each other. Instead, communications between them are broken and the factional conspiracy breaks apart. This distrust, Madison hypothesizes, increases as the number in the majority increases.

This discussion brings us to the principal question and criticism that has been raised against Madison's argument for extent of territory: how do the 'obstacles' present in the extended republic prevent majority factions from forming, communicating and concerting their schemes of oppression without also preventing nonfactious majorities from forming, communicating and concerting their goals?[105] This question, in turn, also raises a more general question: what role did Madison believe that nonfactious popular majorities would play when or if they were able to form? This first question can be answered succinctly as follows. Two of the four 'obstacles' raised by the extended republic act neutrally on both factious and nonfactious majorities. The other two, however, block only factious majorities. The greater distance between citizens and the greater number of individuals present in the extended republic do act neutrally on the formation of both factious and nonfactious popular majorities. The third and fourth 'impediments' to the communication and concert majorities factions — the greater diversity of interests and the civic consciousness that is embedded in the society — however act as barriers only to communications and coalitions among the citizenry when they pursue purposes that are unjust or contrary to the common interest. These obstacles act as a filtering element which distinguishes factious from nonfactious majorities. More specifically, nonfactious majorities are able to overcome the obstacles raised by the diversity of interests because diversity no longer exists. The common interest serves as a standard independent of the demands of any factions and when factions give up their selfish aims and cooperate in pursuit of the common interest they can communicate, form coalitions and act in concert. Similiarly, communications between citizens which have the principles of right, of reason and of the Constitution on their side should be expediated rather than blocked by the civic consciousness that is present in the

[104] Madison made this same point in 1785 when he wrote, 'as the wills [in the society] multiply so will the chances against a dangerous union of them'. Madison to Lafayette, 20 March 1785, *PJM*, VIII, p. 252. This belief that it becomes more difficult to work in concert for purposes of corruption as the number needed increases is an axiom for Madison. See also *The Federalist*, No. 55, p. 374; 'Speech of 20 July 1787', In Constitutional Convention, *PJM*, X, p. 108.

[105] This question, which George Carey has called 'the filter problem', was first raised by Robert Dahl and has bedevilled Madison scholars ever since. Indeed, Garry Wills is so frustrated by this question that he rejects the idea that the multiplicity of interests found in the extended republic is the central argument of the Tenth *Federalist*. The most prudent discussion of this question is offered by Carey. He reaches many of the same conclusions that I present below. See Robert Dahl, *A Preface to Democratic Theory*, pp. 29–30; George Carey, *The Federalist: Design for a Constitutional Republic*, pp. 28–30, 38–44.

society.[106] At any rate, as George Carey has noted, Madison 'certainly does believe that nonfactious majorities can overcome the obstacles posed by extensiveness'.[107] Indeed, the obstacles present in the extended republic are best thought of as means, like the system of separation of powers and checks and balances in the Constitution, of disciplining or channelling the kinds of popular majorities that would be able to form rather than as a means of blocking the formation of all majorities.

Once this is said, however, the role that nonfactious popular majorities play in Madison's constitutional system is not at all clear.[108] On the one hand, Madison's writings provide no evidence that he expected a substantial number of public policies to result from the transfer of popular majorities into legislative majorities. Instead, Madison seemed to have believed that most public policies would be formed by representatives who consulted the views and interests of their constituents and then compared and related these to the public good. In this case, nonfactious popular majorities that formed would probably already be supported by representatives anyway. Furthermore, the many references that Madison made to popular majorities are hardly flattering. He seems to have believed that collective action by the citizenry would most often be the result of public passions and that it would result in the formation of factious majorities.[109] On the other hand, the nonfactious popular

[106] In *The Federalist*, No. 58, pp. 392–3 and *The Federalist*, No. 51, p. 353, Madison explicitly states that combinations among the people which are based on the common interest and have the principles of right, reason and the Constitution on their side can be formed. The idea that the diversity of interests present in the extended republic would block the formation of both factious and nonfactious majorities seems to revert to the pluralist interpretation. Pluralists envision a community composed simply of self-interested groups. To pluralists, the republican vision of a common interest prior to and independent of group interests is a metaphysical spook. Pluralists believe that groups share no underlying common or national interest and that such claims are only projected rationalizations of group demands. Thus, a pluralist believes that any coalitions and communications between groups are problematic and involve bargaining and compromising. But to Madison, groups or factions were by definition combinations of citizens opposed to the common interest. Thus, unlike pluralists, Madison can argue that the diversity of selfish aims of these groups will neutralize unjust combinations, but that these groups can communicate, form coalitions, and act in concert on matters upon which they pursue the common interest — an entity which again is independent of any group.

[107] Carey, *The Federalist: Design for a Constitutional Republic*, p. 29.

[108] Compare and contrast this discussion to Carey's discussion of the role of popular majorities. *Ibid.*, pp. 42–4.

[109] The only condition under which Madison believed that collective action by the citizenry was imperative was when they engaged in a 'defensive concert' against 'the oppression of those entrusted with the administration'. This, however, was a rare — indeed revolutionary — action which involved using the state legislatures to sound the alarm against oppression and eventually resulted in the purgation of oppressive representatives from the public councils. When this happened, Madison maintained, 'one spirit would animate and conduct the whole [body of the people]'. The ordinary diversity of interests is stifled and a coalition of the people can take place because it is prompted by common interest. Indeed, the psychological dynamic that I have outlined above is reversed. Discontent is no longer isolated. As more and more people realize that they share a common interest in opposing the tyrannical policies of the government, public opinion consolidates and results in a change of representatives. The phrase 'defensive concert' is from Madison to Jefferson, 24 October 1787, *PJM*, X, p. 214. For Madison's discussion of the way that a defensive concert would be conducted and the other quotes above see *The Federalist*, No. 44,

majorities which were able to overcome the extended republic might have some role even within the more limited conception of representative republicanism that Madison envisioned. Communications and coalitions among the citizenry may inform or even transform their views and interests. These changes should then eventually be transferred into a change in the representatives' understanding of their constituents' views and interests, a change in the representatives' understanding of the content of the aggregate interest, or even the election of different representatives. Certainly, if the public is aggressive, persistent and unanimously or nearly unanimously in support of a policy, they should be able to ensure that it is enacted. Again, however, it is doubtful that Madison expected many public policies to form in this manner.[110]

Now consider the second major question which I promised to address in this section: how did Madison believe that impartial legislative majorities would form in Congress even in the absence of enlightened statesmen? Here an important caveat is necessary. As Jack Rakove has recently noted, 'the actual basis on which Madison expected legislative majorities to form in Congress remains less than clear'.[111] The reason for this lack of clarity is that Madison's writings contain only limited clues for addressing this question. The discussion that follows is based upon the few statements that Madison made about coalitions and the formation of legislative majorities, upon study of Madison's conduct as a legislative leader in the Virginia House of Delegates and the First Federal Congress, and upon a projection or application of the logic underlying his argument for impartial administration. With this said, we must realize that there are at least three necessary conditions that must be met if impartial majorities are to form in Congress. First, no majority interest or faction can be present in the national councils. Obviously, if a majority faction gains control of Congress, then it becomes a judge in its own cause and has the power to pass laws contrary to individual and minority rights and the permanent and aggregate interest of the nation. This is rendered 'very improbable, if not impracticable' by extent of territory.[112] Second, the claims of all interests must be understood in the national councils. This is important because impartial representation and arbitration

p. 305; *The Federalist*, No. 46, p. 320; *The Federalist*, No. 58, p. 392; and especially 'Consolidation', *PJM*, XIV, pp. 138–9.

110 This whole discussion raises the broader question of whether Madison actually achieved his goal of reconciling majority rule with impartial administration and the protection of private rights. Certainly if majority rule is defined as the rule of a majority of the citizenry no matter what their views or interests, then Madison was *not* successful. His system ensures that *legislative* majorities are congruent with the public good and private rights — he explicitly observes that *factious* popular majorities will be blocked. See 'Vices of the Political System of the United States', *PJM*, IX, pp. 356–7. Also in 1790, Madison explicitly observed that by majority rule he did not mean rule by a simple majority of the citizenry: 'If we are to take', he wrote to Benjamin Rush, 'for the criterion of truth the majority of suffrages, they ought to be gathered from those philosophical and patriotic citizens who cultivate their reason, apart from the scenes which distract its operations, and expose it to the influence of the passions.' Madison to Benjamin Rush, 7 March 1790, *PJM*, XIII, pp. 93–4.

111 Rakove, 'Madisonian Moment', p. 485.

112 *The Federalist*, No. 51, p. 351.

require that the representative understands the claims of each party in order to judge the content of the aggregate interest, to determine a just balance between interests, and to avoid violating the rights of any interest. This condition is met because the national councils will include an adequate number of representatives to ensure a proper understanding of and sympathy with the claims of the nation's interests, and because in Congress representatives will acquire a knowledge of all the interests of the nation.[113] Third, representatives must be willing and able to act independently from that part of their constituents interests that are incongruent with the public good.

Once these conditions are met, impartial majorities form differently depending upon the situation. If the question before Congress involves the rights of some interest or if it can be decided by reference to the rules of the Constitution, then impartial representation involves protecting that right or adhering to that rule. Here, the formation of impartial legislative majorities is possible because the national councils are purged of a factious majority. When factious majorities are neutralized before they are reflected in Congress, then no group has the votes to violate the rights of other groups or to overrun the rules of the Constitution. The Virginia church–state struggle provides an excellent example of how Madison believed that this would work. During this struggle, several attempts were made to pass a 'Bill Establishing a Provision for Teachers of the Christian Religion'. This bill, which Madison considered a flagrant violation of freedom of religion, passed two readings in the House of Delegates. Still, support for this bill was built on an unstable coalition between the Presbyterian and Episcopalian sects. When this coalition broke apart, the Christian Teachers bill failed. In general, the antagonism between Virginia's many religious sects prevented them from gaining a legislative majority. Eventually, the assembly passed Jefferson's Bill for Establishing Freedom of Religion which provided equal protection for the religious freedom of all groups.[114]

In a second scenario, impartial majorities can sometimes also easily be formed in the legislature because not all representatives are equally effected by all questions that come before the legislature. When a question comes before the legislature which affects the interests of only a small number of representatives, majorities may form around the representatives who are interested parties in the question. The representatives who are intensely affected by the claim may advance the interests of their constituents too strongly. Still, the other representatives form a kind of impartial jury[115] and decide the question based on deliberations about its merits. In this

[113] *The Federalist*, Nos. 52–3, pp. 353–66; *The Federalist*, Nos. 55–8, pp. 372–97.

[114] For the Virginia church–state struggle as an experience which led Madison to believe that diversity could protect individual rights see: Lance Banning, 'James Madison, the Statute for Religious Freedom, and the Crisis of Republican Convictions', in *The Virginia Statute for Religious Freedom: Its Evolution and Consequences in American History*, ed. Merrill D. Peterson and Robert C. Vaughan (Cambridge, 1988), pp. 109–38; Ralph Ketcham, 'James Madison and Religion — A New Hypothesis', *Journal of the Presbyterian Historical Society*, XXXVIII (1960), pp. 65–90.

[115] The analogy of the disinterested majority to a jury is useful because it highlights the fact that impartiality is not achieved by virtue of the élite qualities of the representatives. Instead, this majority is expected to be able to achieve impartiality for the same reason that a jury of common citizens is able to achieve impartiality — neither is immediately affected by or interested in the case at hand.

scenario, which is the counterpositive of logrolling, there are shifting majorities in Congress. But these majorities shift away from the representatives most directly interested by the measure at hand. Instead of supporting the demands of other Congressmen in order to gain future support, representatives judge these claims on the basis of their merit and in turn expect that their claims will be judged on their merits. Among Madison's contemporaries, Thomas Jefferson gave this interpretation of Madison's argument. A republic, Jefferson wrote, should be 'so extensive that local egoisms may never reach its greater part; *that on every particular question, a majority may be found in its council free from particular interests, and giving, therefore, an uniform prevalence to the principles of justice*'.[116] More recently, John Murrin has proposed this same interpretation:

> Madison recognized that most Americans would pursue their self-interest most of the time, but he still believed that gentlemen at the nation's capital could identify and pursue the common good. By enlarging the sphere of the government while keeping the number of legislators small, majority factions would be able to form only with great difficulty. *Every Congressman would be an interested party on some issues, but most representatives would be disinterested on any given question at any given time.*[117]

The problem with this example of how impartial majorities are formed is that many questions of public policy — including most of the questions which involve the distribution of burdens and benefits — intensely affect all interests. In this case, no representative is impartial by virtue of not being affected by the outcome of the legislation. Here, a third scenario arises in which representatives become arbiters. In cases which affect broad areas of interest, the representatives' job is to determine a just balance between the various interest in the absence of a formula or rule for making such decisions. Here, impartial coalitions can only be formed from 'mutual concession[s]' or 'equitable sacrifices to the general weal'.[118] Still, this willingness

[116] Thomas Jefferson to Monsieur D' Ivernois, 6 February 1795, *The Writings of Thomas Jefferson*, ed. Andrew A. Lipscomb (Washington, DC, 1905), IX, pp. 299–300.

[117] Murrin, 'Gordon S. Wood and the Search for Liberal America', p. 600. George Carey and Harold Schultz have reached somewhat similar interpretations. Carey speaks of a 'mediating' or 'impartial' group of representatives who have no 'immediate self-interest in the resolution of the issue at hand' and thus can decide the question on its merits. Carey, *The Federalist: Design for a Constitutional Republic*, pp. 38–42. Quotes are on pp. 39–40. Meanwhile, Schultz writes: 'A national Congress selected by the people, he [Madison] argued, would be more likely than a state legislature to represent numerous and varied interests. On any given issue the probability would therefore be greater that some of the legislators would be impartial. The impartial legislators, possessing a balance of power between self-seeking minorities, would determine the formation of each new majority by joining with whatever minority came nearest to the just position. Underlying his whole argument were the assumptions that legislators would vote according to the interests of their constituents without regard to justice for minorities and that legislators who represented constituencies having nothing to gain or lose from a given piece of legislation would be impartial in their judgments. The validity of his argument depended upon the universality of these assumptions.' Schultz, *James Madison*, p. 59.

[118] 'Speech of 9 April 1789', In Congress, *PJM*, XII, p. 70; *The Federalist*, No. 58, p. 397.

to equally bear the public burden and equally distribute the benefits of government is not promoted because representatives display 'heroic impartiality', but because all representatives are in an equal position within a legislative body in which there is a commitment to the collective interest. Within this scenario, representatives may advance the interests of their constituents. After all, these interests have a claim in relation to the public good. Nevertheless, even as they advance such claims, representatives retain an awareness that the public interest limits these claims. In general, public policies congruent with the common interest emerge from deliberations and mutual concessions.

An example of this kind of policy formation occurred in the debate on impost duties in the First Congress.[119] Madison and his colleagues realized that taxes could not be distributed impartially if they were laid on only one or even a few items. Obviously, if only one item were taxed, then the interests which were most directly concerned with this item would bear a disproportionate weight of the public burden. To alleviate this problem, Madison and his colleagues developed a 'system' of taxation which distributed the burden over a multiplicity of items, each of which concerned some interest.[120] Throughout the debate on impost duties, some representatives tried to prevent the interests that they represented from bearing any of the public burden. Still, Madison's admonitions against these representatives and the understanding by all representatives in the legislature that the public burden should be fairly distributed led to the passage of just legislation.

In a final scenario, which seemingly demands the greatest degree of independence and disinterestedness from representatives, one or a few interests might have to be advanced at the expense of the claims of other interests in order to advance the public good. But here, unlike the scenario in which representatives act as arbiters, representatives could not necessarily expect to have any of the demands of the interests they represented met. Here, impartiality would be measured as an attachment to the public good and would require that many representatives advance the claims of interests that were not in their district. Obviously, in legislation such as this majorities could only form when representatives shared a common understanding of the public good and were ready to sacrifice for it.

These possible ways that impartial majorities would be formed within Congress are of course not exhaustive. They are meant as hypothetical examples which suggest how disinterested or impartial majorities can form in the legislature in the absence of enlightened statesmen. This 'Madisonian' approach to the formation of impartial majorities should, in turn, be contrasted with the pluralist conception of the formation of 'moderate' legislative majorities through the bargaining of representatives and the coalescing of interests.[121] Furthermore, this discussion is not meant to suggest that

119 See especially 'Speech of 9 April 1789', In Congress, *PJM*, XII, pp. 69–74; and 'Speech of 28 April 1789', *ibid.*, pp. 118–19.

120 'Speech of 11 June 1788', In Virginia Ratifying Convention, *PJM*, XI, p. 113.

121 The pluralist theory of the formation of legislative majorities is anti-Madisonian on at least three points. First, the pluralist conception of coalition-building presupposes that representatives will act as agents or advocates for the interest groups dominant in their district. As I stress throughout the second section of

Madison was unaware of the tendencies of representatives and legislative bodies to act contrary to the public good. Madison never argued that extent of territory and a greater variety of interests would *guarantee* that legislation passed in the national councils would be just or concerned exclusively with the public good. Indeed, at times he was quite apprehensive that a local spirit would prevail in the national government.[122] Madison was also well aware of the tendencies of representatives to practice logrolling and to barter votes.[123] He argued only that this structure of government would have a 'salutary influence on the administration of the Government'.[124] An extended republic, in other words, would promote the formation of better public policies. It was not an elixir. If a majority of representatives bargained their votes, engaged in logrolling, or stubbornly clung to the interests of their constituents at the expense of the public good, then nothing would prevent unjust and partial legislation from being formed. But again these were precisely the kind of legislative practices that Madison's constitutional system was designed to prevent.

---

this essay, Madison opposed this conception of representation and designed his constitutional system to help prevent it. Second, pluralist theory rests on the concept of unintended effects — pluralists believe that competition between interest groups will be guided by an invisible hand. Ideally, according to pluralist theory, interest groups engage in a face to face struggle over scarce resources, but because no group has the political forces to win the contest, each group is forced to bargain and to compromise. Public policy is then formed which includes some of the demands of each group, but which does not reflect the exact intentions of any group. This policy, according to classic pluralist doctrine, should reflect an equilibrium between the interests. This equilibrium is considered the public interest. In contrast, Madison's writings suggest that he believed that individuals or interests can aggregate only when all parties pursue some common interest. Madison does not apply the invisible hand argument to the interaction of interests. Heterogeneous interests and groups are able to form coalitions only when they all make sacrifices to the national interest (which again is not the product of the interaction of interest groups). When groups pursue self-interested goals, the efforts of all groups are neutralized. In short, Madison's theory of coalition-building is based on the idea of counterpoise, not unintended effects. (See *The Federalist*, No. 58, p. 392; 'Speech of 28 June 1787', In Constitutional Convention, *PJM*, X, p. 80; 'Speech of 11 June 1787', In Virginia Ratifying Convention, *PJM*, XI, p. 115 for the logic underlying Madison's belief that competitive interests are neutralized but groups are able to combine when they pursue a common interest. Still, there are no explicit references to the formation of legislative majorities by coalition-building.) Third, Madison specifically rejected the idea that the public good could emerge from the conflict of rival interests and parties. In the Tenth *Federalist* he writes that the 'public good is disregarded in the conflicts of rival parties' (*The Federalist*, No. 10, p. 57). In 'Majority Governments', written in 1833, Madison argued that the public policies had been formed by compromising and bargaining in the state government during the crisis of republican governments in the mid-1780s. But this pernicious practice, Madison argued, was not as frequently practiced in the national councils under the new Constitution as it had been in the states. 'Majority Governments', *c.*1833, in *Mind of the Founder: Sources of the Political Thought of James Madison*, ed. Marvin Meyers (New York, 1973), p. 525. See also similar quotations by Alexander Hamilton in *The Federalist*, No. 75, p. 511; *The Federalist*, No. 77, p. 518.

122 See for example *The Federalist*, No. 46, pp. 318–19; *The Federalist*, No. 42, p. 283. See also Madison to Jefferson, 29 March 1789, *PJM*, XII, p. 38.

123 See Wood's discussion of the nature of legislative practices in the state legislatures during the mid-1780s and their effect on Madison. Wood, 'Interests and Disinterestedness', especially pp. 73–7.

124 *The Federalist*, No. 37, p. 238.

IV
The Madisonian Model: Impartial Representation, Popular Sovereignty and Liberal Republicanism

> The great desideratum in Government is, so to modify the sovereignty as that it may be sufficiently neutral between different parts of the Society to controul one part from invading the rights of another, and at the same time sufficiently controuled itself, from setting up an interest adverse to that of the entire Society. In absolute monarchies, the Prince may be tolerably neutral towards different classes of his subjects, but may sacrifice the happiness of all to his personal ambition or avarice. In small republics, the sovereign will is controuled from such a sacrifice of the entire Society, but is not sufficiently neutral towards the parts composing it. In the extended Republic of the United States, The General Government would hold a pretty even balance between the parties of particular States, and be at the same time sufficiently restrained by its dependence on the community, from betraying its general interest.[125]

In the final section of this essay I address broader questions raised by the 'impartial representation' or 'disinterested umpire' interpretation of the Tenth *Federalist* Paper. This can perhaps best be done by first showing how the adoption of this interpretation is closely associated with a broader reinterpretation of the historical background and theoretical foundations of the constitutional system developed by Madison and his Federalist colleagues. Once I have recounted our understanding of the Madisonian model, I will then turn my attention to two closely related and equally perennial questions which surround scholarship on the Tenth *Federalist* Paper. First I will address the question, how democratic was the constitutional system developed by Madison and his colleagues? Second I will ask, should Madison's theory of an extended republic be thought of as a species of liberalism or republicanism?

Briefly, the effect of the last twenty-five years of scholarship on the political thought of the Framers has been to gradually (and in some cases incompletely) replace the pluralist interpretation of the Madisonian model with a reading that suggests that the principal goal of Madison and his colleagues was the reconciliation of popular sovereignty and impartial or disinterested administration.[126] This problem was pressed upon Madison and other Federalists by the necessity of controlling what

[125] Madison to Jefferson, 24 October 1787, *PJM*, X, p. 214.

[126] The interpretation of Madison's understanding of representation, separation of powers, and checks and balances that I present in this section can be traced to Gordon Wood's magisterial study, *The Creation of the American Republic*, especially pp. 344–564, 593–615. *The Creation of the American Republic*, however, can and has been read as presenting a pluralist reading of the 'Federalist Persuasion'. (See Wood, *Creation of the American Republic*, pp. 605–6; and J.G.A. Pocock, 'Virtue and Commerce in the Eighteenth Century', *The Journal of Interdisciplinary History*, III (1972), pp. 126–8.) Nevertheless, Wood removed any ambiguity he had left in *The Creation of the American Republic* with his essay 'Interests and Disinterestedness', especially pp. 83–93. This essay clearly contrasts the Federalists' efforts to establish the national government as a disinterested umpire with modern interest group liberalism. Other studies have either consciously or unconsciously built upon and modified Wood's theses. These include Rakove, 'The Madisonian Moment', pp. 473–505; Wills, 'Introduction', pp. vii–xxiv; Wills, *Explaining*

they believed to be an excessive wave of democratization that had taken place in the state legislatures during the mid-1780s *without* violating the Revolutionary principles that the people are sovereign and that governments are founded and rest on their consent. More specifically, the history of British rule had taught the colonists that monarchies or Parliamentary governments administered by 'virtual' representatives rarely ensured a fidelity to the interests of the people. Instead, as events from the Sugar and Stamp Acts to the Coercive Act seemed to verify, such governments inevitably violated the rights of their subjects and set up 'an interest adverse to that of the entire Society'.[127] The principal guarantee against such violations of individual rights and the general interest by rulers became the institutionalization of government by the direct consent of the governed. Following independence, Americans therefore established state governments which minimized the role of the executive branch and lodged power principally in the legislative branch. They also increased the number of representatives and provided for annual elections, used petitions and instructions to insure the direct accountability of representatives, minimized suffrage and office-holding requirements, and established residency requirements for representatives. In short, they moved to institutionalize legislative supremacy and localistic conceptions of representation.[128]

As Gordon Wood has so masterfully shown,[129] by the mid-1780s Madison and his future Federalist allies perceived that the direction of despotism had been reversed. The democratic excesses of the state administrations had led Madison and other Federalists to argue that a commitment to the rule of law, the protection of individual rights, and the promotion of the public interest could not be achieved by rule by popular majorities within a small geographic area. In 'Vices of the Political System of the United States', Madison decried the multiplicity, mutability, and especially the injustices, of the state laws. These 'vices', he argued, brought into question 'the fundamental principle of republican Government, that the majority who rule in such

America; Morgan, *Inventing the People*, pp. 267–82; J.G.A. Pocock, *The Machiavellian Moment: Florentine Political Thought and the Atlantic Republican Tradition* (Princeton, 1975), pp. 519–24. I consider the interpretation that I present in this essay as a refinement of this interpretation of the Madisonian Model. Whereas Wood, Wills and others have linked the idea of disinterested representation to the election of élite representatives from expanded electoral districts, I have argued that Madison's principal concern was to use the barriers established by extent of territory to purge the national councils as much as possible of faction. This, in turn, would help ensure that decisions were made by impartial or disinterested majorities.

127 Madison to Jefferson, 24 October 1787, *PJM*, X, p. 214.

128 Aspects of this interpretation of the historical background behind Madison's theory of an extended republic can be found in Wood, *Creation of the American Republic*; Morgan, *Inventing the People*, pp. 239–67, and Donald Lutz, 'The Theory of Consent in the Early State Constitutions', *Publius,* XI (1979), pp. 11–42; Yarbrough, 'Representation and Republicanism: Two Views', pp. 77–98.

129 Wood, *Creation of the American Republic*, pp. 396–425. See also Wood, 'Democracy and the Constitution', in *How Democratic Is the Constitution?*, ed. Robert A. Goldwin and William Schambra (Washington, DC, 1982), pp. 7–10.

Governments, are the safest Guardians both of public Good and of private rights'.[130] Rule by interested popular majorities, Madison argued, only re-established 'under another name and a more spec[i]ous form, force as the measure of right'.[131] Indeed, as Professor Wood has taught us, Madison and many of his Federalist colleagues rethought the entire question of the relationship of power and liberty. No longer was it believed that licentiousness among the people would lead to anarchy or that the danger to liberty sprang from independent acts of the rulers. Instead, in the American context the problem became popular despotism in which the rights and interests of minorities and individuals were sacrificed to the majority.[132] 'Wherever the real power in a Government lies', Madison wrote, 'there is the danger of oppression. In our Government the real power lies in the majority of the Community, and the invasion of private rights is *cheify* [sic] to be apprehended, not from acts of Government contrary to the sense of its constituents, but from acts in which the Government is the mere instrument of the major number of the constituents'.[133]

By 1787, then, the essential goal for Madison and his Federalist colleagues — his 'Great Desideratum' — became to reconcile popular sovereignty and majority rule (which would prevent rulers from establishing an interest independent of the society) with the impartial protection of the rights of individuals and minorities and the disinterested promotion of the public good (the ends of government which had been violated in the state governments during the mid-1780s).[134] Towards this end, the Federalists' developed a system of constitutionalism in which each branch of the national government was elected either directly or indirectly by the people, and therefore could be defended as an emanation from the fountain of popular sovereignty.[135] Madison and his colleagues then argued that expanded electoral districts, indirect elections, extent of territory, separation of powers, the system of checks and balances, a strong and independent Executive and Senate, and judicial review would provide protection of individual rights and help reconcile temporary and partial manifestations of the public will with the permanent and aggregate interests of the community.

More precisely, in the system of constitutionalism that Madison and James Wilson, in particular, developed and refined over the course of the Philadelphia Convention, indirect elections and the election of representatives from expanded electoral districts were designed to promote the election of disinterested representatives and to purge local bias from the legislature. Extent of territory established obstacles to the

[130] 'Vices of the Political System of the United States', *PJM*, IX, pp. 353–7. Quote is on p. 354.

[131] Madison to Monroe, 5 October 1786, *PJM*, IX, p. 141.

[132] Wood, *Creation of the American Republic*, pp. 409–13.

[133] Madison to Jefferson, 17 October 1788, *PJM*, XI, p. 299.

[134] This goal is brought out especially well in Madison's statements about 'the Great Desideratum' in the 24 October 1787 letter to Jefferson, *PJM*, X, p. 214 and 'Vices of the Political System of the United States', *PJM*, IX, p. 357.

[135] See especially *The Federalist*, No. 39, pp. 251–3.

formation of factious popular majorities and their reflection into the legislature. This helped to ensure that legislative majorities were qualitatively different from the popular majorities that might form or be present in the society at any given moment, and that would almost certainly gain control of the legislature in a small republic. Furthermore, the teachings of mixed government were no longer conflated with the doctrines of checks and balances and separation of powers. Instead, the system of checks and balances was based on the reality of legislative supremacy.[136] In part as a result of their experiences in the state governments during the mid-1780s and in part because their understanding of the nature of republican governments, Madison and his allies viewed the House of Representatives as passionate, powerful and ever encroaching.[137] The qualified executive veto, life tenure for judges, and especially bicameralism, were therefore necessary as defensive powers which would prevent the House from encroaching on the weaker branches.

Finally, American society could not accurately be described as divided between the people, the aristocrats, and the monarch. The American people were better thought of as belonging to a single social order and divided among themselves into a multiplicity of factions or interests groups. It therefore also made no sense to apply the teachings of mixed government to the Constitution and design the system of separation of powers so that the branches of government incorporated distinct social orders and performed the function for which they were believed to be peculiarly qualified. The Federalists, in other words, did not conceive of the House of Representatives as the sole representative of the people; they did not structure the Senate to represent either property or the aristocratic element of the society; nor was the President equated with the British monarch. Instead, each branch of the government spoke for the interest of the whole people, and the system of separation of powers was built upon the principle of functional distribution of powers among the branches and had the primary goal of efficient administration.[138] For example, since Senators served six-year terms, the Senate provided stability and had an institutional memory that made it qualified to participate in the conducting of foreign affairs through the negotiation of treaties and the selection of ambassadors. As the embodiment of unity and responsibility, the President provided energy, secrecy and dispatch to the government, and was therefore qualified to execute and administer the laws. The

[136] See especially Wills, 'Introduction', pp. xv–xvi; and Wills, *Explaining America*, pp. 117–25; Ann Stuart Diamond, 'The Zenith of Separation of Powers Theory: The Federal Convention of 1787', *Publius*, VIII (1978), pp. 45–70; Judith A. Best, 'Legislative Tyranny and the Liberation of the Executive: A View From the Founding', *Presidential Studies Quarterly*, XVII (1987), pp. 697–709.

[137] 'Speech of 17 July 1787', In Constitutional Convention, *Notes of Debates in the Federal Convention*, pp. 312–13; *The Federalist*, No. 48, pp. 333–4; *The Federalist*, No. 51, p. 350; Wood, *Creation of the American Republic*, pp. 403–9.

[138] Stuart Diamond, 'The Zenith of Separation of Powers', pp. 45–70; Wood, *The Creation of the American Republic*, pp. 446–63; Wills, 'Introduction', pp. xvi–xviii; Wills, *Explaining America*, pp. 97–116; Louis Fisher, 'The Efficiency Side of Separated Powers', *Journal of American Studies*, V (1971), pp. 113–31.

judiciary was best qualified by virtue of its insulation from popular passions to expound and interpret the laws.

Was this 'unmixed and extensive'[139] republican government democratic? The best way to address this question is to compare and contrast the Madisonian model with several standard models or conceptions of democracy, and simultaneously to try to get at what Madison and other Federalists meant by 'popular sovereignty' or 'the sovereignty of the people'. Once this is done, it becomes clear that Madison and his Federalist colleagues did not accept the models of democracy developed by the ancients or the model developed by radical English Whigs and continued in the thought of many Anti-federalists. Nor can Madison and his Federalist allies properly be considered either populists or pluralists. Madison of course explicitly differentiated his system of representative republicanism from the classical conception of a 'pure democracy' 'consisting of a small number of citizens, who assemble and administer the government in person'. This form of government, he noted in *The Federalist*, No. 10, offered no cure for the mischiefs of faction.[140] Thus, the people were totally excluded in their collective capacity from governing in the American republic.[141] Unlike radical English Whigs and the Anti-federalists, Madison and other Federalists fought against constitutional reforms which were designed to tie representatives directly to their constituents. More specifically, they fought against annual elections, unduly increasing the number of representatives, and binding representatives to the instructions and petitions of their constituents.[142] Unlike populists, Madison and his colleagues sought to minimize rule by popular majorities which, they believed, were most often tyrannical and irrational. Finally, unlike pluralists, Madison hoped to prevent the penetration of interests into Congress and to ensure the election of representatives who were disinterested statesmen, not mere brokers for their constituents' views and interests. Furthermore, Madison and his Federalist colleagues did not believe that the public good would emerge from the compromising and bargaining of representatives in Congress, but would be ensured only through the conscious adoption of specific policies.

Actually, the Madisonian model is best characterized as a form of representative republicanism resting on the sovereignty of the people. But far from being congruent with either participatory democracy or pluralism, the concept of popular sovereignty was coupled with a cosmopolitan and disinterested conception of representation by Madison and his colleagues and used to prevent the development of participatory schemes of democracy (such as those that had developed in the state governments during the mid-1780s) and interest-based forms of representation. More specifically, Madison and his allies defined popular sovereignty as the belief that all power was

[139] *The Federalist*, No. 14, p. 84.

[140] *The Federalist*, No. 10, p. 61.

[141] *The Federalist*, No. 63, p. 428.

[142] For Madison's opposition to annual elections see *The Federalist*, No. 52, pp. 355–9; *The Federalist*, No. 53, pp. 359–66; Madison's position on the number of representatives necessary can be found in *The Federalist*, No. 55, pp. 372–8; and *The Federalist*, No. 58, p. 396; For Madison's opposition to the instruction of representatives see note 58, above.

derived from and ultimately rested in the people.[143] They then used this concept as the cornerstone for a series of closely related arguments. First, the Federalists argued the people could at any time alter or abolish and replace any government under which they lived. This 'vital' or 'revolutionary' principle[144] (as James Wilson called it) provided justification for the Federalists' radical decision to abandon the Articles of Confederation. As Madison noted in the Convention, 'the people were in fact the fountain of all power, and by resorting to them, all difficulties (concerning the authority to dissolve the existing Confederation) were got over'.[145] Second, Madison and other Federalists defined 'the people' as the people of the whole United States and argued that they formed a unitary sovereign. They thus simultaneously rejected the idea that sovereignty rested in any branch of the government or in the state governments. These points set up the defence (which I have outlined above) of the government established under the Constitution as an emanation of popular sovereignty and in turn allowed the Federalists to defend the Constitution as 'strictly republican', 'wholly popular', and thus congruent with the principles of the Revolution.[146] The system of direct and indirect elections also allowed the Federalists to establish a direct relationship between the national government and the citizenry without the intervention of the state legislatures. This helped to give the national government the authority and broad base of support it needed to counteract the power and influence of the state governments. As Edmund Morgan has said, Madison invented 'a sovereign American people to overcome the sovereign states'.[147] Third, the Federalists' decisions to transfer substantial powers to the national government and to define 'the people' as the people of the whole United States had the practical effect of reducing the influence of popular majorities in the formation of public policies. To have an effect, popular majorities now had to be national majorities. They thus had to overcome some of the obstacles established by the extended

143 Perhaps the clearest version of the Federalist's conception of popular sovereignty was given in an amendment that Madison proposed in the initial version of the Bill of Rights but was later rejected. This amendment read: 'That all power is originally vested in, and consequently derived from the people. That government is instituted, and ought to be exercised for the benefit of the people; which consists in the enjoyment of life and liberty, with the right of acquiring and using property, and generally of pursuing and obtaining happiness and safety. That the people have an indubitable, unalienable, and indefeasible right to reform or change their government, whenever it be found adverse or inadequate to the purposes of its institution.' 'Amendments to the Constitution', 8 June 1789, *PJM*, XII, p. 200.

144 James Wilson, *An Introductory Lecture to a Course of Law Lectures* (Philadelphia, 1791), pp. 31–6. Quotes are on pp. 31, 36. See also Garry Wills, 'James Wilson's New Meaning for Sovereignty', in *Conceptual Change and the Constitution*, ed. Ball and Pocock, pp. 99–106.

145 'Speech of 31 August 1787', In Constitutional Convention, *Notes of Debates in the Federal Convention*, p. 564.

146 Quotes are from *The Federalist*, No. 14, p. 84; and *The Federalist*, No. 39, p. 250.

147 Morgan, *Inventing the People*, pp. 267–77. Quote is on p. 267. See also Joshua Miller, 'The Ghostly Body Politic: *The Federalist* Papers and Popular Sovereignty', *Political Theory*, XVI (1988), pp. 99–119.

republic.[148] Fourth, for Madison and many of his colleagues the concept of the sovereignty of the people was inseparably wed to the concepts of constitutionalism and representation, and thus ironically also to the series of methods and institutional devices which channelled and checked the will of the people.[149] The Federalists, in other words, ask the people to accept restrictions on their own power. As Garry Wills has argued, this argument sprang from the eighteenth-century axioms that a legitimate sovereign, as opposed to a tyrant, accepted limitations on his rule and did not act as a judge in his own cause. In the United States the people were sovereign. In order to rule legitimately they therefore had to accept separation of powers as a method of preventing popular tyranny and representation as a means of ensuring just arbitration of popular disputes.[150] In short, the concept of popular sovereignty, which had been used by the colonists during the Revolution as a justification for opposition to England and for the formation of participatory democracies in the states, became in the hands of Madison and the Federalists a basis for the formation of a truly national government which lodged ultimate control in the people but greatly reduced the role of popular majorities. If democracy is defined as the immediate participation of the citizenry in the formation of public policies, then the Federalists were not democratic.

The final question that I want to address in this essay is whether Madison's theory of an extended republic points towards an understanding of his political philosophy as a species of liberalism or republicanism. Clearly, the interpretation that I have advanced shows that this question — and thus the approach taken in much of the scholarship on the political thought of the Framers over the last twenty years — rests on a false opposition. As several scholars are now beginning to observe,[151] such an interpretation 'assumes a sharp dichotomy between two clearly identifiable traditions that eighteenth-century reality will not support'.[152] The Federalists in particular simply did not believe that they were choosing between liberalism and republicanism. Instead, the 'Madisonian Model' or 'Federalist Persuasion' was built by combining contractual and natural rights arguments about the origins and legitimate ends of

[148] Miller, 'The Ghostly Body Politic', pp. 99–119, makes this point forcefully.

[149] Madison made this point explicitly in the First Federal Congress when an amendment was proposed which allowed constituents to bind their representatives with instructions. 'My idea of the sovereignty of the people', Madison argued, 'is that the people can change the Constitution if they please, but while the Constitution exists, they must conform themselves to its dictates'. 'Amendments to the Constitution', In Congress, 15 August 1789, *PJM*, XII, p. 341.

[150] Wills, 'Introduction', pp. xvii, xxi; Wills, *Explaining America*, pp. 179–247, especially pp. 213–15. See also Wills, 'Taking Ourselves Out of a Fight', *WMQ*, XLIV (1987), pp. 625–6.

[151] Wood, 'Ideology and the Origins of Liberal America', *WMQ*, XLIV (1987), p. 634; Ketcham, 'Publius: Sustaining the Republican Principle', pp. 579–82; Lance Banning, 'Jeffersonian Ideology Revisited: Liberal and Classical Ideas in the New American Republic', *WMQ*, XLII (1986), pp. 11–19; Robert Shalhope, *The Roots of Democracy: American Thought and Culture, 1760–1800* (Boston, 1990), especially pp. xi–xii; Jean Yarbrough, 'Republicanism Reconsidered: Some Thoughts on the Foundation and Preservation of the American Republic', *Review of Politics*, XLI (1979), pp. 61–95; Sunstein, 'Beyond the Republican Revival', especially p. 1541, pp. 1547–58. I borrow the phrase 'liberal republicanism' from Sunstein.

[152] Wood, 'Ideology and the Origins of Liberal America', p. 634.

government with a republican commitment to disinterested representation and a substantive conception of the public good. Specifically, Madison's theory of an extended republic should be thought of as a constructive synthesis of liberal and republican ideas, of modern and premodern thought.

On the one hand, Madison argued that factions were unavoidable in free and civilized governments, and thus rejected the classical belief that they should somehow be suppressed. He also maintained that this unavoidable diversity could have positive effects — it could promote social stability and provide protection for individual rights.[153] Furthermore, in the Tenth *Federalist* Paper, Madison called the protection of the faculties of acquiring property the first object of government[154] — a statement which has long been read to show the strain of natural rights liberalism in his thought.[155] Finally, as many commentators have noted, Madison completely inverted the classical definition of a republic and revealed his distance from the ancients' understanding of the importance of political participation when he suggested that a republic was a form of government in which a scheme of representation takes place and in which the people do *not* 'meet and exercise the government in person'.[156] On these points and others, scholars have clearly been correct to see the Tenth *Federalist* Paper as a harbinger of modern, liberal political theory.

On the other hand, on several essential points the Tenth *Federalist* Paper remains a republican document. First, Madison's acceptance of the inevitability of faction was hardly a glorification or justification of self interest either in the citizenry or their representatives. As Lance Banning has recently observed, even as Madison argued that faction and self-interestedness were unavoidable products of liberty and human nature, he also continued to maintain that virtue was the foundation of republics and that the American people possessed enough virtue to maintain a republican form of government.[157] The reconciliation of these seemingly contradictory statements comes through a more subtle understanding of what Madison and other Framers meant by their insistence on the necessity of virtue than has been presented in much of the existing scholarship on the Framers. They did not, Banning correctly asserts, unrealistically expect citizens to voluntarily and totally surrender their interests to an abstracted public good. Such an act would not have been an act of virtue but one of self-abnegation. Instead, the Framers began with the supposition that citizens would, and indeed should, try to advance their interests. They however also expected individuals to remain conscious of the interests of others, to be obedient to laws and decisions that were made collectively, and to hold a proper degree of deference for leaders. Simultaneously, the Federalists hoped to use representation,

153 *The Federalist*, No. 51, pp. 351–2.

154 *The Federalist*, No. 10, p. 58.

155 For an excellent analysis of this component of Madison's thought see Jack Rakove, 'The Madisonian Theory of Rights', *William and Mary Law Review*, XXXI (1990), pp. 245–66.

156 *The Federalist*, No. 10, pp. 63–4; *The Federalist*, No. 14, p. 84.

157 See especially 'Speech of 20 June 1788', In Virginia Ratifying Convention, *PJM*, XI, p. 163. See also *The Federalist*, No. 55, p. 378.

governmental mechanisms and economic reform to help minimize overly aggressive acts of self-interest and reconcile them to the broader common interest.[158]

Beyond this, Madison's conception of disinterested representation and his understanding of the public good as the 'permanent and aggregate interests'[159] of the community were also distinctly republican. Madison, in other words, did not leap from the belief that self-interestedness was inevitable to the modern, liberal axioms that the public good was a residue that would somehow emerge from the uncertain combinations of individuals or interest groups. Instead, Madison's hard-headed realization that factions were inevitable was parallelled by an equally hard-headed belief that the public good was an independent entity (beyond the aggregation of individual preferences) which could only be realized if it were consciously promoted by government through its representatives.[160] Thus, Madison still expected 'disinterestedness' from political leaders and still defined the promotion of the public good as one of the chief ends of government.

In general, then, Madison's political thought was highly synthetic. One strain of his political philosophy focused on the inevitability of self-interest and the necessity of having government serve as an impartial guardian of individual rights; a second strain, however, included republican commitments to disinterested representation and the promotion of the public good as an end of government.[161] In the first instance, Madison's goals parallelled those of Locke, Kant and later liberals such as John Rawls. But unlike these liberal theorists, Madison's conception of impartiality was not a means of avoiding decisions about the public good. His conception of impartiality was pregnant with the republican idea of 'disinterestedness', of decisions made by public officials based on a substantive understanding of the public good. The agenda for Madison scholars is to ferret out the tensions, relationships and resolutions that exist in this synthesis.

Alan Gibson UNIVERSITY OF NOTRE DAME

[158] Banning, 'Some Second Thoughts on Virtue', pp. 194–212. See also Yarbrough, 'Republicanism Reconsidered', pp. 61–95. These essays serve as excellent modifications of the discussions of the transformation of virtue from the Revolution to the Constitutional Convention presented by Wood in *Creation of the American Republic* and by John Agresto in 'Liberty, Virtue, and Republicanism, 1776–87', *The Review of Politics*, XXXIX (1977), pp. 473–504.

[159] *The Federalist*, No. 10, p. 57.

[160] This point is made particularly well by Ralph Ketcham in 'Publius: Sustaining the Republican Principle', pp. 578–82.

[161] In his writings, Madison consistently identified two ends of government: the protection of private rights and the promotion of the public good. As their juxtaposition suggests, neither of these ends was reducible to the other.

Part IV
Republican or Democrat?

[9]

THE REPUBLICANISM OF JAMES MADISON

Neal Riemer

BECAUSE modern scholarship has not yet assimilated the brilliant work of certain recent students of James Madison he remains one of the least understood of major American political thinkers.[1] The frequently distorted picture of his political philosophy as a whole is not attributable to total neglect but rather to a myopic preoccupation with certain aspects of his thought at the expense of his dominant republican ideology.

This article emphasizes an extremely important but usually ignored or minimized component of Madison's political thought—that relating to the anti- and pseudo-republican danger. In it I will try to correct the undue concentration on Madison's criticism of republican vices and the Confederation's "mortal diseases"; the partial misunderstanding of his "puzzling shift" from Federalism to Republicanism; and the misreading of his alleged states' rights philosophy. I will seek to demonstrate that, if Madison's dominant republican orientation and his life-long recognition of the dangers of anti- and pseudo-republicanism are brought into clearer perspective, any basic inconsistency between his Federalism and his Republicanism disappears. I will attempt to make clear that his early effort to strengthen and invigorate the powers of the central government, his later fight against some of the leading features of the Federalist program, and his still later—and much neglected—opposition to the doctrines of nullification and secession appear as parts of a common and conscious endeavor to establish and maintain

[1] See especially the works of Irving Brant: *James Madison: The Virginia Revolutionist* (New York, 1941); *James Madison: The Nationalist* (New York, 1948); *James Madison: Father of the Constitution* (New York, 1950); *James Madison: Secretary of State* (New York, 1953); "James Madison and His Times", *American Historical Review*, LVII (July 1952), 853–870. See also Douglass Adair, "The Intellectual Origins of Jeffersonian Democracy", unpublished doctoral dissertation (Yale, 1943); *id.*, "The Authorship of the Disputed Federalist Papers", *William and Mary Quarterly*, 3d. ser., I (April and July 1944), 97–122, 235–264; and *id.*, "The Tenth Federalist Revisited", *ibid.*, 3d. ser., VIII (January 1951), 48–67; Adrienne Koch, *Jefferson and Madison: The Great Collaboration* (New York, 1950); Edward McNall Burns, *James Madison: Philosopher of the Constitution* (New Brunswick, 1938); and Abbot E. Smith, *James Madison: Builder* (New York, 1937)

republican government in a federal state. I will indicate some plausible grounds for calling Madison "The Philosopher of Jeffersonian Democracy" (if anyone can be so called). And, finally, I will suggest another—a fuller—sense in which Madison should be viewed as Father of our republican Federal Union.

I

For Madison[2] a republic was a government which derived "all its powers directly or indirectly from the great body of the people" and which rested "on the capacity of mankind for self-government."[3] In republican theory, if not always in republican practice, it was "politic as well as just that the interests and rights of every class should be duly represented and understood in the public Councils."[4] It was also a fundamental republican principle "that men can not be justly bound by laws in making which they have no part."[5] A republican government was one which was "administered by persons holding their offices during pleasure, for a limited period, or during good behavior."[6] Even during this "short duration of their appointments" to government "the trust should be placed not in a few, but [in] a number of hands."[7]

The "fundamental" and "vital" principle of such republican government was "*lex majoris partis*, the will of the majority";[8] and the "majority who rule in such governments" were regarded

[2] The most complete edition of Madison to this date is *The Writings of James Madison*, edited by Gaillard Hunt (New York, 1900–1910). This edition, hereinafter cited as Hunt, is by no means complete and should be supplemented by *Letters and Other Writings of James Madison* (hereinafter cited as Cong. Ed.) (Philadelphia, editions in 1865 and 1884); *The Papers of James Madison* edited by H. D. Gilpin (1840); *The Federalist;* pertinent volumes of E. C. Burnett's *Letters of Members of the Continental Congress;* Henry Adams' edition of *The Writings of Albert Gallatin* (Philadelphia, 1879); and material recently reprinted in the *William and Mary Quarterly.*

[3] *The Federalist*, No. 39, p. 243. All page references are to the Modern Library Edition.

[4] *The Debates in the Federal Convention of 1787*, edited by Gaillard Hunt and J. B. Scott (New York, 1920), p. 329 (hereinafter referred to as *Debates*).

[5] *Ibid.*, p. 619, note 1.

[6] *The Federalist*, No. 39, pp. 243–244.

[7] *Ibid.*, No. 37, p. 227.

[8] Hunt, IX, 528, probably unsent letter on "Majority Governments", 1833.

as "the safest Guardians both of public Good and private rights."[9] Such majority rule, however, must be reasonable and just; the government was not to be one of unlimited power. It was instituted to secure "life and liberty, with the right of acquiring and using property, and generally of pursuing and obtaining happiness and safety." Whenever the government should be "found adverse or inadequate to the purposes of its institution" the people had "an indubitable, unalienable, and indefeasible right to reform or change" it.[10]

Much of this general republican philosophy sounds like familiar echoes of the Declaration of Independence, of the Virginia Bill of Rights, of John Locke, of the English Bill of Rights of 1689, and of James Harrington. This observation, however, is less important than the recognition that Madison's deep and abiding commitment to republican government ensured that he would devote his energies to adapting the traditional republican house to fit the unique American scene: a comparatively huge geographic entity, newly arrived at independence, organized as a confederation, with its political components—the states—exercising substantial sovereignty. He would so devote his energies despite grave problems and sore trials that might well have altered the orientation of a weaker or a more ambitious man, a more pliant or a more dictatorial man, a more faithless or a more dogmatic man.

II

As Madison analyzed the situation, four interconnected problems confronted those who would help establish and maintain sound republican government in America. These were: (1) the potent forces of disunion inherent in the jealously "sovereign" thirteen states;[11] (2) the self-destructive features of republican government itself, either at the state level or in the government

[9] Hunt, II, 366, "Vices of the Political System of the United States", April 1787.

[10] Hunt, V, 376–377, "Amendments to the Constitution", June 8, 1787.

[11] In general, see Hunt, II, 361–369, "Vices . . ."; *The Federalist*, Nos. 18, 19, and 20; Madison's letters to Jefferson (March 18), Randolph (April 8), and Washington (April 16) on the eve of the Convention, Hunt, II, 326–328, 337–340, 344–349.

of the Union;[12] (3) the potentially dangerous remnant of anti- or pseudo-republicans, hostile in theory and disaffected in practice to republican government. Tying these three problems together was (4) the geographic size of America, which discouraged most other advocates of a more perfect republican union and encouraged both the centrifugal forces of confederation and the centripetal forces of consolidation.[13] To keep the record clear one should note, parenthetically, that Madison was to turn the supposed vices of a large state into the redeeming virtues of an extensive republic. This paper, without losing sight of the close connection of these four problems with each other, will deal chiefly with the third.

Madison was well aware that no republican government could claim political immortality. Degeneration was a disease inherent in all governments and a republic was not immune. Government was dynamic; and movement was not necessarily upward, ever onward toward a republican utopia. Anti- and pseudo-republican forces existed, constantly exerted their pressures, made their appeals; they would exploit republican degeneration—in terms of weakness, inefficiency, abuse of power, lack of vigilance—and would bid for and wield power whenever possible. Consequently, those who would both establish and maintain a republican government must make it just, stable and popular, and its people alert.

Madison's hatred of anti- and pseudo-republicanism was as natural as his first conscious (or, indeed, unconscious) and perhaps overzealous thought and action in the turmoil of the Revolution.[14] Certain of his basic premises were eloquently stated as early as 1785, in his protest against a Virginia bill requiring payments by all for the support of Christian religion. The danger here was that the dominant legislative majority would

[12] See, for example, Madison's essay on the "Vices . . .", *loc. cit.*; his famous speech on the floor of the Convention, June 6, in *Debates*, pp. 64–65; *The Federalist*, No. 10, No. 51, p. 337, No. 49, p. 329, No. 55, p. 361; his speech in the Virginia Constitutional Convention, December 2, 1829, Hunt, IX, 358–364.

[13] See, in particular, *The Federalist*, No. 14, p. 80; and "Majority Governments", Hunt, IX, 520–528 (1833).

[14] In general, see Brant, *James Madison: The Virginia Revolutionist;* in particular, see Madison's youthful letters to William Bradford in *ibid.* and in Hunt, I, 18–21, 22–25.

not respect the republican principle of religious liberty (as Madison understood that concept) as an unalienable right. In his *Memorial and Remonstrance Against Religious Assessments,* Madison's sense of the danger might have seemed exaggerated, but the episode illustrates excellently his typical reaction to anti-republican danger. The republican principle of the unalienable right to religious liberty must be maintained lest all our precious rights become insecure. If the legislature were permitted to exercise this power, the legislature might not stop with this violation. Indeed, the legislature might transform itself into "an independent and hereditary assembly."[15]

Actually, however, Madison's rôle as Republican Savior had been adumbrated even before his famous *Memorial and Remonstrance.* As early as 1780, in the midst of the Revolution, he had noted that a weak financial structure endangered the success both of the Revolution and of republican government. A weak financial structure weakened faith in the effectiveness of republican institutions and thus played into the hands of their enemies and false friends.

> One or two millions of guineas, properly applied, would diffuse vigor and satisfaction throughout the whole military departments, and would expel the enemy from every part of the United States. It would also have another good effect. It would reconcile the army and everybody else to our republican forms of government; the principal inconveniences which are imputed to them being really the fruit of defective revenues.[16]

Here in 1780 is the germ of one of Madison's central political themes, expressed in the Congress of the Confederation, enunciated on the eve of the Constitutional Convention, treated on the floor of the Convention, in *The Federalist* and in the Virginia ratifying Convention, *and repeated over and over again throughout Madison's whole life:* that anti-republican and pseudo-republican "innovations" might be "intruded" unless the government were organized in a just, efficient, stable way. Thus the republican experiment would be imperiled—imperiled by those forces that overtly or covertly sought a different brand of government.

[15] Hunt, II, 191, "Memorial and Remonstrance Against Religious Assessments" 1785.

[16] Hunt, I, 93.

Because of the real danger that such men posed for the establishment and maintenance of the Republic, the Union must be so organized as to blunt their criticism. This is the major factor explaining Madison's valiant efforts to strengthen and invigorate the powers of the central government.

On the eve of the Convention he wrote: "The mortal diseases of the existing Constitution [of the Confederation] have tainted the faith of the most orthodox republicans, [and] challenge from the votaries of liberty every concession in favor of stable Government not infringing fundamental principles, as the only security against an opposite extreme of our present situation."[17]

Read out of context the foregoing might perhaps be construed as a pseudo-republican plea for concessions. But the genuineness of Madison's concern is indicated by the following remarks on the floor of the Convention:

> What we wished was to give to the Government that stability which was everywhere called for, and which the Enemies of the Republican form alledged to be inconsistent with its nature . . . . He [Madison was writing of himself in the third person] conceived it to be of great importance that a stable and firm Government organized in the republican form should be held out to the people. If this be not done, and the people be left to judge of this species of Government by the operation of the defective systems under which they now live, it is much to be feared the time is not distant when, in universal disgust, they will renounce the blessing which they have purchased at so dear a rate, and be ready for any change that may be proposed to them.[18]

In this connection one should reread the first paragraph of the Tenth *Federalist* where Madison explicitly indicates his anxiety over "the favorite and fruitful topics from which the adversaries to liberty derive their most specious declamations." Overemphasis on Number 10, as a pre-Marxist or semi-Marxist explanation of the anti-democratic, anti-majoritarian motives of the Constitutional Fathers, has tended to make many observers—erroneously I believe—view Madison's genuine concern with the "adversaries of liberty" and "a republican remedy" as clever rationalization by a frightened conservative which should

[17] Hunt, II, 326.

[18] *Debates*, pp. 95–96.

not fool the penetrating critic long emancipated from patriotic historicism.

Finally, a statement in 1821 makes Madison's intention unmistakable:

> Such indeed was the aspect of things that in the eyes of all the best friends of liberty a crisis had arrived which was to decide whether the American Experiment was to be a blessing to the world, or to blast forever the hopes which the republican cause had inspired; and what is not to be overlooked, the disposition to give to a new system all the vigour consistent with Republican principles, was not a little stimulated by a backwardness in some quarters towards a Convention for the purpose [of invigorating a genuinely republican system], which [backwardness] was ascribed to a secret dislike to popular Government and a hope that delay would bring it more into disgrace, and pave the way for a form of Government more congenial with Monarchical or Aristocratical Predilections.[19]

Because, then, of Madison's awareness of the existence, leanings, and potential strength of anti-republican forces, he sought to forestall an anticipated reaction by establishing a more nearly perfect Union. If his fears of the anti- and pseudo-republicans did not, at the time of the writing and adoption of the Constitution, bulk as large in his utterances as his jeremiads against disunion and faction, it was perhaps because the latter were more immediately real and more immediately threatening. But not for a single moment did Madison lose sight of the fact that disunion, faction, and a comparatively large geographical area provided ammunition to the enemies and false friends of the republican experiment and strengthened their case against it.

With the adoption of the Constitution, the pressing dangers of disunion and faction, inherent largely in the injustice of state action, seem to have been faced and at least momentarily overcome. But other dangers had not been overcome, as Madison, appraising key aspects of the Federalist program, keenly perceived. Before the adoption of the Constitution, Madison had sought to forestall an anticipated reaction against republican government by establishing a more nearly perfect Union. Now he had to contend with the worst possible threat: the *actual*

[19] Hunt, IX, 72–73.

effectuation of a factional program by what he deemed an anti-republican party!

This party arose, Madison contended, with the "regular and effectual establishment of the federal government in 1788." It consisted of "those, who . . . are more partial to the opulent than to the other classes of society; and having debauched themselves into a persuasion that mankind are incapable of governing themselves, it follows with them . . . that government can be carried on only by the pageantry of rank, the influence of money and emoluments, and the terror of military force." Indeed, the anti-republican party believed that to the "stupid, suspicious, licentious" people one should pronounce "but two words—*Submission* and *Confidence*."[20]

Throughout Madison's arguments against such measures and actions as the funding of the debt, the bank bill, Washington's neutrality proclamation as defended by Hamilton, Adams' supposed "monarchical principles" and "heretical politics", and the Alien and Sedition Acts, there runs the common thread of the danger to republicanism. He feared the corruption of the public interest to the advantage of special interests, the conversion of a limited government into an unlimited one, the obliteration of basic civil liberties, the consolidation of the states into one sovereignty, the undue extension of presidential power, and—eventually—the transformation of "the present republican system of the United States into an absolute, or, at best, a mixed monarchy."[21]

It is only in the light of the actual effectuation of a factional program by an anti-republican party that Madison's somewhat restricted interpretation of those two key clauses of the Constitution—the "necessary and proper" clause and the "general welfare" clause—can be squared with his early nationalism. His natural disposition to "write large" the consequences of deviation from republican principles is unmistakable.

[20] Hunt, VI, 113–116, "A Candid State of Parties", September 26, 1792; and pp. 120 and 122, "Who Are the Best Keepers of the Peoples' Liberties?" December 20, 1792.

[21] The best summary is Madison's "Address of the General Assembly to the People of the Commonwealth of Virginia", Hunt, VI, 332–340. The direct quotation is from the "Resolutions of 1798", *ibid.*, p. 327.

Thus he accepted as indispensable the "necessary and proper" clause but opposed any construction of it that would give Congress an "unlimited discretion". Implied powers must naturally, obviously, appropriately, directly, evidently, and immediately pertain to the Constitution's delegated powers. The tie between the delegated power and the implied power must be obvious if the government is to remain one of enumerated, limited powers. Implied powers that are merely convenient or conducive to the exercise of delegated powers are not necessary and proper. The "necessary and proper" clause should not be used to legitimatize a "distinct", "independent", "substantive", "great and important" power—in contrast to "an accessory or subaltern" power.[22]

In connection with the "general welfare" clause Madison held that there was no blanket power to spend for measures related to the general welfare but only a power to spend for the general welfare as the general welfare is explained and limited by the specifically enumerated powers of the Constitution. To Madison it made little difference whether the "general welfare" clause authorized every measure directly or whether it would merely authorize every measure for which money could be expended. Both interpretations would transfer a limited government into an unlimited government.[23]

The universal tendency to abuse power was serious enough. To allow an expansive interpretation of federal power by antirepublican forces to go unchallenged was to court suicide.

Madison's diagnosis was not, of course, limited to "misinterpretations" of the "necessary and proper" and "general welfare" clauses. For example, in protesting against the Alien and Sedition Acts, his attack virtually ran the gamut of constitutional argument. The Acts, he said, represented an exercise of power not delegated; contravened explicit prohibitions of the federal Bill of Rights; violated the principle of separation of powers; would "inflict a deathwound on the sovereignty of the States"; subverted the "general principles of free government";

[22] See Madison's speech against the bank bill. February 2, 1791, Hunt, VI, 29–34; and "Report on Resolutions", *ibid.*, pp. 383–385.

[23] Hunt, VI, 28, and 354–357.

were not authorized by a Constitution which, it was said, embodies common law by implication; could not be sanctioned by the Preamble to the Constitution; were not a legitimate exercise of "preventive justice"; were not justified by any governmentally inherent power of self-preservation; stifled liberty under the guise of controlling the licentiousness of the press; could not be used to justify domestic tyranny under the pretext of combating foreign danger.[24]

The anti-republican danger manifest in the Alien and Sedition Acts was now clear for all to see. Madison's earlier parade of horribles, mobilized against such measures as the first bank bill, and which earlier might have been discounted as partisan exaggeration, was now too meaningful to Republicans throughout the country. The Sedition Act, in particular, was a dramatic illustration of "a power which, more than any other, ought to produce universal alarm, because it is levelled against the rights of freely examining public characters and measures, and of free communication among the people thereon, which has ever been justly deemed the only effectual guardian of every other right." The objective of Madison's attack on the wisdom and constitutionality of such legislation as the Alien and Sedition Acts, the first bank bill, and other special interest legislation, remained the preservation of a republican Federal Union, including—of course—the vital republican rights of free speech, free press, and free communication.[25]

If a touch of partisan exaggeration did characterize Madison's analysis of the Federalist party as "anti-republican", there can be no doubt that his efforts helped greatly to maintain the pure republican faith (sometimes even against Washington himself). What is more significant, Madison helped to maintain this faith in the light of the candid antipathy to some of the fruits of republican principles that appeared in America (and in strategic quarters) with the reaction against the French Revolution.[26]

[24] See Madison's lengthy "Report on the Resolutions", *loc. cit.*

[25] See the "Resolutions of 1798", Hunt, VI, 326–331. The direct quotation is on pp. 328–329.

[26] See, for example, Hunt, VI, 117, note, and 193, note. For one example of Madison's opposition to Washington, see Madison's attack on Washington's denunciation of "self-created Societies", Hunt, VI, 222–223, note.

Later in his life, after he had retired from the Presidency, and when the "republican ascendency" seemed assured, Madison again went forth to battle against the anti-republican forces: this time against the anti-republican principles inherent in the ideology of nullification and secession. In this connection he cannot be accused of partisan exaggeration. However, his characteristic tendency to "write large" anti-republican principles, designs and actions is again unmistakable. Those who hold majority government to be the most oppressive of all governments he believed to be anti-republican. Such a "doctrine strikes at the roots of Republicanism, and if pursued into its consequences, must terminate in absolute monarchy, with a standing military force. . . ." Those who hold such a doctrine in order to attack the tariff "must either join the avowed disciples of aristocracy, oligarchy or monarchy, or look for a Utopia exhibiting a perfect homogeneousness of interests, opinions and feelings nowhere yet found in civilized communities."[27]

The consequences of the twin heresies of nullification and secession were also "writ large" in one remarkably prophetic passage which also demonstrates how inseparable, in Madison's mind, were the problems of disunion, faction, and the anti- and pseudo-republican reality. He foresaw

> . . . a rupture of the Union; a Southern confederacy; mutual enmity with the Northern; the most dreadful animosities and border wars, springing from the case of slaves; rival alliances abroad; standing armies at home, to be supported by internal taxes; and federal Governments, with powers of a more consolidating and monarchical tendency than the greatest jealousy has charged on the existing system.[28]

From the beginning of his political life to the end of his physical life, Madison was painfully aware of the dangers besetting the republican experiment. In the Virginia ratifying Convention he had declared: "From the first moment that my mind was capable of contemplating political subjects, I never, till this moment, ceased wishing success to a well regulated republican government." The last words of his last testament reveal the depth both of his fears and of his devotion to a Republican

[27] Hunt, IX, 520, 526. [28] Cong. Ed., IV, 273.

Union: "Let the open enemy to it be regarded as a Pandora with her box opened; and the disguised one, as the serpent creeping with his deadly wiles into Paradise."[29]

III

When Madison's devotion to republican union coincided with his devotion to national union—as in the Constitutional period and in the controversy over nullification—his position was fairly consistent and extremely persuasive. When, in his opposition to key features of the Federalist program in general, and to the Alien and Sedition Acts in particular, claims made on behalf of national union conflicted with his concept of republican union, Madison retreated somewhat from his earlier nationalism and adopted a more confined view of national power. This view (despite some nationalistic shifts in the period of the Republican Ascendency) permanently conditioned key portions of his political outlook. Despite these shifts—inevitable perhaps in the realm of practical politics—Madison remained opposed not only to the selfish friends of republicanism but also to its scheming foes. Certain key premises of his republican solution remained remarkably consistent.[30]

Early in his political career, in his *Memorial and Remonstrance Against Religious Assessments* (1785), he had utilized successfully the technique of strong popular protest to rally a popular and then a legislative majority against actions threatening republican liberties. His strategy was "to take alarm at the first experiment on our liberties"; to blast the first deviation from the republican faith. Such "prudent jealousy" was

> the first duty of citizens, and one of [the] noblest characteristics of the late Revolution. The freemen of America did not wait till usurped power had strengthened itself by exercise, and entangled the question in precedents. They saw all the consequences in the principle, and they avoided the consequences by denying the principle.[31]

During his service in the Congress of the Confederation,

[29] Hunt, V, 197; and Hunt, IX, opposite 610.

[30] For Madison's defense of his consistency see his letter to N. P. Trist, December 1831 in Cong. Ed., IV, 204–211.

[31] Hunt, II, 185–186.

and prior to, during, and immediately after the Constitutional Convention, Madison had sought to meet the anti-republican danger by establishing a strong, just, stable, popular government, which would disarm reaction by depriving it of legitimate grounds for criticism.

Despite the failures of the government under the Articles of Confederation, and even though Madison was gravely disturbed by the possibility of unjust majority rule—primarily in the states—he worked faithfully and diligently for a new, yet republican, constitution. He always held that certain republican principles and devices were necessary in order to guard against monarchy, aristocracy, oligarchy and plutocracy—as well as against mobocracy. Thus, he advocated popular ratification of the new Constitution.[32] He favored the principle of limited tenure of office.[33] He endorsed the guarantee of a republican form of government to the states, in order to "defend the system against aristocratic or monarchical innovations" and to make sure that the states "shall not exchange republican for anti-republican Constitutions."[34] He defended an electoral system which would permit the electors to be the great body of the people. "Not the rich, more than the poor; not the learned, more than the ignorant; not the haughty heirs of distinguished names, more than the humble sons of obscurity and unpropitious fortune." Similarly, speaking of the requirements of candidates for the House of Representatives, he declared that no "qualification of wealth, of birth, of religious faith, or of civil profession is permitted to fetter the judgment or disappoint the inclination of the people."[35] Fairly consistently, he supported what he called the republican principle of majority rule and firmly op-

[32] See, again, his letters to Jefferson, Randolph and Washington on the eve of the Convention, note 11 *supra;* and *Debates*, pp. 59, 497. It should be clear that Madison advocated popular ratification not only to secure a more legitimately republican union, but also a more effectively republican union.

[33] *The Federalist*, No. 37, p. 227; No. 39, pp. 243–244. Here, again, one should note that, although Madison favored this principle, he sought, in the Convention, longer terms for both Representatives and Senators in the interest of stability and competence. *Debates*, pp. 91 and 167–168.

[34] *The Federalist*, No. 43, pp. 282–283.

[35] *Ibid.*, No. 57, p. 371.

posed minority rule based on force, money, or blood.[36] A bill of rights, which Madison was to introduce in the first Congress, was to provide yet additional protection against anti-republican onslaughts.[37] Laws, unlimited in their duration, were opposed as "dangerous to republican principles."[38] Even titles for the President and Vice-President were opposed as "degrading appendages". This was meant to "shew to the friends of Republicanism that our new Government was not meant to substitute either Monarchy or Aristocracy, and that the genius of the people is as yet adverse to both."[39]

By 1790 Madison was clearly in opposition to key features of the Federalist program. By 1792 the battle lines were clearly drawn, in Madison's mind and writings, between republicans and anti-republicans.[40] The Federalist program thus provided Madison with the spur necessary to formulate and develop more fully his theory of republican opposition, a theory which he was also to use later against the advocates of nullification and secession.

Madison's theory of opposition deserves more attention than it has received. Most students now consider the rôle of the opposing party to be as important for a political theory—especially a republican or democratic theory—as the rôle of the governing party. Although Madison attacked both the wisdom and the constitutionality of certain Federalist measures, his use of and emphasis on constitutional argument helped greatly to establish in the American political firmament the idea of peaceful change: change in accord with basic republican principles; change based on public opinion functioning through constitutional machinery; peaceful republican change which was

[36] See, for example, Hunt, II, 363, "Vices . . ."; *Debates*, p. 124; *The Federalist*, No. 43, pp. 283–284.

[37] Hunt, V, 370–389.

[38] Hunt, V, 359.

[39] Hunt, V, 355, note.

[40] See, for example, Hunt, VI, 113–119, 120–123. Too many observers have overlooked, ignored, or explained away as clever propaganda Madison's closing sentence in the Tenth *Federalist* which indicates clearly the grounds for Madison's desertion of the Federalist party: "And according to the degree of pleasure and pride we feel in being *republicans*, ought to be our zeal in cherishing the spirit and supporting the character of Federalists." [Italics added]

impossible if the right to freedom of speech, press and communication were denied.

The very ambiguity and unorthodoxy of Madison's extreme constitutional remedy—"ultra constitutional interposition"—and his sometimes tortured construction of key constitutional clauses illustrate the lengths to which this sober-minded, scholarly man of political life would go to defend crucial civil rights against the anti-republican danger. In the *Memorial and Remonstrance* Madison had stressed the necessity of denying anti-republican principles to avoid anti-republican consequences. Now that the anti-republican consequences were dangerously manifest, he did not flinch from constitutional interpretation—albeit somewhat strained—to counter such consequences.

Madison, himself, did not take the plunge into constitutional nullification. And he later used his defense of his position in the Virginia Resolutions as a scalpel to dissect and excise the doctrine of nullification and secession. The republican opposition must still remain loyal to those principles of majority rule and aggregate popular sovereignty without which republican government could not endure.

Madison's theory of republican opposition, as he finally defended it, envisaged reliance on argument within the check-and-balance structure of our system of separated powers; fell back on orthodox constitutional intervention—impeachment, elections, repeal, amendment; retreated next to ultraconstitutional interposition—to the people in the states as the source of all legitimate constitutional authority. Beyond this appeal lay the call to revolution—which, though outside the framework of constitutional Union, was the *really* ultimate appeal by the republican opposition in defense of rights against intolerable oppression. The central purpose of such opposition was the preservation of constitutional, federal, republican Union.[41]

Madison hoped that argument—based on the merits and constitutionality of a given measure—might kill such anti-republican measures before passage. If such argument failed,

[41] The most important documents are the 1799 "Report on the [Virginia] Resolutions", Hunt, VI, 341–406; letter to Edward Everett, August 28, 1830, Hunt, IX, 383–403; and 1835 "Notes on Nullification", Hunt, IX, 573–607.

however, Madison was prepared to fight against such measures after passage. He held, despite what may seem a suggestive flirtation with a less respectable doctrine, that public opinion, if enlightened (here with the aid of state initiative), would respond to such anti-republican measures by using legitimate techniques of electoral opposition. Petition by state legislatures to Congress for repeal of obnoxious and unconstitutional measures, requests by state legislatures to the state's own congressmen to propose constitutional amendments, petition by sufficient state legislatures to Congress to call a convention to propose amendments to the Constitution—these were some of the techniques that might be used to rid the nation of unconstitutional, anti-republican measures. Impeachment could be used against a President violating his trust. And as public opinion could result in a legislative change of mind it could also result in a judicial change of mind. Hence, the Virginia Resolutions—asking the other states to concur with Virginia in declaring the Alien and Sedition Acts unconstitutional, and calling for "interposition" and "necessary and proper measures" by other states "for cooperating" with Virginia in "maintaining unimpaired the authorities, rights, and liberties reserved to the States respectively, or the people"—could mean simply those techniques of opposition which are quite orthodox by today's standards.[42]

It must not be forgotten, however, that Madison's defense of these techniques must be appraised in the light of a contemporary denial of the right of the states to protest against the constitutionality of federal legislation; and a denial of the right and propriety of appealing a constitutional question beyond the federal judiciary. In this context Madison's defense of the freedom of the states to communicate ideas challenging the constitutionality of federal legislation, and to take the initiative in seeking change via repeal, elections and amendment, becomes not a commonplace defense of the obvious but a vindication of republican principles under challenge.[43]

Madison contended, however, that these (now orthodox)

[42] "Report on the Resolutions", Hunt, VI, 394, 402. The direct quotation from the Virginia Resolutions is on p. 331.

[43] See Madison's "Notes on Nullification", Hunt, IX, 574, 582, 594–596.

means did not exhaust the possibilities open to the sovereign people of the states, as parties to and creators of the Constitution who could, therefore, explain, amend and remake the Constitution.[44] He maintained that ultraconstitutional interposition remained as a last resort in "those great and extraordinary cases in which all the forms of the Constitution may prove ineffectual against infractions dangerous to the essential rights of the parties to it.[45] The exact nature of this ultraconstitutional remedy—this extreme remedy to be employed only in very rare cases—still remains mysterious, ambiguous and unorthodox. Madison never spelled out its exact nature. He did indicate that such a remedy must secure a peaceful and effective decision. It cannot be employed when the oppressed are a minority and the oppressors a majority. In other words, there is no ultimate, constitutional power on the part of a minority to explain, amend, or remake a constitution. Apparently, only a majority (presumably a majority of people in a majority of states) possess this ultimate, constitutional power as the parties to and creators of the Constitution. So long as the minority stays within the Union and under the Union's Constitution, not even its desperate, oppressed position enables it constitutionally to invoke Madison's doctrine of ultraconstitutional interposition.[46]

Later, in the midst of the nullification controversy, Madison insisted that the interposition called for by the Virginia Resolutions would not justify South Carolina's nullification of federal legislation, even until such single-state nullification was overridden by three fourths of the other states in the Union. Rather, interposition called for the collective, aggregate, concurrent action of the sovereign people of the *states*.[47]

It is also extremely important to bear in mind, apropos of the nullification imbroglio, the scope of Madison's endeavor to heal the sectional breach—before the extremists could gain control and jeopardize republican Union. He relied not only on a sound republican theory—based on the concepts of the

[44] *Ibid.*, pp. 575, 583, 592, 594.
[45] "Report on the Resolutions", Hunt, VI, 351.
[46] "Notes on Nullification", Hunt, IX, 575, 592, 597–598, 606–607.
[47] *Ibid.*, pp. 576, 579, 580.

extensive republic and republican opposition and on a united and functioning Republican party—but also on other factors. Among these were: the binding and cohesive forces of patriotic sentiment, common religious denominations, social and geographic ligaments, mutual economic self-interest, and enlightened statesmanship. Such statesmanship involved more moderate Southern leadership, a realistic and honest understanding of the true causes of the South's distress, a sane reduction of the tariff, and an equitable bearing of necessary economic burdens.[48] Unfortunately, Madison's remarkable grasp of the issues was not shared by any statesman—North or South—who commanded the ability to translate this analysis into public policy.

Madison had been willing to go pretty far in countering the anti-republican danger presented by the Alien and Sedition Acts. But always he kept his eye on the danger, using his theory of republican opposition now against the Alien and Sedition Acts, now against the doctrine of nullification and secession, but still able to face the sectional crisis constructively. In 1787, and in the nullification controversy, Madison's appraisal of the anti-republican danger spurred him on to superlative analysis and statesmanlike solution.

Madison was a strong believer in constitutional government and in constitutional resistance to anti-republican measures. But he never abandoned that republican orientation which justified revolution as the *really* ultimate remedy against intolerable oppression. In taking this stand he was simply endorsing an orthodox philosophy immortalized in the Declaration of Independence. But Madison clearly recognized that this really ultimate remedy of revolution was a natural right and not a constitutional right. It was a natural right because "intolerable oppression" of the people by government, and "abuses or usurpations" by government, released the sovereign people in the states from their obligations under the Constitution. They were thus, in good Lockean fashion, back in a state of nature because of the government's violation of the people's trust embodied in the constitutional compact. Clearly, as far

[48] See Hunt, IX, 432–433 (1831), 481–482 (1832), 520–528 (1833), 610 (1836); Cong. Ed., IV, 567–568 (1833), 298 (1833).

as those who were intolerably oppressed were concerned, government was dissolved, the parties were in a state of nature, and might therefore use their "natural right of self-preservation" to revolt against governmental tyranny. Madison conceded that nullification was such a natural right.[49]

He was less radical in intellectual temperament than Jefferson, and it is not surprising that Madison should issue no impetuous call to revolt against intolerable oppression. Even under such conditions, he felt, one must carefully weigh the consequences of resistance and oppression. Should "power usurped be sustained in its oppressive exercise on a minority by a majority, the final course to be pursued by the minority must be a subject of calculation, in which the degree of oppression, the means of resistance, the consequences of its failure, and the consequences of its success must be the elements."[50]

Madison's central rôle as Republican Savior emerges as a cardinal conclusion of this paper. This rôle is crucial to an understanding of his thought and action. Here, indeed, is the driving force of Madison's political theory: his republican faith. Without an appreciation of this rôle, Madison's theory remains distorted and his genuine contribution to republican constitutionalism imperfectly understood. Republican ideology—not economic interest, not social class, not sectional outlook—is the key to his political thought and actions. Theoretically and practically, he was always hostile to anti- and pseudo-republicanism. He was the most original, most understanding, and most effective champion of republicanism against its enemies. For this alone, Jeffersonian Democracy owes Madison a debt which has not been sufficiently acknowledged.

Madison emerges, too, in a new light as the Father of our *republican* Constitution *in the first five decades of our national life.* He stands forth not only as a major architect and champion of the strengthened instrument of 1787. He appears also as Father of a republican constitutionalism which embraces the concept of equal rights for all and special privileges for none;

49 "Notes on Nullification", Hunt, IX, 574, 588–591.

50 *Ibid.*, p. 597.

a government of broad but limited powers; a Constitution within the framework of which a vigilant, hard-hitting but loyal opposition might function; a Constitution dedicated to federal Union because union was the necessary condition of the Republican Experiment.

Neal Riemer

The Pennsylvania State University

[10]

DEMOCRACY AND *THE FEDERALIST*: A RECONSIDERATION OF THE FRAMERS' INTENT*

MARTIN DIAMOND

Claremont Men's College

It has been a common teaching among modern historians of the guiding ideas in the foundation of our government that the Constitution of the United States embodied a reaction against the democratic principles espoused in the Declaration of Independence. This view has largely been accepted by political scientists and has therefore had important consequences for the way American political development has been studied. I shall present here a contrary view of the political theory of the Framers and examine some of its consequences.

What is the relevance of the political thought of the Founding Fathers to an understanding of contemporary problems of liberty and justice? Four possible ways of looking at the Founding Fathers immediately suggest themselves. First, it may be that they possessed wisdom, a set of political principles still inherently adequate, and needing only to be supplemented by skill in their proper contemporary application. Second, it may be that, while the Founding Fathers' principles are still sound, they are applicable only to a part of our problems, but not to that part which is peculiarly modern; and thus new principles are needed to be joined together with the old ones. Third, it may be that the Founding Fathers have simply become; they dealt with bygone problems and their principles were relevant only to those old problems. Fourth, they may have been wrong or radically inadequate even for their own time.

Each of these four possible conclusions requires the same foundation: an understanding of the political thought of the Founding Fathers. To decide whether to apply their wisdom, or to add to their wisdom, or to reject it as irrelevant or as unwise, it is absolutely necessary to understand what they said, why they said it, and what they meant by it. At the same time, however, to understand their claim to wisdom is to evaluate it: to know wherein they were wise and wherein they were not, or wherein (and why) their wisdom is unavailing for our problems. Moreover, even if it turns out that our modern problems require wholly new principles for their solution, an excellent way to discover those new principles would be to see what it is about modernity that has outmoded the principles of the Founding Fathers. For example, it is possible that modern developments are themselves partly the outcome of the particular attempt to solve the problem of freedom and justice upon which this country was founded. That is, our modern difficulties may testify to fundamental errors in the thought of the Founding Fathers; and, in the process of discerning those errors, we may discover what better principles would be.

The solution of our contemporary problems requires very great wisdom indeed. And in that fact lies the greatest justification for studying anew the

* An earlier version of this was written at the request of the Fund for the Republic; the Fund's generous assistance is here gratefully acknowledged.

political thought of the Founding Fathers. For that thought remains the finest American thought on political matters. In studying them we may raise ourselves to their level. In achieving their level we may free ourselves from limitations that, ironically, they tend to impose upon us, *i.e.*, insofar as we tend to be creatures of the society they founded. And in so freeing ourselves we may be enabled, if it is necessary, to go beyond their wisdom. The Founding Fathers still loom so large in our life that the contemporary political problem of liberty and justice for Americans could be stated as the need to choose whether to apply their wisdom, amend their wisdom, or reject it. Only an understanding of them will tell us how to choose.

For the reflections on the Fathers which follow, I employ chiefly *The Federalist* as the clue to the political theory upon which rested the founding of the American Republic. That this would be inadequate for a systematic study of the Founding Fathers goes without saying. But it is the one book, "to which," as Jefferson wrote in 1825, "appeal is habitually made by all, and rarely declined or denied by any as evidence of the general opinion of those who framed and of those who accepted the Constitution of the United States, on questions as to its genuine meaning." As such it is the indispensable starting point for systematic study.

I

Our major political problems today are problems of democracy; and, as much as anything else, the *Federalist* papers are a teaching about democracy. The conclusion of one of the most important of these papers states what is also the most important theme in the entire work: the necessity for "a republican remedy for the diseases most incident to republican government."[1] The theme is clearly repeated in a passage where Thomas Jefferson is praised for displaying equally "a fervent attachment to republican government and an enlightened view of the dangerous propensities against which it ought to be guarded."[2] *The Federalist,* thus, stresses its commitment to republican or popular government, but, of course, insists that this must be an enlightened commitment.

But *The Federalist* and the Founding Fathers generally have not been taken at their word. Predominantly, they are understood as being only quasi- or even anti-democrats. Modern American historical writing, at least until very recently, has generally seen the Constitution as some sort of apostasy from, or reaction to, the radically democratic implications of the Declaration of Independence—a reaction that was undone by the great "democratic breakthroughs" of Jeffersonianism, Jacksonianism, etc. This view, I believe, involves a false understanding of the crucial political issues involved in the founding of the American Republic. Further, it is based implicitly upon a questionable modern approach to democracy and has tended to have the effect, moreover, of relegating the political teaching of the Founding Fathers to the pre-democratic past and thus of making it of no vital concern to moderns. The Founding

[1] *Federalist,* No. 10, p. 62. All references are to the Modern Library edition, ed. E. M. Earle.

[2] *Federalist,* No. 49, p. 327.

Fathers themselves repeatedly stressed that their Constitution was wholly consistent with the true principles of republican or popular government. The prevailing modern opinion, in varying degrees and in different ways, rejects that claim. It thus becomes important to understand what was the relation of the Founding Fathers to popular government or democracy.

I have deliberately used interchangeably their terms, "popular government" and "democracy." The Founding Fathers, of course, did not use the terms entirely synonymously and the idea that they were less than "democrats" has been fortified by the fact that they sometimes defined "democracy" invidiously in comparison with "republic." But this fact does not really justify the opinion. For their basic view was that *popular government was the genus, and democracy and republic were two species* of that genus of government. What distinguished popular government from other genera of government was that in it, political authority is "derived from the great body of the society, not from . . . [any] favoured class of it."[3] With respect to this decisive question, of where political authority is lodged, democracy and republic—as *The Federalist* uses the terms—differ not in the least. Republics, equally with democracies, may claim to be wholly a form of popular government. This is neither to deny the difference between the two, nor to depreciate the importance *The Federalist* attached to the difference; but in *The Federalist's* view, the difference does not relate to the essential principle of popular government. Democracy means in *The Federalist* that form of popular government where the citizens "assemble and administer the government in person."[4] Republics differ in that the people rule through representatives and, of course, in the consequences of that difference. The crucial point is that republics and democracies are equally forms of popular government, but that the one form is vastly preferable to the other because of the substantive consequences of the difference in form. Those historians who consider the Founding Fathers as less than "democrats," miss or reject the Founders' central contention that, while being perfectly faithful to the *principle* of popular government, they had solved the *problem* of popular government.

In what way is the Constitution ordinarily thought to be less democratic than the Declaration? The argument is usually that the former is characterized by

[3] *Federalist*, No. 39, p. 244. Here Madison speaks explicitly of the republican form of government. But see on the same page how Madison compares the republican form with "every *other popular* government." Regarding the crucial question of the lodgement of political authority, Madison speaks of republic, democracy and popular government interchangeably. Consider that, in the very paper where he distinguishes so precisely between democracies and republics regarding direct versus representative rule, Madison defines his general aim both as a search for "a republican remedy" for republican diseases *and* a remedy that will "preserve the spirit and the form of *popular* government." (p. 58.) Interestingly, on June 6 at the Federal Convention, Madison's phrasing for a similar problem was the search for "the only defense against the inconveniences of democracy consistent with the *democratic* form of government." Madison, *Writings*, ed. G. Hunt, Vol. 3 (G. P. Putnam's Sons, New York, 1902), p. 103. Italics supplied throughout.

[4] *Federalist*, No. 10, p. 58.

fear of the people, by preoccupation with minority interests and rights, and by measures therefore taken against the power of majorities. The Declaration, it is true, does not display these features, but this is no proof of a fundamental difference of principle between the two. Is it not obviously possible that the difference is due only to a difference in the tasks to which the two documents were addressed? And is it not further possible that the democratic principles of the Declaration are not only compatible with the prophylactic measures of the Constitution, but actually imply them?

The Declaration of Independence formulates two criteria for judging whether any government is good, or indeed legitimate. Good government must rest, procedurally, upon the consent of the governed. Good government, substantively, must do only certain things, *e.g.*, secure certain rights. This may be stated another way by borrowing a phrase from Locke, appropriate enough when discussing the Declaration. That "the people shall be judge" is of the essence of democracy, is its peculiar form or method of proceeding. That the people shall judge rightly is the substantive problem of democracy. But whether the procedure will bring about the substance is problematic. Between the Declaration's two criteria, then, a tension exists: consent can be given or obtained for governmental actions which are not right—at least as the men of 1776 saw the right. (To give an obvious example from their point of view: the people may freely but wrongly vote away the protection due to property.) Thus the Declaration clearly contained, although it did not resolve, a fundamental problem. Solving the problem was not its task; that was the task for the framers of the Constitution. But the man who wrote the Declaration of Independence and the leading men who supported it were perfectly aware of the difficulty, and of the necessity for a "republican remedy."

What the text of the Declaration, taken alone, tells of its meaning may easily be substantiated by the testimony of its author and supporters. Consider only that Jefferson, with no known change of heart at all, said of *The Federalist* that it was "the best commentary on the principles of government which was ever written."[5] Jefferson, it must be remembered, came firmly to recommend the adoption of the Constitution, his criticisms of it having come down only to a proposal for rotation in the Presidency and for the subsequent adoption of a bill of rights. I do not, of course, deny the peculiar character of "Jeffersonianism" nor the importance to many things of its proper understanding. I only state here that it is certain that Jefferson, unlike later historians, did not view the Constitution as a retrogression from democracy. Or further, consider that John Adams, now celebrated as America's great conservative, was so enthusiastic about Jefferson's draft of the Declaration as to wish on his own account that hardly a word be changed. And this same Adams, also without any change of heart and without complaint, accepted the Constitution as embodying many of his own views on government.

The idea that the Constitution was a falling back from the fuller democracy

[5] *The Works of Thomas Jefferson*, ed. Paul L. Ford (The Federal Edition), Vol. 5 (G. P. Putnam's Sons, New York, 1904), p. 434.

of the Declaration thus rests in part upon a false reading of the Declaration as free from the concerns regarding democracy that the framers of the Constitution felt. Perhaps only those would so read it who take for granted a perfect, self-subsisting harmony between consent (equality) and the proper aim of government (justice), or between consent and individual rights (liberty). This assumption was utterly foreign to the leading men of the Declaration.

II

The Declaration has wrongly been converted into, as it were, a super-democratic document; has the Constitution wrongly been converted in the modern view into an insufficiently democratic document? The only basis for depreciating the democratic character of the Constitution lies in its framers' apprehensive diagnosis of the "diseases," "defects" or "evil propensities" of democracy, and in their remedies. But if what the Founders considered to be defects *are* genuine defects, and if the remedies, without violating the principles of popular government, *are* genuine remedies, then it would be unreasonable to call the Founders anti- or quasi-democrats. Rather, they would be the wise partisans of democracy; a man is not a better democrat but only a foolish democrat if he ignores real defects inherent in popular government. Thus, the question becomes: are there natural defects to democracy and, if there are, what are the best remedies?

In part, the Founding Fathers answered this question by employing a traditional mode of political analysis. They believed there were several basic possible regimes, each having several possible forms. Of these possible regimes they believed the best, or at least the best for America, to be popular government, but only if purged of its defects. At any rate, an unpurged popular government they believed to be indefensible. They believed there were several forms of popular government, crucial among these direct democracy and republican—or representative—government (the latter perhaps divisible into two distinct forms, large and small republics). Their constitution and their defense of it constitute an argument for that form of popular government (large republic) in which the "evil propensities" would be weakest or most susceptible of remedy.

The whole of the thought of the Founding Fathers is intelligible and, especially, the evaluation of their claim to be wise partisans of popular government is possible, only if the words "*disease*," "*defect*," and "*evil propensity*" are allowed their full force. Unlike modern "value-free" social scientists, the Founding Fathers believed that true knowledge of the good and bad in human conduct was possible, and that they themselves possessed sufficient knowledge to discern the really grave defects of popular government and their proper remedies. The modern relativistic or positivistic theories, implicitly employed by most commentators on the Founding Fathers, deny the possibility of such true knowledge and therefore deny that the Founding Fathers *could* have been actuated by knowledge of the good rather than by passion or interest. (I deliberately employ the language of *Federalist* No. 10. Madison defined faction, in part, as a group "united and actuated by . . . passion, or . . . interest." That is, factions are groups *not*—as presumably the authors of *The Federalist* were—actuated by reason.) How this modern view of the value problem supports the conception of the Constitution as less democratic than the Declaration is clear. The Founding Fathers did in fact seek to prejudice the outcome of democracy; they sought to alter, by certain restraints, the likelihood that the majority would decide certain political issues in bad ways. These restraints the Founders justified as mitigating the natural defects of democracy. But, say the moderns, there are no "bad" political decisions, wrong-in-themselves, from reaching which the majority ought to be restrained. Therefore, ultimately, nothing other than the specific interests of the Founders can explain their zeal in restraining democracy. And inasmuch as the restraints were typically placed on the many in the interest of the propertied, the departure of the Constitution is "anti-democratic" or "thermidorean." In short, according to this view, there cannot be what the Founders claimed to possess, "an *enlightened* view of the dangerous propensities against which [popular government] . . . ought to be guarded," the substantive goodness or badness of such propensities being a matter of opinion or taste on which reason can shed no light.

What are some of the arrangements which have been considered signs of "undemocratic" features of the Constitution? The process by which the Constitution may be amended is often cited in evidence. Everyone is familiar with the arithmetic which shows that a remarkably small minority could prevent passage of a constitutional amendment supported by an overwhelming majority of the people. That is, bare majorities in the thirteen least populous states could prevent passage of an amendment desired by overwhelming majorities in the thirty-six most populous states. But let us, for a reason to be made clear in a moment, turn that arithmetic around. Bare majorities in the thirty-seven least populous states can pass amendments against the opposition of overwhelming majorities in the twelve most populous states. And this would mean in actual votes today (and would have meant for the thirteen original states) constitutional amendment by a minority against the opposition of a majority of citizens. My point is simply that, while the amending procedure does involve qualified majorities, the qualification is not of the kind that requires an especially large numerical majority for action.

I suggest that the real aim and practical effect of the complicated amending procedure was not at all to give power to minorities, but to ensure that passage of an amendment would require a *nationally* distributed majority, though one that legally could consist of a bare numerical majority. It was only adventitious that the procedure has the theoretical possibility of a minority blocking (or passing) an amendment. The aim of requiring nationally distributed majorities was, I think, to ensure that no amendment could be passed simply with the support of the few states or sections sufficiently numerous to provide a bare majority. No doubt it was also believed that it would be difficult for such a national majority to form or become effective save for the decent purposes that could command national agreement, and this difficulty was surely deemed a great virtue of the amending process. This is what I think *The Federalist* really means when it praises the amending process and says that "it guards equally against that extreme facility, which would render the Constitution too mutable;

and that extreme difficulty, which might perpetuate its discovered faults."[6] All I wish to emphasize here is that the actual method adopted, with respect to the numerical size of majorities, is meant to leave all legal power in the hands of ordinary majorities so long as they are national majorities. The departure from simple majoritarianism is, at least, not in an oligarchic or aristocratic direction. In this crucial respect, the amending procedure does conform strictly to the principles of republican (popular) government.

Consider next the suffrage question. It has long been assumed as proof of an anti-democratic element in the Constitution that the Founding Fathers depended for the working of their Constitution upon a substantially limited franchise. Just as the Constitution allegedly was ratified by a highly qualified electorate, so too, it is held, was the new government to be based upon a suffrage subject to substantial property qualifications. This view has only recently been seriously challenged, especially by Robert E. Brown, whose detailed researches convince him that the property qualifications in nearly all the original states were probably so small as to exclude never more than twenty-five per cent, and in most cases as little as only five to ten per cent, of the adult white male population.[6a] That is, the property qualifications were not designed to exclude the mass of the poor but only the small proportion which lacked a concrete—however small—stakein society, *i.e.*, primarily the transients or "idlers."

The Constitution, of course, left the suffrage question to the decision of the individual states. What is the implication of that fact for deciding what sort of suffrage the Framers had in mind? The immediately popular branch of the national legislature was to be elected by voters who "shall have the qualifications requisite for electors of the most numerous branch of the State Legislature." The mode of election to the electoral college for the Presidency and to the Senate is also left to "be prescribed in each State by the legislature thereof." At a minimum, it may be stated that the Framers did not themselves attempt to reduce, or prevent the expansion of, the suffrage; that question was left wholly to the states—and these were, ironically, the very hotbeds of post-revolutionary democracy from the rule of which it is familiarly alleged that the Founders sought to escape.[7]

In general, the conclusion seems inescapable that the states had a far broader suffrage than is ordinarily thought, and nothing in the actions of the Framers suggests any expectation or prospect of the reduction of the suffrage. Again, as in the question of the amending process, I suggest that the Constitution represented no departure whatsoever from the democratic standards of the Revolu-

[6] *Federalist*, No. 43, p. 286.

[6a] *Middle Class Democracy and the Revolution in Massachusetts, 1691–1780.* (Cornell University Press, Ithaca, 1955).

[7] Madison must have thought that he had established this point beyond misinterpretation in *The Federalist*, No. 57. "Who are to be the electors of the federal representatives? Not the rich, more than the poor; not the learned, more than the ignorant; not the haughty heirs of distinguished names, more than the humble sons of obscurity and unpropitious fortune. The electors are to be the great body of the people of the United States. They are to be the same who exercise the right in every State of electing the corresponding branch of the legislature of the State." (p. 371.)

tionary period, or from any democratic standards then generally recognized.[8]

What of the Senate? The organization of the Senate, its term of office and its staggered mode of replacement, its election by state legislatures rather than directly by the people, among other things, have been used to demonstrate the undemocratic character of the Senate as intended by the Framers. Was this not a device to represent property and not people, and was it not intended therefore to be a non-popular element in the government? I suggest, on the contrary, that the really important thing is that the Framers thought they had found a way to protect property *without* representing it. That the Founders intended the Senate to be one of the crucial devices for remedying the defects of democracy is certainly true. But *The Federalist* argues that the Senate, as actually proposed in the Constitution, was calculated to be such a device as would operate only in a way that "will consist . . . with the genuine principles of republican government."[9] I believe that the claim is just.

Rather than viewing the Senate from the perspective of modern experience and opinions, consider how radically democratic the Senate appears when viewed from a pre-modern perspective. The model of a divided legislature that the Founders had most in mind was probably the English Parliament. There the House of Lords was thought to provide some of the beneficial checks upon the popular Commons which it was hoped the Senate would supply in the American Constitution. But the American Senate was to possess none of the qualities which permitted the House of Lords to fulfill its role; *i.e.*, its hereditary basis, or membership upon election by the Crown, or any of its other aristocratic characteristics.[10] Yet the Founding Fathers knew that the advantages of having both a Senate and a House would "be in proportion to the dissimilarity in the genius of the two bodies."[11] What is remarkable is that, in seeking to secure this dissimilarity, they did not in any respect go beyond the limits permitted by the "genuine principles of republican government."

Not only is this dramatically demonstrated in comparison with the English House of Lords, but also in comparison with all earlier theory regarding the division of the legislative power. The aim of such a division in earlier thought is to secure a balance between the aristocratic and democratic elements of a polity. This is connected with the pre-modern preference for a *mixed* republic, which was rejected by the Founders in favor of a *democratic* republic. And the tradi-

[8] This is not to deny the importance of the existing property qualifications for the understanding of the Founders' political theory. The legal exclusion from the franchise of even a very small portion of the adult population may have enormous significance for the politics and life of a country. This is obvious in the case of a racial, ethnic or religious minority. And the exclusion of otherwise eligible adult males on the grounds of poverty may be equally important. The property qualification clearly praises and rewards certain virtues, implies that the voter must possess certain qualities to warrant his exercise of the franchise, and aims at excluding a "rabble" from the operations of political parties. But important, therefore, as the property qualification was, it does not demonstrate that the Founding Fathers departed radically from the most important aspects of the principle of majority rule.

[9] *Federalist*, No. 62, p. 403.

[10] *Federalist*, No. 63, p. 415.

[11] *Federalist*, No. 62, p. 403.

tional way to secure this balance or mixture was to give one house or office to the suffrages of the few and one to the suffrages of the many. Nothing of the kind is involved in the American Senate. Indeed, on this issue, so often cited as evidence of the Founders' undemocratic predilections, the very opposite is the case. The Senate is a constitutional device which *par excellence* reveals the strategy of the Founders. They wanted something like the advantages earlier thinkers had seen in a mixed legislative power, but they thought this was possible (and perhaps preferable) without any introduction whatsoever of aristocratic power into their system. What pre-modern thought had seen in an aristocratic senate—wisdom, nobility, manners, religion, etc.—the Founding Fathers converted into stability, enlightened self-interest, a "temperate and respectable body of citizens." The qualities of a senate having thus been altered (involving perhaps comparable changes in the notion of the ends of government), it became possible to secure these advantages through a Senate based wholly upon popular principles. Or so I would characterize a Senate whose membership required no property qualification and which was appointed (or elected in the manner prescribed) by State legislatures which, in their own turn, were elected annually or biennially by a nearly universal manhood suffrage.

The great claim of *The Federalist* is that the Constitution represents the fulfillment of a truly novel experiment, of "a revolution which has no parallel in the annals of society," and which is decisive for the happiness of "the whole human race."[12] And the novelty, I argue, consisted in solving the problems of popular government by means which yet maintain the government "wholly popular."[13] In defending that claim against the idea of the Constitution as a retreat from democracy I have dealt thus far only with the easier task: the demonstration that the constitutional devices and arrangements do not derogate from the legal power of majorities to rule. What remains is to examine the claim that the Constitution did in fact remedy the natural defects of democracy. Before any effort is made in this direction, it may be useful to summarize some of the implications and possible utility of the analysis thus far.

Above all, the merit of the suggestions I have made, if they are accurate in describing the intention and action of the Founders, is that it makes the Founders available to us for the study of modern problems. I have tried to restore to them their *bona fides* as partisans of democracy. This done, we may take seriously the question whether they were, as they claimed to be, wise partisans of democracy or popular government. If they were partisans of democracy and if the regime they created was decisively democratic, then they speak to us not merely about bygone problems, not from a viewpoint—in this regard—radically different from our own, but as men addressing themselves to problems identical in principle with our own. They are a source from within our own heritage which teaches us the way to put the question to democracy, a way which is rejected by certain prevailing modern ideas. But we cannot avail ourselves of their assistance if we consider American history to be a succession of democratizations which overcame the Founding Fathers' intentions. On that view it is easy

[12] *Federalist*, No. 14, p. 85.
[13] *Ibid.*, p. 81.

to regard them as simply outmoded. If I am right regarding the extent of democracy in their thought and regime, then they are not outmoded by modern events but rather are tested by them. American history, on this view, is not primarily the replacement of a pre-democratic regime by a democratic regime, but is rather a continuing testimony to how the Founding Fathers' democratic regime has worked out in modern circumstances. The whole of our national experience thus becomes a way of judging the Founders' principles, of judging democracy itself, or of pondering the flaws of democracy and the means to its improvement.

III

What was the Founding Fathers' view of the good life? Upon what fundamental theoretical premises did that view of the good life depend? How comprehensive was their understanding of the dangers against which popular government was to be guarded? How efficacious were their remedies and what may have been the unanticipated costs of those remedies? These questions are clearly too vast to answer here and now. What follows is only a series of notes which bear upon the problems raised, and which I think may serve as general guides to what it is important to seek in studying the Founding Fathers.

The Federalist does not discuss systematically, as would a theoretical treatise, the question of the ends or purposes of government. That is, it does not deal systematically with philosophical issues. This is not to say that its authors did not have a view in such matters. But what that view was, and what are its implications for the understanding of the Constitution, is a subject on which I find it difficult to speak with confidence. I must still regard as open the question whether the authors of *The Federalist*, or the other leading founders, had themselves fully reflected on these matters, or whether they treated them as settled by thinkers like Locke and Montesquieu, or whether crucial premises in their thought were unreflectively taken for granted. But men cannot act on a political scale so vast as they did without having and employing a view of the politically fundamental; and it is this view which provides the crucial perspective for the understanding of their particular actions and thoughts.

Perhaps the most explicit fundamental utterance of *The Federalist* is the statement regarding

> the great principle of self-preservation . . . the transcendent law of nature and of nature's God, which declares that the safety and happiness of society are the objects at which all political institutions aim, and to which all such institutions must be sacrificed.[14]

But self-preservation, it is made clear, includes more than mere preservation. This passage, which interestingly echoes the Declaration of Independence on the "laws of nature and of nature's God," emphasizes that preservation includes "happiness" as well as "safety." That is, *The Federalist* is aware of and explicitly rejects the kind of regime that would follow from a narrower view of self-preservation. For example, *The Federalist* seems explicitly to be rejecting Hobbes when, in another context, it rejects the view that "nothing less than the chains of despotism can restrain [men] from destroying and devouring one an-

[14] *Federalist*, No. 43, p. 287.

other."[15] But while it rejects the "chains of despotism," *i.e.*, the Hobbesean solution to the problem of self-preservation, it nonetheless seems to accept the Hobbesean statement of the problem. As it were, the primary fears of *The Federalist* are Hobbesean, that is, fears of "foreign war and domestic convulsion." Rejecting a despotic solution, the great aim of *The Federalist* is to supply a liberal and republican solution to the same problem. But while there is a great difference, never to be underestimated, between a liberal and a repressive, a republican and a monarchical solution, it may be that in making the same dangers and their solution *the* desideratum for the structure and functions of government much of the Hobbesean view is preserved.

The main object of *The Federalist* was to urge the necessity of a firm and energetic Union. The utility of such a Union, and therefore the chief ends it will serve, is that it will strengthen the American people against the dangers of "foreign war" and secure them from the dangers of "domestic convulsion." These functions of government are the most frequently discussed and the most vehemently emphasized in the whole work. To a very great extent, then, *The Federalist* determines the role of government with reference only, or primarily, to the extremes of external and internal danger. It is to avoid the pre-civil forms of these dangers that men form government and it is the civil solution of these dangers which, almost exclusively, determines the legitimate objects of government. But again, *The Federalist* repeatedly emphasizes that a "novel" solution is at hand. The means now exist—and America is uniquely in a position to employ them—for a republican solution which avoids the extremes of tyranny and anarchy. But notice that, on this view, liberalism and republicanism are not the means by which men may ascend to a nobler life; rather they are simply instrumentalities which solve Hobbesean problems in a more moderate manner. It is tempting to suggest that if America is a "Lockean" nation, as is so often asserted, it is true in the very precise sense that Locke's "comfortable preservation" displaces the harshness of the Hobbesean view, while not repudiating that view in general.

To be sure, *The Federalist* does make other explicit statements regarding the ends of government. For example: "Justice is the end of government. It is the end of civil society."[16] But this statement, to the best of my knowledge, is made only once in the entire work; and the context suggests that "justice" means simply "civil rights" which in turn seems to refer primarily to the protection of economic interests. That justice has here this relatively narrow meaning, as compared with traditional philosophical and theological usage, is made more probable when we take account of the crucial statement in *Federalist* No. 10. There the "first object of government" is the protection of the diverse human faculties from which arise the "rights of property" and the unequal distribution of property. The importance of this statement of the function of government is underscored when it is recalled how large a proportion of *The Federalist* deals with the improvements in "commerce" made possible by the new Constitution.

[15] *Federalist,* No. 55, p. 365.
[16] *Federalist,* No. 51, p. 340.

For example, in a list of the four "principal objects of federal legislation,"[17] three (foreign trade, interstate trade, and taxes) deal explicitly with commerce. The fourth, the militia, also deals with commerce insofar as it largely has to do with the prevention of "domestic convulsion" brought on by economic matters.

The very great emphasis of *The Federalist* on commerce, and on the role of government in nurturing it, may not be at all incompatible with the theme of "happiness" which is the most frequently occurring definition of the "object of government." The most definite statement is the following:

> A good government implies two things: first, fidelity to the object of government, which is the happiness of the people, secondly, a knowledge of the means by which that object can be best obtained.[18]

The Federalist is not very explicit in defining happiness. But there are firm indications that what it had in mind has little in common with traditional philosophical or theological understandings of the term. At one place, *The Federalist* indicates that happiness requires that government "provide for the security, advance the prosperity, [and] support the reputation of the commonwealth."[19] In another, happiness seems to require "our safety, our tranquility, our dignity, our reputation."[20] Part of what these words mean is made clear by the fact that they summarize a lengthy indictment of the Articles of Confederation, the particulars of which deal in nearly every case with commercial shortcomings. Happiness, "a knowledge of the means" to which *The Federalist* openly claims to possess, seems to consist primarily in physical preservation from external and internal danger *and* in the comforts afforded by a commercial society; which comforts are at once the dividends of security and the means to a republican rather than repressive security.

What is striking is the apparent exclusion from the functions of government of a wide range of non-economic tasks traditionally considered the decisive business of government. It is tempting to speculate that this reduction in the tasks of government has something to do with *The Federalist's* defense of popular government. The traditional criticism of popular government was that it gave over the art of government into the hands of the many, which is to say the unwise. It would be a formidable reply to reduce the complexity of the governmental art to dimensions more commensurate with the capacity of the many. I use two statements by Madison, years apart, to illustrate the possibility that he may have had something like this in mind. "There can be no doubt that there are subjects to which the capacities of the bulk of mankind are unequal."[21] But on the other hand, "the confidence of the [Republican party] in the capacity of mankind for self-government"[22] is what distinguished it from the Fed-

[17] *Federalist*, No. 53, p. 350–51.

[18] *Federalist*, No. 62, p. 404.

[19] *Federalist*, No. 30, p. 186.

[20] *Federalist*, No. 15, p. 88.

[21] Letter to Edmund Randolph, January 10, 1788.

[22] Letter to William Eustis, May 22, 1823. The letters to Randolph and Eustis were brought to my attention by Ralph Ketcham's article, "Notes on James Madison's Sources for the Tenth Federalist Paper," *Midwest Journal of Political Science*, Vol. 1 (May, 1957).

eralist party which distrusted that capacity. The confidence in mankind's capacities would seem to require having removed from government the subjects to which those capacities are unequal.

IV

So far as concerns those ends of government on which *The Federalist* is almost wholly silent, it is reasonable to infer that what the Founders made no provision for they did not rank highly among the legitimate objects of government. Other political theories had ranked highly, as objects of government, the nurturing of a particular religion, education, military courage, civic-spiritedness, moderation, individual excellence in the virtues, etc. On all of these *The Federalist* is either silent, or has in mind only pallid versions of the originals, or even seems to speak with contempt. The Founders apparently did not consider it necessary to make special provision for excellence. Did they assume these virtues would flourish without governmental or other explicit provision? Did they consciously sacrifice some of them to other necessities of a stable popular regime—as it were, as the price of their solution to the problem of democracy? Or were these virtues less necessary to a country when it had been properly founded on the basis of the new "science of politics"? In what follows I suggest some possible answers to these questions.

The Founding Fathers are often criticized for an excessive attention to, and reliance upon, mechanical institutional arrangements and for an insufficient attention to "sociological" factors. While a moderate version of this criticism may finally be just, it is nonetheless clear that *The Federalist* pays considerable and shrewd attention to such factors. For example, in *Federalist* No. 51, equal attention is given to the institutional and non-institutional strengths of the new Constitution. One of these latter is the solution to the "problems of faction." It will be convenient to examine *Federalist* No. 10 where the argument about faction is more fully developed than in No. 51. A close examination of that solution reveals something about *The Federalist's* view of the virtues necessary to the good life.

The problem dealt with in the tenth essay is how "to break and control the violence of faction." "The friend of popular governments never finds himself so much alarmed for their character and fate, as when he contemplates their propensity to this dangerous vice." Faction is, thus, *the* problem of popular government. Now it must be made clear that Madison, the author of this essay, was not here really concerned with the problem of faction generally. He devotes only two sentences in the whole essay to the dangers of *minority* factions. The real problem in a popular government, then, is *majority* faction, or, more precisely, *the* majority faction, *i.e.*, the great mass of the little propertied and unpropertied. This is the only faction that can "execute and mask its violence under the forms of the Constitution." That is, in the American republic the many have the legal power to rule and thus from them can come the greatest harm. Madison interprets that harm fairly narrowly; at least, his overwhelming emphasis is on the classic economic struggle between the rich and the poor which made of ancient democracies "spectacles of turbulence and contention." *The* problem for the friend of popular government is how to avoid the "domestic convulsion" which results when the rich and the poor, the few and the many, as is their wont, are at each others' throats. Always before in popular governments the many, armed with political power, invariably precipitated such convulsions. But the friend of popular government must find only "a republican remedy" for this disease which is "most incident to republican government." "To secure the public good and private rights against the danger of . . . [majority] faction, and at the same time to preserve the spirit and the form of popular government, is then the great object to which our inquiries are directed."

Without wrenching Madison's meaning too greatly, the problem may be put crudely this way: Madison gave a beforehand answer to Marx. The whole of the Marxian scheme depends upon the many—having been proletarianized—causing precisely such domestic convulsion and usurpation of property as Madison wished to avoid. Madison believed that in America the many could be diverted from that probable course. How will the many, *the* majority, be prevented from using for the evil purpose of usurping property the legal power which is theirs in a popular regime? "Evidently by one of two [means] only. Either the existence of the same passion or interest in a majority at the same time must be prevented, or the majority, having such co-existent passion or interest, must be rendered, by their number and local situation, unable to concert and carry into effect schemes of oppression." But "we well know that neither moral nor religious motives can be relied on" to do these things. The "circumstance principally" which will solve the problem is the "greater number of citizens and extent of territory which may be brought within the compass" of large republican governments rather than of small direct democracies.

Rather than mutilate Madison, let me complete his thought by quoting the rest of his argument before commenting on it:

> The smaller the society, the fewer probably will be the distinct parties and interests, the more frequently will a majority be found of the same party; and the smaller the number of individuals composing a majority, and the smaller the compass within which they are placed, the more easily will they concert and execute their plans of oppression. Extend the sphere and you take in a greater variety of parties and interests; you make it less probable that a majority of the whole will have a common motive to invade the rights of other citizens; or if such a common motive exists, it will be more difficult for all who feel it to discover their own strength, and to act in unison with each other.

I want to deal only with what is implied or required by the first of the two means, *i.e.*, preventing the majority from having the same "passion or interest" at the same time. I would argue that this is the more important of the two remedial means afforded by a large republic. If the majority comes to have the same passion or interest and holds to it intensely for a period of only four to six years, it seems certain that it would triumph over the "extent of territory," over the barriers of federalism, and separation of powers, and all the checks and balances of the Constitution. I do not wish to depreciate the importance of those barriers; I believe they have enormous efficacy in stemming the tide Madison feared. But I would argue that their efficacy depends upon a prior weakening of the force applied against them, upon the majority having been fragmented or deflected from its "schemes of oppression." An inflamed Marxian proletariat would not indefinitely be deterred by institutional checks or extent of territory. The crucial point then, as I see it, is the means by which a majority bent upon oppression is prevented from ever forming or becoming firm.

Madison's whole scheme essentially comes down to this. The struggle of classes is to be replaced by a struggle of interests. The class struggle is domestic convulsion; the struggle of interests is a safe, even energizing, struggle which is compatible with, or even promotes, the safety and stability of society. But how can this be accomplished? What will prevent the many from thinking of their interest as that of the Many opposed to the Few? Madison, as I see it, implies that nothing can prevent it in a small democratic society where the many are divided into only a few trades and callings: these divisions are insufficient to prevent them from conceiving their lot in common and uniting for oppression. But in a large republic, numerous and powerful divisions will arise among the many to prevent that happening. A host of interests grows up "of necessity in civilized nations, and divide[s] them into different classes, actuated by different sentiments and views." "Civilized nations" clearly means here large, commercial societies. In a large commercial society the interest of the many can be fragmented into many narrower, more limited interests. The mass will not unite as a mass to make extreme demands upon the few, the struggle over which will destroy society; the mass will fragment into relatively small groups, seeking small immediate advantages for their narrow and particular interests.

If the Madisonian solution is essentially as I have described it, it becomes clear that certain things are required for the solution to operate. I only mention several of them. First, the country in which this is to take place will have to be profoundly democratic. That is, all men must be free—and even encouraged—to seek their immediate profit and to associate with others in the process. There must be no rigid class barriers which bar men from the pursuit of immediate interest. Indeed, it is especially the lowly, from whom the most is to be feared, who must feel most sanguine about the prospects of achieving limited and immediate benefits. Second, the gains must be real; that is, the fragmented interests must from time to time achieve real gains, else the scheme would cease to beguile or mollify. But I do not want to develop these themes here. Rather, I want to emphasize only one crucial aspect of Madison's design: that is, the question of the apparently narrow ends of society envisaged by the Founding Fathers. Madison's plan, as I have described it, most assuredly does not rest on the "moral and religious motives" whose efficacy he deprecated. Indeed there is not even the suggestion that the pursuit of interest should be an especially enlightened pursuit. Rather, the problem posed by the dangerous passions and interests of the many is solved primarily by a reliance upon passion and interest themselves. As Tocqueville pointed out, Americans employ the principle of "self-interest rightly understood."

> The principle of self-interest rightly understood is not a lofty one, but it is clear and sure. It does not aim at mighty objects, but it attains . . . all those at which it aims. By its admirable conformity to human weaknesses it easily obtains great dominion; nor is that

dominion precarious, since the principle checks one personal interest by another, and uses, to direct the passions, the very same instrument that excites them.[23]

Madison's solution to his problem worked astonishingly well. The danger he wished to avert has been averted and largely for the reasons he gave. But it is possible to question now whether he did not take too narrow a view of what the dangers were. Living today as beneficiaries of his system, we may yet wonder whether he failed to contemplate other equally grave problems of democracy, or whether his remedy for the one disease has not had some unfortunate collateral consequences. The Madisonian solution involved a fundamental reliance on ceaseless striving after immediate interest (perhaps now immediate gratification). Tocqueville appreciated that this "permanent agitation . . . is characteristic of a peaceful democracy,"[24] one might even say, the price of its peace. And Tocqueville was aware of how great might be the price. "In the midst of this universal tumult, this incessant conflict of jarring interests, this continual striving of men after fortune, where is that calm to be found which is necessary for the deeper combinations of the intellect?"[25]

V

There is, I think, in *The Federalist* a profound distinction made between the qualities necessary for Founders and the qualities necessary for the men who come after. It is a distinction that bears on the question of the Founding Fathers' view of what is required for the good life and on their defense of popular government. Founding requires "an exemption from the pestilential influence of party animosities";[26] but the subsequent governing of America will depend on precisely those party animosities, moderated in the way I have described. Or again, founding requires that "reason" and not the "passions," "sit in judgment."[27] But, as I have argued, the society once founded will subsequently depend precisely upon the passions, only moderated in their consequences by having been guided into proper channels. The reason of the Founders constructs the system within which the passions of the men who come after may be relied upon.

Founders need a knowledge of the newly improved "science of politics" and a knowledge of the great political alternatives in order to construct a durable regime; while the men who come after need be only legislators who are but interested "advocates and parties to the causes they determine."[28] *The Federalist* speaks, as has often been observed, with harsh realism about the shortcomings of human nature, but, as has not so often been observed, none of its strictures can characterize the Founders; they must be free of these shortcomings in order to have had disinterested and true knowledge of political things. While

[23] *Democracy in America*, ed. Phillips Bradley (Knopf, New York, 1951) Vol. 2, pp. 122–23.

[24] *Ibid.*, p. 42.

[25] *Idem.*

[26] *Federalist*, No. 37, p. 232.

[27] *Federalist*, No. 49, p. 331.

[28] *Federalist*, No. 10, p. 56.

"a nation of philosophers is as little to be expected as the philosophical race of kings wished for by Plato,"[29] it is tempting to speculate that *The Federalist* contemplates a kind of philosopher-founder the posthumous duration of whose rule depends upon "that veneration which time bestows on everything,"[30] and in particular on a regime well-founded. But once founded, it is a system that has no necessary place and makes no provision for men of the founding kind.

It is clear that not all now regarded as Founding Fathers were thought by the authors of *The Federalist* to belong in that august company. Noting that "it is not a little remarkable" that all previous foundings of regimes were "performed by some individual citizen of pre-eminent wisdom and approved integrity,"[31] *The Federalist* comments on the difficulty that must have been experienced when it was attempted to found a regime by the action of an assembly of men. I think it can be shown that *The Federalist* views that assembly, the Federal Convention, as having been subject to all the weaknesses of multitudes of men. The real founders, then, were very few in number, men learned in the new science of politics who seized upon a uniquely propitious moment when their plans were consented to first by a body of respectable men and subsequently, by equally great good fortune, by the body of citizens. As it were, America provided a rare moment when "the prejudices of the community"[32] were on the side of wisdom. Not unnaturally, then, *The Federalist* is extremely reluctant to countenance any re-opening of fundamental questions or delay in ratifying the Constitution.

This circumstance—wisdom meeting with consent—is so rare that "it is impossible for the man of pious reflection not to perceive in it a finger of that Almighty hand."[33] But once consent has been given to the new wisdom, when the government has been properly founded, it will be a durable regime whose perpetuation requires nothing like the wisdom and virtue necessary for its creation. The Founding Fathers' belief that they had created a system of institutions and an arrangement of the passions and interests, that would be durable and self-perpetuating, helps explain their failure to make provision for men of their own kind to come after them. Apparently, it was thought that such men would not be needed.

But does not the intensity and kind of our modern problems seem to require of us a greater degree of reflection and public-spiritedness than the Founders thought sufficient for the men who came after them? One good way to begin that reflection would be to return to their level of thoughtfulness about fundamental political alternatives, so that we may judge for ourselves wisely regarding the profound issues that face us. I know of no better beginning for that thoughtfulness than a full and serious contemplation of the political theory that informed the origin of the Republic, of the thought and intention of those few men who fully grasped what the "assembly of demi-gods" was doing.

[29] *Federalist*, No. 49, p. 329.
[30] *Ibid.*, p. 328.
[31] *Federalist*, No. 38, p. 233.
[32] *Federalist*, No. 49, p. 329.
[33] *Federalist*, No. 38, p. 231.

[11]

The Commercial Republic & the Pluralist Critique of Marxism: An Analysis of Martin Diamond's Interpretation of *Federalist* 10

Alan Gibson

University of Wisconsin at Milwaukee

Martin Diamond's "commercial republic" interpretation of Federalist *10 is widely embraced by political scientists, especially Straussians, but this article challenges it. It argues that Madison was not a "commercial republican" and that his conception of political economy is not, as Diamond insists, implicit in Madison's understanding of an extended republic. The author argues as well that Diamond misinterprets Madison's understanding of the nature and purposes of representation and that he also systematically transforms Madison's republican remedy for the problems of faction into the pluralist critique of Marxism. The author concludes by challenging Diamond's claim that Madison's political thought should be interpreted as a species of the "New Science of Politics."*

Alan Gibson is Bradley Foundation Assistant Professor of Politics at the University of Wisconsin at Milwaukee. A specialist in American political and constitutional thought, he has published previously in the History of Political Thought.

> The unexpressed assumption upon which the arguments of the tenth *Federalist* paper rests is that the United States remain predominantly agricultural. Indirect elections and the extensive area of the United States guarantee a purely republican form because the people whose will ultimately prevails are virtuous farmers. In large part, Madison's passionate faith in a workable republican government sprang from his agrarianism.
>
> Douglass Adair[1]

1. Douglass Adair, "The Intellectual Origins of Jeffersonian Democracy: Republicanism, the Class Struggle, and the Virtuous Farmer" (unpublished doctoral dissertation, Yale University, 1943), p. 277.

"The history of modern interest in the tenth *Federalist,*" the Jeffersonian scholar Lance Banning observes, "is too nearly a tale of the replacement of one misreading by another."[2] Beneath this tale of errors, Banning might have added, lies a multiplicity of anti-Madisonian political purposes for which Madison's masterpiece has been evoked. The problems and political motivations behind the most common of these misreadings—the "economic determinist" reading—have been well documented.[3] The same, however, cannot be said of Martin Diamond's "commercial republic" interpretation of *Federalist* 10.[4] In a series of essays published between 1959 and 1976,[5] Diamond set forth an interpretation of *Federalist* 10 that, in the words of one prominent scholar, has "over the course of the past few decades come to prevail in most sectors of the academy, and has molded several generations of students who

2. Lance Banning, "The Hamiltonian Madisonian: A Reconsideration," *Virginia Magazine of History and Biography,* 90 (January, 1984): 12, n. 14.

3. The "economic determinist" reading was popularized by Charles Beard, *An Economic Interpretation of the Constitution of the United States of America* (New York: The MacMillian Company, 1913, reprinted 1939), pp. 14–16. For a critique of Beard, see Douglass Adair, "The Tenth Federalist Revisited," in *Fame and the Founding Fathers: Essays by Douglass Adair,* ed. Trevor Colbourn (New York: W. W. Norton & Company, 1974), pp. 86–87 and n. 25; Robert E. Brown, *Charles Beard and the Constitution: A Critical Analysis of "An Economic Interpretation of the Constitution"* (Princeton, NJ: Princeton University Press, 1956), pp. 29–30.

4. Several scholars have criticized the view that Madison held a pluralist conception of representation, but no one has fully explored other aspects of Diamond's interpretation. For a summary of the criticisms, see Alan Gibson, "Impartial Representation and the Extended Republic: Towards a Comprehensive and Balanced Reading of the Tenth *Federalist* Paper," *History of Political Thought,* 12 (Summer, 1991), esp. pp. 3–5 and the citations in notes 8, 10, and 11.

5. For a preliminary version of Diamond's "commercial republic" interpretation, see Diamond, "Socialism and the Decline of the American Socialist Party" (unpublished doctoral dissertation, University of Chicago, 1956), pp. 47, 72, 91–92. A comprehensive version of this interpretation was subsequently presented in five essays: Martin Diamond, "Democracy and *The Federalist:* A Reconsideration of the Framers' Intent," *American Political Science Review,* 53 (March, 1959): 52–58; "The Federalist, 1787–1788," in *History of Political Philosophy,* ed. Leo Strauss and Joseph Cropsey (Chicago: University of Chicago Press, 1963), pp. 589–93; "Ethics and Politics: The American Way," in *The Moral Foundations of the American Republic,* ed. Robert Horwitz (Charlottesville, VA: University Press of Virginia, 1986), esp. pp. 84–98; "The American Idea of Man: The View from the Founding," in *The Americans, 1976: An Enquiry in Fundamental Concepts of Man Underlying Various U.S. Institutions,* ed. Irving Kristol and Paul Weaver (Lexington, MA: Lexington Books, 1976), pp. 11–15; and *The Democratic Republic: An Introduction to American National Government* (Chicago: Rand McNally, 1966), pp. 91–98, or as reprinted in Diamond, *The Founding of the Democratic Republic* (Itasca, IL: F. E. Peacock Publishers, 1981), pp. 71–78.

have gone on to employ it, as citizens and as scholars, in the making and analysis of American public policy."[6] In general, Diamond argues that the theory Madison presents in *Federalist* 10 "anticipated and refuted Marxism."[7] More specifically, Diamond argues that Madison's principal purpose is to promote competition between economic interests and thus to diffuse the possibility of a class struggle. This purpose, according to Diamond, "implied or required" the establishment of an advanced, prosperous, commercial, or industrial society.[8] Furthermore, Diamond maintains, Madison is a thoroughgoing pluralist who believed that public policies would be formed from the compromising and bargaining of representatives who act as spokesmen for the interests that are dominant in their districts.

This essay challenges this reading of *Federalist* 10 and shows the political implications that lie beneath it. My argument divides into four sections. First, I will summarize the "commercial republic" interpretation of *Federalist* 10 as it appears in the works of Diamond. Second, through textual analysis of *Federalist* 10 and Madison's writing and a broader interpretation of Madison's conceptions of political economy and representation, I will show that Diamond is incorrect to claim (1) that Madison's theory of the extended republic "implied or required" the establishment of an advanced commercial or industrial republic and (2) that Madison was a pluralist. Third, I will show that these errors are part of a systematic restructuring of the argument in *Federalist* 10 whereby Diamond replaces Madison's two-part scheme for promoting impartial representation with the critique of Marxism and defense of the welfare state that was held by many social theorists in the 1950s and 1960s. In other words, Diamond combines two misreadings—that *Federalist* 10 shows Madison to be a pluralist and that Madison hoped to establish a "commercial" republic—and, in doing so, he transforms Madison's argument for social and institutional stability into the pluralist defense of the American system. Finally, I will address Diamond's claim that Madison's political philosophy, especially as it was presented in *Federalist* 10, is a quintessential expression of the "New Science of Politics." This interpretation, which was first presented by Diamond and has subsequently been reaffirmed by many Straussians, stresses the continuity of the political thought of Madison and the Framers to the liberalism of

6. Charles Kesler, "*Federalist* 10 and American Republicanism," in *Saving the Revolution: The Federalist Papers and the American Founding* (New York: MacMillan Publishing Company, 1987), p. 16.

7. Diamond, *The Democratic Republic,* p. 94.

8. Diamond, "Democracy and *The Federalist,*" p. 65.

Machiavelli, Locke, and Hobbes. This last section will briefly examine the problems that arise in interpretations that attempt to reduce Madison's political thought to a species of liberalism.

Two caveats are necessary at the outset. First, in arguing that Diamond incorporates central components of the pluralist critique of Marxism into his interpretation of *Federalist* 10, I am *not* arguing that he accepts the pluralist approach to the *study* of politics. Diamond was certainly not an empiricist or positivist and he would not have accepted many aspects of the methodology or epistemology on which postwar pluralism was based. Diamond was, of course, a student of Leo Strauss and was profoundly influenced by Strauss's teachings on the normative basis of politics and the unity of fact and value.[9] Nevertheless, I will contend that Diamond consciously uses *Federalist* 10 to integrate the pluralist critique of Marxism into the broader Straussian interpretation of the Framers as proponents of the "New Science of Politics." Specifically, Diamond accepts the pluralist beliefs that interest group competition is an alternative to class polarization, that commercialization and industrialization help to foster a politics of interests over ideology, and that public policies in the American system are formed from the process of coalition building among interest groups. Furthermore, he believes that these aspects of pluralism are principles upon which the American political system was founded, that they constitute an accurate description of how it operates, and that they form the foundation of a political system that is worth defending and preserving. My criticisms will be directed at showing that the foundations of the American political system are not rooted in pluralism and that Diamond's contention to the contrary is motivated by his intense opposition to Marxism and Progressivism and by his desire to defend the American system and way of life.

Second, while I will contend that Diamond's argument that Madison's theory of an extended republic "implied or required" an advanced commercial or industrial republic is ahistorical and not based on Madison's writings, I do not deny that a moderate version of the "commercial republic" interpretation can be a useful paradigm for intepreting the political and economic thought of *some* of the Framers. As it has been developed in the writings of such scholars as Albert O. Hirshman, Ralph Lerner, and Hiram Caton, the commercial republican interpretation is a sound reading of the conceptions of political economy held by such

9. See Diamond's essay "The Dependence of Fact Upon Value," *Interpretation: A Journal of Political Philosophy*, 2/3 (Spring, 1972): 226-35. For a more general Straussian critique of pluralist methodology, see *Essays on the Scientific Study of Politics*, ed. Herbert Storing (New York: Holt, Rinehart, and Winston, 1962).

important Framers as Alexander Hamilton and John Marshall.[10] As I will show in the conclusion, however, even this version of this interpretation does not accurately describe the theories of political economy held by Madison.

I. A Commercial or Industrial Republic

Diamond begins his reading of *Federalist* 10 by noting that Madison is trying to find a cure for the perennial pathology of democracies: their vulnerability to the violence of majority factions. Democratic governments contained within a small geographic area, Madison observes in *Federalist* 10 and 14, have ever been short-lived, turbulent, and incompatible with personal security and property rights. But as Diamond observes, Madison is principally concerned with the "domestic convulsion" caused by economic factions.[11] Economic interests, Madison maintains, were "the most constant and durable" source of factions.[12] Madison's specific fear, Diamond argues, is that the "great mass of the little propertied and unpropertied" would use the political supremacy they enjoyed in a popular government to vote for a division of the property of the rich.[13] This kind of conflict was the classic struggle between the rich and the poor that had plagued ancient democracies. Yet, Madison did not want to solve this problem by rendering the government undemocratic. In "Democracy and the *Federalist*," Diamond poses the problem he believes Madison faced in this way:

> *Without wrenching Madison's meaning too greatly* the problem may be put crudely this way: Madison gave a beforehand answer to Marx. The whole of the Marxian scheme depends upon the many—having been proletarianized—causing precisely such domestic convulsion and usurpation of property as Madison wished to avoid. Madison believed that in America the many could be diverted from

10. Albert O. Hirschman, *The Passions and the Interests: Political Arguments for Capitalism before Its Triumph* (Princeton, NJ: Princeton University Press, 1977); Ralph Lerner, "Commerce and Character," in *The Thinking Revolutionary: Principle and Practice in the New Republic* (Ithaca, NY: Cornell University Press, 1979), pp. 195–221; Hiram Caton, *The Politics of Progress: The Origins and Development of the Commercial Republic, 1600–1835* (Gainesville: University of Florida Press, 1988).

11. Diamond, "Democracy and *The Federalist*," p. 65.

12. *Federalist* 10, p. 59 in *The Federalist Papers*, ed. Jacob Cooke (Middletown, CT: University Press of New England, 1961). All subsequent citations of *The Federalist Papers* are to this edition.

13. Diamond, "Democracy and *The Federalist*," p. 64.

> that probable course. How will the many, the majority, be prevented from using for the evil purpose of usurping property the legal power which is theirs in a popular regime?[14]

As Diamond notes, Madison argues that there are two means by which to remedy the problems caused by majority factions without violating the principles of popular government: (1) the existence of the same passion or interest in a majority at the same time can be prevented, or (2) if such a coexistent passion or interest exists, the majority can be rendered, by its number and local situation, unable to concert and carry into effect their schemes of oppression.

At this point, Diamond begins to reconstruct Madison's argument substantially. Here and elsewhere in *The Federalist,* Madison argues that the best means for preventing the existence of the same passion or interest in the majority at the same time *and* for preventing such a majority from executing its schemes of oppression were extent of territory, representation, federalism, and the constitutional system of checks and balances. Diamond, however, focuses on Madison's suggestion that the same passion or interest should be prevented from existing in the majority at the same time. This remedy was the more important of the two proposed, Diamond argues, because it is better to prevent a majority faction from ever coalescing than to rely on institutional mechanisms to prevent one from executing its schemes of oppression after it had formed. "An inflamed Marxian proletariat," Diamond hypothesizes, "would not indefinitely be deterred by institutional checks or extent of territory." Other *"sociological"* factors are *"implied or required"* for first "weakening the force" of the majority and thus insuring that it was adequately "fragmented and deflected" before institutional checks would be effective.[15] But how could the conjunction of a common impulse of passion or interest in the majority be deflected or rendered unlikely?

In general, Diamond answers this question by arguing that Madison hopes to promote the diversification of economic interests in order to mute the effects of factions resulting from other causes. More specifically, he identifies three independent causes of factions within Madison's analysis of the causes of faction: opinion, passion, and interest. Interests are then subdivided into those that result from the diverse kinds of property and those that result from the unequal distribution of property.[16] As

14. Ibid., p. 65, emphasis added.

15. Ibid., pp. 64–66 for quotes; emphasis added.

16. Diamond, "Ethics and Politics," pp. 88–90 for Diamond's analylsis of Madison's typology of factions.

Diamond notes, Madison rejects the idea that the causes of factions could be removed, and instead argues that the effects of faction must be controlled. Controlling the effects of faction, according to Diamond, is to be achieved by a science of faction which would bring certain kinds of faction into high degree of activity, while muting other kinds.[17] Throughout history, Diamond continues, philosophers have tried to combat factionalism by refining the religious or political opinions of the society to promote salvation or disinterested virtue. But Madison had seen that such arguments over principles of justice and salvation had too often resulted in civil wars. Similarly, factionalism resulting from passions, especially those passions which lead men and women to an attachment to political figures, were also too volatile to encourage. But according to Diamond, factions resulting from interest are completely different. Madison is "far from seeking to diminish the efficacy" of factions based on interest, but instead wants to *"magnify"* the operation of interests because this is where the new cure for the "mischiefs of factions" can be found.[18] But even here, according to Diamond, Madison does not hope to encourage all forms of economic interest. Instead, Madison hopes to replace the factional strife over the unequal distribution of property by "causing to flourish a new kind of economic faction derived from a *variety* of property."[19]

In each of the versions of this interpretation, Diamond argues that this flourishing or magnification of the various kinds of property was "uniquely the product of a large modern *commercial* society."[20] Here, Diamond uses the word commercial as synonymous with industrial and capitalistic and conflates the division between agrarian commercial economies and industrial or manufacturing economies.[21] Madison's extended republic, according to Diamond, depends upon an economic system that fosters mass production, a high division of labor, and specialized "industries" and occupations, and contains a large market area. This kind of diversity, he argues, is present for example in the transportation industry, where the bus, truck, train, aircraft, and maritime

17. Ibid., pp. 87–88.
18. Ibid., p. 90, emphasis added.
19. Ibid., emphasis in original.
20. Ibid., emphasis added.
21. That Diamond means an advanced industrial economy by his use of the term "commercial" is supported by the language and examples he uses in setting forth this interpretation. It is also noteworthy that Walter Berns and other Straussians have used the term "industrial" to refer to the kind of society required to make the extended republic operative and have linked Madison's theory of an extended republic to Hamilton's "Report on Manufacturing." See Berns, "The Constitution as Bill of Rights," pp. 62–64.

industries are highly splintered and compete with each other rather than encouraging a single class of workers.[22] Such an advanced economy is necessary, Diamond contends, because "tremendous area does not of itself" produce the necessary diversity of interest.[23] "A large Saharan republic," Diamond apparently once maintained, "would be divided by the Marxist-like class struggle between date pickers and oasis landholders."[24] The necessary diversity would only be secured if the large nation was a large advanced commercial nation with a highly complex economy. This, Diamond further argues, is what Madison meant when he said that a diversity of interests "grow up of necessity in civilized nations." "Civilized" here means a commercial nation with a highly advanced economy.[25] The "assumption" that Madison makes, Diamond continues, is that small nations have fewer interests because they have less complex economies. But a large nation would have a complex economy, a high division of labor, and a great diversity of interests because it would be an advanced commercial or industrial nation. "This," Diamond contends, "is an idea straight out of Adam Smith,"

> who showed that a modern, highly differentiated economy depends upon a large market area. Mass markets make mass production possible. And mass production is highly specialized production—the division of labor into many specialized industries and specialized occupations and hence specialized interests. Thus, largeness is valuable because it makes possible the large commercial republic which proliferates economic interests. This proliferation is the variety of property which produces the moderate conflict upon which the constitutional system depends.[26]

In short, in a large commercial society, "the mass will not unite as a mass to make extreme demands upon the few." Instead "the mass will fragment into relatively small groups, seeking small immediate advantages for their narrow and particular interests."[27]

All of this, Diamond argues, depends on a number of prerequisites. First, the country has to be profoundly democratic, by which Diamond

22. Diamond, *The Democratic Republic,* pp. 94–96.

23. Ibid., p. 94.

24. This is attributed to Diamond by Walter Berns. See Berns, "The Constitution as Bill of Rights," p. 63.

25. Diamond, "The Federalist," p. 590.

26. Diamond, *The Democratic Republic,* pp. 94–95.

27. Diamond, "Democracy and *The Federalist,*" p. 66.

means that individuals should be encouraged "to seek their immediate gain and to associate with others in the process." Thus, there should be no class barriers to the acquisition of immediate benefits. Second, Diamond argues, individuals in the republic must at least sometimes achieve real gains; there must be a rising gross national product. Without this, the "scheme ceases to beguile or mollify." Third, the government must protect the property of all, the "little propertied so that they may cleave to their little as their fundamental concern, and of the much propertied so as to make their property seem beyond the reach of envy." Fourth, laws must forbid acts tampering with the value of money and acts impairing the obligation of contracts.[28]

Finally, Diamond connects this argument to the pluralist conception of representation and legislative coalition building.[29] In Madisonian democracy, according to Diamond, representatives enter Congress as "spokesmen for the interest groups dominant in his state or district" and "may be loyally prepared to sacrifice the national interest to their extreme demands."[30] But representatives soon learn that no clear majority is present in Congress and that they do not have the votes to pass such particularistic legislation. They are therefore required to cooperate and compromise with other representatives. As representatives moderate their demands, legislative coalitions form which include the demands of numerous interest groups. Ultimately, only laws and policies roughly congruent with "justice and the general good" are passed.[31] This system of "heterogeneous and fluctuating majorities" is in Diamond's estimation a "stable and decent democracy" based on a realistic assessment of human nature.[32]

II. Diamond's Interpretation: Untangling and Critiquing the Argument

What are we to make of all of this? First, on one important point, Diamond is *partially* correct. Madison is addressing the problem of class conflict in *Federalist* 10. He and many of his Federalist allies saw the ancient struggle of the rich against the poor replayed in the populist uprisings and widespread demands for debtor relief and paper money that took place in the state governments during the mid-1780s.[33] More-

28. Diamond, "The Federalist," pp. 591–92.
29. Diamond, *The Democratic Republic,* pp. 91, 98.
30. Ibid., p. 98.
31. Diamond takes the phrase "justice and the general good" from *Federalist* 51, p. 353.
32. Diamond, "Ethics and Politics," pp. 104, 90.
33. See *Federalist* 10, p. 59, and "Speech of June 6," in Convention, *The Papers of James Madison,* ed. William T. Hutchinson, et al. (Chicago: University of Chicago Press,

over, Madison hopes to use the *existing* multiplicity of economic interests which he believes would form *naturally* in the American republic as the *immediate* solution for preventing class conflict. Still, on this point, as in many aspects of this interpretation, Diamond moves from a solid insight into a series of fallacious conclusions. Madison's belief that the existing multiplicity of interests in the extended republic can be used to stabilize the republic and prevent the polarization of American society did not lead him to the conclusion that the operation of interests should be magnified or that individuals should be encouraged to seek their immediate benefit. Nor is an advanced commercial or industrial economy with mass markets, mass production, a high division of labor, and a rising gross national product "implied or required" by Madison's theory of an extended republic.

It is noteworthy that Diamond's contention that an advanced commercial economy is implied or required by Madison's theory of an extended republic does not derive from a careful textual analysis of Madison's conception of political economy. Diamond's argument is that size alone does not produce diversity and that only a commercial republic can achieve the diversity about which Madison writes. But Madison does not believe nor does the argument of *Federalist* 10 rest on the premise that tremendous area *produces* diversity. *Federalist* 10 rests on an explicit analogy: The states are analogous to the small republic and the union to the extended republic.[34] The reforms on which the Constitution is based are designed to convert the confederation of independent states into an extended republic and thus to form a truly national government. The union of course already contained a much greater variety of interests than any of the states. The point here is that increasing the area of land over which the national government exercises control does not *produce* diversity: it embraces the greater diversity which already exists.[35]

Indeed, Diamond's reading of this section of *Federalist* 10 renders Madison's argument nugatory. This may be shown in several ways. Madison not only argues that an extended republic will contain a greater variety of economic interests than a small republic, he also argues that it will contain a greater variety of religious sects than a small republic. But now apply Diamond's criticism. Size alone does not produce religious

---

and Charlottesville: University Press of Virginia, 1962–), X, pp. 32–33 (hereafter cited as *PJM*). See also Adair, "The Intellectual Origins of Jeffersonian Democracy," pp. 96–186, esp. pp. 111–29, 184–86.

34. *Federalist* 10, p. 64.

35. See *Federalist* 37, pp. 237–38; *Federalist* 53, pp. 362–63; *Federalist* 56, p. 381.

diversity either. But what prerequisites are implied or required to insure a high degree of religious diversity? Using Diamond's method of argumentation, one would be free to supply any factors that seemed plausible for creating greater religious diversity. Another problem with this line of reasoning is that, even if we accept Diamond's criticism that size alone does not create diversity, it does not follow that commercialization is necessary to produce diversity. Actually, we could attribute to Madison any political program that would produce diversity. We could, for example, argue that "tremendous area of itself does not create diversity." Thus, the nation must have a large immigrant population. Finally, to read this section of *Federalist* 10 this way actually makes extent of territory unnecessary. If commercialization, not extent of territory insures diversity, then why have an extended republic at all? Why not simply commercialize a small republic? What these kinds of arguments illustrate is that the only reasonable way to read Madison's argument is to conclude that he hopes to extend the sphere of the republic over an already existing diversity of interests. Interpreters therefore do not need to add factors that produce diversity.

Second, Diamond also supports his view that Madison favors a commercial republic by arguing that Madison is *assuming* that large nations have more complex economies than small nations. But if Madison makes this assumption, he is making a simplistic and false one. As Diamond concedes in a footnote, the size of a nation is not related to its level of economic development.[36] Similarly, there simply is no evidence that Madison favors an extended republic because he believes, like Adam Smith, that a large territory will serve as a large market area in which mass production and a high division of labor will be realized. Simply noting that Madison and Adam Smith both favored a large territory does not establish that they favored one for the same reason. The explicit reason Madison gives for favoring an extended republic is that it will help to control the effects of unjust majorities. Additional evidence—which Diamond does not provide—is necessary to establish that Madison links the extended republic to the development of a high division of labor. As we shall see, Madison's writings on political economy show that exactly the opposite of what Diamond proposes is true. Madison favors land expansion to prevent the development of an advanced commercial economy and explicitly opposes the undue division of labor because he believes that wage labor, a high division of labor, and the manufacturing of unnecessary luxuries make one class of citizens dependent on another

36. Diamond, *The Democratic Republic,* p. 94 and note 16.

and make the worker dependent on public taste that constantly changes.

Third, it is not true, as Diamond contends, that a multiplicity of interests is "uniquely the product of a large modern commercial society," if by commercial Diamond means an industrial or manufacturing society.[37] An *agrarian* society can be quite diverse. Madison made this point in 1829 in the last presentation of his argument for an extended republic:

> *As a source of discordant interests within particular States, reference may be made to the diversity in the applications of agricultural labor, more or less visible in all of them.* Take for example Virginia herself. Her products for market are in one district Indian corn and cotton; in another, chiefly tobacco; in another tobacco and wheat; in another, chiefly wheat, rye, and live stock. *This diversity of agricultural interests, though greater in Virginia than elsewhere, prevails in different degrees within most of the states.*[38]

Finally, the few textual references that Diamond cites to support his argument that Madison favors an advanced commercial republic are evidence only that Madison believes that the commercialization of the economy will follow inevitably from increases in population of the United States. Such references were common among the Framers of the Constitution and followed from the belief, derived from the Scottish Enlightenment, that societies naturally advance through stages of civilization.[39] Thus, when Madison argues that a diversity of interests "grow up of necessity in civilized societies,"[40] or when he argues that time and increases of population would "give a variety and complexity to the affairs of the nation,"[41] he means simply that a commercial and eventually a manufacturing economy are the *natural* product of social development. Such quotations do not support the claim that Madison advocates artificially advancing the commercialization of the economy any more than saying "death and taxes are inevitable" makes one an advocate of shortening life and increasing taxes. Again, as we shall see, Madison believes that undue commercialization would unavoidably result from increases in population and would bring with it corruption,

37. Diamond, "Ethics and Politics," p. 90.

38. "Majority Governments," 1833, in *Mind of the Founder: Sources of the Political Thought of James Madison,* ed. Marvin Meyers (Hanover, NH: University Press of New England, 1981), p. 413, emphasis added.

39. See Forrest McDonald, *Novus Ordo Seclorum: The Intellectual Origins of the Constitution* (Lawrence: University Press of Kansas, 1985), pp. 132–35.

40. *Federalist* 10, p. 59.

41. *Federalist* 56, p. 382.

misery, and the very class struggle that Diamond contends that it would alleviate.

Similar problems arise when Diamond's interpretation of Madison's analysis of the causes of faction is examined. The first part of Diamond's analysis of Madison's typology of factions is solid and insightful. Diamond carefully analyzes the text of *Federalist* 10 and draws out three kinds of factions from Madison's analysis: factions caused by opinion, by passion, and by interest, which are in turn subdivided between differences over degree and differences over kinds of property. But there is no evidence for Diamond's next assertion that Madison believes that factions arising from the variety of interests are benign or that Madison hopes to magnify their operation in order to mute the factionalism caused by opinion or passion. It certainly does not follow from the truism that Madison believes interests are inevitable or unavoidable that he hopes to magnify their operation and believes that the public interest naturally results from their free interaction. As Garry Wills notes, "Madison described interest as faction, which was an evil to be overcome, not an instrument of the invisible hand to be given maximum play. Since interest could not be extinguished, it should be countered, but certainly not encouraged."[42]

In general, all of Diamond's arguments are really only a veil for his real point, namely that only advanced commercial or industrial societies can be stable because only they produce the necessary divisions that will prevent workers from grasping their unity as members of a common class. To raise this point is acceptable, but to maintain that it is required by Madison's theory and then to cite Madison's theory in support of it is to engage in a circular argument.

Moreover, Diamond's contention that Madison's theory rests on a pluralist conception of representation and of coalition building is equally erroneous. Madison never explicitly argues that public policies will be formed from the compromising and bargaining of representatives in Congress. Like Arthur Bentley, Robert Dahl, and others who contend that Madison was a pluralist, Diamond *infers* that this must be case based on a series of selectively chosen and disconnected quotations. Specifically, in *Federalist* 10, Madison observes that an extended republic will reach out to embrace a greater variety of parties and interests than will a small republic. He also observes that the regulation of interests is the "principal task of modern legislation and involves the

42. Wills, "Introduction," Garry Wills ed., *The Federalist Papers* (New York: Bantam Books, 1988), p. xix.

spirit of faction in the necessary and ordinary operations of Government."[43] Diamond reads this as evidence that Madison believes the multiplicity of interests in the extended republic will be reflected in the national councils by representatives advancing the claims of the dominant interests in their districts. He then points to Madison's statement in *Federalist* 51 that "among the great variety of interests, parties and sects which it [the extended republic] embraces a coalition of a majority of the whole society could seldom take place on any other principles than justice and the general good."[44] This statement, Diamond insists, is evidence that Madison believes moderate and just majorities would emerge from the coalescing of interests in Congress.

In fact, the three principal assertions on which this interpretation rests are incorrect. First, Diamond's contention that Madison believes representatives would enter Congress "as the spokesman for the interest groups dominant in his state or district" and would be "loyally prepared to sacrifice the national interest to their extreme demands"[45] is refuted by the series of statements that Madison made about representation from 1782 to 1792 and by the design and purpose of the extended republic.[46] Throughout this period, Madison espoused a conception of representation that is best described as impartial or disinterested. Briefly, what this meant was that representatives should impartially protect the rights of all, should equally distribute public benefits and burdens among the nations' interests, and should impartially advance the public good when decisions between interests had to be made. In this conception of representation, representatives acted at times as a judge who discovered and enforced the rights of interests, at times as an arbitrator effecting a just balance between parties, and at times as a disinterested statesman who made decisions about which interests to advance in order to promote the

43. *Federalist* 10, pp. 64, 59.

44. *Federalist* 51, pp. 352–53.

45. Diamond, *The Democratic Republic,* p. 98. In places, Diamond notes that Madison believed representatives might occasionally transcend the particular interests of their constituents and act in the national interest, but he argues that this will be rare and come about because the "jostling of innumerable interests" in Congress gives representatives the freedom necessary to pursue the national interest; Ibid., p. 98.

46. For examples of Madison's conception of disinterested or impartial representation, see Madison to Jefferson, Oct. 3, 1785, Ibid., VIII, p. 374; *Federalist* 10, p. 62; 43, p. 294; and 57, p. 384; "Observations on Jefferson's Draft of a Constitution for Kentucky," Oct. 15, 1788, *PJM,* XI, pp. 286–87; Madison's statements in the First Congress during debate on impost duties, *PJM,* XII, pp. 85–86, 119; "Notes on William Loughton Smith's *Politicks and Views,*" ca. Nov. 4, 1792, *PJM,* XIV, pp. 398–99.

public good.[47] Most important, impartial or disinterested representation required that the representative remain attached to the national interest and in fact *not* be willing to sacrifice this to the particular interests of their constituents. In *Federalist* 10, for example, Madison argues that representatives elected from expanded electoral districts will "refine and enlarge the public views" and have the wisdom to "best discern the *true* interest of their country" and not sacrifice the national interest to "temporary or partial considerations."[48] Later in the Virginia Constitutional Convention, he argued that in the national councils "the sense of all America would be drawn to a single point. The collective interest of the union at large, will be known and pursued. No local views will be permitted to operate against the general welfare."[49]

Second, the quotes that Diamond and other scholars use to support the idea that Madison hoped the multiplicity of interests in the republic would be reflected in the national councils, where fluctuating and heterogeneous coalitions would form, support a quite different interpretation. Consider how Diamond selectively quotes the central argument of *Federalist* 10.

> Extend the sphere and you take in a greater variety of parties and interests; you make it less probable that a majority of the whole will have a common motive to invade the rights of other citizens; or if such a common motive exists, it will be more difficult for all who feel it to discover their own strength and to act in unison with each other. *Besides other impediments it may be remarked that where there is a consciousness of unjust and dishonorable purposes communication is always checked by distrust in proportion to the number whose concurrence is necessary.*[50]

When the italicized sentence is added, the paragraph changes meaning. Here, Madison is simply arguing that majority factions will be neutralized before they are able to take over Congress because communications between them will become more difficult as the number of citizens in the republic increases. The principal reason for this is that the members of unjust majority factions do not trust each other. Instead, communica-

47. For more on these aspects of Madison's theory of representation, see Gibson, "Impartial Representation and the Extended Republic," especially pp. 14–17.

48. *Federalist* 10, p. 62, emphasis added.

49. "Power to Levy Direct Taxes," in the Virginia Ratifying Convention, June 11, 1788, *PJM*, XI, pp. 109-10.

50. *Federalist* 10, p. 64, emphasis added.

tions between them are broken and the factional conspiracy breaks apart. This distrust, Madison hypothesizes, increases as the number in the majority—"the number whose concurrence is necessary"—increases.[51]

Moreover, Madison's statement that the regulation of interests involves the spirit of party and faction in the operations of Government is not a concession toward pluralism, but simply a sober admission that while the extended republic is designed to reduce the probability that interests will be introduced into the national councils, interests or factions cannot be completely purged from them. The introduction of factions or interests causes "instability, injustice and confusion"[52] and is to be prevented, not encouraged. Perhaps most important, both components of Madison's scheme of representation—expanded electoral districts and extent of territory—are designed to minimize the reflection of factions or interests in the public councils. Expanded electoral districts insure that representatives are responsible for a greater number and variety of interests and help insure that they pay greater attention to the national interest. Meanwhile, extent of territory acts to prevent unjust combinations of interests and thus prevents majority factions from gaining control of the legislature.

Third, Madison does not espouse the pluralist theory of coalition building or believe that just legislation will result from the free interplay of self-interested groups. Unlike pluralists, Madison believes that a public good—a "permanent and aggregate interest"—exists which is not the product of the bargaining of interest groups or the least common denominator of these groups.[53] Madison envisions two possible types of coalitions among citizens and representatives: factional coalitions and coalitions designed to promote the public interest. In *Federalist* 51 and in his other writings, Madison argues simply that extent of territory and the diversity of interests helps to prevent factional combinations from forming and concerting their actions, enabling coalitions and combinations based on the public good to overcome the obstacles raised by the extended republic.[54] In other words, whereas pluralists envision society as composed exclusively of competing interests and believe that any

51. *Federalist* 10, p. 64.

52. *Federalist* 10, p. 59. See also *Federalist* 15, p. 96 and *Federalist* 27, p. 172.

53. *Federalist* 10, p. 56.

54. For insights into Madison's understanding of coalition building, see *Federalist* 10, p. 64; 51, pp. 352–53; and 58, p. 392; Madison, "Speech of June 28, 1787" [in Constitutional Convention], *PJM*, X, p. 80; and "Speech of June 11, 1788 [in Virginia Ratifying Convention], *PJM*, XI, p. 115.

coalitions between these interests involve conflict, bargaining, moderation, and compromise, Madison believes that interests are able to act in unison and form coalitions only when all pursue the common interest—an entity which, to borrow Gordon Wood's description, is "prior to and distinct from the various private interests of groups and individuals."[55] Indeed, when Madison speaks of competition between interest and parties, he maintains that it will prevent the public good from being realized. "The public good," he writes, "is disregarded in the conflicts of rival parties."[56]

All of this is made clearer when Diamond's reading of *Federalist* 10 is contrasted with a republican interpretation of Madison's conception of political economy and his solution to the class struggle. Throughout his life, Madison was a republican, not an advocate of advanced commercialization or a pluralist. Like Thomas Jefferson, Madison believed that the farmer was the most virtuous type of citizen in a republic and that institutional and social stability were ultimately linked to the preservation of an agrarian economy.[57] More specifically, as Drew McCoy has shown, Madison believed with many of his contemporaries that societies naturally and unavoidably evolved through stages from hunting and gathering societies to subsistence agrarian societies and eventually commercial societies (first commercial agrarian societies and then eventually manufacturing societies).[58] Each stage was believed to be characterized by a different set of human relationships and by different patterns of

55. Gordon Wood, *The Creation of the American Republic, 1776–1787* (Chapel Hill: University of North Carolina Press, 1969), p. 58.

56. *Federalist* 10, p. 57.

57. See Madison's essay "Republican Distribution of Citizens," *PJM*, XIV, pp. 244–46. See also Adair, "The Intellectual Origins of Jeffersonian Democracy," pp. 27–30, 65–95, 272–96.

58. See Drew McCoy, *The Elusive Republic: Political Economy in Jeffersonian America* (Chapel Hill: University of North Carolina Press, 1980), pp. 120–35. See also Forrest McDonald, *Novus Ordo Seclorum*, pp. 134–35; Colleen Sheehan, "Madison's Party Press Essays," *Interpretation: A Journal of Political Philosophy*, 17 (Spring, 1990): 355–77; Paul Eidelberg, *A Discourse on Statesmanship: The Design and Transformation of the American Polity* (Urbana: University of Illinois Press, 1974), pp. 131, 201–05.

For the primary source material in which Madison sets forth this theory of political economy see especially Madison to Jefferson, Aug. 30, 1784, *PJM*, VIII, pp. 107–08; Madison to Lafayette, March 20, 1785, *PJM*, VIII, pp. 250–54; Madison to Thomas Jefferson, June 19, 1786, *PJM*, IX, pp. 76–77; "Speeches of June 26, July 26, August 7," in the Constitutional Convention, *PJM*, X, pp. 76–77, 117, 139; "Observations on Jefferson's Draft of a Constitution for Virginia," October 15, 1787, *PJM*, XI, pp. 287–88; "Speech of June 12, 1788," in Virginia Ratifying Convention, *PJM*, XI, pp. 125–26; "Speech of April 9, 1789," in First Federal Congress, *PJM*, XI, pp. 69–74.

behavior. Furthermore, the advanced stages were characterized by the civilizing influence of commerce, a high division of labor, and the desire for conveniences and luxuries. This manufacturing stage was reached when the population became dense and when adequate land was no longer available for tillage.

This much Hamilton, Madison, and Jefferson agreed upon. The fundamental differences in their visions of American society were based on whether they hoped to forestall or to promote the progress of society. Hamilton, of course, hoped to expedite the movement of America through these stages of development by government sponsorship of manufacturing, whereas Madison and Jefferson relished the agrarian base of the American economy. They likened manufacturing societies to the corrupt and decaying societies of Europe, decried the effects that industrialization would have on the character of the citizenry, and believed that manufacturing and undue commercialization eventually led to the formation of a propertyless poor who would seek refuge in the cities and eventually become a threat to the property rights of landed interests. Madison, Jefferson, and Jeffersonians in general believed that Hamiltonian policies would create a class struggle, a war of the poor against the rich.

Well before the Constitutional Convention, Madison wrestled with the question of how best to promote an agrarian republic and thus preserve the character of its citizenry against the increasing pressures of population and development. After sifting through the problem with characteristic thoroughness, he developed a plan of political economy and a solution to the class struggle that was an integral part of his nationalistic reform program. Madison's general aspiration was to delay the modernization of society beyond the point of the commercial agrarian stage. Commercial—not subsistence—farming would insure that the citizenry was energetic, independent, and virtuous. Commercial farming would also allow the United States to benefit from the civilizing benefits of commercialization without suffering the ill effects characteristic of manufacturing societies. Like Benjamin Franklin and Jefferson, Madison believed this kind of society would be promoted best by a policy of landed and commercial expansion. Expansion across space, according to Madison, could delay development through time. If the growing population of the United States was allowed to settle western lands, then the manufacturing stage of society could be delayed, a propertyless poor would not develop, and social stability would be secured. Furthermore, Madison realized that commercial farmers would naturally produce surplus crops. These surplus crops in turn could be sold in European markets in exchange for manufacturing goods, most of which would therefore not have to be produced in the United States. This plan required a strong national governent that could promote internal improvements in order to make surplus crops available for market, protect American navigation rights on the Mississippi, and engage in whatever commercial retaliation was necessary to open international markets.

To describe this conception of political economy as anti-commercial is inaccurate. Commercialism—understood here principally as international trade—is an important element in Madison's agrarian vision. But to use *Federalist* 10 to give Madison's name to the vision of an advanced commercial-business republic with mass production and a high division of labor or to say that he deliberately sought to exacerbate greed and acquisitiveness is quite simply irresponsible scholarship. Indeed, Madison is not a "commercial republican" at all if that phrase carries the connotations given it by Straussian scholarship. Instead, Madison's conception of political economy is best viewed in its ambiguity. As Drew McCoy argues, "Madison was still caught between conflicting claims of classical republicanism and modern commercial society"; he struggled "to define and implement a viable synthesis that was relevant to the American experience."[59]

III. The Pluralist Critique of Marxism

If Diamond misrepresents Madison's argument in *Federalist* 10, then a new question arises: What was Diamond defending? The "beforehand answer to Marx,"[60] which Diamond attributes to Madison, is in fact the critique of socialism and defense of the welfare state that Diamond had espoused in his 1956 dissertation. This set of arguments, in turn, is very much akin to the pluralist critique of Marxism and the "end of ideology" literature that was common among social scientists in the 1950s and 1960s.

Theodore Lowi, John Manley, Edward Purcell, and especially Michael Rogin have shown that pluralist theory, as developed and defended after World War II, was a unified argument for social and institutional stability with industrialization as a key factor.[61] For our purposes, the pluralist

59. McCoy, *Elusive Republic,* p. 134.

60. Diamond, "Democracy and *The Federalist,*" p. 65.

61. Theodore Lowi, *The End of Liberalism: Ideology, Policy, and the Crisis of Public Authority* (New York: W. W. Norton & Company, 1969), pp. 29-97; John F. Manley, "Neo-Pluralism: A Class Analysis of Pluralism I and Pluralism II," *The American Political Science Review,* 77 (June, 1983): 368-83; Edward A. Purcell, *The Crisis of Democratic Theory: Scientific Naturalism & the Problem of Value* (Lexington: University Press of

defense of democracy within industrial-capitalist societies may be thought of as a bundle of three closely related propositions. First, pluralism is a critique of the Marxist conception of the structure of society. Here, pluralists reject the Marxist view of society as polarized between workers and owners and instead insist that modern societies are composed of a multiplicity of groups, each of which is engaged in the rational pursuit of its interest.[62] When individuals identify with and join interest groups, society becomes horizontally differentiated between competing interests rather than stratified between classes, and interest group bargaining replaces class conflict. As Lowi notes, pluralists need not reject the Marxist axiom that workers despise owners in order to reject the inevitability of class conflict.[63] True, workers are in conflict with owners, but they also are in conflict with workers in other industries and those in the lower classes. Thus, rather than uniting to deliver a knockout blow to institutions, Americans join interest groups and jab one another into equilibrium.

Second, from this view of the structure of society, pluralists fashion a corresponding theory of "democratic" politics. At its core, the pluralist conception of the political process stresses the importance of instrumental rationality and the voluntary association. Instrumental rationality is central to the pluralists because a politics of self-interest is seen as more stable than moralistic or ideological politics. If individuals can be encouraged to pursue their own interest rationally, pluralists reason, then political debate can be channeled into discussions about the distribution of resources and the *means* for implementing policies, and away from high-toned and potentially explosive discussions about the ends or goals of the society.[64] The voluntary association is central as the vehicle of this conception of politics, for membership in voluntary associations constitutes a viable form of democracy. Voluntary associations act as points of access to government through which individuals can gain a voice, a hearing, and also a means to discipline government officials who do not support the group's interests. Furthermore, voluntary groups

---

Kentucky, 1972), pp. 235–72; Michael Rogin, *The Intellectuals and McCarthy: The Radical Specter* (Cambridge, MA: M.I.T. Press, 1967), pp. 9–31.

62. Manley, "Neo-Pluralism," p. 370. Manley notes that both Arthur Bentley and David Truman saw interest group analysis as an alternative to class analysis. See Bentley, *The Process of Government: A Study of Social Pressures* (Chicago: University of Chicago Press, 1908), pp. 465–68; and Truman, *The Government Process: Political Interests and Public Opinion* (New York: Alfred A. Knopf, 1951), pp. 165–67.

63. Lowi, *End of Liberalism*, pp. 42–44.

64. Rogin, *Intellectuals and McCarthy*, pp. 12–15, 17–18.

channel self-interest, prevent individuals from becoming isolated and alienated, and buffer citizens from the multiple sources of coercion that exist in industrial society.[65]

In the formation of public policies, pluralists conceive of elected representatives as brokers for the interest groups that are dominant among their constituents and of the government as a neutral receptacle for public preferences. But because society is made up of such a great diversity of interests, no one interest can be dominant in Congress. Representatives, therefore, must bargain; they must moderate the demands made in the interests of their constituents before they can coalesce with other groups. In general, public policies are formed, not by deliberation about content or social impact of the policy at hand, but by a *process* in which coalitions expand to take in more and more groups until a necessary majority is formed.[66] Here, pluralists set forth the idea of a self-regulating political system in which competition between interest groups is guided by an "invisible hand" and the "public interest" emerges as a residue of group conflict.

Third, a commitment to industrial capitalism underscores both the pluralist critique of mass politics and the understanding of a pragmatic politics of competing groups. First, industrialization creates the social diversity necessary to prevent the polarization of society into two classes and thus leads to the formation of interest groups which discipline members with respect to the dominant values of the society. Second, industrialization insures the dominance of instrumental rationality and thus of nonideological politics. Whereas traditional communities were held together by shared values, industrialization leads to the creation of capitalistic and bureaucratic structures that are both the product and the progenitor of instrumental rationality. In short, as Rogin writes, industrialization creates "both capitalistic and bureaucratic structures and an instrumental orientation; these make rational politics possible. It creates as well the groups that integrate individuals into the rational order. Weber's [capitalistic and bureaucratic] society solves Durkheim's problem [of the isolation of the individual following industrialization]; Modern pluralism grows out of this synthesis."[67]

Together these propositions were the DNA of a unified defense of the

65. Rogin, *Intellectuals and McCarthy*, p. 15; Richard H. Pells, *The Liberal Mind in a Conservative Age: American Intellectuals in the 1940's and 1950's* (New York: Harper and Row, 1985), pp. 130–62.

66. Lowi, "American Business, Public Policy, Case-Studies, and Political Theory," *World Politics*, 16 (July, 1964): 678–79.

67. Rogin, *Intellectuals and McCarthy*, pp. 10–16; quote is on p. 14.

values, procedures, and institutions of American democracy and welfare state which was standard among political scientists during the 1950s and 1960s. Deradicalized by the experience of Nazism, the unveiling of Stalinism, and the threat of McCarthyism, pluralists praised voluntary associations, ad hoc alliances, bargaining and compromising, the rational pursuit of economic goods, and the multi-centered structure of American society because these were the stuff of moderate and non-ideological politics. Furthermore, social scientists punctuated their prose with Augustinian-like references to the limitations of human nature and concluded that change had to take place incrementally and within the system. Finally, social scientists spurned formalistic analyses and instead documented the "sociological factors" they believed lay beneath the mystery of the tensile strength of American institutions. Among these factors, economic abundance and a diverse social structure created by industrial capitalism were considered paramount.

The central components of this critique of Marxism and defense of the welfare state were presented in Diamond's 1956 dissertation and then integrated into the interpretation of *Federalist* 10 that he first presented in full form three years later.[68] In his dissertation, Diamond argues that the "millennial" hopes of the American socialist movement had been deflated by twentieth century reality. American workers, Diamond contends, had never been revolutionary. Instead, in America, democratic procedures had insured the orderly pursuit of nonrevolutionary goals, and tremendous wealth had insured that workers could expect to satisfy their economic needs and desires. These factors—in addition to the lack of a feudal heritage, the presence of a broad middle class, the possibility of social mobility, the tendency of the American political system to promote intgration and compromise, and the consensus among Americans to a democratic and commercial society—insured that American workers scrambled for immediate gains through interest groups and elections and did not unite as a class to challenge the existing order. Furthermore, according to Diamond, the New Deal and the establishment of the

68. Diamond, like many in the 1950s and 1960s who defended the American system based on pluralist principles, was a radical during the 1930s and 1940s who later became a fervent anti-Marxist. Specifically, Diamond (then Martin Dies) was a member of the American Socialist Party from 1937 to 1952 and eventually served as a member of the national executive committee. He began his political career as the member of an "ultra-revolutionary youth group" but ended as "an extreme 'right wing' member" of the Socialist Party. Diamond, "Socialism and the Decline of the American Socialist Party," p. 1. See also Marvin Meyers, "The Least Imperfect Government: On Martin Diamond's Ethics and Politics," *Interpretation: Journal of Political Philosophy,* 8 (May, 1980): 5; and William Schambra's comments in "Preface," *Founding of the Democratic Republic,* pp. v–x.

welfare state had civilized capitalism by incorporating the viable suggestions of the socialist program while repudiating its millennial expectations and revolutionary character.[69]

Three years after he completed his dissertation, Diamond used *Federalist* 10 as a vehicle to teach the conclusions he had reached and that he and others were unifying into the critique of Marxism and defense of the American system outlined above.[70] Consider the following parallels between Diamond's interpretation of *Federalist* 10 and the pluralist critique of Marxism. Diamond's general contention, that "Madison's whole scheme essentially" involved replacing the class struggle with the "safe, even energizing struggle" of interest groups directly, parallels the vision he and others had of interest group politics as an alternative to the class struggle.[71] Diamond's assertion that Madison's theory implies or requires a large, complex, advanced economy that would create a high division of labor, increase economic diversity, and fragment the mass into interest groups seeking small immediate advantages for their narrow and particular interests, is also congruent with the conclusions that he and pluralist theorists reached about the importance of industrial capitalism for creating social diversity and instrumental politics. Diamond's argument that Madison hoped to mute the fatal causes of faction that resulted from ideology, passion, and class interest by magnifying the operation of particular interests parallels the emphasis he and others placed on the need to replace ideological politics with a pragmatic interest-based politics.

Other themes in Diamond's dissertation and the pluralist critique of mass politics also resonate in his interpretation of *Federalist* 10. In the first version of the "commercial republic" interpretation, Diamond defines democracy, not in terms of citizen participation, but as freedom for individuals "to seek their immediate profit and to *associate* with

69. Diamond, "Socialism and the Decline of the American Socialist Party," esp. pp. 65-101, 136-64. See also Diamond, "The Problems of the Socialist Party After World War One," in *Failure of a Dream?: Essays in the History of American Socialism*, ed. H. M. Laslett and Seymour Martin Lipset (Garden City, NY: Doubleday, 1974), pp. 362-79 and 390-93.

70. The relationship between Diamond's conclusions in his dissertation about reasons for the failure of the Socialist Party in the United States and his interpretation of *Federalist* 10 is direct. Indeed, the "prerequisites" (democracy and prosperity) he adds to Madison's theory are precisely the ones he cites in his dissertation as the factors preventing American workers from joining the Socialist Party. Compare "Socialism and the Decline of the American Socialist Party," pp. 65-101, esp. 70-71, with *The Democratic Republic*, pp. 91-98, esp. 96-97.

71. Diamond, "Democracy and *The Federalist*," p. 66.

others in the process."[72] Diamond also integrates the pluralist conception of representation and coalition building into Madison's theory, and argues that interest group politics is a "stable and decent [form of] democracy."[73] Diamond also adds "sociological" or noninstitutional factors such as economic abundance to Madison's theory in order to defend the Framers against the charge that their constitutional system rested on a mechanistic system of checks and balances and ignored the social factors that insure institutional stability. Finally, Diamond contends that the unity—the consensus—that Americans held with respect to a democratic and commercial society is the premise of Madison's argument for an extended republic.[74]

In general, this interpretation of *Federalist* 10 serves a series of closely related strategic purposes. First, it allows Diamond to turn *Federalist* 10 against Charles Beard and the Progressive historians. Beard of course had labelled Madison an economic determinist based on a selective reading of *Federalist* 10, and then used this interpretation as the foundation for his argument that the Framers lived in a class-divided society and consciously adopted an anti-democratic Constitution that would protect the property rights of the few. In contrast, Diamond points to the diversity of interests that Madison identifies, and contrasts this structure of society with class polarization. He also points to the pluralist model of representation and coalition building as evidence that the Framers established a system that was "fundamentally democratic."[75] Third, these specific interpretations also served a broader purpose as arguments for the legitimation and preservation of American institutions. Progressive historians and political scientists had sought to expose the self-interested and anti-democratic intentions of the Framers in order to clear a path for reform of the Constitution, whereas Diamond argues that the Framers sought a system that was "decent, even though democratic," in order to maintain support for the Constitution while combatting what he believes to be ill-conceived reforms. Finally, this interpretation provides Diamond with a forum for teaching his life experiences about the reasons for the failure of socialism in the United States and about why a class struggle did not come about in the United States.

72. Ibid., p. 66, emphasis added.
73. Diamond, "Ethics and Politics," p. 90.
74. Diamond, "Socialism and the Decline of the American Socialist Party," pp. 91–92.
75. Diamond, *The Democratic Republic*, 85.

IV. Madison, Commercial Republicanism, and the "New Science of Politics"

Defenders of Diamond's interpretation might still try to include Madison's conception of political economy and his system of constitutionalism within a broad paradigm of capitalism and liberalism. They might, in other words, say: "Sure, Madison hoped to preserve an agrarian society, but agrarian societies can be quite commercial and Jeffersonian political economy was very much a species of commercial capitalism. Similarly, the Madisonian system of checks and balances and separation of powers was very much a modern, liberal solution to the problem of faction. Unlike the ancients, Madison did not try to use education, character-forming laws, and community opinion to try to suppress factions among the citizenry. Instead, he used extent of territory and institutional arrangements to make faction a check upon faction and to pit ambition against ambition. All of this is what Diamond really meant when he argued that Madison's political philosophy was a quintessential expression of the 'New Science of Politics.' "

Certainly, Diamond supports the "commercial republic" reading of *Federalist* 10 by linking it with the broader paradigm of the rise of classical liberalism as developed and taught by Leo Strauss.[76] Diamond's application of this interpretive framework to the political thought of the Founders has subsequently been followed and expanded upon in the scholarship of such influential Straussians as Walter Berns, Ralph Lerner, and, most recently and forcefully, Thomas Pangle.[77] At its core, this interpretation rests on the belief that the political philosophy of Madison and the Framers should be analyzed as part of the revolt against classical political philosophy that had begun with Machiavelli and continued with Hobbes, Bacon, Locke, and others. In this interpretation, modern political philosophy is different from ancient political philoso-

76. Strauss's teaching on the rise of liberalism is found in *Natural Right and History* (Chicago: University of Chicago Press, 1953).

77. Berns, *Taking the Constitution Seriously,* pp. 173–80; Lerner, "Commerce and Character," pp. 195–221; Thomas Pangle, *The Spirit of Modern Republicanism: The Moral Vision of the American Founders and the Philosophy of Locke* (Chicago: University of Chicago Press, 1988). To my knowledge, Leo Strauss never included the American Framers among the disciples of "the New Science of Politics," and there is some reason to doubt that he would have accepted this application of his teaching. See for example his comment in the introduction to *History of Political Philosophy* suggesting that *The Federalist* reflects back to classical political philosophy (*History of Political Philosophy,* p. 6). But contrast this with his comments in *Natural Right and History,* p. 245. See also the discussion in Eidelberg, *A Discourse on Statesmanship,* pp. 101–31 and 101, notes 2 and 3.

phy in several key ways. Ancients, like Plato and Aristotle, believed that man was by nature a political or social animal who could develop his humanness fully only within the *polis*. They therefore designed comprehensive sets of laws that regulated religious belief, established stern educational programs, and limited economic activity, in order to develop a common character among the citizenry. Beyond this, the ancients did not believe that men were created equal. Instead, they believed that a select few within each community had the "right to rule" and that it was the obligation of the regime to develop the excellence of these men while simultaneously maintaining a just regime for those who did not have exceptional ability. The "moderns," such as Hobbes and Locke, on the other hand, envisioned a fictitious, prepolitical "state of nature" in which man in his essence was free, equal, independent, and dominated by a concern for self-preservation and material comfort. Most important, perhaps, this different understanding of the essence of man led the moderns to profoundly different conclusions about the proper role of the government. Whereas the ancients designed rigorous laws to mold the character of the citizenry, the moderns believed that the passions and interests of men were ineradicable. Thus they accepted man "as he was" and believed that the government should be shrewdly designed to channel and counterpoise newly liberated passions and interests. Finally, the moderns believed that the ends of government should be limited by the condition of men in state of nature. They therefore believed that government should be restricted to the protection of life, property, and individual rights. In short, the moderns, including the Framers of the American Constitution, "lowered the aims and expectations" of political life by giving "primacy to the efficacy of means rather than to the nobility of ends."[78]

Beyond this, this interpretation also stresses the acceptance by the Founders of an early form of commercial capitalism. The Founders are said to be "commercial republicans" who rejected the perfectionist pretenses of classical and theological regimes in favor of the realistic alternative of incremental economic growth. These commercial republicans praised commerce and the market model because they believed that, while men could not be expected to exercise virtue consistently or to pursue salvation, men could be expected to pursue systematically the satisfaction of their physical and material desires. More broadly, this was said to introduce constancy and predictability into society, to encourage

78. A concise expression of this paradigm of interpretation may be found in Diamond, "Ethics and Politics," esp. pp. 75–85; quote is on p. 83.

an interdependent and peaceful world, and to provide a humane, prosperous, and stable polity. Specifically, stability would be achieved because individuals would pursue their "enlightened" self-interest rather than warring over frivolous religious and political principles. Further, the tension between private and public good (so important in classical and Christian philosophy) was dissolved into the belief that individuals need only pursue their individual interests in order inadvertently to serve the public good.[79]

Whatever value this broad interpretative paradigm has for illuminating some aspects of the political thought of some of the Founders, it has obfuscated important dimensions of Madison's political philosophy, created widespread misunderstandings about other aspects of it (especially his conception of political economy), and unnecessarily erected broad barriers to understanding the path of Madison's political career. The first of these errors results primarily from the Straussian tendency to split the history of political thought into two sweeping alternatives. Within the interpretative paradigm of "the New Science of Politics," the common teachings of Medieval and Classical political philosophy are emphasized and then differentiated from liberalism which, in turn, is said to have sprung fully armed from the heads of Machiavelli, Hobbes, and Locke. Since Madison's political thought was certainly not a species of classical or Medieval political thought as the Straussians understand it, it therefore must be reducible to liberalism.[80]

Such an interpretation, however, masks the complexity and synthetic quality of Madison's political philosophy.[81] In general, Madison's political philosophy is a subtle synthesis of contractual and natural rights arguments about the origins and legitimate ends of government with republican conceptions of virtue, the public good, disinterested representation, and political economy. Madison rejects the small *polis* and the use of comprehensive sets of laws to repress faction, to develop a common character among the citizenry, and to educate the few differently from the many. He also espouses contractual theory about the legitimate origins and limitations of government and believes that *one* of the principal ends of government is the protection of individual rights. Finally,

79. See Lerner, "Commerce and Character," pp. 195–221. Lerner does not include Madison among the "commercial republicans" he analyzes.

80. On the problems of understanding the political thought of the Framers as a revolt against modernity, see Marvin Meyers's sympathetic criticisms in "The Least Imperfect Government," pp. 11–15.

81. See Lance Banning, "Jeffersonian Ideology Revisited: Liberal and Classical Ideas in the New American Republic," *The William and Mary Quarterly*, 42 (January, 1986): 3–19.

Madison's experiences with the state governments under the Articles of Confederation and his exhaustive study of ancient republics led him to believe that the classical conception of participatory republicanism is too turbulent and will result in violations of individual rights and the neglect of the public good.

Nevertheless, Madison is hardly an unqualified proponent of liberalism. Contrary to Diamond's assertions, Madison's acceptance of the inevitability of faction is neither a glorification or justification of self-interest nor a concession that virtue had exited the American republic. Furthermore, Madison does not propose a mechanistic or self-regulating political system that simply absorbed and channelled (let alone risked deliberately magnifying) interests and passions in the hope that the public good would somehow emerge from the compounding and counterpoising of ambitions and interests. While Madison dispassionately diagnoses "men as they are" and begins his reasoning about the structure and content of the political system from this basis, he does not neglect the conditions under which the character of the citizenry will be best developed and sustained. In other words, Madison begins with a complex, subtle, and realistic assessment of human nature, then moves to an equally complex and subtle account of the conditions necessary to perpetuate a republican character among the citizenry.

Specifically, Madison continues to hold fast to four clusters of republican concepts. First, he believes that virtue is the foundation of republican governments, that no system of separation of powers can substitute for it, and that Americans possess sufficient virtue to maintain a republican form of government.[82] As Lance Banning argues, to reconcile Madison's many statements about the inevitability of self-interested actions by the citizenry with his concern for virtue requires a subtle understanding of what Madison meant by virtue. He did not, Banning argues, believe that citizens had to surrender their interests totally in obedience to an abstracted public good in order to act virtuously. Each interest had a legitimate claim within the common interest and thus could —and indeed should—be advanced. A commitment to virtue among the citizenry, however, did require that interests be advanced only to the degree they were compatible with the public good, that obedience be given to laws and policies made collectively, and that deference be shown for established elites.[83]

82. See Madison's quote from "Speech of June 20, 1788," in Virginia Ratifying Convention, *PJM,* XI, p. 163. See also *Federalist* 55, p. 378.

83. Lance Banning, "Some Second Thoughts on Virtue and the Course of Revolutionary Thinking," in *Conceptual Change and the Constitution,* ed. Terence Ball and J. G. A. Pocock (Lawrence: University Press of Kansas, 1988), pp. 194–212.

Second, Madison holds to a republican conception of representation, believes that the public good can only be secured through deliberate acts of the government made by its representatives (not through the mysterious workings of a self-regulating political system), and believes that citizens should participate in governing the nation beyond simply electing their representatives.[84] As noted earlier, "disinterested" or "impartial" representation meant that representatives could neither use office to advance their personal interests nor advance the interests of their constituents at the expense of the public good. What is most important here is that this conception of representation illustrates that, while Madison rejects the classical model of participatory republicanism in which the citizens "assemble and administer the Government in person,"[85] he embraces representation because, among other things, it helps to secure the republican goal of promoting the public good or common interest. Representation is the means by which the interests and views of the whole nation can be brought together.[86] Representation also makes it possible for the wisest and most virtuous men in the republic to deliberate about the ends and goals of public policy.[87] In short, representation is the means by which the nation's many interests are reconciled with the common interest.

Third, Madison holds a substantive conception of the public good and believes that the promotion of the public good is one of the chief ends of the government. Madison did not believe that the public good is a "by-product of self interest in the same way Locke viewed private acquisition as a public benefit." Nor did he believe that the public good is the "middle ground" resulting from the accommodation and compromise of competing interests.[88] Instead, Madison's understanding of the public good—his understanding of the set of policies that are in the "*permanent* and aggregate" interests of the nation—is linked to his belief in the many

84. On the idea that Madison and other Framers believed the government should actively promote the public good, see Ralph Ketcham, "Publius: Sustaining the Republican Principle," *The William and Mary Quarterly,* 44 (July, 1987): 578–81; Cass R. Sunstein, "Beyond the Republican Revival," *The Yale Law Journal,* 97 (1988): 1539–90, and "Interest Groups in American Public Law," *Stanford Law Review,* 38 (November, 1985): 29–87.

85. *Federalist* 10, p. 61.

86. "Speech of June 30, 1787," in Constitutional Convention, *PJM,* X, p. 90; "Speech of July 26, 1787," in Constitutional Convention, *PJM,* X, p. 117.

87. On the importance of deliberation to Madison and the Framers, see Joseph M. Bessette, "Deliberative Democracy: The Majority Principle in Republican Government," in *How Democratic Is the Constitution?,* ed. Robert A. Goldwin and William A. Schambra (Washington, DC: American Enterprise Institute, 1980), pp. 112–16.

88. Erler, "The Problem of the Public Good in *The Federalist,*" pp. 654, 665.

benefits of agrarianism.[89] He argues that the preservation of an agrarian society is sound policy, both economically and politically. Since there is a natural abundance of land in the United States, the agrarian interest deserves to be promoted based on strictly economic considerations. The U.S. would always have cheap land and thus be able to sell its surplus crops at lower prices than Europeans. Conversely, the Europeans had a well-developed system of manufacturing with which the U.S. could not compete effectively.

Still, as Douglass Adair notes, Jefferson and Madison "were not primarily interested in the agrarian way of life as the producer of abundant crops and as the source of wealth; they were interested in the agrarian way of life as the producer of the ideal type of citizen for a republic."[90] Here Madison's understanding of the public good takes on an enlarged and more classical dimension. Again, Madison believes that because landed farmers were beholden to neither an employer nor the government, they were "the best basis of public liberty, and the strongest bulwark of public safety."[91] Madison also clearly connects his desire to perpetuate an agrarian republic to his belief that husbandry was the best way of life. The independent farmer, Madison argues, enjoyed the benefits of health, virtue, intelligence, and happiness that were less evident in other occupations.[92] The important point is that, far from forming a republic whose representative citizen is the acquisitive individual who exercises "bourgeois virtues," Madison hopes to use landed expansion to insure the perpetuation of a "republican distribution of citizens" composed primarily of independent farmers who exercise "agrarian virtues."

Fourth, and related to Madison's agrarianism, Madison's conception of political economy is pregnant with republicanism. Indeed, this is the dimension of Madison's political thought most misunderstood by Straussian interpretations derived from the "New Science of Politics." These misunderstandings spring from the tendency of Straussians to read *The Federalist* as a "Great Book" with a unified teaching on the benefits of commercial republicanism. Hamilton's economic policies are then viewed as the prerequisites for the actualization of the government created by the Constitution.[93] In fact Madison's system of political

89. *Federalist* 10, p. 57, emphasis added.

90. Adair, "The Intellectual Origins of Jeffersonian Democracy," p. 29.

91. "The Republican Distribution of Citizens," *PJM,* XIV, p. 246.

92. Ibid., pp. 244–46.

93. See Rossum, "Statesmanship and the Future of the American Commercial Republic," *The American Founding,* pp. 157–70. For the kinds of errors that result from reading *The Federalist* as a unified exposition on commercial republicanism, see Berns, "The Constitution as Bill of Rights," pp. 62–64.

economy fused Adam Smith's principles of free trade and a natural system of commerce among nations into a republican commitment to preserve an agrarian society. Again, this conception of political economy rests on a commitment to commerce and certainly contains liberal dimensions. Like most eighteenth century agrarian sympathizers, Madison is a "friend to a very free system of commerce" and believes that "commercial shackles are generally unjust, oppressive and impolitic."[94] But again, to explode Madison's advocacy of unrestricted international commerce into an acceptance of commercial capitalism, unrestricted economic growth within the United States, and Hamilton's policies is anachronistic and misleading. Madison opposes industrialization, urbanization, wage labor, broad inequalities of wealth thought to result from increasing commercialization, artificially increasing the division of labor, and efforts to facilitate the growth of capital and centralize it in the national government. He does not believe that individuals can serve the public good simply by advancing their own interests. Within Madison's system of political economy, commerce is the handmaiden of agriculture, not an end in itself. Similarly, Madison certainly does not oppose economic growth, but neither does he believe that it is the central goal of government. Economic growth is a secondary consideration, to be guided by other *political* considerations.[95] All of these commitments and beliefs are opposed to commercial republicanism as the Straussians characterize it. All are held firmly and explicitly by Madison.

Finally, interpretations that treat Madison's political philosophy as a species of commercial capitalism simply cannot explain the path of his political career. During the mid-1780s and throughout the period surrounding the formation of the Constitution, Madison is said to have reacted to the paper money crisis and Shays' rebellion with a nationalistic reform program designed to protect property rights in order to promote a ceaseless striving for gain among the citizenry. He is also said to have endorsed a Constitution that was "clearly a vehicle for modern commerce that could empower another Walpole."[96] In the 1790s, however, Madison served as the organizer and principal theorist of the Republican Party. He vehemently opposed Hamilton's fiscal policies, emphasized federalism and strict construction of the Constitution (constitutional

94. "Speech of April 9, 1789," in First Federal Congress, *PJM,* XII, p. 71.

95. In addition to McCoy's works and Adair's dissertation, see John Ashworth, "The Jeffersonians: Classical Republicans or Liberal Capitalists?" *Journal of American Studies,* 18 (December, 1984): 430–32.

96. Robert Eden, "Republicanism & the American Founding, 1600–1789," *Polity,* 22 (Winter, 1989): 367.

principles that the Anti-Federalists had used to oppose adoption of the Constitution), and extolled the virtues of the independent yeoman farmer. As Colleen Sheehan observes, for scholars "who grew up understanding Madison as Publius, and Publius as the father of the commercial republic, the Madison of the 1790s is rather startling."[97] Indeed, scholars who contend that Madison was a "commercial republican" during the calling of the Constitutional Convention are simply led to the conclusion that, for whatever reasons, Madison drastically changed course.[98] But was Madison really so inconsistent or is the charge of inconsistency the result of faulty interpretations of the political and economic doctrines that Madison believed were at the foundation of the Constitution? It is beyond the scope of this essay to explore this question thoroughly, but political scientists should take a lesson from the historian Drew McCoy who argues convincingly that the conceptions of political economy that Madison and Hamilton presupposed at the adoption of the Constitution were drastically different.[99] Armed with the understanding that Madison believed the Constitution would be interpreted to promote the preservation of an agrarian republic, scholars may then explain his turn to oppose Hamiltonian policies in the name of the Constitution. Most important, the persistent and puzzling question about the path of Madison's political career would begin to clear.

97. Colleen Sheehan, "Madison's Party Press Essays," p. 374.

98. See Peterson, "The Problem of Consistency in the Statesmanship of James Madison," pp. 122–34; Walter Berns, *The First Amendment and the Future of American Democracy* (New York: Basic Books, 1976), pp. 115–16; Erler, "The Problem of the Public Good in *The Federalist*," pp. 648–50, 665–67; Caton, *The Politics of Progress*, pp. 459–511, especially 485–88.

99. McCoy, *The Elusive Republic*, pp. 120–35.

[12]
Madisonian Democracy

Robert A. Dahl

I

Democracy, it is frequently said, rests upon compromise. But democratic theory itself is full of compromises—compromises of clashing and antagonistic principles. What is a virtue in social life, however, is not necessarily a virtue in social theory.

What I am going to call the "Madisonian" theory of democracy is an effort to bring off a compromise between the power of majorities and the power of minorities, between the political equality of all adult citizens on the one side, and the desire to limit their sovereignty on the other. As a political system the compromise, except for one important interlude, has proved to be durable. What is more, Americans seem to like it. As a political theory, however, the compromise delicately papers over a number of cracks without quite concealing them. It is no accident that preoccupation with the rights and wrongs of majority rule has run like a red thread through American political thought since 1789. For if most Americans seem to have accepted the legitimacy of the Madisonian political system, criticism of its rather shaky rationale never quite dies down; and as a consequence, no doubt, the Madisonian theses must themselves be constantly reiterated or even, as with Calhoun, enlarged upon.

It would be misleading to ascribe all the propositions that follow directly to James Madison himself. For though Madison articulated most of the basic elements of the theory, before and at the Constitutional Convention and later in certain of the "Federalist Papers," his relation to the propositions that follow must be qualified in three ways.

First, despite dissents of varying sorts, much of what he set forth or implied was widely shared by other political leaders of his time. Madison, however, had the rare gift—doubly rare among political leaders—of lucid, logical, and orderly exposition of his theoretical argument; perhaps in no other political writing by an American is there a more compactly logical, almost mathematical, piece of theory than in Madison's *The Federalist*, No. 10. Hence it is both convenient and intellectually rewarding to turn to Madison to discover a basic rationale for the American political system.

Second, even Madison did not always articulate his assumptions as to fact, definition, or value. I have therefore found it necessary from time to time to supply what seem to me these implied assumptions. This is a risky business, and in defense I can only say that in every instance I have sought to make his position as orderly and coherent as possible and not to weaken it. In brief, I rely on Madison where he seems to make his own case most logical, consistent, and explicit, but in all other cases I try to formulate a proposition that seems to me more logical, consistent, and explicit. It is a style of argument I am concerned with, not a perfect reproduction of Madison's words.

Third, it is a little unfair to treat Madison as a political theorist. He was writing and speaking for his time, not for the ages. He was up to his ears in politics, advising, persuading, softening the harsh word, playing down this difficulty and exaggerating that, engaging in debate, harsh controversy, polemics, and sly maneuver. He was a great man, intelligent, principled, successful; and he built well. To take his ideas apart and examine them piece by piece is, undoubtedly, a little unfair. As an admirer of Madison the man and statesman, I would be content to let Madison the theorist lie in peace—if it were not for the fact that he so profoundly shaped and shapes American thinking about democracy.

The central proposition of the Madisonian theory is partly implicit and partly explicit, namely:

Hypothesis 1: If unrestrained by external checks, any given individual or group of individuals will tyrannize over others.

This proposition in turn presupposes at least two implied definitions:

DEFINITION 1: An "external check" for an individual consists of the application of rewards and penalties, or the expectation that they will be applied, by some source other than the given individual himself.[1]

DEFINITION 2: "Tyranny" is every severe deprivation of a natural right.

Three comments need to be made about the definition of tyranny supplied here. First, it is not the same as Madison's explicit definition of tyranny in *The Federalist*, No. 47, where he states that "the accumulation of all powers, legislative, executive, and judiciary, in the same hands, whether of one, a few, or many, may justly be pronounced the very definition of tyranny."[2] It seems to me that Madison's explicit definition has been derived from Definition 2 by the insertion of an empirical premise, i.e., the accumulation of all powers in the same hands would lead to severe deprivations of natural rights and hence to tyranny. It seems reasonable, therefore, to reconstruct Madison's explicit argument into the following Madisonian reasoning:

Hypothesis 2: The accumulation of all powers, legislative, executive, and judiciary in the same hands implies the elimination of external checks (empirical generalization).

The elimination of external checks produces tyranny (from Hypothesis 1).

Therefore the accumulation of all powers in the same hands implies tyranny.

As it stands Madison's explicit definition is unnecessarily arbitrary and argumentative, and since it can be derived from a definition that is not only highly congenial to the whole cast of Madison's thought

1. Hypothesis 1 and Definition 1 are a paraphrase, but I think a reasonably accurate paraphrase, of numerous references in Madison's writings. My language may be more modern, but the ideas are, I think, expressed by Madison, e.g., in his "Observations" of April, 1787, in *The Complete Madison, His Basic Writings*, ed. Saul K. Padover (New York: Harper & Bros., 1953), pp. 27–29. Cf. also his letter to Jefferson, October 24, 1787, pp. 40–43.

2. *The Federalist*, ed. Edward Mead Earle ("The Modern Library" [New York: Random House, n.d.]), p. 313. For another analysis of Madison see Mark Ashin, "The Argument of Madison's 'Federalist' No. 10," *College English*, XV (October, 1953), 37–45.

but, as will be shown in a moment, helpful to the logic of his argument, I propose to adhere to Definition 2.

Second, the natural rights are not clearly specified. Among Madison's contemporaries as among his predecessors there was by no means a perfect agreement as to what "rights" are "natural rights." Such agreement as existed was on a high level of abstraction and left wide opportunities for disagreement in specific cases.[3] As will be seen, the absence of an agreed definition of natural rights is one of the central difficulties of the Madisonian theory.

Third, I have used the expression "severe deprivation" to cover an ambiguity in the thought of Madison and his contemporaries. How far could governments go in limiting natural rights without becoming tyrannical? Here again, neither Madison nor any other Madisonian, so far as I am aware, has provided wholly satisfactory criteria. However, Madison no doubt agreed with his contemporaries that, at a minimum, any curtailment of natural rights without one's "consent" was a sufficiently severe deprivation to constitute tyranny.[4] The ambiguity is so deep-seated, however, that I doubt whether any phrasing can patch it up.

As corollaries of Hypothesis 1 two additional hypotheses need to be distinguished:

Hypothesis 3: If unrestrained by external checks, a minority of individuals will tyrannize over a majority of individuals.

Hypothesis 4: If unrestrained by external checks, a majority of individuals will tyrannize over a minority of individuals.

Or as Hamilton put it more succinctly, "Give all power to the many, they will oppress the few. Give all power to the few, they will oppress the many."[5]

3. Clinton Rossiter has summarized the state of agreement on natural rights at the time of the Revolution in *Seedtime of the Republic* (New York: Harcourt, Brace & Co., 1953), chap. xiii.

4. *Ibid.*, p. 383. Rossiter describes the consensus on this point.

5. *The Debates in the Several State Conventions on the Adoption of the Federal Constitution as Recommended by the General Convention at Philadelphia, in 1787, Together with the Journal of Federal Convention*, etc., ed. Jonathan Elliot (2d ed.; Philadelphia: Lippincott, 1941), V, 203. Hereafter this will be referred to as *Elliot's Debates*.

Let us now turn to the proof of Hypothesis 1, and hence also of Hypotheses 3 and 4.

II

Clearly Hypothesis 1 is an empirical proposition. Its validity can therefore be tested only by experience. Madison's own methods of validating the hypothesis seem to be representative of the widespread American style of thought that in this book is called "Madisonian." Madison's first method of proof is to enumerate historical examples drawn, for example, from the history of Greece and Rome.[6] His second method of proof is to derive the hypothesis from certain psychological axioms that were widely accepted in his day—and perhaps are now. These axioms are Hobbesian in character and run something like this: Men are instruments of their desires. They pursue their desires to satiation if given the opportunity. One such desire is the desire for power over other individuals, for not only is power directly satisfying but it also has great instrumental value because a wide variety of satisfactions depend upon it. The flavor of these axioms is conveyed in remarks at the state and federal conventions from both supporters and opponents of the Constitution:

Lenoir, in the North Carolina debates: "We ought to consider the depravity of human nature, the predominant thirst of power which is in the breast of everyone, the temptations rulers may have, and the unlimited confidence placed in them by this system."[7]

Franklin, at the Federal Convention: "There are two passions which have a powerful influence on the affairs of men. These are ambition and avarice; the love of power and the love of money."[8]

Hamilton, at the Federal Convention: "Men love power."[9]

Mason, at the Federal Convention: "From the nature of man, we may be sure that those who have power in their hands . . . will always, when they can, . . . increase it."[10]

III

If Hypothesis 1 is accepted as validated by these two methods (or others), then Hypotheses 3 and 4, which are merely derived from

6. E.g., Madison's remarks at the Convention, *ibid.*, p. 162.

7. *Ibid.*, IV, 204.

8. *Ibid.*, V, 145.

9. *Ibid.*, V, 200.

10. *Ibid.*, V, 294.

Hypothesis 1, are also valid. Nevertheless, Hypothesis 4 seems to play a special role in Madisonian thought.[11]

Neither at the Constitutional Convention nor in the "Federalist Papers" is much anxiety displayed over the dangers arising from minority tyranny; by comparison, the danger of majority tyranny appears to be a source of acute fear. The "Federalist Papers," for example, reveal no deep-seated distrust of the executive branch, which was regarded by the authors (wrongly, as it turned out) as the strong point for the minority of wealth, status, and power.[12] By contrast, a central theme of Madison's is the threat from the legislature, supposedly the stronghold of the majority. Thus: "It is against the enterprising ambition of this department that the people ought to indulge all their jealousy and exhaust all their precautions."[13]

And it follows from Definition 2, as well as from Madison's own explicit definition of tyranny, that legislative or majority tyranny is not any less tyrannical than executive or minority tyranny. They are equally undesirable. Thus: "The founders of our republics . . . seem never to have recollected the danger from legislative usurpations which, by assembling all power in the same hands, must lead to the *same* tyranny as if threatened by executive usurpations."[14] Madison buttressed his position by calling upon Jefferson, who in his *Notes on Virginia* had said, "One hundred and seventy three despots would surely be as oppressive as one . . . an *elective despotism* was not the government we fought for."[15]

Both majorities and minorities, then, are weighed on the same scales. For the objective test of non-tyranny is not the size of the ruling group;

11. For example, see Padover, *op. cit.*, pp. 28, 37–38, 41, 45–47. But see also Madison's "comment" in 1833, *ibid.*, p. 49. In later years Madison seems to have had a more tender regard for the majority principle. Like most Americans, Madison seems never to have felt any logical contradiction in his position.

12. Hamilton appears to have written the relevant papers, Nos. 67–77; given his political views, he might be expected to deprecate the dangers of tyranny from this branch. Moreover, it must never be forgotten that the "Federalist Papers" were polemical and propagandistic writing, reflecting a highly partisan viewpoint.

13. *The Federalist*, No. 48, p. 323.

14. *Ibid.*, p. 322. (Italics added.)

15. *Ibid.*, p. 324.

it is whether the ruling group, whatever its size, imposes severe deprivations on the "natural rights" of citizens.

IV

So far, the propositions in the Madisonian system are definitional or empirical. With the admission of one more definition, it now becomes possible to state the goals to be used in guiding the choice among possible political systems.

What is needed at this point is a definition of "democracy." However, in Madison's day the term "democracy" was less common than in ours. To some extent it was associated with radical equalitarianism; it was also ambiguous because many writers had defined it to mean what we today would call "direct" democracy, i.e., non-representative democracy. The term "republic" was frequently used to refer to what we would be more inclined to call "representative" democracy.[16] It will do no harm, therefore, to adhere to Madison's own term "republic," which he defined as follows:

> DEFINITION 3: A republic is a government which (*a*) derives all of its powers directly or indirectly from the great body of the people and (*b*) is administered by persons holding their office during pleasure, for a limited period, or during good behavior.[17]

It is now possible to state the central ethical goal of the Madisonian system, which can conveniently be called the Madisonian axiom:

> The goal that ought to be attained, at least in the United States, is a nontyrannical republic.

This goal was taken as a postulate. Because it was not seriously questioned at the Constitutional Convention or elsewhere and has never been seriously questioned in this country since that time, the goal has pretty much remained an unexamined axiom.[18] Hence one cannot

16. On this question, however, see the comment of Elisha P. Douglas, *Rebels and Democrats* (Chapel Hill: University of North Carolina Press, 1955), p. viii.

17. *The Federalist*, No. 39. "It is *essential* to such a government that it is derived from the great body of society, not from an unconsiderable proportion, or a favored class of it. . . . It is *sufficient* for such a government that the persons administering it be appointed, either directly or indirectly, by the people; and that they hold their appointments by either of the tenures just specified. . . ."

18. Cf. Louis Hartz, "The Whig Tradition in America and Europe," *American Political Science Review*, XLVI (December, 1952), 989–1002.

state unequivocally the rationale that may lie behind this postulate. To Madison and many others, however, the axiom was probably deduced implicitly from a more basic ethical postulate with the assistance of an empirical premise, as follows: (1) Natural rights ought to be attained (axiom); (2) attainment of natural rights is non-tyranny (from Definition 2); (3) a republic is a necessary although not a sufficient condition for non-tyranny (empirical generalization). Q.E.D.—the Madisonian axiom.

Although the first two of these propositions were widely accepted, some well-known Federalists like Hamilton denied the validity of the third. Hamilton, who had a frank but by then unrealistic preference for monarchy, said in effect that a republic might be a possible but it was assuredly not a necessary condition for non-tyranny; among the possible conditions for non-tyranny he would have included a constitutional monarchy. Fortunately for the stability of the American political system, but unfortunately for political theory, Hamilton's challenge was treated as a gigantic irrelevancy.

V

After this short excursion into ethical theory, the remainder of the Madisonian system consists of predictive statements, definitions, and inferences derived from what has been given so far. For, given the Madisonian axiom, the question now becomes: What conditions are necessary for attaining the goal of a non-tyrannical republic?

Hypothesis 5: At least two conditions are necessary for the existence of a non-tyrannical republic:

First Condition: The accumulation of all powers, legislative, executive, and judiciary, in the same hands, whether of one, a few, or many, and whether hereditary, self-appointed, or elective, must be avoided.[19]

Second Condition: Factions must be so controlled that they do not succeed in acting adversely to the rights of other citizens or to the permanent and aggregate interests of the community.[20]

VI

In attempting to prove that the first condition is an essential prerequisite of every non-tyrannical republic, the Madisonian system be-

19. *The Federalist*, No. 47, p. 313.

20. *The Federalist*, No. 10, pp. 57 ff.

comes so deeply ambiguous that it is difficult to know precisely how to do justice to the argument.

We are faced at the outset with two alternative possibilities. The first I rejected a moment ago as essentially trivial. For if we accept Madison's explicit definition of tyranny, and if we postulate that tyranny is to be avoided, then the first condition is necessary merely by definition: (1) Tyranny means the accumulation of all powers, etc. (definition). (2) Tyranny is undesirable (axiom). (3) Therefore the accumulation of all powers, etc., is undesirable. Yet to solve the problem by definition leaves open many major questions. For example, if one asks, "Why is tyranny as you define it undesirable?" the explicit Madisonian system proves no answer. For surely "the accumulation of all powers, legislative, executive, and judiciary, in the same hands" is not obviously or intuitively undesirable. The undesirability of such a state of affairs must then flow from certain predicted consequences. What are these consequences? To keep the Madisonian system intact, I took the liberty of specifying what these consequences must be, namely, "the severe deprivation of natural rights."[21]

Another possibility, therefore, is to accept Madison's implicit definition that tyranny is every severe deprivation of natural rights and to propose the empirical hypothesis that the accumulation of all powers, etc., will eliminate external checks (Hypothesis 2) and hence produce tyranny (by Hypothesis 1 and Definition 2).

Yet if we now attempt to retrieve the Madisonian system from a trivial argument by the addition of these implicit hypotheses and definitions, we are faced with a dilemma. For if by "power" we mean constitutionally prescribed authority, then the First Condition is demon-

21. Although the definition is not explicit in Madison's writings, so far as I can discover, it is clearly implied. For example, he argues in many places that in "a just and a free government . . . The rights both of property & of persons ought to be effectually guarded." But if there were universal suffrage and if the majority of citizens lacked property, then property rights might not be protected. Hence government must be so contrived as to prevent property rights from being infringed by majorities (Padover, *op. cit.*, pp. 37–38). Otherwise the government would not be "just & free." I have simply made "just & free" equivalent to "non-tyranny" and "tyranny" equivalent to non-"just & free," i.e., to deprivation of natural rights. If Madison's concept of "majority tyranny" has any other possible meaning than this, I have been unable to discover it.

strably false, for it is pretty clearly not necessary to every non-tyrannical republic, as an examination of parliamentary, but certainly non-tyrannical, democratic systems like that of Great Britain readily prove. Let us suppose, then, that by "power" we mean to describe a more realistic relationship, such as A's capacity for acting in such a manner as to control B's responses. Then it is plain that "legislative, executive, and judiciary" by no means comprise all the power relations or control processes in a society. For example, electoral processes make it possible for some individuals to control others; certainly they assist non-leaders in controlling leaders. Hence it is not obvious that the mere accumulation of legislative, executive, and judicial power must lead to tyranny, in the sense of severe deprivation of rights. Popular elections (and competing parties) might be sufficient to prevent such invasions of basic rights. That is, Madison's argument now seems to require proof of at least one additional hypothesis, namely:

Hypothesis 6: Frequent popular elections will not provide an external check sufficient to prevent tyranny.

For if this last hypothesis is false, and frequent popular elections will provide an external check sufficient to prevent tyranny, then Madison's argument about the need to keep the legislative, executive, and judicial powers constitutionally or otherwise separate in order to prevent tyranny is also patently false.

Now the explicit Madisonian system in effect tries to prove the validity of this hypothesis by assuming the validity of Hypothesis 2, that is, that the accumulation of all powers, legislative, executive, and judiciary, in the same hands implies the elimination of external checks. If we assume this hypothesis, then Hypothesis 6 on the inadequacy of popular elections must be true. But having proved Hypothesis 6 by assuming Hypothesis 2, we cannot now turn around and prove Hypothesis 2 by assuming the validity of Hypothesis 6.

The Federalist, No. 49,[22] to be sure, does attempt to prove that the

22. Although the authorship of this paper was once contested, it is now established that Madison, not Hamilton, was the author. (Irving Brant, *James Madison*, Vol. III: *Father of the Constitution, 1787–1800* [New York: Bobbs-Merrill Co., 1950], p. 184.)

check provided by electoral processes is inadequate to prevent all powers, legislative, executive, and judiciary, from accumulating in the same hands. Two observations can be made about this argument. First, even if the proposition is valid, it cannot establish the necessity of the First Condition except by the trivial definitional route rejected above. For, except by definition, it does not follow that the accumulation of "all powers, legislative, executive, and judiciary" leads to tyranny. Second, the specific arguments in support of the proposition in *The Federalist*, No. 49, seem to me patently invalid or highly inconclusive. They are (1) that frequent appeals would indicate defects in government and so weaken the veneration necessary to stability; (2) that public tranquillity would be dangerously disturbed by interesting public passions too strongly; (3) that being few in number, members of the executive and judiciary can be known only to a small part of the electorate; the judiciary are far removed, the executive are objects of jealousy and unpopularity. By contrast, members of the legislature dwell among the people and have connections of blood and friendship. Hence the contest for power would be an unequal one in which the legislature would swallow up the others.[23]

I am afraid, then, that the validity of the First Condition is not established.

Yet the necessity for this condition for a non-tyrannical republic is an article of faith in the American political credo. From it Madison, and successors who out-Madisoned Madison, have deduced the necessity for the whole complicated network of constitutional checks and balances: the separate constituencies for electing President, senators, and representatives; the presidential veto power; a bicameral Congress; presidential control over appointments, senatorial confirmation; and, in part, federalism. Over the years still other checks and balances within the political system have developed and have been

23. Madison also appends an argument more common among antidemocrats, namely, that issues in popular elections would not be decided on "the true merits of the question" but on a partisan basis. Unlike the first three, which seem to me plainly false, this one is merely meaningless—at least without a very considerable philosophical and empirical inquiry not attempted by Madison. Cf. *The Federalist*, No. 49, pp. 327–32.

rationalized by the same arguments: judicial review, decentralized political parties, the Senate filibuster, senatorial "courtesy," the power of committee chairmen, and indeed almost every organizational technique that promises to provide an additional external check on any identifiable group of political leaders.

VII

Let us now turn to the Second Condition: Factions must be so controlled that they do not succeed in acting adversely to the rights of other citizens or to the permanent and aggregate interests of the community.

How is this state of affairs to be attained? In answering this question, Madison produced one of the most lucid and compact sets of political propositions ever set forth by an American: the now familiar argument of *The Federalist*, No. 10.[24] I shall here attempt no more than to set forth the bare skeleton of his argument.

Obviously a definition is needed at the outset:

DEFINITION 4: A faction is "a number of citizens, whether amounting to a majority or a minority of the whole, who are united and actuated by some common impulse of passion, or of interest, adverse to the rights of other citizens, or to the permanent and aggregate interests of the community."[25]

Given this definition, it is easy to show from Hypothesis 1 that a faction will produce tyranny if unrestrained by external checks. Thus the Second Condition is proved to be necessary.

How, then, can factions be controlled? In brief, Madison argues with elegant rigor and economy that the latent causes of faction are sown in the nature of man: they stem from differences of opinion based on the fallibility of man's reason, from attachments to different leaders, and from differences in property, that are in turn a result of "the diversity in the faculties of men." If people cannot be made alike, the causes of faction could be controlled only by destroying liberty—a solution obviously barred to anyone seeking a non-tyrannical republic.

24. This represents a refinement of ideas Madison had already expounded at the Convention and earlier. Cf., for example, *Elliot's Debates*, V, 242–43.

25. *The Federalist*, No. 10, p. 54.

Hence it follows that factions cannot be controlled by eliminating their causes. In this fashion Madison proves the validity of

Hypothesis 7: If factions are to be controlled and tyranny is to be avoided, this must be attained by controlling the effects of faction.

Can the effects of faction be controlled so as to avoid tyranny? Yes, Madison tells us, provided two further conditions are present:

Hypothesis 8: If a faction consists of less than a majority, it can be controlled by the operation of "the republican principle" of voting in the legislative body, i.e., the majority can vote down the minority.

Hypothesis 9: The development of majority faction can be limited if the electorate is numerous, extended, and diverse in interests.

The validity of Hypothesis 8 must have seemed self-evident to Madison, for he made no effort to prove it. Yet it is an assumption of crucial importance to the Madisonian system; for if it can be shown that the operation of the "republican principle" will not in all cases prevent severe deprivations from being inflicted on the majority by the minority, then the Madisonian system will not produce a non-tyrannical republic. We shall return to this point.

Hypothesis 9 is proved by an argument that contains a number of exceedingly doubtful statements and some that, if true, raise serious questions as to the validity of other basic hypotheses in the Madisonian system. Madison argues that there are only two possible ways of controlling the effects of a majority faction. First, the existence of the same passion or interest in a majority at the same time must be prevented. But because in this case no majority faction would exist, Madison seems to have reversed his earlier argument that the causes of faction cannot be controlled. Second, even though a majority faction exists, its members must be made incapable of acting together effectually.

Both ways of controlling the effects of a majority faction, Madison argues, are provided by a large republic. There ensues an extremely dubious and probably false set of propositions purporting to show that representation in a large republic will provide "better" politicians and reduce the probability of success of "the vicious arts by which elections are too often carried." Then Madison states a final and exceptionally important proposition: "Extend the sphere, and you take in a greater variety of parties and interests; you will make it less probable that a majority of the whole will have a common motive to invade the rights of other citizens; or if such common motive exists, it will be more difficult . . . to act in unison."[26] Let us then paraphrase Madison:

Hypothesis 10: To the extent that the electorate is numerous, extended, and diverse in interests, a majority faction is less likely to exist, and if it does exist, it is less likely to act as a unity.

VIII

In the course of attempting to give meaning to the First Condition, it has already been necessary to examine its validity. Let us now turn to a brief appraisal of the validity of some of the other hypotheses and the utility of some of the definitions in the deliberately formalized Madisonian style of thought I have set forth so far.

The first hypothesis, it will be recalled, is implicit rather than explicit in the Madisonian argument, and it was formulated as follows:

Hypothesis 1: If unrestrained by external checks, any given individual or group of individuals will tyrannize over others.

DEFINITION 1: An external check for any individual consists of the application of rewards and penalties, or the expectation that they will be applied, by some source other than the given individual himself.

Inter alia, the first hypothesis implies:

1. That control over others by means of governmental processes is a highly valued goal, i.e., such control is believed to be either directly or indirectly rewarding to those who exercise it.

2. That it is impossible by social training to create through conscience a self-restraint sufficient to inhibit impulses to tyranny among political leaders. Madison in fact says as much: "Conscience—the only remaining tie—is known to be inadequate in individuals; in large numbers, little is to be expected from it."[27]

3. That the range of sympathetic identification of one individual with another is too narrow to eliminate impulses to tyranny.

Many political theorists prior to Madison placed heavy emphasis on the role of social indoctrination and habituation in creating attitudes,

26. *The Federalist,* No. 10, p. 61. Cf. also the last paragraph of *The Federalist,* No. 51, pp. 339 ff.

27. *Elliot's Debates,* V, 162.

habits, and even personality types requisite to a given type of political system. Machiavelli, who on the whole was not a soft-headed observer of human behavior, evidently believed that the basic check to tyranny was not so much a set of legal formulas about the prescribed distribution of certain controls—i.e., a formal constitution—as a network of habits and attitudes inculcated in the society. Surely this view is more in keeping with modern concepts of behavior than the one implicit in the Madisonian system. A contemporary social scientist would be inclined to assume that the prevailing type of family relationship, for example, would be at least as important a determinant of political behavior as the constitutionally prescribed system of governmental controls. Family structure, belief systems, myths, heroes, legitimate types of behavior in primary groups, prevailing or modal personality types, these and other similar factors would be crucial in determining the probable responses of leaders and non-leaders and hence the probability of tyranny or non-tyranny. Although scientific inquiry into this area has barely begun, it is clear that some personality types or predispositions are much more likely than others to lead to favorable or unfavorable attitudes toward authoritarian leaders. In the United States these predispositions may be related to such factors as class, education, and age.[28]

In other words, present evidence suggests that "internal checks"—the conscience (super-ego), attitudes, and basic predispositions—are crucial in determining whether any given individual will seek to tyrannize over others; that these internal checks vary from individual to individual, from social group to social group, and from time to time; and that the probability of tyranny emerging in a society is a function of the extent to which various types of internalized responses are present among members of that society.

Yet we should make Madison and his present-day followers seem

28. Morris Janowitz and Dwaine Marvick, "Authoritarianism and Political Behavior," *Public Opinion Quarterly*, XVII (summer, 1953), 185; also T. W. Adorno *et al.*, *The Authoritarian Personality* (New York: Harper & Bros., 1950). I am indebted to my colleague, Professor Robert Lane, for calling my attention to the fact that if socioeconomic class is held constant, the other correlates do not appear to be statistically significant. Cf. his "Political Personality and Electoral Choice," *American Political Science Review*, XLIX (March, 1955), 173–90.

fools if we were to assume that they were oblivious to these or similar facts. Long before modern inquiry on authoritarian and democratic personality types, Jefferson, for example, insisted on the importance of a predominantly agricultural milieu for creating the kinds of behavior necessary to the operation of a democracy. Pre-Revolutionary writers had insisted upon moral virtue among citizens as a necessary condition for republican government. Virtue in the citizenry, they felt, in turn required "hortatory religion, sound education, honest government, and a simple economy."[29] In his explicit argument, however, Madison seems to have ignored or played down what must have been a common assumption of his time; no doubt here, as in many other points of the argument, we are confronted by a position oversimplified for purposes of debate and controversy. (Madison had more important tasks at hand than to satisfy the logic of critics a century and a half later.) Thus we might try to save one of Madison's basic implicit hypotheses by casting it in probability terms:

Hypothesis 1': The probability that any given individual or group will tyrannize over others if unrestrained by external checks is sufficiently high so that if tyranny is to be avoided over a long period, the constitutionally prescribed machinery of any government must maintain some external checks on all officials.

That is, it seems reasonable to propose that even if internal checks might frequently inhibit impulses to tyranny, they may not always do so with all individuals likely to be in a position to tyrannize. Hence, if tyranny is to be avoided, external checks are required. And these external checks must be constitutionally prescribed.

IX

Before we accept the reasonableness of the last sentence, however, let us examine some of the kinds of external checks that are used to control behavior. Let us assume that behavior is a product of one's conscious or unconscious expectations of rewards and penalties for one's socially modified drives.[30] What kinds of external checks does the Madisonian have in mind as restraints on tyranny?

29. Rossiter, *op. cit.*, pp. 429–32.

30. Note that when cast in psychological terms, the distinction between internal and external controls over behavior becomes somewhat hazy. Even in the case of

> A mere demarcation on parchment of the constitutional limits of the several departments [he tells us] is not a sufficient guard against those encroachments which lead to a tyrannical concentration of all the powers of government in the same hands.[31]
>
> To what expedient, then, shall we finally resort, for maintaining in practise the necessary partition of power among the several departments, as laid down in the Constitution? The only answer that can be given is, that as all these exterior provisions are found to be inadequate, the defect must be supplied, by so contriving the interior structure of the government as that its several constituent parts may, by their mutual relations, be the means of keeping each other in their proper places.
>
> . . . The great security against a gradual concentration of the several powers in the same department, consists in giving to those who administer each department the necessary constitutional means and personal motives to resist encroachments of others. . . . Ambition must be made to counteract ambition. The interest of the man must be connected with the constitutional rights of the places.[32]

Now the more we examine these passages, the more they seem to dissolve before our eyes like the Cheshire cat. Why is the separation of powers necessary to prevent tyranny? Because it provides an external check on the tyrannical impulses of officials. Why does it provide an external check? Because it guarantees that the ambitions of individuals in one department will counteract those in another. Why will these countervailing ambitions be effective? Presumably because individuals in one department can invoke the threat of rewards and penalties against tyrannical individuals in another department. What then are these rewards and penalties?

Here we come to the core of the question. Presumably they are not such things as loss of status, respect, prestige, and friendship—unless it be argued that the mere fact of constitutional prescription will

internal control by conscience, the cue that evokes the expectation of punishing guilt feelings or "an attack of conscience" may well be an external object or action. Further, even when rewards and penalties are manipulated by a source outside the given individual, e.g., in the case of income or respect, it is the inner expectation or actual sensation of gratification or deprivation that is controlling. Here again, Madisonian theory probably cannot be satisfactorily converted into modern political science without such extensive surgery that the result would not be consistent with the style of thought we have here labeled "Madisonian."

31. *The Federalist*, No. 48, p. 326.

32. *The Federalist*, No. 51, pp. 335–37.

itself convey legitimacy and illegitimacy to certain actions; that officials who undertake illegitimate actions will suffer loss of status, respect, prestige, and friendship; and that these penalties are sufficient to prevent tyranny. But certainly this is not Madison's argument. Nor can the rewards and penalties depend on money, for the Constitution was contrived to restrict this means of control, lest the legislature become all powerful.

Do the rewards and penalties then involve the threat of physical coercion? In this category might be impeachment and conviction, and use of the armed forces. But in this case, a republic must always be on the verge of violence and civil war; for if physical coercion is the central restraint on tyranny, and if tyranny is the basic danger the argument assumes it to be, then the threat of physical coercion and therefore of violence can never be far removed from the operation of politics. Furthermore, if the main restraint is the threat of physical coercion, why would the leaders of a majority ever refrain from tyrannizing over a minority—at least if the majority were thought to be physically more powerful than the minority? Taking a more modern look at the way in which coercive control is distributed, why would a minority with control over the instruments of violence and coercion refrain from tyrannizing over a majority?

The fact is that in some nations powerful minorities have not refrained and tyranny has resulted; yet in other nations they have refrained. And whether or not powerful minorities or mass-based dictatorial leaders have refrained from establishing tyranny is clearly not related to the presence or absence of constitutional separation of powers. Many variables are involved in such a situation, but the constitutional separation of powers cannot be established as one of them.

Thus the Madisonian style of argument provides no satisfactory answer to the fundamental questions it raises. Madison evidently had in mind a basic concept, namely, that of reciprocal control among leaders. But in several ways, the Madisonian argument is inadequate:

1. It does not show, and I think cannot be used to show, that reciprocal control among leaders, sufficient to prevent tyranny, requires con-

stitutionally prescribed separation of powers, as in the American Constitution.

2. Either the significance of constitutional prescription as an external check is exaggerated or the argument misunderstands the psychological realities implied by the concept of a check on, or control over, behavior. And the inferences from either type of incorrect premise to propositions about political behavior or the requisites of a non-tyrannical democracy are false.

3. The Madisonian argument exaggerates the importance, in preventing tyranny, of specified checks to governmental officials by other specified governmental officials; it underestimates the importance of the inherent social checks and balances existing in every pluralistic society. Without these social checks and balances, it is doubtful that the intragovernmental checks on officials would in fact operate to prevent tyranny; with them, it is doubtful that all of the intragovernmental checks of the Madisonian system as it operates in the United States are necessary to prevent tyranny.

X

In the preceding discussion I have assumed that "tyranny" in the Madisonian system is a meaningful term. By assuming it to be meaningful, it has been possible to show that Hypothesis 1 leads to false conclusions. Now, however, we must ask whether the concept of "tyranny" implicit in the Madisonian system, and basic to the usual rationale of the American constitutional framework, has any operational meaning.

Tyranny, it will be recalled, was defined above as meaning every severe deprivation of a natural right. I have already explained why this definition seems to be required; indeed the idea of majority tyranny, against which the Madisonian system is erected, can only mean that a majority acting through regular processes of elections, legislation, and majority rule may nevertheless act in such a way as to deprive a minority of its natural rights.

Now I wish to avoid here a discussion of the concept of "natural right" and its utility in political theory, for this would take us very far afield into a voluminous and almost endless subject. Nevertheless, if I am right in thinking that by "tyranny" Madison meant to include "every severe deprivation of a natural right," then we cannot very well appraise the utility of this definition without considering the concept of natural right. I think, however, that we can get ourselves out of this dilemma in the following way.

We do not need to settle the question whether individuals have natural rights or, if they do, what these may be. All we need to know is whether anything roughly equivalent to the definition of tyranny I have supplied (the only alternative seemed to lead us into an essentially trivial defense of Madison's key First Condition) provides a useful concept in Madison's system. If it does not, then the idea of tyranny, which of course is central to Madison's argument, will have to be left in a highly unsatisfactory state.

It is self-evident that the definition of tyranny would be entirely empty unless natural rights could somehow be defined. It can be shown, I think, that we must specify a process by which specific natural rights can be defined in the context of some political society. To specify this process creates some dilemmas for the Madisonian.

If a natural right were defined, rather absurdly, to mean the right of every individual to do what he wishes to do, then every form of government must be tyrannical; for every government restrains at least some individuals from doing what they wish to do. For example, in this sense every government tyrannizes over criminals, whether these are defined by our own government or that of the U.S.S.R. A non-tyrannical republic would therefore be impossible. So this meaning of tyranny must be excluded.

It follows that tyranny must be defined to mean that severe penalties are inflicted only on some kinds of behavior. How are these kinds of behavior, which it is tyrannical to restrain, to be specified in practice? One possibility is to restrain only those kinds of behavior that every individual (or every adult) in the community believes to be undesirable. But this would require unanimity for governmental actions and would thereby make government impossible. For example, under this rule, if one murderer were to deny that murder is undesirable, the community could not punish murder. The unanimity rule of the United Nations Security Council would be the rule of all republics. Clearly the Madisonian system does not demand this.

The typical political situation is one in which individuals in a group or a society disagree as to the desirability of penalizing or rewarding certain kinds of behavior. Governmental processes are then employed to adjudicate the dispute. But when individuals disagree, what rule is to be employed to determine whether the punishing of some specified act would or would not be tyrannical? One possibility is to permit the majority to decide. I will examine some of the problems associated with this rule in chapter 2. Yet since this operating rule is precisely what Madison meant to prevent, and moreover would make the concept of majority tyranny meaningless, we must reject it. The only remaining possibility, then, is that some specified group in the community, not defined as the majority, but not necessarily always in opposition to it, would be empowered to decide. But if Hypothesis 1 is correct, then any group in the community with such a power would use it to tyrannize over other individuals in the community. Hence, in practice, no one could have the power to decide this question. Hence this definition of tyranny seems to have no operational meaning in the context of political decision-making.[33] And, of course, it follows further that, if tyranny has no operational meaning, then majority tyranny has no operational meaning.

Lest it be said that I have first rejected Madison's definition of tyranny and then deliberately substituted a definition that leads to foolish consequences, and have thus only set up a straw man in order to demolish him, let me say in defense: first, that for the reasons already given, Madison's own definition is a trivial one; second, that the definition I have given is implicit in his system; and third, that no alternative definition consistent with and necessary to the argument of his system as a whole can, I believe, escape the difficulties involved in the definition I have supplied.

33. It might be said that each individual would decide himself, upon consulting his own value system, whether or not a given act was tyrannical. But this is merely a prescription for individual behavior and provides no rule for a collective decision.

XI

If we turn to Madison's explicit concept of faction, we find that it suffers from the same difficulties as the implicit concept of tyranny. It would hardly be worth while to examine Madison's explicit concept of faction, however, if it were not for the fact that some such thought is implicit in many other attempts to defend the idea of constitutionally prescribed checks on "majorities."[34] The reader will recall Definition 4: A faction is "a number of citizens, whether amounting to a majority or a minority of the whole, who are united and actuated by some common impulse of passion, or of interest, adverse to the rights of other citizens, or to the permanent and aggregate interests of the community."

The difficulty with this definition of a faction is similar to the difficulty encountered with "tyranny." How can one use this concept? We can read it to mean that a faction is any group of citizens bent on invading the natural rights of others. Because such an action is tyrannical (by definition, even if the definition is a troublesome one), then obviously factions must be restrained if a non-tyrannical republic is to exist. A republic that avoids tyranny must avoid tyranny.

The definition would cease to be redundant if it could help us in some way to distinguish a "number of citizens" who make up a "faction" from any other number of citizens. Unless we can make such a distinction, the important subsequent propositions that depend upon the distinction are meaningless. Do factions have recognizable stigmata?

It is easy to see that so long as we do not know either the "rights of other citizens" or the "permanent and aggregate interests of the community," we are helpless. In the face of this difficulty, one might suggest a different approach. Instead of asking for the definitional characteristics of a faction, we might try to imagine some political process by which factions could be designated as situations arose. Admittedly

34. The quotation marks reflect my belief that in the usual sense intended, majorities rarely, if ever, rule in any country or social organization at any time. Thus the fear of majority rule, as well as the advocacy of it, is founded upon a misconception of the probabilities permitted by political reality. For discussion of this point, see chap. 5.

this is not what Madison had in mind, but it may be helpful to pursue this path, since Madison himself has left us without a guide.

Now if everyone always agreed what specific actions were "adverse to the rights of other citizens, or to the permanent and aggregate interests of the community," then a faction could be specified by unanimity. But both of these criteria are highly ambiguous, and unanimity is most improbable. Nearly all governmental actions deprive some individuals of legal rights they had previously possessed, and nearly all political groups seek some kind of governmental action that will deprive some individuals of certain existing legal rights. Hence rights must be read to mean natural rights; but as we have shown, consensus is lacking on what kinds of behavior are included in natural rights, particularly in concrete instances. As to the "permanent and aggregate interests of the community," so far as I am aware no political group has ever admitted to being hostile to these.

But if unanimity is not required, then something less than unanimity be sufficient. Yet if a majority is permitted to decide what constitutes a faction, and to invoke the appropriate machinery against that faction, then in practice a majority would never be a faction. For example, in practice a legislative majority might be permitted to determine what policies are "adverse to the rights of other citizens, or to the permanent and aggregate interests of the community." It might then simply vote down any such proposed policy. But it is highly improbable that a majority in favor of a given policy would ever decide that its own policy was factional and thereupon vote it down. Indeed, such an action is entirely inconceivable within the Madisonian framework of political behavior, and it is hardly conceivable within any other. Hence if majority factions are held to be a genuine danger, as Madison and his contemporary followers insist, then the determination of the meaning of faction by the majority itself would make the concept useless within the Madisonian context.

If determination by unanimity and by majority vote are both ruled out, it follows that the only remaining alternative is determination by the decision of some minority. But the preceding argument against resting this power in a majority certainly applies to any minority; if

Hypothesis 1 is correct, then we should expect any minority with this power at best to employ it in its own favor and at worst to tyrannize over other minorities and any majority.

XII

It is not part of my purpose to examine every detailed aspect of the Madisonian viewpoint. Yet one more major point is worth considering.

Protection against factions and therefore against tyranny, it will be recalled, requires two conditions:

Hypothesis 8: If a faction consists of less than a majority, it can be controlled by the operation of "the republican principle" of voting in the legislative body, i.e., the majority can vote down the minority.

Hypothesis 9: The development of majority faction can be limited if the electorate is numerous, extended, and diverse in interests.

Because, as we have seen, the terms "factions" and "tyranny" have been given no specific meaning, as they stand these two hypotheses also have no specific meaning, i.e., no conceivable way exists by which we can test their validity. Hence they remain mere untestable assertions.

To dispatch them in this ruthless way would no doubt leave many readers as unsatisfied as it does me. For one cannot escape the feeling that these propositions are at least worthy of examination if they could somehow be recast so as to overcome the deficiencies of their key terms. What repairs can we make in these concepts in order to test Hypotheses 8 and 9, so far as they may be tested at all?

It might be thought that the difficulties could be escaped in the following way. Let us first postulate that deprivations of freedom should be minimized. Let us then define the "freedom" of an individual as the opportunity to achieve his goals without external restraints. We now propose the following rule: the process of governmental policy-making will be so constructed that every group of a "significant" size will have an opportunity to veto threatened deprivations of its freedom. In this way no group's freedom is likely to be curtailed, except through ignorance, guile, etc.

This formulation involves several difficulties, one of the most important of which is that probably very few people would regard it as reasonable to concede the veto to every group of significant size. Most people, for example, would not grant the veto to criminals even if criminals were a group of significant size. If exceptions must be made, some individuals must make the exceptions; and we then find ourselves running through the maze of dilemmas already witnessed in the preceding discussions of tyranny and faction.

Let us suppose, however, that this problem could somehow be solved and made consistent with Madisonian principles, and that some but not all minorities could be given an effective veto. (As will be seen in chapter 5, something like this actually seems to operate in the American political system.) We may now test the validity of Hypothesis 8. According to this hypothesis, a minority bent on imposing severe deprivations on some majority could simply be voted down in the legislative body. Hence no minority could ever curtail the freedom of a majority through governmental action.

If we leave to one side the difficulties arising out of the majority's customary political passivity about issues at the policy-making stage, then Hypothesis 8 is valid provided that it is narrowly interpreted. By narrowly interpreted, I mean the hypothesis must specify that the majority needs to be larger than the minority by only one person. If a qualified majority is required to pass legislation—that is, a majority greater than the minority by more than one, as when a two-thirds or a three-fourths majority is necessary—then it can easily be shown that Hypothesis 8 will meet threats to the majority only if these threats arise from proposed government action. For if more than a bare majority is required to enact policy, then a minority of the appropriate size can veto any policy it dislikes. If the freedom of some majority is already curtailed in a such way that only positive governmental action will eliminate that deprivation, and if a minority with a veto dislikes the measures proposed to increase majority freedom, then by exercising its veto a minority can maintain deprivations of the freedom of a majority and hence can tyrannize over it.[35]

35. Although Madison seems never to have distinguished this situation clearly, I think he understood it and assumed the narrower meaning of Hypothesis 8. Thus in 1830 he opposed the nullification doctrine if it meant that "the decision of the state is to be presumed valid, and that it overrules the law of the United States,

Thus a majority might believe that child labor, low wages, bad housing, and the absence of effective trade-unions, social security, and slum clearance all represented severe deprivations of their freedom. In this case, the immediate deprivations would be inflicted by private individuals rather than governmental officials. Therefore if action by governmental officials is one necessary condition to eliminate child labor, low wages, and bad housing and to create effective trade-unions, social security, and decent housing; and, if, further, a minority, consisting, say, of employers (or officials responsive to or sympathetic with employers) can veto every government action intended to eliminate these privately imposed deprivations, then Hypothesis 8 is false. For in this case the "republican principle" would not be sufficient to protect a majority against the deprivations imposed by a minority.

XIII

Hypothesis 9 asserts that the effects of majority faction can be controlled if the electorate is numerous, extended, and diverse in interests. Here again, the absence of any definite meaning of the word faction is an obstacle to testing the prediction. Yet if we examine the arguments that Madison himself used to prove the validity of this hypothesis, it is clear that the hypothesis must be read to mean that the effectiveness of any majority whatsoever is severely limited if the electorate is numerous, extended, and diverse in interests. Whether or not the majority is factional is irrelevant to the operation of the restrictions imposed by the existence of a numerous, extended, and diverse electorate. Furthermore, so far as I am aware, no modern Madison has shown that the restraints on the effectiveness of majorities imposed by the facts of a pluralistic society operate only to curtail "bad" majorities and not "good" majorities; and I confess I see no way

---

unless overruled by three-fourths of the states." For, he argued, "to establish a positive and permanent rule giving such a power to such a minority, over such a majority, would overturn the first principle of free government. . . ." (Padover, *op. cit.*, pp. 157–58.) The concept of "minority veto" or "concurrent majorities" is not, strictly speaking, of Madison's creation. This view associated with the name of John C. Calhoun nevertheless seems to have become a fundamental element in the American ideology, and it is frequently defended in essentially Madisonian language.

by which such an ingenious proposition could be satisfactorily established.[36]

Hence the net effect of Hypothesis 9 seems to be this: because majorities are likely to be unstable and transitory in a large and pluralistic society, they are likely to be politically ineffective; and herein lies the basic protection against their exploitation of minorities. This conclusion is of course scarcely compatible with the preoccupation with majority tyranny that is the hallmark of the Madisonian style of thought.

XIV

The absence of specific meaning for terms like "majority tyranny" and "faction" coupled with the central importance of these concepts in the Madisonian style of thinking has led to a rather tortuous political theory that is explicable genetically rather than logically. Genetically the Madisonian ideology has served as a convenient rationalization for every minority that, out of fear of the possible deprivations of some majority, has demanded a political system providing it with an opportunity to veto such policies.[37]

At the formation of the Constitution, the Madisonian style of argument provided a satisfying, persuasive, and protective ideology for the minorities of wealth, status, and power who distrusted and feared their bitter enemies—the artisans and farmers of inferior wealth, status, and power, who they thought constituted the "popular majority." Today, however, it seems probable that for historically explicable reasons a preponderant number of politically active Americans believe themselves to be members, at least part of the time, of one or more minorities—minorities, moreover, whose goals might be threatened if the prescribed constitutional authority of majorities were legally unlimited. Hence, whatever its defects of logic, definition, and scientific utility, the Madisonian ideology is likely to remain the most prevalent and

36. Cf. chap. 4.

37. Calhoun's transparent defense of the southern slavocracy by his doctrine of concurrent majorities seems to me prone to all the weaknesses of the Madisonian system, which in many respects it parallels. But I have not tried to deal specifically with Calhoun's special variant on Madison. Cf. his *Disquisition on Government*, ed. R. K. Cralle (New York: Peter Smith, 1943), esp. pp. 28–38.

deeply rooted of all the styles of thought that might properly be labeled "American." One would be foolish indeed to suppose that an examination of its illogicality would significantly diminish its acceptance. Ideologies serve a variety of needs—psychological, socio-economic, political, propagandistic—that transcend the need of pedants for scientific cogency.

Nevertheless, as political science rather than as ideology the Madisonian system is clearly inadequate. In retrospect, the logical and empirical deficiencies of Madison's own thought seem to have arisen in large part from his inability to reconcile two different goals. On the one hand, Madison substantially accepted the idea that all the adult citizens of a republic must be assigned equal rights, including the right to determine the general direction of government policy. In this sense majority rule is "the republican principle." On the other hand, Madison wished to erect a political system that would guarantee the liberties of certain minorities whose advantages of status, power, and wealth would, he thought, probably not be tolerated indefinitely by a constitutionally untrammeled majority. Hence majorities had to be constitutionally inhibited. Madisonianism, historically and presently, is a compromise between these two conflicting goals. I think I have shown that the explicit and implicit terms of the compromise do not bear careful analysis. Perhaps it is foolish to expect them to.

In searching for a theory about democracy that will bear up under examination, two alternatives suggest themselves, each centered on achieving one of the two basic goals so dangerously allied by Madison's compromise. One possibility is to concentrate one's argument on Madison's worry that the majority will prevent the minority—or a particularly worthy minority—from achieving what it has a "right" to achieve, whether this be property, status, power, or the opportunity to save mankind. Following this line of thought, one would postulate that the goals of some particular set of individuals are inherently right or good, and the process of making decisions should insure the maximization of these goals. Ironically the worry about the dangers of majorities has been shared not only by aristocratic elites but also by political adventurers, fanatics, and totalitarians of all kinds, so that this style of thought takes many forms and finds advocates as different as Plato and Lenin. If we carry one aspect of Madison's argument to its logical limit, then, we can easily place him in the camp of the great antidemocratic theorists. But since Madison recoiled from pushing his premises to their limits, it would be unfair, foolish, and pointless to force his argument so far. Moreover, whatever one may think about the desirability of one or another of the political systems proposed by these theorists, it seems to me that unless we wish to eliminate some very useful distinctions among political systems, we cannot regard these systems, centered on the goal of avoiding majority control, as democratic. Madison, it seems to me, goes about as far as it is possible to go while still remaining within the rubric of democracy. Because of this, I do not propose to explore this alternative development out of Madison's argument.

The other alternative is to lay down political equality as an end to be maximized, that is,to postulate that the goals of every adult citizen of a republic are to be accorded equal value in determining government policies. If this were our objective, what basic conditions should exist for making government decisions? This is the alternative to which we now turn.

APPENDIX TO CHAPTER 1

Summary of the Madisonian argument

I. The basic definitions:

DEFINITION 1: An "external check" for any individual consists of the application of rewards and penalties, or the expectation that they will be applied, by some source other than the given individual himself.

DEFINITION 2: "Tyranny" is every severe deprivation of a natural right.

DEFINITION 3: A republic is a government which (*a*) derives all of its powers directly or indirectly from the great body of the people, and (*b*) is administered by persons holding their office during pleasure, for a limited period, or during good behavior.

DEFINITION 4: A faction is "a number of citizens, whether amounting to a majority or a minority of the whole, who are united and actuated by some common impulse of passion, or of interest, adverse to the rights of other citizens, or to the permanent and aggregate interests of the community."

II. The basic axiom: The goal that ought to be attained, at least in the United States, is a non-tyrannical republic.

III. The argument:

Hypothesis 1: If unrestrained by external checks, any given individual or group of individuals will tyrannize over others.

Hypothesis 2: The accumulation of all powers, legislative, executive, and judiciary, in the same hands implies the elimination of external checks.

Hypothesis 3: If unrestrained by external checks, a minority of individuals will tyrannize over a majority of individuals.

Hypothesis 4: If unrestrained by external checks, a majority of individuals will tyrannize over a minority of individuals.

Hypothesis 5: At least two conditions are necessary for the existence of a non-tyrannical republic:

First Condition: The accumulation of all powers, legislative, executive, and judiciary, in the same hands, whether of one, a few, or many, and whether hereditary, self-appointed, or elective, must be avoided.

Second Condition: Factions must be so controlled that they do not succeed in acting adversely to the rights of other citizens or to the permanent and aggregate interests of the community.

Hypothesis 6: Frequent popular elections will not provide an external check sufficient to prevent tyranny.

Hypothesis 7: If factions are to be controlled and tyranny is to be avoided, this must be attained by controlling the effects of faction.

Hypothesis 8: If a faction consists of less than a majority, it can be controlled by the operation of "the republican principle."

Hypothesis 9: The development of majority factions can be limited if the electorate is numerous, extended, and diverse in interests.

Hypothesis 10: To the extent that the electorate is numerous, extended, and diverse in interests, a majority faction is less likely to exist, and if it does exist, it is less likely to act as a unity.

[13]

James Madison: Republican or Democrat?

Robert A. Dahl

Although James Madison is best known for the views he expressed in the *Federalist*, as he gained greater experience in the new American political system he rejected some of these early views and increasingly emphasized four propositions: (1) the greatest threat in the American republic comes from a minority, not the majority; (2) to protect their rights from minority factions, members of the majority faction must organize their own political party; (3) the danger that majorities might threaten property rights could be overcome by enabling a majority of citizens to own property, a feasible solution in America; and (4) in a republic, majorities must be allowed to prevail. Even Madison's post-1787 constitutional views, however, were flawed in at least three serious ways: (1) as an empirical proposition, his conjecture that increased size reduces the danger of factionalism is contradicted by subsequent experience; (2) in his conception of basic rights, Madison excluded more than half the adult population: women, African Americans, and American Indians; and (3) he actively supported the provision in the Constitution that gave to slave states an increase in representatives amounting to three-fifths of the slave population.

Nearly half a century ago I published a lecture that was highly critical of what I called "Madisonian Democracy."[1] Now I find myself both more sympathetic with Madison and more critical. I'm more sympathetic because I've come to understand how experience with the rapidly emerging American democracy led James Madison to views that I would regard as somewhat more democratic than those he expressed at the Constitutional Convention of 1787 and soon thereafter in the *Federalist*. I'm more critical because of his willingness to exclude a very large part of the adult population from enjoying the rights of citizens in the political system he helped to create.

Despite my criticisms of Madison, I bear a deep respect for the depth and range of his understanding of political life and his constant search for propositions that rose above the level of description to reach a higher level of generality. In this sense he was a distinguished political scientist. Even more, his capacity for modifying his earlier conclusions through later observations gave him the perspective of a true scientist of politics.

Yet his view of politics went beyond empirical observations. For his interest in politics was profoundly anchored in concerns not only for what was, but also, in his view, what ought to be. His lifelong effort to understand politics was clearly motivated by a desire that Americans might achieve a good polity.

In Madison's view, a good polity for Americans would necessarily be a government that derived its just powers from the consent of the governed, or, as we might say today, a democracy. His role in the evolution of democratic ideas and institutions was extraordinary. By his creative leadership at the American Constitutional Convention in 1787 and his persuasive contributions to the *Federalist* immediately thereafter, he helped to inaugurate one of the most fundamental changes in democratic ideas and practices that has occurred over the entire history of this ancient form of government. Henceforth, "government by the people" would no longer be restricted to assemblies of citizens in small units like city-states. Nor would the right to choose representatives to legislatures in larger units be restricted to an exceedingly tiny number of men drawn from the privileged few, as it then was in the parliaments of Britain and Sweden. Judged from this perspective, Madison was, in his own cautious fashion, a revolutionary.

Robert A. Dahl is the Sterling Professor Emeritus of Political Science at Yale University (robert.dahl@yale.edu). A past president of the American Political Science Association, his numerous publications include A Preface to Democratic Theory; Who Governs? Democracy and Power in an American City; Democracy and Its Critics; *and* How Democratic is the American Constitution? *The author expresses his appreciation to the Political Science Departments of the University of Indiana and Stanford University for providing opportunities to offer a lecture on the subject of this essay and to profit from the discussions that followed. Thanks also to Professors Jack Rakove, Richard Mathews, and Lyman T. Sargent for their helpful criticisms and suggestions on a draft of this paper.*

Yet if we were to judge Madison by standards widely used today in determining whether a large political system possesses all the institutions minimally necessary for it to be considered a democracy, we would have to conclude that when he attended the American Constitutional Convention and wrote his essays for the *Federalist* in 1787, he was not much of a democrat. As readers of his well-known contributions to the *Federalist* are aware, he even insisted that the term democracy was not appropriate for the government he envisioned. Instead, it should be designated a republic.

In the years following the convention and the *Federalist*, as he engaged in the ongoing project of creating institutions necessary for a people to self-govern, Madison began to express views that were more "democratic" than those he had announced earlier. We might think of the views he presented at the convention and in the *Federalist* as composing his constitutional theory of 1787, while his later views expressed his post-1787 constitutional theory.[2] A stunning instance of the shift from the first constitutional theory to the second is his role in the formation of the Republican Party.

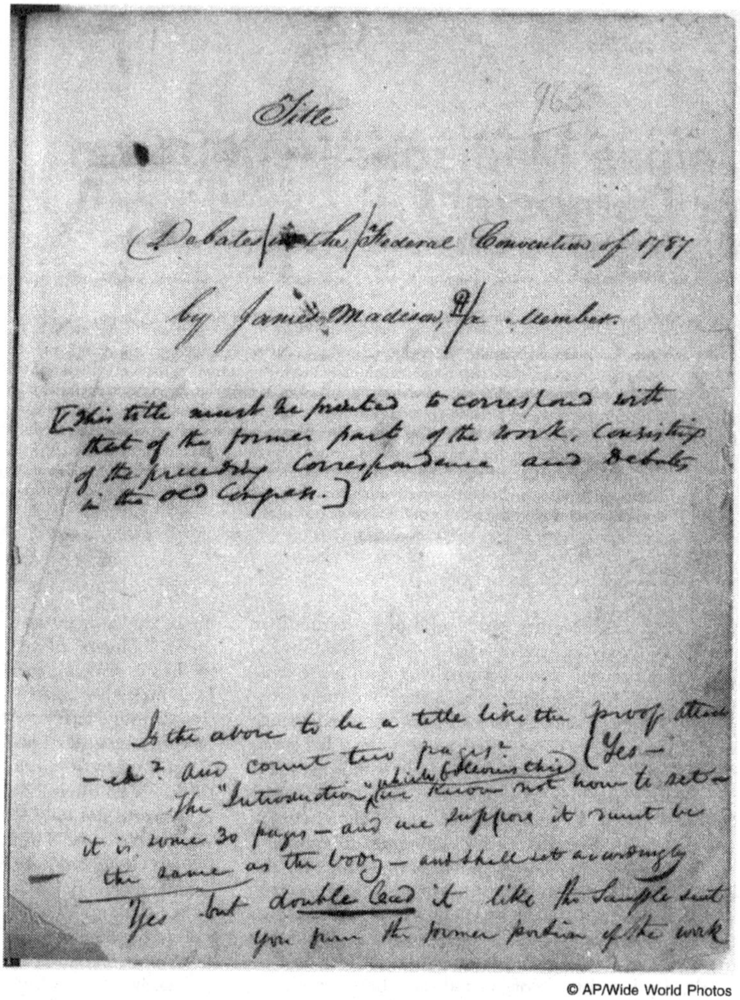

Title

Debates in the Federal Convention of 1787

by James Madison a member.

[This title must be printed to correspond with that of the former part of the work, consisting of the preceding Correspondence and Debates in the Old Congress.]

Is the above to be a title like the proof sheet — eh? And count two pages? {Yes —

The "Introduction" which I know not how to set — it is some 30 pages — and we suppose it must be the same as the body — and shall set accordingly

Yes but double lead it like the sample sent you from the former portion of the work

Yet even in his post-1787 constitutional theory, the more democratic Madison endorsed views and practices that were far less acceptably democratic than those that would come to prevail during the next two centuries.

The Man

When the Constitutional Convention assembled in 1787, Madison was only thirty-six. "At five feet six and less than 140 pounds," one historian has written, "'little Jemmy Madison' had the frail and discernibly fragile appearance of a . . . schoolmaster, forever lingering on the edge of some fatal ailment."[3] With his modest stature and rather high-pitched voice, he was hardly an imposing orator. Yet the knowledge he brought persuasively to bear on the issues, together with his gentleness and fair-mindedness, made him probably the single most influential member of the convention.

With a BA at twenty from the College of New Jersey (Princeton), at twenty-five he was a delegate to the Virginia Convention, at twenty-seven acting secretary and member of the Virginia Council of State, at twenty-nine a delegate to the Continental Congress, at thirty-three a member of the Virginia House of Delegates, and at thirty-five an appointee to the Annapolis Convention. In preparation for the Constitutional Convention at Philadelphia, he undertook a study of "ancient and modern republics [and] ancient and modern confederacies,"[4] wrote a brief note entitled "The Vices of the Political System of the United States," and drew up the essentials of what would shortly be introduced at the convention as the Virginia Plan for the new constitution.[5] At the age of thirty six, James Madison was better prepared for a constitutional convention than most American political leaders of later generations would be at fifty-six or sixty-six.

Madison's Four Questions

Madison's most influential views were, and are today, those he expressed in the *Federalist*, notably in *Federalist* 10 and 51. Few persons, including most political scientists, I believe, have paid sufficient attention to the important ways in which he modified these views as he gained experience with the political system that he helped so much to create.[6]

At the Constitutional Convention, in the *Federalist*, and in letters and other writings of the time, Madison regularly sought to answer four questions:

1. What is the new system of government to be called?
2. Does a common good exist and, if so, can we know what it is?
3. What are the major threats to achieving the common good?
4. Can these threats be overcome and, if so, how?

A Republic or a Democracy?

By "pure democracy," Madison said, he meant "a society consisting of a small number of citizens, who assemble and administer the government in person. . . ." Democracy thus defined—pure democracy—stands in contrast to "a republic, by which I [Madison] mean a government in which the scheme of representation takes place . . . [and] . . . the delegation of the government . . . [is granted] to a small number of citizens elected by the rest . . ."[7]

In advancing this definition, Madison confronted a genuine problem. In the eighteenth century no generally accepted name existed for the kind of government that he and his contemporaries were struggling to create: a government that acquired its legitimacy from the sovereignty of the people, but in which the people would govern indirectly by electing representatives with the power to enact the laws. Although classification schemes from Aristotle to Montesquieu were often presented with more nuance and subtlety than I need to explore here, a common practice was to divide constitutions or political regimes into the rule of the one, of the few, or of the many, each of which might be divided in turn into good and bad forms, depending on whether the rulers sought to achieve the common good or merely their own interests. The good and bad forms of rule by the one were monarchy or despotism. Rule by the few would be aristocracy or oligarchy. What about rule by the many? Should the good form be called a democracy or a republic? What about the bad form?

Around 400 BCE the Athenians, drawing, naturally, on their own language, chose to call their system a "democracy," from *demos* ("the commons," or "the people") and *kratos* ("rule," "sway," or "authority"). At about the same time, the Romans called their system a republic, from the Latin *res*, thing, affair, and *publicus*, public. In the thirteenth century, when the Italian city-states of Venice, Florence, Siena, Lucca, Genoa, Bologna, and Perugia adopted constitutions providing for a measure of self-rule, they all, of course, drew on their own language and history and called their governments republics.

The difference in word usage boiled down to language, not political institutions. Yet whether called democracies or republics, the political systems of Athens, Rome, and the Italian city-states were totally inappropriate for eighteenth-century America. To be sure, along with their citizen assemblies, the Athenian democracy and the Roman republic had some elements of representation. But by no stretch could their political systems serve as models for a representative government in the United States of America. As for the Italian republics, they may have been aristocratic or oligarchic republics, but they were definitely not democratic republics.[8]

To add to the confusion, the two terms—democracy and republic—were, it appears, commonly used more or less interchangeably among Americans in the eighteenth century.[9] My guess is that Americans who were more favorable toward rule by the people tended to use the term democracy, while those who were more dubious preferred the term republic.

In any case, Madison's famous distinction between the terms democracy and republic was somewhat arbitrary and ahistorical. Even some of his contemporaries, like James Wilson, referred to the new representative system as a democracy.[10]

The term democracy soon came into general usage.[11] The Republican Party, founded by Jefferson and Madison, was swiftly renamed the Democratic Republican Party and its successor, in 1828, the Democratic Party. Tocqueville's famous volumes published in 1835 and 1840 were, as we all know, named *Democracy in America*.[12]

The plain fact is that James Madison has decisively lost the battle of terminology.[13] I would dismiss the whole question as trivial if it were not for the frequency with which I have encountered the assertion that the founders created a republic, not a democracy. One could interpret this to mean that by excluding more than half the adult population from the rights necessary for a system to meet today's democratic standards, the founders created an oligarchy—an oligarchic republic, if you will, not altogether unlike the medieval Italian republics. But it is my impression that those who make this claim want to use the authority of the founders to reject the legitimacy of "democracy" as an appropriate standard for contemporary America. To which I would like to reply, if the United

States is not, and should not be, a democratic republic, then what kind of republic is it or should it be? An aristocratic republic? An oligarchical republic?

Let me now turn to Madison's response to the second question; Does a common good exist and, if so, can we know what it is? Adopting a view that was common in his time, Madison assumed that a common good existed and could be definitely known, at least by some. Yet despite Madison's confidence, after two millennia philosophers continue to disagree over two central issues. Just how can we *know* what the public good truly is? And what *persons* would be most likely to know and actually seek to achieve the public good? As to the first issue, is knowledge of the public good self-evident? If not, can it be derived by pure reason, and perhaps only by pure reason, as Kant would assert? If pure reason is insufficient, does knowledge of the public good depend on intuitions? On feelings and emotion? Experience? All of these?

Madison's position was unequivocal: he came down firmly on the side of reason and, like Kant, refused to allow any place for emotions and passions.[14] Here, Madison's understanding of human nature seems to have deserted him, which is particularly surprising because his view flatly contradicted that of David Hume, whose work he had reread before attending the convention and whose argument on the advantages of size for reducing the evil effects of faction anticipated Madison's.[15] Because the physiological connections between reason and emotion were largely unknown until the late twentieth century, aseptic views like Madison's and Kant's were beyond effective refutation. In light of what is known today, however, the assumption that reason can be wholly separated from emotion appears to represent a fundamentally mistaken view of human nature.[16]

As to the second issue, Madison appears to have believed, not unlike Plato, Confucius, and many of his contemporaries, that certain persons of greater wisdom and public virtue might know better than others what the public good truly is, and would also be more inclined to act on it. A crucial advantage of a representative republic over direct or assembly democracy, Madison asserted, is that the requisite wisdom and virtue are more likely to exist among the elected representatives than among the people who elect them. In *Federalist* 10 he wrote that the effect of elections is

> to refine and enlarge the public views, by passing them through the medium of a chosen body of citizens, whose wisdom may best discern *the true interests of their own country,* and whose patriotism and love of justice will be least likely to sacrifice it to temporary or partial considerations. Under such a regulation, it may well happen that the public voice, pronounced by the representatives of the people, will be more consonant to the public good than if pronounced by the people themselves convened for the purpose. (My italics)

Madison was too experienced in the ways of politics and politicians to assume that this desirable outcome was inevitable, and he immediately adds a realistic qualifier:

> On the other hand, the effect [of elections] may be inverted. Men of fractious tempers, of local prejudices, or of sinister designs, may, by intrigue, by corruption, or by other means, first obtain the suffrages, and then betray the interests, of the people.[17]

Before turning to Madison's solution to this dilemma, I want to underscore his implicit assumption that the "public good," the "interests of the people," could be definitely known and described. If Madison were alive today, I find it hard to believe that he would advance this assumption as if it needed no further justification. Today's Madison would surely ask a question like this: In concrete situations when people disagree about the public good, as they commonly do, how can we know what is best? In Madison's own time, didn't the interests of slave owners, including enlightened slave owners like Madison himself, conflict with the interests of others—not least, of course, those who were enslaved? Don't basic human rights trump property rights? Or are property rights inviolable even when they violate fundamental human values?

If some citizens believe that their interests conflict with the interests of others, how should the matter be decided? What is the proper place of public deliberation, and how is it to be achieved? When interests conflict, should we be guided by the utilitarian formula of "the greater good of the greater number," and if so just who constitutes the "we" entitled to make that decision? Or, given the pitfalls hidden in that formula, should the decision follow some other moral principle? If so, what? And just what is the legitimate role of majority rule?

Even if Madison's assumptions about the public good may have been persuasive in his own time, today his contention that the public good can be definitely known by elected representatives would scarcely be debated.

This leads me to my third question. In Madison's view, what are the major threats to achieving the common good? In his 1787 constitutional theory Madison was primarily concerned, I think, with two of these. One I have already mentioned: "Men of fractious tempers, of local prejudices, or of sinister designs, may, by intrigue, by corruption, or by other means, first obtain the suffrages [votes], and then betray the interests, of the people." His main solution to this problem of leadership—a solution widely supported by his colleagues at the convention—was the famous separation of powers into the different branches of government that would serve as checks and balances. Because I want to focus here on some changes in the views Madison came to express as he, the country, and indeed the world gained more experience with large-scale representative government, I'll say no more about this solution and instead turn briefly to the other major threat: factionalism. "By a faction," he wrote, "I understand a number of citizens, whether amounting to a majority or minority of the whole, who are united and actuated by some common impulse of passion, or of interest, *adverse to the rights of other citizens, or to the permanent and aggregate interests of the community.*" Where liberty exists, factions are inevitable. "As long as the reason of man continues fallible, and he is at liberty to exercise it, different opinions will be formed. . . . The diversity in the faculties of men. . . . [is] an insuperable obstacle to a uniformity of interests. . . . The latent causes of faction are thus sown in the nature of man . . . . *[T]he most common and durable source of factions has been the various and unequal distribution of property.*"[18]

How might the dangers of faction be mitigated? "If a faction consists of less than a majority," Madison wrote, "relief is supplied by the republican principle, which enables the majority to defeat [the minority's] sinister views by regular vote."[19] But what if the faction were itself a majority? "In our Governments," he wrote to Jefferson in 1788, "the real power lies in the majority in the Community, and the invasion of private rights is chiefly to be apprehended, not from acts of Government contrary to the sense of its constituents, but from acts in which the Government is the mere instrument of the major number of the Constituents."[20] Like many of his colleagues at the convention, and the classic writers from Aristotle onward who had helped to shape their views,[21] Madison believed that the greatest threat to fundamental rights would come from majorities of citizens who possessed little or no property. For if the many lacked property, they would, driven by the overpowering force of self-interest, surely attempt to infringe on the property rights of the few who did own property.

Turning to Madison's fourth question, if factions that threaten the basic rights and liberties of others are inevitable, what is to be done? A Bill of Rights, Madison believed, might be helpful, but it was not sufficient. "My own opinion," he wrote in his letter to Jefferson in 1788, "has always been in favor of a bill of rights . . . At the same time I have never thought the omission a material defect, nor been anxious to supply it even by subsequent amendment, for any reason other than that it is anxiously desired by others. I have favored it because I supposed it might be of use, and if properly executed could not be of disservice." He was lukewarm about its necessity and doubtful about its effectiveness because "experience proves the inefficiency of a bill of rights on those occasions when it is most needed. . . . Repeated violations of these parchment barriers . . . have been committed by overbearing majorities in every state."[22]

Was Madison's early fear of majorities influenced by the possibility that they might threaten the one form of property—slavery—that was essential to his livelihood? Whatever the reasons, in his earlier years Madison clearly feared that government by majorities might seriously endanger the rights of minorities.

So what was to be done? Madison's solution included several elements: federalism, a constitution of limited enumerated powers, and, as I have mentioned, the election of representatives.[23] But Madison's most original contribution, the one for which he is probably best known and for which he has been cited endlessly, was to enlarge the size of a republic. "Extend the sphere," he asserted, "and you take in a greater variety of parties and interests; you make it less probable that a majority of the whole will have a common motive to invade the rights of other citizens; or if such a common motive exists, it will be more difficult for all who feel it to discover their own strength and to act in unison with each other."[24] Increasing the size of the system, then, was "a republican remedy for the diseases most incident to republican government."[25] Was Madison correct? I'll return to this question in a moment.

Like everyone else in 1787, Madison confronted a challenge for which historical experience provided little guidance. Given that a large-scale representative democracy had never before existed in human history, his conjectures were probably as well founded as they could possibly have been.

Yet the constitutional system that Madison and his colleagues had helped to create would swiftly change in response to the powerful democratic impulses that soon emerged. Madison himself helped to strengthen these democratic impulses and their impact. For the three decades after the convention, he was deeply immersed in political life. Elected to the new House of Representatives in 1789, he quickly assumed a major leadership role. Whatever his reservations may have been, he introduced and quickly gained the passage of the Bill of Rights. In 1788, shortly after retiring from the House, he wrote the Virginia Resolutions, attacking the Alien and Sedition Acts, and the following year, after returning to the Virginia House of Delegates, he defended the Resolutions. In 1801 he was made secretary of state, where he remained throughout Jefferson's tenure. On Jefferson's retirement in 1808, he was elected president, as he was again in 1812. Ten years after retiring from the presidency he succeeded Jefferson as rector of the University of Virginia. In 1829 he was a delegate to the Virginia Constitutional Convention. During his final years he staunchly opposed nullification and defended the union. He died in 1836 at the age of eighty-five.

Madison's experience from 1790 onward led him, I believe, to develop somewhat greater trust in majorities—majorities consisting, of course, exclusively of white males—and a greater distrust of minorities that, in his view, threatened the interests of the majority. Put simply, Madison, I believe, rapidly moved toward answers that were different from, or at least had a much different emphasis than, those he presented at the convention and in the *Federalist.* Madison increasingly emphasized four propositions:

1. The greatest threat in the new American republic came from a minority, not the majority. (By majority I'll continue to mean a majority of white male citizens.)

2. To protect their rights, liberties, and entitlements from minority factions, a majority needed to organize a political party.
3. To ensure that majorities would not threaten property rights, it was necessary (and perhaps sufficient) that a majority of citizens owned property. As property owners, they would have an interest in protecting—not invading—the rights of property.
4. In the end, in a democratic republic, majorities must be allowed to prevail.

I want to illustrate Madison's change in views by noting very briefly some well-known historical developments bearing on each of these new propositions. Like his close ally Jefferson, Madison swiftly concluded that representatives of the Federalist Party were supporting and even achieving policies harmful to the interests of a majority of citizens. These included the pernicious Alien and Sedition Acts, the assumption of state debts, Hamilton's successful effort to establish a national bank, and his support for Britain in its conflicts with France.

It became obvious that to be effective the opposition needed its own political organization. Thus Jefferson, Madison, and other like-minded opponents of the Federalists created the Republican Party, which soon came to be called the Democratic-Republican Party, and finally, with Andrew Jackson, simply the Democratic Party. Like virtually all advocates of democracy, Madison had come to see, as he put it much later, that "no free Country has ever been without parties, which are a natural offspring of Freedom."[26] Creating a political party, however, represented a step away from *Federalist* 10. For a political party is a kind of faction, a faction that is organized by party leaders to win votes in elections. The word party itself, as Giovanni Sartori emphasized some years ago, derives from the Latin verb meaning to divide. Though party was sometimes seen as less derogatory than "faction," the two terms were often used interchangeably. A party is but a "part of a political society," not the whole.[27] In effect, then, organized political parties competing against one another in elections are important elements of the solution to the twin problems of faction and the defense of majority interests.[28]

But competition between political parties would not necessarily diminish, and might even intensify, the danger to property rights if the suffrage were extended to those without substantial property, particularly those without landed property—in Madison's terms, "non freeholders." That danger would be reduced, of course, if most members of the electorate owned or expected to own property, and thus had an interest in protecting property rights. Though a solution along these lines was difficult, if not impossible in, say, Britain, in America the availability of land to the west provided a solution—to be sure, at the expense of the indigenous population. A westward movement that Madison had perhaps not clearly foreseen in 1787 was rapidly resulting in a large population of independent farmers who, as property owners themselves, would have little interest in threatening property rights.

Although Madison's later views were hardly those of a passionate supporter of universal suffrage and political equality, a note he wrote in 1821 begins with the comment that his "observations in 1787 do not convey the speaker's [that is, Madison's] more full & matured view" of the right to suffrage, which is "a fundamental Article in Republican Constitutions." After considering the alternatives, he concluded that extending the suffrage to those without (landed) property was preferable, on grounds of feasibility and justice, to any more restrictive alternative. "In a just & a free, Government," he wrote, ". . . the rights both of property & persons ought to be effectually guarded. Will the latter be so in case of a universal & equal suffrage? . . . . Confining the right of suffrage to freeholders. . .violates the vital principle of free Govt. that those who are to be bound by the laws, ought to have a voice in making them." After examining four alternative arrangements that would deprive or limit the suffrage of those without property, Madison concluded:

> Under every view of the subject, it seems indispensable that the Mass of Citizens should not be without a voice. . . . and if the only alternative be between an equal & universal right of suffrage for each branch of Govt. and a confinement of the entire right to part of the Citizens, it is better that those having the greater interest at stake namely that of property & persons both, should be deprived of half their share in the Govt.; than those having the lesser interest, that of personal rights only, should be deprived of the whole.[29]

Political equality means that the majority must be allowed to prevail. Although Madison may never have fully overcome his worries about the potential threats to property rights arising from voters with little or no landed property, as he observed the expansion in property ownership among his fellow citizens, he seems to have become somewhat more committed to the fundamental principle of majority rule.

Toward the end of his life, particularly after John C. Calhoun had begun his attacks on the principle of majority rule, Madison's defense of the principle was forceful and unambiguous. In a letter written in 1833, Madison contended:

> [W]hatever opinions may be formed on the general subject of confederal systems, or the interpretation of our own, every friend to Republican Government ought to raise his voice against the sweeping denunciation of majority Governments as the most tyrannical and intolerable of all Governments . . . .
>
> [T]he general question must be between a republican government in which the majority rule the minority, and a Government in which a lesser number or the least number rule the majority. . . . Those who denounce majority Governments altogether because they may have an interest in abusing their power, denounce at the time all Republican Government and must

> maintain that minority governments would feel less of the bias of interest or the seductions of power.[30]

That same year in a "Memorandum on 'Majority Government,'" he wrote:

> If majority governments . . . be the worst of Governments those who think and say so cannot be within the pale of the republican faith. They must either join the avowed disciples of aristocracy, oligarchy or monarchy, or look for a Utopia exhibiting a perfect homogeneousness of interests, opinions and feelings nowhere yet found in civilized communities.[31]

I find it regrettable that Madison is almost entirely known for his 1787 constitutional theory, for there can be little doubt that as he and the American political system both evolved, he revised his views in ways that were far more democratic. Yet even Madison's revised constitutional theory contained at least three serious flaws.

The first is his argument in the *Federalist* that increased size reduces the dangers of factionalism. At the convention itself he had—rightly, I believe—"contended that the States were divided into different interests not by their differences in size, but by other circumstances; the most material of which resulted partly from climate, but principally from (the effects of) their having or not having slaves. These two causes concurred in forming the great division of interests in the U. States."[32]

His much better known argument in the *Federalist* (especially in essays 10 and 51) may well have been useful as a rhetorical point that would help to reduce fears expressed at the convention, and outside the convention by Anti-Federalists, that the interests of the people in small states would suffer in the proposed federal system.[33] But if we consider the latter argument as an empirical proposition in political science, two comments seem to me justified. It could not possibly have been tested adequately in his own time. And two centuries of experience since then flatly contradict his proposition.

Among the representative democracies of our time, the smaller countries are no more vulnerable to faction than the larger ones: consider the three Scandinavian countries, together with Finland, the Netherlands, Switzerland, and New Zealand. Or consider that among the seventy or so countries of the world that meet today's standards for democracy—rather higher standards, by the way, than Madison's—countries with populations under a million are much more prevalent than larger countries.[34] Or if we move to a much smaller scale, an analysis of town meetings in Vermont reveals a remarkable combination of vigor, civility, participation, and respect for the direct democracy. Indeed, the smaller the town, the more these qualities tend to appear.[35]

Madison was right in thinking that diversity tends to increase with size.[36] But he overlooked the costs of heterogeneity and the advantages of homogeneity.[37] For example, until immigration recently created new cultural diversities in Sweden, its extraordinary homogeneity enabled Swedes to negotiate national policies with a very high degree of consensus in the cabinet, the parliament, and the entire country.[38] At the other extreme, consider the difficulties the European Union now faces in creating a constitution, given the diverse and conflicting interests, views, values, and political cultures that continue to exist among Europeans.

It is difficult, even impossible, to reconcile Madison's seeming optimism about the beneficial affects of size with his clear recognition of the crucial difference in interests among property owners in different states stemming "from (the effects of) their having or not having slaves." Didn't the framers make the Civil War virtually inevitable by incorporating into the union the Southern states with economies, social systems, and cultures based on slavery? Whether separation rather than union would have been more desirable in the long run is a question too complex to examine here. My point simply is that enlarging the sphere might just set the stage for irresoluble conflict.

I have sometimes wondered whether Madison stressed the advantages of size in order to counter the objections of the Anti-Federalists, perhaps the most vigorous opponents of the new federal system. If so, it was a shrewd move. But that does not make his conjecture empirically valid.

The second major flaw that remained in Madison's revised constitutional theory is the tacit exclusion from full citizenship of an enormous share of the adult population. Like other men of his time, Madison seems to have taken for granted that suffrage should be restricted to men, and that there was no question of the right to vote, as well as many other fundamental rights, being extended to women. And while women had few rights as citizens, slaves had no rights at all. Like Washington, Jefferson, and many other eminent Virginians, Madison owned slaves, which he had inherited from his father. Like Washington and Jefferson, he believed that slavery was an evil,[39] and he seems to have treated humanely those he possessed. Like his fellow Virginians, however, he chose not to free his slaves during his own lifetime or to contest the institution publicly.[40] Nor did he follow Washington's example and emancipate them at his death. Instead, no doubt fearing his wife's impoverishment, he willed them to her.[41] Like Jefferson, he supported schemes of gradual emancipation "and the colonization of freedmen in Africa or some other remote region." In 1819 he even proposed that money obtained from the sale of western lands be used to purchase enslaved persons from their masters—after which they would be shipped to Africa.[42] Of course, the scheme went nowhere.

The third major flaw in his post-1787 constitutional theory had been mainly overlooked by biographers, historians, political scientists, and constitutional lawyers until Garry Wills called it forcefully to our attention.[43] This was the infamous two-fifths rule, according to which, in the words of Section 3, Article I: "Representatives and direct Taxes shall be apportioned among the several states . . . according to their respective Numbers, which shall be determined by adding to the whole Number of free Persons . . . . three fifths of all other Persons." Who were these "other Persons"? Slaves, of course.[44] Wills argues, rightly, I believe, that the extra seats in the House—and therefore in the electoral college—had, in Wills's words, "a great deal to do with the fact that for over half a century, right up to the Civil War, the management of the government was disproportionately controlled by the South."[45] It even "undermined the very possibility of debating or changing the status of slaves—as the gag rules of the 1830s and 1840s would demonstrate."[46] Although Madison seems not to have played a big part in the adoption of this constitutional provision, he supported it at the convention and throughout his life.

Madison was limited in important ways by his time and place, yet he helped to launch the world's first experiment in what would later come to be called representative democracy. The political institutions, practices, and ideas about popular government to which he contributed contained dynamic—even revolutionary—elements that, once set in motion, would continue to evolve, sometimes quite rapidly.

Madison was a part of that evolution. In his 1787 constitutional theory, a fear of majorities required that barriers to their power be imposed by constitutional and other means. In his post-1787 theory, he came to defend majorities. Yet many of the crucial elements of the constitutional system that reflected his earlier, and not his later, views have remained in place to the present day.

I sometimes wonder what further revisions Madison would make in his constitutional theory if he were alive today. I'm inclined to think that after he had reflected at length on the changes since his time in democratic ideas and practices, both in his own country and elsewhere, he might well prove to be a vigorous contemporary critic of the Constitution he helped so much to create.

Notes

1 Dahl 1956.

2 The extent to which Madison expressed his real views in the *Federalist* is a matter of some disagreement. See note 7, below.

3 Ellis 2001, 53.

4 Miller 1992, 15.

5 Padover 1953, 22.

6 Samuel Kernell (2003) argues that "the Madisonian model was formulated after the fact, specifically in *Federalist* 51 and its companion essays, in order to promote the Constitution's ratification" (p. 93). If his interpretation is correct, then Madison's first constitutional theory was simply "campaign rhetoric" (p. 114), and his later views might be interpreted as an expansion of views he actually held earlier but had suppressed in his public rhetoric.

7 *Federalist* 10 (Hamilton, Jay, and Madison 2000, 58–59).

8 In the words of a leading historian, they were "constitutional oligarchies" (Martines 1979, 148).

9 Adams 1980, 99–117.

10 Speaking at the Pennsylvania ratifying convention in November 1787, a mere two months after the convention ended, James Wilson, who was Madison's ally at the Convention and, like Madison, one of its most influential members remarked: ". . . [T]he three species of simple governments. . . . are the monarchical, aristocratical and democratical. In a monarchy, the supreme power is vested in a single person; in an aristocracy . . . . by a body formed upon the principle of representation, but enjoying their station by descent, or election among themselves, or in right of some personal or territorial qualifications; and lastly, in a democracy, it is inherent in a people, and is exercised by themselves *or by their representatives*. . . . [O]f what description is the Constitution before us? In its principles, Sir, it is purely democratical: varying indeed in its form in order to admit all the advantages, and to excluded all the disadvantages which are incidental to the known and established constitutions of government. But when we take an extensive and accurate view of the streams of power that appear through this great and comprehensive plan . . . we shall be able to trace them to one great noble source, THE PEOPLE. [sic]" (Bailyn 1993, 802–3, emphasis added). The following June, at the Virginia ratifying constitution, responding to the criticisms of Patrick Henry, John Marshall contended that "The Constitution provided for 'a well regulated democracy,' where no king, or president, could undermine representative government" (Simon 2002, 25).

11 An interesting deviation from this pattern persisted in presidential inaugural addresses. I find that throughout the nineteenth century, if a president referred to the American political system in an inaugural address, he used the terms republic or republican and, with only one exception, never democracy or democratic. The exception was the ill-fated William Henry Harrison who in 1841 said of the Framers that "there were in it [the Constitution] features which appeared not to be in harmony with their ideas of a simple representative democracy or republic." From this we can infer that the terms "republic" and "representative democracy" were understood as equivalent. I need hardly add that during the twentieth century, in their inaugural addresses presidents frequently referred to the United States as democratic or a democracy. In his four inaugural

addresses, FDR used these terms twenty times and "republic" not once. Reagan and the first Bush used both in equal numbers, while Clinton and the second Bush employed only the term "democracy" in their inaugural addresses.

12 In Europe, as the *Oxford English Dictionary* reminds us, "republic" came to mean "without a monarch," as in France, Germany, and elsewhere. Thus the Scandinavian countries, along with Holland and Spain, are not republics; but, as in the rest of the world, their people rightly call them democracies.

13 An authoritative example: The *Oxford English Dictionary* defines democracy as "government by the people; that form of government in which the sovereign power resides in the people as a whole, and is exercised either directly by them (as in the small republics of antiquity) or by officers elected by them."

14 Matthews 1995, 81.

15 Miller 1992, 53ff.

16 Damasio 1995.

17 *Federalist* 10 (Hamilton, Jay, and Madison 2000, 59).

18 Ibid., 54–56 (emphasis added).

19 Ibid., 57.

20 Padover 1953, 254.

21 Richard 1994.

22 Padover 1953, 254. At the Virginia Ratifying Convention in June, 1788, Patrick Henry gave a lengthy and passionate criticism of the Constitution for, among other things, its omission of a Bill of Rights that would protect the freedom of religion, trial by jury, and "the other great rights of mankind" that were, he noted, preserved by "our own Constitution" (i.e., the Constitution of the Commonwealth of Virginia). In his reply, Madison argued, "If there were a majority of one sect, a Bill of Rights would be a poor protection for liberty. Happily for the States, they enjoy the utmost freedom of religion. This freedom arises from a multiplicity of sects, which pervades America, and which is the best and only security for religious liberty in any society" (Bailyn 1993, 678, 690).

23 I am grateful to Richard Matthews for calling my attention to the first two of these. In *If Men Were Angels*, he provides an excellent account of Madison's views on these and other important constitutional issues.

24 *Federalist* 10 (Hamilton, Jay, and Madison 2000, 61).

25 Ibid. (Hamilton, Jay, and Madison 2000, 64).

26 Farrand 1987, 3:452, appendix A.

27 Sartori (1976, 5ff.), provides an excellent account of the evolution of the term "party" and its distinction from "faction."

28 For a carefully presented view of the evolution of Madison's views on parties, see Riemer 1968, 173–74.

29 Farrand 1987, 3:450–55, appendix A, punctuation as in original. His continuing concerns for property are revealed by his unwillingness to reject one alternative: "Confining the right of electing one Branch of the Legislature to freeholders, and admitting all others to a common right with holders of property, in electing the other branch." He points out that this had been tried and abandoned in New York but "is still on trial in N. Carolina . . . It is certain that the trial, to be satisfactory ought to be continued for no inconsiderable period; untill [sic] in fact the nonfreeholders should be a majority" (p. 454).

30 Madison, *Writings*, 9:520–28, cited in Meyers 1973, 525.

31 Madison, *Writings*, 9:526, cited in Riemer 1968, 157.

32 Farrand 1987, 1:486.

33 This is clearly the case in his response to the (ultimately successful) insistence by delegates of the small states on equal representation in the Senates. Three large states—Virginia, Massachusetts, and Pennsylvania—were, he argued, deeply divided by their different interests. For example, in "staple productions they were as dissimilar as any three other States in the Union" (Ibid., 447).

34 Diamond 2002, 26, table 1.

35 Bryan 2004, 69–81, 136, 231, 296–97. See also Bryan and McClaughry 1989.

36 For evidence and discussion, see Dahl and Tufte 1973, 91ff.

37 Alesina and Spolaore (2003) propose that "the sizes of national states (or countries) are due to the trade-offs between the benefits of size and the costs of heterogeneity of preferences over public goods and preferences provided by government. . . . Our main argument [is] that democratization, trade liberalization, and reduction of warfare are associated with the formation of small countries, whereas historically the collapse of free trade, dictatorships, and wars are associated with large countries" (pp. 6, 15).

38 Lewin 1988, 195–206.

39 Rakove 1996, 337. Ralph Ketcham (1990) writes: "Though brought up among slaves and dependent on their labor, he abhorred the institution of slavery and sought to have as little as possible to do with it" (p. 148).

40 An exception was one Billey. "In 1783, as Madison prepared to return to Virginia from Philadelphia, he discovered that, after nearly four years in the company of free servants, Billey was 'too thoroughly tainted to be fit companion for fellow slaves in Virginia.' . . . Why, Madison asked his father, should Billey be punished 'merely for coveting the liberty for which we have paid the price of so much blood, and have proclaimed so often to be right, and

worthy the pursuit, of every human being'" (Ketcham 1990, 148). All of Madison's pronouncements about the evils of slavery are in private letters or documents.

41 "[I]n his will Madison said of his slaves merely that none of them should be sold without the slave's consent as well as Dolley Madison's. A lifetime of opposition to slavery had thus been reduced in Madison's will to a gesture, likely to be ineffectual, not of freedom, but only of decent treatment. As happened again and again in slave states, the demands of creditors and estate legatees subverted Madison's intentions" (Ketcham 1990, 629).

42 Meyers 1973, 398; Ketcham 1990, 625–29.

43 Wills 2003.

44 When Madison discussed the conflict of interests between property owners in free and slave states early in the Convention, he had proposed that instead of the two-fifths rule, slaves "should be represented in one branch according to the number of free inhabitants only; and in the other according to the whole no. counting the slaves as (if) free. By this arrangement the Southern Scale (sic—States?) would have the advantage in the House, and the Northern in the other. He had been restrained from proposing this expedient by two considerations: one was his unwillingness to urge any diversity of interests on an occasion when it is but too apt to arise of itself—the other was the inequality of powers that must be vested in the two branches, and which wd. destroy the equilibrium of interests" (Farrand 1987, 1:486–87).

45 Wills 2003, 6.

46 Ibid., 4.

References

Adams, Willi Paul. 1980. *The first American constitutions: Republican ideology and the making of state constitutions in the Revolutionary era.* Chapel Hill: University of North Carolina Press.

Alesina, Alberto, and Enrico Spolaore. 2003. *The size of nations.* Cambridge: MIT Press.

Bailyn, Bernard, ed. 1993. *The debate on the Constitution, Federalist and Antifederalist speeches, articles, and letters during the struggle over ratification.* New York: Library of America.

Bryan, Frank. 2004. *Real democracy: The New England town meeting and how it works.* Chicago: University of Chicago Press.

Bryan, Frank, and John McClaughry. 1989. *The Vermont papers: Recreating democracy on a human scale.* Chelsea, VT: Chelsea Green Publishing Co.

Dahl, Robert A. 1956. *A preface to democratic theory.* Chicago: University of Chicago Press.

Dahl, Robert A., and Edward Tufte. 1973. *Size and democracy.* Stanford: Stanford University Press.

Damasio, Antonio. 1995. *Descartes' error: Emotion, reason, and the human brain.* New York: Avon Books.

Diamond, Larry. 2002. Thinking about hybrid regimes. *Journal of Democracy* (April): 21–50.

Ellis, Joseph. 2001. *Founding brothers: The revolutionary generation.* New York: Alfred A. Knopf.

Farrand, Max, comp. 1987. *Records of the federal convention of 1787.* Rev. ed. 4 vols. Ed. James H. Hutson. New Haven: Yale University Press.

Hamilton, Alexander, John Jay, and James Madison. 2000. *The Federalist.* New York: Modern Library. (Orig. pub. 1787.)

Kernell, Samuel. 2003. "The true principles of republican government": Reassessing James Madison's political science. In *James Madison: The theory and practice of republican government,* ed. Samuel Kernell, 92–125. Stanford: Stanford University Press.

Ketcham, Ralph. 1990. *James Madison: A biography.* Charlottesville: University Press of Virginia.

Lewin, Leif. 1988. Majoritarian and consensus democracy: The Swedish experience. *Scandinavian Political Studies* 21 (3): 195–206.

Martines, Lauro. 1979. *Power and imagination: City states in Renaissance Italy.* New York: Alfred A. Knopf.

Matthews, Richard K. 1995 *If men were angels: James Madison and the heartless empire of reason.* Lawrence: University Press of Kansas.

Meyers, Marvin, ed. 1973. *The mind of the founder: Sources of the political thought of James Madison.* Indianapolis: Bobbs-Merrill.

Miller, William Lee. 1992. *The business of May next: James Madison and the founding.* Charlottesville: University Press of Virginia.

Padover, Saul K., ed. 1953. *The forging of American federalism: Selected writings of James Madison.* New York: Harper Torchbooks.

Rakove, Jack N. 1996. *Original meanings: Politics and ideas in the making of the Constitution.* New York: Alfred A. Knopf.

Richard, Carl J. 1994. *The founders and the classics: Greece, Rome, and the American Enlightenment.* Cambridge: Harvard University Press.

Riemer, Neal. 1968. *James Madison.* New York: Washington Square Press.

Sartori, Giovanni. 1976. *Parties and party systems: A framework for analysis.* Cambridge: Cambridge University Press.

Simon, James F. 2002. *What kind of nation? Thomas Jefferson, John Marshall, and the epic struggle to create a United States.* New York: Simon and Schuster.

Wills, Garry. 2003. *"Negro president": Jefferson and the slave power.* Boston: Houghton Mifflin.

Part V
The *Federalist* and Federalism

[14]

Madison and Modern Federalism

Jean Yarbrough

The question, How federal is the Constitution? is both legal and political. It is legal because the Constitution prescribes certain federal features. In a more important sense, however, it is political, since the Constitution does not delineate precisely the extent of the powers to be exercised by the state and national governments, but leaves that practical determination to politicians acting in accord with popular wishes. When we reflect upon this question, we must consider not only the text itself, but also the meaning of those broad silences in the intentions of the men who framed it and who implemented its provisions during the early formative years of the republic. In creating our unique federal system, the framers were compelled to consider the more crucial question, How federal *should* the Constitution be?

Examining the views of the framers provides us with insight into the nature of the American republic. As we shall see, the men of 1787 held views surprisingly current today about how federal the republic should be. The chief architects of the Constitution were radical nationalists who had little patience or sympathy with the arguments in favor of states' rights. Their experience under the Articles of Confederation had persuaded them that the safety and liberty of the people depended not upon the state governments, or even upon a balance between the states and the central government, but upon a preponderance of power in the national government. From this perspective, the framers' understanding of federalism seems surprisingly relevant: they anticipated the steady expansion of the national government into state affairs and approved of it, holding it essential to the preservation of liberty and the common good.

In a consideration of the framers' intentions, the views of James Madison are especially significant, since he is widely regarded as the

I thank my colleague, Professor Raymond Tatalovich, for his helpful comments and suggestions.

Father of the Constitution and is a principal author of *The Federalist*. Yet concentrating on Madison's political thought raises a problem. Within a few years after the Constitution was ratified, Madison began to retreat from the ultranationalist position he espoused in 1787 and broke with this position completely in 1798. The enactment of the Alien and Sedition Laws changed Madison from a vigorous nationalist to a genuine supporter of the newly invented modern federal principle embodied in the Constitution. In the Virginia Resolutions of 1798, Madison defended the states as bulwarks of liberty in an extended republic. Although Madison was later to regret some of the more ambiguous and incendiary language of the resolutions, he never repudiated the document (at least as he clarified it in 1800), and in fact, at the height of the Nullification Crisis during the 1830s, he insisted that the Virginia Resolutions were consistent with his understanding of the Constitution. (For good reason he remained silent on the question of the compatibility of the resolutions with his views at the Federal Convention.)

In this defense of the modern federal over the national principle, there is an even more recent parallel. Just as Madison repudiated the nationalist policies of the Federalist administrations as inconsistent with republican liberty, so too, and for similar reasons, did the Reagan administration seek to dismantle the nationalizing policies of the New Deal and the postwar period. Consequently, Madison's political thought takes on special significance. In considering Madison's intentions as a framer, we cannot limit ourselves to his views in 1787, which he later explicitly rejected as an authoritative explication of the Constitution. We must also consider his emerging views of federalism as he sought "to adapt an untried instrument of government to a new country"[1] and, in the light of his experience, as he reflected upon the institutions necessary to preserve republican government.

Madison the Nationalist: *The Federalist*

Students of the American republic are frequently surprised to learn that the leading framers of the Constitution vehemently opposed the compromises that led to the creation of the modern federal principle. The failure of the states to protect against the evils of majority faction under the Articles of Confederation led supporters of free government to try to replace the confederal form with an energetic national government in which the powers of the states would be greatly diminished. To this end, Madison proposed that the states be stripped of their political representation in the national government and that the national legislature be equipped with an absolute veto over all state acts.[2]

Had Madison's original proposals succeeded, the Constitution would have established a basically consolidated national government in which the states were no more than administrative agencies, stripped of all vestiges of sovereignty. As "corporations dependent upon the General Legislature," the states would continue to perform "beneficial" tasks and to be "subordinately useful," but they would have no power to challenge the national government. This is the relationship that municipal governments now bear to the states, and Madison recommends it as the model for relations between the states and the national government.[3]

Clearly, then, Madison cannot be credited with having invented the modern federal principle. Rather, modern federalism seems to have resulted from compromises that made it unsatisfactory to nationalists and federalists alike. As Martin Diamond has persuasively shown,[4] however, political thinkers in the eighteenth century understood federalism very differently from the way we do. We see federalism as a unique principle whereby political power is constitutionally divided between the states and the national government, each sovereign in its own sphere. In contrast, the earlier thinkers considered federalism synonymous with confederacy, consequently requiring political arrangements more closely resembling a league of nations than a government. For this reason, nationalists like Madison saw the federalism of the Constitution as an unsteady compound of irreconcilable confederal and national elements. They fought to secure the ratification of the Constitution in spite of its federal elements and in the hope that the nationalist principle would ultimately prevail.

In *The Federalist* papers, Madison joined forces with another radical nationalist, Alexander Hamilton, to explain the text of the Constitution in a way that would allay the fears of its critics. To this end, the authors employed a number of rhetorical devices that exaggerate the powers reserved to the states and minimize those entrusted to the national government. Thus, it is not surprising that Madison later sought to qualify the authority of *The Federalist* to explain the principles of the federal Constitution. As he put it, *The Federalist* "did not foresee all the misconstructions which have occurred; nor prevent some that it did foresee."[5] Although he does not mention any specific misconstructions, a careful reading of *The Federalist* suggests that its view of federalism is a prime candidate.

The Federalist exaggerates the significance of the states in several ways. In No. 45, for example, Madison insists that the powers reserved to the states are so "numerous and indefinite" that the states, rather than the national government, pose a threat to liberty. Moreover, since these powers touch on "all those objects which, in the ordinary course of affairs, concerned the lives, liberties, and properties of the people," the citizens were likely to remain more attached to their state governments, thus ensuring their primacy within the federal system. Finally, in No. 44, Madison argues that the states may play an important role in restraining encroachments by the national government. Defending the constitutional grant of implied powers, Madison argues that should the Congress exceed its trust and "exercise powers not warranted by its true meaning," the state legislatures "will ever be ready to mark the innovation, to sound the alarm to the people, and to exert their local influence in effecting a change of federal representatives."[6]

This, then, is the surface argument of *The Federalist* regarding the scope of state powers. It is an argument Madison and Hamilton could make, partly because of their genuine fear that the states did indeed retain too many powers. Madison and Hamilton did not doubt the power of combined states, or even of a single great state, to act. What they feared was that the states would be ruled by majority factions and would therefore endanger the rights of the minority and the common good.[7] But it is also an argument they could make, in spite of their preference for a more consolidated government, because they expected these dangerous centrifugal tendencies to diminish in the future. *The Federalist* makes this argument circumspectly, for obvious reasons.

To the careful reader, however, *The Federalist* suggests that as the people become more familiar with the workings of the national government and experience the benefits of its superior administration, they will see that their rights are better secured by the national government and will welcome its extension to "what are called matters of internal concern."[8] In this way, the people will gradually overcome their natural tendency to love best what is near and transfer their loyalty and affection to the national government. The subtle message of *The Federalist* is that the states will gradually decline, not because the national government will usurp their powers, but ironically because "in republics strength is always on the side of the people."[9] And in the future, the people are more likely to look to the national government to provide for their safety and happiness.

The Federalist hints at its true opinion of federalism in a different way as well. In other papers, where one expects to find a discussion of federalism, there is sometimes silence, or at best a grudging recognition. Speaking in No. 62 of the equal participation of the states in the Senate—a key feature of the old federalism that Madison opposed at the Federal Convention—Madison dismisses it as "the lesser evil," "evidently the result of compromise," "not call[ing] for much discussion."[10] In keeping with assertions made elsewhere in *The Federalist,* Madison here describes his support for the federal elements of the Constitution as a "sacrifice," which he prudently makes expecting that in the future popular support for the federal elements of the Constitution will wane. (To a considerable extent, of course, *The Federalist*'s expectations have been borne out. The Seventeenth Amendment provides for the direct election of senators by the people of each state. More recently, constitutional amendments have been proposed to abolish the partly federal Electoral College in favor of a national popular election. Whether the widespread popular indifference to federalism has resulted in the beneficial results *The Federalist* anticipated, however, remains to be seen.) Similarly, *The Federalist* quickly passed over Article IV, which guarantees the constitutional existence of the states as political associations, and Article V, which protects the equality of state suffrage in the Senate, placing it beyond even the mostly federal amending process.

Even the radically nationalistic Madison nevertheless recognized that there were limits to how far these consolidating tendencies could go. If in the future the people did become more attached to the national government, Madison understood, the states would still be necessary—not because they are vital to liberty, but because there are limits to how far national power can be effectively administered in a large republic.[11] In other words, Madison believed the utility of the states served primarily the purpose of good administration rather than the purpose of federalism. This is but a more cautious restatement of Madison's own observation at the Federal Convention that if it were possible for the national government "to extend its care to all the minute objects which fall under the cognizance of the local jurisdictions,"[12] there would be no need to retain the states at all. In this view, the role of the states is purely administrative.

At first glance this distinction between federalism and administrative decentralization may not seem significant, but in fact the differences between these two modes of decentralization are rooted in opposing views of how republican liberty and the common good are best secured. Modern federalism rests on the assumption that a large consolidated government is itself a danger to liberty, since it dangerously strengthens the executive branch and threatens to transform the republic into monarchy—if not in name, at least in principle. Federalism further assumes that, despite the internal checks provided by the separation of powers and the representative principle, the national government may also infringe upon the rights of the people and the powers of the states. Accordingly, advocates of federalism support the *constitutional* division of power between the states and the national government, so that each may stand guard against the undue accumulation and abuse of power by the other.

Administrative decentralization, by contrast, rests on the assumption that the states as political associations are the primary threat to republican liberty because they are too small to encompass the diversity of interests and opinions necessary to preserve freedom. Consequently, advocates of administrative decentralization oppose the division of sovereignty upon which federalism rests as a needless invitation to discord and faction.[13] They prefer instead to reduce the states to local corporations, whose sole purpose is to carry out the legislative projects mandated by the national government. According to this view, liberty is best secured by a preponderance of power in the national government, provided its powers are properly distributed and its representatives accountable to the people. The states play no major part in preserving republican liberty.

Although these latter views are only hinted at in *The Federalist*, they are consistent with Madison's proposals a few months earlier at the Federal Convention. We find a problem, however, if we rely on the views of leading framers such as Madison at the Federal Convention or in *The Federalist* to explain the federal principle: their nationalist recommendations were not incorporated into the plan of government that emerged from the Philadelphia convention and that *The Federalist* is supposedly elucidating. The Constitution does not reduce the states to mere creatures of the national government but preserves them as political bodies with a considerable portion of sovereignty. As Harry Jaffa observes, the effect of these federal provisions upon the nature of the union is significant:

> The Constitution as originally ratified and subsequently amended seems to have pledged, even against the constituent powers of the people, as embodied in the amending article, to maintain the states in their prescribed constitutional role, as indestructible components of the Union. However flexibly this role might be interpreted, there would appear to be a design in the Constitution destined forever to prevent the people of the United States from becoming a mere numerical aggregate.[14]

Granting that the allocation of these powers is largely a political question, there is still a difference between what *The Federalist* prefers and what the Constitution authorizes.

Moreover, if *The Federalist* exaggerates the powers reserved to the states (while subtly indicating its own preferences), it tends to minimize the powers entrusted to the national government, making them appear more consistent with the constitutional division of sovereignty required by the federal principle. Nowhere is this more evident than in its treatment of implied powers. Critics feared that a broad construction of the "general welfare" and "necessary and proper" clauses would become the "pernicious engines by which their local governments were to be destroyed and their liberties exterminated."[15]

Against the abuse of implied powers in particular, and the totality of powers vested in the national government in general, *The Federalist* offers three arguments. First, the national government will have no incentive to encroach upon the powers reserved to the states because the objects of state legislation are so slight: "the regulation of the mere domestic police of a state appears to me to hold out slender allurements to ambition."[16] This, however, is a curious assurance. Second, the proper distribution of powers and representative accountability will ensure that the national government stays within its bounds. In this regard, Madison suggests that the states may play a role in preserving liberty, but he also implies that resort to the state governments to arouse the citizens to elect new and more faithful representatives is a last resort and will probably be unnecessary.[17] Finally, proper rules of constitutional interpretation will restrain the national government. Implied powers extend only to those objects that the Constitution entrusts to the national government, and the Constitution does not give the national government power over all objects. Nevertheless, within its rightful sphere, Madison takes an almost Marshallian view of implied powers. As he wrote in No. 44,

> No axiom is more clearly established in law, or in reason, than that wherever the end is required, the means are authorized; wherever a general power to do a thing is given every particular power necessary for doing it, is included.[18]

Upon reflection, such a construction of implied powers seems more consistent with Madison's nationalism than it does with the federal principle.

Through these rhetorical devices, *The Federalist* helped to secure the ratification of the Constitution. But it did so at the cost of obscuring the nature of the union. By simultaneously exaggerating the federal and minimizing the national elements of the new Constitution, *The Federalist* managed to suggest one answer to the question, How federal is the Constitution? and an altogether different response to the question, How federal *should* (and, in the future, will) the Constitution be? Because these two views are at odds with each other, however, we must determine which view is the wiser one. On this question, the later political thought of James Madison is instructive.

Madison's Move toward Federalism

Although it is customary to view the framing and ratification of the Constitution as the culmination of the revolutionary era, these activities would have been of no avail if the men of the revolution had not been able to make the new constitution work. Moreover, on the all-important issue of how the Constitution would be used to shape the new republic, the chief authors of *The Federalist* parted company almost immediately over the funding of the national debt and the national assumption of state war debts. Although this issue is not directly related to the federal-national controversy, it is important because it suggests that what Madison initially objected to was not simply an energetic national government but the oligarchic tendencies of Hamilton's nationalism.[19] Madison objected to Hamilton's schemes because he feared they would undermine republican government by creating a powerful economic interest based on speculation rather than on industry. In other words, Madison's initial concern was with preserving republican government through the encouragement of a certain kind of citizen.

Like his fellow Virginian Thomas Jefferson, Madison believed that the agrarian way of life was most suitable for maintaining republican institutions, but unlike Jefferson he never dogmatically opposed commercial and manufacturing interests.[20] Indeed, he supported the imposition of a tariff to raise revenue and promote infant industry during the First Congress and continued to back such measures throughout his career. He was opposed not to commerce, but to speculation, for he thought the latter rewarded the nonindustrious and encouraged the formation of habits and character inimical to the preservation of the republic.[21]

In the dispute over the National Bank, Madison's fears of oligarchy and consolidation came together. Again, as in the funding issue, Madison feared the creation of a speculative moneyed interest tied to the national government.[22] Perhaps for this reason Madison began to fear the strengthening of the national government through a broad construction of implied powers. Whereas Madison had seen no danger from consolidation in 1787, as early as 1791, he began to worry that the centralization of powers would strengthen the executive branch and transform the republic into monarchy. Madison no doubt feared this process would be aided by the antirepublican forces created by Hamilton's economic policies. In another essay written during this period for the *National Gazette,* the Republican party newspaper, Madison described American society as currently divided into two parties, the republican and the antirepublican. The antirepublicans are "those who, from particular interest, from natural temper, or from habits of life, are more partial to the opulent than to other classes of society." Such men are dangerous because they are persuaded "that mankind are incapable of ruling themselves" and can be ruled only by rank, money, or force. Consequently, they seek to direct the government "by degrees" into fewer hands until it approximates "an heredity form."[23]

To repeat, Madison's opposition to the policies of the Federalist party can be explained chiefly as a rejection of the oligarchic thrust of Hamilton's economic program. It was not a wholesale repudiation of an energetic national government. For the extent that the administration's vigorous policies did not threaten the preservation of republican mores and institutions, Madison continued to support them. As we have seen, he favored the tariff and argued that the encouragement of manufacturing was a legitimate exercise of Congress's power to regulate trade. Similarly, Madison's support for the Bill of Rights during the First Congress was not meant to weaken the national government. On the contrary, Madison sought to extend the Bill of Rights to prohibit *state* abridgement of the rights of press, conscience, and trial by jury.[24] Moreover, in the debates, Madison made it clear that the purpose of the Ninth and Tenth Amendments was not "to change the principles of government." For this reason, he opposed the addition of the word "expressly" to the Tenth Amendment, which would have reserved to the states "the powers not *expressly* delegated to the United States by the Constitution." As Madison argued, "It was impossible to confine a government to the exercise of express powers; there must necessarily be admitted powers by implication."[25] In other words, Madison did not object to the principles of implied powers, although his position, beginning in the 1790s, recognized the tension between a broad construction of such powers and republicanism, especially federal republicanism.

Madison attempted to resolve this dilemma by arguing that the Constitution be amended rather than broadly interpreted whenever additional powers were necessary. And although this solution proved too cumbersome and was not adopted, Madison's predictions about the effect of broad construction have proved true.

Momentous as these issues were in shaping "what form of government and what type of society were to be produced in this country,"[26] by far the greatest controversy—and the one that proved decisive in changing Madison's political thought—was not over Hamilton's economic policies,[27] but over John Adams's politics. Although Hamilton's programs obviously prepared the way, the turning point for Madison was the Alien and Sedition Acts of 1798. Opposing these laws in the Virginia Resolutions written in the same year, Madison for the first time fully acknowledged the advantages of modern federalism in sustaining republican government.

The main point of the Virginia Resolutions is that the Constitution creates a national government of specific and enumerated powers. These powers result "from the compact to which the states are parties." Whenever the national government oversteps its bounds by construing its powers too broadly, the states must restrain it. In such cases the states, as parties to the compact,

> have the right and are in duty bound to interpose for arresting the progress of the evil and for maintaining in their respective limits the authorities, rights and liberties appertaining to them.[28]

That Madison here decisively breaks with his ultranationalist principles of 1787 does not, however, mean that he became an advocate of states' rights. The change in Madison's political thought is seemingly less radical, but actually more so. The states' rights position is a restatement of the old confederal-national dichotomy that insists that sovereignty cannot be divided. According to this view, the states as political bodies are sovereign, and the Constitution is a compact uniting sovereign states. Consequently, in all disputes arising under the Constitution, each state, as a sovereign party to the Constitution, has the right to judge the issue for itself.[29] Modern federalism, by contrast, holds that it is not the states as political units that are sovereign, but the people in the states. Acting in their sovereign capacity, they establish a constitution that divides sovereign power between the states and the national government to secure their safety and happiness. In this view, the Constitution is supreme over both governments and the people over the Constitution. It is the recognition that sovereignty can be divided among different governments that makes possible the emergence of modern federalism as a distinct political principle, rather than a compound of warring confederal and national principles.

Yet as Madison himself belatedly recognized, his argument in the Virginia Resolutions was ambiguous and could be (indeed, it later was) read, however mistakenly, as a defense of states' rights. The resolutions do maintain that the powers of the national government result from a compact among the states and that, "in case of a deliberate, palpable, and dangerous exercise of other powers not granted by the compact," the states have the right and duty to "interpose." These inflammatory phrases led every state from Maryland north to reject the constitutional theory enunciated in the Virginia (and even more radical Kentucky) Resolutions.[30] Consequently, Madison found it necessary to issue "A Report on the Virginia Resolutions" in 1799–1800, clarifying his position.

In the report, Madison acknowledges that the expression "states" is vague and ambiguous, but he insists that in the resolutions the term refers to "the people composing those political societies in their highest sovereign capacity." This is the sense in which the Constitution was submitted to the "states," in which the Constitution was ratified by the "states," and in which the "states" are the parties to the compact under which the national powers arise.[31] Accordingly, when the national government exceeds its rightful powers, only the parties to the compact, that is, the people in the states in their highest sovereign capacity, can determine that the Constitution has been breached. It is true that the judicial branch is the "last resort" as far as the three branches of government go, but it is not the last resort "in relation to the rights of the parties to the constitutional compact" because it too is a delegated trust.[32] Moreover, the judiciary may also overleap its rightful bounds, and in such cases the parties to the Constitution must judge. Still, Madison explains, there is nothing unconstitutional in these "great and extraordinary cases" when the people assert their ultimate right. For their views as embodied in the declarations of their respective state legislatures are merely "expressions of opinion."[33] They are not intended to supplant the judgment of the courts, but to arouse the citizens to "promote a remedy according to the rules of the Constitution."

Madison does not prescribe what the remedy should be, leaving the particular choice to the states. His discussion, however, makes clear that he means repealing the Alien and Sedition Acts, either by electing new representatives or by amending the Constitution according to the procedure set forth in Article V. In this way, the Virginia Resolutions are not only consistent with the Constitution, but are actually "expedient." As Madison points out, most state constitutions recommend "a frequent recurrence to fundamental principles . . . [to] safeguard against the danger of degeneracy." The Virginia Resolutions preserve the Constitution by returning to these first principles in speech. As a "declaratory recurrence to the principles of the Revolution,"[34] the resolutions alert the people of the United States to dangerous encroachments upon their rights in time to avoid an actual return to first principles.

The Virginia Resolutions mark a turning point in Madison's political thought because they signify his recognition (made only rhetorically in *The Federalist*) that the states can play a role in maintaining liberty in a large republic. As constitutionally protected political societies, they possess the power to resist the tendency toward consolidation. Moreover, although ultimately it is the people in the states who are sovereign, the states contribute to the happiness of the people by preserving the constitutional balance necessary to protect republican liberty.

As we have already seen, there is another aspect to modern federalism. Insofar as modern federalism derives from the constitutional division of sovereignty between two levels of government, it means not only a political role for the states, but also a more restrictive interpretation of implied powers for the national government. Here too Madison modified his views to make them compatible with his emerging appreciation of federal theory. In contrast to the position he held as late as 1791 in the debate on the constitutionality of the bank, Madison came to view the mere existence of the states as a limitation on national powers (despite his opposition to the bank, he observed that "interference with the power of the States was no constitutional criterion of the power of Congress"[35]). This is apparent in a letter to Judge Roane in 1819, following the *McCulloch* decision, in which Madison reversed his earlier position and argued that "the very existence of these local sovereignties is a controul on the pleas for a constructive amplification of the powers of the General Government." Nevertheless, Madison made it clear that his intention was not to hamstring the national government. What he sought was a prudent middle ground:

> There is certainly a reasonable medium between expounding the Constitution with the strictness of a penal law, or other ordinary statute, and expounding it with a laxity which may vary its essential character, and encroach on the local sovereignties with which it was meant to be reconcilable.[36]

These principles of modern federalism were to guide Madison's political actions and writings for the rest of his life. As president, he followed, in most of his policies, the lines he laid down while in opposition to the Federalists. He sought to reconcile the need for an energetic national government with his commitment to preserve the powers and authorities of the states. As in 1789, he supported a moderate tariff to aid the development of manufacturing after the War of 1812. He also continued to hold that internal improvements were not authorized by the Constitution. Accordingly, he again proposed that the Constitution be amended to provide Congress with a clear grant of power for such projects.[37] Madison's federalism, then, did not prevent him from seeking to enlarge the powers of the national government in those areas he considered its proper domain. But it did keep him from relying upon a broad construction of the Constitution to justify such policies. In only one area during his presidency did Madison reverse himself, and that was on the issue of the Second National Bank. As Professor Marvin Meyers points out, however, Madison's endorsement of the bank in 1816 was not based on a new reading of the Constitution, but on precedent, public opinion, and congressional policy.[38]

Madison's political career is commonly seen as divided into three periods: an early nationalist stage, a middle states' rights period, and a final reaffirmation of nationalist principles. It is true that Madison did not systematically spell out the principles of modern federalism, or distinguish them carefully enough from states' rights, on the one hand, and nationalism, on the other. As we have already argued, though, the break in Madison's political thought, embodied in the Virginia Resolutions, does not rest upon states' rights, but upon modern federalism. We shall now argue that Madison's late political thought, that is, 1830 onward, can be understood not as a return to his nationalism of the 1780s, but as consistent with the federalist principles he enunciated in 1798.

Madison and Modern Federalism

In the 1830s when opponents of the tariff invoked the Virginia (and Kentucky) Resolutions in defense of nullification, Madison responded by publishing his letter to Edward Everett in the *North American Review*, denouncing any connection between the resolutions of 1798 and the South Carolina doctrine. Madison explained that the Constitution spells out the procedures by which unconstitutional usurpations of power may be overturned: first, an appeal to the judiciary and then a change of government by electing more faithful representatives. If these ordinary provisions fail, the proper course is to amend the Constitution. If this too is unsuccessful, a state may resort to force, but this is an extraconstitutional step. There is no constitutional sanction for defiance of the law by a single state. Indeed, such a doctrine reverses the express provisions of the amending article, which require three quarters of the states to change the law. According to the proponents of nullification, one state may invalidate a federal law unless overruled by three quarters of the states. The doctrine of nullification is not sound constitutional interpretation because it fails to distinguish between: (1) the state governments and the states in their capacity as parties to the Constitution; (2) the rights of the parties individually and collectively; and (3) constitutional and unconstitutional modes and objects of interposition.[39]

In his final reflections on the nature of the union, written in 1835–1836, Madison even more emphatically defended the Virginia Resolutions against the claims of states' righters. It is there that he drew the theoretical distinction between states' rights and modern federalism most clearly:

> The main pillar of nullification is the assumption that sovereignty is a unit, at once indivisible and unalienable; that the states therefore individually retain it entire as they originally held it, and consequently that no portion of it can belong to the United States.[40]

If it is correct to say that the early Madison was also inclined to doubt that sovereignty could be divided and, consequently, to champion a consolidated national government, his discovery that it *could* be divided became the guiding principle of his political life after 1798.

Indeed, far from returning to these early nationalist views, Madison implicitly rejected them by repudiating the authority of the Federal Convention to explicate the meaning of the Constitution. Madison gives us an early hint of this thinking in the Report on the Virginia Resolutions. Here he does not openly reject the authority of the Federal Convention but instead invokes the intentions of those who *ratified* the Constitution.[41] Later, Madison made the point explicit:

> As a guide in expounding and applying the provisions of the Constitution, the debates and incidental decisions of the Convention can have no authoritative character. . . . [T]he legitimate meaning of the Instrument must be derived from the text itself; or if a key is to be sought elsewhere, it must not be in the opinions or intentions of the Body which planned and proposed the Constitution, but in the sense attached to it by the people in their respective State Conventions where it received all the authority it possesses.[42]

In Madison's view, the opinions of the framers at the Federal Convention should not be authoritative because they were wrong and, more particularly, he was wrong about the dangers facing republican government. As he explained in a letter to J. G. Jackson, written in 1821:

> That most of us carried into the Convention a profound impression produced by the experienced inadequacy of the

> old Confederation, and by the monitory examples of all similar ones ancient & modern, as to the necessity of binding the States together by a strong Constitution is certain. . . . This view of the crisis made it natural for many in the Convention to lean more than was perhaps in strictness warranted by a proper distinction between causes temporary as some of them doubtless were, and causes permanently inherent in popular frames of Govt. . . . For myself, having from the first moment of maturing a political opinion, down to the present one, never ceased to be a votary of the principle of self-Govt: I was among those most anxious to rescue it from the danger which seemed to threaten it; and with that view was willing to give a Govt resting on that foundation, as much energy as would ensure the requisite stability and efficacy. It is possible that in some instances this consideration may have been allowed—a weight greater than subsequent reflection within the Convention, or the actual operation of the Govt. would sanction.[43]

In other words, the change in Madison's political thought is largely a response to the changing political situation. In 1787, Madison saw the chief danger to liberty arising from a central government too weak to control the factious designs of the states. Accordingly, at the Federal Convention, he advocated a national government with far greater powers than the Constitution created.

By 1798, however, the situation had changed. So successful had the Federalist administration been in asserting the powers of the national government that Madison recognized that the principle of federalism embodied in the Constitution against his wishes could in fact play an important role in preserving republican institutions. It was this revised view of the dangers to republican liberty that led Madison to reject the authority of the nationalist Federal Convention in favor of the more federal ratifying conventions—conventions that, he also believed, represented the authentic sense of the people of the United States about the nature of the union.

In summary, there is only one significant change in Madison's political thought, and that is from his consolidationist nationalism to modern federalism. After 1788, Madison's political thought may be understood as a fairly consistent attempt to resolve political issues within the framework of modern federalism. Such a position allowed him to support a vigorous national government, but it also required him to reconcile this position with the rights and authority of the states. Modern federalism gave him the flexibility to move between national and state demands, depending upon his assessment of a particular issue. But because he did not systematically choose the national government over the states, or the states over the national government, or elucidate sufficiently the principle that allowed him to defend the legitimate spheres of both, he is sometimes accused of inconsistency or even opportunism. Most of these criticisms lose their force, however, when we consider Madison's political thought from the perspective of modern federalism.

Madison on Slavery

In one area, however, Madison's political judgment in asserting the rights of the states over the national government is indefensible: the issue of slavery. Then as now, the issue of race relations proves to be the least susceptible to federal solutions, perhaps because, as Tocqueville recognized, it is the most difficult political problem.

The specific issue on which Madison's federal principle falters is the Missouri Compromise. Asked by Robert Walsh, the Philadelphia journalist, for his views on the constitutionality of the issues involved in the compromise, Madison replied that the Constitution did not give Congress the power to control the migration of slavery within the United States or to make opposition to slavery a condition for the admission of a new state to the union. He even went so far as to question whether Congress had the power to prohibit slavery in the territories. Although Madison acknowledged that Congress did have the power "to make provisions *really* needful or necessary" in the territories,[44] he questioned whether slavery belonged in this category:

> It may be inferred that Congress did not regard the interdict of slavery among the needful regulations contemplated by the constitution; since in none of the Territorial Governments created by them, is such an interdict found.[45]

As Marvin Meyers points out, however, this tortured interpretation ignored "the sweeping grant of federal power in the territorial clause and the long-standing precedent of the Northwest Ordinance as reenacted by the First Congress."[46] In defense of his reading of the Constitution, Madison recurs to the proceedings of the state ratifying conventions, though the one speech he cites by James Wilson in the Pennsylvania debates suggests that Wilson did believe Congress had such a power.[47] Thus, Madison's interpretation does violence not only to the Constitution, but also to the intentions of the men who ratified it.

In his letter to Walsh, Madison argued for the constitutionality of his position, as well as for its "expediency." He speculated that the spread of slavery, by reducing the number of slaves in any one territory, might hasten their emancipation. Madison rejected the possibility that such a policy might eventually lead to a majority of slaveholding states with the power to rescind the limitations imposed on slavery in the Constitution. In this instance it is impossible to escape Meyers's conclusion that "the problem of slavery demanded a kind of political genius and daring and conviction beyond the capacity even of Madison."[48] Meyers brilliantly describes the irony of Madison's position and shows how it ultimately led to the crisis that culminated in the Civil War:

> Madison and Jefferson—the most distinguished spokesmen for the Revolutionary tradition in the South—concluded that the real issue in the Missouri debates was not the spread of slavery across the Mississippi but rather the creation of a sectional party by disguised Federalists who appealed to Northern anti-slavery sentiments in order to divide and conquer the Republicans. The ultimate price of injecting slavery into national politics, they warned, would be the disruption of the Union.
>
> The Compromise of 1820 admitted Missouri without anti-slavery conditions and, contrary to Madison's advice, banned slavery in the Louisiana Territory north of 36° 30′. The *reversal* of that policy of exclusion by Congress and the Supreme Court in the 1850's finally precipitated the division that Madison had feared: the formation of a new Republican party in the North out of the anti-slavery elements of the major national parties.[49]

If Madison's federalism resulted in perverse consequences for the greatest moral and political crisis facing the union, we are justified in asking whether his earlier nationalist views were not in fact wiser, even if they do not accurately describe the government created by the Constitution or reflect the sense of the nation as expressed in the Ratifying Debates.

Reflection upon this matter raises two questions. The first is clearly a matter of speculation: would not the reduction of the states to something like administrative agencies of the national government have averted the Civil War? At first glance, this suggestion seems plausible, for the particular way in which the crisis developed was inextricably bound up with federalism and the question of sovereignty. But the issue of slavery—especially in the early nineteenth century, after Southerners had ceased to view "the peculiar institution" as a necessary evil in irreconcilable tension with the principles of the Declaration of Independence and had begun to defend it as a positive good—cut so deeply into the moral and political fiber of the republic that it seems unlikely that the South would have acquiesced in any scheme to limit slavery, even if the national government had the clear-cut power to do so. In that case, the Civil War would have been a strictly sectional, rather than sectional and federal, affair.[50]

The second question raised is, Would not administrative decentralization preserve the rights of the people better than our system of divided sovereignty? Here again, it seems at first as if the rights of the minority might be better protected if the national government were equipped with an absolute veto over all state laws. The national government may also infringe upon the rights of the people, however, and this danger increases where there are no limits upon the expansion of national power. *The Federalist*'s confident prediction that the national government would be restrained from undue encroachment upon the rights of the people has been belied by the growth of the national bureaucracy, the willingness of the Supreme Court to uphold, and in many cases augment, the scope of national powers, and a firm conviction on the part of public opinion leaders that such developments are both beneficial and irresistible. Even with their status constitutionally protected, the states have not been able to resist the steady expansion of national powers into areas historically reserved to them. This is because, as we suggested at the outset, the distribution of powers between the states and the national government is not set in stone but can be flexibly interpreted to meet the political demands of the time. Why power has shifted to the national government and what this shift means for President Reagan's New Federalism and for the preservation of republican institutions in general, we shall now consider.

Reagan's New Federalism

In his late political thought, Madison cast the states as bulwarks of liberty, jealousy guarding against encroachments by the national government. In our own day, the states have become more like the administrative agencies Madison envisioned in his early nationalist period. Moreover, far from resisting this development, as Madison hoped they would, the states have for the most part welcomed it.[51] The reason for this change is simple and has more to do with economics than political theory.

According to James Q. Wilson, massive federal involvement in state affairs was made possible with the passage of the Sixteenth Amendment in 1913. The Sixteenth Amendment "allowed the federal government to levy an income tax on citizens and thereby to acquire access to vast sources of revenue." The consequences were immediate and enormous: "Between 1914 and 1917, federal aid to states and localities increased a thousandfold. By 1948, it amounted to over one tenth of all state and local spending; by 1970, to over one sixth."[52]

In other words, the relationship of the states to the national government began to shift when the states became the recipients of federal dollars. At first, the states determined the purposes for which these grants would be used; in this way, airports, highways, and other such programs were funded. This period of "cooperative federalism," as it was called, allowed the states the best of both worlds—it increased political power and autonomy, without increasing costs. In the 1960s, however, the federal relationship began to change. Increasingly, the president and his advisers defined the purposes of the grants and targeted money for specific "national" programs on poverty, ecology, and the like. As Wilson points out, all this was done "not necessarily over the objections of the states, but without any initiative from them."[53]

At the same time, state autonomy was more seriously eroded by the expansion of the federal bureaucracy and judiciary into its affairs. As Nathan Glazer explains, the bureaucracy, which is charged with the responsibility for implementing legislation, has increasingly substituted its own more activist view of what the law should accomplish, rather than being guided by the intentions of Congress.[54] Moreover, because the bureaucracy lacks the "power of the purse," the states must bear the burden of these additional requirements and procedures. Similarly, the federal courts have ordered the states to implement costly programs in prison reform, public housing, welfare, and other such areas, leaving the states to raise money.[55] President Nixon's Revenue-Sharing program attempted to return to the states a measure of autonomy by replacing grants-in-aid for specifically defined projects with bloc grants, which would allow them greater leeway in spending federal funds. The program failed to contain encroachments by the federal bureaucracy and judiciary, however.

In contrast with these recent Democratic and Republican efforts, President Reagan's New Federalism is actually an attempt to restore what he believes to be the original meaning of federalism, by returning to the states the responsibility for administering and ultimately *for funding* some of the more controversial programs of the Great Society. For this reason, the states have been reluctant to endorse it. They are understandably reluctant to choose between raising taxes and alienating taxpayers, or eliminating programs and angering organized interests.[56] From the point of view of the states, the issue is not primarily one of liberty or autonomy, but of expense. As long as the people expect the government to maintain—to say nothing of increase—its present level of services, the states will continue to insist upon a more generous federal "partnership," and the provisions of the Constitution are sufficiently flexible to sustain such an interpretation if this is what the people want. Moreover, the New Federalism does not directly redress the principal complaints the states have against the national government. Although the New Federalism may curb bureaucratic encroachments, it cannot immediately restrain judicial activism.[57]

Aside from the issue of cost, which, however important, is not and never can be the animating principle of a free society, are there any advantages to be gained from a renewed respect for the federal principle?

Let us consider briefly the three arguments made on behalf of federalism. First, throughout most of its history, federalism has been important for its role in promoting civic virtue. According to the republican tradition, which stretched from ancient Greece and Rome through the Renaissance republics to the seventeenth-century English commonwealth and up to America in 1776, the primary purpose of federalism was to secure the advantages of a small republic while providing for defense through confederal association. It was thought that republican governments had to remain small in order to secure civic virtue. By civic virtue was meant a willingness to sacrifice private interests for the sake of the common good. This individual dedication to the whole was achieved in part through the active participation of the citizens in public affairs; direct democracy taught them to care for what they held in common. Federalism made direct democracy possible by allowing the republic to remain small; consequently, federalism was essential to the republic because it promoted civic virtue.[58]

This aspect of the republican tradition Madison and the framers of the Constitution consistently and emphatically rejected. Indeed, Madison's defense of the American republic in *Federalist 10* rested upon precisely the opposite assumption: it was not smallness, but largeness that would rescue republican government, and it would do so by substituting representation for direct participation. As Madison explained in *Federalist 63*, "The true distinction between . . . [the ancient republics] and the American governments lies *in the total exclusion of the people in their collective capacity* from any share in . . . their government." He then adds,

> This distinction however qualified must be admitted to leave a most advantageous superiority in favor of the United States.

> But to ensure to this advantage its full effect, we must be careful not to separate it from the other advantage, of an extensive territory. For it cannot be believed that any form of representative government could have succeeded within the narrow limits occupied by the democracies of Greece.[59]

The large republic, based on representation and modern federalism, may be superior to the small republic, but not because it promotes civic virtue in the traditional sense. Although modern federalism does bring the government "closer" to the people (and thus encourages civic virtue in a looser sense), it does not provide the citizens with an active and continuing opportunity to participate in public affairs. Direct democracy is no more possible at the state level than it is at the national level.[60]

The one place where direct democracy is possible in the extended republic is in the localities. Local governments have always been schools for civic virtue. By providing ordinary citizens with the opportunity to share in the activities of the republic within their competence, these political associations mitigate the worst effects of liberal individualism. Moreover, these self-governing communities put teeth into the claim that the people are the source of all political power, for alone among the institutions of the republic they allow men and women to exercise political power and responsibility jointly with their fellow citizens. But the federal system extends only to the constitutional division of sovereignty between the states and the national government; it does not include the localities, which are legally "creatures of the states." Consequently, federalism promotes civic virtue in this sense only indirectly, by further decentralizing political power to the localities. Moreover, since the localities have no constitutional power to resist state encroachments, even the indirect role of federalism in promoting civic virtue is problematic.[61]

Federalism as embodied in the American Constitution cannot, then, be understood primarily within the framework of the classical republican tradition, though it continues to promote such ends in an attenuated way. Rather, modern federalism must be judged by its role in preserving the *liberal* republic, with its commitment to the protection of individual liberty through largeness and diversity. In other words, modern federalism must be judged by how well it promotes pluralism on the one hand and liberty on the other.

Modern federalism strengthens diversity, by providing the different cultures generated in the large republic with the political power to preserve their social, moral, and political differences.[62] It is federalism that makes possible the astounding diversity of state laws on gambling, drinking, marriage, the family, divorce, education, and criminal law, to name some of the more important areas reserved to the states. Thus, federalism permits Nevada's liberal laws on gambling, drinking, and divorce to coexist with the stricter views of neighboring Utah, without offending the dominant culture of either.

Closely related to the role of federalism in preserving our national diversity is the opportunity it affords the states to experiment in public policy, thereby confining the damage if unsuccessful, and serving as a model if successful. This experimentation does not preclude some degree of federal oversight to ensure that the constitutional rights of individuals are not violated, but it does require the national government to respect the heterogeneity and experimentation generated by the federal principle as essential elements of preserving the extended republic.

Finally, and most important, modern federalism is necessary for republican government because it helps prevent the concentration of political power in the national government. For, to a much greater degree than Madison recognized when he warned against the dangers of consolidation, the nationalization of public policy has shifted political power from elected representatives in Congress to an unelected bureaucracy within the executive and to the courts. This is because "it is hard for Congress, owing to its clumsy and complex procedures, to control implementation of legislation by the executive, and it is impossible for Congress to control the interpretation by the judiciary of that implementation."[63] Consequently, we have national policy increasingly made by unelected officials, often against the wishes of the majority. Seen in this light, the rediscovery of the federal principle (though not necessarily in the form of the New Federalism) is long overdue. Federalism, to be sure, does not guarantee the protection of individual rights. Those who oppose federalism because they fear a majority tyranny in the states, however, are advised to consider that a national tyranny is also possible—and more dangerous.

Notes

1. Joseph Charles, *The Origins of the American Party System* (New York: Harper & Row, 1961), p. 3.
2. James Madison to George Washington, April 16, 1787, in Marvin Meyers, ed., *The Mind of the Founder: Sources of the Political Thought of James Madison* (Indianapolis: Bobbs-Merrill Company, Inc., 1973), pp. 94–98. Also, Max Farrand, ed., *The Records of the Federal Convention*, 4 vols. (New Haven: Yale University Press, 1937), vol. 1, pp. 27, 165.
3. Farrand, *Records of the Federal Convention*, vol. 1, pp. 357–58.
4. Martin Diamond, "*The Federalist*'s View of Federalism," in George C. S.

Benson, ed., *Essays in Federalism* (Claremont, Calif.: Institute for Studies in Federalism, 1962), pp. 21–64.

5. Madison to Jefferson, Feb. 8, 1825, in Meyers, *Mind of the Founder*, pp. 444–45.

6. James Madison, Alexander Hamilton, and John Jay, *The Federalist*, ed. Jacob B. Cooke (Middletown, Conn.: Wesleyan University Press, 1961), No. 45, p. 313; No. 44, p. 305.

7. *Federalist* No. 10.

8. *Federalist* No. 27, p. 174, and No. 46, p. 317. Also, Diamond, "*Federalist*'s View of Federalism."

9. *Federalist* No. 31, p. 198.

10. *Federalist* No. 62, pp. 416–17.

11. *Federalist* No. 46, p. 317; also, Diamond, "*Federalist*'s View of Federalism," pp. 56, 61, 64.

12. Farrand, *Records of the Federal Convention*, vol. 1, pp. 357–58.

13. Diamond, "*Federalist*'s View of Federalism," p. 60n., but cf. *The Founding of the Democratic Republic* (Itasca, Illinois: F. E. Peacock Publishers, Inc., 1981), p. 131.

14. Harry V. Jaffa, "Partly Federal, Partly National: On the Political Theory of the American Civil War," in *The Conditions of Freedom* (Baltimore: The Johns Hopkins University Press, 1975), pp. 161–62.

15. *Federalist* No. 33, p. 204.

16. *Federalist* No. 17, p. 105.

17. *Federalist* No. 44, p. 305.

18. Ibid., pp. 304–305; cf. Marshall's reasoning in McCulloch v. Maryland, 4 Wheat. 316, 4 L. Ed. 579 (1819).

19. Charles, *American Party System*, p. 6ff. Also, Paul C. Peterson, "The Problem of Consistency in the Statesmanship of James Madison: The Case of the Virginia Report," in Ralph A. Rossum and Gary L. McDowell, eds., *The American Founding: Politics, Statesmanship, and the Constitution* (Port Washington, N.Y.: Kennikat Press, 1981), pp. 122–34.

20. Cf. Madison's essay, "A Republican Distribution of Citizens," in Meyers, *Mind of the Founder*, pp. 241–43, and Jefferson, Query No. XIX, in William Peden, ed., *Notes on the State of Virginia* (Chapel Hill: University of North Carolina Press, 1954), p. 165.

21. See Madison's comment in *The Writings of James Madison*, ed. Gaillard Hunt, 9 vols. (New York: G. P. Putnam's Sons, 1906), vol. 6, p. 86, where he supports "withholding unnecessary opportunities from a few, to increase the inequality of property by an immoderate, and especially unmerited accumulation of riches."

22. Harry V. Jaffa, "The Nature and Origin of the American Party System," in *Liberty and Equality* (New York: Oxford University Press, 1965), p. 27; also, Peterson, "Problem of Consistency," p. 123.

23. Meyers, *Mind of the Founder*, esp. p. 247.

24. Ibid., p. 217. See also, Herbert Storing, "The Constitution and the Bill of Rights," in Robert A. Goldwin and William A. Schambra, eds., *How Does*

the Constitution Secure Rights? (Washington, D.C.: American Enterprise Institute, 1985), pp. 15–35.

25. As cited in Alpheus T. Mason and William M. Beaney, *American Constitutional Law: Introductory Essays and Selected Cases* (Englewood Cliffs, New Jersey: Prentice-Hall, Inc., 1964), p. 105.

26. Charles, *American Party System*, p. 6.

27. Nathan Schachner, *The Founding Fathers* (New York: Capricorn Books, 1961), p. 467. On the Sedition Acts, Schachner quotes Hamilton as saying they contained provisions "which, according to a cursory view, appear to me highly exceptionable. . . . I hope sincerely the thing may not be hurried through. Let us not establish a tyranny. Energy is a very different thing from violence."

28. Henry Steele Commager, ed., *Documents of American History* (New York: Appleton-Century-Crofts, Inc., 1948), vol. 1, p. 182.

29. Jaffa, "Partly Federal, Partly National," esp. p. 173.

30. Commager, *Documents of American History*, vol. 1, p. 184.

31. Meyers, *Mind of the Founder*, pp. 302–3.

32. Ibid., p. 306.

33. Ibid., p. 346.

34. Ibid., p. 307.

35. Cited in Walter Berns, "The Meaning of the Tenth Amendment," in Robert A. Goldwin, ed., *A Nation of States* (Chicago: Rand McNally, 1962), p. 157n.

36. Meyers, *Mind of the Founder*, p. 461; also, p. 328.

37. Ibid., pp. 379, 390.

38. Ibid., pp. 390–91.

39. Ibid., p. 543.

40. Ibid., p. 568.

41. Ibid., p. 327.

42. Madison to Thomas Ritchie, September 15, 1821, in Farrand, *Records of the Federal Convention*, vol. 3, pp. 447–48.

43. Ibid., p. 449.

44. Meyers, *Mind of the Founder*, p. 410 (emphasis added). The Constitution grants the power to "make all needful rules and regulations respecting the territory . . . of the United States." Cf. Madison's opposition to the addition of "expressly" to the Tenth Amendment, and his additional qualification "*really*" in this matter.

45. Ibid.

46. Ibid., p. 405.

47. Farrand, *Records of the Federal Convention*, vol. 3, p. 437. Professor Meyers gives the full text of the letter, but omits the footnote referred to here.

48. Meyers, *Mind of the Founder*, p. 398.

49. Ibid., p. 406.

50. Daniel J. Elazar, "Civil War and the Preservation of American Federalism," *Publius: The Journal of Federalism*, vol. 1, no. 1.

51. Morton Grodzins and Daniel J. Elazar, "Centralization and Decentral-

ization in the American Federal System," in Goldwin, *Nation of States*, p. 18ff.

52. James Q. Wilson, "The Rise of the Bureaucratic State," in Nathan Glazer and Irving Kristol, eds., *The American Commonwealth, 1976* (New York: Basic Books, Inc., 1976), p. 91.

53. Ibid., p. 92. This section draws heavily on Wilson's analysis.

54. Nathan Glazer, "Towards an Imperial Judiciary?" in ibid., p. 113.

55. Ibid., esp. pp. 117–19.

56. Especially since it was the national government that created these "clients" (Wilson, "Rise of the Bureaucratic State," p. 92). Moreover, owing to judicial activism, the states would be obliged to maintain a far greater range of services than they did in the 1950s.

57. Glazer, "Towards an Imperial Judiciary?" pp. 112–23. Here, however, the judicial self-restraint and respect for federalism exhibited in recent opinions of Justices Rehnquist and O'Connor is a hopeful sign.

58. John Agresto, "Virtue and Republicanism, 1776–1787," *The Review of Politics*, vol. 39, no. 4, pp. 473–504.

59. *Federalist* No. 63, p. 428.

60. *Federalist* No. 9, pp. 52–53.

61. *Federalist* No. 44, p. 305.

62. Meyers, *Mind of the Founder*, pp. 431–32. Also, Daniel J. Elazar, *Cities of the Prairie* (New York: Basic Books, Inc., 1970).

63. Glazer, "Towards an Imperial Judiciary?" p. 113.

Part VI
Madison's Bill of Rights

[15]

THE MADISONIAN THEORY OF RIGHTS

JACK N. RAKOVE*

In April 1988, I paid my first visit to the estate of James Madison at Montpelier. The tour is far less elaborate than what one sees at Mr. Jefferson's house at Monticello—and in this, as in so many other things, our fourth president still lags a step or two behind his friend and immediate predecessor. The van that takes visitors from the mansion to the parking lot some distance away swings by the family plot where Madison is buried. I was the only passenger who took up the driver's invitation to view the grave; but then I was the only Madison biographer on the bus, and it was late in the afternoon. In any event, there was little to linger over. The stone simply reads, "James Madison, 1751-1836." Once again, I found it hard to ignore the contrast with another marker not so far away, where Thomas Jefferson, by his own wish, is remembered as the "Author of the Declaration of American Independence, of the Statute of Virginia for Religious Freedom, and Father of the University of Virginia."

Any epitaph written for Madison today would probably recall him as the principal author of the Constitution of 1787, of *The Federalist*, and of the constitutional amendments we know as the Bill of Rights. Among these three achievements, Madison would doubtless be most proud of the first and most surprised by the great intellectual reputation he has gained from the second. But perhaps he would be most puzzled by the enormous influence that the Bill of Rights has acquired over modern American constitutionalism. For, although Madison the founder was very much the libertarian, he was highly skeptical of the value of bills of rights. Indeed, in August 1789, at the height of the congressional debates over his proposed amendments to the Constitution, he privately described his efforts as a "nauseous project"[1]—though by this he

---

* Associate Professor of History, Stanford University. A.B., Haverford College, 1968; Ph.D. Harvard University, 1975.

1. Letter from James Madison to Richard Peters (Aug. 19, 1789), *reprinted in* 12 THE PAPERS OF JAMES MADISON 346, 346 (1979).

probably alluded to the feelings of his colleagues in Congress rather than his own.

Among the members of the First Congress, Madison was almost alone in believing that prompt action on amendments was a political necessity. Nearly everyone else favored postponing the entire subject until the new government was operating safely—by which point, many congressmen hoped, the perceived need for a bill of rights itself might have evaporated. Madison's insistence that Congress act sooner, not later, insured the incorporation of a bill of rights in the Constitution.

On balance, however, Madison's prior and subsisting doubts about the value of bills of rights seem far more interesting than his expedient reasons for proposing the amendments of 1789. He based his position on this question on considerations far more substantial than the standard Federalist argument that a bill of rights was unnecessary and even dangerous. Madison's reservations were rooted instead in his fundamental criticism of what he called the "Vices of the Political System of the United States"[2] and in his general theory of republican government—especially as that theory coalesced during the late 1780s, the Madisonian moment of American constitutionalism. Recognizing, as a good originalist should, that the intentions and understandings prevailing at the time of the legal adoption of the Constitution should guide later interpretations, I propose to pay particular attention to the conclusions Madison drew during this crucial period. At the same time, as a card-carrying historian concerned with describing change over time, I want to identify the evolutionary elements in his thought, and in doing so, to suggest something of the difficulty of trying to isolate a pure or pristine Madisonian understanding of the problem of rights.[3]

By way of introduction, one can identify three critical propositions that lie at the heart of Madison's thinking about bills of rights and the larger problem of the protection of individual and minority rights:

2. Madison, *Vices of the Political System of the United States*, *reprinted in* 9 THE PAPERS OF JAMES MADISON 345 (1975).

3. For a more general discussion of Madison's political thought in the late 1780s, see Rakove, *The Madisonian Moment*, 55 U. CHI. L. REV. 473 (1988).

1. In a republic, claims of rights were to be asserted most directly not against the coercive authority of the state per se, but against the wishes and desires of interested popular majorities who could, in effect, control the uses to which the legal power of the state could be put.

2. Consistent with the arithmetical logic of his general theory of faction, Madison believed that the greater dangers to individual and minority rights would continually arise within the smaller compass of the states and local communities rather than within the extended sphere of the national republic itself.[4] Seen in this way, the most Madisonian element of the Constitution is arguably the fourteenth amendment, which was, of course, adopted a full three decades after his death.

3. Madison's reservations about the dangers inherent in any enumeration of rights rested on a profound perception of the plasticity of legislative power. The enumeration of rights was problematic because the delegation of specific powers was unlikely to restrain lawmakers who knew how to exploit the suppleness of legislative power itself.

I

As we all know, it is no easy matter to define exactly what we mean by rights; but however open or complex our definitions, we think of rights as durable claims that individuals and groups may maintain against the political will of the community or the state. Rights are permanent and inalienable. New rights may be created, but old rights should never be abolished once their legitimacy is accepted. Yet we also know from our own experience that our particular conceptions of rights, and our conceptions of particular rights, vary all the time.

As it is today, so it was in the era of the American Revolution. Ideas of rights figured powerfully in the political movements that led to the writing of both the Declaration of Independence in 1776, and the Constitution and Bill of Rights in 1787 and 1789 respectively. Certain principled notions of rights and liberties remained fixed throughout the period. Yet no one could possibly claim that

4. *See* Madison, *supra* note 2, at 353-57; Letter from James Madison to George Washington (Apr. 16, 1787), *reprinted in* 9 The Papers of James Madison 382, 383-84 (1975).

the Revolutionaries' understanding of rights was static and unchanging, or beyond the realm of political debate and heated controversy. Like every other element in the matrix of American constitutional thought, definitions of rights and notions of their protection shifted with the progress of the republican project.[5]

No one illustrates better the dynamic and nuanced character of American thinking about rights than James Madison. Precisely because Madison was such an original thinker, he may not be the most representative figure to single out in an effort to reconstruct the true "original understanding" of the Bill of Rights. As its principal mover in 1789, however, his intentions and ideas deserve special notice.

The evolution of Madison's thinking about the general problem of rights took place in four stages, which I will block out before going on to examine the distinctive elements of his general theory. The first phase is the easiest to describe. It dates roughly from the early 1770s, when Madison returned to Virginia from his collegiate studies at Princeton, to 1785-86, when he played the crucial political role in the defeat of the religious assessment bill and the subsequent passage of the celebrated Statute for Religious Freedom that his friend Thomas Jefferson had drafted in 1779. This was the Madison whose commitment to broad principles of religious liberty predated the development of his interest in either politics or constitutional theory. His first known comments on political issues of any kind expressed his abhorrence of the persecution of Baptist ministers for preaching without a license in pre-Revolutionary Virginia.[6] His early letters to his college friend William Bradford contain several comparisons between the enlightened condition of religious liberty in Bradford's Pennsylvania and the benighted situation in his own colony.[7] Madison's first notable action in public life was to secure an amendment to the Virginia Declaration of Rights of 1776, altering an article that originally proposed allowing

---

5. The most important work on pre-Revolutionary conceptions of rights is J. REID, CONSTITUTIONAL HISTORY OF THE AMERICAN REVOLUTION: THE AUTHORITY OF RIGHTS (1986). *See* J. REID, THE CONCEPT OF LIBERTY IN THE AGE OF THE AMERICAN REVOLUTION (1988).

6. *See* Letter from James Madison to William Bradford (Apr. 1, 1774), *reprinted in* 1 THE PAPERS OF JAMES MADISON 111-13 (1962).

7. *See* Letters from James Madison to William Bradford (Dec. 1, 1773, Jan. 24, 1774, and Apr. 1, 1774), *reprinted in* 1 THE PAPERS OF JAMES MADISON 100, 104, 111 (1962).

the "fullest Toleration in the Exercise of Religion" to a broader recognition that "all men are equally entitled to the free exercise of religion, according to the dictates of conscience."[8]

Madison stated his own position on religious liberty most explicitly in his *Memorial and Remonstrance against Religious Assessments* of 1785.[9] Precisely because Madison strains to deploy every argument he can against the idea of a general assessment, no one reading the *Memorial* could conclude intelligently that its author was anything but a strict separationist. Nothing sustains the claim that Madison actually favored what we now call nonpreferentialist support for religion in general. "Who does not see," he asked, "that the same authority which can establish Christianity, in exclusion of all other Religions, may establish with the same ease any particular sect of Christians, in exclusion of all other Sects?"[10]

As much as the *Memorial* reveals about the depth of Madison's unequivocal commitment to religious liberty, its treatment of the general problem of rights offers a curious mixture of original and conventional ideas. In its most explicitly political passages, the *Memorial* casts the question of religious liberty in the familiar terms of a struggle between overreaching rulers and a citizenry that needs to be roused to protect its rights. The rights in question belong to the ruled; the danger they face arises specifically from the rulers. Madison thus uses much the same language that Revolutionary leaders had directed against Parliament a decade earlier:

> The Rulers who are guilty of such an encroachment [on the rights of the people], exceed the commission from which they derive their authority, and are Tyrants. The People who submit to it are governed by laws made neither by themselves nor by an authority derived from them, and are slaves.[11]

---

8. Madison, *Declaration of Rights and Form of Government of Virginia*, *reprinted in* 1 THE PAPERS OF JAMES MADISON 173, 175 (1962). The progress of dis-establishment in Virginia has been extensively studied. *See* T. BUCKLEY, CHURCH AND STATE IN REVOLUTIONARY VIRGINIA, 1776-1787 (1977); THE VIRGINIA STATUTE FOR RELIGIOUS FREEDOM: ITS EVOLUTION AND CONSEQUENCES IN AMERICAN HISTORY (M. Peterson & R. Vaughan eds. 1988) (collected essays).

9. Madison, *Memorial and Remonstrance against Religious Assessments* (1785), *reprinted in* 8 THE PAPERS OF JAMES MADISON 298 (1973).

10. *Id.* at 300.

11. *Id.* at 299-300.

Thus wrote Madison in point two of the *Memorial*. The next point made the appeal even more explicit. The general assessment should be opposed, Madison continued,

> [b]ecause it is proper to take alarm at the first experiment on our liberties. We hold this prudent jealousy to be the first duty of Citizens, and one of the noblest characteristics of the late Revolution. The free men of America did not wait till usurped power had strengthened itself by exercise, and entangled the question in precedents. They saw all the consequences in the principle, and they avoided the consequences by denying the principle.[12]

In his concluding point Madison returned to the greater danger that would arise from a failure to check the rulers in this one instance: If the rulers could violate this one right, why could they not "sweep away all our fundamental rights" as well?[13] Samuel Adams could not have put the point any better in opposing the Stamp Act or the Declaratory Act or any of the other parliamentary measures that led to the Revolution.

If the rhetoric of rights sounds familiar, however, in other respects Madison's position was not entirely conventional. The rulers against whom these claims were to operate were no longer the politically unaccountable members of Parliament or the agents of the British crown; they were the elected representatives of the citizens of Virginia. In the traditional view, they were the men who were supposed to defend popular rights and liberties against the arbitrary claims of the other main branch of government—the executive. The novelty of the question Madison and others faced was to understand how claims of rights could be maintained against the political institution long regarded as the great bulwark of liberty. Insofar as Madison could locate the assessment struggle within the familiar rubric of rulers and ruled, however, his thought remained, in a sense, conventional.[14]

The second phase in the evolution of Madison's thinking about the problem of rights overlaps the first. By 1785, Madison was worrying more and more about the problem of legislative misrule

---

12. *Id.* at 300.
13. *Id.* at 304.
14. *See* G. WOOD, THE CREATION OF THE AMERICAN REPUBLIC, 1776-1787 268-73 (1969).

within the states. Indeed, his mounting concern with the character of state legislation, state legislatures and state legislators was the engine that drove the development of his constitutional thinking in the mid-1780s. Much of his concern was a reaction to his experience in the Virginia Assembly in the mid-1780s. As Gordon Wood has nicely put it, "Really for the first time, Madison found out what democracy in America might mean."[15] What it meant, he now knew, was that "[n]ot all the legislators were going to be like him or Jefferson; many of them did not even appear to be gentlemen."[16] Repeatedly, his "parochial" colleagues in the Assembly mangled or rejected the useful, enlightened bills that Madison drafted or supported. "What could he do with such clods?" Wood asks.[17]

Madison's initial discontent centered more on general questions of public policy than on matters of rights, and more on the failings of legislators than on the shortcomings of their constituents. By 1785, however, he was clearly sensitive to the need to protect individual rights against legislative abuse. In his August 1785 letter discussing a constitution for Kentucky, Madison argued that

> [t]he Constitution may expresly [sic] restrain [the legislature] from medling [sic] with religion—from abolishing Juries[,] from taking away the Habeus corpus—from forcing a citizen to give evidence against himself, from controuling the press, from enacting retrospective laws at least in criminal cases, from abridging the right of suffrage, from seizing private property for public use without paying its full Valu[e,] from licensing the importation of Slaves, from infringing the Confederation.[18]

Yet even this list of rights seems fairly conventional.

It was between August 1785 and March 1787 that Madison developed the two absolutely crucial elements defining his great goals for the Federal Convention. The first derived from his conviction that state laws were not simply poorly crafted or ill considered or

15. Wood, *Interests and Disinterestedness in the Making of the Constitution*, in BEYOND CONFEDERATION: ORIGINS OF THE CONSTITUTION AND AMERICAN NATIONAL IDENTITY 69, 74 (1987).

16. *Id.*

17. *Id.*

18. Letter from James Madison to Caleb Wallace (Aug. 23, 1785), *reprinted in* 8 THE PAPERS OF JAMES MADISON 350, 351 (1973).

unwise on grounds of policy, but that they were unjust because they violated fundamental private rights. The second component that is also difficult to locate in Madison's thought before 1787 is the recognition that the deeper sources of this injustice lay not in the guile or ambition of legislators, but in their very responsiveness to the wishes of their constituents.

The great moment of discovery came when Madison drafted his remarkable memorandum *Vices of the Political System of the United States* in April 1787.[19] For it was here that he first recognized that the "multiplicity," "mutability," and most importantly, the "injustice" of the laws that the states had enacted since independence, had called "into question the fundamental principle of republican Government, that the majority who rule in such Governments, are the safest Guardians both of public Good and of private rights."[20] In explaining why this was true, Madison developed the central ideas of his constitutional theory and his new understanding of the problem of rights.

In 1787, Madison was still ready to blame the sorry condition of public affairs on the characters of state legislators. All too often they sought office only for motives of "ambition" and "personal interest," rather than from sincere considerations of "public good." But the greater danger arose, he now concluded, not from the legislators themselves, but from their constituents. "A still more fatal if not more frequent cause" of unjust legislation, he wrote, "lies among the people themselves."[21] Madison designed his famous theory of faction to explain why this was so.

For all the midrashic commentary this theory has evoked, its central points are readily stated. First, factions are inevitable in "[a]ll civilized societies" because the diversity of interests and the fallibility of human reason and passions generate endless sources of division.[22] Second, a republic's peculiar danger is that "[w]henever . . . an apparent interest or common passion unites a majority," few effective checks exist to "restrain them from unjust violations of the rights and interests of the minority, or of individ-

19. Madison, *supra* note 2, at 354.
20. *Id.*
21. *Id.* at 355.
22. *Id.*

uals."[23] Third, because the ease with which such factious majorities form varies inversely with the size of a society, a national republic will be more resistant to the mischiefs of faction than the existing states of the American union.[24] Fourth, because much of the burden of governance will continue to rest with the states, however, individual and minority rights will remain exposed to violation by state legislatures and the majorities they represent.[25] The only adequate solution to this problem, Madison believed, was to give the reconstituted national government an absolute veto over all state laws. The national government would serve as a "disinterested & dispassionate umpire in disputes between different passions & interests in the State"—that is, within the individual states—and curb "the aggressions of interested majorities on the rights of minorities and of individuals."[26] The proposed national veto on state laws was thus the central innovation of Madison's entire scheme of reform.[27] This, rather than the adoption of a comprehensive bill of rights, was the measure that Madison regarded as indispensable to the preservation of civil liberty in America.

Madison's new understanding of rights was also clearly based on his growing fear that fundamental rights of property were becoming increasingly vulnerable to abuse by legislators spurred on by the factious majorities they represented.[28] By 1787, the need to protect property had become almost an obsession for Madison, and this concern carried his thought far beyond his longstanding commitment to religious liberty and the more conventional civil liberties of the Anglo-American tradition. The force of this attachment to the rights of property alone explains just how radical, or reactionary, his thought had become.

The rejection of the veto so gravely disappointed Madison that he left Philadelphia in September 1787, fearful that the Constitution would "neither effectually *answer* its *national object* nor pre-

---

23. *Id.*

24. *See id.* at 356-57.

25. *See id.*

26. Letter from James Madison to George Washington (Apr. 16, 1787), *reprinted in* 9 THE PAPERS OF JAMES MADISON 382, 384 (1975).

27. On this point, see Hobson, *The Negative on State Laws: James Madison, the Constitution, and the Crisis of Republican Government*, 36 WM. & MARY Q. 215 (1979).

28. *See infra* text accompanying notes 51-58.

vent the local *mischiefs* which every where *excite disgusts* ag[ain]st the *state governments*."[29] The third stage of his thinking about the problem of rights dates from the adjournment of the Convention to Madison's successful campaign to push the Bill of Rights through the First Federal Congress in 1789. Its significance rests on Madison's efforts to balance intellectual consistency with his perception of the public discussions of the Constitution. Far from abandoning the conclusions he had drawn during the months before the Convention, Madison remained convinced that his reasons for dismissing bills of rights as useless "parchment barriers"[30] were still sound. Yet from his intense involvement in the ratification campaign of 1787-88 and the first federal elections that followed, he also came to recognize that public opinion demanded the addition of some amendments to the new Constitution.[31]

Just how little had changed in Madison's private thinking about rights is evident from two remarkable letters he sent to Jefferson on the subject. Written a year apart, the letters are entirely consistent with the analysis and conclusions he had drawn in his preparations for the Federal Convention. Madison's defense of his proposed absolute veto on state laws in the first letter cannot be dismissed as a reflective rationalization of an idea whose impracticality he now recognized. It was instead a spirited defense of a measure whose rejection would leave the new government under the Constitution unable either to defend itself against the interference of the states or to protect individual and minority rights against unjust state legislation.[32]

Equally important, Madison still believed that the worst threats to liberty would arise "not from acts of Government contrary to the sense of its constituents, but from acts in which the Government is the mere instrument of the major number of the constitu-

29. Letter from James Madison to Thomas Jefferson (Sept. 6, 1787), *reprinted in* 10 The Papers of James Madison 163, 163-64 (1977).

30. Letter from James Madison to Thomas Jefferson (Oct. 17, 1788), *reprinted in* 11 The Papers of James Madison 295, 297 (1977).

31. *See* Editorial Note, *Madison's Election to the First Federal Congress Oct. 1788 - Feb. 1789*, *reprinted in* 11 The Papers of James Madison 301, 302 (1977).

32. Letter from James Madison to Thomas Jefferson (Oct. 24, 1787), *reprinted in* 10 The Papers of James Madison 206 (1977).

ents."[33] The popular character of these majorities was the crucial factor that led Madison to dismiss bills of rights as mere "parchment barriers." Why would a majority bent on injustice be dissuaded from its evil purposes by the mere existence of a bill of rights? Madison's analysis of the sources of faction and the nature of public opinion was bent toward demonstrating why rational appeals to higher principles would prove unavailing. In a monarchy, the existence of a bill of rights might serve as "a signal for rousing & uniting the superior force of the community"[34] against tyrannical acts of government; but in a republic "the political and physical power"[35] of government rested with the people at large, and a bill of rights could hardly work to rouse the community against itself.

These comments appeared, however, in the same letter in which Madison informed Jefferson that he would be willing to accept the addition of a bill of rights to the Constitution.[36] Madison soon publicly affirmed this position during his contest with James Monroe for a seat in the House of Representatives.[37] Explaining this shift as a "campaign conversion" is easy enough.[38] Yet Madison had a more principled basis for his reluctant acceptance of the need for amendments. A bill of rights might be useful, Madison conceded, if "[t]he political truths declared in that solemn manner acquire by degrees the character of fundamental maxims of free Government, and as they become incorporated with the national sentiment, counteract the impulses of interest and passion."[39]

The experience of the ratification campaign itself probably made this educative aspect of bills of rights more appealing to Madison

33. Letter from James Madison to Thomas Jefferson, *supra* note 30, at 298.

34. *Id.*

35. *Id.* This opinion tracks his earlier explanation in The Federalist No. 49 of the reasons why appeals to public opinion could not provide an effective remedy against the abuse of legislative power.

36. Letter from James Madison to Thomas Jefferson, *supra* note 30, at 297.

37. Editorial Note, *supra* note 31, at 302-03.

38. As Robert Morris put the point in 1789, when Madison was struggling to get Congress to consider his amendments, he "got frightened in Virginia and 'wrote a Book.'" Madison issued public letters announcing his revised views. Letter from Robert Morris to James Wilson (Aug. 23, 1789) (Willing, Morris, and Swanwick Papers, Pennsylvania Historical and Museum Commission, Harrisburg, Pa.).

39. Letter from James Madison to Thomas Jefferson, *supra* note 30, at 298-99.

in 1788 than earlier. The popular clamor for amendments indicated, perhaps, that public opinion was less "vicious" or misguided than Madison imagined. A bill of rights framed in response to popular demands would acquire more authority precisely because of the exceptional political circumstances under which it was adopted. To future generations, it would provide evidence of how deeply Americans had cared about preserving rights at the great moment of the Constitution's adoption. When Madison prodded a reluctant Congress in 1789 to take up his amendments, he took care to explain that he was responding, first and foremost, to the legitimate call of public opinion.[40]

When Madison first informed Jefferson of his willingness to accept a bill of rights, he added one other reason to justify his change of heart. "Altho' it be generally true . . . that the danger of oppression lies in the interested majorities of the people rather than in the usurped acts of the Government," he noted, "yet there may be occasions on which the evil may spring from the latter sources; and on such, a bill of rights would be a good ground for an appeal to the sense of the community."[41] He did not think this was a likely scenario, but he could not rule out the possibility that a government insulated from popular control might abuse liberty, even in a republic.

Madison came to accept the real force of this danger during the fourth phase in the evolution of his thinking about the problem of rights. This phase can be dated to the decade of the 1790s—the period after the first ten amendments were framed and ratified. As Madison and Jefferson began to oppose the programs of Alexander Hamilton, they regarded the ruling Federalist party not as the instrument of a true popular majority, but as a quasi-aristocratic clique that had gained control of the national government. Confidence in their belief that a popular majority would eventually rally to their own Republican standard sustained the two Virginians through the repeated political reverses they suffered in the 1790s. By the end of the decade, however, Madison realized that Jefferson had been right all along to insist that "a bill of rights is what the people are entitled to against every government on earth, general

40. 1 ANNALS OF CONG. 427-28 (J. Gales ed. 1789) (speech by Madison before Congress).
41. Letter from James Madison to Thomas Jefferson, *supra* note 30, at 299.

or particular."[42] For in the opposition to the Sedition Act of 1798, the first amendment did provide "a good ground for an appeal to the sense of the community" against "usurped acts of the Government."[43] At the same time, Madison also recognized that dangers to liberty could arise as easily at the national level of government as at the state level.

II

If nothing else, this brief effort to trace the evolution of Madison's thinking about rights should illustrate the difficulty, if not the absurdity, of attempting to freeze a moment of historical time as the point when he possessed a true original understanding of exactly how the Constitution was to protect rights. The general problem of rights concerned Madison continuously, but his ideas of which rights most needed protection, and how they were to be protected, varied over time. Certain recurring concerns and insights, however, gave the Madisonian theory of liberty its power and brilliance, and remain instructive today.

To some extent, Madison did accept the clever arguments against a bill of rights that James Wilson offered in a widely reported public speech in Philadelphia, delivered only three weeks after the adjournment of the Constitutional Convention. The explicit reservation of certain rights in the Constitution, Wilson declared, "would have been superfluous and absurd" because the new government had not been given the power to regulate the various activities that most deserved protection.[44] Madison further accepted the basic Federalist argument that the positive declaration of certain rights might relegate to inferior status other rights left unmentioned but equally valuable. He was also aware that any attempt to reduce a general right to a specific textual formula could prove self-defeating if, for political reasons, "a positive declaration of some of the most essential rights could not be obtained in the

42. Letter from Thomas Jefferson to James Madison (Dec. 20, 1787), *reprinted in* 10 The Papers of James Madison 335, 337 (1977).

43. Letter from James Madison to Thomas Jefferson, *supra* note 30, at 299.

44. Speech by James Wilson before Public Meeting in Philadelphia, Pennsylvania State Courthouse Yard (Oct. 6, 1787), *reprinted in* 13 The Documentary History of the Ratification of the Constitution 339, 339-40 (J. Kaminski & G. Saladino eds. 1981).

requisite latitude."[45] The very act of reducing a conception of one right or another to any specific form might limit rather than expand the basis for its protection. Better, in other words, not to have any bill of rights than to incorporate in the Constitution weak textual statements that might leave room for the violation of liberties the bill of rights was meant to protect.

Yet, as Jefferson argued, "Half a loaf is better than no bread. If we cannot secure all our rights, let us secure what we can."[46] This was the sensible objection Madison remained reluctant to accept. The problem was not that he was incapable of enumerating a whole range of rights; he could have done so readily at the dip of a quill, and had done so in a 1785 letter concerning a constitution for Kentucky, for example.[47] He had no problem recognizing the benefits of an outright prohibition of legislative power over matters of religion. Nor would he have found it difficult to codify the essential civil and political liberties necessary to protect the citizen against the coercive power of the state. And indeed, as Leonard Levy has noted, in 1789 Madison sought to incorporate expansive notions of rights into the provisions that became the fourth amendment's protection against "unreasonable searches and seizures" and the fifth amendment's protection from self-incrimination.[48]

Madison's opposition to the enumeration of rights rested on a more profound and complex set of considerations. At the heart of his thought lay two overarching concerns. One involved his substantial fears about the security of property; the other involved his analysis of the nature of legislative power itself.

The best way to develop these points may be to examine the relation between Madison's views of religious liberty and the near obsession with property rights that affected him so strongly in 1787. We know that Madison's appreciation of the liberty-preserving benefits of diverse economic interests owed a great deal to his grasp of the way in which multi-denominationalism fostered religious liberty. He said as much in a famous passage in *The Federalist No. 51*:

45. Letter from James Madison to Thomas Jefferson, *supra* note 30, at 297.

46. Letter from Thomas Jefferson to James Madison (Mar. 15, 1789), *reprinted in* 12 THE PAPERS OF JAMES MADISON 13, 14 (1979).

47. Letter from James Madison to Caleb Wallace, *supra* note 18, at 352-56.

48. L. LEVY, ORIGINAL INTENT AND THE FRAMERS' CONSTITUTION 242-45, 247-49 (1988).

> In a free government, the security for civil rights must be the same as that for religious rights. It consists in the one case in the multiplicity of interests, and in the other, in the multiplicity of sects. The degree of security in both cases will depend on the number of interests and sects; and this may be presumed to depend on the extent of country and number of people comprehended under the same government.[49]

Diversity begets jealousy, and jealousy begets security. This was a lesson Madison drew from experience as well as observation and reflection. In the struggle over the religious assessment bill of 1784-85, Madison and his allies had appealed to the mutual jealousies of the various sects of Protestant Virginia. Even though those sects arguably had a common interest in the bill, which would have supported all teachers of Christianity, its opponents managed to parlay their diverse opinions and their fear that one or more denominations might benefit excessively into a final decision validating an essential principle of liberty.[50] Had the denominational map of Virginia looked less complex, the bill probably would have passed.

In at least two other respects, however, the differences between the case of religious liberty in 1785 and the issues that Madison sought to resolve in 1787 are as striking as the similarities. First, the apparent lesson that Madison could have drawn from the defeat of the assessment bill in 1785 was exactly the lesson he rejected in 1787. In 1785, Madison could have concluded that appeals to public opinion could work in a liberty-preserving way. His *Memorial*, after all, was not a mere tract espousing religious liberty, but an actual petition designed to sway the votes of popularly elected legislators. That appeal, coupled with other petitions that garnered even more support, had worked, successfully mobilizing public opinion in Virginia in behalf of liberty.

Far more important, however, was the fundamental difference between issues of religious liberty and other areas of governance in which Madison feared that factious majorities stood ready to trample individual and minority rights. At the core of Madison's sup-

---

49. THE FEDERALIST No. 51 (J. Madison), *reprinted in* 10 THE PAPERS OF JAMES MADISON 476, 478-79 (1977).

50. THE FEDERALIST No. 10 (J. Madison), *reprinted in* 10 THE PAPERS OF JAMES MADISON 263, 265-66 (1977).

port for free exercise and dis-establishment lay the radical conviction that the entire sphere of religious practice could be, in a word, deregulated. In this one area, at least, Madison and Jefferson were the Friedrich von Hayek and Milton Friedman—dare one say the Richard Epstein?—of their day. They believed not only that religious conviction and practice were private matters, but also that religion, like capitalism, flourished best when unregulated.

Because religion could be seen as a matter of opinion only, it marked the one area of traditional governance in which a flat constitutional denial of legislative jurisdiction seemed able to enlarge the realm of private rights. No such clarity emerged, however, when the Madison of 1787 turned to the other area in which he feared that private rights were most vulnerable to violation. When rights of property were at stake, Madison believed, neither the positive and specific delegation of legislative power, nor its explicit denial and limitation would prove adequate. The clearest statement of his reasoning on this point is in *The Federalist No. 10*, in the paragraph that follows the description of the sources of faction. It deserves careful explication.

After noting how different forms of property divided society into different "interests," Madison closed his account of "[t]he latent causes of faction" with this observation: "The regulation of these various and interfering interests forms the principal task of modern legislation, and involves the spirit of party and faction in the necessary and ordinary operations of government."[51] But Madison then proceeded to challenge the very idea that acts of economic regulation are truly legislative in character. "[W]hat are many of the most important acts of legislation," he asked, "but so many judicial determinations, not indeed concerning the rights of single persons, but concerning the rights of large bodies of citizens; and what are the different classes of legislators, but advocates and parties to the causes which they determine?"[52]

Madison's examples of such "determinations" reveal how much he regarded decisions of economic policy as implicating questions of private rights. Laws relating to creditors and debtors, to the protection of domestic manufactures and the restriction of foreign

51. *Id.* at 266.
52. *Id.*

goods, and to the apportionment of taxes all involve questions of justice, and thus of rights.[53] In contrast to the modern cry against judges acting as legislators, Madison suggested that legislators inevitably act as judges, without needing, however, to maintain a pretense of judicial impartiality. Economic rights, then, were fundamentally different from rights of conscience in this one critical sense: Government could safely abstain from regulating matters of religion, but it could never avoid having to regulate the "various and interfering interests" of which modern societies were composed.

The new and creative elements in Madison's understanding of the problem of rights were thus rooted in his mounting concern about the security of property. To reduce Madison's notions of rights to economic questions alone would, of course, be wrong. Yet clearly the Madison of 1787 was intensely worried that populist forces in the states might pass all kinds of laws endangering property rights.

That concern was not entirely original in 1787. In 1785, for example, Madison endorsed the idea that the electors of the upper house in the states should be limited to those holding a significant, though unspecified, amount of property.[54] Events since 1785 made this somewhat abstract concern more urgent. Paper money laws, debtor stay laws, and Shays' Rebellion in Massachusetts all alarmed him terribly. So did the grim prospect that he sketched at the Federal Convention. Even in the United States, he warned, a factious majority might eventually form, made up "of those who will labour under all the hardships of life, & secretly sigh for a more equal distribution of its blessings."[55] The constitution writers of 1776, Madison believed, had erred in assuming that by protecting "the rights of persons" they would also protect "those of property."[56] Now he understood "that in all populous countries"—the United States not excepted—"the smaller part [of society] only

53. *Id.*

54. Letter from James Madison to Caleb Wallace, *supra* note 18, at 353.

55. Speech by James Madison before the Federal Convention in Philadelphia (June 26, 1787), *reprinted in* 10 THE PAPERS OF JAMES MADISON 76, 77 (1977).

56. Madison, Observations on Jefferson's Draft of a Constitution for Virginia (Oct. 15, 1788), *reprinted in* 11 THE PAPERS OF JAMES MADISON 285, 287-88 (1977).

can be interested in preserving the rights of property."[57] Efforts to protect the rights of property had to be made now, while "the bulk of the people" were still attached to the rights of persons and property alike.[58]

These comments belie the optimistic forecast we associate with *The Federalist Nos. 10* and *51*. Madison could be fairly certain that Protestant sectarianism would remain a constant in American life, protecting religious liberty through its fruitful multiplication of irresolvable opinions on theology, ecclesiology and forms of worship. Indeed, nothing better illustrated the way in which mere opinion could generate division within a community, even when its members shared other interests. He was less confident, however, that economic change would produce divisions equally complex. True, an extended republic would prevent or discourage the wrong kinds of majorities from forming at the national level of government, but the catch lay in the residual power that the states would necessarily exercise over the economy. Even in his most expansive moments, Madison never pretended that a reconstituted national government could superintend the daily affairs of the entire union. Most legislation affecting property would continue to be enacted at the state level.

Moreover, according to the arithmetical logic of his theory of faction, the creation of an extended national republic would not prevent the continued formation of factious majorities within the individual states, which was why the entire Madisonian scheme of 1787 required the national veto on state laws. Madison may have hoped that a reformed national Congress would set examples of sound lawmaking that even the "clods" in the state assemblies could learn to imitate. Even then, however, his perception of the populist character of state politics did not encourage him to conclude that state legislators would prove suddenly resistant to the "vicious" impulses of their constituents. The factious majorities that he feared would continue to coalesce in the states were popular majorities, not simple coalitions of sleazy legislators.

---

57. *Id.*

58. *Id.* Madison thus well illustrates Gordon Wood's description of the transformation of property as a Lockean right pertaining to all men into a peculiar interest deserving protection. *See* G. Wood, *supra* note 14, at 214-22.

Madison's doubts about the wisdom of enumeration had another and more profound source. Legislators themselves were no longer the sole or chief defendants in Madison's indictment of the political sources of faction. Instead, his analysis of the constitutional problem of rights placed great emphasis on the nature of legislation—especially on what he later called its "plastic faculty."[59] He put the point most directly in his letter to Jefferson of October 24, 1787,[60] but in striking ways it recurs elsewhere in his writings. In defending his proposed national veto, Madison called attention to the supple and amorphous character of legislative power. He spoke, for example, of "the impossibility of dividing powers of legislation, in such a manner, as to be free from different constructions by different interests, or even from ambiguity in the judgment of the impartial."[61] Close off one avenue of legislative excess, and an artful legislature would only slip down another alley to do its insidious work. This was why the "partial provision[s]" the Constitution offered for the protection of economic rights through the contract clause and the prohibition against state emission of paper money would prove inadequate. "Supposing them to be effectual as far as they go, they are short of the mark. Injustice may be effected by such an infinitude of legislative expedients, that where the disposition exists it can only be controuled by some provision which reaches all cases whatsoever."[62] This was why the veto had to be unlimited.[63]

In the realm of economic legislation, then, Madison doubted that any enumeration of legislative powers would work. The interests to be regulated were so complex, and the ends and means of legislation so intertwined, that no simple formula seemed likely to defeat a legislative ingenuity spurred on by the passions and interests of popular majorities. Nor could one rely safely on the good offices of

59. Letter from James Madison to Spencer Roane (May 6, 1821), *reprinted in* 9 THE WRITINGS OF JAMES MADISON 58 (1910).

60. *See* Letter from James Madison to Thomas Jefferson, *supra* note 32, at 211.

61. *Id.*

62. *Id.* at 212.

63. That is also why the Madison of the 1790s must have told himself a thousand times that he should have paid more attention to the "necessary and proper" clause, whose broad interpretation by Alexander Hamilton proved how right Madison had been only a few years earlier. *See* Hamilton, *Opinion on the Constitutionality of an Act to Establish a Bank* (Feb. 23, 1791), *reprinted in* 8 THE PAPERS OF ALEXANDER HAMILTON 63, 101-07 (1965).

the executive and judiciary to counteract the improper impulses of the dominant branch. By its very rulemaking powers, the legislature could circumscribe the best efforts of the two weaker branches of government to correct the injustices of legislation. The legislature could always "mask under complicated and indirect measures, the encroachments which it makes, on the co-ordinate departments,"[64] Madison wrote in *The Federalist No. 48*. "It is not unfrequently a question of real nicety in legislative bodies, whether the operation of a particular measure, will, or will not extend beyond the legislative sphere,"[65] he said.

As Jefferson was quick to note, Madison seemed to ignore the possibility that a bill of rights might actually provide an independent judiciary with a "legal check" against improper acts of legislation.[66] Madison had reached exactly the opposite conclusion. An enumeration of rights, he feared, would prove far more effective in limiting the judicial protection of rights than an enumeration of legislative powers would in preventing their violation.

Madison's resistance to the enumeration of rights was thus merely the opposite side of his fear that legislative power could never be confined. The enumeration of rights, in other words, might prove restrictive in a way or to an extent that the enumeration of legislative powers could not. He believed it better to give the two weaker branches something of the free play that the dominant lawmaking branch could enjoy by manipulating its "infinitude of legislative expedients."[67] If many legislative decisions were truly judicial in nature, Madison reasoned, why not bring the judiciary into the legislative process so that judicial advice could hopefully prevent the legislature from committing its unjust mischief in the first place? This was the point of Madison's other great proposed innovation of 1787: the joint executive-judicial council of revision, which would be charged with the duty of advising Congress of the merits of legislation before it was enacted, and which could back up its advice by wielding a limited veto. The fact that the

---

64. THE FEDERALIST No. 48 (J. Madison), *reprinted in* 10 THE PAPERS OF JAMES MADISON 456, 457 (1977).

65. *Id.*

66. Letter from Thomas Jefferson to James Madison (Mar. 15, 1789), *reprinted in* 12 THE PAPERS OF JAMES MADISON 13 (1979).

67. Letter from James Madison to Thomas Jefferson, *supra* note 32, at 212.

Philadelphia Convention found this proposal no more acceptable than the absolute veto on state laws did not shake Madison's belief in its essential value. As late as October 1788, in commenting on Jefferson's draft of a constitution for Virginia, he modified his views only to suggest that bills should "be separately communicated to the Exec[utive] & Judic[iar]y depts." before their enactment.[68]

One can thus make the case that James Madison's thinking about rights in the late 1780s fused radical and reactionary elements. What other conclusion can we reach when we move beyond the familiar formulas of *The Federalist No. 10* to map the larger contours of his thought? Here was a man who thought that virtually all matters of religion could be put safely beyond the reach of the state, yet who also thought that all questions of economic regulation involved questions of rights; who was prepared to argue that because many legislative acts were really judicial in nature, the judiciary might just as well be involved in the business of legislation; who felt that the only reliable security for rights lay in giving an insulated national government an absolute veto over the acts of the officials most directly accountable to the people, their representatives in the state legislatures. Yet as acute and powerful as Madison's positions were, many of them were only positions—points that he was prepared to reinforce, modify or even abandon as he continued to revolve the problem of rights in the light of experience and events.

Among all the problems of rights that he had to consider, none seemed more ominous or less tractable than the single form of oppression that Madison had observed most closely. He was frank to include "the case of Black slaves in Modern times" as a potent example of "[t]he danger of oppression to the minority from unjust combinations of the majority."[69] At the Federal Convention, he had noted that "the mere distinction of colour has been made . . . a ground of the most oppressive dominion ever exercised by man over man."[70] Yet for all his virtues, which were many, Madison was

68. Madison, *supra* note 56, at 292-93.

69. Madison, *Notes for the National Gazette Essays*, *reprinted in* 14 The Papers of James Madison 157, 160 (1983).

70. Speech by James Madison before Federal Convention in Philadelphia (June 6, 1787), *reprinted in* 10 The Papers of James Madison 32, 33 (1977).

no better prepared to imagine a solution for the problem of slavery than were any of his contemporaries. In his own way, he was part of the problem. Madison defended the republican guarantee clause in part because it would allow the national government to aid in the suppression of slave rebellions, and the three-fifths clause because the ownership of slaves was a peculiar form of property right that deserved special protection.[71]

One Madisonian puzzle yet remains. I have argued that the unlimited national veto on state laws was the crucial proposal for the protection of rights that Madison favored in 1787 and 1788. Could he seriously imagine that his own constituents would ever accept such a proposal once they understood that its reach would extend to the regulation of slavery? Or did he somehow hope that the veto would provide an entering wedge with which the national government might work to weaken the hold of slavery and all of its evil effects? If he at least glimpsed the latter possibility, can we not conclude that the Civil War amendments, especially the fourteenth, are the most Madisonian elements of our Constitution?

So I like to think; but nothing better exposes the limits of Madison's analysis of the problem of rights, and the reasons why we must assess his thought critically, than his inability to articulate—or perhaps even perceive—the conclusions to which his proposals led.

71. Madison's thoughts about slavery, especially during his long period of retirement after 1817, are the subject of poignant analysis in D. McCoy, The Last of the Fathers: James Madison and the Republican Legacy (1989).

[16]

JAMES MADISON AND THE BILL OF RIGHTS: A RELUCTANT PATERNITY

PAUL FINKELMAN

In May 1789, when the first Congress was just two months old James Madison indicated his intention to introduce a series of amendments to the Constitution. A month later Madison finally found an opening in the agenda to propose his amendments.[1] He faced opposition from all sides.[2] Former federalist allies, like Fisher Ames and Roger Sherman, dismissed Madison's call for amendments as unnecessary, imprudent, or worse yet, an attempt by Madison to gain popularity.[3] In private correspondence they were even more critical of Madison's proposals.[4]

Paul Finkelman is Visiting Associate Professor of Law, Brooklyn Law School.

AUTHOR'S NOTE: I wish to thank Willi Paul Adams, Kenneth Bowling, Michael Kent Curtis, Peter Hoffer, Ralph Ketcham, Knud Krakau, Sanford Levinson, Pauline Maier, Jack Rakove and Frank Rohmer for their very useful comments on this article. Portions of this paper were read at the Organization of American Historians, the American Society for Legal History, and the colloquium of the John F. Kennedy Institute at the Free University of Berlin.

[1]Speeches of Madison, Annals of Congress, 1st Cong., 1st Sess., (May 4, 1789 and June 8, 1789) 257; 440–469.

[2]William E. Nelson argues that the "Federalists acceded to Antifederalist demands for the protection of personal rights as the price of ratification," Nelson, Reason and Compromise in the Establishment of the Federal Constitution, 1787–1801, 44 Wm. & Mary Q. 477 (3rd ser., 1987). This seems correct only for the ratification conventions, where federalists in Massachusetts, Virginia, and New York voted for recommended amendments after the conventions ratified the Constitution. However, by 1789 many federalists in Congress were no longer willing to support amendments. Only Madison's maneuvering, tenacity, and arguments led them to support the Bill of Rights.

[3]Brant, James Madison: Father of the Constitution, 1787–1800 267–68 (1950).

[4]Bowling, "A Tub to the Whale": The Founding Fathers and the Adoption of the Federal Bill of Rights, 8 J. of the Early Republic 223, 237 (1988).

Many antifederalists were equally unsupportive. Elbridge Gerry, who had refused to sign the Constitution in part because it lacked a bill of rights, was unwilling to support Madison at this time.[5] Aedanus Burke, on the other hand, wanted amendments but not the kind Madison proposed. He thought Madison's were "frothy and full of wind, formed only to please the palate; or they are like a tub thrown out to a whale, to secure the freight of the ship and its peaceable voyage."[6]

Despite this resistance, Madison persisted. Ultimately Congress accepted most of the substance of what Madison suggested.[7] Within five months Congress agreed to twelve amendments, ten of which were ratified by 1791.

For his persistence in the summer of 1789, Madison well deserves his reputation as the father of the Bill of Rights. This may indeed have been "some of his noblest work,"[8] and modern civil libertarians have good reason to claim Madison as one of their own. As Leonard W. Levy has persuasively argued, Madison's "accomplishment in the face of opposition and apathy entitles him to be remembered as 'father of the Bill of Rights' even more than as 'father of the Constitution.'"[9] This article does not challenge the conventional wisdom on this point; rather, it explores the route that Madison took to his well-earned place in the history of liberty.

Despite his eventual support for a bill of rights, Madison had no well thought-out intentions on this subject. Rather, he had well thought-out reservations about a bill of rights. While always sympathetic to the goal of preserving liberty, Madison, even as he introduced the Bill of Rights in the Congress, had little faith in the value

[5]In nine recorded votes on the Bill of Rights, Gerry voted against Madison seven times. They voted together, in the majority only on two minor procedural questions which were overwhelmingly defeated. These votes are compiled in Schwartz, 5 The Roots of the Bill of Rights 1116, 1124–25, 1127, 1132, 1137, 1161, 1163 (1971).

[6]Speech of Burke, Annals of Congress, 1st Cong., 1st Sess. (Debate of August 15, 1789) 774. On this issue, see generally Bowling, note 4 *supra*, at 223–51. George Mason thought Madison's proposals were "Milk & Water propositions," while Senator Richard Henry Lee dismissed them as "not similar" to the amendments proposed by the Virginia ratifying conventions. *Id.* at 233.

[7]Madison proposed that "No State shall violate the equal rights of conscience, or the freedom of the press, or the trial by jury trials in criminal cases." This provision passed the House of Representatives but was eventually struck out by the Senate. Schwartz, note 5 *supra*, at 1027, 1156.

[8]Burns, James Madison: Philosopher of the Constitution 15 (1973).

[9]Levy, The Bill of Rights, in 1 Encyclopedia of the American Constitution 115 (Levy, Karst & Mahoney, eds., 1986).

of what he derisively called "parchment barriers."[10] Madison's paternity of the Bill of Rights was a reluctant one that he accepted only after political realities forced him to rethink long-held positions.

Madison's primary purpose in supporting amendments was twofold: to fulfill promises made to his constituents during his campaign for Congress and to undermine opposition to the Constitution. On this latter point Madison argued that the amendments "would have stifled the voice of complaint, and made friends of many who doubted the merits of the constitution."[11]

I. Madison and the Authorship of the Bill of Rights

The amendments Madison introduced in the House of Representatives were rewritten by a committee, amended on the floor, and then altered again by the Senate. The Congress wisely rejected the very structure of Madison's amendments. Madison proposed that the amendments be imbedded into various sections of the Constitution because "He feared that the placement [of the amendments at the end of the Constitution] would lead to ambiguities about how far the original Constitution had been superseded by the amendments."[12] Had Madison's idea been accepted the "Bill of Rights" would not exist as such, although the rights themselves would still be found in the Constitution. Fortunately, Congress accepted Roger Sherman's suggestion that the amendments be added in a series at the end of the Constitution. It is quite likely that the impact of the Bill of Rights on our society would have been seriously diminished if it had not been one coherent body of rights found in one place in the Constitution.

The Senate categorically rejected Madison's favorite proposal—an amendment declaring that "No state shall infringe the right of trial by Jury in criminal cases, nor the rights of conscience, nor the freedom of speech, or of the press." This amendment would have limited the power of the states to undermine religious liberty, freedom of expression, and due process of law.[13] Such an amendment

[10]James Madison to Thomas Jefferson, October 17, 1788, 11 The Papers of James Madison 295–300, quoted at 297 (Rutland ed. 1977) (cited below as Papers of Madison).

[11]Speech of Madison, Annals of Congress, 1st Cong., 1st Sess. (June 8, 1789), 444.

[12]Bowling, note 4 *supra*, at 242.

[13]4 Documentary History of the First Federal Congress of the United States of America: Legislative Histories 39 (Bickford & Veit, eds., 1986). At the Constitutional Convention

would have radically altered the federal structure of the new government.

Though other members were active in the House and Senate debates, Madison was without question the key player in the adoption of the Bill of Rights. Perhaps "the Bill of Rights would be in place whether Madison had been present or not."[14] It would, however, be a different bill of rights and it certainly would not have been ratified by 1791. Madison was, as Jack Rakove has persuasively argued, "almost alone" in the First Congress "in believing that prompt action on amendments was a political necessity."[15] It may be true that "there was too much pressure from George Mason, Thomas Jefferson, Richard Henry Lee and others for the matter simply to have dropped."[16] But many antifederalists were exerting pressure for amendments that most probably would not have been ratified; they were also exerting pressure for a second Convention, which might have undone the work of the 1787 gathering. Without Madison's boundless energy in supporting amendments, despite his ambivalence about their value, strong anti-federalist pressure might have undermined the new government under the Constitution, leading to unforeseen developments. If there was a "framer" and a "father" of the Bill of Rights, it was Madison.

II. The Bill of Rights and the Constitutional Convention

The Constitutional Convention never seriously considered adopting a bill of rights. Near the end of the Convention the issue was discussed briefly and disposed of summarily. At the same time the delegates defeated various proposals for the protection of specific civil liberties, many of which were eventually incorporated into the Bill of Rights.

On August 20, 1787, Charles Pinckney "submitted sundry propo-

Madison had tried, and also failed, to incorporate greater limitations on the states by giving Congress the power to overrule state legislation. Hobson, The Negative on State Laws: James Madison, the Constitution, and the Crisis of Republican Government, 36 Wm. & Mary Q. 215 (3rd Ser., 1979). See also Banning, James Madison and the Nationalists, 1780–1783, 40 Wm. & Mary Q. 227 (3rd Ser., 1979), for a discussion of Madison's early nationalism, and Banning, The Hamiltonian Madison, 92 Va. Mag of Hist. & Biog. 7 (1984), for Madison's fear, "As late as 1789" that "the necessary powers of the central government would prove vulnerable to the encroachments by the states."

[14]Rutland, The Trivialization of the Bill of Rights, 31 Wm. & Mary L. Rev 287 (1990).

[15]Rakove, The Madisonian Theory of Rights, 31 Wm. & Mary L. Rev. 245, 246 (1990).

[16]Rutland, note 14 *supra*, at 287.

sitions" to the Convention. While some of Pinckney's propositions ultimately were included in the body of the Constitution, the Committee on Detail ignored his proposals to insure freedom of the press and to prohibit the quartering of troops in private homes. On September 12 the Convention rejected a proposal by Elbridge Gerry that the right to a jury in civil cases be guaranteed by the Constitution.[17]

George Mason, Madison's Virginia colleague, then suggested that the entire Constitution be "prefaced with a Bill of Rights." He thought that "with the aid of the State declarations, a bill might be prepared in a few hours." Roger Sherman argued that this was unnecessary because the Constitution did not repeal the state bills of rights. Mason replied that federal laws would be "paramount to State Bills of Rights." This argument, however correct, had little effect on the Convention, which defeated Mason's motion with all states voting no.[18] Within the Virginia delegation Madison opposed this motion.

The next day advocates of a bill of rights made one last attempt to add protections for basic civil liberties. Gerry once again proposed a guarantee of juries for civil trials, and once again the state delegations unanimously rejected this proposal. Pinckney and Gerry then proposed "that the liberty of the Press should be inviolably observed."[19]

Sherman again argued that under a government of limited powers specific protections of liberty were unnecessary because "The power of Congress does not extend to the Press." Five states were unconvinced, and voted for the proposal.[20] It is possible Madison voted for this motion, because we know Mason and Randolph carried at least one other Virginian within their delegation. But a majority of the state delegations sided with Sherman, defeating the motion to protect "the liberty of the Press."[21]

On Saturday, September 15, 1787, the next-to-the-last day of the Convention, George Mason expressed his reservations about the Constitution. He observed: "There is no Declaration of Rights, and the laws of the general government being paramount to the laws and

[17] 2 The Records of the Federal Convention of 1787 587 (Farrand ed. 1966) (cited below as Farrand).

[18] 2 Farrand 587–88.

[19] *Id.* at 5.

[20] Madison recorded the vote as 4 in favor and 7 states opposed. Both the official records and McHenry's notes recorded 5 states in favor and 6 opposed. 2 Farrand 611, 618, 620.

[21] *Id.* at 617–18.

Constitutions of the several States, the Declaration of Rights in the separate States are no security." Mason noted that under this Constitution "the people" were not "secured even the enjoyment of the benefit of the common law."[22]

Mason had other objections to the Constitution. He disliked the commerce power, the treaty-making provisions, the continuation of the African slave trade for *at least* twenty more years,[23] and the power of the President to grant pardons, especially to "those whom he had secretly instigated to commit" crimes and "thereby prevent a discovery of his own guilt."[24] These complaints about the Constitution were magnified by the lack of a bill of rights. Mason feared that the Senate and the President would combine "to accomplish what usurpations they pleased upon the rights and liberties of the people," while the federal judiciary would "absorb and destroy the judiciaries of the several States." He thought the expansive powers of Congress threatened the "security" of "the people for their rights." Without a bill of rights all this was possible. He complained, "There is no declaration of any kind, for preserving the liberty of the press, or the trial by jury in civil causes; nor against the danger of standing armies in time of peace."[25] For these reasons, Mason refused to sign the Constitution.

Another Virginian, Edmund Randolph, also refused to sign. He proposed a second convention to consider amendments, including a bill of rights. Elbridge Gerry of Massachusetts agreed with Mason on many substantive issues, including the dangers posed by the aristocratic nature of the Senate and the centralizing tendencies of the commerce power. He would have been able to "get over all these" defects "if the rights of the Citizens were not rendered insecure" by the virtually unlimited power of Congress under the necessary and proper clause and the lack of a guarantee of jury trials in civil cases.[26] But, without such guarantees, he too refused to sign the Constitution.

---

[22] *Id.* at 637–38.

[23] Finkelman, Slavery and the Constitutional Convention: Making a Covenant with Death, in Beyond Confederation: Origins of the Constitution and American National Identity 218–21 (Beeman, Botein &. Carter, eds., 1987).

[24] 2 Farrand 637–38.

[25] *Id.* at 639–40.

[26] *Id.* at 632–33; Hon. Mr. Gerry's Objections to signing the National Constitution, in 2 The Complete Anti-Federalist 6–7 (Storing ed. 1981).

While Mason, Randolph, Gerry, and Pinckney argued for explicit protections of liberty, James Madison remained oddly silent. Madison was one of the most vocal delegates to the Convention. He said something on virtually every issue raised during the summer-long meeting. Why did Madison fail to support his colleagues from Virginia on this major issue? Why, if he was opposed to a bill of rights, did Madison not speak against their proposals?

There is no immediately satisfactory answer to either question. One explanation for Madison's reticence, and indeed for the majority's refusal to add a bill of rights, is a lack of time. The delegates had spent most of the summer discussing the framework of the new government. Only late in their deliberations did some delegates begin to perceive a threat to liberty from the increasingly centralized government. By then it might seem that the delegates had exhausted themselves creating the machinery of government and had neither the time nor the energy to work on a bill of rights.

Certainly by late August, and even more so by mid-September, most of the delegates were "hurrying toward adjournment" and had little patience for further debate.[27] But this explanation, though plausible, is ultimately unsatisfactory.

The first proposal for civil liberties protections came before the Convention on August 20, when Charles Pinckney suggested libertarian additions to the Constitution. This was late in the Convention, but certainly not too late for action. The contrast with the Fugitive Slave Clause,[28] which was for black Americans the antithesis of a bill of rights, is revealing. Charles Pinckney and Pierce Butler introduced this clause on August 28. The Convention adopted it the next day, after almost no debate, even though Americans had virtually no prior experience with the interstate rendition of fugitive slaves. The delegates, then, were clearly capable of swiftly and decisively expanding the Constitution even at the end of the Convention.[29]

The lack of time argument is especially unpersuasive in Madison's case. On September 14, three days before final adjournment, Madison proposed giving Congress two new substantive powers: to grant charters of incorporation and to create a national university.

---

[27]Ketcham, The Dilemma of Bills of Rights in Democratic Government, in The Legacy of George Mason 29 (Pacheco ed. 1983).

[28]U.S. Constitution, Art. IV, §2, cl. 3.

[29]Finkelman, note 23 *supra*, at 219–24.

That day Madison also supported a change in the wording of Article I to discourage standing armies. Clearly Madison was willing to make changes late in the Convention, but a bill of rights was not on his agenda.

The explanation for Madison's silence may be that on this issue he was uncharacteristically ambivalent. On the one hand, as a firm supporter of individual rights and personal freedom, Madison did not oppose the concept of protecting rights. He was, according to one former editor of the Madison papers, "the only one [among the founding fathers] who could be called a civil libertarian by the rigorous standards of the American Civil Liberties Union."[30] As early as 1774 Madison had considered "the possibility that a 'Bill of Rights' might be adopted by Congress and confirmed by the King or Parliament, such that America's liberties would be 'as firmly fixed and defined as those of England were at the revolution.'"[31] Later he played a role in drafting Virginia's Declaration of Rights.[32] As one historian has argued, "No man of his [Madison's] generation had a broader or deeper commitment to the general principles of civil liberty and procedural justice."[33]

On the other hand, for a variety of theoretical, practical, and political reasons, he was uncertain if the new American Constitution ought to have a bill of rights. Thus, Madison avoided the bill of rights debate. While not speaking out on the Convention proposals to protect individual liberty, Madison voted against most of them. During the ratification debates, when forced to take a stand, he opposed a bill of rights, although not always with great conviction. Even when arguing for amendments on the floor of the House, Madison was never fully convinced that a bill of rights was necessary or even desirable. In fact, for nearly two years—from the end of the Convention in 1787 until Congress endorsed the amendments in 1789—Madison consistently accepted the validity of the federalist arguments against a bill of rights.

---

[30]Hobson, James Madison, the Bill of Rights, and the Problem of the States, 31 Wm. & Mary L. Rev. 267, 268 (1990).

[31]Maier, From Resistance to Revolution: Colonial Radicals and the Development of American Opposition to Britain, 1765–1776 245 (1972).

[32]Rutland, James Madison: The Founding Father 11 (1987), points out that Madison proposed a key amendment to Mason's draft of the Virginia Declaration of Rights, changing religious "toleration" to "full and free exercise."

[33]Meyers, The Mind of the Founder: James Madison xxxvii (1973).

III. Reasons for Federalist Opposition to a Bill of Rights

There are five general reasons why Madison, along with most other federalists, opposed the addition of a bill of rights. These men believed one or more of the following propositions about a bill of rights: that it was 1) unnecessary; 2) redundant; 3) useless; 4) actually dangerous to the liberties of the people; and, 5) violative of the principles of republican government embodied in the Constitution.

1). The lack of necessity argument rested on the twin assumptions that the states were the main guarantors of liberty and that the national government under the Constitution lacked power to interfere with basic rights and liberties.

In the Convention Madison's allies argued that state protections of liberty were adequate. James Wilson asserted that one purpose of the states was "to preserve the rights of individuals." Oliver Ellsworth explained that he looked to the state governments "for the preservation of his rights." Roger Sherman argued that "the State Declarations of Rights are not repealed by this Constitution; and being in force are sufficient." He believed that the national legislature might "be safely trusted" not to interfere with the liberties of the people. Madison joined a majority of the delegates in supporting Sherman's position.[34]

Madison also agreed that as a compact for a government of limited powers, the Constitution did not empower the national government to interfere with liberty. After ratification Madison would assert that "the rights in question are reserved by the manner in which the federal powers are granted."[35]

2). Somewhat inconsistent with the argument that the national government could not interfere with liberty was the claim that the Constitution already protected liberty. Although federalists asserted that the Constitution did not need a bill of rights *per se*, they were quick to point out that the document contained many clauses which protected individual liberties and rights.

The Constitution prohibited any "religious test" for office hold-

---

[34]1 Farrand 354, 492, and 2 Farrand 588. In the debate over a specific protection for a free press Sherman again argued that "The power of Congress does not extend to the Press" and thus the proposal was unnecessary. *Id.* at 618. Here Sherman carried a narrow majority that probably did not include Madison.

[35]Madison to Jefferson, October 17, 1788, 11 Papers of Madison 295–300, quoted at 297.

ing; prohibited government officials from simultaneously holding more than one office; and prohibited the suspension of the writ of habeas corpus except in time of actual invasion or rebellion. Article I prohibited both Congress and the states from adopting *ex post facto* laws and bills of attainder or granting titles of nobility. Article III guaranteed jury trials in criminal cases in the district where the alleged crime took place. Article III also eliminated the old English concepts of treason and constructive treason, by requiring two witnesses to an overt act.

These Constitutional provisions protected many basic liberties and rights. One Madison biographer found "twenty-four elements of a Bill of Rights in a Constitution that is said to contain none."[36] Supporters of the Constitution did not make such a careful count, but they extolled the protections of liberty in the document.

3). A third argument of the federalists conflicted with these first two. Federalists argued that a bill of rights would be useless in stopping the government from trampling on the liberties of the people. Many members of the Convention, including Madison, believed that paper guarantees of basic rights meant very little. During a debate over prohibiting *ex post facto* laws, Daniel Carroll of Maryland and James Wilson argued that "these prohibitions in the State Constitutions have no effect" and thus it was "useless to insert them" in the national constitution.[37] More than a year after the Convention Madison told Jefferson that "experience proves the inefficacy of a bill of rights on those occasions when its controul is most needed. Repeated violations of these parchment barriers have been committed by overbearing majorities in every state." He noted that in Virginia he had "seen the bill of rights violated in every instance where it has been opposed to a popular current." He warned that "restrictions however strongly marked on paper will never be regarded when opposed to the decided sense of the public; and after repeated violations in extraordinary cases, they will lose even their ordinary efficacy."[38]

Madison's views on the inefficacy of "parchment barriers" reflected his fundamental distrust of democratic majorities. In the Vir-

[36]Brant, The Bill of Rights: Its Origin and Meaning 12 (1965).

[37]2 Farrand 376.

[38]Madison to Jefferson, October 17, 1788, 11 Papers of Madison 297–99. For similar views by federalists see Letter of Cassius, No. 8, reprinted in Essays on the Constitution of the United States 28 (Ford ed. 1892), and 2 The Debates in the State Conventions on the Adoption of the Federal Constitution 174 (Elliot, ed., 2nd ed., 1836).

ginia legislature Madison had encountered men who "seemed so parochial, so illiberal, so small-minded, and most of them seemed to have only 'a particular interest to serve.' They had no regard for public honor or honesty" and were "reluctant to do anything that might appear unpopular."[39] Such "clods," as historian Gordon Wood has called them,[40] could not be expected to obey the restrictions of a bill of rights.

4). Federalists, including Madison, also argued that a bill of rights might actually be dangerous. This was based on the legal theory that any rights not enumerated in a bill of rights would have been given up. This argument assumed that a complete enumeration of all rights would be impossible. Thus, in defending the Constitution in the Pennsylvania ratifying convention, James Wilson asked who would "be bold enough to undertake to enumerate all the rights of the people?" He thought no one could, but warned that "if the enumeration is not complete, everything not expressly mentioned will be presumed to be purposely omitted." He asserted that members of the Convention considered a bill of rights "not only unnecessary, but improper."[41] Alexander Hamilton made a similar point in *Federalist* 84, arguing that a bill of rights was:[42]

> not only unnecessary in the proposed Constitution, but would even be dangerous. They would contain various exceptions to powers not granted; and, on this very account, would afford a colorable pretext to claim more than were granted.

Madison agreed with this analysis. He told Jefferson if a bill of rights was added to the Constitution it had to "be so framed as not to imply powers not meant to be included in the enumeration."[43]

Madison further worried that a bill of rights might be dangerous because it would not fully secure rights. He believed "that a positive declaration of some of the most essential rights could not be obtained" because he assumed that New Englanders would weaken any attempt to require a separation of church and state. Thus Madison feared that the "rights of Conscience" would be "narrowed much

---

[39]Wood, Interests and Disinterestedness in the Making of the Constitution, in Beyond Confederation, at 74.

[40]*Ibid.*

[41]3 Farrand 144, 161–61.

[42]Hamilton, Federalist 84, in 4 The Papers of Alexander Hamilton 706 (Syrett ed. 1962).

[43]Madison to Jefferson, October 17, 1788, 11 Papers of Madison 297.

more" by a bill of rights than any government would dare do on its own.[44] An incomplete or limited protection of conscience was, in Madison's mind, worse than none at all.

5). Finally, the very notion of a republican government led federalists to argue that a bill of rights was unnecessary. Part of this argument was based on the notion that Congress lacked the power to legislate on the subjects that would be covered by a bill of rights. But this analysis went beyond the concept of a limited government. Oliver Ellsworth, writing as "Landholder," argued that the theory of the Constitution itself precluded the need for a bill of rights. "Landholder" asserted that a bill of rights was something that the people wrested from the king, thus in America a bill of rights was "insignificant since government is considered as originating from the people, and all the power government now has is a grant *from the people*." Similarly, James Wilson argued that "it would have been superfluous and absurd, to have stipulated with a federal body of our own creation, that we should enjoy those privileges, of which we are not divested." James Iredell argued that in England a bill of rights was necessary because of the Crown's "usurpations" of the people's liberties. But, under the new Constitution the people delegated power to the national government, and thus Iredell argued that such usurpations by the national government were impossible. Iredell asserted that under the Constitution the government could no more "impose a King upon America" than "go one step in any other respect beyond the terms of their institution."[45]

The more sophisticated and skeptical Madison understood that a republican government might threaten liberty, but that such threats would not be by a minority attacking a majority. Rather, the threats to liberty were most likely to emanate from the legislature which represented the majority of the people. Madison further doubted that in a republic a bill of rights would have any effect against a determined legislative majority. In the Virginia ratification debates he asserted that "If there were a majority of one sect, a bill of rights would be a poor protection for liberty." Freedom of religion, he argued, was secured by "that multiplicity of sects, which pervades America, and

[44]Madison to Jefferson, October 17, 1788, *id.* at 297.

[45]The Landholder, No. VI, reprinted in 3 Documentary History of the Ratification of the Constitution: Ratification by the States: Delaware, New Jersey, Georgia, Connecticut 489 (Jensen ed. 1978); Substance of an Address by James Wilson and Answer to Mr. Mason's Objections to the new Constitution, by Marcus [James Iredell], in Pamphlets on the Constitution 161, 335 (Ford ed. 1888).

which is the best and only security for religious liberty in any society."[46] After Virginia had ratified the Constitution Madison made much the same point to Jefferson:[47]

> Wherever the real power in a Government lies, there is the danger of oppression. In our Governments the real power lies in the majority of the Community, and the invasion of private rights is *chiefly* to be apprehended, not from acts of Government contrary to the sense of its constituents, but from acts in which the Government is the mere instrument of the major number of the constituents.

Madison simply did not believe that a bill of rights could forestall a determined majority which might want to act in ways which would trample on the rights of a minority.

IV. Working for Ratification

Madison left the Philadelphia Convention hopeful that the Constitution would be ratified. He initially did not plan to become involved in the ratification struggle, but soon was drawn into it.[48] Once involved, he became dedicated to two related goals: securing ratification and preventing a second convention to amend the Constitution because he believed such a convention would undermine the Constitution.

Madison was clearly ambivalent about the Constitution. It did not create the strong, consolidated government that he had hoped for. Indeed, "The Constitution Madison expounded and defended as 'Publius' was a pale version of the plan he had carefully worked out before the Philadelphia meeting."[49] He thought the plan was a vast improvement over the Confederation. But, whether he thought it a sufficient improvement is another matter. In urging his friends at home to support the Constitution Madison argued that the Convention had succeeded in "blending a proper stability & energy in the Government with the essential characters of the republican Form" while retaining "a proper line of demarcation between the national

---

[46]Madison in the Virginia ratification convention, reprinted in 11 Papers of Madison 130.

[47]Madison to Jefferson, October 17, 1788, *id.* at 298.

[48]Editorial note, 10 Papers of Madison at 259.

[49]Hobson, The Negative on State Laws: James Madison, the Constitution, and the Crisis of Republican Government, 36 Wm. & Mary Q. 217 (3rd Ser., 1979).

and State authorities."[50] But, this seems more like a political posture than an accurate reflection of Madison's true beliefs.

In more private correspondence he argued that the government created by the Constitution was still too weak. Shortly before the Convention ended he wrote in secret code to Jefferson, who was still in France, that the plan of government "will neither effectually answer its national object nor prevent the local mischiefs which every where excite disgusts agst. the state governments."[51] In late October he still bemoaned the fact that the Convention had rejected his proposal to give Congress a "constitutional negative on the laws of the States."[52]

If Madison really believed that the Convention had created a proper but delicate balance between competing interests, as he wrote his friends in Virginia, then he properly feared amendments which would destroy this balance. Similarly, if Madison really viewed the Constitution as creating too weak a government, as he privately expressed to Jefferson, then he certainly did not want any amendments, including a bill of rights, which would have further weakened the national government.

Opposition to the Constitution formed as soon as the document became public. The most common antifederalist complaint was the lack of a bill of rights. Thus, in defending the Constitution Madison was forced to oppose the call for a bill of rights. To do otherwise would have been to admit that the Constitution had a major defect. Madison could not admit this; along with most federalists, he was firmly convinced that ratification of the Constitution was an all-or-nothing proposition, and an admission of the need for a bill of rights would prevent ratification.

Madison's first test of the issue came in the soon-to-be defunct confederation Congress, which received the work of the Convention. Madison was one of over a dozen signers who were also members of Congress. These "fiery zealots"[53] wanted quick action to send the Constitution on to the states without any changes. In accomplishing this, Madison helped defeat a motion by Richard Henry Lee and Melancton Smith to add a bill of rights to the Constitution. The successful arguments in this brief debate were procedural, focusing on

---

[50] Madison to Edmund Pendleton, Sept. 20, 1787, 10 Papers of Madison 171.

[51] Madison to Jefferson, September 6, 1787, *id.* at 163–64.

[52] Madison to Jefferson, October 24, 1787, *id.* at 212.

[53] The term is Richard Henry Lee's, and is quoted in Brant, note 3 *supra*, at 161.

the complications that would arise if Congress added its own proposals to the work of the Convention.[54] Here Madison was able to oppose the addition of a bill of rights without having to take any position on its merits.

For the next two months Madison continued to avoid the question of a bill of rights. In mid-October he commented to Washington about the unfair nature of George Mason's attacks on the Constitution, but he did not mention Mason's demand for a bill of rights. When he reported to Edmund Randolph the growing opposition to the Constitution over "the omission of the provisions contended for in favor of the Press, & Juries &c.," Madison again failed to comment on the validity of the argument or to propose a strategy for combating it.[55]

On October 24 Madison sent Jefferson a seventeen page letter, analyzing the strengths and weaknesses of the Constitution. This important document reveals that the Madison "who later became an indefatigable publicist in support of the new Constitution was in fact profoundly disappointed with the results of the convention."[56] Madison's main objection to the final document was the inability of the national government to veto state legislation. Madison feared that majorities within the states would destroy the liberties of minorities. He thought this problem could be prevented by giving the national government the power to overrule the states. In an argument later developed in *Federalist* 10 and 14, Madison declared that "private rights will be more secure under the Guardianship of the General Government than under the State Governments" because the constituency of the national government would be so diverse that no single group would ever control it.[57]

Madison did not think that a majority in the national government might also oppress the people and deny them basic liberties. Thus, he had nothing specific to say about a bill of rights, except to note that George Mason had left Philadelphia "in exceeding ill humour"

---

[54]Madison to George Washington, September 30, 1787, 10 Papers of Madison 179–81.

[55]Madison to Washington, October 18, 1787, *id.* at 196–97; Madison to Edmund Randolph, October 21, 1787, *id.* at 199–200.

[56]Editorial note, to letter of James Madison to Thomas Jefferson, October 24, 1787, *id.* at 205.

[57]James Madison to Thomas Jefferson, October 24, 1787, *id.* at 212. In 1789, when he drafted what became the Bill of Rights Madison attempted to make certain amendments applicable to the states in one last attempt to secure a federal veto over some state legislation. This provision passed the House but was deleted by the Senate.

and that his chief complaint was that he "considers the want of a Bill of Rights as a fatal objection."[58] Madison did not comment on the merits of this position. At this point in his career Madison thought that the national government needed to be strengthened to protect the people from their state governments, but he saw no reason to think that the people needed a bill of rights to be protected from the national government.

V. Defending the Constitution, Opposing a Bill of Rights, and the Federalist Papers

In mid-November 1787 Madison joined Alexander Hamilton in writing *The Federalist*.[59] This was the beginning of his active involvement in the ratification process. As "Publius" Madison began to articulate more fully—and in public—his opposition to a bill of rights.

In his first contribution to the series, the now-classic *Federalist* 10, Madison argued that the greatest danger to liberty in a Republic came from "the violence of faction" which he defined as "a number of citizens, whether amounting to a majority or minority of the whole, who are united and actuated by some common impulse of passion, or of interest, adverse to the rights of other citizens, or to the permanent and aggregated interests of the community."[60] Madison saw no way to eliminate the causes of faction without destroying political liberty itself. But he argued that political factions might be controlled by increasing the size of an electoral district, thus increasing the number and diversity of the electors, so no single interest could actually obtain a majority. "Extend the sphere, and you take in a greater variety of parties and interests; you make it less probable that a majority of the whole will have a common motive to invade the rights of other citizens; or if such a common motive exists, it will be more difficult for all who feel it to discover their own strength, and to act in unison with each other."[61]

---

[58]Madison to Jefferson, October 24, 1787, *id.* at 215.

[59]The editors of the Papers of Madison suggest that Madison was not brought into the project "until the middle of November, perhaps as late as the seventeenth." *Id.* at 261. Ralph Ketcham argues that the collaboration began just after October 10. Ketcham, James Madison: A Biography 239 (1971).

[60]Federalist 10, in 10 Papers of Madison 264. He had of course developed these arguments earlier, in The Vices of the Political System, reprinted in 9 Papers of Madison 350–54.

[61]Federalist 10, in 10 Papers of Madison, at 269.

Under the theory expressed in *Federalist* 10,[62] a bill of rights was unnecessary to protect people from oppressive majorities, because the majorities themselves would typically take the form of unstable coalitions of different groups. As such, they would be unable to threaten the people's liberties. The theory of *Federalist* 10 turned on the informal structure of the government under the Constitution. Competing and diverse interests would neutralize each other, making a bill of rights unnecessary.

In *Federalist* 51 Madison elaborated on how the Constitution's system of checks and balances combined with the diversity of the people to provide formal defenses against one faction taking power and depriving the citizens of their liberty. Madison argued that "If men were angels, no government would be necessary," but, given human nature Madison believed some formal controls were necessary. He thought the people themselves would "no doubt [be] the primary control on the government" but that "auxiliary precautions" were also useful, including the Constitution's aim "to divide and arrange several offices in such a manner that each may be a check on the other." This, Madison argued, would prevent any single branch of government from threatening liberty. Furthermore, the division between the states and the federal government would provide a "double security to the rights of the people."[63]

In *Federalist* 51 Madison again asserted, as he had in *Federalist* 10, that the competing interests caused by diversity of the people was the key to liberty. As long as the [64]

> society itself will be broken into so many parts, interests and classes of citizens, that the rights of individuals or of the minority, will be in little danger from interested combinations of the majority. In a free government, the security for civil rights must be the same as that for religious rights. It consists in the one case in the multiplicity of interests, and in the other, in the multiplicity of sects. The degree of security in both cases will depend on the number of interests and sects.

As Jack Rakove has succinctly phrased it, Madison's theory rested on the notion that "Diversity begets jealousy, and jealousy begets se-

---

[62]This was a theory of government that Madison had been working on in 1786, when he made Notes on Ancient and Modern Confederacies, and then in the Spring of 1787, when he drafted the memorandum On the Vices of the Political System of the United States. During the Federal Convention of 1787, Madison also argued along the lines later developed in Federalist 10.

[63]Federalist 51, 10 Papers of Madison 477–78.

[64]Federalist 51, *id.* at 478–79.

curity."[65] While not explicitly rejecting the idea of a bill of rights in *Federalist* 51, the implications of his argument are that diversity of interests—not any formal document—would ultimately preserve fundamental rights.

Madison reiterated these points in *Federalist* 57, arguing that the "vigilant and manly spirit which actuates the people of America" would prevent the legislature from usurping its power.[66] Furthermore, ever attuned to turning private interest to the public good, Madison argued that members of the House of Representatives would never betray the liberties of the people because if they did, they would not be reelected. In essence Madison argued in *Federalist* 10, 51, and 57 that the political process, the governmental structures, and the social and demographic diversity of the nation would protect liberty.

In *Federalist* 38 he casually dismissed calls for a bill of rights because the antifederalists could not all agree on what protections of liberty they wanted.[67] Rhetorically asking "Is a bill of rights essential to liberty," he noted the "confederation has no bill of rights."[68] Such arguments were inherently weak. That some antifederalists did not want a bill of rights, or others could not completely agree on its contents, did not diminish the need for one. Madison also well knew that the demand for a bill of rights was a result of the strengthening of the national government by the new Constitution. Thus, it was disingenuous for Madison to argue that the Constitution did not need a bill of rights because the Articles of Confederation lacked one.

In *Federalist* 44 Madison pointed out that the Constitution prohibited the states from passing bills of attainder, *ex post facto* laws, or laws impairing the obligations of contracts, even though such laws were also prohibited in the "declarations prefixed to some of the state constitutions." Here Madison argued that "experience has taught us nevertheless, that additional fences against these dangers ought not to be omitted."[69] Madison did not explain why "additional fences" against the federal government were also not useful.

In *Federalist* 46 he argued that the state governments would prevent the national government from usurping powers not granted in the

---

[65] Rakove, The Madisonian Theory of Rights, 31 Wm. & Mary L. Rev. 245, 259 (1990).

[66] Federalist 57, 10 Papers of Madison 523.

[67] Federalist 38, *id.* at 367–68.

[68] Federalist 38, *id.* at 370.

[69] Federalist 44, *id.* at 421.

Constitution. This implied that the people did not need to fear that their liberties would be taken from them by the national government, and thus, again by implication, that a bill of rights was unnecessary. In *Federalist* 48 he returned to the theory—again by implication—that bills of rights were useless. Here he noted that in Pennsylvania "the constitutional trial by jury had been violated; and powers assumed, which had not been delegated by the constitution."[70] Thus Madison reiterated his belief in the danger and futility of relying on "parchment barriers against the encroaching spirit of power."[71] The same analysis might effectively have shown the potential danger of usurpation of power by the national government under the proposed constitution. But if Madison saw the double-edged nature of his argument, he did not comment on it.

The most direct statement on the bill of rights in *The Federalist* did not come from Madison, but rather from Hamilton, who argued in *Federalist* 84: "Why declare that things shall not be done which there is no power to do? Why, for instance, should it be said that the liberty of the press shall not be restrained, when no power is given by which restrictions may be imposed?"[72] Madison probably subscribed to this position. After all the essays were published, Madison explained that while "the writers are not mutually answerable for all the ideas of each other" the project was carried out "in concert" between the three authors.[73] "In concert" the authors put together a general outline of the project, which probably included some agreement on major issues and strategies. In the absence of evidence to the contrary, it seems reasonable to conclude that Madison did not disagree with Hamilton on this point.

VI. The Private Madison and the Bill of Rights

In his private correspondence during the ratification struggle Madison gave further evidence of his opposition to a bill of rights. This position developed despite pressure from correspondents and friends to recognize the merits of a bill of rights. For George Turber-

70Federalist 48, *id.* at 459.

71Federalist 48, *id.* at 456. Madison would use the term "parchment barriers" somewhat later in a direct reference to the bill of rights. Madison to Jefferson, October 17, 1788, 11 Papers of Madison 297–99.

72Hamilton, Federalist 84, in 4 The Papers of Alexander Hamilton 706.

73Madison to Jefferson, August 11, 1788, 11 Papers of Madison 227.

ville, a minor Virginia politician, he simply laid out his "powerfull reasons that may be urged agt. the adoption of a Bill of Rights."[74] But to his closest friends, like Washington, Jefferson, and Edmund Pendleton, Madison revealed both his opposition to a bill of rights and his hostility to opponents of the Constitution who demanded such an addition.

Most federalists, including Madison, held their opponents in contempt and did not take seriously their demands for a bill of rights. General Henry Knox believed that antifederalists were "Demagogues and vicious characters." In New England federalists described their opponents as "wicked," "malignant, ignorant, and short-sighted triflers." A federalist in North Carolina referred to his opponents as "a blind stupid set, that wish Damnation to their Country," who were "fools and knaves" opposed to "any man of abilities and virtue." A New Hampshire federalist predicted "that none but *fools*, *blockheads*, and *mad men*" opposed the Constitution. In New York the anonymous "Caesar" thought that the demands for a bill of rights were made by "designing croakers" in order "to frighten the people with ideal bugbears."[75]

Madison also buttressed his opposition to a bill of rights by attacking the integrity and motives of his opponents. He divided Virginia's supporters of amendments into two categories: men like Edmund Randolph and George Mason, who "do not object to the substance of the Governt. but contend for a few additional Guards in favor of the Rights of the States and of the people," and others, led by Patrick Henry, who sought amendments that would "strike at the essence of the System."[76] He believed Henry's group had "disunion assuredly for its object" while disunion was the "real tendency" of all oppo-

---

[74]George Turberville to Madison, April 16, 1788, in *id.* at 23. Madison's letter to Turberville, which contained these "powerful reasons," is now lost, but we can assume that they were a summary of arguments in The Federalist and elsewhere.

[75]Rutland, Ordeal of the Constitution: The Antifederalists and the Ratification Struggle, 1787–1788 34, 73, 269, 216 (1966). Letters of Caesar, II, in Essays on the Constitution 289 (Ford ed. 1892). Ford incorrectly identifies the author of this letter as Alexander Hamilton. See 4 The Papers of Alexander Hamilton 278–79.

[76]Madison to Jefferson, December 9, 1787, 10 Papers of Madison 312. In April Madison modified his analysis, informing Jefferson that Randolph "cannot properly be classed with its [the Constitution's] enemies," while Mason was "growing every day more bitter" and had become "outrageous" in his opposition and would "in the end be thrown by the violence of his passions into the politics of Mr. H______y." Madison to Jefferson, April 23, 1788, 11 Papers of Madison 28–29. When the Virginia convention began Madison happily reported Randolph firmly in the federalist camp, noting that "The Govr. has declared the day of previous amendments past. . . ." Madison to Rufus King, June 4, 1788, *id.* at 76.

nents. Thus Madison felt that there could be "no middle ground" between supporters and opponents of the Constitution.[77]

While Madison conceded that some opposition in Virginia came from "men of intelligence, patriotism, property, and independent circumstances," he thought their grass-roots support was from people "much accustomed to be guided by their rulers." In other words, in Virginia a few demagogues, like Patrick Henry, were misleading the people. In most of the rest of the country the educated elite were "zealously attached to the proposed Constitution." He was particularly pleased that in New England "the men of letters, the principle Off[i]cers of Govt. the Judges & Lawyers, the Clergy, and men of property" almost universally supported the Constitution.[78]

He described the Massachusetts antifederalists as including "scarce a man of respectability." They were a combination of supporters of Shays' Rebellion and "ignorant and jealous men, who had been taught or had fancied that the Convention at Philada. had entered into a conspiracy against the liberties of the people at large, in order to erect an aristocracy for the rich, the *well-born*, and the men of Education." On the other hand, "all the men of abilities, of property, and of influence" supported the Constitution.[79]

Such observations help explain Madison's hostility to amendments. He believed the proponents of amendments were either antinationalists, like Henry, out to destroy the Constitution, or men who lacked "intelligence, patriotism, property, and independent circumstances." They were, in other words, not men who Madison thought should govern the republic. Because Madison believed that all who demanded amendments "threaten shipwreck to our liberty,"[80] he could not admit that any of their points might be valid. No wonder Madison condemned the recommended amendments of the Massachusetts ratifying convention as "a blemish" even though he conceded they were "in the least Offensive form."[81]

---

[77]Madison to Edmund Pendleton, February 21, 1788, 10 Papers of Madison 532–33.

[78]Madison to Jefferson, December 9, 1787, *id.* at 312–13. Madison was "persuaded" that some of those supporting amendments, especially in Virginia, did so "with the most patriotic & virtuous intentions." He conceded that "men equally respectable in every point of character" were on both sides of the issue, but nevertheless believed the opposition in his home state would "either dismember the Union" or injure Virginia's pride and "foresight." Madison to Archibald Stuart, December 14, 1787, *id.* at 325–26.

[79]Madison to Edmund Pendleton, February 21, 1788, *id.* at 532–33; Madison to Jefferson, February 19, 1788, *id.* at 519.

[80]Madison to George Washington, December 14, 1787, *id.* at 327.

[81]Madison to Washington, February 15, 1788, *id.* at 510–11.

Echoing *Federalist* 38, Madison was also contemptuous of the antifederalists because they could not agree on what they wanted.[82] He argued that if the antifederalists "were to enter into an explicit & particular communication with each other, they wd find themselves as much at variance in detail as they are agreed in the general plan of amendments." He believed their only agreement would be on "points of very little substance."[83] Their positions were "as heterogeneous as can be imagined."[84]

That federalists were also "heterogeneous" on many points did not seem to trouble Madison. By the spring of 1788 Madison wanted the Constitution ratified at all costs, and he would work with anyone toward that end and similarly opposed any idea which might undermine that goal.

VII. The Virginia Ratifying Convention

In late February Madison began making plans to return to Virginia to seek election to that state's ratifying convention. Mounting hostility to the Constitution made his presence imperative. By the time Madison left New York the debate over a bill of rights had been altered. The critical change came in Massachusetts.

When the Massachusetts ratifying convention opened in January 1788, an antifederalist majority seemed certain to defeat the Constitution. The convention elected John Hancock, an apparent antifederalist, as its president. A key opposition leader was Samuel Adams, the old revolutionary, who was an important and powerful politician in the Commonwealth, and a man who had been committed to bills of rights since the beginning of the Revolution.[85] Many delegates came to the Boston convention with instructions from their constituents to oppose ratification unless a bill of rights was added to the Constitution.

With opponents of ratification in apparent control, the Massachusetts federalists sought a compromise. They suggested that a series of recommended amendments to the Constitution be sent to Congress along with the convention's ratification. John Hancock was persuaded to present these amendments to the convention. Samuel

---

[82] Note 62 *supra*.

[83] Madison to Archibald Stuart, December 14, 1787, 10 Papers of Madison 326.

[84] Madison to Edmund Pendleton, February 21, 1788, *id.* at 532–33.

[85] Maier, The Old Revolutionaries: Political Lives in the Age of Samuel Adams 25 (1980).

Adams offered a counter-proposal that the convention actually add a bill of rights to the beginning of the Constitution, and then ratify both. Had this motion been successful, Massachusetts's ratification would have been conditional, and only gone into effect if the other states accepted the Massachusetts amendments. The danger of prior amendments, which is what Samuel Adams wanted, was that each state would propose different amendments and the Constitution would never be ratified.

When his motion for prior amendments was defeated, Adams joined Hancock in supporting ratification with recommended amendments. A few other antifederalists joined as well, and the Constitution squeaked through, by a vote of 187 to 168. A change of only ten votes would have defeated the Constitution in Massachusetts.

The importance of the Massachusetts compromise—ratification with recommended amendments—was not immediately apparent to Madison and his friends. Edmund Randolph thought the Massachusetts amendments were a "paltry snare" which were either "inadmissible," aimed against the Southern states, or "milk & water."[86] Madison thought the ratification in Massachusetts had "almost extinguished" the hopes of the New York antifederalists. He did not think the proposed amendments mattered one way or the other, although he believed they were a "blemish." Madison's attentions were already focused on New Hampshire and Virginia.[87]

In early March Madison left New York for Virginia. For the first time in his public career Madison was forced to campaign for office. On March 22 Madison probably met with Rev. John Leland, an influential Baptist minister who at the time was hostile to the Constitution. Leland and other Baptists feared that the Constitution would undermine religious freedom in the nation. Madison's long record of supporting religious liberty, and his sincere empathy for Leland's concerns, convinced the minister to support Madison for the Virginia convention.[88]

Madison reached Montpelier on March 23, the day before the election for delegates to the Virginia ratification convention. On the 24th

---

[86]Randolph to Madison, February 29, 1788, 10 Papers of Madison 542–43.

[87]Madison to Randolph, Madison to Washington, and Madison to Edmund Pendleton, all on March 3, 1788, *id.* at 554–55; 555–56; 554.

[88]Butterfield, Elder John Leland, Jeffersonian Itinerant, 62 Proceedings of the American Antiquarian Society 183–96 (1952).

Madison overcame his natural shyness to give his first public speech before the voters. He tried to dispel the "absurd and groundless prejudices against the foederal Constitution" that had been growing in his absence. This brief campaign was successful, as he beat his nearest anti-federalist rival by a margin of almost four to one.[89] Madison was pledged to support the Constitution as written. He was not pledged to prior amendments, or any other alterations of the document.

Madison's meeting with Leland was critical to his election campaign, because Madison believed the support of the Baptists was crucial to his electoral success. Indeed, it seems likely that "Madison owed his presence in the Virginia convention to" Leland and other "dissenters whose trust he had earned in the struggle for religious liberty."[90]

The meeting with Leland was also critical for Madison's eventual support for a bill of rights. Until this time Madison dismissed the antifederalist demand for a bill of rights as a smokescreen for defeating the Constitution. In Leland, however, Madison faced a man who wanted to support the Constitution, but sincerely feared that without a bill of rights freedom of religion would be jeopardized under the new government. Madison could not easily dismiss Leland's arguments as politically motivated because they were not. Thus, for the first time Madison was forced to take seriously the bill of rights argument.

The Virginia voters elected a convention that was almost evenly split between federalists and antifederalists. Almost immediately some of Madison's friends urged that the Massachusetts model be applied to Virginia. George Nichols argued it was the only basis on which compromise "can safely take place."[91] Madison agreed. He did not think amendments were a particularly good idea, but he did believe that proposing them as Massachusetts had done, to be considered after ratification, would blunt antifederalist opposition. The Massachusetts plan was "unquestionably the Ultimatum of the foederalists" while conditional ratification or a second convention would "be fatal."[92]

---

[89]Madison to Eliza House Trist, March 25, 1788, 11 Papers of Madison 5–6.

[90]Kukla, A Spectrum of Sentiments: Virginia's Federalists, Antifederalists, and Federalists Who are For Amendments, 1787–1788, 96 Va. Mag. of Hist. & Biog. 282 (1988).

[91]George Nichols to Madison, April 5, 1788, 11 Papers of Madison 8–9.

[92]Madison to George Nichols, April 8, 1788, *id.* at 11–12.

Madison easily saw the practical value of supporting subsequent amendments as a way of obtaining immediate ratification. He told Edmund Randolph he was ready to support them in Virginia. This was perhaps the bridge that could connect strong federalists, like Madison, with more reluctant supporters of the Constitution, like Randolph. Nevertheless Madison remained skeptical about the effectiveness of this tactic. He believed that in Massachusetts the proposed amendments had been directed at popular sentiment, and had actually done little to sway opponents in the ratification convention.[93]

As the Virginia convention approached, Madison's views firmed. There was a real danger that the Virginia convention would endorse conditional ratification based on subsequent amendments or, worse yet, a demand for a second convention. If Virginia adopted either "the Constitution, and the Union will be both endangered."[94] Madison, who had once given lukewarm support to the Constitution, now equated its success with that of the nation itself.

This change was not the result of his changing views of the Constitution. Rather it reflected his realization of the true nature of politics in America. If a second convention came about, Madison feared there would be "little" of the "same spirit of compromise" of the previous summer. Madison expected that at a new convention it would be "easy also for those who have latent views of disunion, to carry them on under the mask of contending for alterations popular in some but inadmissible in other parts of the U. States."[95] Madison could give no quarter to those who wanted fundamental changes in the Constitution, because they would undermine ratification. At the same time, he had to blunt their demand, growing more popular each day, for a bill of rights. Recommended amendments looked better all the time.

In the Virginia convention Madison gave no immediate indication of his new position. Early in the convention he stressed his argument, previously made in *Federalist* 10, that the greatest threat to liberty came from the "majority trampling on the rights of the minority."[96] He also reiterated the argument made by Wilson in the

---

[93]Madison to Randolph, April 10, 1788, *id.* at 18–19.

[94]Madison to Jefferson, April 23, 1788, *id.* at 28–29.

[95]*Ibid.*

[96]Speech of Madison, June 6, 1788, *id.* at 79.

Pennsylvania convention and by Hamilton in *Federalist* 84 that civil liberties could not be harmed because of the limited nature of the national government. The Congress could create no national religion because "The government has no jurisdiction over it."[97]

Madison then attacked the impracticality of "obtaining previous amendments" to the Constitution. He noted that any amendments Virginia adopted would also have to be submitted to all the other states, which might then submit amendments of their own.[98] This would lead to an endless process that would produce nothing. Significantly, Madison still did not suggest recommended amendments, such as Massachusetts had proposed.

On June 12 Madison argued against a bill of rights because paper guarantees were worth little. Madison asked:[99]

> Is a bill of rights a security for religion? Would the bill of rights in this state exempt the people from paying for the support of one particular sect, if such sect were exclusively established by law? If there were a majority of one sect, a bill of rights would be a poor protection for liberty.

In answering his own questions Madison reiterated his notion that diversity protected liberty. He found that religious liberty was protected by "that multiplicity of sects, which pervades America, and which is the best and only security for religious liberty in any society. For where there is such a variety of sects, there cannot be a majority of any one sect to oppress and persecute the rest."[100] Reminding the Convention that he had always "warmly supported religious freedom," Madison argued that "a variety of sects," not a bill of rights, was the key to religious freedom.[101]

By mid-June Madison privately predicted that opponents of the Constitution would be narrowly defeated in their demand for previous amendments.[102] Confident of ultimate success, for the first time Madison argued against the substance of some rights.

A common antifederalist complaint was that the Constitution did

---

[97] Speech of Madison, June 6, 1788, *id.* at 84.

[98] *Ibid.*

[99] Speech of Madison, June 12, 1788, *id.* at 130.

[100] *Ibid.*

[101] Speech of Madison, June 12, 1788, *id.* at 131.

[102] Madison to Rufus King, June 18, 22, 1788, *id.* at 152, 167. See also, on Madison's confidence, Madison to Hamilton, June 20, 1788, and June 22, 1788, Madison to George Washington, June 23, 1788, and Madison to James Madison, Sr., June 20, 1788, *id.* at 157, 166, 168, 157–58.

not guarantee trials in the district where an alleged crime took place. This complaint would eventually be remedied by the Sixth Amendment. At the Virginia convention Madison argued that such a remedy was unnecessary, and might be decidedly dangerous to the welfare of the nation. He claimed that he would have supported a "provision for a jury from a vicinage" but only if it could be "done with safety." But, Madison argued that in some situations, like a rebellion, a trial "would be impracticable in the county" where the law was violated. Madison noted that even though the jury trial was "sacred" in America, there had nevertheless been numerous "deviations" from it since independence. Madison concluded that the legislature must have "discretion" in setting the rules for trials.[103]

Two days later Madison spoke against ratification with amendments. Now fully expecting to win a vote for ratification, he was also confident the convention would defeat prior amendments. After ratification he was prepared to support "a conciliatory declaration of certain fundamental principles of liberty, in a form not affecting the validity & plentitude of the ratification."[104]

Madison once again argued that previous amendments were impractical and that a bill of rights was unnecessary. The impracticality argument rested on the assumption that a demand for previous amendments by Virginia would lead to similar demands from other states, and require that the ratification process begin again. He then reasserted the long-held federalist position that "every thing not granted" to the federal government by the Constitution "is reserved" to the states or the people. He further argued that "an imperfect enumeration" of rights "is dangerous."[105]

Having dismissed the need for a bill of rights, Madison made one major concession to the opposition. He declared that if Virginia ratified the Constitution, he and other federalists would "freely, fairly and dispassionately consider and investigate your propositions, and endeavour to gratify your wishes." He promised that those amendments which were "not objectionable, or unsafe" could be "subsequently recommended" after ratification. But, he did not admit such amendments might be necessary. Rather, he argued, they would be considered "because they can produce no possible danger,

---

[103]Speech of Madison, June 20, 1788, *id.* at 164.

[104]Speech of Madison, June 24, 1788, *id.* at 174–75; Madison to Ambrose Madison, June 24, 1788, *id.* at 170–71.

[105]Speech of Madison, June 24, 1788, *id.* at 174–75.

and may gratify some gentlemen's wishes."[106] Thus, even as Madison accepted the idea of amendments, he did so as a matter of political expedience and accommodation, rather than as a matter of conviction.

VIII. Madison, Jefferson and the Bill of Rights: Reconsidering the "Great Collaboration"

While Madison was working for ratification, and fighting against a bill of rights, he was involved in a long-distance correspondence with Thomas Jefferson, who was then America's ambassador in Paris. The two had previously been allied in various political enterprises at the state and national level.[107] Now they disagreed over the importance of a bill of rights.

The conventional historical wisdom is that Jefferson pointed out the importance of a bill of rights "in letters persuading Madison to switch positions."[108] But it is not clear whether Jefferson's letters had any effect on Madison's actions or views. Certainly in the short run they did not, because the distance between the two men, and the long time it took for letters to be exchanged, made it impossible for the letters to have any immediate impact. At first glance, for example, Jefferson's well-known letter of December 20, 1787 seems to be an important criticism of Madison's position.[109] But, Madison did not receive this letter until July, 1788, after Virginia had ratified the Constitution and Madison himself had publicly announced his willingness to support future amendments.

Madison often wrote to Jefferson in code, which allowed him the luxury of great candor in an age when mail delivery was erratic and private letters might fall into the wrong hands. Because of the many months that it took for letters to cross the Atlantic, Madison did not fear that his openness would have adverse political repercussions. Thus, this correspondence tells us what Madison really believed about the bill of rights. The letters confirm that Madison's opposition was not simply tactical, but that he truly opposed the adoption of a bill of rights. This investigation also undermines the view that Jefferson "converted Madison to the cause of adding a Bill of Rights

---

[106]Speech of Madison, June 24, 1788, *id.* at 177.

[107]See generally, Koch, Jefferson and Madison: The Great Collaboration 3–32 (1950).

[108]Levy, note 9 *supra*, at 114.

[109]Jefferson to Madison, December 20, 1787, in 12 Jefferson Papers 438.

to the new federal Constitution."[110] The evidence suggests that Madison was converted to a bill of rights by political necessity rather than logical argument and that the conversion, such as it was, took place before Madison received Jefferson's letter of December 20, 1787 or his other letters urging the addition of a bill of rights.

A. JEFFERSON'S VIEWS

The day after the Convention ended George Washington sent a copy of the Constitution to Thomas Jefferson. In mid-October Benjamin Franklin sent Jefferson an official copy of the document. Finally, on October 24, 1787, Madison sent Jefferson a seventeen page letter and a copy of the Constitution.[111]

In late December, 1787, Jefferson finally received Madison's long letter of October 24th. By this time Jefferson had already seen a copy of the Constitution, and already corresponded with his counterpart in London, John Adams, about the lack of a bill of rights.[112]

Madison's October 24, 1787, letter gave Jefferson a short history of the Convention. Madison was guardedly enthusiastic about the Constitution, but thought it did not go far enough in nationalizing power.[113] Jefferson's thoughtful response, his famous letter of December 20, 1787, reflected quite different concerns about the Constitution. After detailing what he liked about the Constitution, Jefferson turned to "what I do not like."[114]

Jefferson's first complaint was "the omission of a bill of rights providing clearly and without the aid of sophisms for freedom of religion, freedom of the press, protection against standing armies, restriction against monopolies, the eternal and unremitting force of the habeas corpus laws, and trials by jury in all matters of fact triable by the laws of the land. . . ." Jefferson disputed James Wilson's arguments "that a bill of rights was not necessary because all is reserved

---

[110]Levy, Jefferson and Civil Liberties: The Darker Side 3 (1st ed. 1963).

[111]Koch, note 107 *supra*, at 39, states that these men "rushed copies" of the Constitution to Jefferson. This is true for Washington, but not for Franklin and Madison, who sent their letters on October 14 and October 24. Washington to Jefferson, Sept. 18, 1787; Franklin to Jefferson, October 14, 1787; 1787 in 12 The Papers of Thomas Jefferson 149, 236, 270 (Boyd ed. 1955) (cited below as Jefferson Papers). Madison to Jefferson, October 24, 1787, 10 Papers of Madison 205–20.

[112]John Adams to Jefferson, November 10, 1787; Jefferson to Adams, November 13, 1787; Jefferson to Madison, December 20, 1787, all in 12 Jefferson Papers 334, 349, 438.

[113]See text at notes 35–39 *supra*.

[114]Jefferson to Madison, December 20, 1787, 12 Jefferson Papers 441.

in the case of the general government which is not given. . . ."[115] Unbeknownst to Jefferson, Madison had taken more or less the same position as Wilson on this question.[116] Jefferson thought Wilson's argument was "gratis dictum" which was "opposed by strong inferences from the body" of the Constitution. Jefferson argued that "a bill of rights is what the people are entitled to against every government on earth, general or particular, and what no just government should refuse, or rest on inference."[117]

This letter, which is useful for an understanding of Jefferson's views on fundamental rights, had no effect on Madison's actions during ratification, because Madison did not receive it until July, 1788, which was after Virginia had ratified the Constitution and, for tactical reasons, Madison had agreed to support amendments. When Madison answered Jefferson's letter of December 20, 1787, he said nothing about a bill of rights, perhaps because Jefferson's points were already moot.[118] Madison had already agreed to support amendments that were "not objectionable, or unsafe,"[119] not because he had been convinced of their virtues by Jefferson's arguments, but rather because he had accepted the political necessity of them.

On July 31, 1788, Jefferson wrote Madison once again, "rejoic-[ing] at the acceptance of our new constitution by nine states."[120] Jefferson apparently knew about New Hampshire's ratification on June 21, but not about Virginia's (the 10th state) on June 25.[121] Nor did Jefferson know that Madison (without the benefit of Jefferson's letter of December 20, 1787) had supported subsequent amendments. Thus, Jefferson once again urged Madison to support a bill of rights.

The Constitution was "a good canvas, on which some strokes only want retouching." Jefferson's brush would paint a bill of rights that would "go to Juries, Habeas corpus, Standing armies, Printing, Religion & Monopolies." Jefferson argued that "the few cases wherein

---

[115]Jefferson to Madison, December 20, 1787, *id.* at 440.

[116]See text *supra* at III.

[117]Madison to Jefferson, October 24, 1787, 12 Jefferson Papers 270–86; Jefferson to Madison, Paris, December 20, 1787, *id.* at 438, 440.

[118]Madison to Jefferson, July 24, 1788, 11 Papers of Madison 196–98.

[119]Speech of Madison, June 24, 1788, *id.* at 177.

[120]Jefferson to Madison, July 31, 1788, *id.* at 212.

[121]Curiously, from the Jefferson Papers it appears that none of Jefferson's many friends in Virginia bothered to write him after the Virginia convention ratified the Constitution on June 25 or finished its deliberations on the 27th.

these things may do evil, cannot be weighed against the multitude wherein the want of them will do evil." He hoped that "a bill of rights will be formed to guard the people against the federal government, as they are already guarded against their state governments in most instances."[122]

B. MADISON'S VIEWS

In August 1788 Madison sent Jefferson two letters which described the ratification struggles in New York and North Carolina. His focus remained on the adoption of the Constitution, and not on the protection of rights under it. He conceded to Jefferson that the Constitution was not perfect and that "A trial for one year [of the workings of the Constitution] will probably suggest more real amendments than all the antecedent speculations of our most sagacious politicians."[123] This indicates that Madison was more concerned with the mechanics of government under the Constitution than a bill of rights, which he viewed as a tactical issue, rather than one of principle.

In mid-October Madison received Jefferson's letter of July 31, in which the latter strenuously argued for a bill of rights. Madison had never responded to Jefferson's arguments set out in his letter of December 20, 1787. Nor had he responded to Jefferson's public letters, which had continued to "criticise . . . the omission of a bill of rights."[124] Finally, on October 17, 1788, Madison faced the criticism of his friend.

His response showed that after a year of calls for a bill of rights, which included two strong appeals from Jefferson, Madison remained basically unconvinced. Madison claimed that his "own opinion has always been in favor of a bill of rights," but he then repeated the litany of federalist arguments against a bill of rights, including: (1) that it was unnecessary under a government of limited powers; (2) that it could not be complete enough, especially because New Englanders would oppose absolute religious freedom; (3) that the inherent tension between the states and the federal government made a bill

[122]Jefferson to Madison, July 31, 1788, 11 Papers of Madison 212, 213.

[123]Madison to Jefferson, August 23, 1788, *id.* at 238–39; see also Madison to Jefferson, August 10, 1788, *id.* at 225. On September 21, and October 8, 1788, Madison again wrote to Jefferson, but did not discuss the substantive questions of a bill of rights. *Id.* at 257–59, 276–77.

[124]Madison to Edmund Randolph, August 2, 1788, *id.* at 215.

of rights unnecessary; (4) that "[r]epeated violations of these parchment barriers" showed that a bill of rights was useless; and (5) that a bill of rights was only needed to protect the people against a monarch, which was not a situation the Americans faced.[125]

Having explained to Jefferson why a bill of rights was unnecessary, Madison offered three reasons why he was now willing to support one. First, he acknowledged that "political truths declared" in a "solemn manner" would "acquire by degrees the character of fundamental maxims of free Government, and as they become incorporated with the national sentiment, counteract the impulses of interest and passion." Second, Madison acknowledged the unlikely event that the government itself might oppress some or even a majority of the people. Although doubtless a depressing scenario for a committed republican, Madison seemed to recognize that even in a republic the elected government might trample on the rights of the people and the people might not immediately resist their own government. Under such circumstances, "a bill of rights will be a good ground for an appeal to the sense of the community." Finally, he conceded a small point to the opposition, noting that perhaps "a succession of artful and ambitious rulers, may by gradual & well-timed advances, finally erect an independent Government on the subversion of liberty," and a bill of rights would be "prudent" "especially when the precaution can do no injury." Not ready to concede too much to the antifederalists (even though they were now thoroughly defeated) Madison immediately added that he saw "no tendency in our governments to danger on that side."[126]

As if he had conceded too much to the opposition, even in this private letter to Jefferson, Madison reiterated his ambivalence about a bill of rights. "Supposing a bill of rights be proper" he wrote, "I am inclined to think that *absolute* restrictions in cases that are doubtful, or where emergencies may overrule them, ought to be avoided."[127] He warned that[128]

> restrictions however strongly marked on paper will never be regarded when opposed to the decided sense of the public; and after repeated violations in extraordinary cases, they will lose even their ordinary efficacy. Should a Rebellion or insurrection alarm

[125]Madison to Jefferson, October 17, 1788, *id.* at 297–98.

[126]Madison to Jefferson, October 17, 1788, *id.* at 298–99.

[127]Madison to Jefferson, October 17, 1788, *id.* at 299.

[128]*Ibid.*

> the people as well as the Government, and a suspension of Hab. Corp. be dictated by the alarm, no written prohibitions on earth would prevent the measure.

Madison's distrust in democracy led him to believe that no legislature would obey either constitutionally or self-imposed limits. The "clods" (as historian Gordon Wood has called them) in the legislature, whether it be state or federal, would do as they pleased.[129]

Well before he received Madison's letter of October 17, 1788, Jefferson made one more plea for a bill of rights. On November 18, 1788, he urged Madison to support a bill of rights, not on ideological or philosophical grounds, but as a matter of practical politics. Jefferson argued that "the minorities [the antifederalists] are too respectable not to be entitled to some sacrifice of opinion in the majority. Especially when a great proportion of them would be contented with a bill of rights."[130] By the time Madison received this letter, in March 1789, he had already adopted this position, and in fact been elected to Congress on the basis of it.[131]

Meanwhile, Madison's letter of October 17, 1788, was delayed even longer than usual for transatlantic correspondence. It did not reach Jefferson until February 1789, and he did not respond until March 15, 1789. In this response Jefferson showed his respect for some of Madison's positions, but continued to argue strenuously for a bill of rights. This letter, however, had little effect on Madison's subsequent conduct—his paternity of the Bill of Rights—because he did not receive it until the end of May. By then Madison had already put Congress on notice of his intention to propose amendments. In response to Jefferson's letter of March 15, Madison wrote that a bill of rights would be introduced into Congress within a week.[132]

IX. Madison Moves Toward His Paternity

Throughout the ratification struggle Madison's opposition to a bill of rights was both tactical and theoretical. In his letter to Jeffer-

---

[129]See text at note 38 *supra*. Wood, Interests and Disinterestedness in the Making of the Constitution, in Beyond Confederation, at 74.

[130]Jefferson to Madison, November 18, 1788, 11 Papers of Madison 353–54.

[131]Madison to Jefferson, March 29, 1789, 12 Papers of Madison 38.

[132]Jefferson to Madison, March 15, 1789; Madison to Jefferson, May 27, 1789, *id.* at 13, 186. Before he received Madison's letter of October 17, Jefferson once more urged his friend to support a bill of rights.

son of October 17, 1788, Madison had detailed his theoretical arguments.[133] His tactical position was one which even Jefferson understood. Simply put, Madison wanted the Constitution ratified without a second convention being called. He felt that even an admission that a bill of rights was necessary might jeopardize this goal, while a concession on prior amendments would certainly have endangered ratification.

Despite his claim in his October 17, 1788, letter that he had "always been in favor of a bill of rights," Madison seems not to have favored one until he introduced his amendments in Congress. Even then, it is not clear that Madison theoretically supported the amendments.

How and why did Madison move to his reluctant paternity? The answers to both questions are tied to the politics of Virginia in 1788–89.

Virginia's ratification of the Constitution was an embarrassing defeat for Patrick Henry. He correctly saw Madison as the chief cause of this outcome. "To humiliate Madison, Henry managed his rejection by the Assembly for a seat in the Senate, referring to him as one 'unworthy of the confidence of the people,' whose election to office 'would terminate in producing rivulets of blood throughout the land.'" In order to "exclude Madison from the House of Representatives as well, Henry, a master of the 'gerrymander' long before that term had been invented, placed Orange County [Madison's home] in a Congressional district otherwise composed of counties considered heavily antifederal."[134] As he had before the ratification convention, Madison was forced to return to Virginia to campaign for office—an activity for which he had little enthusiasm.[135]

Madison arrived home at the end of December, 1788. He faced an uphill election campaign. His opponent was James Monroe, a friend and neighbor, but also a moderate antifederalist who had the support of Patrick Henry and his allies. Henry and his friends had already circulated rumors that Madison opposed any changes in the Constitution, including a bill of rights. Madison was particularly disturbed by allegations that he opposed any amendment protecting religious freedom.

---

[133]Madison to Jefferson, October 17, 1788, 11 Papers of Madison 298–99. See text at note 124 *supra*.

[134]Ketcham, note 59 *supra*, at 275.

[135]Rutland, note 32 *supra*, at 48.

On January 2, 1789, Madison wrote to Rev. George Eve, a leading Baptist minister, to explain his position on the Constitution. As he had a year earlier during the campaign for his election to the ratifying convention, Madison found that Baptist fears about religious liberty were sincere, strongly held, and had to be overcome if he was to win election.

Madison's letter was surprisingly frank for a man seeking votes. He freely admitted his disagreement with Eve; he did not see in the Constitution "those serious dangers which have alarmed many respectable Citizens." Thus while the Constitution was unratified Madison had opposed amendments, because he believed they were "calculated to throw the States into dangerous contentions, and to furnish the secret enemies of the Union with an opportunity of promoting its dissolution." However, with the Constitution ratified he was willing to support "amendments, if pursued with a proper moderation and in a proper mode" because under such circumstances they would "be not only safe, but may well serve the double purpose of satisfying the minds of well meaning opponents, and of providing additional guards in favour of liberty." Madison told Eve that "Under this change of circumstances, it is my sincere opinion that the Constitution ought to be revised, and that the first Congress meeting under it, ought to prepare and recommend to the States . . . provisions for all essential rights, particularly the rights of Conscience in the fullest latitude, the freedom of the press, trials by jury, security against general warrants, &c."[136]

Madison's changing position was partially a function of the calls by his opposition, including Monroe, for a second convention to alter the Constitution. Madison thought a second convention would lead to a disastrous rewriting of the Constitution. With this as a likely alternative, Madison now saw amendments as the best hope for keeping the Constitution more or less as it had been written. Thus, he told Rev. Eve that future amendments were "the safest mode" of changing the Constitution because "The Congress, who will be appointed to execute as well as to amend the Government, will probably be careful not to destroy or endanger it" while a second convention "containing perhaps insidious characters from different parts of America," would "be but too likely to turn every thing into confusion and uncertainty."[137]

---

[136]Madison to George Eve, January 2, 1789, 11 Papers of Madison 404–05.

[137]*Ibid.*

Madison subsequently wrote similar letters to other Virginians, explaining his position on a bill of rights. Two of his letters, which were published at the time, contained his "unequivocal pledge" to work for amendments if elected to Congress.[138] This counterattack turned the tide in his favor. At a meeting of Baptist leaders Rev. Eve defended Madison, reminding his co-religionists that Madison had always supported their interests by fighting for full religious freedom in Virginia.[139] In addition, Madison went to various Baptist meetings, German churches, and numerous courthouses to debate Monroe and explain his new support for amendments. His friends continued to argue his case throughout the district.[140] The campaign paid off with "a resounding federalist victory and remarkable personal tribute to Madison in a district 'rigged' against him."[141]

X. An Ambivalent Advocate

Shortly after his election Madison headed for New York as a Congressman pledged to propose constitutional amendments to protect individual liberty.[142] Although slated to open on March 4, 1789, Congress did not actually begin until April 6, when both houses finally achieved a quorum. When the session finally began a bill of rights was not high on the agenda. Opposition clustered around four different arguments. Some diehard federalists opposed any changes to a Constitution which they thought was beyond improvement. Some antifederalists still hoped for a second convention or substantial amendments that would restructure the new government. They correctly understood that the adoption of a bill of rights would un-

[138]Madison to Thomas Mann Randolph, January 13, 1789, later published in the Virginia Independent Chronicle, January 28, 1789; Madison to "A Resident of Spotsylvania County," January 27, 1789, published in Fredericksburg Virginia Herald, January 29, 1789; Benjamin Johnson to Madison, January 19, 1789, 11 Papers of Madison 415–17, 428–29, 423–24. Madison's letter of Randolph was also published in the Virginia Herald and Fredericksburg Advertiser, January 15, 1789, Ketcham, note 59 *supra* at 276, Rutland, note 32 *supra*, at 48.

[139]Ketcham, note 59 *supra*, at 276. See also Rutland, note 32 *supra*, at 48.

[140]Ketcham, note 59 *supra*, at 276–77; see also Rutland, note 32 *supra*. at 48. See also George Nichols to Madison, January 2, 1789, and January 24, 1789; Madison to Washington, January 14, 1789; Henry Lee to Madison, January 14, 1789, 11 Papers of Madison 406–09, 427–28, 417–18, 420–27.

[141]Ketcham, note 59 *supra*, at 277.

[142]Madison was not willing to support "alterations" to the Constitution that would change the fundamental powers of the government or weaken the power of the national government to control the states. See Bowling, note 4 *supra*, at 225–26.

dermine that goal.[143] They viewed the amendments as a "Tub to the Whale," designed to divert antifederalist s from making more substantive changes in the Constitution.[144] Some members of Congress agreed that a bill of rights might be important, but thought there were greater priorities, such as establishing various executive departments, raising revenue, and creating a judiciary. Finally, many in Congress doubtless sympathized with the position expressed by Georgia's James Jackson, who declared that the Constitution was "like a vessel just launched, and lying at the wharf; she is untried, you can hardly discover any one of her properties." Therefore, he argued that amendments should be delayed until this ship of state could be launched and Congress "guided by the experiment."[145]

Madison now believed that amendments ought to be added to the Constitution. He did not think them necessary to preserve liberty—on that point he had not wavered. But he felt a personal obligation to fulfill his campaign promise of supporting amendments. He also hoped that such amendments would remove the fears of many Americans who had opposed the Constitution. Moreover, he believed that Congressional action on a bill of rights would defeat the call for a second convention. Such a convention, he was convinced, would destroy the new Constitution.[146] As he later told Congress, Madison was "unwilling to see a door opened for a reconsideration of the whole structure of the Constitution—for a re-consideration of the principles and the substance of the powers given because I doubt if such a door were opened, we should be very likely to stop at that point which would be safe to the Government itself."[147]

For Madison, then, the bill of rights was now a question of tactics: how could he get the amendments adopted? His "strategy was to seize the initiative for amendments, to use the Federalist majority in the First Congress to finish the unavoidable business of amendments

---

[143]In North Carolina, which had not yet ratified the constitution, Hugh Williamson believed that some antifederalists also held this position. Williamson to Madison, May 24, 1789, 12 Papers of Madison 184.

[144]The phrase comes from Jonathan Swift, "Tale of a Tub" (1704): "Seamen have a custom, when they meet a whale, to fling him out an empty tub by way of amusement, to divert him from laying violent hands upon the ship." Quoted in Bowling, note 4 *supra*, at 223.

[145]I Annals of Congress, 1st Cong. 1st. Sess., 442.

[146]See, for example, Madison to George Eve, January 2, 1789, 11 Papers of Madison 404–05.

[147]Speech of Madison, I Annals of Congress, 1st Cong., 1st Sess. (debate of June 8. 1789), 450.

in such a way as to remove from the national agenda the major Anti-federalist objections. . . ."[148]

Even before the session began he sought the advice of sympathetic fellow federalists.[149] After Congress convened Madison's first strategic step was to involve President Washington in the campaign for a bill of rights. At this time Madison was Washington's closest advisor and part time speechwriter. In drafting Washington's first address to the Congress, which also served as Washington's inaugural address, Madison inserted a clause reminding Congress of its duty to consider proposing constitutional amendments in response to the "objections which have been urged against the System, or by the degree of inquietude which has given birth to them." Here Washington declined to make any specific recommendation, but placed his "entire confidence" in the Congress's "discernment and pursuit of the public good." The speech did urge that Congress show "a reverence for the characteristic rights of freemen, and a regard for the public harmony. . . ."[150]

On May 1 Madison proposed that the House send a formal response to the President "assuring him of their disposition to concur in giving effect to every measure which may tend to secure the liberties, promote the harmony, and advance the happiness and prosperity of their country." The House then appointed a committee, chaired by Madison, to draft this reply.[151] On May 5 Madison brought the resolution, which he wrote, to the floor. This resolution included the following paragraph: "The question arising out of the fifth article of the Constitution, [the amendment process] will receive all the attention demanded by its importance; and will, we trust be decided, under the influence of all the considerations to which you allude."[152]

This episode was certainly a coup for Madison. He was able to put into Washington's mouth his own views on the need for a bill of

[148]Storing, The Constitution and the Bill of Rights, in Rossum & McDowell (eds.), The American Founding: Politics, Statesmanship, and the Constitution (1981) 32.

[149]Tench Coxe to Madison, March 18 and 24, 1789, Edmund Randolph to Madison, March 26, 1789, 12 Papers of Madison 21, 27, 31.

[150]Address of the President to Congress, April 30, 1789, and Editorial Note, 12 *id.* at 123 & 120. See also 1 Messages and Paper of the Presidents 43–49 (Richardson ed. 1897).

[151]I Annals of Congress, 1st cong., 1st Sess., 242 (May 1, 1789); 12 Papers of Madison 134n.

[152]I Annals of Congress, 1st Cong., 1st Sess., 258 (May 5, 1789); 12 Papers of Madison 132–34. Washington also asked Madison to help him draft a short, formal reply to the House resolution. Washington to Madison, May 5, 1789, reprinted in 30 Writings of George Washington 310, and 310 (Fitzpatrick ed. 1939).

rights. Historian Robert Rutland has suggested that Washington was acting "cautiously"[153] in calling for Congress to act in its own "discernment of the public good." However, it seems more likely that by having Washington ask Congress to act Madison was shrewdly getting the President to endorse amendments without appearing too heavy handed. By writing a speech in which Washington deferred to Congress to work out the details, Madison was not taking any great risk because Madison was already the most effective member of the Congress and was emerging as the "first man" of the House.[154]

Madison then followed this by becoming the prime draftsman of a resolution supporting the speech that he had written for Washington. Through Madison's adroit pen both the President and the House were on record supporting amendments to protect liberty.[155] All Madison had to do now was introduce these amendments and shepherd them through Congress. This, however, was no easy task.

On May 4 Madison told the Congress of his intention to propose amendments later in the month, but on the 25th Madison moved for a postponement. As he explained to Jefferson: "more urgent business" had caused a slight delay, but within a few weeks a "Bill of rights . . . will be proposed."[156]

On June 8 Madison finally had the opportunity to present his amendments. He told the House he was "bound in honor and in duty" to bring the amendments forward. His plan was to "advocate them until they shall be finally adopted or rejected by a constitutional majority of this House."[157] Others in the House wanted a delay, some because they opposed all amendments, some because they thought the Congress had more important work ahead of it. Madison noted that he had already postponed his motion once. In arguing

[153]Rutland, The Birth of the Bill of Rights, 1767–1791 198 (1955).

[154]Editorial Note on Madison at the First Session of the First Federal Congress, 12 Papers of Madison 52–53.

[155]Later in the debates Madison produced a letter from Washington in which the President declared he saw "nothing exceptionable in the proposed amendments" and some were "importantly necessary" while others, while not essential were "necessary to quiet the fears of some respectable characters and well meaning Men." Thus, Washington declared his hope they would receive "a favorable reception in both houses" of Congress. Washington to Madison [ca. 31 May 1789], 12 Papers of Madison 191.

[156]I Annals of Congress, 1st Cong., 1st. Sess., 257; 4 Documentary History of the First Federal Congress of the United States of America: Legislative Histories: Amendments to the Constitution Through Foreign Officers Bill 3 (Bickford & Veit, eds., 1986); Madison to Jefferson, May 27, 1789, 12 Papers of Madison 186.

[157]I Annals of Congress, 1st Cong., 1st Sess., 440–41 (Debate of June 8, 1789).

against further postponements, Madison asserted one of his major points in favor of amendments: that "if we continue to postpone from time to time, and refuse to let the subject come into view, it may well occasion suspicions, which, though not well founded, may tend to inflame or prejudice the public mind against our decisions." Madison feared that the "very respectable number of our constituents" who had asked for amendments might conclude that Congress was "not sincere in our desire to incorporate such amendments in the constitution as will secure those rights, which they consider as not sufficiently guarded."[158] Although about to propose amendments, Madison was still not advocating them for their substance. Rather, he argued he had a moral obligation to present them and that it would be politically expedient for Congress to accept them.

Madison's initial speech led the staunch federalist Roger Sherman to urge the House to delay action until it was "a proper time."[159] Madison responded by reiterating the necessity of calming those who feared the new strong central government. He wanted "the opportunity of proving to those who were opposed to" the Constitution that "those who have been friendly to the adoption of this constitution" were also "sincerely devoted to liberty and a Republican Government" and not attempting to "lay the foundation of an aristocracy or despotism." He reminded the House of those who had "apprehensions" that the new government wished to "deprive them of the liberty for which they valiantly fought and honorably bled." He believed that many who had opposed the Constitution were now ready "to join their support to the cause of Federalism, if they were satisfied on this one point." Furthermore, he argued amendments might lure North Carolina and Rhode Island into the union.[160]

While proposing amendments, Madison remained ambivalent about a bill of rights. Madison did not propose a bill of rights as such. Rather, he proposed a series of changes in the main body of the Constitution which would have been scattered throughout the document. Madison noted that his proposal "relates to what may be called

[158] *Id.* at 440–44.

[159] *Id.* at 444.

[160] *Id.* at 449. Without knowing that Madison had already introduced amendments, William R. Davie of North Carolina wrote him urging that amendments be adopted before the North Carolina convention, which was scheduled for the following November. Davie to Madison, June 10, 1789, 12 Papers of Madison 210–11. See also George Lee Turberville to Madison, June 16, 1789, *id.* at 222–23, explaining that amendments would "tend very much to satisfy the minds of *those who were really fearful of danger* to the Liberties of their fellow citizens" while undermining those who opposed the Constitution for selfish and narrow reasons.

a bill of rights"[161] but he did not call it that, just as he did not present it as a unified package.

Madison did not argue with passion or even much conviction for his proposal. He admitted that he had "never considered this provision so essential to the federal constitution" that it should have been allowed to impede ratification. But, with the Constitution ratified Madison was willing to concede "that in a certain form and to a certain extent, such a provision was neither improper nor altogether useless."[162]

Madison followed this tepid endorsement of his amendments with a balanced assessment of the pros and cons of a bill of rights. He conceded the virtues of the opposition, but found reasons to counter all their points. Madison's most innovative proposal concerned the vexing problem that "by enumerating particular exceptions of the grant of power, it would disparage those rights which were not placed in that enumeration; and it might follow, by implication, that those rights which were not singled out, were intended to be assigned into the hands of the General Government, and were consequently insecure." He argued that this problem could be "guarded against." He had already done so with a provision which became the ninth amendment.[163]

Madison concluded his opening speech on the bill of rights debate by asking that the House appoint a committee to consider the amendments. He argued that "we should obtain the confidence of our fellow citizens, in proportion as we fortify the rights of the people against the encroachments of the government." To Madison's disappointment, the House referred the amendments to a committee of the whole, thus delaying the process of adoption.[164]

Madison had introduced the amendments because he claimed it "was my duty" to do so.[165] His unstated goal was to convince the nation's moderate antifederalists to support the Constitution. His subsequent correspondence indicates that he believed his strategy

[161] I Annals of Congress, 1st Cong., 1st Sess., 453.

[162] *Ibid.*

[163] *Id.* at 456. Madison's original provision read: "The exceptions here or elsewhere in the constitution, made in favor of particular rights, shall not be so construed as to diminish the just importance of other rights retained by the people, or as to enlarge the powers delegated by the constitution; but either as actual limitations of such powers, or as inserted merely for greater caution."

[164] *Id.* at 459.

[165] *Ibid.*

was working. He was certain that the amendments, if adopted, would "be satisfactory to a majority of those who have opposed the Constitution."[166] He was pleased that they were "limited to points which are important in the eyes of many and can be objectionable in those of none." Proudly he noted that "the structure & stamina of the Govt. are as little touched as possible."[167]

Part of Madison's strategy was to avoid controversial political issues so that his amendments would pass as quickly as possible. He thought that "nothing of a controvertible nature ought to he hazarded" in order to avoid a defeat of the amendments. He told Edmund Randolph that he had avoided anything of a "controversial nature" because of the "caprice & discord of opinions" in the House and Senate, which had to approve the amendments by a two-thirds vote, and in the state legislatures, three-fourths of which had to approve the amendments. The amendments had a "twofold object of removing the fears of the discontented and of avoiding all such alterations as would either displease the adverse side, or endanger the success of the measure." In sending them to a North Carolina correspondent he doubtless hoped to push that state toward ratification.[168]

Because the amendments were now in the committee of the whole, Madison had to weigh carefully when he ought to try to bring them up again. Madison's energies, and those of the rest of Congress, were directed at other pending legislation on such matters as the removal power of the President, import duties, western land, and the salaries of congressmen. For the next month most of his correspondence focused on these issues, rather than on the bill of rights. This reflects Madison's low key and deliberate approach to amendments. He had done his "duty" in introducing a bill of rights, and he would continue to fight for the proposal. But, he was not preoccupied with the question.

Tench Coxe, a Philadelphia federalist, agreed with this analysis and happily noted that "the most ardent & irritable among our friends are well pleased" with the amendments, as were "honest" antifederalists. Edmund Randolph, meanwhile, noted that "*strong*

[166]Madison to Jefferson, June 13, 1789, 12 Papers of Madison 218.

[167]Madison to Edmund Randolph, June 15, 1789, *id.* at 219.

[168]Madison to Edmund Pendleton, June 21, 1789, Madison to Edmund Randolph, June 15, 1789, and Madison to Samuel Johnston, June 21, 1789, *id.* at 253, 219, 250. See also Madison to Tench Coxe, June 24, 1789, Madison to George Nichols, July 5, 1789, *id.* at 257, 282.

foederalists" in Virginia supported the amendments, while among diehard antifederalists "nothing, nay not even the abolishment of direct taxation would satisfy those, who are most clamorous." Another Virginia friend was pleased the amendments would protect individual liberty "so far as declarations on paper can effect that purpose" while at the same time "leaving unimpaired the great Powers of the government."[169] Hugh Williamson, a leading North Carolina federalist, liked what he saw, but correctly predicted that his state would not ratify the Constitution until after Congress had approved the amendments.[170]

On July 21, during a brief lull in the legislative business, Madison "begged the House to indulge him in the further consideration of amendments." Madison's colleagues were in no mood for another debate in the committee of the whole. Some, like Roger Sherman, opposed any amendments and wanted to end the entire process but a majority voted for a select committee of one member from each state to consider the amendments.[171]

On August 13 the select committee reported back to Congress. For the next eight sessions the House debated the amendments, finally adopting them on August 22. Although active in these debates, Madison did not dominate them.[172] Madison never spoke directly to the merits of a bill of rights but throughout the debates almost always argued for their expediency. Initially he asked if it was "desirable to keep up a division among the people of the United States on a point in which they consider their most essential rights are concerned?" He argued that consideration of the issue would "promote that spirit of urbanity and unanimity which the Government itself stands in need of for its more full support."[173] Later he argued for a particular clause because "it be desired by three important States." Even on the protection of religious liberty—something he fervently supported—Madison would not affirmatively argue for his amendment. He re-

[169]Tench Coxe to Madison, June 18, 1789; Edmund Randolph to Madison, June 30, 1789; and Joseph Jones to Madison, June 24, 1789, *id.* at 239, 273, 258–59. See also Edward Stevens to Madison, June 25, 1789, *id.* at 261.

[170]Hugh Williamson to Madison, July 2, 1789, *id.* at 274–75. See also Benjamin Hawkins to Madison [July] 3, 1789, *id.* at 275.

[171]I Annals of Congress, 1st Cong., 1st Sess. 685–92.

[172]Madison spoke twenty-three times during these debates, while Elbridge Gerry spoke twenty-nine times. Nine other men spoke at least ten times each, for a collective total of 130 times. This is based on a count of speeches in *id.* at 730–808.

[173]*Id.* at 731.

fused to say "Whether the words are necessary or not" arguing only that members "of the State Conventions . . . seemed to entertain an opinion that under the [necessary and proper] clause of the constitution" Congress might "infringe the rights of conscience, and establish a national religion." He consistently "appeal[ed] to the gentlemen who have heard the voice of the country, to those who have attended the debates of the States conventions, whether the amendments now proposed are not those most strenuously required by the opponents to the constitution?"[174]

During the debates over the Constitution many of the antifederalists had reflected "the traditional politics of consensus, the old quest for unanimity, not the new majoritarian politics of the constitution's promoters."[175] Ironically, in the congressional debates over the bill of rights Madison, who was perhaps America's first modern politician, reflected this older notion of politics. He sought reconciliation by giving the antifederalists the protections of liberty that they valued so highly.

Only twice in these debates did Madison seem to speak about the amendments with great enthusiasm. Both brief speeches showed that Madison remained more committed to limiting the powers of the states than to limiting the power of the national government. Thus, he passionately supported a proposal that would have prohibited the states from infringing "the equal right of conscience . . . freedom of speech or the press, . . . [and] the right of trial by jury in criminal cases." Madison thought this was "the most valuable amendment in the whole list."[176] Although the House approved this clause,[177] the Senate did not and thus these rights did not become applicable to the states until after the adoption of the Fourteenth Amendment and its modern development, starting with *Gitlow* v. *New York*.[178] Similarly, Madison strongly and successfully opposed adding the word "expressly" to what became the tenth amendment. Madison thought this would give the states too much power.[179]

---

[174] *Id.* at 746, 758, 775.

[175] P. Maier, note 85 *supra* at 228.

[176] I Annals of Congress, at 783–84.

[177] See note 7 *supra*.

[178] Gitlow v. New York, 268 U.S. 652 (1925).

[179] I Annals of Congress, 1st Cong., 1st Sess., 790.

XI. A Reluctant Paternity and Modern Interpretation

Madison did not enjoy these debates. He wrote to Richard Peters of the "nauseous project of amendments."[180] This phrase has been subject to contradictory interpretations.[181] Jack Rakove has argued that Madison was "probably allud[ing] to the feelings of his colleagues in Congress rather than his own."[182] In another article Rakove has argued that the essence of the "nauseous project" statement was the fact that Madison's support the Bill of Rights was "only for expedient reasons of politics."[183] Robert Rutland, on the other hand, suggests this statement is an "offhand remark" and should not be taken "as a statement of fact." Rutland argues that this statement has been wrongly interpreted to indicate that Madison's support of the amendments was marred by "a tinge of hypocrisy."[184] In this context, Rutland takes exception to Rakove's comments on political expediency.

Rutland is on solid ground in arguing that this statement does not indicate a "tinge of hypocrisy" in Madison's support for the Bill of Rights. Madison, after all, did not think the substance of the amendments was "nauseous." Moreover, even as Madison fought for the Bill of Rights, he never appeared enthusiastic about the proposals. Given his cool and reserved support for the amendments, it would be impossible to consider him hypocritical, even if one were to interpret his "nauseous project" remark to refer to the substance of the amendments. Similarly, Rakove is correct in seeing Madison's support for the Bill of Rights as fundamentally political. Just because it was political does not mean, as Rutland implies, that the support was hypocritical. Here Rutland apparently misread both Madison and Rakove. Madison's support for the amendments was based on a coherent and rational political analysis of the needs of America under

---

180 Madison to Richard Peters, August 19, 1789, 12 Papers of Madison 346.

181 Kenneth Bowling, in A Tub to the Whale, note 4 *supra*, has ignored the phrase altogether, perhaps because it is so distracting, and so easily misunderstood. This analysis is based on Bowling's public comments on an earlier version of this paper at the Organization of American Historians meeting in 1990.

182 Rakove, The Madisonian Theory of Rights, 31 Wm. & Mary L. Rev. 245–46 (1990).

183 Rakove, Mr. Meese, Meet Mr. Madison, The Atlantic Monthly (Dec., 1986), 77, quoted at 84, col. 1.

184 Rutland, The Trivialization of the Bill of Rights, 31 William & Mary L. Rev. 287, 291 (1990).

the Constitution; such a motivation seems hardly an act of hypocrisy.

Rutland is also wrong, I think, in dismissing the statement as is merely an "off hand remark" or a "slip of the pen."[185] The "nauseous" comment was not an isolated one. Madison also described the debates over the amendments as "extremely difficult and fatiguing"[186] and "exceedingly wearisome."[187] What Madison found to be "nauseous," "fatiguing," and "wearisome" was the process of getting the amendments through Congress. No doubt it was. "Madison was sick and tired of the obstructionism of Roger Sherman, Aedanus Burke, William Loughton Smith, James Jackson, and other congressmen who thought the introduction of a bill of rights was a waste of time."[188] Madison probably found this obstructionism particularly distasteful because of his own ambivalence about the goal he sought.

While never actually opposed to the idea of rights, in 1787–89 Madison was never convinced a bill of rights was either necessary or completely harmless. To the end Madison was uncertain about the value of a bill of rights. A few days before the House endorsed the amendments, Madison observed that "we are so deep in them now, that right or wrong some thing must be done." This was hardly the sentiment of an enthusiastic partisan. But, Madison had not become one, even as he supported the addition of a bill of rights. With victory in sight, he could only marshal a series of weak arguments to support his position: a bill of rights was "a thing not improper in itself;" "had no assurances been given" of subsequent amendments the Constitution might not have been ratified; "as an honest man" Madison felt "bound" to support amendments after the Virginia convention; without his promise to support amendments Virginia would have elected antifederalists to Congress; if Madison had not introduced his amendments, opponents of the Constitution would have presented more damaging ones; once the amendments were adopted they "would kill the opposition every where, and by putting an end to the disaffection to the Govt. itself, enable the administration to venture on measures not otherwise safe"; the amendments would head off a second convention; and the amendments were necessary to bring North Carolina into the Union.[189]

---

[185]*Ibid.* This is also Rutland's terminology.

[186]Madison to Edmund Pendleton, August 21, 1789 12 Papers of Madison 348.

[187]Madison to Edmund Randolph, August 21, 1789, 12 Papers of Madison 348.

[188]Rutland, note 184 *supra*, at 292.

[189]Madison to Richard Peters, August 19, 1789, 12 Papers of Madison 347.

In sum, Madison argued that the bill of rights should be adopted because it might help the country, and could not hurt it. "We have" he told Congress "something to gain, and, if we proceed with caution, nothing to lose."[190]

Despite his ambivalence and misgivings about a bill of rights, Madison fought hard for the amendments. Duty to his constituents, duty to himself as an "honest man," and his keen sense of politics kept him going. But, so too, no doubt, did Madison's libertarian values. Whether opposing amendments during the ratification struggle or giving them lukewarm support in Congress, Madison rarely opposed the idea of protecting basic rights and liberties. He never denied the value of due process, freedom of expression, and religious liberty. If he doubted the value of the amendments, he never doubted the values they stood for. That, in the end, enabled him to support the Bill of Rights, even while uncertain if it was either necessary or prudent. He would, in effect, leave that question up to future generations.

Madison's ambivalence about the Bill of Rights serves to remind the living generation that liberty is ultimately protected, not by parchment barriers, but by the "vigilant . . . spirit which actuates the people of America."[191] The Bill of Rights articulates the goals of that spirit.

---

[190]Speech of Madison, in I Annals of Congress, 1st Cong., 1st Sess., 450 (June 8, 1789).

[191]Federalist 57, in 10 Papers of Madison 523.

Part VII
Religious Liberty

[17]

Madison: On the Separation of Church and State

Irving Brant*

TO James Madison, author of the American Bill of Rights, freedom of religion was the fundamental item upon which all other forms of civil liberty depended. Its maintenance would not automatically preserve the entire liberty of the citizen. But without it the other rights were sure to be destroyed.

In the area of religion, as Madison saw it, the basic element was freedom of conscience. But in the protection of that freedom, the fundamental requirement was a total separation between government and religion. In the first legislative endeavor of his life, when he was 25 years old, he wrote a guarantee of freedom of conscience into the Virginia Constitution of 1776, whence it spread into other state charters. In his second creative action for civil liberty, he wrote separation of church and state into the federal Constitution. Then in his later years, in an "Essay on Monopolies," which was lost and unpublished until 1914, he linked these two defenses to each other and to human rights in general.

For the first expression of his belief in separation of church and state one must go back at least to 1774, when 23-year-old Madison wrote to William Bradford:

> If the Church of England had been the established and general religion in all the northern colonies as it has been among us here, and uninterrupted tranquility had prevailed throughout the continent, it is clear to me that slavery and subjection might and would have been gradually insinuated among us. Union of religious sentiments begets a surprising confidence, and ecclesiastical establishments tend to great ignorance and corruption; all of which facilitates the execution of mischievous projects.[1]

For the germ of this belief one can go still farther back, to the choice in 1769 of Princeton over Williamsburg as the seat of Madison's collegiate studies. Health conditions and alumni loyalties played a part, but only a

* Mr. Brant is the author of the definitive life of Madison now in progress which has dealt with his subject's career 1751-1800. He is writing the fourth and final volume.

[1] James Madison, *The Writings of James Madison,* edited by Gaillard Hunt (New York, 1900-1910), I, 19.

part, in that decision. The Reverend Mr. Horrocks, president of William and Mary College, was the reputed head of a powerful group seeking to establish an American Episcopate with himself at the head of it. Madison's father was an Episcopal vestryman but wanted no authoritarian bishop over him. Church establishment in Virginia was displaying its by-products—the stoning and jailing of Baptist preachers, maintenance of corrupt and dissolute rectors under the tithe law and other statutes. On the contrary side Princeton offered President Witherspoon, newly come from Scotland, whose Presbyterian activities led an observer to write in the summer of 1769: "Our Jersey College is now talking as if she was to be a bulwark against Episcopacy." There is more reason to believe that hostility to church establishment led Madison to Princeton, than that the choice of a school fixed his principles.[2]

Madison was not a church member, but attended church (regardless of denomination) with regularity and reserved the unorthodoxy of his mature years for fireside conversation. In college he traveled with a slightly impious crowd—impious by eighteenth-century standards—the sophisticated American Whigs as opposed to the devout and fervent Cliosophists. All championed religious liberty. His concern over the subject became manifest after he returned to Virginia in 1772. In the following year, he asked Bradford to send him a draft of the origin and principles of the Pennsylvania Constitution, "particularly the extent of your religious toleration." Dr. Samuel Stanhope Smith, taking his bride (Anna Witherspoon) to the Madison home in 1775, was invited to bring also Josiah Tucker's *Apology for the Church of England as by Law Established* and Phil Tumeaux's *Essay on Toleration*—a defense of dissenting ministers. In between these two requests, Madison paid a visit to Philadelphia, desiring (he told Bradford) "again to breathe your free air." In Virginia:

> Poverty and luxury prevail among all sorts; pride, ignorance and knavery among the priesthood, and vice and wickedness among the laity. This is bad

[2] "James Madison's Autobiography," edited by Douglass Adair, *William and Mary Quarterly*, 3d. ser., II (1945), 191-209; William C. Rives, *History of the Life and Times of James Madison* (Boston, 1866-1868), I, 11; Irving Brant, *James Madison* (Indianapolis, 1941-), I, 67-71. Alexander and Thomas Martin, whose persuasions helped send Madison to Princeton, were Episcopalians. Both were graduates of the New Jersey Presbyterian college, which had been as aggressive against church and state under Presidents Davies and Finley as it was later under Witherspoon. Alexander Martin, as governor of North Carolina, opposed the favored position of his own church and defended the "enthusiast" cults, but was less extreme than Madison in his opposition to public financial support of religion.

enough, but it is not the worst I have to tell you. That diabolical, hell-conceived principle of persecution rages among some and to their eternal infamy, the clergy can furnish their quota of imps for such business. . . . There are at this [time] in the adjacent county [Culpeper] not less than five or six well-meaning men in close jail for publishing their religious sentiments which in the main are very orthodox. I have neither patience to hear, talk, or think of anything relative to this matter; for I have squabbled and scolded, abused and ridiculed so long about it to little purpose, that I am without common patience. So I must beg you to pity me, and pray for liberty of conscience to all.

At the time of this writing—the spring of 1774—Baptists and Presbyterians were planning an appeal to the Virginia Assembly, but that body, Madison felt, was "too much devoted to the ecclesiastical establishment to hear of the toleration of dissentients." Again contrasting Virginia and Pennsylvania he wrote to Bradford: "The sentiments of our people of fortune and fashion on this subject are vastly different from what you have been used to. That liberal catholic and equitable way of thinking as to the rights of conscience, which is one of the characteristics of a free people and so strongly marks the people of your province is but little known among the zealous adherents to our hierarchy."[8]

In this, one may note a contrast between the quiet spirit of Madison the student and the spirit of Madison the reformer—a spirit which makes it easy to understand the man's lifelong zeal for religious freedom. Something else, however, becomes notable at this point. In speaking of the polemic literature of religion, and of the struggles waged by others, he refers to *establishment* on the one hand, *toleration* on the other. But in expressing his own conception of the contest, the contrast is between establishment and the *rights of conscience*. As early as 1774, he had come to think of religious toleration (the ultimate goal of most reformers) as only the halfway point on the road to freedom.

With this conviction Madison became an Orange County delegate to the Virginia Convention of 1776. Advised by the Continental Congress to set up a system of civil government, this convention responded by asking Congress to declare the United Colonies free and independent, then proceeded to draft a constitution and bill of rights.

George Mason, liberal Anglican, wrote in his draft of the Declaration of

[8] William Meade, *Old Churches, Ministers and Families of Virginia* (Philadelphia, 1857), II, 99 (lamenting Madison's heterodoxy); Madison, *Writings,* I, 20-21, 23.

Rights that as duty to the Creator can be governed only by reason and conviction, "all men should enjoy the fullest toleration in the exercise of religion, according to the dictates of conscience." In committee, Madison pointed out that "toleration" made freedom a favor sanctioned by the established sect, rather than a natural and inalienable right. The convention accepted his version, which declared that "all men are equally entitled to the free exercise of religion, according to the dictates of conscience."

While securing this amendment, Madison failed to obtain approval of a declaration "that no man or class of men ought, on account of religion to be invested with peculiar emoluments or privileges." This was designed to knock out the tithe system and disestablish the Episcopal church. However, Madison contended steadily thereafter that any form or degree of church establishment violated the rights of conscience, and was unconstitutional under the article actually adopted. That too was the immediate interpretation of Article XVI by Virginia Dissenters. Seeing no automatic relief from Episcopal oppression, they flooded the next legislative assembly with petitions for statutory enforcement of the guarantee of freedom. From Prince Edward County came the appeal of citizens who looked on this article "as the rising sun of religious liberty, to relieve them from a long night of ecclesiastical bondage." They asked that without delay, "all church establishments might be pulled down, and every tax upon conscience and private judgment abolished." Other requests for action came from Albemarle, Amherst, Buckingham, Richmond and Culpeper counties. Over the mountains in Scotch-Irish Augusta County, the militia and other freeholders met to instruct their delegates. Free exercise of religion according to the rights of conscience, they asserted, meant that there should be no "favoring some to the hurt of others." Demanding "that no religious sect whatever be established in this commonwealth," they notified "interested bigots, illiberal politicians" and disguised enemies to freedom that men who had rushed to arms to defend the common cause were not to be trifled with. Deny them their patrimony of equal liberty and the consequences "may shake this continent and demolish provinces."[4]

In the legislature, strategic factors worked for and against Episcopal

[4] Brant, *Madison,* I, 241-248, 293-298; *Journals, Virginia House of Delegates,* October session, 1776; *Virginia Gazette* (Purdie), October 18, 1776; Thomas Jefferson, "Autobiography," *Writings of Thomas Jefferson* (Washington, 1905), I, 57-62.

influence. Thomas Jefferson came home from Congress and took over the House of Delegates leadership relinquished by Patrick Henry (a supporter of the established church) when he became the state's first governor. Dissenters and liberal Anglicans would have had things their own way, except for the "rotten borough" system which built up the conservative tidewater representation and pulled down the West. Even with this handicap, Jefferson, Madison and their allies put through a resolve for the abrogation of laws requiring church attendance and punishing the holding of certain beliefs, and for the repeal of acts for the support of the clergy. When the actual repeal bill came up, church leaders Edmund Pendleton and Robert C. Nicholas were able to cut it to a mere suspension of religious tax levies until the next session of the assembly. That was enough. Once relieved of tithes, the people of Virginia forced a renewal of the suspension year after year, until in 1779 the basic law was repealed.

The established clergy, whose moral delinquencies cut down voluntary financial support from the Episcopalian laity, became terrified at the loss of public funds. Laymen allied with the clergy foresaw the doom of religion and a general wave of licentiousness in the people. At the 1784 spring session of the General Assembly, they made a double move to renew and tighten the links of state and church. A resolution was introduced to levy a general assessment for the support of teachers of religion (each taxpayer to designate the sect to which his money should go). A bill was proposed for the incorporation of the Protestant Episcopal church, including an innocent-looking clause whose purpose (as Madison construed it) was to insure life tenure for clergymen by making it impossible for the lay vestries to remove them. Through the inclusion of all sects in the financial provision, the Anglicans hoped to seduce the Presbyterian clergy to support the assessment plan, leaving the Baptists as the only opponents who were both united and powerful. (Catholics and Quakers were opposed, but weak; Methodists were divided.) The incorporation measure was expected to give the Episcopal church special privilege without giving it a monopoly. The prospect of state support produced such a change in the Presbyterian divines that Madison said he did not "know a more shameful contrast" than between their earlier and later attitudes. However, the Presbyterian laity and the Scotch-Irish preachers in the Shenandoah Valley held to their principles, and so did the Reverend John B. Smith of Hampden-Sydney College, the leading Presbyterian of the state. He termed the incorporation proposal "an express attempt to draw the state into an illicit connection and commerce" with the Anglicans, and was equally vehement against the assessment.[5]

Madison at this time had just re-entered the legislature after four years in the Continental Congress. Jefferson was a diplomat in France. Patrick Henry, following his retirement as governor, had been for five years the undisputed overlord of the General Assembly. Madison named him years later as the sponsor of the assessment bill, but the great orator was a cautious man who never waged an open fight unless he foresaw victory. On this occasion, Madison wrote to Jefferson, the friends of the assessment measure "did not choose to try their strength in the house," while the incorporation bill "was preserved from a dishonorable death by the talents of Mr. Henry. It lies over for another session."[6]

Reconvening in October, 1784, the legislature found on its doorstep a litter of petitions supporting the two measures, and not one against them. Confident now, Patrick Henry came forward with a resolve that the people "pay a moderate tax or contribution annually" for the support of the Christian religion or some Christian church. Madison took the lead against him. Ordinary political lines were wiped out as tidewater conservatives backed their chronic enemy, Patrick Henry, while such Henry-worshipers as French Strother and Spencer Roane joined Madison, the Nicholas brothers and Zachariah Johnston in opposition. Rising to answer the great orator, Madison argued that religion was totally outside the purview of civil authority, and that a law compelling people to support it financially was a violation of the constitutional guarantee of freedom of conscience. To refute Henry's claim that religion was decaying through lack of financial support, he launched a general assault on religious establishments as corrupters of both state and church. The nations whose fall Henry described had state churches. The flourishing eras of the Christian religion were not those in which the state fostered it, but when it was in conflict with the prevailing laws—as in primitive Christianity, in the Reformation, in the reaction of Dissenters against restraint. For declining morals and religion the remedy was not church establishment but laws to cherish virtue, a better administration of justice, personal example, the education of youth. Madison's speech is preserved not in its full text but in topical notes which

[5] John B. Smith to Madison, June 21, 1784, *Writings,* II, 213*n.*

[6] Madison to Jefferson, July 3, 1784, *ibid.,* II, 56-62.

conclude with his instructions to himself for the discussion of Christianity: "Panegyric on it, on our side."[7]

Patrick Henry won the first test of strength on the assessment bill, but the publicity aroused the state and brought hostile petitions. Madison helped maneuver Henry out of the legislature by electing him governor once more. The Episcopal incorporation bill, stripped of its most obnoxious features, was allowed to pass, in order (Madison wrote) to cool the eagerness of its votaries for a much greater evil. Forty-five to thirty-eight, the assessment bill was then postponed till the following November.[8]

The 1795 spring elections, bringing defeat to many advocates of this measure, caused Madison to regard its postponement as akin to death. George and Wilson Cary Nicholas, however, warned him that the rotten tidewater boroughs might give the bill a majority in the legislature which it lacked among the people. Their appeal for an address to the public brought from Madison his famous "Memorial and Remonstrance against Religious Assessments."[9]

Designed for general signature and presentation to the state assembly, the memorial opened with a statement that the subscribers, as faithful members of a free state, were bound to protest against a dangerous abuse of power and to give the reasons for their remonstrance. These were set forth in fifteen numbered paragraphs.

Quoting what he himself had implanted in the Declaration of Rights, Madison declared that religion must be left to the conviction and conscience of every man. That was not only the right of the citizen, but his duty toward the Creator, and was "precedent both in order of time and degree of obligation, to the claims of civil society. . . . We maintain therefore that in matters of religion, no man's right is abridged by the institution of civil society, and that religion is wholly exempt from its cognizance."

Society at large having no control over it, still less could religion be governed by its creatures and vice-regents, the legislature. To preserve a free government, its departments must be held within their proper spheres, but more especially, none of them must "overleap the great barrier which defends the rights of the people. The rulers who are guilty of such an en-

[7] Madison, "Notes of Speech Against Assessments for Support of Religion," *Writings*, II, 88.

[8] After 1784, the Virginia legislature met once instead of twice a year.

[9] Madison, "Memorial and Remonstrance Against Religious Assessments," *Writings*, II, 183-191.

croachment . . . are tyrants. The people who submit to it . . . are slaves."

Such language represented no figurative use of the symbols of force. It was a tangible threat. Armed revolution was but one year past, and had no moral terrors. "It is proper," Madison went on, "to take alarm at the first experiment on our liberties. We hold this prudent jealousy to be the first duty of citizens, and one of the noblest characteristics of the late Revolution. The freemen of America did not wait till usurped power had strengthened itself by exercise, and entangled the question in precedents. They saw all the consequences in the principle, and they avoided the consequences by denying the principle. We revere this lesson too much, soon to forget it."

A state which could establish Christianity, he observed, could with equal ease establish a particular sect. The authority which could force a citizen to pay three pence (the amount of the war-provoking tax on tea) for the support of any one establishment could force him to conform to any other establishment. The memorial then launched into a more specific attack on the bill, denying that civil magistrates were competent to say what societies were Christian, denying the need of the Christian religion for an establishment to uphold it and challenging the value of religious establishments in general. What had been their fruits in fifteen centuries? "Pride and indolence in the clergy; ignorance and servility in the laity; in both, superstition, bigotry and persecution."

No more, Madison argued, was this establishment necessary for the support of civil government. In the past, ecclesiastical societies had erected a spiritual tyranny on the ruins of civil authority, or had upheld the thrones of political tyranny. In no instance had they been the guardians of the liberties of the people. The proposed establishment was a departure from that generous policy which offered "an asylum to the persecuted and oppressed of every nation and religion." It differed from the Inquisition only in degree. It would hasten the emigration of citizens by revoking their liberty. It would destroy that moderation and harmony which religious liberty had produced, and transform Christian forbearance into animosities and jealousies. It was adverse to the diffusion of the light of Christianity. Being too obnoxious for enforcement, it would enervate the laws in general by offering so striking an example of impotency in the government.

In his final paragraph, Madison came back to the Virginia Declaration of Rights. The right to free exercise of religion was held by the same tenure with all our other rights. It was equally the gift of nature, and was set forth in the basic law "with equal solemnity, or rather studied emphasis." Either, then, the legislature "may sweep away all our fundamental rights; or . . . they are bound to leave this particular right untouched and sacred."

Spread hastily throughout the state, and eagerly received, this memorial started such an avalanche of petitions to the legislature that the assessment bill was suffocated beneath them. Under the momentum of their voteless victory, Madison and his allies brought out of its pigeon hole the Bill for Religious Liberty which Jefferson had drafted in 1779 as part of the (as yet unenacted) revisal of state laws. Both in substance and history, the bill represented a statutory implementation of Madison's 1776 constitutional guarantee. It wrote into law the specific protections asked for in the petitions of Virginia Dissenters, which they as well as Madison regarded as implicit in the rights of conscience. Designed by Jefferson to destroy the tithe system and other privileges by anathema as well as by prohibition, it fitted perfectly into the reaction against all religious assessments. "To compel a man to furnish contributions of money for the propagation of opinions which he disbelieves," said the preamble, "is sinful and tyrannical." Neither should he be compelled to support the teachers of his own religious persuasion. By this law, religious tests for office were abolished, old laws against heresy were overridden, and it was guaranteed that no man should be compelled to "frequent or support any religious worship, place or minister whatsoever." The vital clauses of the bill passed without a single alteration, Madison wrote to Jefferson in Paris, "and I flatter myself have in this country extinguished forever the ambitious hope of making laws for the human mind."[10]

Two facts, significant for the future, stand out in this fight against religious assessments. Over and over, Madison termed tax support "an establishment of religion." He also regarded any compulsory contribution to religion, through taxes, as a violation of the individual taxpayer's religious liberty. Hence financial support of religion was unconstitutional if the basic law either forbade an establishment of religion or guaranteed the rights of conscience.

This same issue arose about the same time in the federal field, but far

[10] William W. Hening, *Statutes at Large, being a collection of all the laws of Virginia, from the first session of the legislature in 1619* (Richmond, 1819-1823), XII, 84; Madison to Jefferson, January 22, 1786, *Writings,* II, 214-226.

less pointedly, when a committee of the Confederation Congress offered a western land ordinance which set aside one section in each township for public schools and one section for the support of religion. A vote in the full Congress striking out the religious grant led Madison to write in 1785: "How a regulation so unjust in itself, so foreign to the authority of Congress, so hurtful to the sale of public land, and smelling so strongly of an antiquated bigotry, could have received the countenance of a committee is truly matter of astonishment."[11] The Articles of Confederation contained no specific bar to government support of religion. He did not question the power of Congress to make a grant for public schools in the western territories. The religious grant was regarded as unconstitutional because religion, in his view, was totally outside the cognizance of civil authority.

In the Federal Convention of 1787, Madison took no part in the brief debate over a bill of rights. Impatience to adjourn, he remarked later, was a factor in the scant attention paid to George Mason's demand for guarantees of liberty in the new Constitution. The omission, however, had to be defended when Mason and Patrick Henry, in their campaign against ratification, made it a foremost issue in the Virginia convention of 1788. The discussion centered there on trial by jury and freedom of the press, but Madison made a detailed reply to Henry's alarum (directed chiefly at the Baptists) over the absence of any clause making religion secure. Now, however, depreciating instead of emphasizing the value and validity of a religious guarantee, he pointed to the reckless readiness of legislatures to override the constitutional provision he himself had written for Virginia. Would that state's bill of rights "exempt the people from paying for the support of one particular sect, if such sect were exclusively established by law?" It would be a poor protection, if a majority of the people were of one sect. Religious freedom, he asserted (following Voltaire), "arises from that multiplicity of sects, which pervades America, and which is the best and only security for religious liberty in any society." There was not a shadow of right in the general government to intermeddle with religion. "Its least interference with it would be a most flagrant usurpation"; moreover, as a simple matter of fact, the United States abounded in such a variety of sects that no one of them would be able to overreach that bar and persecute the rest.[12]

[11] *Journals of the Continental Congress,* April 23, 1785; Madison to Monroe, May 29, 1785, *Writings,* II, 143-145.

[12] Madison, *Writings,* V, 176.

To insure ratification of the new federal charter, Madison and his lieutenants finally promised to help plant a bill of rights in it through amendments to be submitted by Congress to the states. Had this promise not been given, he wrote to Richard Peters of Pennsylvania, the Constitution "would have been *certainly* rejected." Patrick Henry then offered a sheaf of twenty libertarian articles for recommendation to Congress by the convention. For strategic reasons, Madison ignored the obnoxious wording of the religious clause, which first guaranteed the rights of conscience and then furnished a loophole for financial support of all churches by providing that "no particular religious sect or society ought to be favored or established by law in preference to others."[18]

This half-hidden sabotage in the article on religious freedom was a warning to Madison of difficulties ahead, but the existing conditions made it a spur rather than a deterrent. A promise for a bill of rights had been given and (he wrote to Peters) "as an honest man I feel bound by this consideration." To Jefferson, who in the fall of 1787 had reacted violently against the omission of guarantees of liberty from the new Constitution, Madison explained his position in detail after the Virginia convention adjourned: "My own opinion has always been in favor of a bill of rights; provided it be so framed as not to imply powers not meant to be included in the enumeration. At the same time I have never thought the omission a material defect, nor been anxious to supply it even by *subsequent* amendment, for any other reason than that it is anxiously desired by others."

To some extent, though not completely, he thought, these civil rights were reserved to the people by the manner in which the federal powers were granted. That and several other factors reduced the importance of the bill of rights in his eyes: "There is great reason to fear that a positive declaration of some of the most essential rights could not be obtained in the requisite latitude. I am sure that the rights of conscience in particular, if submitted to public definition would be narrowed much more than they are likely ever to be by an assumed power."

No less was the danger that declared rights, especially that of religious freedom, would be overridden by governments which were the instrument of an impassioned majority opinion:

> In Virginia I have seen the bill of rights violated in every instance where it has been opposed to a popular current. Notwithstanding the explicit pro-

[18] Jonathan Elliot, *Debates* (Washington, 1836), III, 657-659.

vision contained in that instrument for the rights of conscience, it is well known that a religious establishment would have taken place in that state, if the legislative majority had found as they expected, a majority of the people in favor of the measure; and I am persuaded that if a majority of the people were now of one sect, the measure would still take place and on narrower ground than was then proposed, notwithstanding the additional obstacle which the law has since created.[14]

Madison's desire for a protective clause became more acute when he went home from the Confederation Congress at the end of 1788 and found that to defeat him for the new House of Representatives Patrick Henry's lieutenants were telling the Baptists that he had "ceased to be a friend to the rights of conscience." To the Reverend George Eve, his chief Baptist supporter, he wrote at once that it was his sincere opinion that the Constitution ought to be revised, and the first Congress should submit amendments covering "all essential rights, particularly the rights of conscience in the fullest latitude, the freedom of the press, trials by jury, security against general warrants, etc."[15]

In his paramount emphasis upon religious liberty as the core of all freedoms, Madison differed somewhat from Jefferson, whose mind centered on freedom of the press, trial by jury and habeas corpus, and from Mason, who was steeped in generalities about the original principles of government. So it was with first thought of a comprehensive clause on religion that Madison undertook to redeem the pledge he had given at the Virginia convention to have guarantees of liberty written into the Constitution. On June 8, 1789, he laid a bill of rights before Congress, including this clause: "The civil rights of none shall be abridged on account of religious belief or worship, nor shall any national religion be established, nor shall the full and equal rights of conscience be in any manner, or on any pretext, abridged."

A committee of which he was the No. 2 member (Vining of Delaware chairman), retained both of his major objectives in a shortened revision: "No religion shall be established by law, nor shall the equal rights of

[14] Jefferson to Madison, December 20, 1787, *Writings of Thomas Jefferson,* VI, 385-393; Madison to Jefferson, October 17, 1788, *Writings,* V, 269-275; Madison to Richard Peters, August 19, 1789, Library of Congress, Acq. 1226D1. The law referred to was the Statute of Religious Liberty.

[15] Madison to George Eve, January 2, 1789, *Writings,* V, 319*n.*

conscience be infringed." To a New York congressman who feared that this tended to abolish religion, Madison explained its meaning: "Congress should not establish a religion, and enforce the legal observation of it by law, nor compel men to worship God in any manner contrary to their conscience." From another quarter fear was expressed that it would close the federal courts to suits to collect contributions pledged to churches, since financial support "might be construed into a religious establishment." To meet this apprehension, Madison suggested that the word "national" be inserted before "religion." "He believed that the people feared one sect might obtain a pre-eminence, or two combine together and establish a religion to which they would compel others to conform. He thought if the word 'national' was introduced it would point the amendment directly to the object it was intended to prevent."

Madison withdrew the latter motion when it was pointed out that Antifederalists associated the word "national" with the abolition of state governments. The House then approved a wording offered by Livermore of New Hampshire and modeled after a proposal by that state's ratifying convention: "Congress shall make no laws touching religion, or infringing the rights of conscience."

This broad but ambiguous clause gave way a few days later to a substitute offered by Fisher Ames of Massachusetts: "Congress shall make no law establishing religion, or to prevent the free exercise thereof, or to infringe the rights of conscience."

It is probable that Madison wrote the Ames version and resorted to his common device of submitting it through another. Besides definitely limiting the prohibition to acts of Congress, it deviated from the committee version only by the insertion of language taken from Madison's speech explaining the original proposition. Ames, up to this time, had done nothing but jeer at the whole subject of a bill of rights in his private letters. However, he would have been ready enough to co-operate in promoting a change which would both attain Madison's objective and relieve the fear of New Englanders that the constitutional amendment might interfere with their established state churches.[16]

When the clause reached the United States Senate it passed into the

[16] *Annals of Congress* (House), June 8, August 13, 15, 20, 1789; Fisher Ames to George Minot, June 12, 1789, *Works of Fisher Ames,* edited by Seth Ames (Boston, 1854), I, 53-54.

hands of enemies. Senator Richard Henry Lee of Virginia had been an all-out supporter of the 1784 religious assessment bill.[17] Grayson of the same state was his Antifederalist ally. The clause which the Senate approved and sent back to the House bore all the earmarks of a combination between the established churches of North and South—the Congregationalists and Episcopalians. It protected religious creeds but left the way open to federal financial aid to religion by providing that Congress should "make no law establishing articles of faith or a mode of worship or prohibiting the free exercise of religion." Both of the provisions on which Madison relied for complete separation of state and church were gone.

Madison was chairman of the House members of the conference committee on the Bill of Rights. Since his associates, Vining and Sherman, had shown no interest in the clause on religion, and since the House won a complete victory in conference, there can be little or no doubt that Madison shaped the final draft which came from the committee and became a part of the Constitution. Broadening the previous language of the House and adding the useful part of the Senate clause, it reads: "Congress shall make no law respecting an establishment of religion or prohibiting the free exercise thereof."

When this and the other provisions of the Bill of Rights came before the Virginia legislature for ratification, it ran afoul of the Antifederalist campaign to sabotage the new government through substantive amendments. The House voted almost unanimously for ratification. In the Senate, by a vote of eight to seven, four amendments were stricken out of the House resolution, including the one on freedom of religion and the press. The eight opposition senators then published a signed statement, alleging that the clause on religion did not protect the rights of conscience. It did indeed, they said, forbid establishment of a national religion, but Congress might "levy taxes to any amount for the support of religion or its teachers."

Strangely enough, every senator who had a notorious record of opposition to religious liberty was among the eight who voted against the article and complained that it was not drastic enough. Every conspicuous defender of religious liberty voted to ratify. The explanation can be found in a letter written to Madison by Hardin Burnley, House member from Orange County. The opposition in the Senate, said Burnley, did not result

[17] Richard Henry Lee to Madison, November 26, 1784, *Letters of Richard Henry Lee,* edited by James C. Ballagh (New York, 1911-1914), II, 304-307.

from dissatisfaction with the amendments, but from an apprehension "that the adoption of them at this time will be an obstacle to the chief object of their pursuit, the amendment on the subject of direct taxation." In other words, the most popular amendments were defeated in order to throw the whole subject back on Congress, with a resulting chance to secure a new amendment emasculating the taxing power, and the project was furthered by a public appeal designed to frighten the Baptists and other opponents of religious assessments. Madison predicted that the Senate's obstructive course would recoil on the authors of it rather than inspire the public to a new attack on the Constitution.

"One of the principal leaders of the Baptists," he wrote to George Washington, "lately sent me word that the amendments had entirely satisfied the disaffected of his sect and that it would appear in their subsequent conduct."[18] And so it proved not only in Virginia, but in the other states when the ten amendments became part of the fundamental law in 1791.

What did Madison believe he had obtained in the religious guarantee of the First Amendment? If an establishment of religion covered what he said it did in his "Memorial and Remonstrance," the amendment insured a total separation of church and state in the federal field, including a ban on all forms of financial assistance to religious bodies. But in soothing the fears of congressmen in 1789, he had said in debate that the people feared the pre-eminence of one sect, or that two sects would combine to establish a religion, and the purpose was to prevent Congress from establishing "a national religion." In telling what the people feared, did he cover the entire purpose and effect of the article, as he saw it, or did he confine his explanation to that portion of its scope which was certain to win the needed support of New England congressmen?

There is no need to guess at the answer, for Madison has given it himself. One year later, in 1790, he explained why, in an amendment to the census bill, he had excluded professional men from an enumeration by occupations: "As to those who are employed in teaching and inculcating the duties of religion, there may be some indelicacy in singling them out, as the general government is proscribed from interfering, in any manner

[18] Hardin Burnley to Madison, November 28, December (misdated November) 5, 1789, Madison MSS, Library of Congress; Madison to Washington, November 20, 1789, *Writings,* V, 425-429; Madison to Washington, January 4, 1790, Madison MSS, Library of Congress. For the records of individual state senators, see Brant, *Madison,* III, Chapter XXII, note 16.

whatever, in matters respecting religion; and it may be thought to do this, in ascertaining who [are] and who are not ministers of the gospel."[19]

Here was the broadest conceivable definition of the constitutional guarantee, made publicly by the author of the amendment to the same group of men who had approved it. Nobody challenged his statement. The question of financial support of religion came squarely before Madison as President when Congress in 1811 passed a bill granting certain lands to a Baptist church at Salem, Mississippi. There was ample warrant for the legislation, in simple justice. The church had been accidentally built on public land through an error in surveying, and the grant was designed to correct the error through a trivial gift. But Madison saw a momentous future issue in the question of power to do so. He vetoed the measure "Because the bill in reserving a certain parcel of land of the United States for the use of said Baptist church comprises a principle and precedent for the appropriation of funds of the United States for the use and support of religious societies, contrary to the article of the Constitution which declares that 'Congress shall make no law respecting a religious establishment.' "[20]

A week earlier he had vetoed a bill to incorporate a church within the District of Columbia, holding that this too was an establishment of religion within the meaning of the Constitution. In both of his veto messages, Madison misquoted the Constitution by using the phrase "a religious establishment" instead of "an establishment of religion." This was a significant accident. In two recent cases before the Supreme Court, lawyers upholding the power of government to support religious schools contended that the First Amendment was weakened when the words "make no law establishing religion" were changed to "make no law respecting an establishment of religion." Instead of being broadened by the word "respecting," they argued, the amendment was reduced from a ban on the *establishing* of religion to the prohibition of "a religious *establishment,*" the drafter having in mind "The Establishment" of England. That is, Congress was forbidden to set up a full-fledged state church. Madison's misquotation of the Constitution, however, makes it plain that he gave the word "establishment" the same meaning in both phrases, and made

[19] *Annals of Congress* (House), January 25, February 2, 1790; Madison to Jefferson, February 14, 1790, *Letters and Other Writings of James Madison* (Philadelphia, 1865), I, 507.

[20] James D. Richardson, *A Compilation of the Messages and Papers of the Presidents* (Washington, 1896-1899), I, 490.

both of them synonymous with the ban on "establishing" religion. Any federal financial aid whatsoever to religious institutions would be unconstitutional under any of the wordings, as interpreted by Madison.[21]

During Madison's lifetime there was no federal bar to support of religion by individual states. That prohibition came into being as a by-product of the Fourteenth Amendment, which forbids any state to deprive any person of life, liberty or property without due process of law. In opinions which gained strength gradually through the years, the Supreme Court held that religious liberty, as defined in the First Amendment, is a right protected by the Fourteenth.[22] Thus a prohibition originally directed against Congress alone became binding on state governments also. This was a belated fulfillment of one of Madison's objectives. In the sheaf of amendments which he first submitted to Congress in 1789, No. 5 provided that *no state* should violate the equal rights of conscience, freedom of the press or trial by jury in criminal cases. This, he told the House, was the most valuable of the whole list, but he did not arouse the New Englanders by saying why.[23] In the earlier Virginia fight, he had described the guarantee of equal rights of conscience as a bar to the legal establishment of religion. This proposed federal amendment, if interpreted in line with his views, would have disestablished state churches throughout the Union. It passed the House, but was killed in the Senate.

Religious freedom as a state issue came before Madison in a minor way when he collaborated with Jefferson in creating and organizing the University of Virginia. Theological professorships were almost universal in colleges, and there was a general expectation in church circles that part of the money provided by the legislature to support the university would go to a chair of religion. Opposed to this course and believing it contrary to the Declaration of Rights, but not wishing to raise a public controversy,

[21] *Ibid,* 489-490 (Madison's veto); Everson v. Board of Education, U. S. Supreme Court, October term 1946 (No. 52), brief *amici curiae* of the National Council of Catholic Men and National Council of Catholic Women, 25-26; People of Illinois ex rel. McCollum v. Board of Education, October term 1947 (No. 90), appellees' brief, 56-59.

[22] Dissenting opinions of Justice Field and Justice Harlan in O'Neil v. Vermont, 144 U.S. 323 (1892); Harlan's dissenting opinions in Maxwell v. Dow, 176 U.S. 581 (1900) and Twining v. New Jersey, 211 U.S. 78 (1908); Gitlow v. New York, 268 U.S. 652 (1925); Grosjean v. American Press Co., 297 U.S. 233 (1936); Cantwell v. Connecticut, 310 U.S. 296 (1940); Murdock v. Pennsylvania, 319 U.S. 105 (1943); Everson v. Board of Education, 330 U.S. 1 (1947); Illinois ex rel. McCollum v. Board of Education, 333 U.S. 203 (1948).

[23] *Annals of Congress* (House), August 17, 1789.

Jefferson and Madison induced the Board of Visitors to omit theological professorships. To forestall or at least to reduce the expected criticisms (as Madison explained it to Edward Everett in 1823) the Visitors were "merely authorized to open a public hall for religious occasions, under *impartial* regulations; with the [additional] opportunity to the different sects to establish theological schools so near that the students of the University may respectively attend the religious exercises in them." Or the young men could attend church in the nearby village of Charlottesville. The Board of Visitors' report to the legislature, written by Jefferson, described this proposed arrangement with an enthusiasm for pious exercises not ordinarily expressed by him. His approval of it was cited to the Supreme Court in the recent McCollum case as a justification of the "released time" system of religious teachings in public schools. Madison's letters make it plain, however, that he and Jefferson were employing a lesser evil to escape the greater one. The Fourteenth Amendment being half a century in the future, they had no federal constitutional barrier to help them escape the dilemma. Madison summarized the situation to Everett in these words: "A University with sectarian professorships, becomes, of course, a sectarian monopoly; with professorships of rival sects, it would be an arena of theological gladiators. Without any such professorships, it may incur for a time at least, the imputation of irreligious tendencies, if not designs. The last difficulty was thought more manageable than either of the others."[24]

Two years later he wrote to Frederick Beasley that "public opinion seems now to have yielded" to the incompatibility of theological professorships with a *state* institution. He repeated his account of the use of a public hall for religious exercises which students were free to attend or not as they chose, and said that it presented some difficulties but seemed the best plan of escaping the other problem. At the age of 82, in correspondence with the Reverend Jasper Adams, principal of Charleston College, South Carolina, he reaffirmed his lifelong position by roundly asserting the benefits of a complete separation of religion from all the workings of civil government, except for the preservation of order and the protection of each sect against trespass on its legal rights.[25]

[24] Madison to Edward Everett, March 19, 1823, *Writings,* IX, 124-130; Report of Board of Visitors, University of Virginia, to the president and directors of the Literary Fund (i.e. to the legislature), October 7, 1822, *Writings of Thomas Jefferson,* XIX, 410-416.

[25] Madison to Frederick Beasley, December 22, 1824, *Writings,* I, 210-213; Madison to "Rev. Adams, Charleston S. C.," 1832, *ibid.,* IX, 484-488. Adams sent Madison

It was in his "Essay on Monopolies,"[26] written some time after he retired from the presidency, that Madison most clearly demonstrated the consistency and vigor of his views on separation of church and state, and the broad scope he gave to the First Amendment. Condemning all monopolies except those granted for a limited time to authors and inventors, he warned against the "silent accumulations and encroachments by ecclesiastical bodies." The American states, he said, "have the noble merit of first unshackling the conscience from persecuting laws, and of establishing among religious sects a legal equality." If some states had not gone as far as they should, all of them could instruct the most enlightened states of the old world, "and there is one state at least, Virginia, where religious liberty is placed on its true foundation and is defined in its full latitude."

In the Virginia Statute of Religious Liberty, said Madison, the separation between human laws and natural rights is traced as distinctly as words can admit, and the limits of political authority are established with as much solemnity as the forms of legislation can express. States which retained "any aberration from the sacred principle of religious liberty" should "revise and purify" their systems, making themselves "pure and complete" examples of "freedom of the mind." He then outlined the perils of any measures short of this.

"Strongly guarded as is the separation between religion and government in the Constitution of the United States," asserted Madison, "the danger of encroachment by ecclesiastical bodies may be illustrated by precedents already furnished in their short history." He told of his veto, as President, of bills to incorporate one church and make a land grant to another. The most notable encroachment, he asserted, was that attempted in Virginia, "to establish a general assessment for the support of all Chris-

a printed copy of his sermon before a convention, on the relationship of Christianity to civil government, and asked for his comments on it. The Reverend Jasper Adams was principal and professor of moral and political philosophy of Charleston College, whose trustees included Episcopalian, Congregational and German Lutheran ministers. His zeal for public support of church schools may have been connected with the fact that his own college, after a long shutdown due to lack of funds, had reopened in 1824 and a year later came into competition with the state-supported South Carolina College. Adams then undertook a difficult but successful campaign to raise money for a new building. See Charleston City Directory for 1835-1836, pp. 146-147, 158.

[26] "Monopolies, Perpetuities, Corporations, Ecclesiastical Endowments," in "Madison's 'Detached Memoranda,'" edited by Elizabeth Fleet, *William and Mary Quarterly*, 3d. ser., III (1946), 551-562; Gaillard Hunt, ed., "Aspects of Monopoly One Hundred Years Ago," *Harper's Magazine*, CXXVII (1914), 489.

tian sects." He condemned the excessive wealth of ecclesiastical corporations in Europe, and asked whether the United States was awake to the dangerous tendency of "the multiplied incorporations of religious congregations," many of them unlimited either in duration or in the amount of property they might acquire and hold. Returning then to the Constitution, Madison asked whether the appointment of chaplains to the two houses of Congress was consistent with it, or with the pure principle of religious freedom:

> In strictness the answer on both points must be in the negative. The Constitution of the United States forbids everything like an establishment of a national religion. The law appointing chaplains establishes a religious worship for the national representatives, to be performed by ministers of religion, elected by a majority of them; and those are to be paid out of the national taxes. Does not this involve the principle of a national establishment, applicable to a provision for a religious worship for the constituent as well as of the representative body, approved by the majority, and conducted by ministers of religion paid by the entire nation.

In addition to the conflict with constitutional principles, the essayist contended, the establishment of congressional chaplainships was "a palpable violation of equal rights." Election of chaplains by the majority "shut the door of worship against the members whose creeds and consciences forbid a participation in that of the majority. . . . Could a Catholic clergyman ever hope to be appointed a chaplain? To say that his religious principles are obnoxious or that his sect is small, is to lift the evil at once and exhibit in its naked deformity the doctrine that religious truth is to be tested by numbers, or that the major sects have a right to govern the minor."

Chaplainships in the army and navy, Madison thought, suffer from the same constitutional defect. He doubted, moreover, whether in their appointment, more heed was not given to the temporal interest of the shepherds than the spiritual interest of the flock. If there were situations, like that of navies with insulated crews, where his reflections did not wholly apply, we should nevertheless always "keep in mind that it is safer to trust the consequences of a right principle, than reasonings in support of a bad one." The chaplainships, he granted, were too well fixed to be disturbed. What then? Why, this step "beyond the landmarks of power" must not be treated as a legitimate precedent. Rather, "apply to it the legal aphorism de minimis non curat lex" (the law does not concern itself with trifles), or class it (this too was in Latin) with the blemishes which either carelessness has caused to spread or which human nature too little guards against.[27]

Religious proclamations by the executive, recommending thanksgivings and fasts, were classed by Madison as "shoots from the same root with the legislative acts reviewed. Although recommendations only, they imply a religious agency, making no part of the trust delegated to political rulers. . . . They seem to imply and certainly nourish the erroneous idea of a *national* religion." As President, he recalled, he had intended to issue no religious proclamations, following Jefferson's example in that respect. When this became known, (through his failure to invoke divine help in the War of 1812) Congress passed a resolution asking him to issue a proclamation. "It was thought not proper to refuse a compliance altogether; but a form and language were employed which were meant to deaden as much as possible any claim of political right to enjoin religious observances."

It is astonishing how many controversial questions of fact are answered in this "Essay on Monopolies." Within the last few years books, articles and Supreme Court briefs have said:

1. *That Madison did not intend the First Amendment to be as broad as the Virginia Statute of Religious Liberty, nor to ban tax support of religion.* In the "Essay on Monopolies" he presents both the First Amendment and the Virginia statute as complete guarantees of the separation of church and state, and cites the Virginia assessment bill as the most notable warning of the danger of ecclesiastical encroachment on the federal guarantee.

2. *That the appointment and payment of congressional chaplains is proof of constitutional power to support churches and church schools through taxation.* Madison cites their establishment as a violation of the Constitution—one which can perhaps be disregarded as trivial or the result of negligence, but must never be allowed to "have the effect of a legitimate precedent."

3. *That the presence of the term "national religion" in Madison's first version of the First Amendment, and his suggestion that the word "national" be inserted in a later version, prove that he was aiming only*

[27] Cum maculis quas aut incuria fudit, aut humana parum cavit natura.

at prohibition of the establishment of a national church. But in the "Essay on Monopolies" he discusses the First Amendment as if the word "national" were still in it, yet continues to give it the utmost scope. Chaplainships are said to be unconstitutional because the Constitution "forbids everything like an establishment of a national religion." The naming and payment of chaplains "involve the principle of a national establishment." The President, in his opinion, has no constitutional power to proclaim a day of religious attendance, because it implies or nourishes "the erroneous idea of a *national* religion."

Whatever inconsistencies there may be in Madison's position on other public questions, none can be found in his record upon freedom of religion. As a boy defending jailed Baptist ministers, as a young legislator helping to frame the Virginia Declaration of Rights, as a defender of his state against the devotees of religious establishments, as a member of Congress drafting the national Bill of Rights, as a President enforcing it, and as an elder statesman surveying the country from a Virginia farm, he never once narrowed his objective, and never ceased to think of the dangers that lurked in small deviations. His opinion of the Virginia Statute of Religious Liberty, which he regarded as co-extensive with the First Amendment, reveals the spirit in which he approached every phase of his lifelong self-appointed task, and stands as his permanent message to the American people: "This act is a true standard of religious liberty: its principle the great barrier against usurpations on the rights of conscience. As long as it is respected and no longer, these will be safe. Every provision for them short of this principle, will be found to leave crevices at least through which bigotry may introduce persecution; a monster, that feeding and thriving on its own venom, gradually swells to a size and strength overwhelming all laws divine and human."[28]

[28] "Monopolies, Perpetuities, Corporations, Ecclesiastical Endowments," 551-562.

Part VIII
Political Parties

[18]

THE MADISONIAN SYSTEMS

JOHN ZVESPER
University of East Anglia

"*. . . there would always have to be in the city something possessing the same understanding of the regime as you, the lawgiver, had when you were setting down the laws.*" — Plato, *The Republic*, 497c-d.

JAMES MADISON is widely although somewhat inaccurately known as the "Father of the Constitution" and the founder of pluralism in American political science. He is equally although less widely known as one of the founders of the American party system and an advocate of a more participatory and communitarian theory of politics. Both of these characterizations are well founded. The first is based largely on Madison's career up to 1789, particularly his collaboration with Alexander Hamilton and co-authorship of the *Federalist Papers*; these were the activities connected with what political scientists usually call the "Madisonian system," the theory of which is best known from *Federalist* 10. The second derives from Madison's conduct in the 1790s and his writings for the Republican press, activities which helped to establish a very different political system. The party system is a second Madisonian system, which contradicts the first in both theory and practice. The pluralism of Madison the Federalist favored the multiplication of social and economic interests, in order to facilitate competent governmental control and direction of these interests. The party system of Madison the Republican displayed more confidence in the political competence of citizens outside government, and favored the consolidation of social "interests and affections" to control and direct government. Such consolidation is one of the characteristic purposes of modern political parties, and Madison, one of the leaders of the first such party, clearly understood this (*Writings* 6:67-69; Riemer 1954a and 1954b: 37; Zvesper 1977: 110-19; Jaenicke 1980). The case for pluralism was a case for a system of groups in which (as *Federalist* 10 presupposes) there are no overarching parties, or in which any overarching parties are ideologically promiscuous instruments of consensus. The case for a party system was primarily a case for strong party government, with party (the singular is more appropriate) as a participatory instrument of democratic choice. Both of the major schools of modern democratic theory — both pluralist and participatory democrats — are legitimate heirs of Madison. Both of the major American political parties can trace their origins to Madison.

Madison can be admired for his inventiveness. But what are we to make of his inconsistency? How should this great contradiction in Madison's political theory and practice be understood? Political scientists have generally been tempted to resolve the contradiction by treating the Madison of *Federalist* 10 as the worthier of their consideration, while historians have tended to suggest that Madison's Republican partisanship was more characteristic of the man and his basic political loyalties. Can the political scientists' Madison and the historians' Madison be reconciled?

I shall argue that the circumstances of Madison's use of his main Federalist argument suggest that he consciously deployed political theories to extract their rhetorical usefulness. A broad sketch of Madison's apparently contradictory career will also provide evidence (again suggestive rather than definitive) in favor of this contention. I suggest not that Madison was merely a cynical rhetorician, skillfully manipulating partisan slogans, but that his political vision comprehended the limits of both of the theories that he expressed. He did not emphasize these limits in his public rhetoric, but his comprehension of them controlled his publicly observable attachment to the theories, making him more susceptible than most politicians to the charge of inconsistency.

Interpreting Madison's Contradictions

Madison's enemies have always explained his contradictory words and deeds by saying that they resulted from his defective character and second-rate political abilities (Hamilton, *Papers*, 11: 426-43; Lodge 1892: 47-74). And even Madison's most admiring biographers have found it difficult to explain the way in which his career can be understood as that of a first-rate politician, because they have found it difficult to understand and to articulate the consistency that they have felt in his contradictory career (Hunt 1902: 211-12; Brant 1950: ch. 23 and 1952).

Adrienne Koch (1966: 117-18) tried to explain Madison's contradictions by pointing to changes in circumstances. Like other observers, she noted that in the last part of his career he switched back to an almost Hamiltonian view of federal power. Her explanation of Madison's two great switches was based on the observation that in the 1790s his fear had been "twofold": "that an extension of [federal] power so early in the history of the Republic would establish dangerous precedents with no limits and undermine the constitutional enterprise of limiting federal government," and "that Hamilton had little concern for popular sovereignty." Once the first fear had diminished with the passage of time, and the second and "more substantial" fear that national ends would be advanced by Hamilton's undemocratic means had been removed by the removal of Hamiltonians from power, Madison could take up once more the cause of nationalism. This circumstantial explanation is similar to the view that Madison's contradictions were simply a result of historical drift (Burns 1938: 58-59, 200), but it is superior to that view because it allows that Madison was a swimmer, sometimes with the drift and sometimes against it. However, it does not take into account the logical abyss between Madison's two positions. Even Koch's summary of Madison's "twofold" fear suggests a depth in his contradiction that she did not notice: the fear of Hamiltonian methods leads in the direction of the strong democratic government of a party system; the fear of unlimited government leads in the direction of the Madisonian system of liberty through pluralism. It is true that Madison advocated both, but it is questionable whether they are easily reconcilable.

A similar point can be made about one of the most comprehensive surveys of Madison's politics, by Neal Riemer (1954b: 34-43; 1967: 146). Riemer analyzed some of the elements of Madison's divergent views and policies, but applauded his successful "blending" of these elements:

> . . . although Madison, in his diagnosis of faction, emphasizes the "worst side" of man, his over-all cure [including "his concept of republican opposition"] balances the picture by presenting man's better side, without which — as Madison clearly recognized — republicanism cannot endure. The total effect is a balanced picture of man, the only basis for a constructive, creative, and enduring political theory.

Riemer saw certain residual imperfections in Madison's solution to the problem of balancing pessimism against optimism, the restraint of pluralist liberty against the initiative of party democracy. For example, he had a New Dealer's reservations about Madison's "negative" interpretation of presidential power — reservations which suggest that Riemer himself preferred Madison the optimistic party democrat to Madison the pessimistic pluralist. However, he concluded rather sanguinely that Madison's political philosophy solved the fundamental problem of politics — the problem of faction — "without destroying liberty or impairing authority. Justice and limited government are preserved without sacrificing republican rights and popular rule." It is too generous to credit Madison with the solution to this problem simply because he recognized it as a problem and analyzed it in elegant essays. Or perhaps one should say that it would be even more generous to credit Madison with the capacity to realize that the political elements could never be blended quite so smoothly and finally as Riemer suggested, because these ingredients are more incompatible than Riemer imagined. A blend requires a recipe with guiding principles, and Riemer could not say what these were.

One of the most searching examinations of Madison's inconsistencies in recent scholarship is that of Marvin Meyers (1973: xli-xlv). Meyers concluded that, although there are good explanations for some of Madison's contradictions, especially for those involved in his second switch, there was

> undoubtedly a change in Madisonian principles [in the 1790s] that could be reconciled with his earlier analysis only by straining words. . . . Most dramatically, the analysis of *Federalist* 10 disappeared for a season. . . . Madison changed his earlier views for a modified version of Antifederalism. If he was historically justified, he must have been nevertheless theoretically embarrassed, for his previous case had rested not upon temporary circumstance but on the general nature of man and society under free government
>
> The case, is, I think, that Madison in opposition subordinated his subtle and powerful political analytics to a simpler statesman's rule of thumb.

Meyers had more appreciation than many previous commentators for the irreducible contradiction between Madison the Federalist and Madison the Republican. Yet he seems to have returned to the judgment of Madison's enemies that Madison the Federalist was theoretically superior. The Madison who produced so much anti-Federalist theory and propaganda was an aberration, understandable but a little suspect.

Very able admirers of Madison thus join his detractors in failing to pay sufficient attention to the possibility that Madison's political consistency resided in his skeptical and therefore inconsistent reliance on two political theories each of which is only partially true, and which are too contradictory to be combined. It would be difficult to demonstrate that this is the proper way to appreciate Madison's career. If Madison had furnished us with conclusive evidence that this is what he had in mind, by saying so, he would have given the game away. As Gaillard Hunt pointed out, Madison "was a self-contained man, and the hidden current of his hopes, fears and ambitions he disclosed to no one, and we must judge him by what he said and did and by his surroundings." Demonstrative proof may be out of reach, but the suggested possibility seems probable when one pays close attention to the way in which Madison developed and used his two theories. Because political scientists tend to identify Madison with his pluralist theory, and because they generally fail to notice the reasons for the inadequacy of the theory, this article will concentrate on Madison's development and use of that theory, although it will conclude by questioning the wisdom of the historians' tendency to identify Madison with his republican party theory.

The Purpose of the Extended Republic Argument

Madison's contributions to the improved "science of politics" announced by Hamilton in *Federalist* 9 concerned both the character of modern society and the institutions of enlightened government. However, Madison's arguments in the *Federalist Papers* depend finally more on his social analysis (*Federalist* 10) than on his institutional observations. The politico-economic pluralism of American society was expected to weaken the force of interest groups and thereby to make enlightened government more feasible, while the partial separation of governmental powers and attendant checks and balances were expected to help ensure that government would do the things that social pluralism made it more possible to do. But Madison recognized that these "auxiliary precautions" — the separation of powers, coupled with bicameralism, the executive veto, and federalism — were ultimately dependent on the "primary control on government," popular election, and therefore on the character of the electorate. As Hamilton had already noted in *Federalist* 28, representation "is the essential, and, after all, the only efficacious security for the rights and privileges of the people which is attainable in civil society." One consequence of this is that the legislative branch of government "necessarily predominates." This statement in *Federalist* 51, the culmination of Madison's discussion of the major auxiliary precaution, the separation of powers, suggests that in the long run, one cannot place too much reliance on the merely auxiliary precautions, so Madison ends by reconsidering the social diversification that he had previously described in *Federalist* 10 as the only way to ensure that the "primary control" itself will be reliable. This is why the end of *Federalist* 51 returns to the argument of *Federalist* 10. As Madison admits in *Federalist* 57, the representative and institutional devices that he relies upon to procure wise and virtuous representatives and to keep them virtuous are the same kind of prudential device already used in the state governments; the republican superiority of the new Constitution lies less in its perfection of these devices than in the extensiveness of the territory of the union in comparison to that of each state. The constitutional structure, if it is to remain republican — that is, if it is not to be based on "a will in the community independent of . . . the society itself" (*Federalist* 51) — must depend on the character of this more extensive society. Therefore the social analysis of *Federalist* 10, pessimistic as it is, is nevertheless the keystone of Madison's Federalist science of politics. *Federalist* 10 is the anchor of republican liberty to which Madison's chain of constitutional safeguards is attached (Diamond 1972: 639-40, 646-47).

The case for the "extended republic" in *Federalist* 10 is based on consideration of "the two great points of difference" between a pure democracy and a representative republic, points from which most advantage can be drawn, it is claimed, in large republics. A republic, especially a large one, can include a great number and variety of interest groups, "which renders . . . factious combinations . . . more difficult." The second claim is that the larger size of constituencies in large republics makes it "more difficult for unworthy candidates to practise with success the vicious arts by which elections are too often carried." Both claims rely on the "reprobated axiom of tyrannies," divide and rule (*Papers*, 10: 214): in a divided, pluralistic constituency it is easier for a worthy representative to maneuver and to survive, and in a divided, pluralistic society it is easier for a worthy government to resist the pressure of individual interests.

Examination of the development of this reasoning in Madison's thought will show that, except in the *Federalist Papers*, Madison did not place as much weight on this argument as most commentators have supposed. This is a point in Madison's favor, because the logic of the "extended republic" argument is seriously flawed, as will be seen below. The flaw makes it more appropriate to use the argument in an *ad hoc* fashion, more as a rhetorical device than as a true principle. That Madison did so, and that he did so because he was aware of the flaw, is difficult to prove, but is at least compatible with the fact that less than three years after he developed and used that argument, he busied himself writing and publishing essays which analyzed and denounced that flaw.

Federalist 10 was published in the autumn of 1787. In a letter Madison wrote to Jefferson in March 1787 we can see the seedbed — but, significantly, not the seed — of the extended republic argument. In this letter, Madison (*Papers*, 9: 319) outlined the major changes which he thought should be made in the American system of governments. One of these changes was to arm "the federal head" (the general government) with positive powers of "regulating trade and sundry other matters in which uniformity is proper," and with the power of assenting to or vetoing all state legislation. Madison thought this "negative" power would entail "the participation of the Union in the making of the laws"[1] of individual states — an effect not far short of Alexander Hamilton's plan to give state governors, appointed by the general government, the job of reviewing all bills in state legislatures. This supervisory power would have four effects, Madison wrote to Jefferson. It would help make the general government "the federal head," by making its laws clearly superior to state legislation, to guard "national rights." It would guard "national interests"; the supervisory power would make the positive powers of the general government secure from "invasion by the states." It would make the general government a more effective "federal head," able to make the states cooperate with each other or at least to prevent them from "thwarting and molesting each other." Finally, the fourth and most important effect would be "to restrain the States . . . from oppressing the minority within themselves by paper money and other unrighteous measures which favor the interest of the majority."

The first three effects of the benevolent involvement of the general government in the legislative process of the states can be understood as aspects of that national tilt in the mixture of federal and national which Madison thought necessary in order to avoid a deadlock of federalism. He realized that ultimate political supremacy had to reside in "the federal head," to avoid "the evil of imperia in imperio,"[2] to make the system function as a political system rather than as a series of indecisive battles among states and between state and federal governments, ending either in disunion or in a forced consolidation of the union under a monarch. The key to Madison's understanding of federalism resembles his explanation in *Federalist* 48 and 51 of the key to the separation of powers. Just as the separation of powers in a government will not work unless the separate powers "are so far connected and blended as to give to each a constitutional control over the others," and unless one power (in republics, the legislative branch) ultimately "predominates," neither will the separation of general and local governments work without "a mutuality of dependence between the General and particular authorities," and "a controlling power" in "the federal head," "to prevent an appeal to the sword."[3] This is the great improvement on previous federal systems which Madison discovered, and which he (unsuccessfully) tried to persuade the Constitutional Convention to adopt. Without such an improvement, fed-

[1] Letter to George Washington, 16 April 1787 (*Papers*, 9: 384). See also Madison's speeches of 28 June and 17 July 1787 (*Papers*, 10: 80, 103).

[2] Letter to Thomas Jefferson, 24 October 1787 (*Papers*, 10: 209-12).

[3] Letters to George Washington, 16 April 1787, and to Thomas Jefferson, 24 October 1787; *Federalist* 39. See also Madison's speech of 6 June 1787 (*Papers*, 10: 35). Madison hoped that the new government's need to exercise a constitutionally expressed power of coercion over the states would be obviated by its participation in state legislation: letter to Washington, 16 April 1787, and speech of 31 May 1787 (*Papers*, 10: 21). Hobson (1979) provides a useful narrative of Madison's attempt to secure a national veto, but exaggerates Madison's nationalism when he refers to this veto as "a mechanism for transforming a confederate system into a national one." See note 10 below.

eral government was not true government; it was federalism, resting merely on the faith (*fides*) of the parties. Madison thought national judicial review — the Constitution's version of the controlling power — was a less appropriate form for this power to assume than his scheme of national legislative supervision, because the legislative power, being both prior to and more political than judicial review, was less likely to result in stalemate and "a recurrence to force."[4] But in either case, he could argue that placing the control in the general rather than in the particular governments was a matter of course, "a position not likely to be combated" (*Federalist* 39), once the necessity of such a control is admitted. In other words, Madison did not seem compelled to argue that the general government would be a better repository of the controlling power by arguig that it would be composed of wiser and more disinterested men.

However, Madison was less able to avoid making such an argument in connection with the fourth and most important effect he wanted from the supervisory power. Here it was no longer simply a question of harmonizing the operations of two levels of government. It was rather a case of seizing the opportunity afforded by the answer to that question, to attack a problem only indirectly related to that question — the problem of bad state legislation, which Madison said contributed more than the problems of the federal system "to that uneasiness which produced the Convention, and prepared the public mind for a general reform." Here it became a matter of showing "how private rights will be more secure under the Guardianship of the General Government than under the State Governments" (*Papers*, 10: 212). This was the task of the extended republic argument. But Madison did not yet make that argument, in his letter to Jefferson in March, in which he did already reveal his desire to have that task accomplished.

The Inadequacy of the Extended Republic Argument

It is not sufficiently recognized how inadequate the extended republic argument is to the task assigned to it. Briefly stated, the inadequacy is this: if a free society is as submerged in selfish faction as Madison's familiar argument suggests, then a republican government, derived from that society, is a utopian enterprise, devoid as such a government must be of concern for common interests; if statesmanship for the direction of that society is founded simply on a Machiavellian "love of fame" — the other suggestion typically made in Federalist writings — then the liberal republican character of the government, both its liberty and its dependence on

[4] Letter to Thomas Jefferson, 24 October 1787. Madison thought a Constitutional amendment banning states' violations of civil liberties was necessary to make the Supreme Court more effective in the function that had devolved to it, and was greatly disappointed not to have his proposal of such an amendment included in the Bill of Rights. The effects of the due process clause of the Fourteenth Amendment show how important Madison's proposed amendment would have been.

the will of society, becomes tenuous.[5] In *Federalist* 38, Madison admitted that while the variety of interests in the United States, "for reasons sufficiently explained in a former paper, may have a salutary influence on the administration of the government when formed, yet every one must be sensible of the contrary influence which must have been experienced in the task of forming it." But as students of Machiavelli or Plato would know, the virtues needed to acquire or to found a republic will be required again and again to maintain it, so if extensiveness and variety of interests contributed so little to the former, they could hardly be expected to contribute so much to the latter.

The problem inherent in the extended republic argument was noted by some of Madison's contemporaries. Alexander Hamilton (Madison's *Papers*, 10:34) recorded the inconclusive nature of what he called "Maddison's Theory" when he heard Madison explain it to the Philadelphia convention. For one thing, Hamilton doubted the absence of majority factions in the United States, in spite of the multiplication of factions through the enlargement of the sphere of government. Indeed, Madison's own claim was only that majority factions would be "less probable" in the extended republic (*Federalist* 10). Hamilton also noticed that the "process of election calculated to refine the representation of the People" in Madison's scheme failed to cancel the dominance of faction: "An influential demagogue will give an impulse to the whole. Demagogues are not always inconsiderable persons." Madison's assertion that larger constituencies will choose better representatives is not well argued; men with "the most diffusive and established characters" are not necessarily men who will be good "guardians of the public weal" (*Federalist* 10). Representatives forced to play off one faction against another will not for that reason be obliged or even encouraged to act for the public good. They

[5] This problem in Madison's pluralism has been noticed by Morgan (1974: 860), Zvesper (1977: 24-25), Jaffa (1977) and Erler (1980-81: 658-59). More commonly, Madison has been criticized (for example, by Schattschneider 1942; Dahl 1956; and Burns 1967) for adding unnecessary "auxiliary precautions" such as the separation of powers to the already reasonably adequate system of factional pluralism. For criticism of these critics, see Carey (1978), Wills (1981: Part Three), and Morgan (1981). Carey's view of Madison is superior to the critics' view, because he takes Madison's thoughts more seriously. But his response to the critics goes too far when it argues that the "auxiliary precautions" were addressed not to the problem of majority oppression tackled in *Federalist* 10, but (almost) solely to the problem of governmental tyranny — that is, the problem of governments acting in a self-directed manner, capriciously and arbitrarily, without inspiration from a majority faction. This makes Madison's thoughts on the separation of powers sound more like Jefferson than like "Publius." Cf. Diamond (1972: 641-47) for an account which shows how Madison (as well as Hamilton) used "auxiliary precautions" also to counter the danger of majority oppression, which was "the great object" (*Federalist* 10) of the Federalist science of politics. Diamond's analysis suggests that Madison's critics are wrong not so much because they mistake the purpose of Madison's "auxiliary precautions" as because they (like Carey 1978: 155, 163) overestimate the effectiveness of factional pluralism on its own. As Madison says, extensiveness means "less danger" of majority tyranny (*Federalist* 51); it does not mean no danger. (At the end of his article, pp. 161-62, Carey himself notices Madison's use of auxiliary precautions against majority oppression, but he seems to regard this as a somewhat redundant "bonus" from Madison's point of view.)

might simply be good log-rollers; worse, they might incite some factions into a coalition to victimize others, or they might exploit their relative freedom from factional pressure to act against the interest of all factions but their own. This leads to a third objection to Madison's argument: it is too negative and abstract. It erects plausible (though not wholly adequate) barriers to majority tyranny, but does not even suggest why one should expect positive, substantive, public-spirited policies to be more dependably originated in the extended republic. Madison urges that in the larger territory "a coalition of a majority of the whole society could seldom take place on any other principles than those of justice and the general good" (*Federalist* 51). Even granting the first half of this assertion, that majority factions will be infrequent, one must ask how non-factious forces favoring justice and the general good have suddenly appeared in the political arena. Madison recognizes that such forces are necessary, but it is difficult to see where they are to be nurtured in modern liberal societies, if such societies are accurately described as collections of factions "inflamed . . . with mutual animosity, and . . . much more disposed to vex and oppress each other than to co-operate for their common good" — factions over which "neither moral nor religious motives can be relied on as an adequate control" (*Federalist* 10). The sense of this third and most fundamental objection was expressed by an Antifederalist writer: "If the administrators of every government are actuated by views of private interest and ambition, how is the welfare and happiness of the community to be the result of such jarring adverse interests?"[6] Having abandoned a reliance on republican virtue ("moral motives"), Madison is hard pressed to show how government can be wise and virtuous and still republican, that is, still "derived from and dependent on the society" (*Federalist* 51).

It is therefore not surprising to find Madison privately reflecting that the government of the extended republic, in its supervision of state legislation, could play a role in the federal system similar to the role of a monarch in a mixed regime. The monarchy's independence of society and consequent neutrality make it immune to the characteristic evil of republican governments, of acting in the interests of one part of society in violation of the rights of another part. But how can a republican government imitate this independence without actually being independent and therefore non-republican? Monarchy is properly associated with the absence of politics, republicanism, and mixed regimes with its noisy presence.[7] Accordingly, it was only by emphasizing the negative side of the national supervision of legislation (for example, by referring to it always as the national "negative") that Madison's hope to combine republicanism and monarchy in the same offices could seem reasonable. It was only by denaturing the politics of the general government that Madison

[6] The immediate target of this writer was the mixed regime defended by John Adams, which betrayed the same weakness as the extended republic of factions (Kenyon 1966: 7).

[7] Consider the views of such varied authorities as Aristotle, *Politics*, Bk. III; Machiavelli, *Discourses*, Bk. I, Ch. 4-6; Hobbes, *Leviathan*, Ch. 21, 22, 25, 29; and Locke, *Second Treatise*, Ch. 6-7.

could argue with any plausibility that this government would be both republican and independent from the pressures of the factions of society. The extended republic is in a sense essentially monarchical! Even its limited operation in the supervision of state legislation would depend on the assumption that in that supervision there would be no politics at the national level. There is a contradiction between this assumption and the invigoration and extension of the political power of the general government which Madison was simultaneously advancing.

It is possible to defend Madison's project by assuming that a sharp distinction could be maintained between powers concerning matters of interest to the whole nation (which the central government's politicians can or must be trusted to deal with in a competent way even though they are elected by a faction-ridden society) and powers concerning local policy (which local politicians cannot be trusted to deal with because they are too dependent on the factions interested in the policies, but which the general politicians can be trusted to deal with because they will be impartial, more like judges than politicians, when exercising these powers). This defense is made questionable by Madison's preference for political supervision over judicial review. But in any case, the argument has come full circle. Madison had originally designed the supervisory power precisely as an "expedient" to cope with "the impossibility of dividing powers of legislation, in such a manner, as to be free from different constructions by different interests, or even from ambiguity in the judgement of the impartial" (*Papers*, 10: 211; *Federalist* 37). There was no argument here (although there may have been an unspoken assumption) that the general government would be more impartial than the states in distinguishing federal from local. But Madison went on to suggest the "happy effect" that the supervisory power would have on "the internal vicissitudes of State policy" (*Papers*, 9: 384), and this "happy effect" would depend on the possibility of that clear definition of power, the impossibility of which had made the supervisory power necessary in the first place! In making the case for the necessity of a national predominance in the combination of federal and national, Madison did not seem obliged to argue that an impartial character would be required in political representatives, any more than it could be found in their constituents. It was simply necessary that a decision be made on questions of conflict between general and local jurisdiction, and Madison argued not that the general authorities would be wise judges of such questions, but simply that they were better placed to be decision-makers. One could argue that even this half of Madison's project point in the direction of a fully political extended republic, with a demand — not to say a provision — for statesmanlike representatives in the general government. But the necessity for Madison to make such a provision is more evident in his extension of his demands on the supervisory power, from policing the border between federal and local to preventing local injustice. Before national representatives could act in either of these capacities, they would first have to decide in which capacity they were acting, so they would know whether to act as energetic federal republican politicians (possibly statesmanlike but not apolitically impartial) or as quasimonarchical, "neutral" judges. But that decision itself would be a controversial political decision, if the distinction between federal and local is as difficult to maintain but as necessary to decide as Madison said it is. It may be that if his scheme had been adopted by the Constitutional Convention, Madison would never have written *Federalist* 10; he might never have proclaimed the case for the extended republic and the "happy" fourth effect of the supervisory power. He might have let that effect operate accidentally, as it were, with no formal constitutional recognition. But this would not have ended the possibility of controversy.

Besides, what would have ensured the necessary element of impartiality in federal representatives when they were reviewing state laws? Even if it had been possible for them to determine when to be impartial, why should one have expected them to have either the capacity or the incentive to be so? The great defect of the extended republic is evident even if the "negative" power exercised against bad state laws could have been separated somehow from the politics of positive exercises of power and purely federal exercises of the "negative" power. There is no provision for a source of public-spirited statecraft. The multiplication of factions in the extended republic does not provide such a source, nor does it make it more likely that politicians who possess such statecraft, if they exist, would be elected. The case for the extended republic simply assumes the existence of such politicians, and unreasonably hopes they will find their way to political power. The extended republic may provide more scope than the smaller republic or pure democracy for worthy politicians — should they happen to appear on the scene — but it provides the same or perhaps even more scope for those "men of factious tempers, . . . or of sinister designs" who were recognized in *Federalist* 10 as the unworthy but all too often successful candidates for election. If Madison's characterization of modern, civilized societies as irredeemably factious is accepted, the case for the extended republic can be saved only by supplementing it with a case for an energetic executive, the leading feature of which would be an unrepublican independence from the will of society. Madison would soon be accusing Hamilton of attempting to fashion such a supplement. The alternative is the party system, which depends on the discovery or creation of a source of statecraft in society itself.

The super-political, monarchical tendency of the extended republic can be seen in its first surviving written version, in a paper on the "Vices of the Political System of the U.S." This paper, which was not published in Madison's lifetime, was one of his preparations for the Philadelphia Convention. Here Madison considered the problem of faction in the light of the differences not (as in *Federalist* 10) between pure democracies and representative republics, but between absolute monarchies and small republics. He suggested that one needed to combine the advantages of the two regimes, but it is not clear that the small republic added any advantage to the combination that he contemplated:

> The great desideratum in Government is such a modification of the Sovereignty as will render it sufficiently neutral between the different interests and factions, to controul one part of the Society from invading

> the rights of another, and at the same time sufficiently controuled itself, from setting up an interest adverse to that of the whole Society. In absolute Monarchies, the prince is sufficiently neutral towards his subjects, but frequently sacrifices their happiness to his ambition or his avarice. In small Republics, the sovereign will is sufficiently controuled from such a Sacrifice of the entire Society, but is not sufficiently neutral towards the parts composing it. As a limited Monarch tempers the evils of an absolute one; so an extensive Republic meliorates the administration of a small Republic. (*Papers*, 9: 357)

In monarchy, government can control society in a neutral manner, but might not control itself; in republics, government is controlled so that it will not act against the whole society, but it might not control society in a neutral manner. By limiting monarchy — whether by the rule of law or by the admixture of a balancing republican element — one attacks the characteristic evil of monarchical government, the tendency to act against the interest of the whole society. Likewise, by extending republics, Madison argues, "The Society becomes broken into a greater variety of interests, of pursuits, of passions, which check each other, whilst those who may feel a common sentiment have less opportunity of communication and concert." By multiplying factions, one attacks the characteristic evil of republican governments, the tendency to act in the interest of only part of society — the interest of a faction. The "enlargement of the sphere" does not require a mixture of republics. It tries to combine the principles of monarchy and republic. The problem of monarchy is the weakness of liberty or society, against the will of government independent of society. The problem of the republic is the weakness of power or government, because of that very dependence on society which makes it proof against the evils of monarchy. These problems are so intrinsic to the regimes that Madison describes that one must doubt that the "modifications" he suggests are solutions to these problems so much as they are, as he says, devices which can "temper" and "meliorate" the evils. "The great desideratum" remains a thing desired rather than a thing achieved. A monarchy ultimately cannot be made dependent without destroying the nature of monarchy and its advantages: a limited monarchy tends to become a republic. Nor can the government of a republic be detached finally from the society without destroying the nature of the republic and its advantages: an extensive, factious republic tends to become a monarchy. In any case, in combining the two forms, one would combine the evil tendencies as well as the advantages.

The federal combination of large republic and small republics — which was what Madison was trying to perfect with the aid of all these arguments — appears from the point of view of the extended republic in a false light, as a datum rather than a desideratum. The combination may seem to provide a method of ensuring that the combination of republic and monarchy would contain advantages without evils, but the method is inadequate, partly because the republican principle contributes none of the advantage. The republican principle appears only as a source of typical republican evils — the vices of state politics. The advantage comes from the monarchical independence from state politics which it is presumed federal representatives would enjoy in their supervision of state legislation. They would have also a republican attribute in their "dependence on the community" (*Papers*, 10: 214) in their other capacity, as directors of federal affairs. Although this republican aspect of federal representatives was not yet (as in *Federalist* 10) defended — and thereby destroyed — by the extended republic argument, this republican contribution to the general government was already couched in negative terms which point towards *Federalist* 10, and which contaminate that contribution with the anti-republican implications of that argument. Their "dependence on the community" (not yet, as in *Federalist* 10, their independence from a factious, uncommunal society) is to restrain them "from betraying its general interests" (*Papers*, 9: 384; 10: 214). But what is to make them able and willing positively to advance those general interests? What is to make them "feel most strongly the proper motives to pursue the end of their appointment, and be most capable to devise the proper means of attaining it?"[8] If Madison had been asked in the spring of 1787 (as he had to assume he was being asked six months later, when he was writing *Federalist* 10) to defend his opinion that federal representatives would be good at their positive tasks, would he not have had to trot out the extended republic argument again?

Madison's Use of the Extended Republic Argument

Madison's first statement of the extended republic argument appeared in his paper on the "Vices of the Political System of the U.S." This statement did not indicate that he wanted to limit the application of that argument (as he did otherwise limit it, until he wrote *Federalist* 10) to supporting his claim that the supervisory power's effects on state laws would be benevolent. Perhaps Madison was aware of the argument's resistance to this limitation. The separate and previous statement of this claim (in the letter to Jefferson in March), and the unlimited nationalism that it would be easily possible to see in this first description of the extended republic (in April) help confirm the suggestion that Madison had some appreciation for the defects of the extended republic argument, which led him to use it in an *ad hoc* manner, as a supporting argument rather than as a principle.

When Madison used the extended republic argument at the Philadelphia Convention, in the summer of 1787, it seems immediately to have been understood by some listeners as a nationalist argument (*Papers*, 10: 34). Perhaps Madison's listeners were more acute than he had hoped they would be; they saw that if Madison was enhancing (or, as he thought, creating) the political nature of the general government, his argument must be that more political competence would exist in that government

[8] This is the "auxiliary desideratum" called for in "Vices" (*Papers*, 9: 357). The first statement in Madison's writings of the principle of safety through multiplicity, noted by Coniff (1980: 391), is couched in extremely negative terms; "complexity" and "diversity" do not make just action more likely, they merely make any action at all less likely.

than in the state governments. The argument was not intended by Madison to be understood in this way. It was not yet used by him except to defend his proposals for the perfection of the federal system of governments — proposals which he had made before he developed that plausible supporting argument.

In Madison's first (and last) public use of the extended republic argument, in *Federalist* 10 and 51, he was compelled to reverse his true view of the priority of federalism and extensiveness; "the federal principle" — the "proper structure of the Union" — now appeared as a means to rather than (as before) an end of the "extent" of the Union: for "the larger the society, provided it lie within a practicable sphere, the more duly capable it will be of self-government. And . . . the practicable sphere may be carried to a very great extent by a judicious modification and mixture of the *federal principle*." At the same time Madison was making this argument, he acknowledged in a letter to Jefferson that, apart from considerations of practicability, the extensive sphere of a republic should be limited so that "a defensive concert" will not be "too difficult against the oppression of those entrusted with the administration." (*Papers*, 10: 214). In *Federalist* 63, in Madison's determined efforts to proclaim the bright side of the compromise over the principle of representation (he had not wanted equality of states' representation in the Senate), he pointed to this same defect: "the same extended situation which will exempt the people of America from some of the dangers incident to lesser republics will expose them to the inconveniency of remaining for a longer time under the influence of those misrepresentations which the combined industry of interested men may succeed in distributing among them." Madison saw very clearly that there were good reasons not to rely on that oversimple formula of *Federalist* 10, the larger and more diverse the better.

In his private letter to Jefferson, as in the private deliberations of the Constitutional Convention, Madison's defense of the extensiveness of the republic was limited to making national supervision of state legislation seem reasonable. But of course, in practice Madison could no longer maintain such a limitation, and in his only public statement of the case for the extended republic he had to abandon the limitation, because the Constitution's "modification and mixture of the federal principle" were less "judicious" than Madison had hoped they would be. Besides the unsound compromise over representation, there was the lack of provision for political linkage between general and state governments, to reduce the friction of their concurrent operation and to secure national supremacy with less trouble than Madison believed federal judicial review would encourage. These deficiencies led Madison to hazard the opinion that the new government "will neither effectually answer its national object nor prevent the local mischiefs which every where excite disgusts agst. the state governments" (*Papers*, 10: 163-64). These deficiencies also stopped Madison from using his clever argument for extensiveness in the limited way that he wished to use it.

But Madison nevertheless believed that, however imperfect the Constitution was, the Articles of Confederation were "more imperfect," and, as he said in *Federalist* 38, "No man would refuse to give brass for silver or gold, because the latter had some alloy in it." So he chose to defend the Constitution, even with that brilliant, though insufficiently republican and potentially dangerous, extended republic argument. The government of the Constitution was more federal and less national than Madison had wanted it to be, but he had to defend it with a less federal and more national version of his extended republic argument. The first assumption of that argument, in both its straightforward national (*Federalist* 10) form and its earlier federal form, is that "civilized societies" are properly characterized by their inability to learn to act on the basis of prudent, enlightened self-interest, respect for moral character, or safe religious considerations (*Papers*, 9: 355-56; 10: 213-14; *Federalist* 10). Madison treated this assumption as he treated the argument: when he had no use for it, he abandoned it, and embraced the opposite assumption of the second Madisonian system, the Republican party. In fact, like Jefferson (Zvesper 1977: 91-92), Madison later adapted the extended republic argument to fit this second system: "in a confederal system, if one of its members happens to stray into pernicious measures, it will be reclaimed by the frowns and the good examples of the others" (*Writings*, 9: 520-21) — that is, by the frowns and good examples of the Republican party.[9] Madison displayed a remarkable detachment from the large republic, pluralist theory that is so often identified as the "Madisonian system."

Reinterpreting Madison's Contradictions

One cannot avoid the judgement that in opposing the policies of Hamilton, Madison opposed his earlier self as well — not only his *Federalist* essays, but also the assumption which those essays shared with Madison's freer and less simply nationalist thoughts during his Federalist period. The shared assumption was that decent republican government can be constructed and maintained without relying very much on the influence of the public-spiritedness and political competence of the people. The great difference between Madison the Federalist and Madison the Republican was not the former's nationalism and the latter's defense of states' rights; Madison could defend himself from the charge of inconsistency on this score. As he claimed in a famous letter in defense of his consistency, he never veered from his loyalty to a composite system, "partly federal and partly national" (*Writings*, 9: 473-75). This was "a system of Government emphatically sui generis" (*Writings*, 9: 177), and therefore a suitably flexible principle for a skeptical politician to defend.[10]

[9] Contrast the penultimate paragraph of *Federalist* 10, where Madison necessarily overlooks the possibility of the "good examples of the others" (for all are motivated by the same selfish passions), and looks to the "national councils" (not to a popular party) for a cure, or at least for the absence of the disease.

[10] Hobson (1979: 228) points out that Madison objected to the phrase "partly federal and partly national" when it was introduced into the Constitutional debates at Philadelphia. But this was only in connection with the *source* of the new government's powers and the *method* of their operation, both of which Madison thought should be wholly national

Madison's emphasis on the dominance of the national element in the Constitution naturally diminished when the extra-Constitutional party system — potentially a powerful national force — became part of the actual constitution; it made sense to defend states' rights more when those rights came to be more threatened. But there remains an important inconsistency: Madison the Federalist had tried to associate republican dependence on the people with the absence of popular virtue, and Madison the Republican returned to a more traditional and a truer association of republicanism and the necessity for popular virtue. The political party which Madison helped to construct was meant to embody that virtue, and to erect over the formal constitutional system "one paramount Empire of reason, benevolence, and brotherly affection" (*Writings*, 6: 67-69). In 1823 looking back on the first party system, Madison not inaccurately placed the basis of the difference between the Republican and the Federalist parties in "the confidence of the former, in the capacity of mankind for self Government and in a distrust of it by the other or by its leaders" (*Writings*, 9: 136). The leaders of the Republican party saw that republican politics must rely primarily on society, not on government. The Federalists, agreeing with *Federalist* 10, had been too ready to dismiss the possibility that elements of "pure democracy" might assist the "cure for the mischiefs of faction," and that "the people themselves" might be more able than their representatives to reach conclusions "consonant to the public good."

That Madison himself was aware of this great self-contradiction is perhaps best shown by the degree of self-parody in the essays against Federalism which he published in 1792. (Henry Adams read too literally when he failed to see any trace of Madison's sense of humor in his published writings.) His essays for the Republican party press, in contrast to those he wrote as "Publius," favored social solidarity rather than diversity, and the cultivation of unified public opinion rather than the raising of barriers to communication by extending the sphere of government. He now stressed the naturalness and inevitability of political parties (parties of principle and opinion) rather than of economic factions (parties of interest). He defined the "republican party" as those who "are naturally offended at any public measure that does not appeal to the understanding and to the general interest of the community." (*Writings*, 6: 113-18) The series of essays culminated in a dialogue between an "Anti-republican" and a "Republican" — often resembling the dialogue between Madison the Federalist and Madison the Republican — disputing the question "Who Are the Best Keepers of the People's Liberties?" Republican proposes "The people themselves." Anti-republican objects: "They cannot safely trust themselves." Republican replies that the correct remedy is not to accept and to perpetuate popular political incompetence, but to en-

---

(*Papers*, 10: 88-89, 100-102); he already recognized (as he later spelled out in *Federalist* 39) that the *extent* of these powers would be limited by the separate sovereignty of the states, and in this sense his own scheme was partly federal, although less so than the scheme that emerged from the convention.

lighten, to awaken, and to unite the people. Republican refuses to admit that the people's flightiness and "centrifugal tendency" can be a political problem, requiring a boost to the power of government rather than attention to the liberty of the people. In response, Anti-republican can caricature the Madison of four years before (see Madison to Jefferson, 17 October 1788): "Wonderful as it may seem, the more you increase the attractive force of power, the more you enlarge the sphere of liberty" (*Writings*, 6: 120-23).

Madison could reconcile his "nationalist" and "states' rights" positions; he could not reconcile his rejection and then acceptance of the necessity for republican virtue — the basic difference between his pluralist and his party government theories. Here Madison appears not only to have been guilty of inconsistency, but almost to have admitted his guilt. The explanation of this major inconsistency could begin by remembering the elementary rhetorical principle that one can sometimes be much more persuasive if one appears to adopt opinions which are more "realistic" than one's true opinions. It may be counterproductive to be known to adhere to an unpopular idealism when a realistic argument can be used to advance the end of that idealism (Aristotle, *Rhetoric*, I: vii, 36-38). During the years when Madison was known and respected for his adherence to realistic Federalist opinion, he saw that this realism was powerful. In 1790, he wrote to Jefferson (in a passage which he wanted to be deleted from his published papers): "The evils suffered and feared from weakness in Government, and licenciousness in the people, have turned the attention more towards the means of strengthening the powers of the former than of narrowing their extent in the minds of the latter" (*Papers*, 13: 24-25). Madison thus recognized the drift of American political thinking in the 1780s toward postwar disenchantment with Revolutionary ideals of republican virtue (Wood 1969: ch. 10). He saw the necessity of advancing his political schemes with this theoretically questionable but nonetheless practically powerful movement of opinion. He could follow or even lead this movement and still act in accordance with the true guiding principles of his career: his desire to promote the federal union as a means to human safety, liberty, and happiness (*Papers*, 10: 21). His consistent ends were these goals of liberalism, which could be advanced at times with the realistic, pluralist rhetoric of Federalism.

Such an explanation of Madison's statecraft would have to apply to his Republican, party government phase as well as to his Federalist phase. When public opinion and Madison's rhetoric were less concerned to encourage more powerful government and became more focused on popular virtue, Madison did not lose sight of the partial truth — and partial falsity — of both that old realism and this new idealism. He knew that "in every political institution, a power to advance the public happiness involves a discretion which may be misapplied and abused" (*Federalist* 41). This applied to party institutions as well as to the more formal constitution. Thus, he eloquently and effectively championed the cause of constitutionalism as well as the cause of party. He consciously avoided becoming a "folk hero" President (Smelser 1968: 318).[11] He puzzled his contemporaries and later historians by his apparently strange insistence that a Constitutional amendment precede the use of federal funds for roads and canals. Popular, party opinion was favorable to the policy, and Madison himself thought it was advisable. However, he insisted on sticking to legal forms. He had often enough been compelled to countenance the opposite doctrine, *vox populi vox dei*. Even then, he was often able, as in his explanation for his approval of the second national bank, to insist that *vox populi* had to prove its endurance in order to be proclaimed *vox dei*.[12] Madison saw that the association of republicanism and popular virtue is truer than the assumption of the extended republic, because it recognizes the moral preconditions of republican politics. (Koch was right: the "more substantial" of Madison's fears was of Hamilton's undemocratic methods; Meyers was wrong: it was Madison's Federalist "science of politics" that was the less satisfactory of his two theories.) But he also saw that it is not the whole truth, because it suggests that those preconditions are always actual, and that its limits on individual statecraft are always reasonable. He saw that the jump from the pluralism and constitutionalism of the first "Madisonian system" to the social solidarity and activism of the second was in some ways a jump from the frying pan into the fire, so he kept jumping. It is this principled inconsistency rather than the pluralism of *Federalist* 10 or the party system of Jefferson and Madison that constitutes Madison's true system.

At the end of his *Reflections on the Revolution in France*, Edmund Burke offered a defense of the consistency of one like himself, "who would preserve consistency by varying his means to secure the unity of his end;

[11] The consequence was "that in crises the constitutional separation of powers enfeebled the government," because the President did not "seize and exercise majority-party leadership" (Smelser 1968: 319). Riemer's New Dealish complaint, described in the text above, was similar, and he too failed to explain how Madison could have maintained his constitutionalism if he had imitated Jefferson or anticipated Jackson. As Smith (1942) says, Madison should at least be given "credit for an attempt to conduct policy strictly according to the letter and spirit of the Constitution." Young (1966: Ch. 9) points out that even Jefferson, the strongest of the Jeffersonian Presidents, lacked the ideological climate and institutional structures needed to sustain his "experiment in party government under presidential leadership," which therefore "withered on the vine." But he also notes that such success as Jefferson enjoyed in this experiment owed much to his "liberation" from the doubts entertained by Madison, Monroe and Adams about the extent to which Presidents should steal the initiative from Congress and soil their hands by grubbing for power in order to do so.

[12] ". . . the question of the constitutional authority of the Legislative to establish an incorporated bank . . . being precluded in my judgment by repeated recognitions under varied circumstances of the validity of such an institution in acts of the legislative, executive, and judicial branches of the Government, accompanied by indications, in different modes, of a concurrence of the general will of the nation . . ." (*Writings*, 8: 327); ". . . a course of authoritative, deliberate, and continued decisions, such as the Bank could plead was an evidence of the Public Judgement, necessarily superseding individual opinions." (*Writings*, 9: 476-77) See also the reference to "insufficient precedents" in Madison's veto of the internal improvements scheme, 3 March 1817 (*Writings*, 8: 388); Adams (1889-91, 9: 152-53); and Brant (1961: 469).

and, when the equipoise of the vessel in which he sails may be endangered by overloading it upon one side, is desirous of carrying the small weight of his reasons to that which may preserve its equipoise." Madison's consistency requires a slightly different defense. Burke would explain changes of allegiance by reference to changed circumstances. Madison's changes were based on his recognition of the intrinsic weakness of both of the political theories with which he allowed himself to be identified, apart from any extrinsic circumstance. He regarded both of the theories as sources of possible but imperfect means of securing liberal rights. Madison did not share Burke's project to remove the political influence of abstract theories, to make all parties conservative parties. He helped usher in an age of party ideology which Burke fought against. Perhaps he did share Burke's view that such theories were dangerous elements in political practice, but he seems to have thought they were unavoidable dangers.

Whether Madison's system served good purposes, and how successfully, is another matter. Is the liberal goal of securing the rights to life, liberty and the pursuit of happiness a good end? Were Hamilton's policies not better means to that end than Jefferson's and Madison's (even if Hamilton was too unappreciative of the wisdom of their policy-making methods)? But one can more profitably raise such questions after one has fathomed the system behind Madison's two more obvious systems. Behind the rival theories of pluralism and party government is a systematic effort to subordinate both to the dictates of a liberal prudence. Madison's most important message to the twentieth-century heirs of his theories might well be a reminder that the theories are "inventions of prudence" (*Federalist* 51). Madison was more consistently attached to the principles of liberalism and prudence than to the devices of pluralism and party government.

REFERENCES

Adams, Henry. 1889-1891. *History of the United States During the Administrations of Thomas Jefferson and James Madison*, 9 vols. New York: Charles Scribner's Sons.

Brant, Irving. 1950. *James Madison: Father of the Consitution, 1787-1800*. Indianapolis: Bobbs-Merrill.

———. 1952. "James Madison and His Times." *American Historical Review* 57: 853-70.

———. 1961. *James Madison: Commander in Chief, 1812-1836*. Indianapolis: Bobbs-Merrill.

Burns, Edward McNall. 1938. *James Madison: Philosopher of the Constitution*. New Brunswick, N.J.: Rutgers University Press.

Burns, James MacGregor. 1967. *Deadlock of Democracy*. Englewood Cliffs: Prentice-Hall.

Carey, George W. 1978. "Separation of Powers and the Madisonian Model: A Reply to the Critics." *American Political Science Review* 72: 151-64.

Coniff, James. 1980. "The Enlightenment and American Political Thought: A Study of Madison's *Federalist Number 10*." *Political Theory* 8: 381-402.

Dahl, Robert. 1956. *A Preface to Democratic Theory*. Chicago: University of Chicago Press.

Diamond, Martin. 1972. "The Federalist." *History of Political Philosophy*. Leo Strauss and Joseph Cropsey, eds. 2nd ed. Chicago: Rand McNally.

Erler, Edward J. 1980-1981. "The Problem of the Public Good in *The Federalist*." *Polity* 13: 649-67.

Hamilton, Alexander. 1961-1979. *The Papers of Alexander Hamilton*, 26 vols. Harold C. Syrett and Jacob E. Cooke, eds. New York: Columbia University Press.

Hobson, Charles F. 1979. "The Negative on State Laws: James Madison, the Constitution, and the Crisis of Republican Government." *William and Mary Quarterly* (Third Series) 36: 215-35.

Hunt, Gaillard. 1902. *The Life of James Madison*. New York: Doubleday Page.

Jaenicke, Douglas. 1980. "Party Against Constitution: Madison v. Madison." Paper delivered at the Annual Conference of the American Politics Group of the United Kingdom Political Studies Association, Manchester.

Jaffa, Harry V. 1977. "A Phoenix from the Ashes." Paper delivered at the Annual Meeting of the American Political Science Association, Washington, D.C.

Kenyon, Cecelia M., ed. 1966. *The Antifederalists*. Indianapolis: Bobbs-Merrill.

Koch, Adrienne. 1966. *Madison's "Advice to My Country."* Princeton: Princeton University Press.

Lodge, Henry Cabot. 1892. *Historical and Political Essays*. Boston: Houghton, Mifflin.

Madison, James. 1900-1910. *The Writings of James Madison*, 9 vols. Gaillard Hunt, ed. New York: Putnam.

Madison, James. 1962 to date. *The Papers of James Madison*, 13 vols. to date. William T. Hutchinson, William M. E. Rachal, Robert A. Rutland and others, eds. Chicago: University of Chicago Press and Charlottesville: University Press of Virginia.

Meyers, Marvin, ed. 1973. *The Mind of the Founder*. Indianapolis: Bobbs-Merrill.

Morgan, Robert J. 1974. "Madison's Theory of Representation." *Journal of Politics* 36: 852-85.

———. 1981. "Madison's Analysis of the Sources of Political Authority." *American Political Science Review* 75: 613-25.

Riemer, Neal. 1954a. "The Republicanism of James Madison." *Political Science Quarterly* 69: 56-64.

———. 1954b. "James Madison's Theory of the Self-Destructive Features of Republican Government." *Ethics* 65: 34-43.

———. 1967. *The Democratic Experiment*. Princeton: Van Nostrand.

Schattschneider, E. E. 1942. *Party Government*. New York: Farrar and Rinehart.

Smelser, Marshall. 1968. *The Democratic Republic*. New York: Harper and Row.

Smith, Abbot. 1942. "Mr. Madison's War: An Unsuccessful Experiment in the Conduct of National Policy." *Political Science Quarterly* 57: 229-46.

Wills, Garry. 1981. *Explaining America: The Federalist*. New York: Doubleday.

Wood, Gordon S. 1969. *The Creation of the American Republic 1776-1787*. Chapel Hill: University of North Carolina Press.

Young, James Sterling. 1966. *The Washington Community, 1800-1828*. New York: Harcourt, Brace.

Zvesper, John. 1977. *Political Philosophy and Rhetoric: A Study of the Origins of American Party Politics*. Cambridge: Cambridge University Press.

[19]

Madison v. Madison: The Party Essays v. The Federalist Papers

DOUGLAS W. JAENICKE

ABSTRACT

The most authoritative commentary on the Constitution remains 'The Federalist'. Yet 'The Federalist's' explanation and defence of the Constitution was always somewhat suspect, since, as the authors themselves admitted, 'The Federalist' was a polemic, written to promote the ratification of the Constitution, as well as a work of political philosophy. Moreover, Alexander Hamilton and James Madison, its main authors, soon parted political company, with Madison in the House of Representatives leading a party in opposition to Hamilton's policies as Secretary of the Treasury. Madison, known as the 'Father of the Constitution', was also the father of the party system, grafted onto the Constitution soon after the government went into operation. This chapter displays the departures that Madison's thinking as party leader made from the thinking of Madison the co-author of 'The Federalist', and argues that these departures comprised a very different and in some ways a superior way of conceiving of America's form of government.

While the United States is celebrating the bicentennial of its Constitution, it might be salutary to reflect upon James Madison's second thoughts regarding his original arguments on behalf of that document. Most historians and political scientists and indeed many ordinary Americans identify Madison with the Constitution and especially its defence by 'Publius' – the pseudonym adopted by Madison, Alexander Hamilton and John Jay – in *The Federalist Papers*. Few, however, are aware that in a series of articles published in *The National Gazette* between December 1791 and September 1792 Madison repudiated many of the arguments of *The Federalist Papers*. Marking the beginning of Madison's attempt to organise the republican opposition as a national political party, these essays contained arguments which resembled those of his previous Anti-Federalist opponents.[1]

Norman Jacobson has contrasted the warm fraternal thought of the Articles of Confederation and Thomas Paine's *Common Sense* with the cold, rational, impersonal proceduralism of the Constitution and *The Federalist*. The former abounded with expressions of friendship, affection, American uniqueness and a disdain for mere interest. The latter spoke the harsh language of coercion, interests, threats and calculating rationality.[2] Yet, no sooner had the Constitution been ratified than Madison, one of its principal architects and defenders, in an astonishing act of self-criticism, assailed his previous position as Publius.

Some authors either explicitly[3] or implicitly[4] deny that the thought of Madison as party organiser is significantly different from that of Madison as Publius. Other scholars have asserted that a fundamental antagonism exists; but only John Zvesper has argued the case in any detail, and even he has not delineated the full extent of Madison's transformation in 1791–2 into a trenchant critic of *The Federalist*.[5] This chapter will document the fundamental incompatibility between the thought of the two Madisons. It will also challenge those scholars who concede the contradiction but assume the theoretical superiority of Publius and slight the theoretical worth of Madison's party writings.[6] Madison's essays in *The National Gazette* not only criticised his earlier position as Publius but also adumbrated, if not fully developed, an alternative theory of liberal politics.

Where Publius had sought the greatest possible social heterogeneity as a *sine qua non* of republican government, Madison the party organiser of 1791–2 urged greater homogeneity as essential for preserving a republican regime. Unlike Publius with his expediential defence of equal rights and republican government, Madison as founder of the Republican party sought to touch the soul of Americans by nurturing a principled attachment to republican government and political equality. Furthermore, the extended orbit praised by Publius was now seen as threatening rather than perfecting republican government. What is more, the two Madisons prescribed fundamentally different methods of maintaining the constitutional balance. Finally, Madison's later description of the partisan conflict between republicans and anti-republicans bears no resemblance to the factional politics of *The Federalist*.

HETEROGENEITY VERSUS HOMOGENEITY

For Madison as Publius, the social pluralism generated by a large population inhabiting a large territory provided the principal means of ensuring that a republican government would not become tyrannical. He preferred the greatest possible social heterogeneity in order to fracture public opinion and fragment organised political life, thereby obviating the chief problem of a republic – a majority faction. According to Publius, no faction could be trusted with government power; given the opportunity, it would use government power to advance its own interest at the expense of the national interest or the private interests of others. But removal of the causes of faction would be inexpedient – as it would entail the destruction of liberty, if not impossible – as one could not give citizens 'the same opinions, the same passions, and the same interests'.[7] The answer, then, was to control the effects of faction to ensure that no faction could appropriate government power to benefit itself.

But whereas a minority faction is rendered harmless by 'the republican principle which enables the majority to defeat its [a minority's] sinister views by regular vote', the same principle exacerbates rather than solves the problem of a majority faction. 'When a majority is included in a faction, the form of popular government ... enables it to sacrifice to its ruling passion or interest both the public good and the rights of other citizens.'[8] As events at the state level had demonstrated, even 'auxiliary precautions' such as federalism, separate institutions sharing powers, different terms of office, and different modes of election and selection were unlikely to thwart a majority faction since it would be capable of sweeping aside all such institutional complexity.[9] Furthermore, Madison disparaged any suggestion that virtue could be relied upon to protect Americans from the dangers posed by a majority faction.

> If the impulse and the opportunity be suffered to coincide, we well know that neither moral nor religious motives can be relied on as an adequate control. They are not found to be such on the injustice and violence of individuals, and lose their efficacy in proportion to the number combined together, that is, in proportion as their efficacy becomes needful.[10]

Hence Publius proposed the extensive social pluralism generated by the country's extended orbit as the primary solution to the problem of majority faction. 'Extend the sphere,' Madison wrote, and you take in a greater variety of parties and interests; you make it less probable that a majority of the whole will have a common motive to invade the rights of other citizens.'[11] Given sufficient heterogeneity, a governing majority would be a coalition of minorities, each compelled to compromise, if not abandon, its particularistic demands. Thus, 'in the extended republic of the United States, and among the great variety of interests, parties, and sects which it embraces, a coalition of a majority of the whole society could seldom take place on any other principles than those of justice and the general good'.[12]

Shifting his ground in 1791, Madison now argued that political moderation derives from the people's affection for and confidence in one another, not from the exigencies of coalition-building within a pluralist society. 'The greater the mutual confidence and affection of all parts of the Union, the more likely they will be to concur amicably, or to differ in moderation, in the elective designation of the chief magistrate.'[13] If shared republican values do not remove all political differences, at least they minimise them and assure a defeated minority that their rights will be respected. Secure in their knowledge of their fellow citizens' principled commitment to republican liberty, the citizens' mutual concord, sympathy and confidence enable them to trust one another with their interests and rights. Even earlier, Madison had argued that social pluralism and free political institutions were inadequate to preserve republican government if a large number of citizens distrusted the new order. Hence, Madison recommended adoption of a bill of rights to reassure Anti-Federalists that their Federalist opponents were committed to republicanism.[14]

Although *The Federalist* had opposed any possibility of a popular majority acting as a concerted political force, Madison in 1791–2 urged the American people to 'be united' so that they could effectively watch over the national government; greater political and social homogeneity were needed to facilitate common political action in defence of republican government.[15] Adopting the approach of those 'theoretic politicians' disparaged in *Federalist* no. 10, Madison now worked to unify most, if not all, Americans around common interests and opinions; hence the greater substantive homogeneity he now advocated transcended a procedural consensus on the rules of the game. While eschewing any utopian expectation that Americans could share exactly the same interests, he sought to discourage the multiplication of different interests and to reduce differences of interest.

In 1791–2, Madison favoured increased social homogeneity in order to deflect arguments for increased executive discretion. 'In the first place, in proportion as uniformity is found to prevail in the interests and sentiments of the several states, will be the practicability of accommodating legislative regulations to them, and thereby of withholding new and dangerous prerogatives from the executive.'[16] By reducing the difference between the states, Madison hoped to obviate the need for executive discretion in implementing legislation and consequently to confine the executive branch to a narrow sphere of activity.

Ignoring his earlier warnings against a majority faction, Madison now recognised that only a people united by republican sentiment and interest could vouchsafe the efficacy of the fragmented government structure. The American people no longer were to be divided by their different factional interests and the distrust which necessarily accompanied them, but rather were to be united by warm fraternal feelings nurtured by an identity of interests. Madison urged Americans to

> employ their utmost zeal, by eradicating local prejudices and mistaken rivalships to consolidate the affairs of the states into *one harmonious interest*; and let it be the patriotic study of all, to maintain the various authorities established by our complicated system, each in its respective constitutional sphere; and to erect over the whole one paramount Empire of *reason, benevolence, and brotherly affection*.[17]

Madison the party organiser sought to unite the citizenry by inner bonds of fellowship which would supersede the impersonal justice secured by the Constitution's external procedural safeguards.

In pursuit of this republican unity, Madison in 1791–2 began organising the Republican party which he intended to become such a vast majority, that it would not only defeat Hamilton's Federalists electorally, but also obliterate Federalism as a viable political alternative and overwhelm the constitutional structure by securing control of all branches and levels of government. Although describing the division between republicans and anti-republicans as 'natural to most political societies',[18] Madison did not accept the Federalists as a legitimate opposition and consequently did not envisage a party system in which they and Republicans rotated in office, While tolerating Federalism, Madison expected the Republican party to banish its opponents to the political wilderness.[19]

Transcending the heterogeneity produced by the extended sphere, 'the republican party ... will naturally find their [*sic*] account in burying all antecedent questions, in banishing every other distinction than that between enemies and friends to republican government, in promoting a general harmony among the latter wherever residing, or however employed'. By contrast, the anti-republicans would exploit the nation's heterogeneity in order to disrupt the Republican party and advance their aristocratic purposes. 'It will be equally their [the anti-republicans'] true policy to weaken their opponents by reviving exploded parties, and taking advantage of all prejudices, local, political, and occupational, that may prevent or disturb a general coalition of sentiments.'[20] Far from being a necessary condition for republican government, social heterogeneity was now perceived as a resource available to anti-republicans and hence as a serious danger to a republican regime.

In 1791–2, recognising that the actualisation of republican fraternity required more than exhorting Americans to be friendly towards one another, Madison urged a diminution of social differences in order to encourage fraternal bonds. Unlike Publius who sought political salvation in the multiplication of different interests, Madison now preferred to reduce differences of interest which bred distrust and animosity.

> The less the supposed difference of interests, and the greater the concord and confidence throughout the great body of people, the more readily must they sympathize with each other, the more seasonably can they interpose a common manifestation of their sentiments, the more certainly will they take the alarm at usurpation or oppression, and the more effectively will they *consolidate* their defense of the public liberty.[21]

Now Madison mordantly caricatured his previous advocacy of maximum heterogeneity.

> In all political societies, different interests and parties arise out of the nature of things, and the great art of politicians lies in making them checks and balances to each other. Let us then increase these *natural* distinctions by favoring an inequality of property; and let us add to them artificial distinctions, by establishing *kings* and *nobles* and *plebeians*. We shall then have the more checks to oppose each other; we shall then have the more scales and the more weights to protect and maintain the [constitutional] equilibrium. This is as little the voice of reason, as it is of republicanism.[22]

Although interest groups or factions which are promoted or created by government are qualitatively different from factions which are voluntary creations,[23] Madison as Publius had simply sought the greatest possible social diversity in order to obviate the likelihood of a majority faction. While he had never urged the creation of hereditary classes, Publius had certainly favoured 'the more scales and more weights' in order to forestall the danger of a majority faction.

In contrast to Publius who had insisted that the 'first object of government' is the protection of 'the different and unequal faculties' which produce 'different degrees and kinds of property',[24] Madison as party organiser now urged an approximate substantive equality of condition. To overcome differences of interest so that affection and sympathy might find fertile soil in which to take root, the essay 'Parties' proposed a diminution of economic inequalities although not an absolute equality of condition: '2. By withholding unnecessary opportunities from a few to increase the inequality of property, by an immoderate, and especially unmerited, accumulation of riches. 3. By the silent operation of laws, which, without violating the rights of property, reduce extreme wealth towards a state of mediocrity, and raise extreme indigence towards a state of comfort.'[25] Madison now sought to provide poor citizens with sufficient property in order to secure their political independence and to deprive the rich of excessive wealth in order to prevent them from wielding disproportionate political influence. Although Madison's proposals were marked by moderation and ambiguity, his new determination to reduce economic inequality contradicted Publius' view that inequality was natural. Madison's new concern with attaining a rough substantive equality is apparently traceable to a recognition that large economic inequalities might impede the creation of genuine political community with its inner bonds of affection and trust.[26] It might be easier to subordinate differences of economic interest to common republican values if those differences were negligible.

Unlike Publius, who had simply sought to multiply the number of occupations in order to prevent the existence of a majority faction, and consequently had adopted a stance of moral neutrality towards different occupations, Madison the party organiser favoured greater occupational homogeneity. Abandoning Publius' neutrality, Madison the party organiser now preferred those economic occupations which he considered to be favourable to republican liberty.

The goodness or badness of an occupation now resided in its relation to republican values, not in the individual; 'the best distribution [of citizens into employment] is that which would most favor *health, virtue, intelligence* and *competency* in the *greater number* of citizens'.[27] According to Madison, husbandry nurtures such characteristics but manufacturing and commerce injure them. While the agricultural work of yeoman farmers fosters 'solid utility', factory work stunts the intellectual and physical development of the operatives; sailors lead morally and physically unhealthy lives; and the fashion industry degrades workers by subjecting them to the whim and caprice of the wealthy followers of fashion. Regarding the fashion industry, Madison asked rhetorically: 'Can any despotism be more cruel than a situation, in which the existence of thousands depends on one will, and that will on the imagination?' Employment in the fashion industry produces a 'servile dependence of one class of citizens on another class' which is inappropriate for republics.[28]

In 1791–2, Madison acknowledged that some occupations benefit a republic by nuturing qualities necessary for active participation in republican politics, while others are harmful since they produce citizens who are less capable, if not incapable, of self-government. Yet Hamilton's financial policies were benefitting and encouraging precisely those occupations which Madison considered injurious to republican citizens. Consequently, Madison now concluded that greater occupational homogeneity rather than increased heterogeneity would be more favourable to republican government. 'The class of citizens who provide at once their own food and their own raiment ... are the best basis of public liberty, and the strongest bulwark of public safety ... The greater the proportion of this class to the whole society, the more free, the more independent, and the more happy must be the society itself.'[29] Although Hamilton's economic policy increased the number of social interests as Madison had recommended in *The Federalist*, Madison now opposed Hamilton's measures because he judged them to be incompatible with the preservation of republican government.

THE EXTENDED ORBIT: A PROBLEM, NOT A SOLUTION

For Madison as Publius, the extended orbit of the United States provided the primary defences against the problem of a majority faction. In addition to increasing social heterogeneity and therefore making it unlikely that a majority would share a common interest, the extended orbit, by posing almost insurmountable problems of communication and co-ordination, would make it less likely that a majority faction could organise around a shared interest if such an interest existed despite the country's heterogeneity.[30]

Representation made an extensive republic possible, and the extended sphere in turn perfected representation. According to Publius, 'the two great points of difference between a democracy and a republic are first, the delegation of the government, in the latter, to a small number of citizens elected by the rest; secondly, the greater number of citizens and greater sphere of country over which the latter may be extended'.[31] Many Anti-Federalists preferred direct democracy and only reluctantly accepted representation as an unavoidable necessity in a large country. In contrast to many Anti-Federalists who favoured a large number of representatives elected for short terms from small districts in order to approximate direct democracy, Madison welcomed the additional safeguards created by the election of relatively few representatives from large electoral districts. Madison rejected direct democracy as inherently flawed since it 'can admit of no cure for the mischiefs of faction'.[32] Because direct democracy could only be practised by a relatively small population concentrated in a compact territory, a pure democracy lacked sufficient heterogeneity to guard against a majority faction. Therefore, even where possible, direct democracy was never desirable; representative government was always preferable since it excluded '*the people in their collective capacity*' from government while still permitting free political institutions.[33]

According to *The Federalist*, representation was a necessary but not sufficient condition to preserve republican government; events in the states had demonstrated that in a small country representation alone could not sufficiently insulate government officials from popular pressure.[34] Additional safeguards were necessary. In order to weaken the immediate pressure of public opinion, to keep popular passions at bay and to favour the election of the better qualified members of the 'conventional' aristocracy who were assumed to be members of a 'natural' aristocracy of talent, representation had to be combined with a large territory, large electoral districts, and a relatively few representatives.[35]

In *The Federalist*, Madison concluded that large republics are most favourable to the election of proper guardians of the public weal'.[36] The larger the electoral district, the greater was the likelihood that well qualified individuals would be elected and appointed to national office. In large districts, the absolute number of talented individuals would be greater,[37] merely local reputations would count for less, and unworthy candidates would be less able 'to practice with success the vicious arts by which elections are too often carried'.[38] As electoral units increase in size and as voters consequently possess less personal knowledge of the candidates, voters increasingly rely upon the education, wealth, status, family connections, and reputations of candidates when deciding between them. Hence regarding both elective and appointive office, the large territory advantages members of the 'conventional' aristocracy at the expense of ordinary citizens because the social position of the former endows them with the extensive reputations necessary for election and selection.[39] In a large country with large constituencies, national legislators, executive officials and judges would be better able than the majority of citizens to identify the national interest, and maximum social pluralism would free them to act according to their conception of the public good. Consequently Madison expected Congress and the entire national government to act as a 'filter' which would improve public opinion.[40]

To help remove government officials from ordinary citizens, Madison as Publius relied upon not only representation and the country's extended orbit but also a wholly formal theory of representation[41] which contrasted with the mirror or reflection theory of representation espoused by many Anti-Federalists. Rejecting Publius' 'filter' theory of representation as 'aristocratic', many Anti-Federalists wanted to make the legislature into a portrait in miniature of society so as to best approximate direct democracy and thereby reduce the distance between officials and citizens. To ensure that representatives would think, act and feel like their constituents, these Anti-Federalists prescribed frequent elections, small districts, and short terms of office.[42] They argued that electoral accountability was insufficient and that a representative would faithfully represent his constituents only if he also resembled them in their occupations, status and opinions. But Publius insisted that the electoral connection was sufficient.

In *Federalist* nos. 35 and 36, Hamilton rejected the Anti-Federalists' 'idea of an actual representation of all classes of the people by persons of each class'[43] and concluded that electoral responsibility, not any resemblance to the voters, ensured the representatives' fealty to their duty. According to Hamilton, there was no need for any organic connection between representatives and represented since the electoral connection sufficed. Echoing Hamilton, Madison as Publius rejected the Anti-Federalists' prescriptions for bringing representatives and represented closer together. Furthermore, when Madison argued in *Federalist* no. 56 that Representatives would have sufficient knowledge of the laws and interests of their states in order to legislate appropriate national taxation, he said nothing to suggest that they should be aware of or pay heed to the opinions of their constituents. Madison assumed that the social pluralism of large electoral districts would free representatives from any need to consult regularly with their constituents.

While emphasising its beneficial effects, Madison did concede that the nation's extended territory might 'expose [Americans] to the inconvenience of remaining for a longer time under the influence of those misrepresentations which the combined industry of interested men may succeed in distributing among them'. To overcome this disadvantage, Madison at this time recommended reliance upon institutional 'auxiliary precautions' to ensure that a single diseased branch would not be fatal to republican liberty. If one branch of the new national government succeeded in manipulating public opinion and hence escaping from popular control, the institutional complexity of the new government would prevent that branch from governing tyrannically.[44]

In contrast to his earlier perception of the nation's large territory as an essential element of republican government, Madison as creator of the Republican party portrayed the nation's extended orbit as a danger. He now argued that the nation's large size endangered republican government by removing government from popular control, by impeding the concerted action of republicans, by thwarting the formation of genuine national public opinion, by encouraging abuses of government power and by vitiating fraternal feelings. Consequently in 1791–2 he sought to diminish the distance between the national government and the governed.

Now as party organiser, Madison perceived a new danger not identified by Publius: 'The more extensive a country, the more insignificant is each individual in his own eyes. This may be unfavorable to liberty.'[45] In a large republic, an individual citizen is likely to conclude that his voice is politically unimportant and hence might become politically apathetic. To encourage political participation by ordinary citizens, Madison's new Republican party mobilised Americans into a common political movement so that a citizen would see himself, not as a weak isolated individual, but rather as an active member of a powerful collectivity.

According to Madison, 'monarchies' suffered from two disadvantages: '1st, That the eyes of a good prince cannot see all that he ought to know – 2nd, That the hands of a bad one will not be tied by the fear of combinations against him.' These disadvantages increased as the size of the country increased.[46] Since Madison alleged that Hamilton's and the Federalists' preference for enhanced executive power betrayed their preference for 'monarchy', Madison was warning that the United States would fall prey to these disadvantages if Hamilton and the Federalists succeeded. Unfortunately, the country's extended orbit favoured Hamilton's designs. In an earlier essay, Madison had argued that an extensive territory contributed to the expansion of executive power by weakening popular control of the legislature which provided the only possible institutional check to executive usurpation.[47] Hence the extended territory jeopardised republican government either because a well-intentioned executive would lack sufficient knowledge of the country or because a tyrannically-inclined executive would exploit the weakness of the legislature.

Although as Publius he had advocated distancing government officials both physically and psychically from the people, Madison the partisan now argued that such removal endangered republican government by providing government with the opportunity to counterfeit public opinion. In a large country where it is more difficult to ascertain genuine public opinion, the government can more easily influence and mould opinion for its own purposes and could even inject its surrogate into the vacuum which results from the people's inability to fashion and discern an independent public opinion. A government's interference in opinion formation, and even outright substitution of its own surrogate for genuine public opinion, threatens republican government since 'public opinion sets bounds to every government and is the real sovereign in every free one'.[48] Laying aside his previous fear that popular passions might overwhelm republican government, Madison acknowledged in a letter to Edmund Pendleton a new fear that the nation's large territory might weaken popular control of government. 'In all

Governments the public censorship is necessary in order to prevent abuses. In such a one as ours, where the members are so removed from the eye of their Constituents, an easy and prompt circulation of public proceedings is peculiarly essential.'[49]

While Publius had praised the obstacles to organisation and communication created by an extensive territory and opted for the institutional 'auxiliary precautions' to safeguard against the problem he associated with it, Madison the party organiser now adopted an anti-institutional solution which proposed to bring the public and government closer together. Although still not adopting the Anti-Federalists' mirror or reflection theory of representation, Madison as party organiser did embrace their anti-institutionalism; he now advocated a regular interchange between representatives and constituents so that the representative's opinions would more closely reflect those of his constituents. To forestall the danger posed by the country's extended orbit, Madison in 1791–2 urged that the government and people be brought into closer proximity. Although the physical territory of the country could not be reduced literally, a figurative shrinkage could be effected.

> Whatever facilitates a general intercourse of sentiments, as good roads, domestic commerce, a free press, and particularly a *circulation of newspapers through the entire body of the people*, and *Representatives going from, and returning among every part of them*, is equivalent to a contraction of territorial limits, and is favorable to liberty, where these may be too extensive.[50]

Repudiating Publius, Madison now hoped to reduce the distance between government and governed in a republic. Far from desiring 'a general intercourse of sentiments', Publius had been hostile to any such intercourse because it could facilitate the formation of a majority faction. However, Madison now played the leading role in organising a national Republican party and establishing a leading republican newspaper in order to facilitate 'a general intercourse of sentiments'.

Unlike Edmund Burke's parliamentary party of family connections, Madison's Republican party reached out into the citizenry in order to mobilise and concentrate a general public opinion, not the fragmented opinions of multifarious factions. Its roots lay in the spontaneous democratic–republican societies which acted out-of-doors to agitate political issues, to arouse public opinion and to pressure elected and appointed officials.[51] While Publius had cautioned against involving the public too strongly in political affairs, Madison's party now sought to unite citizens in all parts of the country in a common endeavour to ensure that genuine public opinion would not only ultimately confine the government, but also govern.

While Publius had favoured an impersonal electoral mechanism to link representatives and represented, Madison now began creating a party in the electorate which rested on face-to-face personal relationships. With its roots in local life, Madison's political party rewarded and favoured exactly those individuals and characteristics scorned by *The Federalist*. Publius had recommended the extended orbit precisely because it would thwart the election and selection of individuals with purely 'local' reputations. Now as party organiser, Madison emphasised inner bonds of affection, sympathy, friendship and trust; however, the nation's large territory prevented the personal knowledge upon which those inner bonds depend for their existence. Requiring proximity among participants, those particularistic qualities can appear only if the participants possess direct personal knowledge of one another. While the Jeffersonian Republican party could not bring all citizens into immediate contact with one another, it could encourage citizens to participate in a common political organisation where they could develop the inner bonds of trust, confidence, and friendship. By providing citizens with the political space where they could develop inner, fraternal bonds, Madison's party helped overcome one deleterious consequence of an extensive territory.[52]

Madison's competing accounts of representation and the extended sphere found in *The Federalist* and his later partisan essays were located at opposite ends of what Samuel P. Hays has termed the 'community–society continuum'.[53] As Publius, Madison had praised the extended territory for removing national politics from the local community and consequently reconstituting the national political arena as one of secondary, impersonal relationships. But Madison's Republican party was rooted in the local life of primary interpersonal relationships. Occupying the 'society' end of the spectrum, Publius spoke the universal language of interest and sought to insulate a wholly popular government from immediate popular control. As a state-builder, the earlier Madison defended the creation of free political institutions which were as separate from and independent of the citizenry as popular government would allow.[54] Yet Madison the party organiser adopted a more anti-institutional approach which blurred the line of demarcation between government and people.

REPUBLICANS FROM EXPEDIENCY OR PRINCIPLE?

In *Federalist* no. 51, Madison explained that self-interested calculation or expediency would induce Americans to endorse the proposed Constitution with its supposedly neutral decision-making process. Since no faction wanted to see any other faction armed with government power, and since each desired protection from the others, all could agree to a government that would ensure minimal justice by punishing crime, enforcing contracts and repelling foreign attacks.

> In a society under the forms of which the stronger faction can readily unite and oppress the weaker, anarchy may as truly be said to reign as in a state of nature, where the weaker individual is not secured against the violence of the stronger; and as, in the latter state, even the stronger individuals are prompted by the uncertainty of their condition, to submit to a government which may protect the weak as well as themselves; so, in the former state will the powerful factions or parties be gradually induced, by a like motive, to wish for a government which will protect all parties, the weaker as well as the more powerful.[55]

Although every faction desires to tyrannise, calculations of self-interest or expediency, especially the impossibility of becoming a tyrant and the fear of being tyrannised over, lead weak and strong alike to edorse an impartial government guaranteeing equal protection of the laws. According to *Federalist* no. 51, Americans, who are divided by their competing factional interests, accept as a second-best compromise a republican government which impartially protects the rights of the weak as well as the strong. Lacking a principled commitment to republican government, Americans still consent to it for expediential reasons.

However, if given an opportunity, an individual who only consented to impartial republican government for expediential reasons would be only too eager to deprive his fellow citizens of their liberty and to govern tyrannically. As Publius, Madison did not attempt to remove such tyrannical desires, but instead relied upon free government and the minority status of all factions to prevent Americans from acting upon those desires. Only if a governing majority was a coalition of minorities would liberty be safe. In a republic, the minority status of all factions would preserve liberty.

> In a free government the security for civil rights must be the same as that for religious rights. It consists in the one case in the multiplicity of interests, and in the other in the multiplicity of sects. The degree of security in both cases will depend on the extent of country and number of people comprehended under the same government.[56]

For Madison, neither the weak parchment barriers of a bill of rights nor, by implication, any principled commitment, but rather a plethora of minority religious sects in the context of free political institutions preserved religious liberty in Virginia and the United States. Madison insisted that if a majority belonged to a single religious sect that majority would inevitably institutionalise its religious practices and beliefs as the state church and state religion since no sect had principled objections to such establishments.

> Is a bill of rights a security for religion? Would the bill of rights in this state [Virginia] exempt the people from paying for the support of one particular sect, if such sect were established by law? If there were a majority of one sect, a bill of rights would be a poor protection for liberty. Happily for the states, they enjoy the utmost freedom of religion. This freedom arises from that multiplicity of sects, which pervades America, and which is *the best and only* security for religious liberty in any society. For where there is such a variety of sects, there cannot be a majority of any one sect to oppress and persecute the rest. Fortunately for this commonwealth [Virginia], a majority of the people are decidedly against any exclusive [religious] establishment – I believe it to be so in the other states ... It is better that this security should be depended upon from the general legislature, than from one particular state. A particular state might concur in one religious project. But the United States abound in such a variety of sects, that it is a strong security against religious persecution, and is sufficient to authorise a conclusion, that no one sect will ever be able to out-number or depress the rest.[57]

According to Madison's analysis, despite every sect desiring to establish itself as the state church, religious freedom survives in Virginia and the United States for two reasons: extensive social pluralism ensures that no religious sect can claim the allegiance of a majority of citizens; and in a republic, a majority will always have the power as well as the motive to prevent any minority from establishing its beliefs and practices as the official religion and church. Since its more extensive territory encompasses a greater variety of religious sects than the individual states and therefore increases the probability that all sects will be minorities, the United States better protects religious liberty than does a single state. Since minority status and republican government prevent each sect from attaining its first preference of establishing itself as the official church, all sects can and do agree on a second-best alternative of religious freedom and equality.

Madison's insistence that republican government could not survive without virtue in the people[58] and his declaration that 'republican government presupposes the existence of these qualities ['which justify a certain portion of esteem and confidence'] in a higher degree than any other form'[59] apparently contradict this view that Madison thought that Americans lacked any principled commitment to republican government. Yet even if officials and citizens in *The Federalist* might be capable of transcending narrow self-interest and acting so as to realise a broader public interest, Americans still are not virtuous in the sense of possessing a principled commitment to free government. At this time, Madison mistakenly equated an expediential American preference for republican government with virtue, although this preference originated in unvirtuous expediency and self-interest and was devoid of any principled commitment. Hence Madison confused an expediential preference with a virtuous motive; but a reluctant, expediential acceptance of republican government is not equivalent to a virtuous, principled commitment to it.

The 'virtue' of the rulers and the more limited 'virtue' of the ruled which Madison invoked to rescue the essentially mechanical system of *The Federalist* are the products of placing officials and ordinary Americans in an institutional context where it is in their interest to act according to a broader public interest.[60] Hence, Publius derives the virtue of officials from their electoral incentive in a heterogeneous society to behave themselves and to act in the public interest since various factional interests cancel one another; but electoral calculation is hardly equivalent to virtue. Similarly, if voters in a sufficiently heterogeneous society must turn to representatives who can discern a broader public interest and eschew electing potential despots because they do not want to become subjects, their expediential decision hardly makes the voters virtuous in the conventional sense; rather these voters are merely prudential. According to Publius' mistaken logic, an individual who is deterred from committing a crime because he fears punishment is just. However while the behaviour may be just, the individual is not.

Madison's ideological rebirth began in late 1788 during the movement for adoption of a national bill of rights. Although he continued to think that parchment barriers were ineffective in resisting a tyrannical majority, he now acknowledged that a bill of rights had an expressive role which might significantly impede the appearance of a majority with despotic intentions; within three short years, he perceived the Jeffersonian Republican party as a united majority whose commitment to republicanism innoculated it against any desire to deprive its Federalist opponents of their rights.[61]

While advocating a national bill of rights a few months after the Virginia ratifying convention, Madison continued to adhere to his previous arguments that social pluralism was the best guarantor of religious liberty and that a bill of rights could not prevent a majority from depriving a minority of its rights. However, he now appreciated that a bill of rights could positively shape public opinion so that a united majority might never desire to violate the rights of a minority.

> What use ... can a bill of rights serve in popular Governments? 1. The political truths declared in that solemn manner acquire by degrees the character of fundamental maxims of free Government, and as they become incorporated with the national sentiment, counteract the impulses of interest and passion. 2. Altho' it be generally true as above stated that the danger of oppression lies in the interested majorities of the people rather than in usurped acts of the Government, yet there may be occasions on which the evil may spring from the latter sources; and on such, a bill of rights will be a good ground for appeal to the sense of the community.[62]

Madison's advocacy of a national bill of rights manifested a new anti-institutional concern for the formation of the citizenry's political beliefs. By symbolising the entire nation's commitment to shared republican values, a bill of rights would encourage a firmer, more general attachment to liberty so that Americans would not desire to deprive their fellow citizens of liberty. Although a bill of rights could be employed as a standard by which to limit executive power or even to check a usurping minority, it primarily functioned in a republic to safeguard minorities against a tyrannical majority, not by legally checking a majority, but by instilling republican beliefs and thereby forestalling the formation of 'interested majorities' which desired to tyrannise. Hence the ultimate value of a bill of rights extended beyond its legal properties to its role in politically educating the citizenry. Despite Publius' conclusion that constitution-makers could only strive to control the effects of faction,[63] Madison now recommended a bill of rights as an antidote to 'the impulses of interest and passion'.

Unwilling to rest republican government upon the insecure foundation of expediential calculation, Madison the party organiser relied upon 'good' citizens[64] who possessed a firmer, more principled commitment to liberty and republican government. 'As the metes and bounds of government, they [charters of government] transcend all other land-marks, because every public usurpation is an encroachment on the private right, not of one, but of all.'[65] Since Publius' expediential calculators are only too eager to encroach upon the rights of others, this assertion that 'every public usurpation is an encroachment on the private right, not of one, but of all' holds only if citizens are committed to liberty and republican government from firm principle. Free of the trammels of prudential calculation, Madison's good citizens oppose all abuses of government power, regardless of whether such abuses rebound to their private advantage.

While Publius' self-interested calculator measured all government action against the standard of his private interest, principled republicans 'are naturally offended at every public measure that does not appeal to the understanding and to the general interest of the community, or that is not strictly conformable to the principles, and conducive to the preservation of republican government'.[66] Although a faction might object for self-interested reasons to partial legislation which benefits another faction, factions are not 'naturally offended' by '*all*' partial legislation; rather the factions of *The Federalist*, and especially a majority faction, are a problem precisely because they seek and welcome partial legislation which will benefit themselves.

While Publius' factions with their hunger for governmental favours are willing to sacrifice impartial republican government to their self-interest, the good citizen of Madison the party organiser does not calculate whether a government policy which encroaches upon the rights of others benefits or injures himself. Possessing a principled commitment to republican government, a good citizen will not sacrifice the liberty of others for his own advantage; he disinterestedly subordinates his private interest to the value of liberty. His firm, strong attachment to liberty becomes part of his second nature so that he 'naturally' opposes all narrowly self-interested legislation even when it would benefit his own private interest.

Good citizens reject selfish advantage as a proper motive or as a legitimate criterion for evaluating governmental activity. They insist that public policies should 'appeal to the understanding and to the general interest of the community'. Hence good citizens or principled republicans repudiate partial legislation even when it appeals to their own selfish interest. Madison complained that by appealing 'less to the reason of the many than to their weakness',[67] anti-republicans lured citizens away from their attachment to liberty by promising private economic benefits. Such anti-republican appeals tempted citizens with only an expediential preference for republicanism to sacrifice the liberty of others to their private advantage.

Having previously co-authored *The Federalist* with Alexander Hamilton, Madison now opposed the new Secretary of the Treasury's economic policies which sought to create a class of citizens who would have a strong economic interest to support the new national government. Worried that such an appeal to naked self-interest reduced the grand republican experiment to nothing more than an economically profitable arrangement, Madison objected that Hamilton's economic policy transplanted the English system of corruption to the United States.[68] Yet Hamilton's proposal to provide economic incentives to entice some individuals to defend the national government simply made Madison's earlier expediential calculus in *Federalist* no. 51 and in the Virginia ratifying convention more concrete.

PUBLIC OPINION AND THE CONSTITUTIONAL BALANCE

As Publius, Madison insisted that the preservation of liberty depended upon the maintenance of the constitutional balance; hence he described as despotic popularly elected state legislatures which overwhelmed the other branches and appropriated all effective government power. He defined tyranny procedurally: 'The accumulation of all powers, legislative, executive, and judiciary, in the same hands, whether of one, a few, or many, and whether hereditary, self-appointed, or elective, may justly be pronounced the very definition of tyranny.'[69] Madison formulated the political equivalent of Adam Smith's 'invisible hand' of the free market which was supposed to produce the public interest from the individual pursuit of self-interest; Publius counted upon the self-interested competition of officials in independently powerful government institutions to preserve the constitutional balance although no political actor actually willed its preservation.

When disputes between the different branches and different layers of government occurred, how would those disputes be resolved without disrupting the constitutional equilibrium? Who or what would adjudicate? To preserve the constitutional balance, Publius could not simply rely upon the Constitution's formal demarcation of the separate government institutions and their respective powers, since events at the state level had demonstrated the inefficacy of mere parchment barriers.[70]

Federalist nos. 49 and 50 also disparaged the suggestion that public opinion could be safely entrusted with the delicate task of preserving the constitutional balance whenever a conflict arose over the power of the different branches or levels of government. *The Federalist* feared that appeals to public opinion would inflame dangerous passions, thereby generating additional turmoil and fanning unrest: 'The danger of disturbing the public tranquility by interesting too strongly the public passions is a still more serious objection against reference of constitutional questions to the decision of the whole society.' Furthermore, Publius heeded the lesson learned at the state level that public opinion usually favoured the legislature whenever it came into conflict with the other branches: 'But the greatest objection of all is that the decisions which would probably result from such appeals would not answer the purpose of maintaining the constitutional equilibrium of the government. We have seen that the tendency of republican governments is to an aggrandizement of the legislative at the expense of the other departments.'[71] Hence Publius concluded that both mere parchment barriers and public opinion were inadequate to protect the constitutional balance between the different levels and branches of government.

Fashioning an institutional solution internal to the Constitution, Publius counted upon social pluralism, the fragmentation of governmental power and the self-interest of officials to maintain the dynamic equilibrium of the constitutional structure. Publis expected self-interest to motivate officials to assert the independent power of their institutions when confronted by challenges from other levels or branches of government. To preserve the Constitution's distribution of power, Madison relied upon a 'policy of supplying by opposite and rival interests, the defect of better motives'.[72] Although officials would not have to be public-spirited, their self-interested defence of the power of their offices would still contribute unintentionally to the maintenance of the constitutional balance.

> But the great security against a gradual concentration of the several powers in the same department consists in giving to those who administer each department, the necessary constitutional means and personal motives to resist encroachments of the others ... Ambition must be made to counteract ambition. The interest of the man must be connected with the constitutional rights of the place.

Therefore, within the constitutional structure, 'the private interest of every individual may be a sentinel over the public rights'.[73] Publius concluded that constitutional liberty could survive and even flourish although no individual consciously upheld it. The private pursuit of interest within the Constitution's elaborate structure was supposed to protect liberty as an unintended consequence, just as the pursuit of self-interest in Adam Smith's free market ostensibly served the public good unintentionally.

Although later worried by the threat of executive, rather than legislative, usurpation, Madison in 1791–2 agreed with Publius about the necessity of maintaining the constitutional balance: 'Power being found by universal experience liable to abuses, a distribution of it into separate departments, has become a first principle of free governments.'[74] Still associating the Constitution's institutional balance with republican government and liberty, Madison now eschewed Publius's reliance upon self-interested officials and his political version of the invisible hand. Instead, he argued that the regime of republican liberty could be maintained only if citizens willed its defence. Hence Madison the party organiser substituted an anti-institutional reliance upon virtuous public opinion for Publius' mechanical solution. 'To secure all the advantages of such a system [that is, a confederated republic], every *good citizen* will be at once a centinel over the rights of the people; over the authorities of the federal government; and over both the rights and the authorities of the intermediate governments.'[75] Although Publius had confidently expected the self-interested competition of office-holders in separate institutions with overlapping powers to preserve constitutional liberty, Madison the party organiser declared: 'Let it be the *patriotic* study of all, *to maintain the various authorities* established by our complicated system, each in its respective constitutional sphere.'[76] Abandoning Publius' political version of the invisible hand, Madison now sought citizens who would consciously act to preserve the constitutional balance. In order for a citizen to be a 'centinel over the rights of the people', he now had to be 'good' and 'patriotic'; but Publius had only required them to be self-interested or ambitious. Madison now expected Americans to possess those 'better motives' which Publius had thought superfluous.

Expounding a new anti-institutionalism, Madison in 1791–2 subordinated institutional arrangements to public opinion as the ultimate guarantor of republican government and denigrated the importance of the Constitution's institutional complexity: 'In bestowing the eulogies due to the particular and *internal checks* of power, it ought not the less to be remembered, that they are *neither the sole nor the chief palladium* of constitutional liberty. The people who are authors of this blessing, must also be its guardians.'[77] Madison the party organiser belittled institutional arrangements as sterile and inefficacious unless supported by republican opinion. Madison now contended that public opinion, not the social pluralism and 'internal checks' celebrated by Publius, determined whether governments respected liberty.

According to Madison the party organiser, republican opinion constrains even tyrannical governments; and the best, most elaborately constructed republican government will go awry if republican opinion ceases its active oversight.

> All power has been traced up to opinion. The stability of all governments and security of all rights may be traced to the same source. The most arbitrary government is controlled where the public opinion is fixed ... *The most systematic governments* are turned by the slightest impulse from their regular path, where public opinion no longer holds them in it.[78]

Since the new United States Constitution obviously qualified as one of 'the most systematic governments', Madison now disparaged his earlier overweening concern for mechanical solutions. Not only are institutional arrangements inferior to republican opinion in protecting republican government, but also even the most perfected and developed institutional arrangements alone cannot preserve republican government. Only the citizenry's republican opinion, not the social pluralism and 'auxiliary precautions' of *The Federalist*, determines the republican character of American government.

At this time, Madison offered a new anti-institutional explanation of the preservation of English liberty. Institutionally-inclined thinkers like Publius attributed the existence of liberty in Britain to the equilibrium of the British constitution, with its tripartite division and the association of each branch with a different social order. According to this Whig analysis, the social complexity of three distinct estates conjoined with institutional complexity to generate a dynamic equilibrium protective of liberty. Derisively dismissing this argument which, with the necessary modifications to accommodate the absence of three permanent social orders (or estates), had served as the model for the new United States Constitution, Madison now declared: 'The boasted equilibrium of this [the British] government (so far as it is a reality) is maintained less by the distribution of its power, than by the force of public opinion.'[79] Madison's new position echoed Thomas Paine's heretical *Common Sense*. Repudiating the Whig constitutionalism of the pre-Independence resistance literature,[80] Paine had written: 'It is wholly owing to the constitution of the people, and not to the constitution of the government, that the crown is not as oppressive in England as in Turkey.'[81]

PARTIES BEYOND FACTION

Publius had accepted an interest-based factional politics as natural in a free society: 'The latent causes of faction are thus sown in the nature of man.' Furthermore, while acknowledging the multitude of differences which generated political divisions, Publius had concluded: 'the most common and durable source of factions has been the various and unequal distribution of property.'[82] Earlier Madison had avowed an even more extreme position by distinguishing 'natural' divisions based on economic interest from 'artificial' cleavages arising from political or religious opinions.[83]

In contrast, Madison the party organiser distinguished partisan conflict from the factional competition of *The Federalist*; by linking parties to ideological disagreements which transcended economic differences, Madison defined political parties as qualitatively different from factions. The two concluding essays in his series postulated the ideological antagonism between republicans and anti-republicans as the essential core of American political conflict.

As party organiser, Madison sought to make political parties respectable by divorcing them from mere factional squabbles. Madison periodised American history into four periods of partisan conflict, but 'general' or national parties existed in only three of these periods. The conflict between the supporters and opponents of independence defined the first period; but Madison implied that the latter might not qualify as a proper political party since there were so few members of that 'disaffected class'. The peace treaty with Britain ushered in the second period from 1783–7 which lacked 'general' parties although there were 'local' 'parties in abundance'.[84] The third period witnessed the reappearance of 'general' parties which were divided by their support for and opposition to the new Constitution. The struggle for ratification, however, did not mark a resumption of fundamental political conflict since most of the members of both these national parties were good republicans, although both also contained some opponents of republican government. While 'the great body [of Federalist supporters of the Constitution] were unquestionably friends to republican liberty', they also contained 'some who were openly or secretly attached to monarchy and aristocracy; and hoped to make the constitution a cradle for these hereditary establishments'. Similarly, the 'great body' of the Anti-Federalist opponents of the Constitution 'were certainly well affected to the union and to good government, tho' there might be a few who had a leaning unfavourable to both'.[85]

Resembling the first party period, the fourth period renewed the original conflict between republicans and anti-republicans. This current conflict was far different from the local divisions of the second party period and from the less fundamental differences of the third. In both the first and fourth periods, the friends and enemies of free republican government were segregated into competing, even if unequal, national parties.

Contradicting his earlier teaching about the naturalness of factional politics, Madison described the conflict between republicans and anti-republicans as 'natural to most political societies';[86]

this partisan division was at heart an ideological disagreement. Abandoning Publius' earlier emphasis upon (economic) self-interest as the mainspring of political conflict, Madison defined the anti-republican party ideologically as that party which

> consists of those, who from particular interest, from natural temper, or from the habits of life, are more partial to the opulent than to the other classes of society; and having debauched themselves into a persuasion that mankind are incapable of governing themselves, it follows ... that government can be carried only by the pageantry of rank, the influence of money and emoluments, and the terror of military force. Men of those sentiments must naturally wish to point the measures of government less to the interest of the many than of the few, and less to the reason of the many than to their weaknesses.[87]

Although some anti-republicans were self-interested and some anti-republican ideas benefitted a few wealthy individuals, anti-republicans could not be accurately described in terms of factional interest.

According to Madison, the anti-republicans sought to rule by imitating the British use of 'place' and force. Fearful that 'the people are ever ready to fly off from the government', the anti-republicans recommended that the national government be supplied with additional military capacity for compelling obedience and increased financial resources to bribe some citizens to be loyal.[88]

Distrusting the people's capacity for self-government, the anti-republicans urged that the protection of the people's liberty be entrusted to 'their wise rulers'.[89] As Publius, Madison had argued that the election and selection of relatively few national officials from an extensive territory and population would transform the national government into a 'filter' by ensuring the elevation of the virtuous and wise to government posts. But as party organiser, Madison now identified as anti-republican the teaching that the people should trust 'their wise rulers' to protect their liberty.

Acknowledging that the people had often erred in self-government, Madison the party leader refused to accept such error as sufficient reason for proscribing self-government.

> Too true it is, that slavery has been the general lot of the human race. Ignorant – they have been cheated; asleep – they have been surprised; divided – the yoke has been forced upon them. But what is the lesson? That because the people *may* betray themselves, they ought to give

> themselves up, blindfold, to those who have an interest in betraying them? Rather conclude that the people ought to be enlightened, to be awakened, to be united, that after establishing a government they should watch over it, as well as obey it.[90]

Madison now identified the latter as the republican course, but it hardly resembles the path taken by Publius four years earlier. Publius had never proposed to enlighten the people, had feared a united citizenry, and had argued that the citizenry could not be relied upon to preserve the constitutional order. Although in less extreme form, Madison as Publius had opted for the former 'anti-republican' solution.

Just as Madison described the anti-republican party in terms of its political ideas so he also defined republicans, not in terms of their interests, but rather by their commitment to free government. Republicans have faith in the people's capacity to govern themselves and to preserve their liberty. The republican party

> consists of those who believing in the doctrine that mankind are capable of govering themselves, and hating hereditary power as an insult to the reason and an outrage to the rights of man, are naturally offended at every public measure that does not appeal to the understanding and to the general interest of the community, or that is not strictly conformable to the principles, and conducive to the preservation of republican government.[91]

Not just their preference for republican government but also their principled commitment to it distinguishes republicans from their anti-republican opponents.

CONCLUSION

Madison as Publius endorsed maximum heterogeneity, but as party organiser he favoured greater homogeneity. While Publius praised the beneficial consequences of the extended sphere, Madison in 1791–2 emphasised its deleterious effects. The later Madison's call for a principled devotion to republican liberty rejected Publius' expediential logic. Publius thought that the constitutional balance could be preserved as the unintended by-product of political competition mediated by a complex institutional structure; but Madison the party organiser recognised that Americans would have to will its preservation. Madison's later description of the partisan conflict between republicans and anti-republicans hardly accords with the factional politics of *Federalist* no.10.

In part, these differences are attributable to the two Madisons responding to different political problems. Confidently assuming that majority rule automatically prevents minority factions from gaining and abusing government power, Madison as Publius had emphasised that in a republic a majority faction posed the real danger to liberty. Contradicting this assumption, Madison the party organiser stressed that a minority had usurped government power. Similarly, Publius had sought to prevent the legislature from unilaterally exercising legislative, executive and judicial powers; but in 1791–2, unchecked, expanding executive power worried Madison.

Another, more important reason for the differences between Madison as Publius and as party organiser was their competing conceptions of a liberal politics. John Zvesper has suggested that Madison's commitment to liberalism provides the continuity in his thought. As Publius and as party organiser, Madison offered different defences of a liberal political order, but at all times he 'was more consistently attached to the principles of liberalism and prudence than to the devices of pluralism and party government'.[92] However, Zvesper's cogent conclusion should not obscure the fact that Madison's twin devices defended two fundamentally different liberal regimes.

As Publius, Madison had accepted economic inequality as the inevitable outcome of the individual pursuit of interest; but Madison the party organiser sought greater equality of condition. While Publius simply sought the greatest possible number of social interests, Madison in 1791–2 evaluated different occupations according to their compatibility with republican politics. Transcending the usual point that individuals who desire to pursue their self-interest must be willing to respect the right of others to do the same, Madison the party organiser now deemed some occupations to be harmful and others beneficial, not because the former (criminally) violated, and the latter respected, the rights of others, but because some occupations stunt and others nurture the capacities needed by self-governing republican citizens. The earlier, institutionally-inclined Madison had placed his primary faith in the extended republic, the 'auxiliary precautions', and expediential calculation; but emphasising that only a principled commitment to republican government ensured its survival, the later Madison concerned himself with the moral health of Americans.

Revealing that a liberal consensus does not necessarily preclude fundamental political conflict, the later argument between Stephen Douglas and Abraham Lincoln about how best to deal with the slavery extension issue recapitulated this earlier intra-liberal antagonism between Madison as Publius and as party organiser. On behalf of a procedural politics divorced from questions of ultimate value, Stephen Douglas refused to judge slavery as immoral and condemned Lincoln's willingness to interject moral considerations into politics. Douglas insisted that private opinions about the morality and immorality of slavery should not intrude into politics. In contrast, Lincoln called upon Americans to give political force to the moral judgement that slavery was sinful. While Douglas proclaimed that he was indifferent to whether the people of a territory decided to permit or prohibit slavery, Lincoln argued that a liberal republic could survive only if its members publicly judged slavery to be immoral and incompatible with free government. Like the two Madisons, Douglas and Lincoln not only disagreed about how to preserve a liberal political order but also offered competing liberal visions.[93]

Despite the disagreement between the two Madisons, Madison in 1791–2 never directly criticised the Constitution; however, his criticism of Publius' defence of it implied a criticism of the document itself. In 1791–2, Madison expected his national Republican party to embody the virtue needed to ensure the proper functioning of the Constitution. If, according to Madison the party organiser and even according to some of Publius' comments, virtue in the people and statesmanship in the leaders are necessary to preserve republican government, then Madison's loyalty to the Constitution seems misplaced, since that document does not attempt to ensure the availability of the required virtue and statesmanship. If, as Madison the party organiser thought, the moral health of the citizenry is more important than institutional arrangements, can one praise a Constitution which eschews responsibility for nurturing inner virtue?

NOTES

The author thanks Paul Cammack and John Stachniewski for their assistance.

1 Marvin Meyers (ed.), *The Mind of the Founder: Sources of the Political Thought of James Madison*, Indianapolis, Bobbs-Merrill, 1973, p. xliv.
2 Norman Jacobson, 'Political science and political education', *American Political Science Review*, 57, 1963, pp. 561–9.
3 Neal Riemer, *James Madison*, New York, Washington Square Press, 1968; and 'James Madison's theory of the self-destructive features of republican government', *Ethics*, 65, 1954, pp. 34–43.
4 Robert J. Morgan, 'Madison's analysis of the sources of political authority', *American Political Science Review*, 75, 1982, pp. 613–25.
5 Meyers, *Mind of the Founder*, pp. xliii–xlvi; Edward J. Erler, 'The problem of the public good in *The Federalist*', *Polity*, 13, 1980–81, pp. 649–67; Harry V. Jaffa, 'A phoenix from the ashes', a paper delivered at the annual meeting of the American Political Science Association, Washington, D.C., 1977; John Zvesper, *Political Philosophy and Rhetoric: A Study of the Origins of American Party Politics*, Cambridge, Cambridge University Press, 1977, pp. 110–19.
6 Meyers, *Mind of the Founder*, pp. xliii–xlvi; Adrienne Koch, *Madison's 'Advice to My Country'*, Princeton, Princeton University Press, 1966.
7 Alexander Hamilton, John Jay and James Madison, *The Federalist Papers*, ed. Clinton Rossiter, New York, New American Library, 1961, no. 10, p. 78. Henceforth, all citations from *The Federalist* refer to this – the Rossiter – edition.
8 *The Federalist*, no. 10, p. 80. See letter to Jefferson, 17 October 1788, *The Papers of James Madison*, eds. William T. Hutchinson, William M. E. Rachal, Robert A. Rutland, *et al.*, Chicago, University of Chicago Press and Charlottesville, University Press of Virginia, 1962 to date, 11, p. 298. Henceforth this source is cited as *Papers*.
9 The defenders of the new Constitution interpreted stay laws and paper money as unjust infringements of property rights perpetrated by majority factions; state constitutions with the greatest institutional complexity had proved inadequate to check these tyrannical actions by unified majorities. Even the institutionally complex constitution of Massachusetts which served as a model for the new federal constitution had failed to protect property rights. When poor farmers led by the Revolutionary War captain Daniel Shays had resorted to illegal direct action to close the state courts in western Massachusetts with the aim of preventing mortgage foreclosures, the state government had used the militia to quell the rebellion; but then the Shaysites discovered that they could achieve their factional objective legally. Defeated militarily, the Shaysites triumphed electorally, and their duly elected representatives then enacted stay laws prohibiting mortgage foreclosures. Gordon Wood, *The Creation of the American Republic, 1776–1787*, New York, W. W. Norton, 1969, pp. 463–7; Isaac Kramnick, 'Editor's introduction', in Alexander Hamilton, John Jay and James Madison, *The Federalist Paper*, New York, Penguin Books, 1987, pp. 55–6.
10 *The Federalist*, no. 10, p. 81.
11 *The Federalist*, no. 10, p. 83.
12 *The Federalist*, no. 51, p. 325.
13 James Madison, *The Writings of James Madison*, ed. Gaillard Hunt, New York, Putnam, 1900–10, VI, p. 68. Henceforth this source is cited as *Writings*.
14 Meyers, *Mind of the Founder*, p. 213. Also see *Papers*, 11, pp. 404, 415.
15 *Writings*, VI, p. 120.
16 *Writings*, VI, p. 68.
17 *Writings*, VI, pp. 68–9, emphasis added.
18 *Writings*, VI, p. 114.

19 The later Jacksonian Democrats developed the idea of a party system. Richard Hofstadter, *The Idea of a Party System: The Rise of a Legitimate Opposition in the United States, 1780–1840*, Berkeley, University of California Press, 1970, esp. pp. 84–6; Michael L. Wallace, 'Changing concepts of party in the United States: New York, 1815–1828', *American Historical Review*, 74, 1968, pp. 453–91.
20 *Writings*, VI, p. 119.
21 *Writings*, VI, p. 68, original emphasis.
22 *Writings*, VI, p. 86, original emphasis.
23 See Theodore J. Lowi, *The End of Liberalism: The Second Republic of the United States*, New York, W. W. Norton, 2nd edn, 1979; and Grant McConnell, *Private Power and American Democracy*, New York, Vintage, 1966.
24 *The Federalist*, no. 10, p. 78.
25 *Writings*, VI, p. 86.
26 Jean Jacques Rousseau, *The Social Contract and Discourses*, tran. G. D. H. Cole, New York, E. P. Dutton, 1950, p. 50.
27 *Writings*, VI, p. 96, original emphasis.
28 *Writings*, VI, p. 100.
29 *Writings*, VI, pp. 98–9.
30 *The Federalist*, nos. 10 and 63.
31 *The Federalist*, no. 10, p. 82.
32 *The Federalist*, no. 10, p. 81.
33 *The Federalist*, no. 63, p. 387, original emphasis.
34 *The Federalist*, no. 10, pp. 82–3; Wood, *Creation of the American Republic*, ch. 10.
35 *The Federalist*, nos. 10 and 63.
36 *The Federalist*, no. 10, p. 82. See no. 10, pp. 82–3; no. 3, p. 43.
37 *The Federalist*, no. 10, p. 82.
38 *The Federalist*, no. 10, pp. 82–3.
39 Jean Yarbrough, 'Thoughts on *The Federalist's* view of representation', *Polity*, 12, 1979, pp. 65–82; Wood, *Creation of the American Republic*, pp. 475–83, 495–9.
40 *The Federalist*, no. 10, p. 82. See Yarbrough, 'Thoughts', pp. 68–73; Kramnick, 'Editor's introduction', pp. 41–3; Wood, *Creation of the American Republic*, pp. 506–18.
41 *The Federalist*, nos. 35, 36, 56, 57; Yarbrough, 'Thoughts'.
42 Kramnick, 'Editor's introduction', pp. 43–6.
43 *The Federalist*, no. 35, p. 214.
44 *The Federalist*, no. 63, p. 385.
45 *Writings*, VI, p. 70.
46 *Writings*, VI, p. 80.
47 *Writings*, VI, p. 67.
48 *Writings*, VI, p. 70.
49 Letter to Edmund Pendleton, 6 December 1792, *Writings*, VI, p. 121.
50 *Writings*, VI, p. 70, original emphasis.
51 Eugene Perry Link, *The Democratic-Republican Societies, 1790–1800*, New York, Columbia University Press, 1942; Richard Buel, Jr., *Securing the Revolution: Ideology in American Politics, 1789–1815*, Ithaca, N.Y., Cornell University Press, 1972, pp. 97–105, 129–34.
52 According to Eldon Eisenach, except for its possession of government coercion, Jefferson's proposed 'ward system' of government resembled Madison's Republican party. 'The American Revolution made and remembered', *American Studies*, 20, 1979, p. 89.
53 Samuel P. Hays, 'Political parties and the community–society continuum', ch. 6 in William Nisbet Chambers and Walter Dean Burnham (eds.), *The American Party Systems*, New York, Oxford University Press, 1967.
54 Kramnick, 'Editor's introduction', pp. 67–75.
55 *The Federalist*, no. 51, p. 325.

56 *The Federalist*, no. 51, p. 324.
57 Speech, 12 June 1788, *Papers*, 11, pp. 130–31, emphasis added. Madison repeated this argument in a letter to Jefferson dated 17 October 1788. *Papers*, 11, p. 298.
58 *Papers*, 11, p. 163.
59 *The Federalist*, no. 55, p. 346. Also see nos. 10, 51, 57. Some scholars see no difficulty in reconciling Madison's description of self-interested factional politics and his assumption of virtue in the rulers and ruled. However, other, more sceptical scholars doubt that *The Federalist*'s sudden shifts from self-interested factional politics to disinterested republican virtue are compatible. Erler, 'Problem of the public good'; Jaffa, 'A phoenix from the ashes'; Zvesper, 'The Madisonian systems', *Western Political Quarterly*, 37, 1984, pp. 236–56.
60 *The Federalist*, nos. 51, 55, 57.
61 *Writings*, VI, p. 123.
62 Letter to Jefferson, 17 October 1788, *Papers*, 11, pp. 297–9.
63 *The Federalist*, no. 10, p. 80.
64 *Writings*, VI, p. 82.
65 *Writings*, VI, p. 84.
66 *Writings*, VI, p. 118.
67 *Writings*, VI, p. 117.
68 *Writings*, VI, pp. 94, 120–23.
69 *The Federalist*, no. 47, p. 301.
70 *The Federalist*, no. 48.
71 *The Federalist*, no. 49, pp. 315–16.
72 *The Federalist*, no. 51, p. 322.
73 *The Federalist*, no. 51, pp. 321–2.
74 *Papers*, 14, p. 217; *Writings*, VI, p. 91.
75 *Writings*, VI, p. 82, emphasis added.
76 *Writings*, VI, p. 68, emphasis added.
77 *Writings*, VI, p. 93, emphasis added.
78 *Writings*, VI, p. 85, emphasis added.
79 *Writings*, VI, p. 87.
80 Thomas Paine, *Common Sense and Other Writings*, Indianapolis, Bobbs-Merrill, 1953, p. 9.
81 Stephen Newman has demonstrated how Paine's *Common Sense* broke radically with the Whig constitutional theory of the resistance literature. 'A note on *Common Sense*', *Political Theory*, 6, 1978, pp. 101–8.
82 *The Federalist*, no. 10, p. 79.
83 *Writings*, V, p. 29.
84 *Writings*, VI, pp. 109–10.
85 *Writings*, VI, pp. 112–13.
86 *Writings*, VI, p. 114.
87 *Writings*, VI, pp. 114–17.
88 *Writings*, VI, pp. 94, 120–23.
89 *Writings*, VI, p. 120.
90 *Writings*, VI, p. 120, original emphasis.
91 *Writings*, VI, p. 118.
92 Zvesper, 'The Madisonian Systems', p. 254.
93 See J. David Greenstone, 'Political culture and American political development: liberty, union and the liberal bipolarity', in Karen Orren and Stephen Skowronek (eds), *Studies in American Political Development: An Annual*, New Haven, Yale University Press, 1986, I, pp. 1–49; Harry V. Jaffa, *The Crisis of the House Divided: An Interpretation of the Lincoln–Douglas Debates*, Seattle, University of Washington Press, 1959; and Major L. Wilson, *Space, Time and Freedom: The Quest for Nationality and the Irrepressible Conflict, 1815–1861*, Westport, Conn., Greenwood Press, 1974.

Part IX
Interpreting The Constitution: What's Wrong With "Original Intent"?

[20]

Constitutional Interpretation and Conceptual Change

Terence Ball

My aim in this essay is to take another look at a current, or rather recurring, hermeneutical controversy. That controversy centers around a set of questions about what the Constitution "means" and how it should be interpreted. Is the meaning of this particular (or perhaps any) text extensionally equivalent to a (re)statement of its authors' beliefs and intentions? Or does the meaning of this (or any) text change over time and vary with the changing perspectives and interests of its interpreters? Various versions of the doctrine of "originalism" answer the first question affirmatively and the second negatively. Critics of originalism tend to answer the first negatively and the second affirmatively.

Interesting as these questions (and answers) are to scholars, they are not, needless to say, purely academic. Such questions constitute what I have elsewhere called "deadly hermeneutics"—deadly inasmuch as how they are answered has an important bearing on people's lives and well-being.[1] I want here to take a critical second look at one way of addressing and answering these questions. That perspective—once called "strict constructionism" and, more recently, "originalism" or, in one particular version, "original intent"—holds that the meaning of a text or utterance, generally speaking, is whatever its author initially intended or could conceivably have intended it to mean. In the case of the Constitution the task of the interpreter or "interpretive community"[2]—consisting not only of legal scholars, lawyers, judges, and Supreme Court justices, but ultimately of ordinary citizens as well—is to discover what the founders originally meant by this or that word, article, phrase, or passage.[3] Much has been said in defense and in criticism of this doctrine.[4] My aim here, however, is not to retread these well-traveled and by now deeply rutted roads but to suggest an alternate route to a familiar destination.

I propose to criticize originalism by advancing and defending two claims. The first, which I take to be straightforward and noncontroversial, is that discovering an author's beliefs and intentions requires that one recover or reconstruct the language or idiom in which those beliefs and intentions were framed in the first place. Although fraught with difficulties, this task can be, and has been, performed by conceptual historians.[5] My second and more controversial claim is that there are compelling reasons why judges and Supreme Court justices—and ordinary citizens—are not now and should not become conceptual historians bent on reconstructing the world of words within which the framers expressed their beliefs and framed their intentions.

My argument proceeds in the following way. I begin by sketching, very roughly and with the fewest possible strokes, a picture of the kind of un- or half-articulated beliefs that underlie and give point and meaning to human action and intention. This crude picture I then attempt to connect with current concerns about conceptual change and commensurability in anthropology and elsewhere. These concerns, I argue, also have their counterpart in constitutional interpretation. The background beliefs and the discursive or linguistic conventions within which the founders framed their intentions are in many respects remarkably different from our own. To recover and reinstate their intentions would require that judges not only recover but that they (and we) accept as valid and legitimate the outdated or even discredited theoretical discourse of an earlier epoch. This approach, however, is a retrograde move that we cannot rationally make. Next, I suggest that although one can of course sometimes discern the intentions of any particular individual founder, one commits the "single-author" fallacy if one attempts to impute a unique or univocal intention to the founders as a group. Finally, I conclude by suggesting that the most persuasive critic of originalism is none other than the Father of the Constitution himself.

BACKGROUND BELIEFS AND THE PROBLEM OF COMMENSURABILITY

It might be best to begin by stating the obvious. Our intentions are necessarily framed against the backdrop afforded by our understanding of the world and how it works. This understanding includes not only beliefs about causal connections (if you wish to bring about *Y*, you must first do *X* because *X* causes *Y*) but also certain assumptions about human nature—what kinds of creatures human beings are, what moves or motivates them, what ends they seek, and so on. These causal beliefs and these assumptions about human nature are in their turn part of a larger picture of the world and our place in it. As Isaiah Berlin observes:

> Men's beliefs in the sphere of conduct are part of their conceptions of themselves and others as human beings; and this conception in its turn, whether conscious or not, is intrinsic to their picture of the world. This picture may be complete and coherent, or shadowy or confused, but almost always . . . it can be shown to be dominated by one or more models or paradigms: mechanistic, organic, aesthetic, logical, mystical, shaped by the strongest influence of the day—religious, scientific, metaphysical or artistic. This model or paradigm determines the content as well as the form of beliefs and behaviour.[6]

To correctly characterize an agent's action—or an author's text—requires that one be able to identify the world picture that informs the language within which his or her intentions are (or were) framed in the first place.[7] One must, in other words, see them as somehow fitting in with a whole network of background beliefs about the world and how it works.

Yet this task often proves to be an extraordinarily difficult one to perform. Even in cases involving contemporaries with whom we presumably share a culture and a common language, we are often at a loss to say what they are doing, much less why they act as they do. One need only think, for example, of the difficulties facing a secular observer who wishes to give an account of the actions and self-understandings of someone who has undergone a religious conversion. One can of course ask what this person is doing, or intends to do, and why. But one is unlikely to accept at face value any self-understanding in which even the most ordinary events are seen as evidence of divine providence.[8]

These difficulties are doubled when observer and subject share neither a culture nor a common language. In such circumstances the so-called commensurability problem becomes both obvious and acute.[9] The epistemological perils facing anthropologists are notorious, and the opportunities for mistranslation and other forms of cross-cultural miscommunication are legion.[10] How—to take merely one example among many—can one talk about self-interested behavior in a culture or a people whose language lacks the (modern Western) concept of "economic man" or even of the individual self or "person"? After all, as Clifford Geertz notes,

> [t]he Western conception of the person as a bounded, unique, more or less integrated motivational and cognitive universe, a dynamic center of awareness, emotion, judgment, and action organized into a distinctive whole and set contrastively both against other such wholes and against a social and natural background is, however incorrigible it may seem to us, a rather peculiar idea within the context of the world's cultures.[11]

The very terms that we take to be descriptive or even constitutive of who and what we are or aspire to be are not always readily translatable into what we might call the moral languages of other cultures (nor theirs into ours). And even those terms for which translations are readily available—birth, death, marriage, friendship, worship, God, prayer, play, and a hundred others—have very different meanings in different cultures.

Such problems of translation and interpretation—of grasping the meaning or point of alien practices and actions—are perhaps most fully evident in anthropology and other disciplines that deal with other cultures and languages. But those problems are by no means unique to those disciplines. I want to suggest that the art of constitutional interpretation is fraught with dangers and difficulties at least as great, and possibly as intractable, as those facing any anthropologist.

Now this might seem absurd on its face. After all, we do—so the argument might run—share with the founders a continuous culture and a common language. We are able to recover and understand their intentions because they are, or were, framed in the very language that we still speak. It is of course true that we, like the founders, are speakers of English. But it is no less true that that language has changed in several crucial respects. First, and most obviously, many of the "same" words have quite different meanings for us than they did for the Founders. Garry Wills gives the following example:

> "Your argument is obnoxious, but it will be liquidated once its specious character is discovered." That sentence would not be considered friendly if spoken today. But its terms were not hostile in the eighteenth century. We need to translate: "Your argument, though exposed to malice, will become clear when its attractive distinction is revealed."

"Minor misunderstandings," Wills continues, "can, cumulatively, become major if we forget the many small differences in usage between [the founders'] time and our own."[12]

Still, this problem, important as it is, is readily remediable with the aid of a good glossary or translation manual. But there is a second and perhaps more profound sense in which our language differs from the language in which the founders framed their intentions. What we call "our language" (or theirs, for that matter) is not all of a piece. It is instead compounded of those specialized sublanguages or idioms that we might for want of a better term call *discourses.*[13] Such discourses would today include, though by no means be restricted to, those that are conventionally termed legal, literary, political, ethical, educational, scientific, economic, artistic, and athletic. Such sublanguages or discourses are not, of course, hermetically sealed, much less mutually exclusive. Each tends at times to transgress on the other. (One need only think, for example, of the ways in which the discourse of sports is used today to describe and appraise political actions and practices.) Such transgressions are, indeed, one of the main sources of conceptual change and innovation.

The language of the founders resembles ours in at least one respect: it was compounded of a number of different discourses. But the important point to remember is that the discourses of which it was compounded are in many respects quite different from those with which we are familiar. If we are to understand the meaning of their actions—in this case those linguistic actions or speech acts that make up the arguments out of which and on the basis of which the Constitution was constituted—then we must know what their beliefs and intentions were. But these we cannot know without knowing something about the language in which those beliefs were expressed and intentions framed and made meaningful and intelligible in the first place. The conceptual and moral universe that the founders inhabited is of course connected with—and is indeed partially constitutive of—the one that we now inhabit; but it does not coincide with our world at all possible points. To borrow a phrase from Gadamer, their historically specific "prejudices" (or prejudgments or standpoints: *Vorurteile*) are not wholly unrelated to ours, but neither are they entirely equivalent. Originalist claims to the contrary notwithstanding, the task of legal and constitutional interpretation is not to suspend or forego our own prejudices in favor of theirs, but to recognize, and if possible reconcile, our different understandings of how political society works and ought to be structured and governed.[14]

ORIGINALISM AND WILLFUL IGNORANCE

The founders subscribed to a particular view of politics and human nature. And this view in its turn provided the backdrop against which "power" was conceived (and checked), "liberty" understood (and promoted), and "ambition" feared (and countered). It was within this theoretical horizon or discourse that they framed their intentions and couched their arguments in defense of the new design.

That much, at least, is part of a familiar story. But the story is incomplete without a more precise and detailed account of the connection between a particular kind of discourse and the intentions capable of being formulated within it. What was the founders' discourse, and what intentions did it make possible and intelligible? Like all apparently simple questions, this one admits of no easy answer. Part of the difficulty is due to their having access to a number of discourses, not all of which were of a piece, must less mutually compatible. For the sake of simplicity I shall focus on only two, the first being the political discourse of the republican tradition, the second the scientific discourse of "faculty psychology."

Historians have of late rediscovered the remains (perhaps one should say the ruins) of an identifiable "republican" tradition that stretched from Aristotle and Polybius up through Machiavelli and Harrington to Montesquieu and the American Founding Fathers.[15] Very roughly, republicanism was the theory that viewed the *bios politikos*, the life of active citizenship, as the highest human calling and that, as a corollary, viewed the self-interested pursuit of private gain as an "idiotic" (from the Greek *idion*) way of life unfit for free human beings. Not surprisingly, then, the concepts constitutive of the discourse of republicanism—"liberty," "virtue," and "corruption" among them—had different meanings for say, Machiavelli or even for Montesquieu than they do for us. "Liberty," for example, referred to the free citizen's ability and opportunity to take an active part in political affairs; "virtue" to making full use of this liberty; and "corruption" to the inability or unwillingness to use—and if necessary, to take up arms to defend—one's liberty, choosing instead to pursue private gain and to lead a life of luxury and ease.[16]

The concepts of classical and Renaissance republicanism form scarcely any part of the discourse of latter-day capital-*R* Republicans like Ronald Reagan, of course; but neither are the rest of us on intimate terms with that tradition. We live, as Alasdair MacIntyre maintains, "after virtue"; our ethics are not the ethics of virtue, nor are our politics the politics of *virtù*.[17] Confronted with an author or a text in which "virtue" appears, we are likely to react much as Thomas Mann's Hans Castorp reacted to Settembrini's reliance on the discourse of "virtue":

> What a vocabulary! and he uses the word virtue just like that, without the slightest embarrassment. What do you make of that? I've never taken the word in my mouth as long as I've lived; in school, when the book said "virtus," we always just said "valour" or something like that. It certainly gives me a queer feeling inside to hear him.[18]

This indeed is how modern readers might at first react to the proceedings of the Constitutional Convention and the various tracts and broadsides of the Ratification Debate. In the late 1780s "Brutus," "Publius," and other latter-day mock Romans spoke of virtue, corruption, and liberty in ways that Machiavelli would have readily understood but that we can scarcely comprehend. That this may be our loss, I do not deny; but what cannot be denied, I think, is that this discourse has been largely lost to us and is unlikely to be recovered, rehabilitated, and used once again as the common coin of communication. Yet it is on our capacity to carry out just this sort of recovery and rehabilitation that originalism rests. That doctrine, as we shall see shortly, would require a Canute-like attempt to turn back the tide of conceptual change and would doubtless meet with just about as much success.

The political and moral discourse of republicanism is not the only language lost to us; so too is at least one of the theoretical discourses employed by the founders. Emphasizing "the importance of the intellectual conventions of an age in defining an author's intentions," Daniel Walker

Howe has recently reconstructed the discourse in which the founders talked and thought about human nature. The authors of the Constitution and the *Federalist* papers, Howe reminds us, had ready recourse to the concepts of "faculty psychology."[19] Faculty psychology holds that human beings are endowed with certain species-specific powers or "faculties" that, taken together, constitute human nature. Human nature is therefore teleological in that each faculty impels us toward certain sorts of ends. This teleological psychology constitutes the theoretical model or background beliefs (or, in Berlin's sense, the paradigm) within which the founders framed their intentions and argued their case.

To reread the Constitution, the records of the Constitutional Convention, and the *Federalist* papers in the light cast by this recently recovered theoretical idiom is to better understand where the founders stood and how they thought. But it is one thing to arrive at such historical understanding and quite another to put it to present-day judicial use. To take the originalist position seriously enough to put it into (interpretive) practice would require that lawyers and judges accept that particular background theory as valid, or at any rate unproblematic, in arguing their cases and arriving at legal decisions. Were they to do so, however, they would be out of step with their contemporaries, including those whom we now call psychologists. No psychologist now subscribes to the tenets of faculty psychology, as though Freud (and even Skinner) had never lived or written a word. We can of course recognize and appreciate that the founders considered this particular theory persuasive. But human knowledge has grown; too much has transpired to allow us to accept this theory as authoritative, still less true. To the extent that the founders framed their intentions in the idiom of this theory, we can recover those intentions, but we cannot return to them and make them our own. Anyone attempting to do so would be in a position analogous to a modern sailor who steers his ship by relying on old navigational charts and maps drawn in the belief that the earth was flat.

To understand what the founders intended to convey or communicate requires that we recognize, as some say nowadays, "where they're coming from." It turns out that in the two aforementioned respects the founders were coming from a place that no longer exists on modern maps of knowledge. To reconstruct earlier cartographic theories, and the maps drawn with their aid, is often illuminating; but we would not want to put those theories and maps to present-day navigational use. Yet that is precisely what originalists propose that we do, or at any rate aspire to do.

My contention is not that judges and the rest of us cannot adopt an originalist strategy—far from it. For certain purposes—to arrive at a better understanding of the founders' historical context, for example—originalism functions as an admirable (if not readily attainable) regulative ideal. My contention is, rather, that originalism in its several versions is defective, unwieldy, and probably unworkable as a guideline for arriving at judicial decisions. Originalism is not so much impossible as it is misguided in its aims and unworkable in practice.[20] Since in our present political climate this is a contentious claim, I want to restate and illustrate it by placing it in a more distant and, I hope, somewhat less contentious historical context.

A DISTANT MIRROR

The current call for a return to the beliefs and intentions of the founders is hardly novel. It is a call issued periodically by fundamentalists in different domains, whether literary, legal, religious, or otherwise. It appears at first glance to provide an attractively simple solution to an otherwise very complex problem: How do we moderns understand a text produced by predecessors who did not fully share our world, our language, our beliefs and presuppositions? Answer: we simply read the text as a statement of (actual or at any rate conceivable) authorial intent, which in turn fixes the meaning of the text then, now, and forever after. In fact, however, the purported answer turns out to be extraordinarily complicated not only for the logical and conceptual reasons to which I have alluded already but for several eminently practical reasons as well. The two turn out, moreover, to be quite closely connected.

We can look, by way of illustration, not at the Bible or the Constitution or the Qurʾān—texts around which passionate and protracted hermeneutical controversies continue to swirl—but at the distant mirror provided by the civil jurisprudence of late medieval and early modern Europe.[21] The story, in a nutshell, is this: Roman law, as codified by Justinian in the sixth century and subsequently glossed by Bolognese jurists in the twelfth, was synthesized in Accursius's Great Gloss of the midthirteenth century. The work of Accursius and other "Glossators" was necessary because without their commentaries, clarifications, and cross-references the text of the Justinian code was well-nigh incomprehensible. Accordingly, Accursius's Gloss was widely regarded as enjoying equal authority with the Code. In the fourteenth century the commentators who came to be known as "Bartolists" (after their most renowned representative, Bartolus of Saxoferrato) devised cumbersome but workable techniques for interpreting and applying Roman law to the judicial problems being addressed in late medieval European society. This they did not only by looking at the letter of the law but by teasing out premises or principles believed to be latent in the law. Out of the archaic Code and accompanying Gloss they constructed a *ius commune*, a common law more attuned to the needs of their era.

By the fifteenth century, however, Renaissance grammarians challenged the Bartolists by claiming, with considerable justification, that newly refined philological techniques made it possible to rediscover and recover the original meaning of Roman law. Ancient texts could be restored to their original, and presumably authoritative, meaning. With the aid of this new broom, they claimed, much of the excess verbiage of "interpretation" or "commentary" could be swept away and the original meaning of the Roman law reinstated.

This approach seemed at first sight to be eminently sensible. But it was not long before the so-called Neo-Bartolists countered by pointing out that the original discourse of the Roman lawgivers, and the intentions it made possible, presupposed beliefs, legal contexts, and linguistic conventions far removed from those of sixteenth-century Europe. To interpret the law in the light of an earlier lawgiver's "original intent" would therefore mean removing the law from the contexts in which it did its unwieldy work. Sundered from the language of the modern marketplace and contemporary morality, the law would cease to be "common," becoming not only more unwieldy and less workable but largely unintelligible to those to whose conduct it was supposed to apply. The law would, in other words, cease to reflect the beliefs, inform the intentions, and regulate the actions and activities of those who were not legal scholars and specialists. The Neo-Bartolists accordingly acknowledged that although the historical reconstruction or recovery of original meaning or initial intent had its place in judicial reasoning, jurists were not to attempt the impossible feat of recovering the past in order to return to it.

There is in this sixteenth-century case, I think, a lesson to be learned by late-twentieth-century Americans—and a warning for those willing, ready, and even eager to return to the original intent of the founders. The lesson is not that such a return is impossible either in principle or in practice. Far from it: modern conceptual historians, like Renaissance grammarians, can and regularly do restore the world of words within which intentions were initially framed, whether by lawgivers in Rome or in Philadelphia. Theirs is, to be sure, an exceedingly difficult task; but it can be, has been, and is still being performed—and sometimes at a very high level.[22] The difficulty that needs to be recognized and addressed by both proponents and critics of originalism is of a rather different sort. Even supposing that one can arrive at some approximation of the founders' intent or original meaning, what weight, if any, is it to be given? This question becomes especially important in light of the fact that the recovery of the founders' beliefs and intentions requires that one not only understand but presumably *accept as authoritative* the discourse(s) in which their intentions were framed in the first place. Of course, conceptual historians have no difficulty in "accepting" such theoretical idioms; theirs is acceptance for the sake of argument and for the sake of historical understanding: they wish, that is, to restore the contexts that render intelligible the beliefs, intentions, arguments, and actions of agents long dead. The arguments in which they engage are, however, largely—and nonpejoratively—academic.

The judge or Supreme Court justice, by contrast, is faced with a very different and distinctly nonacademic task. His or hers is not the task of recovering and restoring the idioms and intentions of lawgivers long dead but of rendering decisions that apply to law benders and breakers now living—and of doing so, moreover, in terms that are more or less intelligible to those whose conduct is being judged. Of course, this remains a regulative ideal to which reality all too rarely corresponds. No one could fail to recognize that there are exceptions, breakdowns, and failures aplenty: many a criminal goes to prison with only the vaguest understanding of the letter of the law under which he has been charged, tried, and sentenced. The larger point, however, is that the criminal's contemporaries should be able to understand the law even if the criminal does not. It is in the final analysis a question of criminal intent, not original intent, and of the intelligibility of the law to those whose conduct or conscience is being appealed to. An originalist jurisprudence is blind and deaf to considerations of either sort. And that, I submit, is only one of its flaws.

THE SINGLE-AUTHOR FALLACY

Another of the flaws afflicting originalism is to be found in its treatment not of texts in general but of the Constitution in particular. Originalists who look to the intent of the framers propose to treat the Constitution as if it were the product of a single author. But in fact it is possible to give only the most minimal and abstract characterization of the (shared) intention(s) of the founders: they intended the Constitution to be the binding legal basis of a system of government in which each branch would balance and check the others and in which there was a division of powers between the federal government and the several states. Beyond that, agreement ends and intentions differ. As the Record of the Constitutional Convention clearly shows, the articles, sections, clauses, sentences, and even single words that make up this text were originally the result of often contentious and even quarrelsome collaboration and an almost endless series of compromises among its many authors.[23] And if the diaries, memoirs, and correspondence of individual founders are any indication, few were fully satisfied with the final result.[24]

To attempt to treat the Constitution as one would a text by a single author is to commit the single-author fallacy. To see just what relevance this fact has for contemporary constitutional interpretation, particularly from the standpoint of original intent, I want to examine a case that has, as of this writing, captured considerable interest.

The case I wish to examine—*Perpich et al. v. Department of Defense*—involves a gubernatorial challenge to the constitutionality of section 522 of the Defense Authorization Act for fiscal year 1987.[25] Section 522, popularly known as the Montgomery Amendment, severely restricts the grounds on which state governors may withhold consent to permit their National Guard units from participating in training missions outside the United States. The Montgomery Amendment was added when several state governors balked at the Pentagon's decision, late in 1986, to expand its practice of sending National Guard units to Central America on expeditions rather euphemistically described as "training" missions. Led by Governor Rudy Perpich of Minnesota, the governors filed suit in federal district court. The gist of the plaintiffs' suit was that the Montgomery Amendment violates the militia clause (article 1, section 8) of the Constitution, which reserves to the states the right to oversee the training of their respective militias. On 6 December 1988 the Eighth U.S. Circuit Court of Appeals found for the plaintiffs, citing in its decision "the intent of the Founders" in drafting the militia clause.

Among the many ironies in this case was that the Reagan administration—which, in the persons of Attorney General Edwin Meese III, Solicitor General Charles Fried, and at least one unsuccessful nominee for the Supreme Court (Judge Robert Bork), had been a staunch advocate of the doctrine of original intent—had the tables turned on it. For the Court of Appeals' decision was couched precisely in terms of the intentions of the founders. It turns out that a judicial strategy of original intent, far from being the consistently conservative blade that Bork and Meese expected it to be, can cut in quite unexpected directions. At this writing it seems certain that the case will be appealed to the Supreme Court. And since this could prove to be a landmark case, its historical origins may be worth reviewing here.[26]

Coming as it did in the bicentennial year of 1987, the governors' lawsuit was well-timed, for it reopened one of the questions so heatedly debated in Philadelphia during the hot summer months of 1787. That question was, who is to control the individual state "militias"—the federal government or the states themselves?[27]

On the one side were the centralizers like Alexander Hamilton, who favored nationalizing the state militias by putting them under the control of the central government. They feared that the irregular state militias might take up arms against neighboring states and even against the federal government itself.[28] Their fears were not without foundation. The memory of Shays's Rebellion (1786–87) was still fresh in their minds. And their worst fears would be realized seventy-four years later when the Southern states seceded from the Union and turned their respective militias against the federal government. On the other side were those who wanted the states to retain exclusive control over their own militias. They feared that an all-powerful central government would ride roughshod over the rights reserved to the states, using federally controlled state militias to stifle dissent.

As so often happened during the Constitutional Convention, neither side carried the day entirely, and a compromise was eventually reached. The results of that compromise can still be seen in article 1, section 8, which empowers the Congress to "raise and support armies" and to "provide and maintain a navy," both of which are to be under the exclusive jurisdiction of the federal government. As for the state militias, the new Constitution gave Congress the power "to provide for calling forth the militia to execute the laws of the union, suppress insurrections, and repel invasions."

This wording still did not satisfy skeptical decentralizers, who insisted that the extent of congressional control over the state militias be spelled out more fully and more precisely. And so in the succeeding paragraph of article 1, section 8 we see the further fruits of that heated debate. It begins by specifying that the Congress is "[t]o provide for organizing, arming, and disciplining the militia, and for governing such parts of them as may be employed in the service of the United States" and concludes by "reserving to the states respectively, the appointment of the officers, and the authority of training the militia according to the discipline prescribed by congress." In short, the centralizers who favored federal control of the militias succeeded in giving the Congress some measure of control over the state militias. And the states'-rights minded decentralizers succeeded in limiting the extent of congressional control. Each side got the proverbial half-loaf.

The governors' lawsuit claimed—and the court of appeals has now agreed—that the Montgomery Amendment reneges on the crucial compromise of 1787 by giving an additional and arguably unconstitutional slice to the federal government. Article 1, section 8 specifies that "the authority of training the militia" is to be left to the individual states, provided that this training accords with congressional guidelines regarding the appropriate regimen or "discipline." Citing "the intent of the Founders," the court of appeals agreed with Governor Perpich's claim that the Montgomery Amendment goes well beyond this. By forbidding states to withdraw their militias from foreign countries without declaring an official state emergency, that amendment is inconsistent with the original intent of the founders.

Yet, I think, the appeals court decision did not go as far as it might have had it considered the language in which the founders framed their (several) intentions and their final (univocal) compromise. A close reading of article 1, section 8 scarcely suggests that the Congress can deploy state militias outside of our borders for any purposes whatsoever, whether they be engaged in actual combat or in training exercises. After all, "the laws of the union" do not apply outside of our borders; an "insurrection," in the eighteenth-century parlance of the founders, was a domestic, not a foreign, uprising; and an "invasion" can by definition be "repelled" only after an invader has already crossed our borders. All this suggests that the original intent of the founders—or, at any rate, the result of their compromise—is that state militias are only to be deployed *domestically*, that is, intranationally, not internationally. If so, not only the Montgomery Amendment but the governors' lawsuit and the court of appeals' decision are alike in resting on a constitutionally false premise.

More than that, the decision of the court of appeals commits the single-author fallacy. For while the judges were surely right in their recovery and reconstruction of the intentions of some founders, they did not succeed in recovering and respecting the intentions of Hamilton and others who wished to place the several state militias under federal control. But of course to raise questions about the particular intentions of individual founders is perforce to undermine the entire thrust—and (dare I say it?) the intent—of the original intent variant of originalism.

MADISON'S CRITIQUE OF ORIGINALISM

If the foregoing arguments against originalism should prove to be less than completely convincing, let me turn, finally, to that last refuge of scoundrels and scholars, the argument from authority. My authority is none other than the Father of the Constitution himself, James Madison. I choose Madison simply because he, in his role as founder, is one of those to whose beliefs and intentions originalists are duty-bound to look for advice and guidance. Ironically, however, Madison sides with those who hold that the reader or interpreter must have some say in determining what a text "means." To put the point in a slightly more sophisticated (though admittedly anachronistic) way, we might say that Madison, like modern "reception" theorists, holds that texts are by their very nature essentially incomplete: even though a particular text has an author(s), it nevertheless needs a reader(s) or interpreter(s) to round it out and give it its full meaning.[29] It is, I submit, something like this position to which Madison himself subscribed and for reasons that might best be termed conceptual or linguistic.

In *Federalist* 37 Madison remarks, "All new laws, though penned with the greatest technical skill, and passed on the fullest and most mature deliberation"—as the document drafted in Philadelphia surely was—"are considered as more or less obscure and equivocal, until their meaning be liquidated [i.e., clarified] and ascertained by a series of particular discussions and adjudications."[30] Madison then goes on to enumerate three reasons for subscribing to this reception-theory account of constitutional meaning. The first has to do with "the obscurity arising from [the] objects" of constitutional deliberation. The more complex the object, the greater the possibility of mistake or misunderstanding. The second has to do with "the imperfection of the human faculties." The powers of human reason and understanding are by nature imperfect, occasionally defective, and invariably limited and must therefore be checked or compensated for. Important as they are, however, these two reasons for a reception-theory approach get short shrift in comparison to the third.

Madison's third and weightiest reason has to do with the nature of language itself. "[T]he medium through which the conceptions of men are conveyed to each other," he complains, "adds a fresh embarrassment. The use of words is to express ideas. Perspicuity therefore requires not only that the ideas should be distinctly formed, but that they should be expressed by words distinctly and exclusively appropriated to them. But," he adds,

> no language is so copious as to supply words and phrases for every complex idea, or so correct as not to include many equivocally denoting different ideas. Hence, it must happen, that however accurately objects may be discriminated in themselves, and however accurately the discrimination may be considered, the definition of them may be rendered inaccurate by the inaccuracy of the terms in which it is delivered. And this unavoidable inaccuracy must be greater or less, accordingly to the complexity and novelty of the objects defined. When the Almighty himself condescends to address mankind in their own language, his meaning, luminous as it must be, is rendered dim and doubtful by the cloudy medium through which it is communicated.

Madison maintains that the medium through which human beings communicate is not contingently but necessarily a "cloudy" one. Not only is perfect clarity impossible for human beings using human language; it would be impossible even for God, were he to deign to talk to us in any human tongue.

Now if God cannot make his meaning perfectly clear, it follows that even the most godlike human legislator cannot frame and communicate his intentions with perfect precision and clarity. Not only can he not do it, says Madison, he cannot even *hope* to do it, given the nature of human language itself. The opacity of language is not, Madison insists, a failure or shortcoming of any particular language; it is, rather, an ineliminable feature of all language and hence, by implication, of all authors and speakers and therefore of all utterances and texts.

Madison's reflections on language and meaning are, I believe, fatally damaging to the doctrine or originalism. For that doctrine assumes that language is (or is at any rate capable of being) a transparent medium in which meanings and intentions can be framed and communicated in an absolutely unambiguous way. But such transparency, according to Madison, is impossible. Language is not, and can never be, a wholly transparent medium. Thus, that doctrine rests on what Madison might have termed the Fallacy of Perfect Clarity.

Originalist doctrine also depends on another doubtful assumption, the one that Nietzsche called the Dogma of Immaculate Perception and that I call the Dogma of Immaculate Reception. That dogma holds that a reader or listener or interpreter is, or can (or should) be, an empty vessel—a veritable tabula rasa on which a speaker, author, or text imprints its message. But human communication, as Madison certainly acknowledged, is a two-way street. It involves not only speakers and authors but also listeners and readers. The speaker or author is not simply the active agent and the listener or reader an inactive patient or passive receptacle. Both are and must be participants in any act of communication. As Madison puts it, the meaning of even the most carefully drafted law will be "more or less obscure and equivocal, until [its] meaning be liquidated and ascertained by a series of particular discussions and adjudications." And these discussions and adjudications can, and arguably must, begin in and be mediated through the theoretical, moral, legal, political, and/or scientific discourse of our day, and not simply that of the founders alone. So it would appear that Madison foresaw—and arguably attempted to forestall or, failing that, to add his own voice to—the debate over originalism.

CONCLUSION

The thrust of the foregoing account, if correct, is that the doctrine—or perhaps one should say the dogma—of originalism is specious in the eighteenth-century sense of that term: flashily attractive. Its obvious attractions aside, that doctrine, I have argued, is afflicted with a number of heretofore unnoticed difficulties. But if past experience is any guide, it is unlikely that this doctrine will be dislodged by argument, much less dropped altogether, at least as long as it satisfies some influential faction's rhetorical requirements. And that, arguably, is what accounts for the continuing appeal of originalism.

NOTES

An earlier and rather different version of this essay was presented to the Roundtable on Legal Hermeneutics at the 1987 meeting of the American Political

Science Association. I am grateful to the roundtable's organizer and chair, Gregory Leyh, to my fellow panelists Fred Dallmayr and Michael Perry, and to Lief Carter for commenting critically on that first version. The present version was further and very helpfully criticized by James Farr, Russell Hanson, and Gregory Leyh. I am also grateful to John R. Tunheim, chief deputy attorney general of Minnesota, for his help in explaining the intricacies of *Perpich et al. v. Department of Defense.*

1. See my "Deadly Hermeneutics; or, *Sinn* and the Social Scientist," in *Idioms of Inquiry,* ed. Terence Ball (Albany: State University of New York Press, 1987), 95–112.

2. On the notion of "interpretive communities," see Stanley Fish, *Is There a Text in This Class? The Authority of Interpretive Communities* (Cambridge: Harvard University Press, 1980), esp. chap. 15.

3. The U.S. Constitution's interpretive community, as Francis Lieber averred, includes not only the lawyers, judges, and courts but the entire citizenry, as James Farr points out in "The Americanization of Hermeneutics: Francis Lieber's *Legal and Political Hermeneutics,*" in this volume.

4. Strictly speaking, originalism is not a single doctrine but a fairly close-knit family of doctrines sharing a common assumption: viz., that judges and other interpreters must return to and regard as authoritative the original source, whether that source be construed as author, authorial intent, text, or, more broadly, the moral, historical, legal, and political context in which the author worked and/or the text was composed. For present purposes I shall be dealing mainly with the "original intent" version of originalism. For a useful taxonomy of types of originalism, see Paul Brest, "The Misconceived Quest for Original Understanding," *Boston University Law Review* 60 (1980): 204–38. In defense of originalism, see, inter alia, Robert Bork, "Neutral Principles and Some First Amendment Problems," *Indiana Law Journal* 47 (1971): 1–35, and "Tradition and Morality in Constitutional Law," in *Views from the Bench: The Judiciary and Constitutional Politics,* ed. Mark Cannon and David O'Brien (New York: Chatham House, 1985); Raoul Berger, *Government by Judiciary* (Cambridge: Harvard University Press, 1977); Henry Monaghan, "Our Perfect Constitution," *New York University Law Review* 56 (1981): 353–96. For criticisms of originalism from several perspectives, see, inter alia, Ronald Dworkin, *A Matter of Principle* (Cambridge: Harvard University Press, 1985), chaps. 6 and 7; Dworkin, "The Bork Nomination," *New York Review of Books,* 13 August 1987, 3–10; Gregory Leyh, "Toward a Constitutional Hermeneutics," *American Journal of Political Science* 32 (1988): 369–87; Michael J. Perry, "The Authority of Text, Tradition, and Reason: A Theory of Constitutional 'Interpretation,' " *Southern California Law Review* 58 (1985): 552–602; and Perry, *Morality, Politics, and Law* (New York: Oxford University Press, 1989). Unlike many other critics, Perry believes originalism to be both coherent and plausible, but less so than nonoriginalist approaches to interpretation.

5. On the methods and justifications for constructing "conceptual histories," see Reinhart Koselleck, *Futures Past: On the Semantics of Historical Time,* trans. Keith Tribe (Cambridge: MIT Press, 1985). For the execution of particular conceptual histories, see the mammoth *Geschichtliche Grundbegriffe: Historisches Lexikon zur Politisch-Sozialer Sprache in Deutschland,* ed. Otto Brunner, Werner

Conze, and Reinhart Koselleck (Stuttgart: Klett-Cotta, 1972–), 5 vols. to date; and *Handbuch politisch-sozialer Grundbegriffe in Frankreich, 1680–1820*, ed. Rolf Reichardt and Eberhard Schmitt (Munich: Oldenbourg Verlag, 1985–), 2 vols. to date. For more anglicized and americanized versions of conceptual history, compare *The Languages of Political Theory in Early-Modern Europe*, ed. Anthony Pagden (Cambridge: Cambridge University Press, 1987); *Political Innovation and Conceptual Change*, ed. Terence Ball, James Farr, and Russell Hanson (Cambridge: Cambridge University Press, 1989); *Conceptual Change and the Constitution*, ed. Terence Ball and J. G. A. Pocock (Lawrence: University Press of Kansas, 1988); and Terence Ball, *Transforming Political Discourse: Political Theory and Critical Conceptual History* (Oxford: Basil Blackwell, 1988).

6. Isaiah Berlin, *Concepts and Categories* (Harmondsworth, Eng.: Penguin, 1981), 154.

7. See, e.g., E. M. W. Tillyard, *The Elizabethan World Picture* (New York: Random House, Vintage Books, n.d.). The point applies not only to law and literature but to the natural sciences as well. See E. A. Burtt, *The Metaphysical Foundations of Modern Science*, rev. ed. (New York: Humanities Press, 1952); Alexandre Koyré, *From the Closed World to the Infinite Universe* (Baltimore: Johns Hopkins University Press, 1957); and Stephen Toulmin, "The Construal of Reality: Criticism in Modern and Postmodern Science," in *The Politics of Interpretation*, ed. W. J. T. Mitchell (Chicago: University of Chicago Press, 1983), 99–117.

8. Here I think of the amusing and instructive tale of the "born-again" Christian outfielder, Pat Kelly, as told by Fish, *Is There a Text*, 269–72.

9. On various versions of the commensurability problem as it appears in the discourses of anthropology and other disciplines, see Richard J. Bernstein, *Beyond Objectivism and Relativism* (Philadelphia: University of Pennsylvania Press, 1983), esp. part 3.

10. See, e.g., Clifford Geertz, "From the Native's Point of View: On the Nature of Anthropological Understanding," in *Interpretive Social Science*, ed. Paul Rabinow and William M. Sullivan (Berkeley and Los Angeles: University of California Press, 1979), chap. 6; and Peter Winch, "Understanding a Primitive Society," in *Rationality*, ed. Brian R. Wilson (Oxford: Basil Blackwell, 1970).

11. Geertz, "Native's Point of View," 229.

12. Garry Wills, *Explaining America: The Federalist* (New York: Penguin, 1981), 280. Wills quite appropriately appends a glossary of terms for the *Federalist Papers*.

13. For an explication of the notion of discourses, see J. G. A. Pocock, "The Concept of a Language and the *Métier d'Historien:* Some Considerations on Practice," in *Languages of Political Theory*, chap. 1; James Boyd White, *Justice as Translation: An Essay in Cultural and Legal Criticism* (Chicago: University of Chicago Press, 1990), esp. chap. 3; and my *Transforming Political Discourse*, chap. 1.

14. On the historicity of human existence and the inescapable necessity to start—though not to stay—with our present "prejudices," see Hans-Georg Gadamer, *Truth and Method* (New York: Seabury, 1975). Some of the legal and constitutional implications of Gadamer's hermeneutics are traced by Leyh, "Toward a Constitutional Hermeneutics."

15. The scholar who has done most to reconstruct the history of an identifiable "Atlantic Republic Tradition" is J. G. A. Pocock, particularly in *The Machia-*

vellian Moment: Florentine Political Thought and the Atlantic Republican Tradition (Princeton: Princeton University Press, 1975).

16. See my *Transforming Political Discourse*, chap. 3, esp. 48–54.

17. Alasdair MacIntyre, *After Virtue* (Notre Dame: University of Notre Dame Press, 1981).

18. Thomas Mann, *The Magic Mountain*, trans. H. T. Lowe-Porter (New York: Knopf, 1966), 101.

19. Daniel Walker Howe, "The Language of Faculty Psychology in *The Federalist Papers*," in *Conceptual Change and the Constitution*, chap. 7.

20. Although I take a somewhat dimmer view of originalism than does Perry ("Authority of Text" and *Morality, Politics, and Law*), I agree with his conclusion that its primary defects are practical ones.

21. What follows is a much abbreviated and simplified version of the tale told by Donald Kelly in "Civil Science in the Renaissance: The Problem of Interpretation," in *Languages of Political Theory*, chap. 3. See also Ball and Pocock, introduction to *Conceptual Change and the Constitution*, esp. 9–11.

22. See above, n. 4.

23. Cf. *The Records of the Federal Convention of 1787*, ed. Max Farrand (New Haven: Yale University Press, 1966); and *The Founders' Constitution*, ed. Philip B. Kurland and Ralph Lerner (Chicago: University of Chicago Press, 1987).

24. Though not alone among the founders, Hamilton came to believe the Constitution a failure. "Perhaps no man in the United States," he wrote in 1802, "has sacrificed or done more for the present Constitution than myself; and contrary to all my anticipations of its fate . . . I am still laboring to prop the frail and worthless fabric." Quoted in John C. Miller, *Alexander Hamilton: Portrait in Paradox* (New York: Harper and Brothers, 1959), 543. Others among the founders, including John Adams, arrived at almost equally critical if less gloomy conclusions. See John R. Howe, Jr., *The Changing Political Thought of John Adams* (Princeton: Princeton University Press, 1966). See further and more generally, Michael Kammen, *A Machine That Would Go of Itself: The Constitution in American Culture* (New York: Knopf, 1986).

25. Cf. 10 United States Codes 672 (f), Sec. 522.

26. Decision and eighty-one-page opinion in U.S. Court of Appeals for the Eighth Circuit, No. 87-5345 (6 Dec. 1988). In 1990, the Supreme Court ruled against Perpich et al.

27. See *Records of the Federal Convention* 2:129–37, 158–59, 323, 353, 380–83, 570, 595; and *Founders' Constitution* 1:173–211.

28. In addition to the debates noted in n. 23 above, see Hamilton, *Federalist* 29.

29. For different variants of reception theory, see, inter alia, Fish, *Is There a Text; The Reader in the Text: Essays on Audience and Interpretation*, ed. Susan R. Suleiman and Inge Crosman (Princeton: Princeton University Press, 1980); Hans Robert Jauss, *Toward an Aesthetic of Reception*, trans. Timothy Bahti (Minneapolis: University of Minnesota Press, 1982); and, more generally, Robert C. Holub, *Reception Theory: A Critical Introduction* (London: Methuen, 1984).

30. This and all following quotations come from Madison, *Federalist* 37.

Name Index